The World
and the Word

Nongenile Masithathu Zenani. "Kwathi ke kaloku ngantsomi. . . ." "It happened in a fantastic tale. . . ."

The World and the Word

Tales and Observations from the Xhosa Oral Tradition

Nongenile Masithathu Zenani

Collected and edited, with
an introduction, commentaries,
and annotations by

Harold Scheub

The University of Wisconsin Press

The University of Wisconsin Press
114 North Murray Street
Madison, Wisconsin 53715

3 Henrietta Street
London WC2E 8LU, England

5   4   3   2   1

Printed in the United States of America

Library of Congress Cataloging-in-Publication Data
Zenani, Nongenile Masithathu.
The world and the word: tales and observations from the Xhosa
oral tradition / Nongenile Masithathu Zenani ; collected
and edited, with an introduction, commentaries,
and annotations by Harold Scheub.
512 pp.   cm.
Includes bibliographical references and index.
ISBN 0-299-13310-9
1. Xhosa (African people)—Folklore. 2. Tales—South Africa.
3. Xhosa (African people)—Social life and customs.
I. Scheub, Harold. II. Title.
GR359.2.X64Z46   1992
398.2'089'963985—dc20   92-50261

"These are the storyteller's materials:
the world and the word."
Nongenile Masithathu Zenani

Contents

Illustrations

Preface

This collection of stories and observations by Nongenile Masithathu Zenani provides an unprecedented view, by a gifted intellectual and artist, of an oral society from within. During a period of two years, from 1968 to 1969, and again from 1972 to 1973, I worked with Mrs. Zenani, taping and filming her repertory of imaginative tales, along with autobiographical and ethnographic material, identified here as "Commentaries." In the commentaries as in the tales, I have taken great care not to interfere with her words and thoughts: I have not altered the material in any way. These translations are as close to the originals as possible. Any interpolation by me is provided in bracketed notes in the text or in footnotes. I did break some of Mrs. Zenani's commentaries into segments, but again I emphasize that these are her words. These materials were taped in their entirety and filmed in part. The introductions and the headnotes preceding the tales are based on conversations I had with Mrs. Zenani after her performances. I have attempted to retain the substance and the style of her observations. These conversations were not taped; after my discussions with the storyteller, I wrote down her analyses.

I worked closely with four Xhosa speakers on these translations, with A. C. Jordan, Gideon Mangoaela, Durward Ntusi, and, especially, with Wandile Kuse, who guided me through many of the intricacies and beauties of the Xhosa language. In my many discussions with her, Mrs. Zenani also provided me with many insights into metaphorical and symbolic meanings of words, images, and expressions.

The introductions, commentaries, and tales have been organized into broad categories. The volume is in four parts—Birth, Puberty, Marriage, Maturity—with a prologue, Origins, and an epilogue, Destiny. Each of the four major parts is divided into two sections: one includes nonfictional commentaries by Mrs. Zenani and the other is composed of a number of imaginative tales related in some way to her nonfictional observations. The reader is thereby provided a background of realistic images of the world, as expressed in her commentaries, against which the storyteller constructs her story.

Specific information on the dates, locations, and audiences for each of Mrs. Zenani's performances can be found preceding each commentary and following the headnote for each tale, and occasionally in the notes.

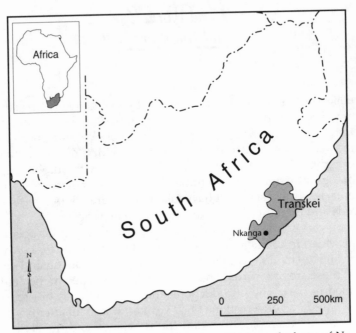

Map of South Africa, showing the location of Nkanga, the home of Nongenile Masithathu Zenani. Map courtesy of the University of Wisconsin–
Madison Cartography Laboratory.

The World
and the Word

INTRODUCTION

Storytellers have always been innovative, and they have always been imitative. This need not be seen as a contradiction. Oral performers have routinely relied on tradition, as they have typically worked within two realms, the world of the immediately perceptible and the world of the imagination. The latter is the link to the past—a grandly mythicized past, the journey to its essence essayed by generations of estimable artists. The genius of the storyteller is to be discovered in her ability to work within the tradition, the imitative part of her art, as she simultaneously gives her audiences new insights into ancient images by using them to give form to their contemporary world, the innovative part of her performances.

Every age has surely produced its masters, storytellers who have moved the tradition into new areas, always within contexts inherited from those who have come before. The materials and methods of composition have remained constant through the centuries—images from past and present, representations of fantasy and reality, worked together and artfully crafted into rich metaphorical parallels in performances that enlist the emotions of the members of audiences. The storytelling tradition has kept the members of the society in harmony with an antiquity that only vaguely resembles fact. That past, the paradigm of the culture, continues to exert its influence on the shaping of the present, giving it a mythic heart, a traditional context, and a nascent form.[1] "These are the storyteller's materials," Mrs. Zenani contended: "the world and the word." This combination of the real world and the imaginative word controls the narrative performance and streams unerringly to the essence of a culture. The stories have a predictability and a familiarity that enable the members of the audience to enter them with facility and without confusion. The performer then proceeds to manipulate the members of the audience, as they are willingly and pleasurably made a part of the dynamics of metaphor, which is the basis of all storytelling.

"When those of us in my generation awakened to earliest consciousness," Mrs. Zenani told me, "we were born into a tradition that was already flourishing. Narratives were being composed by adults in a tradition that had been established long before we were born."[2] She was refer-

1. Stories in the oral tradition were never meant to be memorized, Mrs. Zenani argued, nor were they meant to be frozen in time. The storyteller is constantly in the process of linking the present and the past: it is therefore crucial that the images be flexible, that their union be evanescent.

2. A San storyteller, //kabbo, says, ". . . I sit in the sun, sitting and listening to the stories that come from out there, stories that come from a distance. Then I catch hold of a story that floats out from the distant place—when the sun feels warm and when I feel that I must visit

ring to an oral tradition that is simultaneously ancient and contemporary, composed of images from the past and the present.[3]

Mrs. Zenani has her home on the slope of a ridge some thirty miles from the Indian Ocean on the southeastern coast of Africa. For as long as she can remember, she has been a creator of Xhosa *iintsomi*, oral narratives. This tall, erect woman, regal in her bearing and her face a mask of disdain, is seemingly indifferent to, even contemptuous of, the members of her audience. She pulls her red ochre cape around her, ignores the audience and its banter, and proceeds to detail the colorful world of the *intsomi*. At times, her body movement is brightly flamboyant, but she is not always given to broad dramatic gesticulation, and one is apt to miss the extraverbal character of her production if one is not attentive, an attitude that she fully expects. One might also fail to discern the developing and warming intimacy between the artist and her audience during the process of the performance, and overlook the skill with which Mrs. Zenani exploits the considerable tension that arises between her and its members. Slowly and smoothly, she moves into the narrative, usually a lengthy one, pronouncing the opening formula in a casual manner that conceals the seriousness with which she is about to evoke her images. She provides motivation for the crisis that lies in the future, avoiding the eyes of those in her audience, seeking beyond them ancient motifs, employing the creative tools that will conspire to create her work of art. A network of relationships organizes the body of images, a network that is frequently complex when it seems most obvious, understated even when it appears most apparent, submerged thoughts briefly realized.

Her face and body are in controlled harmony: a slight grimace, a flash of

---

and talk with my fellows" (quoted in W. H. I. Bleek and L. C. Lloyd, *Specimens of Bushman Folklore* [London: George Allen and Co., Ltd., 1911], pp. 300–301).

3. A San storyteller, //kabbo, expresses it poetically: "A story is like the wind: it comes from a distant place, and we feel it" (quoted in W. H. I. Bleek and L. C. Lloyd, *Specimens of Bushman Folklore* [London: George Allen and Co., Ltd., 1911], 300–301). Walter Benjamin, having read an African tale, commented, "This story from ancient Egypt is still capable after thousands of years of arousing astonishment and thoughtfulness. It resembles the seeds of grain which have lain for centuries in the pyramids shut up air-tight and have retained their germinative power to this day." A story, he concluded, "does not expend itself" the way information does. "It preserves and concentrates its strength and is capable of releasing it even after a long time" (*Illuminations*, tr. Harry Zohn [Glasgow: William Collins Sons and Co., 1973], p. 90). A Xhosa storyteller, A. C. Jordan, argued that performers "gave artistic utterance to their deepest thoughts and feelings about those abstract and concrete things that came within their experience. . . ." With these images, artists speculated about "the origin of things, including man himself and the universe," they interpreted "the struggle between man and the mysterious forces that surround him," they expressed their admiration "for those individuals of the human race to whom legend gave credit for the triumph of man over such forces" (*Towards an African Literature, The Emergence of Literary Form in Xhosa* [Berkeley: University of California Press, 1973], p. 3).

fear, anger, joy. Her hands work softly, serenely, deftly, molding the performance, giving a nuance to a character, adding depth to another, her red cloak catching a flashing ray of the setting sun as her body moves rhythmically to the poetry of her narrative.

She has known these stories for years, she told me. She learned them in no formal way, for the *intsomi* tradition, with its dependence on nuclear images for transmission through the generations, requires no such apprenticeship. She learned her craft the way all Xhosa performers do: she heard stories in her neighborhood, observed performances presented by an aunt, a grandmother, a friend of her parents; she picked up a detail here, a useful stylistic device there. She found elements of production that she appreciated when she was a member of an audience, that she cherished and remembered, then made her own. Mrs. Zenani is an amalgam of all the performers she has met; her performances have their roots in the countless stories she has heard, as a child, a teenager, and as a mature woman. But she is more than that, of course; she is a skilled artist with an extraordinary ability to work with these *intsomi* images, to transform them into unique, glimmering, evanescent moments of color and movement. Under her guidance and control, the images become reflections of her society and of her own opinions and thought.[4]

She employs the finite number of images in the *intsomi* repertory as a poet uses language. She is faithful to the traditional images, to a controlling metaphor that pictures a society of order, of an equilibrium best exemplified in symbols of nature, but she is in no way confined by them. Her art demonstrates how wide are the curbs of the tradition, how a competent artist can make the tradition work for her. Like any poet or visual artist, she is tied to the conventions of her time. Her basic aesthetic equipment consists of the ancient mythic images, and her genius is in the way she brings them together into new combinations; more than that, she gives the images new interpretations.

The members of her audiences are emotionally involved in the *intsomi* images when she is in the midst of a performance, taking their cues from this artist who has firm control over all aspects of the production, and so they become psychologically and rhythmically a part of the performance. They may have heard the narratives many times, but in form and development of theme they know that there are few artists of the stature of this one.

---

4. Her sense of personal sorrow and her pride in her medical profession (when she was still a young woman, she became a healer) are frequent themes in her stories.

THE ART OF THE STORYTELLER

Performance Note
Time: 3 August 1972 in the afternoon. *Place:* Outside, near Mrs. Zenani's home in Nkanga, Gatyana District, the Transkei. *Audience:* Six women and twelve teen-agers and children. (NS-22.)

The art of composing imaginative narratives is something that was undertaken by the first people—long ago, during the time of the ancestors. When those of us in my generation awakened to earliest consciousness, we were born into a tradition that was already flourishing. Narratives were being performed by adults in a tradition that had been established long before we were born. And when we were born, those narratives were constructed for us by old people, who argued that the stories had initially been created in olden times, long ago. That time was ancient even to our fathers; it was ancient to our grandmothers, who said that tales had been created years before by their grandmothers. We learned the narratives in that way, and every generation that has come into being has been born into the tradition. Members of every generation have grown up under the influence of these narratives.

But those ancient stories were quite different from those of the present age. The current stories, those that we hear now, tend to be written down. As if from nowhere, we suddenly find that they are being written.

But the genuine stories were never, at any time, written down. They were composed orally by the old people. And when we too asked how this tradition came into existence, we were told that it was a craft that had been practiced at the very beginning, in the old times. Such tales go back as far as ancestral time, to the age of the first people. But these works did not resemble what we have in contemporary times.

At first, nothing was bought. People ate food very unlike the food that is eaten today. At first, for example, pumpkins were not eaten. In the same way, ancient stories were not like the stories of today. When we ask how it came about that there are now such things as edible pumpkins, the old people say that initially pumpkins were not cultivated. A pumpkin was merely a thing over there on the hillsides, growing wild like all the other plants. It was domesticated because of the enlightenment of the people of later generations; they saw that it was edible, this thing that they had previously regarded as simply a wild plant. In the beginning, a pumpkin was just a thing that was in the forest, something that one might knock against with his foot and not even know what he should do with it. This was also the case with maize. It was not regarded as something edible in

7

the beginning. A plant that seems to date from the beginning is millet; they say that millet was the first food.

All these things have followed this pattern. So it is with oral narratives: their origin is with the ancestors, the ancient grandmothers. Such narratives were a part of an active tradition when we were born. In the old days, when we performed these stories, the old people would listen to us. Then they would say, "This child knows the stories!" Or, "This one does not know them! He speaks a thing that he does not know. There's no story like this one. This child is just chattering about his own things." It would be clear that the good storyteller was composing a story that was really ancient—a really genuine narrative. So we children continued to be separated like that, repeatedly, separated in that way into two groups by the old people.

PROLOGUE—ORIGINS

Performance Note

Time: 12 August 1972, at 2:00 P.M. *Place:* In a fallen rondavel near Mrs. Zenani's home in Nkanga, Gatyana District, the Transkei. *Audience:* Five women, three teenagers, and two children. (NS-158.)

Here are the first reports that we have regarding our emergence as a people. Our elders, our ancestors, describe the origin of humans in this way.

In the beginning, it is said, the first human came into being naturally. He achieved form as a human being; he quite clearly was a person. He came to be regarded as the archetype, the first human being. That was the beginning of what came to be known as a human being among the Xhosa.

That first person, the archetypal human being as far as the Xhosa are concerned, was Tshawe.

Now the Xhosa divided themselves, and increased. In the beginning, this man, Tshawe, sired many male children by his first wife: the elders say that he had ten male children. These children of his grew up, and, when they were older, it is said that the first child made a wife of his sister. The children born of this woman were said to be the real children of the home.

Then this sister produced male children again, a second generation of them. These children also grew up; all of them became princes. Because they were children of this home, they were referred to as princes.

Nobody thought much of this in those days; no one made an issue of such activities. No one wondered who the father of these children was.

Nor did anyone question matters the second time she bore children; no one wondered by whom she had begotten these children.[1] In those days, it was not yet known that such a thing [incest] was right or wrong. In the end, of course, the people awakened into the knowledge that, really, this thing seems to be wrong.

The woman's children grew. When she was quite old, and they were men, she died; she died at the appropriate time—she died a natural death.

It is said that in those days death was unlike the death that we know today. It used to be that a person's throat would be narrowed as he grew older; swallowing would become more and more difficult for him. Finally, he would be able only to drink milk, to swallow but a spoonful. But that

---

1. According to Ms. Zenani, it might be considered questionable enough that the first generation of children was sired by the mother's brother, but the second one too? Still, in those days, she noted, no one raised this moral issue.

9

would be sufficient for him. So it went, until such a person could breathe no more.[2]

He would then be taken and put into a secret place. No hole was dug in those days; no one said that a "burial" had taken place.

The people would see that he was no longer breathing. He had grown old and was no longer able to get up. But his death was not caused by aches and pains; he just died gently. He became old; then, because of his age, he was unable to walk. And when his breath was no more, he was taken away and put in a hidden place, far from home.

That is the way things were.

In those days, many people were being born into this homestead. Death was uncommon at that time; a person's time would come to an end, nothing would afflict him while he was still young.

According to the ancient accounts, it had become clear that the children who were the offspring of that woman in that homestead should be provided with another clan name: they should not be called Tshawe. The first man was no longer there; only his offspring were living now—the first generation of men, together with the young men who made up the second generation. It was decided that all those who had been borne by that woman should have a name other than Tshawe.

What should they be called? The matter was discussed, and it was determined that they would be called the Wangu,[3] and the place where the Wangu reside should become known as the place of the Wangu, to distinguish it from the place of the Tshawe. They should now establish their own place, they should multiply their numbers and increase—as Wangu. Everything, it was decided, should be divided; the division of the cattle would symbolize this apportionment.

So it was that things were divided, and the Wangu established themselves in their own place. They produced their own offspring. It was said that women should be taken from the Tshawe royal residence, that they should become wives of the Wangu, so that the Wangu would have offspring. The exchange took place, the women of the royal residence of the Tshawe were married by the Wangu. They married, the Wangu married these Tshawe women, and they themselves gave birth to Tshawe. And so it went on.

In time, one of the Wangu—a man who wanted to return here to the

2. That is, death was gentle then.
3. In Perf. 624 (*Time:* 13 September 1967, in the early evening; *Place:* Outside, in a kraal in Nkanga, Gatyana District, the Transkei; *Audience:* Fifty men, women, and children), Mrs. Zenani created this exchange: "But the uncle insisted that this man could not rule, because he was a Wangu. He asked, 'What is a wangu?' He said, 'I say you are a Wangu! You don't belong to this homestead, because you're the child of an unmarried woman!' " See also the companion tale under Tale 6.

royal residence of the Tshawe—set out. When he had returned, they decided to settle him in yet another area, so that he could be a councillor in it. Because he was a councillor, he required a homestead. He was alone, he had no wife: a homestead was therefore built for him, then a young woman from the royal residence became his wife. This man's name was Ngwevu. As his village increased in size, it became known as the place of Ngwevu, again, to distinguish it from the place of the Tshawe. The Ngwevu thereby became an esteemed line from which the councillors of the Tshawe royal residence would come.

There was a general increase in population, and the question rose, "What shall we call all these people?" They became known as the Xhosa. All of the various groups, taken together, are Xhosa.

Time passed, and a child was fathered by that Ngwevu fellow. But this child did not resemble any of his own people; the child looked like no one but himself.

People said of this child, "Where did he get him from?"

"Did he get him from some place we know nothing of?"

"He certainly doesn't look like anyone here!"

It was said that the child was unique, "so exceptional that we just can't figure him out."

"This child is a presence!"

"A completely unfamiliar one!"

They said, "We don't understand where such a child has come from!"

As the child grew up, the people talked about him, but they did not address him directly. As frequently happens, things get discussed, people come together and talk about something; it is given a certain form, and opinion is thereby shaped.

At length, it was said, "This child is a man now. A home should be built for him over there, far away."

"This is a Mfengu."

"This is a Mfengu, he's not a Xhosa."

The name "Mfengu" meant that the boy resembled no one in this place.

Because he was a man, they circumcised him before he moved into his new homestead. He wanted to know who would go to that place with him; he wanted a companion. So a young woman was taken from among the Wangu and brought to him. She became his wife. The people increased in numbers over there too, but the headquarters of the Xhosa remained among the Xhosa.

The Ngwevu also increased greatly, the Wangu area also grew.

So it went on. A person who had many male children would get a wife from another area. He would not take his wife from his own area.[4] This

4. She is making a distinction here from the earlier incestuous relationships.

went on, and over a period of time the institution of polygamy developed—wives, wives who go in twos; men who have two wives, maybe three, sometimes just one.

Then, a certain woman of the royal residence gave birth for the first time; her child was named Mpondo. A homestead in another area was constructed for this Mpondo. It was determined that certain men should establish their own subordinate principalities, that a village bearing the name of So-and-so should be set up and should increase in population. The village would become known as So-and-so's village.

Mpondo also fathered children—a wife had been obtained for him from the Ngwevu region. Mpondo sired children, and they were called Mpondo. In time, as the Mpondo increased in their area, they made the claim that "This side is ours! All of us here are Mpondo people!" They, in turn, divided themselves into subsections, in the same way that they themselves had originated, dating from the Tshawe side that had begun the division, that being the early precedent for these divisions.

That exceptional person, Mfengu, the one who had settled over there and increased: his area came to be known as the place of the Mfengu. When that area was referred to, it was said, "At the place of the Mfengu people," because this child's progeny had multiplied. The Mfengu increased in their own way, and then it came about that they were no longer included in the polity of the Tshawe. The Mfengu were industrious, a strong people, but they had no part in the polity of the Tshawe; they increased, and established their own institutions. They too inaugurated the custom of polygamy and such traditions as the right-hand house and the subordinate houses.[5]

That is the way the fission began. The groups were gradually broken up, increasing in population all the while. So the land became populated. In time, each village came to know its origin, where it had come from. And customs began to diverge because of the divisions.

Now, about the establishment of custom. Two things brought custom into being: first, the luxury of having sufficient goods to be able to dream; and second, a reverence for and desire to propitiate the ancestors. A thought would come to a man. He would be pleased with the thought and would begin to carry out the implications of that thought: "This is the way it shall be done in this homestead." But it was not this way in the beginning. Custom is a human thing, a cultural creation; it is not in the nature of things.

5. If a man, a commoner, has two wives, the woman he marries first is called the great wife and her house, the great house. The woman he marries second is called the right-hand wife and her house, the right-hand house. The third wife is the *iqadi*, the supporting house. Such third houses may support either the great house or the right-hand house.

In some ways, custom is a matter of style; it is brought into being by the uniqueness of some person who likes to do a certain thing in a certain way in his own home. He desires to do that thing, and he wants people to come to his homestead because of what he has done. People begin to speak of this, saying, "It was nice at So-and-so's place."

Then, as time goes on, people comment upon the weakness of the person who has not done that thing, who does not observe the custom. He is compared unfavorably to the person who fulfills the custom without being put under any pressure, doing it because he wants to. Even a person who has nothing seeks to fulfill this custom, until it develops into a thing that has a hold on people's minds, until it becomes internalized, and succeeding generations are awakened into the tradition, realizing that "This thing is a custom," that in a certain homestead a certain custom is fulfilled. A name is given to the custom, and the significance of that custom is such that an offering will be made to a person. It is said that a beast is being slaughtered for him, but this person being slaughtered for is not present, he is dead. The beast is seized, people called together, and the thing performed—because it has been done that way in the first homestead, at the royal residence of the Tshawe.

It happened in time that a certain person dreamed of someone who was no longer there—and he had never seen him in person while he was yet alive.

He said, "I dreamed that there was an important man here. This man said that a certain beast should be slaughtered for him. He wants meat [a reinforcement of ritual]."

This was believed, it was really believed. They thought that what was dreamed by a person while he was asleep was indeed the truth. And the man who had dreamed that thing, in his own home, was dreaming of his grandfather, his ancestor, the father of his father.

He said, "No matter when I go to sleep, I dream the same thing. It really seems that he is actually here. But he doesn't eat the meat. I experienced pain, even though I was only dreaming that I was in pain. And I dreamed that it was said, 'To get well, you must slaughter this beast.'"

So the man did it. He called the other men together, telling them, "This thing that I am doing is something I dreamed, while I was asleep. I dreamed that an old man was speaking to me. I had a pain somewhere in my body. I was sick and in pain. Since I wanted to heal the afflicted part of my body, I said to myself, 'I'll do what he says.' Today I am making this offering to that man—my ancestor, my father's father."

When he had done that, the man got well. And others in the homestead who had aches were also healed.

This began to be called "custom," a custom that must be observed by anyone if he is to live well in his homestead. He must make an offering to a certain old person of his homestead, a person who is deceased.

This is how the customs of the Xhosa went, all things followed the pattern: it began with someone doing something that he liked, that he wanted to do. That thing that he did was then admired by others, and they started to do it too. So it developed. Other people began to do the same thing, imitating each other as far as that custom was concerned. Each wanted to do the thing that had been done by So-and-so.

This became known, in the land of the Xhosa, as "custom."

This went on, and ultimately another custom, the ritual of circumcision, was established.

In those days, people did not yet circumcise the youth. Then the king spoke: "A boy must be different from a man. When someone arrives at the stage of manhood, that stage should be marked, commemorated. A distinction must be made between boyhood and manhood."

People asked, "How can this be done?"

In the times before circumcision, when a person became mature, a wife would be procured for him, and then he would have the status of a man. Marriage was the mark of manhood, not circumcision. There was nothing called "circumcision" in the olden times.

Then it was said, "Something [the foreskin of the penis] should be removed, so that there is bleeding first, so that this person is separate from other people and is regarded differently, so that it becomes known formally that he is a man."[6]

The ceremony began at the royal residence. When the ritual of circumcision was adopted, one section—the Mpondo—did not accept it. They wanted no part of it, and the Mpondo were already a large group, having increased greatly. They did not adopt this ritual; they refused to accept it. To this day, they have not accepted the ritual of circumcision. No Mpondo youth goes through the circumcision ceremony; no one has a part of him cut off.

Things went on, and the various sections had been established: the Mfengu were by themselves, the Bhaca by themselves, the Xhosa by themselves, the Mpondo by themselves, the Bomvana by themselves. But from the point of view of origins, they all came from the same source. One house was divided, one person cut up—divided into sections, apportioned in the beginning. In this way, the original human multiplied. The sections divided and increased, and so peoples' customs began to diverge.

Those who were Sotho were called "Sotho," but the origin was identi-

6. She seems to be implying a comparison here with *intonjane*, the female puberty rite. The girl is ready for purification when she first menstruates, and the people seem to be seeking a like sign with men. As the girl undergoes purification when she first bleeds, the boy becomes a man when *he* bleeds in the same area, in the sexual zone, both boy and girl bleeding before passing on into manhood and womanhood. The woman seems to be the model here.

cal. It is Tshawe. He continues to have that breadth, even today. Through-out the Transkei, it is said, "The bull is Tshawe!" In all the land, the bull is Tshawe. But even though that is so, all those places and all those peoples have now increased, and they have their own bulls. Still, they are united, all of them, in the sense that they are less than Tshawe.

That is how it was in the beginning. A way had to be found whereby these people were to become the various separate people they are today. They did not begin by being diverse. They came from one place, like the offspring of a puff adder. Each one built homesteads for himself out there, each received a name other than Tshawe.

Part One: Birth

INTRODUCTION

MASITHATHU ZENANI ON STORYTELLING

Storytelling, said Masithathu Zenani, is a sensory union of image and idea, a process of recreating the past in terms of the present; the storyteller uses realistic images to limn the present, and fantasy images to evoke and embody the essence of the past. These latter, the ancient, fantastic images, are the culture's heritage and the storyteller's bounty: they contain the emotional history of the people. With the culture's most deeply felt, enduring fears and hopes compressed within them, they have the capacity to elicit strong emotional responses from members of audiences: it is the task of the storyteller, Mrs. Zenani contended, to forge the fantasy images into masks of the realistic images of the present. These fantastic images establish and sustain inner cores; they are placed into a context of contemporary and therefore unstable images, enabling the performer to join present and past, to visualize the present within a context of and therefore in terms of the past. Flowing through this potent emotional grid is a collection of ideas that have the illusion of antiquity and ancestral sanction, a grand storyteller's design and illusion made possible by the nature of images and the effect of patterns.

Fusion of the two kinds of imagery is accomplished by means of the crucial contextualizing device, performance, particularly by the patterning of image, body, and emotion. Story occurs within the mesmerizing, unreal realm of performance, a world unto itself—whole, with its own set of laws. Patterning comprises the repetition of fantasy images and their satellite contemporary images. It involves the aesthetics of performance: the body of the performer, the music of her voice, the complex relationship between her and her audience.

The storyteller breaks through the tyranny of the linear movement of the story to move the audience to deeper and more complex experiences. This is done to a great extent by juxtaposing unlike images, then revealing, to the delight, instruction, and development of the members of the audience, the connections between them that render them homogeneous. In this way, the past and the present are blended: ideas are thereby generated, forming an audience's conception of the present. Performance gives the images their context, and it assures the audience a ritual experience that bridges past and present and shapes contemporary life.

Nongenile Masithathu Zenani was always at pains to emphasize that the storytelling tradition is never simply a spoken art; it is an enactment, an event, a ritual, a performance. The patterning of imagery is the most visible artistic activity, involving the blending of the contemporary world and the fanciful fabrication of the tradition; the combining of the images and their transformation into dramatic ritual is the result of metaphor, a poetic recreation of the world.

Oral stories frequently focus on moments of crisis in an individual's life, when a person is undergoing a change of some kind—moving, for example, into adulthood, marriage, death. The stories, engaging as they do the emotions of the members of the audience, maneuver us to the essence of the experience and prepare us to undergo it, or act as mementos of the ordeal. Not only do the tales refer to cultural experiences and transport an audience to the heart of a society, they are imaged ways of reliving those events.[1]

1. The tale, or, in Xhosa society, the *intsomi,* has to do with change on an individual level. In mythic tales, change transpires on a cosmological plane, touching all living things. In epic tales, transformation occurs on a cultural scale, and involves a hero who, bestriding the contemporary world and the envisioned society, moves people from the one state to the next.

COMMENTARIES

THE START IS A MAN, AND A MAN TAKES A WIFE

Performance Note

Time: 2 August 1967, in the morning. *Place:* In the home of Mrs. Zenani, in Nkanga, Gatyana District, the Transkei. *Audience:* Members of Mrs. Zenani's family—her husband, her daughter, a granddaughter. (NS-10.)

The start is a man, and a man takes a wife. When he has a wife, he fathers children. This is the way an African raises children . . .

When a wife becomes pregnant, during the sixth month of her pregnancy she begins to take a purifying medicine. This medicine is usually placed in a gourd-vessel, and it remains there. Long ago, when there were no boxes or chests, it would be put into such a vessel, then covered with a lid woven of grass. Others are cautioned not to look into that vessel into which the medicine has been placed while still in the form of roots. The medicine grows inside that container and develops leaves. If that happens, it is a sign to a Xhosa person that a woman has a live pregnancy. If the fetus is dead, then those roots will indicate this—they will not unfold, the roots will tend to rot. The householder then becomes very sad, realizing that nothing will come of his wife's pregnancy. If the medicine does develop leaves, they will cover the vessel. The husband will cut the leaves and put them just beside the container. The roots will grow again, right up to the ninth month of pregnancy. One woman might deliver in the tenth month, another in the eleventh, yet another in the ninth. When the woman has delivered, that vessel from which she has been drinking during her pregnancy will be taken, and a spoonful of the medicine will be given to the infant she has borne.

When the woman has labor pains, other women are called to be midwives, and then she will deliver her child. Attached to the child's navel is the umbilical cord, which hangs from the stomach after the birth of the child. A stalk of grass is taken, and that cord is then severed and shortened. Then the umbilical cord is buried beneath the very place where the woman has delivered her child. When that is done, water is taken and warmed in the hearth. Then the baby is washed over the spot where the cord has been buried. When the child has been washed, it is put down and covered in its mother's garments. Then more water is added, and that nursing mother washes herself over the place where the umbilical cord is buried. Soil is dug up from the hearth. The stalk of grass with which the umbilical cord has been severed is taken and used to stir the water. It is

21

smeared on the umbilical cord, so that the navel and the cord are separated. The breasts of the nursing mother are then drained onto bark that has been taken from a mimosa tree. When that has been done, the soil is taken and kneaded into that bark. Cooked porridge is then taken; it is to be eaten by the young mother. A portion of the porridge is mixed, and smeared on the child's umbilical cord. After all that, the child can be suckled on its mother's breasts.

WHY DID THE CHILD NOT DRINK MILK FROM ITS MOTHER?

Performance Note

Time: 2 August 1967, in the morning. *Place:* In the home of Mrs. Zenani in Nkanga, Gatyana District, the Transkei. *Audience:* Members of Mrs. Zenani's family—her husband, her daughter, a granddaughter. (NS-10.)

It happened that a certain newly born child did not grasp its mother's breasts and suckle, yet when it was taken by another woman among the midwives the child did take hold of the breast.

What could be wrong? Why did the child not drink milk from its mother, yet it drank from another woman?

This matter was reported to the men: "Over there in that house, the baby does not drink from its mother." The men were alone in another house; they had not yet entered the house in which the nursing mother was staying.

The men then came and asked, "Why is it, Woman, that the child refuses to suckle from you? Yet it suckles from other people."

The woman spoke: the reason the child did not suckle from her breast was because the woman did a thing that is unacceptable in the land of the Xhosa. When she married, she had been sleeping with her father—and that is incest, a taboo. The evidence of this incest was the child's refusal to suckle.

The nursing mother said, "Before I understood what was wrong and what was right, I had already been sleeping with my father. But it was never noticed by anyone, we were very secretive about it."

"Put her to your breast, Woman!"

"That is incest!"

So the men said.

She took the child then and brought it to her breast. Then the child did begin to suckle.

When the child had suckled at its mother's breast, it was reported to her home: "She has confessed to having incestuous relations with her father."

A way to resolve the problem was sought, a way to absolve this act of incest. According to Xhosa tradition, such actions can be purified by the slaughter of "the beast of incest." Her father, over there at her home of birth, had to be brought here to his daughter's home of marriage, brought here to her in-laws, to the assembly of the men of the village. Then that animal was slaughtered—not in the kraal, but outside, below the homestead. The animal was slaughtered below the homestead, a distance from the home. A large fire was kindled there. The nursing mother was naked, her father was also naked; no respect was shown, no deferential language used. The father and his daughter sat facing each other without covering their genitals.

A long strip of meat from that animal was prepared; it was roasted. When it had been roasted, one end was put into the mouth of either the father or the daughter on one side of the fire, and the other end was put into the mouth of the other one on the opposite side of the fire. Then they began to chew the strip of meat until it snapped; they tugged and pulled each other by means of the meat. When that had been done, it was said that the filthy thing that they had done was being purified, it was being exorcised.

It was said, "It has been successful. May a thing like this never happen again."

When the ritual with the piece of meat was at an end, the father and daughter got their garments and covered themselves. Then the rest of the meat was consumed, all of it was eaten out there. None of it went into the house.

THE RECOGNITION OF THE CHILD

Performance Note

Time: 2 August 1967, in the morning. *Place:* In the home of Mrs. Zenani, in Nkanga, Gatyana District, the Transkei. *Audience:* Members of Mrs. Zenani's family—her husband, her daughter, a granddaughter. (NS-10.)

Time passes, the baby suckles at its mother's breast, and it grows up. The navel slowly heals; it is continuously anointed, the remnant of the umbilical cord being smeared with that paste. Then this remnant just falls off, and the child's navel heals. It is then said that the nursing mother should end her confinement and mingle with the rest of the people.

It is said, "Bring the cow dung, Child."

A child brings wet cow dung, and the nursing mother daubs the walls

Exchanging news

and floor of that house. She girds her clothes, then daubs the house. When that is finished, she takes a bucket and goes to the river.

In those days, they still dipped water with clay pots, a traditional Xhosa practice. Such pots were made of clay, molded into vessels with which water was dipped.

When the nursing mother gets to the river, she smears mud over the child's heart, she smears mud over its feet. Then she dips water and goes home. When she gets home, she must cook a meal adequate for all the members of the family. Then they eat.

It is said, "The child's body should be anointed with cow dung."

After the child has grown, about one or two months later, the nursing mother again anoints the child. The men of the village are called together for this purpose. When the men arrive, a goat is taken. The beast is put into the kraal, and the nursing mother is told to apply red ochre to her body and white ochre to her face. She is also told to cover the body of her child with white ochre.[1]

Then the men tell the nursing mother, "Take the baby outside."

The baby is taken by a woman of the homestead who happens to be present. The nursing mother remains seated, and her child is taken outside, carried by this woman. The woman stands in front of the house.

1. Ochre is a clay that is used for ritual purposes. The clay is worked into an ointment or a powder, and parts of the body are anointed with it.

A spokesman among the men over there at the kraal stands up then and says, "Here it is! We recognize today that this child is a boy!"

Or, if the baby is a girl: "We recognize the girl today! We anoint her, that she may be healthy and live well in this home!"

The nursing mother approaches then, and it is said, "Be appeased!"

That is the way this new status is acclaimed. The nursing mother approaches, and the man of the house is carrying a spear with which the ritual beasts of the homestead are pierced. Now the man will stab that goat. When the goat bellows, it is said, "Be appeased!" Then the goat's throat is cut, and it dies.

The meat of the goat's foreleg is taken, and someone orders that a fire be kindled in the nursing mother's home. The fire is built, the meat is placed on a mimosa branch, a mimosa that has been cut down and put in the kraal. After the goat's carcass has been flayed, it is placed on the branches of this tree. Now a small branch of that mimosa tree is taken, along with the meat of the goat's foreleg. A man brings this meat into the house, then cuts a piece from the shoulder and prepares it, cutting it properly. He roasts it in the hearth. He puts it before the nursing mother and cuts it up with a knife.

He says, "Eat this, Nursing mother."

The nursing mother takes the meat and puts it into her mouth; she smears the meat on the baby's mouth. Then the nursing mother herself eats it, she eats that first piece of meat.

When she finishes, it is said, "She has done it."

Then the men quickly cook the goat meat; they also cook the liver, and so on, and the men eat it. The viscera are brought into the house, along with the tripe and the duodenum. These are cut up by the women.

It is said, "This meat will be cooked tomorrow."

So that meat is cooked. When the men's liver is ready, they ask if the women's meat is finished yet. The women eat their meat, even if it is still raw because it is necessary that all the meat be taken from the fire at the same time.

Time passes for the members of this household.

The next day, they go to cook the carcass of the goat. It is taken out just as it has been left in the house, and it is cut up by the men. The meat of the women is left in the house, where the women cut it up.

Those meats are quite distinct. There is the meat of the breast—that is the men's portion. There is the meat of the leg—that is the men's portion. There is the meat of the neck—that is the men's portion. The pieces of meat are designated in that way. A whole side goes to the women; a whole side, together with the breast and the head and hooves, goes to the men. The foreleg of one side of the beast is special; it is a meat that will be cooked the next day, when the bones have been burned. The bones of this carcass are not thrown away.

When the meat of the men has been cooked, if the women's meat is not yet ready, the men say, "Please go over there, Young man!"

A young man goes over and says, "I have been told, Mothers, to come and see if your meat is cooked yet. It is time."

"It is done."

That meat, the foreleg from which that first meat eaten earlier by the nursing mother had been cut, belongs to the nursing mother. The rest of the meat belongs to the women. The foreleg is taken from the fire for the young mother. Then the women take the meat off the fire for the men. That meat is eaten, and they make certain that no bone is carried off by a dog. All of the bones are carefully preserved; they are placed over there on the goat's skin. That includes the bones from the meat of the men as well as those from the meat of the women. Then they all disperse.

The next day, the people rise early and begin an important part of these activities. The foreleg belonging to the nursing mother and the head of the animal are cooked. The head is removed from the fire and assigned to the men. The men supply the boys with portions of meat. It is the women who supply the girls with meat.

When the eating of the meat is finished, the bones are taken, together with the branches of the mimosa tree, and all that is burned in the kraal.

TALES

Tale 1

THE FROG AND THE CHILD WITHOUT LIMBS

Masithathu Zenani's Analysis: The image is the basic unit of storytelling. Typically, the images, real and fantastic, are visualized or sensed actions, concrete and vivid, that the performer seeks to evoke in the imaginations of the members of the audience.

Images are ordered in linear ways, as the storyteller moves her characters from conflict to resolution; they are also organized in cyclical forms, patterns. These patterns or models are the central theme-generating units of the story. The simplest form of storytelling involves the repetition of a single model at the heart of which is a memorable fantastic image. In such stories, one pattern is established, then repeated. In a more complex pattern, the storyteller creates a model, then repeats it. The repetition of the model is slightly changed, and the point of the story is to be discovered in the alterations. In other stories, a variety of patterns will interact with each other to produce meaning. As stories become more involved, the images themselves are not repeated in any obvious way, so that it is not always easy to discern the patterning. In such cases, the functions of the characters, not the characters themselves, reveal the similarities produced by patterns.

"The Frog and the Child Without Limbs"[1] is a tale with a single such pattern: it has to do with the relationship between Nginingini and her brother, the frog, and includes the restoration and removal of the girl's limbs by the frog. When she has her limbs, she does the work of a girl in the household, and so fulfills her social function.

It is the story of the forming of the child. As that child grows into an adult, the performer plots the way; each major step, each significant transformation, in a human life is being fully dramatized in story form, providing a cultural context for the child's biological movement toward adulthood and beyond. The storyteller does not, however, seek to duplicate these transitions in realistic detail; rather, she reorders them, working them into a series of images that she has inherited from the past. The mixture, a judicious selection of relevant contemporary images placed within an imaginative context inherited from the past, creates the story. The effect is to provide a regular, culturally sanctioned commentary on and guide for the young person's movement from birth to puberty to adulthood and old age.

Storytellers frequently use the graphic language of the storytelling tradi-

---

1. The three tales in this section are puberty rite of passage stories as much as they are stories of birth. They are placed in this part of the collection because birth and its immediate aftermath are developed at some considerable length.

27

tion to suggest an incomplete person.[2] Nginingini is without arms and legs. The storyteller thereby suggests an unfinished being: the child is not yet fully grown. She achieves her status as a human with the assistance of a frog, a creature of nature. Nginingini, unlike other members of her household, is in harmony with nature. Stories having to do with the rites of passage have to do with cultural harmony, one of the preoccupations of the storytelling tradition. Harmonious relations with nature is another of the significant themes of the African oral tradition, and sometimes, as in this tale, the two ideas are blended. Storytellers, emphasizing the harmony with nature theme, will sometimes show that adults have lost that primal relationship with nature. Children have it, but the movement from childhood to adulthood often means the loss of an innocence that brings a human into close linkage with nature. Nginingini's ties with the frog—not just a remote creature of nature, but her brother—make it possible for her to move beyond childhood and into a new relationship with culture and with nature.

Performance Note

Time: 15 September 1967, in the morning. *Place:* Along a path in Nkanga, Gatyana District, the Transkei. *Audience:* Five women, two men, fifteen children. (Perf. 651.)

A woman was pregnant, she gave birth in her homestead. She bore two unusual children: one child had no legs, she had no arms—there was only a head and a stomach. The other child was a frog, it had the legs of a frog.

The women who were attending the mother said, "This thing is really ugly!"

"It's a frog!"

"Imagine! A human bearing a frog!"

"This frog must be taken outside and buried in the ashes."

The other child was not discarded like that, because, even though she had no legs, even though she had no arms, she was still a human.

"We can't bear to kill her."

"She'll be a burden, but that's the way it'll have to be."

The frog was taken and put into the ashes. A hole was dug, and the frog was covered up.

The mother remained with the other child, and finally her confinement ended.

When her age-mates began to crawl, this child did not crawl as she should have.

Her age-mates began to stand, but she did not stand as she should have.

2. In another story in this collection (Tale 3, "A Father Cuts Off His Daughter's Arms"), for example, a girl has no arms.

Her age-mates began to walk, she did not walk as she should have. She merely remained the thing that she was.

Her age-mates began to work, she did not work as she should have.

Even though she had become older in years, she was a girl who could do nothing. She did not go beyond the nursing stage, because she could not walk; she could not manage anything.

She had no hands, she had no feet.

Long years passed: the girls who were her age-mates were married, they were women now. But she was a thing who was just there: she was fed, she reclined all the time in her characteristic way.

She was just that round thing.

One day, after some time had gone by, the mothers of these children went out to cultivate in the fields. Her mother closed the door of the house; she closed it to make certain that the fowls would not come in because there was no one to drive them out when they entered. This child, after all, could not walk.

So the child stayed there, she remained in that condition. No other person was around.

Suddenly, something was heard at the door, saying to this child, "Nginingini! Nginingini!" That was her name.

She replied, "Hniii?"

"I'm coming in," it said.

She said, "Come in."

The thing entered—it was a frog!

When it had entered, it said, "Nginingini!"

She said, "Hnnii?"

"Why aren't you walking?"

She said, "I can't walk."

"But why aren't you able to walk? Your age-mates are already married. And you're now so old."

"I have no legs."

"Where are your legs?"

"I have none. I've never had them."

"What's the matter with you? Why don't you sweep the house? It's full of dirt—and you're so old."

"I have no arms."

"Where are your arms?"

"I've never had them."

"Really! Were you an only child?"

"I was not an only child."

"Whom were you born with?"

"I was born with a frog."

"And where's that frog?"

"It was taken and buried in the ashes. They said that it was a bad thing, a fearful thing."

"They said it was a bad thing, a fearful thing?"

"Yes."

"How was it disposed of?"

"They dug a hole for it and killed it."

"It died?"

"Yes."

"Why don't you say that? How can you be so detached from it? It's your brother, after all. Your brother died!"

"Well, I never saw it."

"You never saw it?"

"That's right."

"Did you learn about this frog from other people?"

"Yes."

"From whom did you hear that you were born with a frog?"

"I heard about it when my mothers spoke of it. They said two of us were born, and one was a frog. It was said that the frog must be buried."

"Well, I'm that frog, the one you were born with. I'm the one who was taken to be buried in the ashes because, they said, I was subhuman. Yet I'm better off than you. You can't walk, you can't even feed yourself. But I can walk. Look!" Then the frog leapt into the air, and landed. It leapt, and landed. "Do you see? I can walk!" So the frog said, and it leapt over her, it leapt over her. "Can you see that I can walk? And you, what are you? What was the point of throwing me away for your sake? You, you're a thing still wearing diapers, yet you're old. But you're called a person, a human. Not so! I'm the human.

"Still, I must do something for you because I like you; we were born together. It's not really your fault. You're not the one who put me in ashes, in that hole. It's your mothers. And I don't enjoy being parted from my sister.

"Nginingini, let your arms appear."

Her arms appeared. Suddenly, she had her own arms!

"Nginingini, let your legs appear."

And her legs appeared!

Nginingini stood up. She laughed, she ran, she did everything. She went outside, she ran. She went to the cattle kraal, she ran. Then she came back to the house.

She said, "Oh, Child of my mother, you've helped me!" She clapped her hands.

Then she took a broom and swept the house. She went to the dishes; she took water and washed those dishes. She took corn and put it into a pot; she kindled a fire and roasted the corn. When the corn had been roasted, she dipped it out and ground it.

She said, "What do you eat, Child of my mother?"

The frog said, "I have no teeth, so I can't eat roasted maize. Just make some gruel for me."

"I'll make it for you, I'll make it for you, Child of my mother!" So saying, Nginingini took the corn and crushed it on a grinding stone. She crushed the corn. She moistened it with hot water. Then she took the dough and covered it. She ground it deftly. When it was getting the way she wanted it to be, she ground it until it was fine, she ground it until it was fine. She cooked the porridge, then added some salt. She took it outside to cool it.

Nginingini was moving about excitedly—quickly moving about, very pleased with her ability to walk, prizing her new capacity to take anything with her hands, repeatedly staring at her feet and hands, admiring them.

She put the food in front of the frog and said, "Eat now, Child of my mother."

The frog ate; it ate the thin porridge and was satisfied.

It said, "Thank you, you've been good to me. I'll help you on another day. I'll do this again, Nginingini, but now I must go because the people are returning from the fields. I don't want to be here when they arrive. And you, you mustn't tell anyone that I was here. They'll ask you a lot of things; they'll ask who swept the house. Just say that you're the one who did it, that you rolled around and did this. They'll ask who did the cooking. Just say that you're the one who did it, that you rolled about and did it. But don't mention me. If you say anything about me, you'll never have arms again."

"No, I won't mention you."

"I'm going now. I'll take these arms, so that when the people get here, you'll be the thing that you were before."

She said, "All right."

The frog said, "Go to your sleeping-place. Wrap yourself in your blankets because when I've taken your limbs, you won't be able to go over there and get the blankets."

Nginingini got up then, and she sat in her place. She put her blankets on, and she lay there.

The frog said, "Nginingini, let your arms disappear."

Her arms disappeared.

"Nginingini, let your legs disappear."

Her legs disappeared.

She was that round thing again.

The frog departed. It went and stayed in the ashes.

The mothers came home from the fields. While Nginingini's mother was still outside, she was saying, "Who is it, Friends? Who swept the yard?

Who removed all the dirty things here at home? Who is it, Friends? Have the people of my home come to visit?"

She entered the house. When she went in, "Oh! The house has been swept! A pot is on the hearth!" She uncovered the pot. "Corn has been cooked!" The mother said, "Nginingini!"

"Hnn?"

"Who swept here?"

"I did."

"How?"

"Well, I just rolled around."

"But how?"

"I rolled around, I did it that way."

"But how did you do it?"

"I gripped the broom with my mouth."

"No, no, no! Tell me what happened!"

"Leave me alone! I know no more."

"Who cooked?"

"I did."

"How did you do it?"

"I just rolled around."

"No, please tell me, my child! Why aren't you telling me the truth?"

"I say that I did it!"

"Who washed the dishes?"

"I did."

"How did you wash them?"

"I just rolled around."

"No! Tell me! Tell me!"

"I have nothing else to say."

Her mother said no more. But these things made her anxious because she did not know who had come here to her house and swept. She went to sleep, and the next day she journeyed again to the fields. Before she left, she prepared food and fed this child.

She fed her, then said, "Are you satisfied?"

"I am satisfied."

She put the food away. Because there was no one to sweep the house, the mother did so; then she went to the fields.

Some time after the mother had departed, a voice was heard at the door: "Nginingini!"

"Hnnn?"

"Whom are you with?"

"I'm alone."

"Your mother was pressing you so hard. Did you tell her about me? I heard her here as she spoke. I heard her scolding you, saying, 'No, tell me!' "

"I didn't tell her."

"You did right. Don't tell her anything."

"All right."

"Child of my mother, I like you. I want you to cook for me now; make me some gruel. I slept well last night because I was full. Nginingini, let your arms appear."

Her arms appeared.

"Nginingini, let your legs appear."

Her legs appeared.

Nginingini got up and took some corn. She crushed it on a grinding stone, then moistened it with hot water. She set it aside. When the dough was as she wanted it, when it was soft, she took it and ground it. She ground it until it was fine. She ground it until it was fine. She cooked the dough into a thin gruel and sprinkled it with salt. She cooked it and gave it to the frog. It ate the gruel; it ate and was satisfied.

Nginingini said, "I'll go to the river. When my mother returns today, there'll be water here."

She took a bucket—she was very pleased with her legs, she admired her arms, she took pleasure in walking. She went to the river; she arrived and dipped water. She returned with the bucket and put it down. She cooked, she swept. When she had finished sweeping, she took fresh cow dung and coated the floor of the house. Then she sat down.

Nginingini and the frog spent some time together, conversing.

She said, "Child of my mother, don't return to that place. Let's stay together. I don't want to part with you."

"No, that won't do at all, Nginingini. When the people return, they'll say, 'Here it is! Here it is, here's a frog!' and they'll beat me. Remember, they tried to kill me in the past! I don't like them. But I like you. You're not to blame for what happened to me."

"Well, I don't want you to go," Nginingini said to the frog. "When you're not here, my heart is pained."

The frog said, "Don't let your heart be pained. Just remain here. It's all right for me to stay in that place. I shall watch for them, and when they're gone, I'll come. Then you can cook for me, and I'll eat. I can see them when they leave here. They don't see me because they care nothing about me. Well, it's not important. But Nginingini, it seems that they're returning now. I must leave. I'll take back your arms."

"All right."

The frog said, "Nginingini, let your arms disappear."

The arms disappeared.

"Nginingini, let your legs disappear."

The legs disappeared.

The frog departed, it went to its place. When it got there, it watched the people as they returned.

Nginingini's mother started speaking while she was still outside. She said, "No no no! Really, have you ever seen anything like this? Well, the child must tell me what is doing these things here at home! What is it, Nginingini, my child? Why do you continue to refuse to tell me what it is that does these things? This is so beautiful! Why do you hide it?"

"I'm telling you, Mama, I'm the one!"

"How can it be you?"

"I told you. I roll down."

"No, that's impossible! You couldn't possibly do these things with your mouth. Just tell me who dipped the water with this bucket."

"I did the dipping."

"But how did you dip it, Nginingini?"

"I rolled down."

"Who carried the bucket?"

"I kept nudging it along."

"Why didn't it fall down when you nudged it?"

"It didn't fall down. God loves me, so it didn't fall down. It just didn't fall!"

"Please do it while I'm here. Just nudge it while I'm watching."

"No, I shall not be forced to do it. I'll go dip water when you're not here, but I shall not be compelled to do it. I wasn't forced to do it when I dipped this water."

"Please do it so that I can see it. I want to see how you do it."

"No, I won't do it!"

The woman left the child alone.

She said, "Something's going on here. I don't know what it is, but someone is coming here and doing these things for you. It has to be someone! You won't tell me, but you ought to tell me. I wish to thank the person who does such nice things for me in my absence."

"There's no one else, Mama. I'm the one."

"I'll just leave you alone for now." She left her there.

At night, while they were asleep, her mother awoke.

She said, "Nginingini!"

"Hnnnn?"

"Are you awake?"

"Yes."

"My child, we're alone now, just the two of us. Please tell me about this matter."

"What matter should I tell you about, Mama?"

"Tell me who comes here when I'm away from home. Who does these nice things, my child? Tell me."

"No, Mama, please leave me alone! Please leave me alone, I'll tell you. Just leave me alone, I'll tell you some time."

"Where does this person come from, my child, this one who comes here all the time?"

"No, Mama, please leave me alone! I'll tell you, but don't rush me. I'll tell you, but I'm not going to tell you now, while you're pressing me."

Her mother left her alone. In the morning, she went to the fields. She departed that day not having done the things she usually did before leaving. She did not even feed Nginingini as she customarily did. She just left her; she went to the fields.

The child remained behind.

The frog was watching the mother as she went; then it came out and went to the house.

It said, "Nginingini!"

She said, "Hnnn?"

"You almost told about me, didn't you?"

"No, I didn't tell her about you!"

"Well, you almost told about me during the night. I heard you when you said to your mother, 'No, stop! I'll tell you some other time!' Why did you say that? Why did you say you would tell her?"

"I just wanted her to leave me alone. She was harassing me. My mother continually talks about this, and I wanted her to stop. I won't tell her, I won't, Child of my father!"

"If you do tell her, you'll spoil things for yourself. You'll never again have arms and legs. But now I'm hungry, Child of my mother. I've just spoken harshly to you, but I'm hungry. Nginingini, let your arms appear."

The arms appeared.

"Nginingini, let your legs appear."

The legs appeared.

Nginingini took some corn and crushed it on a grinding stone. She moistened it with hot water; then she ground it, she ground it until it was fine. She cooked the thin gruel and sprinkled salt on it. She cooled it and gave it to the frog. The frog ate and was satisfied.

Time passed for them; they were happy.

Nginingini said, "Child of my mother, I want to go and gather some firewood now. When my mother returns, the firewood will be here for her. She usually returns from the fields tired, yet she must go and find firewood. This time she'll be spared that."

"Well, all right. If you don't tell her, it'll be all right."

Nginingini traveled then; she gathered the wood. She gathered firewood; then she returned with it and put it in a pile. When she had done that, she said, "I want the old woman to be able to rest a little." She sat, and she and the frog talked, they talked. She did not want him to leave.

"I'm going. They'll return shortly."

"It's not going to be easy because my mother will be insistent again. She'll ask me things, and I'll feel bad about it. Why don't you just stay, so that when she arrives, you'll be here? I can say that you helped me."

"No, I don't want to do that. I don't want to be here when they arrive. They deliberately buried me! I don't want to be here when they come. Just let your mother live with you in your usual condition."

"All right."

"Nginingini, let your arms disappear."

Her arms disappeared.

"Nginingini, let your legs disappear."

And her legs disappeared.

The frog departed, it went to its place. It was sitting there when the mother arrived.

She said, "I come home today and there is firewood in the woodpile! What is this child hiding here? This is really a wonder! Well, I'm going to gather the men together. I'll gather the men, and the child will be under pressure to tell what has been going on. What she is doing to me is wrong!"

The mother entered. "Nginingini!"

"Hnn?"

"Where did this firewood come from?"

"I gathered it."

"Where did you gather it?"

"In the forest."

"How did you gather it?"

"I rolled."

"You rolled? How?"

"I rolled down."

"You rolled down. Then what?"

"I carried the wood."

"How did you break it up?"

"I broke it with my mouth."

"How did you fasten it?"

"I fastened it with my mouth."

"How did you carry it?"

"I nudged it along."

"What did you nudge it with?"

"With my head."

"How did you move the wood?"

"I rolled on my stomach."

"That's impossible! It's impossible! You're going to tell me today what has been going on here. This is the day! You must tell me!" she said.

"I'll tell you nothing. You might as well kill me!"

"I'm going to call the men."

Her mother departed. She went to summon the men to a nearby homestead.

She said, "Something strange has been going on: whenever I go away from home, much hard work is done here. It seems to be done by this child, but she can't walk. When I ask her what happened, she says that she has done all these things. And she'll tell me nothing more. But it's clear to me that she could not possibly do these things. Just look for yourselves. A girl like this—could she possibly do this work? I even wake the child up at night and threaten her, but she won't tell me. I've just finished asking her again; she refuses to say anything."

These men said to the girl, "Nginingini, please restore your mother to health. Tell her what she wants to know."

"What is it, Child, that you won't tell your mother?"

"Whoever it is who is so helpful—your mother loves him! Why do you hide the truth from your mother?"

"I've told her, I roll around myself and do these things. No one else does them—they're done by me! But my mother won't let me alone. She keeps insisting that I must tell her. There is nothing I can tell her. I'm the one who does these things. I just rolled down and did them."

A man said, "But is such a thing possible?"

"Would you do some of those things while we're here?"

"Just show us briefly how you do these things."

"I don't want to show you. I'll not be forced to do it! It just doesn't happen when I'm forced. In order for it to happen, I must do it on my own."

"Well, please tell us, Child. All these things that you do—you just roll down? When you're coating the floor, you roll around? And when you grind, you roll?"

"That is right."

"But how do you grasp the grinding stone?"

"I nudge it with my head."

"And how does the stone return toward the head?"

"Well, I roll over and approach it from the other side, then I nudge it."

"Just do it, Nginingini. Just do one of those things now, while we're here."

"Just show us how you do it—even if it's just sweeping."

"Just show us—even if it's just taking a dish."

"I won't show anything. I've told you, I do these things when I'm not being compelled to do them. When I'm forced, I don't know how! I want to do them on my own, without being forced by anyone."

"Do you mean that you would rather die than speak?"

"Your mother has called us because she's afraid of what you're refusing to tell her."

"She doesn't know how this thing will end."

"Kill me if you want to kill me. I can only speak what I know. I've told you that I roll down and do these things. I'll say nothing more!"

A man jumped on her. He leapt on her, frightening her, choking her. He seized her by the throat. She struggled vainly. It was clear to the men that she would rather die than speak.

The man left her, saying, "Nginingini, do you mean that you will not talk about this matter?"

She said, "I have said that I won't say anything. I've already said what I'm going to say! I've said that I roll down. That's all."

She was left alone then. They departed with her mother. Nginingini was left behind.

The men said to that woman, "Now, regarding these things that your child is doing, we're going to set a trap. Don't question her anymore, leave her alone now."

"We men must be given a chance to look into this thing."

"You go on with things as usual, but we'll be lying in wait."

"All right then."

The next day, the woman departed, heading for the fields. Again, she did not prepare anything for Nginingini; she just left her behind without having fed her.

When she departed, the frog arrived.

It said, "Nginingini!"

She said, "Hnnn?"

It said, "It's difficult for you!"

"Hnnn?"

"The men of the village were called together because of you. They even choked you, Child of my mother, though you had done nothing wrong. I was concerned when I heard you being choked; my heart ached because of what these men were doing to you. Still, you'll have to endure such treatment here; it's all in vain that they do that to you.

"But now I'm hungry, Child of my mother. Really I am!"

The other said, "Yes, it's time, it's about time for you to be hungry."

The frog said, "Nginingini, let your arms appear."

Her arms appeared.

"Nginingini, let your legs appear."

Her legs appeared.

Nginingini got up.

But over there were the men. They were below the homestead, hidden behind the kraal. They overheard Nginingini conversing with the frog; they heard everything.

The men approached stealthily, walking slowly, slowly, walking sideways.

The frog said, "I'll never part from you. I don't want these women who tried to kill me, but I love you, Nginingini. I would die for you because I love you—we were born on the same day. You knew nothing about what they did to me, you had no part in that."

Nginingini ground the thin porridge. She cooled it, having sprinkled it with salt.

The frog ate.

The men closed in; the frog was now sated. They shut the door to the house; the frog leapt up quickly. When it jumped, one fellow seized it, for it had jumped onto his garment. He seized the frog.

He said, "Nginingini, have you been staying here with this frog?"

"Yes! Please don't kill that child of my mother! I have arms as I do because of him! I have legs as I do because of him!"

"Is it this frog that you've been hiding?"

"Yes, this frog, this is the one I have been hiding! I'm hiding it, but it has nothing to do with you!"

"Why do you hide the frog?"

"Where has this frog come from?"

She said, "I was born with this frog. My mother gave birth to both of us. This is the one that was taken and put in the ashes."

"Oh!"

The men did not release the frog. They asked it, "What is your relationship to Nginingini?"

"She is my sister. We were born on the same day. I was put into the ashes by the women; I was destroyed by them. They said that I was a disgrace because I was not a human. It did not matter to them that this one had no arms. She had to be protected because she was a person, a human—even if she had no arms. She must not be abandoned, this crippled thing. And I was forsaken. But although I was cast off, I did not die. I lived on. From my vantage, I can see what people are doing, even though they cannot see me. I came into this house to visit for a time with my sister. I arrived and found her the thing that she is. I provided her with arms, so that she would be able to move about as I do. I gave her legs, so that she would be able to walk as I do. But I told her that she must never tell anyone about me. The women had already attempted to destroy me once. How could I be sure that they wouldn't try again and succeed this time? This is why I insisted that she conceal my presence here."

"Well, Nginingini, if the frog made this same argument to you, we can see why you sought to hide these things. Today we have seen you; you'll remain here from now on. Sit over there near your sister; don't go anywhere. Let her keep those legs. She'll continue to work for you as you like; she'll do everything for you. You must never eat mud like other frogs. You'll eat elegant food which is prepared for you by your sister in this home. And your mother will also do things for you because if there is anything that we have longed for in this home, it has been that your sister have legs and arms."

That is what this fellow said, and the frog went over and sat near its sister. They looked fondly at one another, gently stroked each other, and the frog sat on her lap. They loved each other.

When the mothers returned from the fields, that frog was still sitting there. The men explained to their mother their meeting with the frog.

"We spoke with the frog and discovered that it is the one who provided the child with her arms and legs."

But her mother heard nothing that was being spoken now: she was admiring her child's legs, admiring her child's arms. Whatever these men were saying, she heard nothing. She ignored them, she did not hear them.

She kept saying, "Please stand up, Nginingini, let me see!

"Please stand!

"Please walk!

"Please come out!"

"We're trying to tell you that we saw this frog and asked—"

"No no no! Please, please, just leave me alone! Please walk, Nginingini! Just bring the firewood here; please draw water for me!"

Nginingini went to draw water.

"Oh, my child, my child!" So this woman said, and she went to the frog and kissed it. She kissed the frog; she put it on her lap, she covered it, she loved it very much. Only then did she acknowledge that she had given birth to this frog.

So it was that the frog no longer lived over there in the ashes. Now it lived in this house. They made porridge for it every day. Every morning, they prepared gruel, and the frog ate it. It could not eat other kinds of food.

The frog became fat, it became huge. It was bigger than other frogs. Its color shone because of the healthy foods that it ate.

Tale 2

MBULUKAZI AND THE RAVEN WIFE

Masithathu Zenani's Analysis: By means of patterns, storytellers will frequently use images to mirror other, ostensibly unlike images. This is a storyteller's way of creating complex metaphorical themes or of providing stream-of-consciousness insights into the characters.

In this story, as in the previous one, a child is identified with a creature of nature—here, with doves. But the storyteller provides a struggle within nature that duplicates the struggle occurring within the character of Mbulukazi: a struggle between the doves, or the positive side of her character, and the ravens, the negative side.

The argument of this story is established in two sets of parallels: the great wife's struggle with a raven wife in part one is paralleled by Mbulukazi's struggle with a raven wife in part two; and a husband's choice between human and raven wives in part one is paralleled by a husband's choice between human and raven wives in part two. These correlations emphasize the struggle between doves and ravens, life and death, Mbulukazi and her mother on the one hand and the raven wife and her mother on the other.

At the heart of the story is Mbulukazi's death to her past and her acceptance of a new life as an adult. She must struggle with and overcome the raven side of herself—what it symbolically represents—to do this. What protects Mbulukazi from the death-dealing parts of her world and that part of her character represented by the ravens is the chain that links gods, ancestors, doves, *imbulu* skins, and the *ubulunga* beast. When, in part two, Mbulukazi is killed by the raven and then given renewed life by the *ubulunga* beast, we see the forces struggling for her soul. The raven and the forces represented by the *ubulunga* beast are these two sides of her. When Mbulukazi dies, the raven side of her is gone (the raven can then conveniently be destroyed and moved out of the way), and the *ubulunga* beast or the life-giving side of her survives.

"Mbulukazi and the Raven Wife" is a story about coming of age in a hostile environment and of the meaning of marriage. Once the problem at Mbulukazi's home of birth has been overcome, and her mother and father are reconciled, she moves to her home of marriage—where, in the character of the *ubulunga* beast, she retains her ties to her home and, beyond home, to God. The beast is protective of her, just as the *imbulu* skin, which it eats, protected her in her childhood.

The raven, which represents antisocial acts and death, just what a young person undergoing her puberty ritual should not be, comes into conflict with the *ubulunga* beast, as they fight over the maturing Mbulukazi. Her death represents her triumph over the raven; she sheds the raven part of her. Life is the result, and that is reinforced when the *ubulunga* beast animates her: the beast stands for life, for her mother, for the ancestors, for God. It stands for life in a real sense: the *imbulu* skin is a part of the beast. The skin saved Mbulukazi from death in her youth, as the beast saves her from death as she moves into adulthood. The storyteller here dramatizes the polar sides of a girl going through her puberty ritual. In real life, the bride is presented with an *ubulunga* beast. As the bride-to-be moves to her home of marriage, the beast is a living symbol of her connection with her home of birth. The beast cannot be destroyed; no one can take it from the young bride. It remains the token of her protection by the home of her ancestors while she dwells in an unfamiliar place.

The *imbulu* is an imaginative character from the oral tradition. It is frequently associated with the rite of passage of a girl. Half beast and half human, it yearns to return to its full humanity, and so it takes over the girl's identity, forcing her to take on its identity as a subhuman. Wearing the *imbulu* skin, she is forced to the fringes of human society and must struggle against what the *imbulu* represents as it moves about masquerading as a human. The *imbulu* skin thus becomes associated with a kind of swallowing: when the girl emerges from the skin of the beast, she has attained full womanhood. The *imbulu* skin signals the end of childhood, the blossoming of the child into the woman. Symbolically, it stands between the rituals of birth and puberty. The doves are clearly tied to god and the ancestors; they give the instructions regarding the *imbulu* skins and thereby include them in this chain.[3] Finally, when the *ubulunga* beast swallows the *imbulu* skins, it becomes a part of a set of relationships having their origins in God.

Performance Note

Time: 14 September 1967, in the afternoon. *Place:* At a large gathering in Gatyana District, the Transkei. *Audience:* About forty women, twelve men, and twenty children. (Perf. 645.)

In the olden times, a man married a young woman. He married her, he made her his wife. But when this woman settled down at his home, she did not become pregnant. The man grieved, and so they grew old.

They grew old, and when they were quite old, this man said, "Wife, I must marry another woman because you're unable to conceive. I've roamed the country, seeking medicines for your barrenness. I've been patient with you, waiting for you, but you don't give birth. Our lives have become difficult—we're old now, and there's no one in the house whom we can send out on errands. We've grown weak in our old age."

The wife said, "All right, Sobani, marry whomever you choose."

The man went to seek a wife in another land. He found a woman and married her. He married that woman, and she conceived. But when she gave birth, this woman bore birds—ravens!

She gave birth to more and more birds, and they completely filled the house. Everytime she became pregnant, she bore a bird. A bird, everytime she became pregnant! The homestead was full of these ravens!

3. The doves give the children names derived from the *imbulu* skins: Mbulukazi is the vocative form of *imbulu* with the feminine -*kazi* ending.

". . . she did not become pregnant." The body of the storyteller is wholly involved in the performance.

This grieved the heart of this man, but he resigned himself to living with a wife who at least gave birth to something—rather than stay with the one who had never been pregnant at all.

He went to live in the new wife's homestead. This other wife lived alone now; she continued to grow old. The man lived with those birds; he lived with those birds—buying food for them, feeding them, eating with them. They were his children, the only children he had fathered.

A long time passed. The old woman, the great wife,[4] was sorrowful. She went to live by the side of the kraal, because there were cattle there at her homestead: they kept cattle. But then the husband took the cattle. He took them over there to the other homestead and milked them for the ravens.

4. The great wife is the first wife. She traditionally had a considerable amount of influence in the home.

This great wife lived alone. Now she was called "a dog" by her husband; she was called "a thing that doesn't give birth." As she considered her plight, the woman wept there by the side of the kraal. She cried, and the sun set. When the sun had set, she went into the house, still crying. And so she remained.

Time passed. She wept in the house too, and the next day she was still weeping. She wondered what she might do; she even thought of killing herself.

One day, her sister came to visit her.

She said, "What's the matter, Child of my mother? Why are you so thin?"

"What would you do if you were in my position? My husband lives over there with that woman who gives birth to birds. And I stay alone here in this house. I have no one to bring me food now. He doesn't even want to look at me!"

She said, "Oh, Child of my mother! It would be better for you to go home than endure this."

The wife said, "I won't go home! I won't go home, I'll die here. I married this man not knowing that I wouldn't be able to bear children." That was the woman's answer; then she went to cry at the side of the kraal. She cried at the side of the kraal.

In the afternoon, some doves arrived, two of them. They perched there and spoke to her.

One of the birds said, "*Vukuthu!*"[5]

The other said, "*Vukuthu!* Please ask this woman why she's crying."

The other bird said, "*Vukuthu!* Why are you crying, Woman?"

The woman said, "I'm crying because I'm unable to bear children."

The dove said to the other, "She says that she's crying because she's unable to bear children."

The other said, "*Vukuthu!*" Then it said, "*Vukuthu!* Please ask her what she would give to the person who enables her to bear children."

The other one said, "*Vukuthu!* He asks you what you would give to the person who enables you to bear children."

The woman said, "I can give such a person corn grains."

The dove said, "*Vukuthu!* He asks if you think we have throats big enough to swallow corn grains."

The woman said, "I can give you sorghum."

The dove said, "*Vukuthu!* He asks if you think we have throats big enough to swallow sorghum."

The woman said, "I can give you seeds."

The dove said, "Let's see them."

5. *Vukuthu* is an ideophone, suggesting the sound made by the doves.

The woman went to the house and took down the seeds that were in a billycan [a tin container]. She went back to the cattle kraal and poured out some of the seeds.

The doves pecked up the seeds.

They finished and said, "*Vukuthu!*"

One of them said, "*Vukuthu!* Please tell her to undress and to expose her thighs."

Even before the other dove had a chance to relay the instructions to her, the woman undressed, so desperate was she to have children. That was the only thing in the world that she wanted.

She sat there, naked.

The doves again said, "*Vukuthu!*"

"Tell her to stretch out her legs."

It said, "*Vukuthu!* Stretch your legs."

The woman stretched her legs. When she had stretched them to their full length, one of the doves began to work on one of her thighs. The other dove went to her other thigh. They rubbed dirt from her thighs, from both sides. When they had finished, one of them said, "*Vukuthu!*"

The other said, "*Vukuthu!* Please ask her if she has a calabash [a container made from a gourd]."

The other said, "*Vukuthu!* Do you have a calabash?"

She said, "I have one."

It was said, "*Vukuthu!* Please bring it."

The woman went to the house to get the calabash.

Then it was said, "*Vukuthu!* Please scrape this calabash. Scrape it, then go and dip some water."

The woman scraped the calabash and put it down. Then she went to dip water. When she had done that, she returned.

It was said, "*Vukuthu!*"

It was said, "*Vukuthu!*"

Then it was said, "Take these two balls"—referring to the dirt from the woman's thighs that had now been molded into two small balls—"and put them into this calabash. Then cover it for a full week. Don't uncover it during that week. Uncover it only during the second week."

The woman took the calabash, and the doves departed. She went to the house, then put the two balls—the dirt from her thighs—into the calabash and covered the dirt with water.

The woman waited. The week was finally over.

At the beginning of the second week, she uncovered the calabash. She uncovered it—and there were two children! A girl and a boy!

When she saw these children, the woman jumped up and hit herself against the wall. She returned to the calabash. She stared. Then she took the children—but just as she was about to touch them, she pulled back.

She uncovered the children, then covered them again hastily. She went to sit at the side of the kraal. She cried. She was crying because of what seemed to her to be a miracle; it seemed to be magic—as if the children had appeared by magic. And they might as suddenly disappear! She was still crying when the doves arrived again.

One of them said, "*Vukuthu!*"

The other said, "*Vukuthu!* Please ask her why she's crying."

The other said, "*Vukuthu!* He asks why you're crying."

The woman said, "No, I'm not crying about anything."

One of the doves said, "*Vukuthu!*"

The other said, "*Vukuthu!* Please ask her how things are going with her?"

The other said, "*Vukuthu!* He wants to know how things are going with you."

She said, "Well, I saw children, two of them. They seem to be a girl and a boy. I saw two children, a girl and a boy. Children! What shall I do with them? They're getting too big for the calabash."

One of them said, "*Vukuthu!*"

The other said, "*Vukuthu!* Tell her to take them out of the calabash. Is there a pot that's big enough to hold them?"

The woman said, "Yes, there is such a pot. I do have one."

One of them said, "*Vukuthu!*"

The other said, "*Vukuthu!* Tell her to put them under the pot. But she must not feed those children. Give us some more seeds." So the doves spoke, a second time.

The woman went to the house. She took the seeds and spread them. The doves pecked up the seeds; then they flew off. When the doves had flown away, one of them returned.

It returned and said, "Let a month go by, then look under the pot a second time."

So it said, and again it flew off.

The woman went to the house, and time passed for her. Again and again, she heard something hovering about her, constantly hovering. Sometimes she heard something cry out. She heard the cries, the cries of children. At such times, she would go to the pot. Then she would resolve not to go to the pot—leaving it alone, not touching it. The children were playing inside the pot, playing, laughing, crying.

The woman sat there; she did not go anywhere, she remained in the house.

During the second month, she uncovered the pot and found that the children were already walking. When she saw the children walking, the woman embraced them with fondness. She took one of the children and put it on her shoulder. She took the other and carried it on her back. Then she took the one and put it on her lap. She kissed the children. They urinated and did everything human, and she recognized them as human children, not as magical creatures. They would stay with her, they were real.

Then she put the children back into the pot and covered it. And she cried again. She cried, thinking, "I wonder when I'll see the doves again? What should I do about these children because they're walking now."

She went to sit at the side of the kraal and she cried.

While she was crying at the side of the kraal, the doves arrived. And when they had arrived, one of them said, "*Vukuthu!*"

The other said, "*Vukuthu!* Please ask her why she's crying."

"*Vukuthu!* He ask why you're crying."

"No, I'm not crying about anything. I see that the children are now grown up, and I've been puzzled. I wonder if I should feed them now. I don't know what to do with them. They're walking, they're tall. They're walking now. I've seen them."

"All right, this is what you must do. Get up early and go to the deep pool over there. When you get to the pool, sit down just above it. Two animals will come out; they'll come to you. Don't be afraid of them. Seize one of them—the first one that comes to you. They'll come out one at a time. When you catch the first one, skin it. Skin it like a bag. Make it into something like a goat-bag. Then, when you've finished making that first bag, another creature will come out of the pool. Skin that one, too. Skin it and make it like a goat-bag too.

"Here's the reason for doing all this: you must put the children into these bags. These animals are called *iimbulu.*[6] Put the children into the bags. The names of your children are Mbulu and Mbulukazi.[7] Now, please give us some seeds."

The woman again went to the house. She returned with some seeds and poured them out. When she had done so, the doves pecked them up, they pecked them up.

Then they said, "We're going now." The doves flew off. The woman was left behind, and time passed for her.

The next morning, she took provisions of bread and went to sit above that pool. She had sharpened her knife; it was sharp. When she got to the pool, she sat there and waited. Then she saw that the water of the pool was shaking—churning, churning. Something suddenly appeared on the surface, emerging through the quaking water. She was afraid, but she remembered the injunction of the doves. And she took courage.

6. The *imbulu* (pl. *iimbulu*) is a fantastic creature, frequently appearing in tales as a subhuman character. It is human, but it cannot walk upright. It has a tough skin, it lisps, and it has a tail that cannot resist milk or meat fat. It is usually found in tales that have to do with girls' puberty rites of passage.

7. By naming the children, the doves, representations of nature and of God, give them their identities.

She seized the animal. When she had seized it, she skinned it. It did not resist. She skinned it; she skinned it well. And she fashioned it into something like a goat-bag. When she had finished doing that, she tanned it.

While she was still in the process of tanning that skin, she saw that the water in the same pool was again agitated. And an animal like the first one appeared. She caught this one also, and it too complied. She skinned it; she tanned it. She tanned both of them, tanned them, and they became soft and supple. Then she went home.

She arrived at home, took her children out of the pot, and closed the door so that no one would see what was happening. No one in this land should see it; no one was to know anything about it.

She said, "Come, Mbulu!" addressing the child who was a boy. She dressed him, she dressed him, and he came to resemble an *imbulu* with a tail.

She said, "Come, Mbulukazi!" and the one who was a girl came to her. She dressed her, she dressed her, and the child came to resemble a female *imbulu*, an *imbulukazi*.

The woman took some corn. She cooked it, then poured some water over the corn—instead of milk, because her cattle had been taken away by her husband. She poured water over the porridge and said, "Pour some salt on it, so that it's got some flavor."

The children ate and were satisfied. They laughed and played here in the house which she had locked. The inside of the house was lit.

She said, "Go in now."

They went into the pot. When they had gone into the pot, she opened the door of the house.

Time passed for this woman.

The children outgrew the pot. The girl developed breasts, and the boy developed the things of boyhood.

"What shall I do now? The children have outgrown the pot; they're old now. And they want to chat with their mother. What shall I do about this?" she cried. "I don't know how to get in touch with those doves. I don't know where they live."

She went to sit at the side of the cattle kraal; she cried there at the side of the kraal. She cried—and the doves suddenly appeared. They arrived and perched there.

One of them said, "*Vukuthu!*"

The other said, "*Vukuthu!* Please ask her why she's crying now."

"*Vukuthu!* He asks why you're crying now."

"I'm crying because my children are old. And because they're old, they've outgrown the pot—the girl has breasts, the boy is stretching toward the things of boyhood. And they keep calling for me: 'Mama! Free us! We're getting stuck here!' I don't know what I should do."

The doves said, "*Vukuthu!*"

One of them said, "*Vukuthu!* Tell her to take the children out. She should close them up in the house during the day. When they are outside, she herself must watch them. Then she should shut them up inside. Please bring some seeds."

The woman went to the house, she took the seeds and spread them about. The doves pecked them up.

"We're going now. Let the children out tomorrow."

And there go the doves, flying away.

Time passed for the woman, and the next day she opened the pot and put it over there. She stayed with her children in the house, at her sleeping place. She closed the door. She opened it at night, and during the entire day she kept it closed. She wanted no one to open it.

She did not see her husband. Whenever he happened to pass by, she would say, "Give me some tobacco," and he would respond, "You fool! Get someone else, stay away from me! I don't know why you're remaining in that homestead! There's no reason for you to remain here—you have no children!"

Time passed for this woman. Time passed for her; then it was ploughing time. Whenever she left to plough in the fields, she said, "Please, Children, do not open the door and go outside!"

The doors in those olden times were made of stakes of wood; they would be closed at dawn, they would be tied shut with a rope. One day, when their mother had departed, the children broke the rope and went outside.

The girl, Mbulukazi, took a billycan.

She said, "Mbulu, please go and dip some water for Mother. She works all the time, we mustn't let things go on in this way. We must dip some water for her. And I want to cook some boiled corn so that when she gets home she can just rest."

The boy said, "No, Mbulukazi! She said that we shouldn't go outside and be seen by other people."

"No, let's do it, Mbulu! We'll keep close to the kraals so that we won't be seen. We won't go by any homesteads."

The boy said, "Well, Mbulukazi, do you know where water is dipped?"

Mbulukazi said, "If we just stay on the path, Mbulu, we'll see the place where the water is dipped."

He agreed to the plan. They broke the ropes on the door and went out. Mbulukazi took the billycan, and they went to the river. They dipped water.

Mbulukazi said, "Mbulu! Let's just wash our bodies. Let's take a bath here. Mother's tired of washing us—we're as big as she is! For once, let her return from work to find us washed."

"Well, all right. How shall we go about it?"

They washed; they washed their bodies. These children were light skinned because they had never been exposed to the sun. Their hair was black and long.

They were still washing when horses abruptly appeared, four of them. Riding these horses were four men who were seeking a wife for one of the four [a king] in various places.

When they came to these children who were bathing, the one in the front said, "Let's just hide here for a while. Let's look at them and find out whose daughter she is. She's so beautiful! Where have these handsome youths come from?"

The children, not seeing the riders, continued to bathe. Then the man could no longer resist; he was burning inside. He had to approach these children, to look at the beautiful children more closely. The men arrived, and they saw Mbulukazi.

She said, "Mbulu! Here are some people!"

They rushed to put their clothes on; they put them on. The garments clung to their wet bodies, to their wet *imbulu* skins. They put the clothes on in a great rush.

Meanwhile, the men continued to approach them.

"Hello, my children! Don't rush so, you'll get hurt!"

"Yes, Father."

"Whose children are you?"

"We don't know our father. We've never seen him. We have seen our mother."

"Where's your home?"

The children pointed to their home.

"And where is your mother?"

"Mother's gone to plough."

"And what are these things that you're wearing, Children?"

"They're *imbulu* skins. Our mother was unable to bear any children. Some doves made it possible for her to give birth."

"She put us in a pot, and we took it on ourselves to come out."

"Go then, my children."

The men went on their way. When they had gone a little way, the man who was seeking a wife said, "Let's turn around, Men! I've seen my wife. Let's go and begin anew at home. I'll proceed no further to our original destination."

They men turned around. As they did so, the children were arriving at their home. When they got home, they remained there. Then their mother arrived.

She said, "What's this? Why is this door broken? Why did you do this, my children?"

Mbulu said, "Mother, it was Mbulukazi! She said that we should go to the river. She was going to cook some corn for you because you've been so overworked. When we got to the river, Mbulukazi suggested that we bathe. We were seen by some men. They asked us who our father is. We said that we don't know our father, but that we do know our mother. Then the men asked us where our home is, and we pointed it out to them. They asked us where our mother is, and we told them that you were out ploughing. Then they left."

"You've done a bad thing, my children! You let yourselves be seen by men whom I don't know! Mbulukazi, you shouldn't do things like this, my child! When I say something to you, you must heed my words!"

"Mother," Mbulukazi said, "we were feeling sorry for you."

Time passed for the woman. She was happy, even considering these circumstances.

In a few days, the men arrived. They went to the homestead in which the father of the ravens was living. They went there and said that they had come to ask for a wife. When that request had been made, the man produced ravens.

He said, "Here are my daughters." He introduced the female ravens. He said, "Here are my daughters. Choose from among them the one that you want."

It was said, "No, how can you give us ravens? We want a woman!"

He said, "These are my daughters! If it is my homestead that you want, if it is me that you want, here are my daughters!" So said this man.

The king took one of the ravens. He said, "All right, I'll marry this one."

"Yes," said the father.

"All right, then," said the king.

"Substantiate your desire to marry, my fellow," said the father.[8] "I want six head of cattle for my daughter."

The father was saying the words, "my daughter," firmly, because he had never begotten anything else. He was certain that this was his daughter: the only daughters he had were these birds.

The six head of cattle were produced then.

The next day, the king returned.

He said, "I want a wife, I want another of your daughters."

"Which one now?"

"I want a daughter from your great house, from the great wife."[9]

"No, no one ever gave birth in that homestead. That's a dog there; she doesn't beget. She's never had a child! I deserted that thing. I don't live with that thing anymore."

---

8. The father is referring to *lobola,* the dowry that the prospective groom must provide.

9. The wife of the great house is the man's first wife. The raven wife is the wife of his right-hand house. The right-hand wife is the second wife of a commoner.

"Well, Father, we do want a woman from there. We have seen her. A woman whose name is Mbulukazi."

"Can such a thing be? Can such a thing be? A daughter in this homestead? You must have seen your wife's sisters."[10]

"No, Father, we want a wife from over there. Please go there for us. Please go for us. We want a wife from over there to be our right-hand wife. This one I've already married will be the great wife. As you know, we kings do sometimes take two women from a single homestead."

"All right. Let's go."

They went there, and the great wife was moving about in the front of the house. She was happy.

The man saw that his wife had now become attractive; her blood was obviously healthy. He wondered what it was that had made her so radiant—since she was living only on grass, after all.

When they arrived, "Nobani! Please come here!"

The strangers were sitting in the courtyard.

"Please come here!"

She came.

"What's all this about a young woman who has been seen here?"

That very Mbulukazi came out immediately.

"Mother, these are those men who approached us over there at the pool."

The father lowered his head in disgrace. He was ashamed; he was humbled when he witnessed this. He saw that below the *imbulu* skin were the feet of a human. He could see that the hands were human hands. Because of the *imbulu* skin, he did not see a human body. But he could see that this being was dressed up in an *imbulu* skin. This person was not what she appeared to be.

"You, Wife."

[Member of audience: "Oh, he has a wife now!"]

His wife said, "Come to me, in the house. You left me in the house. You didn't leave me near that kraal! You didn't leave me in a crowd! I'm still sitting by the hearth just where you left me!"[11]

Her husband got up and nervously pulled his beard. He went into the house and said, "Nobani."

"Mmmhmm."

He arrived, and the children greeted their father.

10. The father's term "your wife's sisters" refers to the suitor's recent decision to marry one of the his raven daughters. The father is saying that the suitor must be in error. He must have seen some of the raven-wife's sisters, also ravens.

11. She is reminding her husband that he walked out on her; he disrupted their relationship. Before we involve other people, she is suggesting, let us settle this matter about us. And she invites him to come into the house: That is where you left me, she seems to be saying, and that is where we must start out again.

"Nobani, these children—"

"I was given the children by God. No one need ask where they came from. It's nobody's business how they got here. Why don't you just go back to your ravens? Don't come to me asking about children who have been given to me by God. Don't think that you left me alone in this house. God gave me children."

"No, no, please approach, Wife! This is a king. He has come to ask for a wife. The king has already taken one of my daughters as a wife—Hlungwana [Little Raven] from the house down below. Now he wants a right-hand wife. He says that he has seen this young woman here—this Mbulukazi. Now how are we going to handle this, Wife?"

She said, "Do it as you wish. I'll not tell you what to do. After all, this is your homestead. I'm still your wife. I've not yet departed from the homestead."

"I'll give him the young woman, Wife."

So the father gave the woman to the king.

The king said, "Go on talking, Father. Whatever you say."

"Well," he said, "I want sixteen head of cattle for this young woman because this wife of mine conceived when she was already old."

The king said, "There is no arguing about the cattle, they're just outside.[12] I shall produce the sixteen cattle. Now, I want this young woman to come with a bridal party to my homestead. We'll do it that way, rather than by the way of abduction."[13]

"All right, let's discuss that."

"We'll come back," the king said.

The strangers departed, the others [the members of Mbulukazi's homestead] remained behind.

The father did not return to that house of ravens. Instead, he slept here, in the house of his great wife.

He slept here at home.

In the morning, his wife said, "Go home! Yes, go home, go to the house of the ravens! You can take care of the marriage negotiations from that place, from the ravens' home. Don't stay in this house!"

Well then, the man did go home. He went to stay in that homestead of his on the following morning.

During the next week, the suitors returned, coming now to begin the marriage ceremonies. Generous amounts of beer were brewed; the suitors arrived, and they began the ritual over there at the ravens' home.

They behaved in the way prescribed for a groom's party when it comes

12. That is, the cattle are as good as present here. They are not here, but the king will get them shortly.

13. Both ways are correct traditionally, but the king prefers the more formal and dignified way.

to the bride's place for a wedding, and they finished that part of the marriage ceremony. A beast was slaughtered for them, and they produced flagons of liquor. They also brought the dowry cattle along.

Then they went to the homestead of Mbulukazi, and they produced the sixteen cattle. They produced vessels of liquor for Mbulukazi's part of the ceremony. And they clothed the girl's mother.

The groom's party departed after setting a date for the arrival of the bridal parties at the home of the groom; it was decided that the two bridal parties should arrive on the same day. When all that was settled, the groom's party departed.

Preparations were then made over there at the ravens' home. The wife who gave birth to ravens did not know that Mbulukazi even existed; she knew nothing about her at all. The husband hid this from her; he did not mention it to the mother of the ravens. In fact, that raven-wife was a little bitter.

[Member of audience: "Why is she so bitter?"]

Yes, she was bitter.

That other wife, who was now a little better off than she had been, was not as resentful as this raven-wife. But, so that the affair could proceed without interruption, they were not discussing Mbulukazi with the raven-mother.

Time passed, and finally all was ready: the preparations for the marriage ceremonies had continued; mats had been plaited, along with baskets and all the wedding vessels—everything, everything, everything. Finally, all things were complete.

Then the girls were assembled, and the men, and the women—people to go with the bridal parties. Over there at the ravens' home, there were six people in the bridal party, two girls, two women, and two men. At Mbulukazi's place, there were four girls, four women, and four men. These people of Mbulukazi's bridal party were brought together. The wagon was inspanned: sixteen cattle were harnessed to the wagon. Mbulukazi's goods were loaded on the wagon. Then Mbulukazi got on as her mother ululated:

> "Ki ki ki ki ki ki ki ki kiiiiiiiiii!
> Go then, little animal of Tese's home[14]—
> You, who have been deliberately designed
> To be the way you are!"[15]

[Member of audience: "Oh!"]

The other young woman also came out over there—that child of the bird!

14. "Tese" may be a name for Mbulu, or it may be the name of a favorite ox.

15. That is, Mbulukazi did not happen naturally. She was created by design, by intention. In this case, she was born by the intervention of the doves.

[Member of audience: "The one with wings!"]

Yes. Then it was said, "Halaalaa! yeha! yeha! Halala! halala!"

They journeyed then. Eeeee! As the bridal parties arrived, Mbulukazi was driving the beast of the bridal party;[16] she was driving the beast of the bride[17]—these beasts were two. [And the raven-bride was driving no such beasts.] Mbulukazi was also carrying the money for the women.[18]

They arrived. Yes, they arrived over there at the groom's homestead. They got there at dusk, and the bridal parties remained on a small hill overlooking the homestead.

[Member of audience: "They arrived on the same day?"]

The dogs barked: "Hawu hawu! hawu hawu! hawu hawu hawu!"

Yo! In the groom's homestead, it was seen that the strangers had arrived.

A person came out and said, "Well, they're here! The people are here. There are many of them. I don't understand. There shouldn't be so many in the bridal party."

The king said, "It's just as it should be. There are two parties here. Those bridal parties left their homesteads at the same time."

"Oh."

"Well, someone must go and interrogate them. Whoever goes should start with the raven's bridal party. He should not start by asking questions of Mbulukazi's party."

Someone went out to the bridal parties.

That person spoke to the raven's party: "Hello!"

"Yes."

"Mm! Where do these people come from?"

"Well, we have come from the other side of the Mbashe River, and we're going to cross the Nciba River [also called the Great Kei River]. But we have a child with us who is limping, and we're asking for a place in which to spend the night."[19]

16. The "beast of the bridal party" was the *impothulo* beast. "This animal was brought by the bridal party for food, for until the nuptial arrangements are completed, it continues independent and self-supporting. Assistance in the killing of the animal is asked for from the men of the kraal. The cutting up and division of the carcase is performed in accordance with a prescribed formula." (John Henderson Soga, *The Ama-Xosa: Life and Customs* [Lovedale: Lovedale Mission Press, 1931], 231.)

17. The "beast of the bride" was the *ubulunga* beast. This was ". . . the cow or heifer given to a woman by her people as a kind of dowry; it is held sacred, and may not be taken, nor even confiscated, by the chief. . . ." (Albert Kropf, *A Kafir-English Dictionary* [Lovedale: Lovedale Mission Press, 1915], p. 222.)

18. Various symbolic gifts are distributed during this period of the marriage ceremony.

19. This is a typical, exaggerated story invented by the bridal party as it creates an excuse to remain at the groom's place overnight during a fictional long journey—in this case, from the Mbashe River in the Transkei to the Nciba River. Note how abruptly the raven's party is treated and with what respect Mbulukazi's party is approached. The person doing the questioning of the raven's bridal party is a woman.

She went back to the house.

"These people say they've come from a place far off. They say they're going to cross places like the Nciba.[20] I don't understand these people. They say they're traveling with a child who's tired."

"Go and get them."

A house had already been prepared—two houses, in fact.

"Go and get them. Put them in that house."

The members of the raven's party were put into one of the houses.

When the raven's bridal party had gone into that house, it was said, "Now let a man go to that other bridal party; let a man go and interrogate them."

A young man who was a councillor in the royal residence went out.

He said, "Hello!"

It was said, "Yes!"

"I've been sent from the house. I was told to come and ask the people who are sitting here above the homestead what the trouble is. What kind of people might they be?"

"Well," the fellow who was in front—the master of ceremonies—answered. "Well, sir, really, these people are on a journey, but they've been overtaken by darkness. They're not familiar with this land. They saw a light in a homestead that happened to be just next to the road on which they were traveling and decided to ask for a place to stay. You see, among us is a person whose chest is somewhat congested."

"Well then, that's all right. I'm going to return to the house." So this person said, as he went back to the house. He got there and explained, "These people say that they have come from far away, that they're traveling with a person who doesn't feel very well. They're asking for a place to spend the night."

"That's all right. Someone should go and take these people; they should be taken to the house that had been smeared with milk."[21]

[Members of audience: "With milk! Wo! Wo!"]

Smeared with milk! Not dung! Milk!

Oh! Well then, this person went there and said, "I've been told to come and take you over there. Come with me."

The people followed him; they entered that house. New mats were spread for them. They were well taken care of. A curtain had been fash-

20. The speaker is purposely vague; she speaks casually, as if she does not care much about the raven's bridal party.

21. The floors are normally smeared with a mixture of dung and earth. The difference between the two houses is meant to emphasize the very distinct attitudes of the king's people, and doubtless of the king himself, to the two brides. The performer has already made a similar distinction, by giving Mbulukazi's bridal party twice the number of participants as in the raven-wife's party.

ioned of an old blanket; it was knotted, knotted on the top. The young women went behind it—the women were on one side of the curtain, the men on the other.

They were sitting like that when a woman entered.

She said that she had come to cause them to urinate.[22] "I have come to cause the bridal party to urinate."

There was a urination then: ten shillings were taken out, and these were given to the woman.

It was said, "We're closing the door now because we're tired and want to go to sleep. Don't come and make us urinate again."

Time passed, and over there in the other house, the house of the raven, nothing was happening. They were just sitting there. No one was saying anything. Not a word was being spoken; there was no progress there at all. And they did not have an ox of the bridal party.

The master of ceremonies of Mbulukazi's bridal party said, "I have a request to make of the groom's people. I have a request. I request a kraal. I have something that I've been driving, something that I'm taking to the country to which I am going. And it might just run away."[23]

"That's all right."

A member of the groom's homestead went to open the gate of the kraal for him, and the master of ceremonies of Mbulukazi's bridal party put into the kraal both of these beasts that he had been driving.

Early in the morning, the master of ceremonies said, "I have another request. I'm asking that someone open the kraal for me. May I also borrow a thong?"

The ox of Mbulukazi's bridal party was slaughtered. This bridal party beast was slaughtered; then it was brought into the house. The bridal party took the portions of meat belonging to the groom's house.

By morning, meat was being cooked, beer was being brewed here at home—this was the celebration of greeting the bridal party. Then all the money had to be produced: the money of the women, the money of the beards, that of the aprons, the entry-into-the-house.[24]

It was determined that the bridal parties should be seen on the very same day. So they were seen—beginning with the bridal party of the raven.

22. This is a part of the marriage ritual. No one really urinates at this stage; this is the "money of the urination," one more of the symbolic gifts that knits the bride to the groom's homestead and family.

23. Again, this is a part of the fiction that the bridal party is only passing through this country. The ritual requires that one of the beasts be reserved for the exclusive use of the bride, it being her symbolic connection with her home of birth; the other beast is to be slaughtered to provide food for the bridal party during the betwixt and between period, when it is still on the outside, not yet fully a part of the groom's home.

24. Again, the various deposits of money are meant to be symbolic of the developing network connecting the homes of the bride and the groom.

It was said, "How beautiful this girl is!" and then she was covered.[25]

Then Mbulukazi's bridal party came out. The party came out in a procession, the person-of-the-meat[26] between the four girls, the fifth one in the middle. Two women were in the front of them and two behind.

[Member of audience: "Why didn't this happen to the bird?"]

And two of the men were in front.

They came to a kraal, and a mat was spread. The bride sat on the mat, dressed in a necklace of beads and shells.

She was seen then. The people of the groom's place heaved; they rose as one.

"What kind of person is this?"

That *imbulu* skin of hers, the skin that had transformed her into Mbulukazi, was now given to that ox of the bride to eat. And that ox of the bride, which they had driven here, did eat the *imbulu* skin.

At dawn on the next day, it was clear that the bridal party must go and get water and gather firewood. The members of the bridal party put on their skin skirts; they were dressed elegantly, and they went to gather wood. Then they put that wood in the homestead.

The next day, the bridal parties went home, and these brides remained in their home of marriage.

It was clear what these brides were like. Mbulukazi knew how to gather wood—she had hands, a head, she had legs. That bride who was a bird knew how to do nothing except peck grains.

[Member of audience: "Yu!"]

Time passed then, and their houses were built. The king built for Mbulukazi a house that had four corners, and it was located on a high ground.[27]

The raven was seen to be just a mindless bird. As time went on, she became jealous because the husband was hers to begin with: she was his first wife. And now he didn't want her. This bird knew how to speak—as you know, it was born among people, so it had learned how to speak—and she was able to understand, too.

"It's become clear now that I am nothing. I'm a laughing stock. Even the children laugh at me." Then she said to Mbulukazi, "Let's go, Sister."

It was as if the raven loved Mbulukazi, she kept so close to her.

"Let's go, Sister. Let's go and cut wood," she said to Mbulukazi.

---

25. This covering and uncovering is done by the master of ceremonies, who thereby teases the members of the groom's party, giving them glimpses of the bride's beauty. In the case of the raven, note how perfunctory this part of the ritual is, in comparison to the elaborate development of the rite for Mbulukazi.

26. The "person of the meat" is the bride, the person for whom the celebration is being held, for whom the cattle are being slaughtered.

27. A house with four corners is a modern house, contrasted with the rondavel type of home, the traditional round home.

Mbulukazi said, "But, Child of my father, how will you do that?"

"Well, let's just go and gather some firewood. I'll break the wood with my beak, and, since you know how to hoist the wood to your head, you will carry it."

"All right then, let's go."

They went; they gathered firewood in the forest. They gathered wood, they gathered the wood. While they were still gathering wood in that way, the raven said, "Ee, Mbulukazi! This branch is a little difficult for me."

"What's the matter with it?"

"I've been trying to twist it off for a long time, but it won't be twisted. Please come. Please come, Mbulukazi, Child of my father!"

So Mbulukazi went to the raven, and when she got there, she said, "Friend, tell me now, how do you come to be gathering wood in a place like this?"

"No, just stand here! Stand in this place and pull the branch that way."

So Mbulukazi stood where the raven asked her to stand and caught hold of the branch. While she was holding onto the branch, the raven leapt at her. It flew into her eyes, flapping its wings, stinging her eyes, momentarily blinding her. It flew into her eyes with its wings. Mbulukazi leapt up in pain, holding her face—and she plummeted over a cliff.

She was smashed down below, her brains were scattered. She was mangled, torn to pieces there.

The bird went home.

When she got home, her husband said, "Where did you leave my wife?"

"She was still stacking wood when I left her. I helped her to gather the wood for a long time, but then I wanted to come home because I don't know how to stack wood. I was helping that wife of yours."

"Since you went together, how could you leave her behind? You left her behind!"

"What else could I do? It was getting late! What could I do? She wanted to take eight months to do it!"

"Well, what you've done is unacceptable!"

Time passed, and all was quiet there in that homestead. No issue was made of the matter. All was quiet.

Then that ox returned, the one that had eaten the *imbulu* skin that Mbulukazi used to wear. It returned from among the other cattle, bellowing, "Mbooooooooo! Mbooooooooo! Mbooooooooo!"

Someone said, "What's the matter with this ox?"

Then the ox charged into the homestead, lunging directly at the raven's house. It stormed into the house. It charged! It raged into the house! It ripped the house apart, it tore the house, it gored, it turned the walls of the house into chunks of earth, and the house fell down.

Someone said, "What's this about?"

"What does it forebode?"

"What is this ox doing?"

The raven flew away.

"Well!"

"Ee!"

"This ox's actions mean something!"

The ox returned. It bellowed. It roared to the front of Mbulukazi's house. It bellowed, standing there in the doorway. It bellowed, it bellowed, and then it departed, still bawling.

The men followed the ox.

Someone said, "This ox's actions have something to do with the fact that this woman hasn't come back yet."

They followed the ox, they followed it. The king also set out with his councillors; they surged after this ox. The ox went into the forest; it went into the forest, and the men followed. It stopped on the cliff where Mbulukazi had been gathering firewood. It stopped there, bellowing, looking down below.

When the men peered over: "Here she is!"

She had been scattered down below. She had been like that for some time—she was dismembered. The ox looked for a place whereby it might get down there; it went back and forth, up and down, until finally it found a place it could cut through in order to get down below. It arrived there and went to Mbulukazi. It licked her, it licked her, gathering her together, gathering her with its horns. It licked, it gathered her together with its horns; it licked, bellowing. It gathered her together with its horns, it licked, it joined her together piece by piece. It joined her together, it licked her. With its horns, it caused her to get up. It made her sit on her buttocks. She was unsteady, so it let her down, licking her; it licked her, it licked her. And finally she did sit on her behind. When she sat up, the ox continued to lick her, bellowing, going round and round her.

Finally, she sat and looked around. She was called by her husband, and she responded and got up. The ox licked her as she stood on her feet. It licked her, the ox went round and round her. Finally, she walked slowly, and the ox walked with her. When she stopped, it would lick her and lick her, so that she slowly became stronger. She walked, she walked about. When she became fatigued, the ox licked her again; it licked her, and finally she was completely restored. She became as she was before.

They went home then.

They took a bundle of grass. That raven-wife was beaten, then taken and put inside a house. The bundle of grass was taken and ignited in this house. The raven burned, and died, and the house fell in. When the house fell in, the raven died.

Mbulukazi remained there, living in happiness with her husband.

Tale 3

A FATHER CUTS OFF HIS DAUGHTER'S ARMS

Masithathu Zenani's Analysis: "A Father Cuts Off His Daughter's Arms" is the Xhosa version of a story that is universally performed.[28] It is essentially a puberty rite of passage tale, but it also has to do with a girl's movement away from her home of birth. It dramatizes three of the rites of passage, birth, puberty, and marriage.

The opening pattern of the story has to do with the father's incestuous advances toward his daughter. His approaches become more and more urgent, but she regularly refuses him. This pattern leads to the separation phase of the girl's puberty ritual, her necessary departure from her home of birth. The main pattern reveals the girl's ordeal or initiation phase. This pattern has to do with her miserable experiences in the forest where, after her father has cut off her arms, she becomes animal-like in her desperate quest for food. She loses her identity as a human in the process and is compared to a pig, a hog, a cow. The pattern is composed of her many efforts to provide for herself, to find something to eat, to survive. This pattern is again invoked when she leaves her in-laws' homestead, when once again she must provide for herself, this time with her child strapped to her back. It is a lengthy struggle, a move to womanhood. She is literally and figuratively incomplete; she is not a whole person. Her physical state, her armlessness, is a reflection of her mental and spiritual states: she is not yet a woman.

A letter-writing pattern, a unique element in an oral tale, reinforces the main pattern. The parents write a letter to their son, pretending to be his wife; the incestuous father writes a letter to his daughter, pretending to be her husband. These letter-writing acts are crude attempts to place the husband-wife relationship at risk, to compromise it and break the marriage tie. This pattern reinforces the girl's isolation and ordeal, and it equates the acts of her father with those of her in-laws. The effect in both cases is to drive her from a home.

In a closing pattern, a fantastic bird restores the girl's arms to her, giving her physical wholeness. This mirrors her spiritual and mental fullness, her coming of age. The father's behavior and the bird's act of rejuvenation, moreover, provide a patterned frame for the tale. With the restoration of her arms, the young woman is reincorporated into human society.

Even though she marries a young man earlier, the marriage is not complete, suggested by the fact that she remains armless. Her conflict with her father and her clash with her in-laws are a part of the story's major pattern, that depicting her ordeal. The struggle with her father is a dramatic suggestion that she must leave her home of birth. She cannot remain there; to do so is tantamount to incest. She cannot fulfill herself as a woman, a wife, a

28. Versions of the story have been recorded in Europe, in Central and South America, and in the Caribbean.

mother at her home of birth. The strife with the in-laws suggests that her rite of passage remains incomplete: she is victimized by them, she cannot do any work, she cannot provide for her child. In the end, it is nature in the form of the bird that gives her an adult identity.

Performance Note

Time: 10 August 1972 in the afternoon. *Place:* Near Mrs. Zenani's home in Nkanga, Gatyana District, the Transkei. *Audience:* Six women, three men, six children. (Perf. NS-141.)

There were a woman and a man. The woman gave birth—she bore a child, a girl.

And time passed for this woman and her daughter; time passed for them. Then the woman died, leaving her daughter behind.

The girl lived with her father, who had no other wife.

The father lived with his daughter, loving her very much.

A long time passed, and the child did all the work that had been done by her mother. She cut short her playtime with other children because of the demands of the labors of her home. She did everything, from the work of an adult to the work of a child.

There were the two of them there, just the child and her father.

After some time, the ploughing season came, and the lands were culti-vated. The child herded the livestock; she helped to plough the fields. She continued to do the cooking, and washing clothes was one of her duties. During the ploughing season, she helped her father to inspan the oxen. Though she was a girl, she also knew how to do the milking. The father, because his daughter did all the work of the house, was free to go places, leaving her at home to tidy up and do all the work of the homestead.

That is the way it was for this girl.

Time passed for her, and she continued to do this demanding work. The other children seldom saw her; they gave up on her in the end because she was always too busy to play with them.

The child was beautiful; she was exquisite. But she did not marry. It was as if she were a married woman of her own home here: she did the work of a married woman here at her home.

Her father became troubled by certain vague but persistent feelings: This child! She looks so much like her mother!

Once, while the daughter was delousing him, delousing his head, her father suddenly turned over and looked intently at her; he looked at this child of his. He looked at her and cried.

The child asked, "Father, why are you crying?"

With her body, Nongenile Masithathu Zenani explores the emotional depths of her story.

"No, it's nothing, my child. It's nothing."

But this became a habitual thing with her father: he would be sitting with the child; he would look at her, he would look at her and cry.

Time passed, and the father's conduct caused the child great anxiety—his staring at her, his tears. She became thin; she could not understand why her father cried like that. Her mother had been dead a long time, so she could hardly have understood that connection.

Time passed, and things went on in this way. The child was disquieted by what her father was doing. She still could not understand his behavior.

Then one day, as she was delousing him, her father again suddenly turned over and stared at her. And he cried.

The child said, "Now what is this, Father? Why do you always cry, then never say why you are crying? There must be a reason, and I'm sure it's bad! Don't you realize how much pain this causes me?"

"My child, I'm crying because my heart aches. My heart is in pain. You resemble your mother so much. Whenever I look at you, I think of your mother."

The child felt terrible about this. She cried now because of what her father had said to her.

He said, "My child, don't cry."

The child was quiet then, and she withdrew. She was no longer a child at that time; she was a big girl, a girl who did everything. She went to herd the livestock; then she came back home. She milked, she cooked, she dished out the food—she did everything.

And she fed her father.

Again, when it was dusk, her father said, "My child—"

"Father?"

"Do you know that you resemble your mother?"

"Yes, Father."

"Only one thing will end my anguish. You must come and share my bed with me."

The child said, "Father! I would never do such a thing!" The child began to cry; her sorrow was great.

He said, "No, be quiet! People will hear you. They'll come to see what's happening here!"

So the child was quiet.

The next day, in the morning, her father got up in a sullen mood. He refused to speak.

The child was silent too. She did her various chores, the usual tasks.

Then, at midday, her father said, "Now what do you have to say about that matter that I mentioned to you?"

The child burst into tears again; she cried and cried.

Again, her father calmed her: "Stop this! Are you swearing that you cannot change your mind and replace your mother?"[29]

The child said, "Never! Never!"

Her father said, "Would you rather die?"

The child said, "I would rather die! That would be better. It would be better to die than to do what you are suggesting!"

Her father became quiet. He took a knife and went to sharpen it at the side of the kraal. He sharpened the knife, and when the knife was sharp, he put it into a bag and kept it with him. He took another bag and cut it in the middle, so that it was no longer a bag but a kind of blanket to be worn. He folded it, and kept that with him, too.

The next day, in the afternoon, he said, "Let's go, my daughter."

The child asked, "Where are we going, Father?"

"You'll see. There's a certain place to which I want to go."

The child departed with her father. They walked and walked, going to a distant land. The sun set. The sun set, and when the day had again dawned, they were still traveling. They had walked all night, and on the next day they continued to travel, again walking until the sun set. It was the third day of their journey, and they ranged on. Finally, they came to a large forest. When they got to the forest, the father entered the wood. Because the father was silent, the child was not speaking at all. She just kept in step behind him as he walked.

When he had gone into the forest, he said, "Now, we've come to the place." As he said this, he spread the bag out on the ground. Then he said, "I say to you, come and share this bed with me."

The child said, "Oh, Father! Never! Never!"

Her father said, "You still say that? Even now?"

"I still say that!"

He took the knife and cut off her arms. Both of them.

He put her arms on the ground, and said, "Stay there then!"

The child was in terrible pain, the garments she wore became bloody— all of them, all of them became bloody. She bled in an extraordinary way, as she sat there beside that bag. She bled, and she suffered from the cold. She was cold because of her wounds. The bleeding, the anguish went on until dawn, and she was still there—in the place she was in when her father had departed.

Time passed; she was in acute pain, tormented by the wounds, suffering from cold and hunger. She had no energy to do anything to help

---

29. "Are you swearing . . . ?" Literally, "Are you making eight?" i.e., eight fingers. Are you making eight fingers stand up? Are you taking an oath?

herself. She sat there all that time, wanting to get up, unable to get up. Finally, because she had no hands with which to grasp things, she moved herself by rolling. At last, she got support from something, and she was able to stand up. When she got to her feet, she found that everything that she had been wearing had become stiff because of the blood. Her clothes shrank, exposing her body. She had bled much, and now the blood had dried on her and coagulated. In the process, it caused her clothes to shrink. Her body was exposed because her clothing had shrivelled up and become stiff.

She walked in the forest, not knowing how to get out of it. She was hungry and without energy, without strength. She walked on; she walked in the forest, descending, ascending. The forest seemed to her endless.

Finally, on the third day of her useless walking, she emerged; she was now on the periphery of the forest. She looked around; she explored the countryside. And she found that she did not know this country at all. She did not know it at all; it was a country she had never seen. She looked around as she walked on the edge of the forest; she kept close to the forest, walking on its fringes, afraid that she might get lost.

She explored, she searched, then saw that "There are some homesteads! With gardens!"

There were plants in those gardens by the homesteads. And as far as she could determine, those plants were edible. There were peaches over there.

"If only I could get there! I would be able to fill my stomach. I'm so hungry!"

She walked, moving herself in the direction of the garden. As she approached it, she looked about carefully. She found that "This garden is walled, there's no entrance." She went around the garden. It was some distance from the house, it was not very close. She went around the garden; she went around it, then discovered a place that the pigs seemed to have dug, under the wall. It was not a proper entrance, but a hole that the pigs had rooted under the wall. She went to this place, then threw herself down. She had to throw herself on the ground, there was no way that she could get down easily because of the pain of the arms that had been cut off on both sides of her body. Those arms that had been cut off: she had left the arms over there, in the place where they had been severed, in the forest. When she threw herself to the ground, she struggled to roll her body. Finally, she managed to get herself through the hole where pigs entered the garden. She struggled all day and eventually got herself into the garden.

While she was attempting to get under the wall, a person from the homestead happened to enter the garden. He came in, looking for something, then he went out again. He did not see her.

She finally got her body into the garden. She found that there was much corn there, corn that had grown very tall. She rolled on, no longer able to stand up as she had before. In the end, she found some corn. She hit her body against the corn; she rolled against some corn that was on the ground, that had fallen to the ground. She got there and ate the corn that had fallen, eating it with her mouth as a hog does. She ate hoggishly, eating everything—leaves, everything. Whatever was in reach of her mouth, she ate—as a cow would. Her hunger was abated; the only thing that remained was the drumming pain.

Time passed. She slept in that garden. No one noticed that something was here in the garden.

Time passed, time passed until the sun set; she slept out there in the cold, with no covering, exposed like that and in deep pain. But her hunger was eased. Her hunger was assuaged because she had swallowed and eaten everything, whatever was in reach.

At dawn the next day, she was still not hungry because she had eaten things that had not been cooked. Her stomach hurt now, it bit her because of the things she had eaten. Another sun set, and the next day was the third day that she had been in this garden, and she felt hungry once more. She had to try again to get some food. But there was no fallen corn here beside her, the corn was high up and beyond her reach. So she rolled herself, she rotated her body, even though it was painful; she persevered because she was hungry. Finally, she came to a place beneath some peach trees. Peaches had fallen from the trees, they were on the ground. She picked them up; she picked them up with her mouth, eating them. When she had picked it up with her mouth, she would swallow a peach whole. She would chew it and swallow it—all of it. And again her hunger was eased. When she was sated, it was difficult for her to stand; she was unable to stand. So she sat there. And while she was sitting there, the owner of the garden, a man, came out.

He said, "Now what's been tramping things down around here? What's been eating things in this garden? Everything's been leveled! What has been trampling around here and eating here? What has come into this garden? Just look around—" speaking to someone else "—see if there's a pig in the garden."

They looked around, seeking a pig. They searched and searched in the garden. Then one of them discovered her—the girl.

That person fled.

"Here's something! Here's something! There's a thing over here, something I've never seen! It's dirty! A thing that's lying under the peach trees!"

The owner of the house went to see this thing. He called his dogs and went over there. He wanted the dogs to attack this thing. He went over there; the dogs barked.

The child said, "No! Come to me, Father, and I'll tell you what has happened! I am not a pig! I am a human being! Come!"

He stopped, then said, "What kind of person are you? What has happened to you? What kind of person is this?"

The girl said, "No, Father, I am a human being! Come here! I can't get up. I've been injured!"

The man stood at a distance from her, apprehensive. He was afraid to approach this creature.

The girl said, "No, I am a human being, Father! The only thing is—my arms were cut off. I got into this garden through that hole there, where the hogs come in. I threw myself to the ground, then crawled through. It is very difficult for me to stand. I can't get up when I'm on the ground. When my wounds are touched, I am in great agony. It's painful—here, in the arms! Both of my arms were cut off!" So said the girl, and she began to cry.

As she cried, this man approached her. He examined her more closely, and when he had done so, he saw that "This person has had both of her arms cut off! She has no arms. Here at the head, she is a human. Here in the face, she is human." And the feet, he could see from the feet that "This is a human." But this human was dirty and stiff. It was clear that this coagulated blood had come out from these arms. But it was not coming out anymore, only the wounds remained.

He said, "Where have you come from?"

The girl said, "I come from such-and-such a place. I was taken there by my father who brought me to a forest that I do not know, in a land that is strange to me. He took me to that forest, then cut off both of my arms. And he left me there in the forest. Three days later, I found my way out. I was forced to come out because of the pain. I was forced to come out because of the pain, and my spirit shriveled because of my bitterness. I saw that I was going to die. I tried to get up. I was finally able to do so when I leaned against a tree. When I made the effort, I managed to stand up. Now that my arms have been cut off, I cannot stand up without support, without something to lean on. The only way I can get up from here, Father, is to be picked up."

The man said, "Your arms. What happened to them?"

The girl said, "My father cut them off."

The man said, "Why did your father do that?"

"My father cut off my arms—My mother died, and the two of us, my father and I, lived there at home for a long time. The two of us lived there many years. One day, my father suddenly turned on me with the idea that I should sleep with him! Because I resemble my mother! He wanted to bring back my mother through me. I did not agree. That's what made him take me and mutilate me. That's why he dismembered me. For two or three days, he kept insisting that I sleep with him, and I kept refusing. When it happened the first time, I was delousing him. He kept looking at me, crying. I saw that he was crying, and I asked him what made him do that. But he would not tell me. He just said, 'It's nothing!' I thought that he was feeling unhappy because of our circumstances—being left behind like that. And I began to lose weight; I became thin because of his behavior. This is not the usual weight of my body, the way you see me here. I've been thinner than usual for a long time because of what my father was doing. On the next day, the second day, at dusk, my father again said that I should go to bed with him. Again, I refused to do so. I cried. He hushed me, saying that people would wonder what was going on. So I stopped crying. On the third day, my father said the same thing, and again I refused. Then he said, 'Are you refusing? Definitely refusing?' Did I prefer to die rather than do what he was proposing? I told him that I would rather die than go to bed with my own father. He said, 'All right,' and he took a knife—I saw him pick the knife up, but I didn't know that he would use it to harm me. He loved me very much. I had no reason to be suspicious of him. He loved me. He used to say, 'My child, you really resemble your mother. When I look at you, I can only think of your mother.' I didn't pay much attention to that. I didn't think that he really felt so seriously about this. He took a sack; I watched him as he tore it, as if it were a blanket. He said to me, 'Let us go!' He knew where we were going, but he did not tell me. I walked with him, asking no questions. This was in keeping with my usual behavior, I always did whatever my father said. We journeyed then, we walked for several days, we traveled night and day. On the third day, we entered a large forest. When we got to the middle of that wood—we never stopped—he made me sit on the ground. Then he spread out the sack that he had torn. He said, 'Let us go to bed!' insisting that I should go to bed with him. I said, 'I'll never do that, Father!' and he asked me if I was still refusing, even then. I said, 'Father, I still refuse to do so!' He asked if I would prefer to die rather than do that thing. I said that I would prefer to die rather than do that. He said that I would not see the daylight again. He took out a knife and cut off both of my arms, then put them down on the ground. When he had done that, he went away. On the third day, I came out of the forest and walked here."

This fellow listened to what she said and concluded that she was telling the truth. He was clearly filled with compassion when he heard what had been related by this dirty child who was covered with sores on both sides of her body, and who had no arms.

He said, "What you've told me is painful." Then he went to the house and asked his wife to come out. She did so; she approached her husband. He said, "Do you see this?"

"What is this? What kind of thing is this? Why are you not fearful of such a thing?"

He said, "Well, just listen. I have heard a sorrowful story. Just look closely: this is a human being."

This wife observed closely then, and she saw that this was indeed a human—it was just that she was very dirty and soiled with blood. The part of her body not covered with blood was very small, but that small portion not clotted with blood was enough to reveal that she was a human being.

This wife said, "Where did you say this thing came from?"

The man said, "It turns out that this is what we thought was the pig that's been eating things in the garden." So said the man, and he peeled the corn off the cob for his wife, to the extent that the girl had peeled it off for him. [He went into the details of the story for his wife to the extent that the girl had related the events to him.] He told her everything: he told her of the girl's departure from her home with her father, of the journey to the forest, the arrival in the forest, until finally on the third day she came to be the person in this garden. These days, when they were all added up, amounted to nine days: she had been in the garden a total of three days; at her home, the period during which her father had sought to persuade her to sleep with him amounted to three days; they journeyed for three days; and she came out of the forest after three days of wandering.[30]

"Now, my wife, take this person. Go with her; see that she's washed. We'll keep her with us. We'll treat these painful wounds and heal her."

The woman took the child then and helped her to stand.

When she was standing, she said, "Leave me alone now, I can walk on my own." So said the girl. "I'm able to walk. What I can't do is stand when I've been lying on the ground. When I have been lying on the ground, I cannot get up again."

They went then, they went out of the garden gate. They entered the house. The girl was undressed, all those dirty things were removed. She was undressed, and the dirty things were put to one side. Garments from this home were put on her; she put them on and was covered. When she had been clothed, she was given something to eat. She ate, and when she had finished eating, water was dipped out for her; she was washed, scrubbed, that blood that was dried and sticking to her was scrubbed off. When those things had been done, when she had been clothed, they started to wash her garments. Her clothes were washed thoroughly; they were made elegant again. Then they were spread out to dry.

The man and his wife conversed with her. She was asked again to tell

---

30. The storyteller, by summarizing the various three day periods, is calling the audience's attention to, equating, and paralleling the various activities of the girl.

the story of how she came to be in this situation. So the girl told the story to the mother of the house—how it was that she came to be here, how it was that "I ended up this way."

Now it happened that, here at this homestead, there was a young man who did not yet have a wife.

It was said to him, "Son, this person should become your wife. No one dare make any comment about her deformity. She must be your wife, she must bear children for you, because she is a human being, a person. She has everything. The only thing she doesn't have is arms. She won't be able to work because she has no arms, but that doesn't really matter. We don't mind that. We only want her to bear children."

The young man agreed, and she became his wife. The son accepted the suggestion. He agreed to the proposal presented to him by his father and mother.

The young man and the young woman were happy.

They saw that she was a beautiful person. "She'll make beautiful children for us."

So it went, the young man repeatedly going to the young woman's house. She became pregnant, this woman who was under the compassionate protection of these people, this woman who had no arms. She became pregnant, her stomach grew; she became that kind of responsibility. As for her arms, she had long been healed, the pain had stopped. She was now a person who seemed to have been born that way, without arms.

Her stomach grew; the time came and she gave birth. She bore a child, a girl once again—just as her own mother had given birth to a girl child.[31]

She bore a child who was beautiful, who resembled her.

She constantly looked at this child. And when the others looked at her, they said, "It's clear that her mother was like this, Dear ones! This baby resembles her mother, even though her mother has no arms."

She too, when she spoke, would say, "You see—my own arms, my own wrists were like these."

Time passed then, time passed in this way. The child was weaned, and, when that had been done, the mother began to realize that "My life is no longer comfortable."

Her husband, the son of this homestead, had taken a train and gone away.[32] She was made uncomfortable because she began to be treated badly by her in-laws, by her mother-in-law and her father-in-law.

They were now suggesting to their son, "Why is it that you make no move to have another wife, to have a woman other than this cripple?"

31. The storyteller will now begin to equate the new born child and her mother, on the one hand, and the armless bride and her own mother on the other.

32. The storyteller here alludes to the realities of life in South Africa, of husbands going to the cities to work, leaving their families behind.

But the son loved this wife, even though she was the way she was. It was his parents who wanted him to seek another wife, a wife who would be able to work. The son paid them no attention, but his parents had begun to dislike this daughter-in-law of theirs. They began to refer to her in this way: "This cripple has wasted this young man's time. He doesn't have a wife."

And in this way: "There's nothing this thing can ever do in this house. She does nothing. Everyone has to do things for her!"

And this: "She doesn't know how to do anything! We have to wash for this thing; we have to cook for this thing. We have to build for this thing. Even water has to be dipped for her!"

And this: "She is able to do nothing! She has to be fed, food must be taken to her mouth, she can't even feed herself because she has no hands!"

It was at this time that the young man boarded the train and went away—he was going to seek work in the land of the white man. He went off to look for a job. This wife of his was left behind, even though her life was difficult, even though she saw that "I'm no longer loved in this house. It was my parents-in-law who first wanted me to be their daughter-in-law. Now they have gone back on their word, even though their son still has a good attitude toward me."

These parents plotted to make it possible for their son to have another wife; their plans for his future excluded his present wife. They wrote a letter; they wrote to their son. In this letter, they pretended to be his wife; they wrote the letter as if it were drafted by his wife. They wrote, "I, your wife, am pregnant. I am pregnant, I came home pregnant. When I came home, no one made reference to this pregnancy. No one objected." [She became pregnant by someone other than her husband and then had the effrontery to return to this home.]

The parents-in-law wrote this letter completely on their own; the wife had nothing to do with it.

When the son received this letter that came from his mother, though his parents pretended that it had been composed by his wife, he wrote an answer to his wife. He asked her if she had received his letter, "the one I wrote first, before the one you wrote to me regarding your pregnancy. And regarding that pregnancy that you reported to me in your letter and have not reported at home: why have I not heard of this from my own people? Why is that? Why should I learn of this from you, and not in the proper way, from my own people?"

When the wife got this letter from her husband, she became suspicious. She said, "There is something menacing me here. I can see that I am no longer in good favor in this house." She was unhappy because she knew that she could never return to her own home, to that father of hers who had killed her. She could not even consider going to him. Ever.

Then she received a letter from that father of hers, from her own father. He was writing from his home. He had heard of a certain woman who had given birth to a child. He had heard that this woman had been picked up in a garden, that she had no arms. He had learned that, in the homestead where she had been found, she had become a person who, when she had been washed, was seen to be beautiful. He had discovered that she had become a worthy person, a person who bore elegant children for them. He had heard that she was living very well. She had her weight back now, she had her beautiful body. This man had thought that she had died; now he realized that she was not dead at all. Therefore, he concocted another plan, something he might do to be certain that she would die.

So it was that he wrote this letter, a letter that purported to come from the land of the white man. It was addressed to her; it called her by the name of her own parents' place, not the name of her husband.

The letter said, "I had better never see you at my home again! I am coming home. If I come and find you there in that house, I am not only going to stab you, I shall kindle a fire and put you in it! And you will burn! That is a better way of doing it, now that I have seen that you are able to rise again when you have been stabbed with a knife. I am certain that if I burn you to ashes, you shall not rise again! I do not want to hear your name. I want no child who comes out of you—not at all! Not at all! Not at all! And I do not want an answer to this."

That letter arrived—it came from her father, who was pretending to be her husband. At the end, the letter said, "I do not even want to sign my name to this letter! You recall what I once said to you, that I do not really care to have a wife who has more arms than you have. Now I wish I had not said that!"

The young woman read this letter when it arrived. Then, in misery, she cried, "I wonder what will happen to me! I thought that I had found a place of refuge [literally, a place to lean against]. I wonder who has turned my husband against me? I always had some idea that this might happen. Nothing ever happens without some foreshadowing, nothing ever happens completely by surprise to anyone. In the beginning, I wasn't badly treated here. I don't know what I've done.

"I was picked up by my father-in-law in the garden. He found me there, then called his wife, my mother-in-law. I told them of my ordeal, how it came about that I had become the thing that had entered the garden through the hole the pigs had made under the wall. And they seemed that day to be very compassionate toward me. But that sympathy ended soon enough. My misfortune, my torment, goes deep. But I must go now—where, I don't know. But if what is in this letter is true—"

Her father-in-law, the father of her husband, took the letter, saying, "Let me see that letter, young woman."

She gave the letter to him. When he had read it, when he had read all the things that were written in it, when he found that the letter contained the things that the young wife had said it included, he said, "This is painful. Even to me. Now really, my child," said the man of this house, "I only wanted him to take another wife, a person who knows how to cook. It's not that I hate you; it's because you're unable to work. I don't hate you, I love you! I just wanted someone to be here in the homestead, someone to help with the work. Your child has to be put on your back, you can't even do that by yourself. That child must be taken from your back by someone; you can't do these things by yourself. But this letter from your husband is painful to me. You must just remain here until he comes home. We'll see what he does when he gets here."

The wife cried in her pain, she said, "No, Father-in-law! I've been told to get out. I've been told that otherwise I'll be hurt. I don't want to stay here until that happens. What will wake me up if I should die?"

Her father-in-law said, "Just allow things to happen, let's see what develops. We'll be here when he arrives."

The young wife said, "No, no, please, let me go! Please, dear ones! When someone from another home says that he's going to kill me, it's not likely than he'll spare me if he'd rather destroy me. If my own father killed me, if my own father did not spare me, then it's even more likely that a stranger will kill me. It's much more likely that one will be killed by a stranger than by one's own father. So please leave me alone. Leave me, let me go. Put the child on my back, let me go."

The father-in-law tried to persuade her to leave the child with him, but she refused. She said, "I can't leave my child behind. Let me go with her, particularly because I've turned into an animal in the eyes of the person who caused me to have the child."

She traveled then, she traveled with the child who had been put on her back. The child had a billycan that contained its food. She was put on the woman's back and buttoned up; she was tied on her mother's back. The woman journeyed, and, when they had gone a great distance, the baby cried. The child cried; she wanted to get down: the child was hungry. But her mother had no arms, she did not know how to get the child down. Both of them cried now. The mother of the child cried; she wept because her child was crying. Her baby was hungry, she wanted to eat, but the mother did not know how to get the child down from her back and feed her.

As a result of all this, the child had to urinate. And she urinated. Then it was obvious that the child wanted to defecate, and she defecated. All this caused the mother to cry; she wept, crying with that child. The mother cried until she became tired.

She slept, then they journeyed on, moving a distance equal to that which they had already traveled.

Then the baby was startled from her sleep. The baby was awakened, she wanted to get down, to suckle so that she would be nourished.

The mother was also tired, she was also hungry.

This occurred on the second day of their journey.

When the sun set, the mother had not yet found a way to resolve the problem: among other things, she was unable to sit down. And she saw no one whom she might call to come and help her in her predicament. That is the way things were through the night.

The next morning, the child was still crying, still hungry. Finally, she went to sleep. She slept, then was startled from her long sleep. It was time for her to awaken again, and she did so, and again she started to cry.

The night had passed, the third day dawned.

On that morning, the mother and child were on a plain. There were no homesteads: the way was barren, there were no villages. The mother crossed rivers, she became thirsty but there was nothing she could do to satisfy her thirst. Were she to throw herself down with the child on her back, the child would be hurt. And she too might be hurt and be unable to get up.

As she contemplated this crisis, she looked ahead and saw a large lake. She could see that there was much water in that lake, and she hurried toward it. She walked and walked, and finally she was very near the lake. When she was a short distance away, she moved quickly, directly to the body of water. She got there, she walked around the lake; she was thirsty, the dam was full. She went around, investigating the possibilities. No matter what method she might try to get water, it would be difficult for her. No matter what she did, she could not solve the problem. No matter what she did, it would be very challenging. No matter what she did, she knew that "I'll be hurt! Anything I do will be futile. No matter what I do, I'll drown. I might as well dive in." But she drew back, fearful of drowning. She went to a place some distance from the lake and cried. Then she returned to the lake. She was able, after a time, to get down on her knees—but she could only do so with abruptness. She went down on her knees, and when she had done so, she tried to bend her head down to the water so that she might drink. But when she tried to bend her head, the water churned, splashing water in her face.

Suddenly, there emerged a bird with long wings. This bird flew above her, it soared through the air, and the woman was terrified. She was still frightened when the bird poised on the brink of the lake. She trembled as the bird dipped its wing into the water and splashed water, suddenly, abruptly.

The bird spoke. It said, "There is your right arm for you, Young woman. You shall have your arms. Your husband is in great sorrow. His parents have written to him, referring to his expulsion of you. But that letter actually came from your father, that devious man, the filthy one who cut your arms off. He is the one who is driving you from your marriage. You really do have a good marriage. You shall live well, my child!"

Her right arm was now there!

Oh! She looked at it! She leaned on it, and was surprised.

"Why, what's happened? I see an arm just like my own!"

The bird again dipped its wing into the water, splashed water, and said, "There's your left arm, my woman! Take the child now and feed her. Then go home, go back to your home of marriage."

And that is what happened.

She had both of her arms again. She took her child's billycan, then sat above the lake. Without getting up, she began to feed her child. When she had finished doing that, she dipped again and again into the lake, and she drank. Her thirst vanished as she drank, her thirst ended.

She began to talk babytalk to her child, bouncing her about, putting her on her lap, hoisting her up, bringing her down, admiring her, putting her on her back, then again taking her and bringing her to her breast. She walked about with her child, hushing her, smacking her child's buttocks, doing many things to show fondness—things she had been unable to do when she had no arms. She did all those things now. She pinched the child, and the child cried. And when the child cried, she hushed her, she wiped the child's tears. She suckled her and fed her. She fondled the child, she cradled her, patted her on the face. And the child cried again, and the mother did all those things once more. When the child urinated, the mother took the blanket and wrung it out.

Then she put the child on her back and went on her way. But she did not return to her home of marriage. Instead, she went to a homestead that was north of her homestead of marriage. She arrived and sat there, asking for a place to stay.

It was said, "So-and-so's wife has arms! How did she get them?"

She said, "How did I get those arms? They just came out! I was given them by the ancestors of my home because I lived in such grief. They suddenly came out, I saw them. That was after I had been expelled from my home of marriage. I'm not going back to that homestead, even now. I've come to stay here. I want to find work so that I can rear my child. At my homestead of marriage, even the child is not desired anymore. My husband wrote to me and said that he was going to kindle a fire and put me into it—because when my father had tried to kill me by cutting off my arms, he had failed. I didn't die, I arose! He's not going to stab me. If he does stab me, I shall not die. He wants to burn me up, to turn me to ashes, so that he shall never see me again. But now the ancestors have made arms for me. I had my arms restored suddenly when I was over there. But there was no one there! After that happened, I decided to turn around, to return, to seek work. I no longer belong at my homestead of marriage. So please help me, keep me, be my friends."

Time passed; she remained in this homestead. They sent a messenger to her homestead of marriage, to explain what had happened to her, to explain that this young woman was here now—with arms.

They sent a person over there to her homestead of marriage, and he arrived with this message: "I've been sent from over there. The third day after she left her homestead of marriage, that young woman was suddenly seen—with arms! I tell you, she has arms!"

"Oh!" those of her homestead of marriage exclaimed. "What are you saying?"

"I say, she has arms! She says that she was expelled from this home. And now she says that she wants to live over there. She's looking for work. She wants to work so that she can feed her child. Because she was expelled from this place. It was said that she would be burned!"

Her father-in-law said, "Yes, that's the way it was. There's a letter from her husband, that's precisely what he says in the letter. I tried to restrain her, to keep her from departing. We've not been happy here since she left. Is it true? Is it true? Does she have arms?"

"Yes, she has arms! Go and see!"

The man got up, he went off hastily with the mother-in-law so that they might observe this thing for themselves.

Can it be true? Does she have arms?

They arrived. The young woman was smiling because she really did love them. But she had become confused on that day in the past. They too had loved her all that time. They too were perplexed—by her departure; they could not understand what their son had done.

The daughter-in-law explained things to her father-in-law: "I was crying, Father, and walking. On the third day after I left your homestead, I came upon a large lake. I was unable to do anything; I was wondering what to do. Should I throw myself into the lake even if it meant that I might drown? And so on. The child was hungry. The child was hungry, and so was I. And there was also in the physical state that I was in.

"Then, when I went down to my knees, when I went down to drink, a bird suddenly came out of the water. It splashed water in my face. I was startled, the bird flew above me. Then it came and dipped a wing into the water; it again came and splashed me. It said, 'There's your right arm, Young woman! Your arms that were cut off by your father are coming out today!' The bird told me about everything that had happened; it told me that no letter had come from my husband. It said that the letter had been sent by my own father; he had heard that I was living well, and he wants me to die. The bird told me to return to my homestead of marriage, but I was afraid to come to you. I was formulating a plan whereby you should see me living in another homestead, Father. I didn't feel that I should presume to return to your homestead."

"Oh, my child," said the father-in-law, "could this be you? This one who has no arms? Just stand up, my child!"

"All right."

"Please take your child."

The daughter-in-law took the child.

He said, "Just put her on your body."

She did so.

He said, "Please take her off your body."

She took the child off.

He said, "Put her on your back."

She put the child on her back.

He said, "Please lower her."

She did so.

He said, "Well, my child truly has arms!"

The mother-in-law was amazed; she was astonished by these events. And she was crying now, a mixture of pity and sadness at the departure of her child. Yet the departure had not been their fault. All they had wanted was another wife who would feed even the crippled woman herself because she did not know how to feed herself on her own.

Now they began to coax her, asking those in this homestead where she was living to allow her to go with them, to go to their home. They would write to their son.

The people in this homestead agreed to the request because they had no part in these affairs. All they knew was what had occurred on this day.

She went with them; she and her parents-in-law arrived at their homestead. The parents wrote to their son, telling him about his young wife: "We have just seen her, and she has arms now." That letter followed another which they had written, the earlier one stating that she had departed, "having been expelled by you." But the letter they were writing to him now would not reach him because he was coming back, returning to all this confusion. He felt that it could not have happened, that his wife would just disappear like that, especially since he had never written anything untoward to her.

Her husband arrived then. He arrived and saw that his wife had arms. When he got there, he said, "It is good that things have turned out like this. Your father was incestuous, and out of his filth he developed your arms once again as he continued to wallow in his perversity. He is in league with the devil. God is on your side, my wife. There was a plan here at home that I should take another wife. Never would I have another wife! I would have employed a servant to do the work for you, but I would never have taken another wife."

Part Two: Puberty

INTRODUCTION

MASITHATHU ZENANI ON STORYTELLING

A performer of oral narratives utilizes the materials of his or her culture much as a painter uses color. The analyst must therefore not mistake the cultural elements found in such narratives for direct reflections of the culture itself. There are few one-to-one relationships between the events in the performances and the artist's society, and it is this poetic truth that Mrs. Zenani routinely underscored in discussions regarding her stories. If the narrative tradition does mirror nature, it does so only in intricate, aesthetically perceived forms, which ultimately have the same effect on an audience as visual art, dance, and music do.

In oral narratives, certain repeated spatial relationships are established which, when the words dissolve, reveal the pure form of the work. The message of such a production is a complex one, generated by the movement of words, delineating the actions of characters, developed within formal patterns that have the effect of guiding the artist's arrangement of images. The fully developed story involves the movements of characters as dictated by these formal patterns. The aesthetic experience is of such felt relationships in addition to, rather than simply of, the verbal aspects of the story.

The plot, the linear movement of characters from conflict to resolution, is a stable element of the tradition, along with the patterns established by means of images trapped in verbal cliches, the patterning of narrative actions, and also nonverbal cliches, the patterning of body movement and sound. The temporal movement of the plotted actions of a story occurs within a set of patterns, making it possible for the inexorable progress toward resolution to be altered without tampering with its chronological unity. It is in this manner that complex relationships, the message of the performance, are experienced by the members of the audience. It is a sensual process, dependent on the elaborate network of relationships that constitutes the narrative production generally, and image and body movement are essential links in this activity. Definable categories of movement correspond to each of the two stable elements. In fact, the audience seems to respond in one way to plotted story, in yet another to rhythmic patterning. While these involved sets of emotions are unified during the performance, the more cognitive concern of the audience is with plot; the response to the patterns is wholly emotional, answering not to words but to verbal and nonverbal repetition.

By means of the repeated patterns, the performer causes an expectation of patterning in the early aesthetic experience of the members of the audience. They take up the repeated patterning, with their bodies, voices, and emotions, as the artist slowly transfers the responsibility for the sustaining of form to them; and a sense of anticipation is created. Once the audience is in apparent control of the rhythmic movement (the performer will repeat the basic patterns until she is certain that it is in control), friction is introduced as the artist purposely neglects to fulfill the audience's expectations by refusing to complete a pattern. The audience, now fully in harmony with the movement of the patterns and finding its expectations frustrated, becomes uncomfortable, reacts anxiously, and this contributes to its aesthetic experience as new relationships are forced upon its members. The introduction of friction makes possible an emotional, aesthetic reorientation, so that initial expectations are shattered, frequently giving way to new patterns and new expectations—and therefore new relationships. There is a concomitant development of complexity in the relationships between the separate image sequences. The combination of repeated forms, anticipation of forms, and friction, that is, incomplete forms, makes possible the audience's sensual experience. With the layering of new and simple narratives in a performance, relationships become more involved, the production developing into an experience of involute links between forms, generating yet a third level of performance, symbol. It is a process, constructed of the interaction of story and pattern, a move from concrete actions to an aesthetic experience of form.

The performance of oral narrative is a confluence of four crucial elements of oral tradition: the performer (and the historian is frequently a performer in such societies); narrative images, inherited from the past, a repertory which all members of the oral community share; images of the contemporary world, with its routine activities, implements, and rituals; and members of the audience, fellows of the artist's world.

Images from the inherited tradition, often fantastic, and from the contemporary milieu are brought together in performance, and any study of the aesthetics of such a system must consider the transmission of the juxtaposed images from an artist to the members of an audience. All four constituents must be present before performance can take place. The ancient images, when joined to the images of the contemporary world, provide a profoundly traditional and formal context for perceiving the objective world; this process endows that world with a design and therefore a meaning that has no existence outside the work of art and the tradition that has fostered it. The performance, depending on the psychological involvement of the members of the audience, exploits the unique combination of images.

The ancient images are obviously no longer reflective of the contemporary world: they are history, experiences once felt, memories of the past.

But those memories have been retained through the generations; since that early time when they did reflect a contemporary world, they have evolved into highly compressed images that no longer have the function of mirroring reality in any direct way. They have become altered, the faces and bodies and actions of the characters depicted by the images becoming allegorical extensions of their emotional content—that is, the emotional reactions to such historical characters and events by the audiences of the past. These early historical characters have come to represent in their physical and psychological representations the expressions with which they were once greeted, heroes becoming paradigms of purity, villains becoming the essence of malevolence. If they no longer have the function of directly depicting reality, they now reflect the experience of reality, as felt by separate generations of the culture and shared by them over the years to the extent that these condensed, symbolic images have developed unique meanings, common to many audiences, thereby becoming culturally significant. These images are therefore steadily retained in the art tradition over the generations because they continue to represent key cultural experiences, emotions, and values. They enable contemporary performers to plumb the cultural past, to relate modern experiences to those of the past. But the images of the past dominate those of the present because ancient images are tied into story, and it is story that gives the images of the present a context that they do not otherwise have. The inherited images continue to evolve, and they fall out of use when they have lost their significance and usefulness. Images are therefore constantly in a state of flux, developing, evolving, falling away, being incorporated. This historical process operates in the individual narrative performance, as characters from the real world become identified with the imagery from the past, as they blur and merge into one another. The performance is the tradition in microcosm.

During performances in present time, the ancient images are juxtaposed with real world images, and the result is a moment of intense emotional recognition, as the audience comes into emotional union with the experiences of the many audiences of the past, those experiences capsuled in the ancient images. The way we have of recalling past experiences differs considerably from the way we experience contemporary reality. The work of art unifies these varying perceptual experiences, and this emotional, formal combination of tradition and the contemporary world controls the emotions of an audience and an artist, and is the ultimate meaning of the artistic experience. The performance gives order to experience by bringing disparate images of the present, which are chaotic, without form, into relationship with a story composed of the condensed images of the past, so that the everyday experiences of the members of the audience are brought into contact with the cultural memory as codified in the imaginative tradition. The present is thereby given form and meaning through the act of juxtaposition.

Doubtless the most significant single characteristic of oral narrative performance is also its most obvious—repetition, in a variety of forms. The repetition of words, of phrases, of full images, and finally of complete narrative segments, whether identical or diverse, is vital to the artistic experience and involves both temporal and spatial elements. The simplest form of image repetition, other than the repeating of single words and phrases, is the expansible image, the recurrence of image sequences consisting of a central action which is similar if not identical with each repetition. But each repetition is not lexically the same; the fundamental narrative unit is a sensually experienced image and not a word rote-memorized. Such images have no place in time until they are objectified in a performance, placed in a linear continuum before an audience.

Each repetition contains new information. The artist fashions a work of art around the repeated action, moving the characters toward a climax, succeeding repetitions adding further new information to the accumulated experience. Each fresh layer and its intensified experience may, however, be an emotional rather than intellectual impression. The plotted images, or story, contain their own dynamics. Frequently, surface themes which support social norms in some way are generated by the imagery. But this plotting of images is also a chief organizing mechanism in the narrative system. It is largely the linear movement, created by the plotted images, that, in effect, turns in upon itself, breaks its own surface through the complex formation of repeated images, and thereby shapes the audience's experiences which have no place in time. Yet, ironically, these timeless experiences are established by a plotting system that has no existence except in time. The plotting mechanism, moreover, is responsible for the precise ordering of the audience's awareness of images, and it therefore plays a crucial role in revealing image relationships.

There is full participation by the members of the audience in the unfolding story. No proscenium arch exists, there is no safety in distance and darkness. Everyone is known: the artist emerges from the audience and, her narrative completed, is again swallowed up by the audience. The separate emotions and experiences of individual members of an audience are worked into the narrative being created. The members of the audience know the images; they have experienced them scores of times. They know the performer intimately, and she knows them. The artist seeks in a variety of ways to involve the audience wholly in her production. With words and gestures, she calls forth those two kinds of experience from the memories of those sitting before her. As she blends the images, she traps the emotions of the audience. While its members know the images well, their separate experiences of such images may not be, and most probably are not, precisely the same. Still, there is a sufficiently common experience of the images to make possible the capturing of the several emotional responses to them. When this has been done successfully, what remains is to trap other emotions in yet other images and image clusters. The final step in the process is the juxtaposition of the images, which now have caught up within them the experiences and emotions of the members of the audience: the images are brought into contact one with the other, and the message is communicated.

An important part of the oral narrative experience is nonverbal; this involves the regular movement of the artist's body and the resulting harmonizing of the body movements of the members of the audience, sometimes physical, always an emotional harmonizing. In some, if not all, narrative performances, the completely nonverbal movements of the artist—those that are not simply complementary to the verbal elements, as is mime, for example, but which supplement the verbal—are involved in the experiencing of the narrative message. The body movements of the performer reveal the basic repeated patterns of complex narratives and in so doing lead the members of the audience to an aesthetic experience of message.

There is a spectrum containing the extremes of mimed nonverbal gesture on the one end and purely abstracted body movement on the other. The abstract movements may or may not have their origins in the mimed activities. In the simple, expansible image performance, the verbal and nonverbal elements are very close to each other, the nonverbal being almost purely complementary to the verbal in both mimed and abstract movements. The rhythmical, musical breaking down of the narrative into its constituent parts is quite obvious in such performances, both verbally and nonverbally. In a southern African narrative, a woman is hurrying with her two children across the bleak veld. A voracious beast assails her, and she delays it by throwing it bits of her baggage. This set of images—flight/confrontation/delay—becomes the repeated action, and there is a song, also repeated, in which the anxious mother asks the importunate beast what it wants. Image plotting and patterning are thoroughly integrated. Repeated gestures accompany the words: the demands of the monster, the woman's fears and deepening terror, the throwing of the bits of baggage, the eating movements, the flight—all are mimed. The combination of these—repeated image sequence, repeated song, repetition of body movement—becomes predictable as the narrative proceeds; in fact, the message of this performance is achieved just through this predictability. Image set is piled on image set, word and gesture united in a repetition that finally has the effect of revealing the emotional plight and confusion, and fate, of the woman as she confronts her mysterious, ever returning adversary.

Patterning through repetition and the resulting predictability involve emotions of anticipation and fulfillment, with suspense a by-product, the artist's whenever she chooses to employ it. These are formal aesthetic aspects of performance, and they are compatible with the conflict-resolution movement of the plotted images, the development of which owes much to the repetition-predictability combination. But in complex performances, these two sets of composition materials (conflict-resolution, repetition-predictability) are not the same thing. Plotting of imagery is broken by the very elements that make possible the flow from conflict to resolution, by means of patterning and its product, predictability. The function of the repeated patterns, to sort out images and show relationships, becomes more critical. Message may now be experienced by means of elements of image plotting that are seemingly not calculated to generate message. As patterning and predictability enable plotting of imagery to move toward resolution, they also assist the artist to liberate herself from such linear plotting and achieve an experience not evident in such plotting.

In narratives in which the expansible image sequences are not at all obvious, the nonverbal elements—abstracted now, having no clear association with the verbal elements of the narrative in the sense of miming them—do the same work of ordering that they do in the simpler narratives in which the nonverbal are more directly aligned with the verbal aspects of the performance. In the tale depicting the actions of the woman and her deadly assailant, the nonverbal elements were so unified with the verbal that a separate function could hardly be assigned to them.

The human body and the music of the language, the nuances of gesture, the combined rhythms of performance, continue to break the narrative into its parts, even when the verbal elements no longer reveal these parts so obviously. Hence, the danger of making analytical judgements based on printed texts alone, and the necessity of considering performance when analyzing oral narrative, poetry, and history. The nonverbal activities perhaps had their alignment with the verbal originally, in these complex performances as in the simpler ones. Now the verbal elements continue to provide the narrative performance with the same harmonic grid, the same rhythmic frame that the nonverbal activities do more directly in the simpler narratives. And the verbal elements continue to have the same function, to demarcate the narrative, to identify its parts clearly so that relationships can be felt and the message experienced. It is not so much a self-conscious process as a felt experience.

The purely rhythmical movement of the body and the voice may reflect the underlying patterns of the narrative. These patterns are themselves composed of the rhythmic elements of the performance: patterns are constructed of the music of the words, but not necessarily the words themselves, the movement of the body, the temporal and spatial characteristics of the image sets. The rhythm that makes up the patterns has its objectification in the body of the artist and the sound of her words. These nonverbal aspects of oral narrative production reveal the texture of the verbally evoked images.

This rhythm, once established, creates an anticipation in the members of the audience that gets tied into nonverbal patterning, or models. When the same pattern reappears in a later image sequence in the performance, even if the verbally expressed images are not the same as those of the earlier sequences, the body, because it now has built into it a memory of the earlier pattern and hence a structural anticipation of the same rhythm, will react in the same way to this identical structure underlying different image sets, and so assist in the collapsing of the persistent linear movement of images, making possible the establishment of nontemporal forms crucial to message.

COMMENTARIES

TIME PASSES, THE BABY GROWS

Performance Note

Time: 2 August 1967, in the morning. *Place:* In the home of Mrs. Zenani, in Nkanga, Gatyana District, the Transkei. *Audience:* Members of Mrs. Zenani's family—her husband, her daughter, a granddaughter. (NS-10.)

Time passes, the baby grows and grows, until it becomes an older child.

When she is a child, a little child, she begins to go to gatherings of children. She visits other homes; occasionally she is scolded. When she is remiss, she is called a vagabond. So it goes on, the children getting together, making cattle of clay, spending time along riverbanks, playing. While they play, they sometimes involve themselves in rather dubious activities, the games of childhood. They sometimes play a game called *undize* [literally, "Shall I come?"; a form of hide-and-seek], during which the girls are mounted by the boys, and there are further scoldings: "These children are naughty!"

THE GAMES OF CHILDHOOD

Performance Note

Time: 18 September 1967, in the afternoon. *Place:* In a home in Gatyana District, the Transkei. *Audience:* Thirty men, women, and children. (Perf. 687.)

A boy and a girl were always quarreling in the presence of their mother and father.

Once, when this girl had contradicted her parents over some matter, her aunt reacted: "My child, why are you always quarreling with your brother about everything? Why do you do it? People will begin to wonder who it is you take after!" She continued her admonition: "You don't listen to what we say here. You refuse to change your behavior; you do whatever you want to do! I shouldn't be the one to speak to you about this, Child of my brother. I should call other people. You're a burden to me, you refuse to follow custom."

The younger child, the girl, said, "No, he's the one who crosses me! I simply said that I wasn't going to the purification ceremony. I won't go to the ceremony while it's raining!"

88

"You won't go to the ceremony while it's raining?"[1]

"That's right."

"If that's your reason, then you ought to tell it to the boys with some respect. If you're not going to the ceremony, just tell the boys. But tell them with respect. What is the right thing for you to do now? Let's go and discuss this matter with Grandfather over there in his house."

"Do you really think we should?"

"Yes, we must go to Grandfather because you promised to go to the ceremony and now you're refusing to keep the appointment."

"My brother talks to me like that because he is older than I am. And things won't change unless I forget that I'm younger than he is because a younger person is supposed to respect someone who is older. The younger must defer to the elder person. When we're with others, he puts on airs, he acts in a haughty way toward me. All right, I'll go to the ceremony. Let's get this over with."

"I was just suggesting that we go to the ceremony," said her brother.

"All right, let's go."

They went, and when they arrived there, someone said, "Let's play *undize*."

"How is *undize* played?" a girl asked.

The boy said, "*Undize*—mats are put into the rooms. Chests and boxes are used as hiding places."

"Then what happens?"

"Well, say I'm the one who hides first. When I have hidden, the one who is to come and look for me says, 'Shall I come? Shall I come?' And I shall say, 'Yes!' and when I've said that, the other one will come and look for me. He responds to the words, 'Shall I come?'"

"And the one who is discovered—what happens then?" the girl asked.

The boy said, "The one who's discovered? Well, the one who's discovered—the one who found him can do whatever he likes to the person he has found."

"Oh, well, I can't play a game like that."

"The game of *undize* is not to be played with a brother and sister. It must be played with other children from the village."

A boy from another village said, "Well, this girl should play the game with me if she doesn't want to play it with her brother."

"All right, play with her then."

They played the game. While they were playing, another youth got up and went to the boy who was hiding himself behind a mat. He hit him, and the boy said, "What're you doing now?"

---

1. The performer abruptly shifts the scene from a conversation between the girl and her aunt to the earlier conversation between the girl and her brother.

The other said, "I'm playing the game."

"Oh, is this how *undize* is played? But what is this? Why are you mounting her?"

The dams dried up. The dams that were filled with water dried up [that is, a fight began].

"Why are you climbing on top of her? From now on, we are no longer friends! You've been like a brother to me. You've been my closest friend. But now I've found you out! I was a little suspicious of you yesterday. You don't want to do anything properly, you refuse to behave properly. Our friendship is at an end, I can see that."

The other said, "But why is our friendship ending?"

"We can't be friends anymore—you got on top of her!"

"But that's how the game of *undize* is played!"

"Well, I'll be the first one to do it to her then. I'll be the first to do this *undize* to her. I want to be sure that the game is really played that way. Where is this *undize* played, anyway?"

"Well, it's played by people at home who love each other; it's played when they're happy. It's played by the children of that place."

"Oh, and this *undize* is not played by strangers? And people don't join the game while it's going on?"

"*Undize* is not a game for guests. It's something that children in a village play."

"I'll play it with you now. When I get tired, it'll be your turn."

"But the game doesn't just involve one girl and one boy. It's usually played by a group of children in a village."

"How would it be if we just skipped this *undize* and played some other game?"

"Which game?"

"Let the girls play the boxing game."

"My friend," one of the boys said, "what is the boxing game?"

"It's a game in which girls box with each other—fight with their fists. And we can play our own game, a boys' game of boxing. We'll take sticks, we'll cushion one of our hands, then we'll fight."

"Do you call that a game?"

"Of course! It's a game because it takes place without a quarrel starting it. It's a game that's played by children of our age."

"I saw a little of this thing that you call a 'game' at So-and-so's place, at the circumcision lodge. I watched the coming out of the young circumcised men.[2] I watched as all the young men of that area divided themselves into sides. I watched them pad their hands, and I saw some of them

---

2. As they return to the village from the circumcision lodge, they are preceded by young men engaged in a stick fight.

knocked to the ground. But no one worried about that; it wasn't taken seriously. No one said that this was a bad thing. Instead, it was praised. One young man was even singled out from the others, and it was said, 'He defeated the entire group.' Yes, I know the kind of game you're describing, I've seen such a game played.

"Now, in the game of boxing, no one goes to the point of drawing blood. Boxing is a game. Those who aren't allowed to play the game just go away. Those who are allowed to play the game are simply accepted. But there are no hard feelings in this game, no blood is drawn. Some people lose, others are victorious. But I won't argue anymore. Whatever the rest of you decide to do, I'll go along with it. I'll play. Let's begin.

"Let's begin with a game of tag. One of you must run. Run up to that place! Then I'll give chase. I'll try to tag you. Now if I'm just about to catch you, and if you're getting tired and don't realize how close I am, all you have to do is say, '*Tyholi!*' [*Umtyholi* is the devil], and I must leave you alone. But if I get to you and tag you first, then you're the one I've tagged."

"No, my friend, I won't play a game like that," said the other boy. "Those games are for very little children! But there is something here that I really want; there's a girl who I want. When we're around other people, she pretends that she doesn't like me. But when there's no one around, then she's well pleased with me. I want to come face to face with her. Then I'm going to do something that'll disturb others from her home because there are young men and boys over there from her village. It'll be said that I'm the cause of trouble. But really, it's that girl who has no respect for me. She's the cause."

"How can you say that?"

"I'm saying it for this reason: only yesterday, I had a date with her. And she didn't keep it. Even though we had an understanding. She said that she does not know what I want from her. Now I'm not naive when it comes to boy-girl relations. I've been dealing with people for a long time, and they go the whole way with me. They keep their appointments."

THE AWAKENING OF THE CHILD

Performance Note

Time: 2 August 1967, in the morning. *Place:* In the home of Mrs. Zenani, in Nkanga, Gatyana District, the Transkei. *Audience:* Members of Mrs. Zenani's family—her husband, her daughter, a granddaughter. (NS-10.)

Then comes "the awakening of the child": a girl is now very sensitive; she resents any reference to herself in her presence.

The child continues to grow older: a boy finally reaches the stage when he attends the night dances; he goes to those parties, he herds the livestock, among other things.

Then there is the girls' puberty ceremony, a ritual during which girls are initiated into womanhood, when the custom of entry into womanhood is performed: young girls become marriageable women. This is an occasion for celebration. The women ululate: "Halala!"

There are also parties for younger children. On festive occasions, the children want to sleep overnight at other places; they do not wish to go home, and these boys and girls sleep overnight—young men, too, people who have experienced the various activities of boyhood. There is frequently somewhat antisocial behavior on such occasions; unwholesome things occur. Sometimes, while the others are sleeping, a child might sneak up on them and do something that began with the game in which the children mount each other. The child might develop a habit of sneaking in while others are sleeping.

The one who is the object of this secretive activity says, "Who is this? What are you doing?"

The other says, "I'm not doing anything."

But it is said that the sneaky one is making improper sexual advances—if he happens to be surprised in the act.

That child will learn. That is how Xhosa practice works.

He will grow older; he will grow until he reaches the stage at which, in proper Xhosa fashion, he speaks to another child and says, "I want you!"

The other replies, "I don't want you."

"What's the matter with me? Why don't you like me?"

"I have put you into a cockroach's leg [a riddling comment]."

"How? Take it out then."

"No, it can't be taken out."

"How did you put it in?"

And the girl says, "I have put you into a cockroach's leg."

They will flirt with one another in that way until one accepts the other's proposition. They will grow in mutual understanding, doing various things but not publicly.

THE DANCE FOR BOYS

Performance Note

Time: 13 August 1972, in the morning. *Place:* In a fallen rondavel near Mrs. Zenani's home in Nkanga, Gatyana District, the Transkei. *Audience:* Two women and one teenaged boy. (NS-169.)

Here in the land of the Xhosa, members of the younger generation from various sections frequently gather in large numbers on Saturdays, going to a dance, a dance for boys. The boys are accompanied by their girlfriends.

There are two grades of the dance for boys. The dance for younger boys is separate and has another name; it is a dance of boys who are still quite young. They too have their girlfriends, chosen from age sets equal to their own. Their dance also takes place on a Saturday, in the evening.

When they have finished eating, the children form a procession that meets with other groups, and they all go to a homestead where they have obtained a house for the dance. They go there and entertain themselves the whole night. The children who attend the younger boys' dance must get home at sunrise to be in time to take the livestock out to the pasture because the boys who are at the older boys' dance will not return until sunset.

REQUESTING AN OLDER BOYS' DANCE

Performance Note

Time: 13 August 1972, in the morning. *Place:* In a fallen rondavel near Mrs. Zenani's home in Nkanga, Gatyana District, the Transkei. *Audience:* Two women and one teenaged boy. (NS-169.)

Then again, there might be a quarrel among the boys. There might be a surprise attack, boys from another area surrounding these boys. Or boys from another area might come along to suggest that "We must get together."

"Let's have another dance party."

That is how it proceeds. Boys who can talk smoothly first talk together, then say, "We want to have a dance party with those particular boys." They send off a request that an older boys' dance be held. Such a request has to be made because if the boys simply go off without making a request things might prove dangerous; there may be a falling out.

So they take counsel. Then four or perhaps as many as eight boys go to request an older boys' dance. They join with the boys of another area; they come together, and the older boys' dance plans unfold. The boys come in, standing over by the door, to one side. Then they sit.

It is observable from the start that "These are not boys with whom we usually have parties."

"They are strangers."

There is a pause, then someone whistles. Conversations are interrupted. There is silence.

Someone asks, "Where are you boys from?"

One of them responds, "We're from such-and-such an area."

"Continue."

"Well, we've come here to request an older boys' dance with you."

"Where have you danced before?"

"Well, we've danced all over, from our own area to that place over there. Now we want to have an older boys' dance with you. We've been wanting to have one with you for a long time. But we have not brought ourselves to mention it to you."

Then it is said, "Well, that's the word, Comrades. You've heard what these boys have said."

They talk it over with each other in low voices. Some of them speak abrasively: "Nonsense! Why have they become tired of their own dances over there?"

"Ee! Well, if you care about their request, go on—answer them."

They talk in the manner of boys—contemptuously.

Then a boy speaks: "Well, Fellows, they've come to ask to join us in an older boys' dance. They should be given a reply."

"If we don't want to accede to their request, then that's it. But if we're going to agree, let's say so."

At length, the request is accepted.

Then it is said, "We have heard them."

Those strangers ask where, the following week, the party is to be held. They are told. This older boys' dance goes in turns; it is held on this side this week, and the next one will be in a different location. The one following that will be somewhere else. The venue is variable, according to some pattern; it is not fixed.

The boys indicate where the older boys' dance is to be held next. They clearly indicate the homestead, carefully telling the strangers precisely where it is.

They ask, "Since you wish to dance with us, how many areas do you represent?"

The boys reply that they are representing only one area. Or, if two areas are involved, they say that.

The next morning, they go home. They return to their homes, having first attended a local stick-fight. But they themselves have not participated in the sport; they have been observers only.

On Saturday of the following week, in compliance with the understanding they have reached, they come to the party. The host boys are expecting them. They are welcomed, according to the prior agreement.

They arrive, and, if the party is a big one, more than one house will have been allocated for the dance. The strangers are assigned a house. If they are satisfied with this arrangement, the party will go on according to its usual pattern.

When these older boys get to their meeting place, they begin at once to dance to the girls' chants. There is a special chant to accompany the sitting-down of the girls; then the boys sit on the girls' laps. And the boys compete in dancing. Boys from the different areas form teams, and one boy from one of those sections steps forward. He engages in a dancing contest with another boy. The boys compete until one boy is clearly the champion dancer, until he has surpassed all the others. When that competition is at an end, all the boys stand up, along with the girls, and they sing and clap their hands, rhythmically moving their feet. This movement is also a competition, and one of the dancers, the one who surpasses the others, is acclaimed the bull, the champion. The dance is a vigorous one: every part of the champion's body quivers, as he exhibits his ability. The others are not quite up to his talent; they might as well be walking, they are by contrast inept. One of them does not even know how to keep the rhythm. Others point to this awkward dancer; they talk to each other about him, complaining that he has spoiled things, that he has caused others to make a muddle of the dance. But that does not really upset anyone.

So it goes on; they continue in this way until the morning. When morning comes, they are all perspiring, going outside again and again to cool off. The girls do the same because they too have been dancing, vigorously, diligently. In the morning, the girls go out in couples, in threes and fours, going to freshen themselves because, as you realize, they have not slept. Their faces are now covered with dust, they are soiled. All of this lively activity has the effect of beating down the floor of the house; dust is raised, and this dust soils them because their bodies are sweaty. In the morning, then, they go out to wash up. They go around to the various homesteads in the neighborhood of the house where they have been dancing, and they ask for water.

When a girl wants to go out and wash up, she first goes to a boy from her section and says, "We want to go and freshen up."

The boy gives them leave to go. If a girl goes out without reporting, she is beaten by the boys and pushed back into the house. Belts are used to scourge the girls. Also, when the boys say, "Sing! Chant, clap your hands!" one of the boys might start out at one end, playfully lashing all the girls with a belt. This is one of the rules of the older boys' dance: the boy does not lash out in anger. It is understood that anyone who feels like it just goes ahead and beats the girls. When that has been done, the girls are told to chant.

A group of girls goes out to request water at some of the homesteads in the vicinity. They ask the woman of the house, "Mother, please give us some water so that we can wash up."

The extent of indulgence to such requests from the young people varies. One woman might dislike the practice; another might give the girls the water. Then they wash.

That boy from whom they have asked permission to go and wash up comes to the girls repeatedly, and says, "Hurry up! It's getting late!"

So the girls freshen their makeup. They wash their faces and their feet too. Then they dry themselves and put on ochre cosmetics to make themselves presentable. They apply to their faces various types of ochre, all of which are produced by rubbing certain stones together. Some apply an ochre known as "Pride." Each girl wears the type of ochre she likes best. They adjust their elegant clothing, putting on various ornaments. Then they look to see if the boy from whom they have asked leave to go is anywhere around. He is seen coming toward them. He plays at lashing them with the belt, and they hurry a little, returning to the dance house. In the end, all of the girls have gone through this activity, going out of the dance house in this way.

In the house, the various groups are gathered according to their places of origin. When the business of washing up is over, the tempo of the dancing seems to increase, along with the chanting. The dance moves to a vigorous climax.

AFTER THE DANCE: STICK-FIGHTING

Performance Note

Time: 13 August 1972, in the morning. *Place:* In a fallen rondavel near Mrs. Zenani's home in Nkanga, Gatyana District, the Transkei. *Audience:* Two women and one teenaged boy. (NS-169.)

When the dance is over, the various sections of boys position themselves. Each boy carries three sticks—there is the stick for defense, the stick for offense, and the stick for fighting in a random, free-for-all contest. That last stick is a knobkerrie [a short wooden club with a knob at one end]. When sitting about casually, each boy has his stick of offense with him, along with the knobkerrie; the stick for defense is stuck into the ceiling of the house while the dancing is going on through the night. This stick for defense is stuck into the ceiling, each boy putting his on the side of the house where he is sitting.

When the dance is about to end, the girls begin removing the ornaments that the boys have been wearing on their heads. These ornaments are varied, diamond-like ornaments. They are removed from the boys. The earrings are also removed from the boys. The girls take the ornaments from the boys who are in their sections.

Bound for work

Now the dance comes to an end, and as it does the boys retrieve those defensive weapons. Each boy gets his fighting stick. Then they take small blankets and wrap them around their knuckles as cushions: they are preparing themselves for stick-fighting. They come out of the dance house, one after the other, and they get ready for the fight. They prepare immediately, in front of the dance house. The girls simultaneously cheer the boys on, urging them to play that sport of theirs. They move a distance from the homestead where the dance has been held and find a place slightly out of view, a place that seems suited to the strategy of their stick-fight. The boys now arrange themselves in various groups. Those who are on the side that has acted as hosts to the others will be by themselves, along with another group. So the sides are formed.

This is how the sport is played: one boy from one of the sides steps forward, then one comes forth from the other side. These two join in battle, fighting each other. This activity is euphemistically referred to as a "sport." But it can happen that a boy will die in such an encounter. The game is not an easy one. The combatants assault each other. The knobkerries remain with the girls. The boys may have a few of them, but the function of the knobkerrie is not connected with this sport.

The boys step out of the sections two by two. One of them fights until he can take no more, until he has been hit and overwhelmed by the force of the continued assaults. Sometimes a fighter has a poor defense, and he is bleeding in many places. At last, he is bested. Under those circumstances, the boy has to concede: "All right, my fellow, you've overcome me!" Those two then sit down. Two others step forward in the same way—one boy from one of the sides, the other from the opposing side. They then meet in battle.

The fighting goes on until two boys who are evenly matched come together. They hit each other equally hard, they exchange blow for blow; each is hurt as badly as the other. But no one wants to call the fight off. Those who are sitting there watching say, "Really, they ought to be stopped."

"But neither of them will give in!"

"They continue hitting each other!"

"That's because they're so hard-headed!"

Finally, they are stopped.

Someone says, "We've called a stop!"

"Now call it off! Sit down!"

They stop. But there is a constant desire for a rematch since neither has conceded, neither has said, "You've overcome me!"

Each says, "I was never overcome by So-and-so!"

"Others intervened and stopped us."

This kind of thing happens in connection with an older boys' dance. They engage in that kind of fighting, beginning with those in the junior age group. Among these older boys, those who attend the older boys' dance, there are also boys who are called juniors. And there are boys who are called the senior boys. So there is an inequality that exists among those who participate in the older boys' dance. In all organizations, there are always those who lag behind the others. Still, they are all supposed to be of the same rank at this dance. But in the older boys' dance as elsewhere, there are boys who are junior to the others. And when the sports events take place, the juniors go first. After that, it is said, "Off with the juniors!" and the seniors take their turns.

"We want the first league now."

A big boy from that side steps out, and a big boy from the other side also comes forward. They come together and fight, and one of them is overwhelmed in the same way as among the juniors. A fight ensues, and it will be a bloody one. When the boys engage in this sport, there is always blood. But that does not upset anyone very much. It is a popular sport, a traditional and ancient Xhosa practice. One grows up accustomed to being hit. It is said, "If one has never been hit on the head and bled, he is uninitiated."

"If you've never bled, not even a little, in the head, you've not been initiated."

The sport is a common one. A boy who is afraid to participate in it is called a coward—the boy who does not play the sport, who is afraid of being hit. He is derided, blankets are piled on top of him until he is covered with sweat, unable even to move. All the boys are told to pile their garments on top of him; he should not even watch the sport because he will never do anything anyway.

While the boys are engaged in their sport, playing their game on the veld, the girls are over there inside the dance house. They are hitting each other in the same way as the boys, except that the girls use their fists, their hands; they even kick each other. Girls of the red ochre people wear certain things on their wrists—bangles; they wear hard bangles on their wrists. And they wear rings on their fingers. When they exchange blows, one throwing her arm against another, this bangle slashes into the opponent's forehead or nose, and the fists pound as well.

In their own way, the girls have taken sides comparable to those of the boys. The girls, corresponding to the separate sides that the boys have taken, so align themselves. Because the knobkerries of the boys have been left behind here in the house, the girls sometimes take these weapons and pound each other with them. The knobkerries are sticks of wood which have been handsomely crafted, so that there is a portion that is rounded. Nails have been carefully arranged around this knob, nailed to the knob so that it becomes heavy. If it should hit someone on the head, it may or may not break a bone, but it does leave an ugly wound on the head, a really vicious one. But if the girls do happen to generate a fight among themselves, they are restrained. These battling girls in the dance house are told to stop.

After a while, the boys' sport ends, and the girls interrupt their activities by looking from time to time to see what the boys are doing. There are occasions when the girls' sparring develops into a general melee, and they will begin fighting in earnest. They pick up the knobkerries, and begin to attack each other. This is reported to the boys, and perhaps two of the boys will come over and scatter the girls, playfully beating them all to stop them from what they are doing. Then the girls play and dance; they are happy and do things in a less chaotic fashion, now comporting themselves with some dignity. But when they were fighting among themselves, they tied up their skirts with their turbans in an unseemly way.

The boys return to the dance house. Then they depart with the girls, returning to the separate areas from which they have originally come. They fan out now, going back to their homes, the girls chatting with these boys, talking about things that are typical conversation topics among girls of these age levels.

They reach their homes at sunset.

A DEEPER DIMENSION TO THE SPORT

Performance Note

Time: 13 August 1972, in the morning. *Place:* In a fallen rondavel near Mrs. Zenani's home in Nkanga, Gatyana District, the Transkei. *Audience:* Two women and one teenaged boy. (NS-169.)

When the dawn has come and the older boys' dance has come to an end, the stick-fight begins. A boy steps forward from his group, and a boy comes from the host group. The sport goes on as usual; they engage each other in stick-play. If, as the game goes on, it becomes clear that there is a deeper dimension to the sport, and the strangers are hitting the hosts with considerable force and overwhelming them, the hosts conclude that "These boys we agreed to accept—they're overwhelming us."

Another strategy is discussed: "We'll have nothing to do with them."

They express their displeasure in this way: "You must never come to a party here again."

"Don't come here again!"

The guests, who were well satisfied while they were overwhelming these host boys, demand to know why they are being denied this privilege. They resist the idea that they might be unwelcome in the future. Having been expelled, however, they depart.

That is how, according to Xhosa protocol, a crisis deepens.

When they have departed, the ousted boys take counsel. They conceive a plan: "Let's go back and surround them."

"We'll close in on them while they're still partying."

"Yes, since we know where the older boys' dance is being held."

So they set out, fully armed, at night. They decide to move out in the middle of the night. They arrive when the night is already far gone; well armed, they approach the site of the party. When these boys get to the older boys' dance, the other boys look at each other—and then they go out of the dance house, one by one.

"These are the boys we told to leave!"

"Why have they come back?"

"Look carefully. See if they're dressed in their finery."

They wonder if the boys are still wearing their beads, those beads that are removed and left in the care of the girls when the older boys' dance is ending.

The interlopers are inspected carefully from a distance, and it can be seen that they are armed—not dressed in their beads. This means that they have come to force the issue, even though they have been instructed to leave.

The host boys therefore prepare themselves; they cautiously ready themselves without making it too obvious, pretending to be moving about casually.

They say to their juniors, "You keep on dancing."

"Don't let on to these boys that we know what they're up to."

"Pretend that we're not aware that they're up to mischief."

So the junior boys continue to dance. The seniors stealthily remove the beadwork that they are wearing; they move about and come back to the party. Everything happens with suddenness. These boys, having signaled each other, close in; they shower blows on those who are in the dance house, trapping them by closing the door.

That is how it happens in the land of the Xhosa.

It is not uncommon that some boys die in the dance house. These boys beat the others, and there is no way out. They push each other back and forth in that house. Some manage to escape in the confusion. Lamps go out. Sometimes, a boy attacks his own comrade, even to the point of killing him, not realizing who he is fighting in all that darkness.

Outside are the younger ones. They can hear the battling, and there is no speaking. No one talks.

What talking there is is done by the girls. And they are screaming. "Yo-o-o! Yo-o!" All of them. There is a din. "Yo-o-o-o!"

"Where has everyone gone?"

"We'll die here!"

"Yuu-u-u!"

"Ooo-o!"

"My mother's child!"

"The darkness!"

This is what the girls say.

At length, the owner of the homestead where the party is being held hears what is going on. He is in his own house; the dance house is the one he has loaned to the boys. He can now hear the screaming and the thuds of the knobkerries as blows fall on heads, the ribs being hit by varieties of offensive weapons. The home owner comes out then and goes to other men, neighbors of his, telling them of the "Boys over there at home! They're involved in an ugly fight! Come, Fellows!"

So those men come. The owner quickly sends one man to go to the royal residence, to the ruler of the area, the headman. And he sends someone to go to the member of the board who is close to the village. The board member comes along with the headman that very night.

The men stand outside the dance house, saying, "You, Boys! Come out of that house!"

The men are also well armed; they are carrying spears. As the boys who have been fighting emerge from the house, each man is on guard. He does not know whether a boy might fall on him and attack him.

The boys come out, and it is said, "Where do these boys come from?"

A boy who has escaped in the darkness without a scratch says, "We're being beaten by boys from such-and-such a place. The ones we had a party with last week."

Then it is said, "You boys from that place, get out of here!"

The men drive them away. They drive those boys off. The boys are told to leave the area, and they stand some distance off in a group. They inspect each other, making certain that they are all present because, as you might guess, during the time that the fight was raging, it was dark. Sometimes, after such a battle, they are all accounted for; there are no casualties. And sometimes, some of them are missing. In that case, they remain there, they will not go away. They stand at a distance, knowing that if they refuse to leave the men might harm them.

Time passes, and lamps are lit to see if there have been any casualties among the boys. When they discover who has been hurt, they turn their attention to those who can be helped. For those who can be treated, Xhosa medicines are applied to the wounds, even on the heads of some of the boys. For some of them, nothing more can be done. Others are found already dead. Some have died in the fight.

Then it is determined, in Xhosa fashion, that there will be a lawsuit because of that activity, because these boys have been attacked by the others. If a member of the attacking group has been killed, there is no dispute over that because they are the aggressors. They are the ones who have attacked these boys who were simply enjoying themselves in their own area. The law will make the attackers responsible for any casualties incurred during this fight.

Even the girls are splattered red with blood because, when a boy is assaulted, he is thrown and falls among the girls. Or he might be wounded, and he runs bleeding, hiding behind the girls in all the confusion.

At the royal residence, the discussion of the lawsuit leads to this conclusion: "This trouble was caused by your boys!" On the other side, the matter is also considered in the royal residence. Then the chiefs discuss the matter between themselves. That is Xhosa procedure.

Sometimes the boys themselves meet—by themselves—demanding reparation because some of their number died in the confrontation. They speak of the matter among themselves; the boys discuss it alone, away from everyone else. It is not referred to in the presence of their parents; the older people know nothing about these discussions. The boys set up the meeting in this way: they send two children to the boys who assaulted them, saying, "We want to meet you at a certain place on a certain day."

Others know of the plan; it is to be a daylight fracas. The boys come together—and fight. But they will not tell the older people about it. The adults will just have to see it happening because that is how the Xhosa do

A girls' dance

it. This custom was also the practice of the boys' forefathers, when they were boys. When boys act this way, it is usually because they are going to a fight. People are quiet. They do not speak because, according to Xhosa tradition, "If you speak, you'll cause the boys to be weak and cowardly. You must say nothing, just keep quiet. If you want to say something, just feel it inside, don't speak it. Even if you're anxious, you must keep quiet because—you don't know—one of the boys of your side might he grievously hurt."

The boys speak of their plan to the others, and an arrangement is reached. A day is fixed, along with a time—early in the morning—because this imbroglio must start in the middle of the day. The boys begin to come together in the place that they have agreed upon. You can see them going, in threes and fives, going to sit at that place. Each boy hurriedly eats something at his home, each boy removes from his body anything that might slow the flow of his blood. Nothing must constrict him in the arms. The boys do not like to sit around in the house; they tend always to be outside. Nor do they walk with women.

Older people recognize on such a day that "Something's going to be done by these boys!"

According to Xhosa custom, it is imperative that the people be alert, prepared. An adult will seem not to care; she will pretend to be calm, unconcerned, but she will tend to walk about anxiously, worried about what her offspring might be involved in, hoping that the cares of her child are not burdensome.

The boys set out, carrying their weapons—the knobkerries, the defensive sticks. They take from the girls some small blankets for cushioning. Then they depart. It is clear where they are to meet. They appear in a certain order: "The wing should be held by someone who's tough, who knows how to fight!" It is done that way on both sides. Some of the boys are on guard; others walk behind them. Behind the boys come their girls.

The girls are chanting, singing of the coming confrontation between the opposing boys. The girls have girded themselves, their upper bodies exposed, uncovered. They are swaggering, singing praises:

> "The fellows will get what they want!
> This is the coming confrontation!
> It is a clear confrontation.
> The milk is in the sun!"

But the girls observe these activities from a distance. They do not come close—only close enough to be able to see what will happen.

When the boys come together in battle, it is not pleasant, I assure you. They begin attacking each other. No one waits for the other to make the move. Confusion is complete. The confrontation is ugly, it is terrible. Some of the boys fall to the ground; they are tramped on by the others because no one is careful about such things in the battle. There is no time for such niceties.

Eventually, the combatants become exhausted, their strength ebbs, their power declines. Each one seeks to bring the boy he has met to his knees; he attempts to bring him to the ground. Each side desires to do that. But finally one of the sides is defeated; it retreats. The boys on the losing side flee. But some of the boys on their side have not noticed that they are in retreat: they only know that whoever has died is dead, that whoever has survived is alive. The retreat goes on, and the victorious boys begin to drive back those who continue to hold on while their comrades are fleeing.

This kind of fight is normally watched as a form of entertainment. After a while, when those boys have dispersed and fled, others intervene. "The boys should all leave now!" Only the casualties should be left behind.

In a situation of that nature in the land of the Xhosa, there is no accountability because it is a confrontation in which no one is assaulted without foreknowledge. There is a mutual invitation; both sides have accepted it. Even if someone is hurt seriously, it is said, "Well, it was a confrontation, and the dead one is the dead one. It was his bad luck."

And that is the end of it.

MONDAYING

Performance Note

Time: 13 August 1972, in the morning. *Place:* In a fallen rondavel near Mrs. Zenani's home in Nkanga, Gatyana District, the Transkei. *Audience:* Two women and one teenaged boy. (NS-169.)

Time passes; after the sun has arisen and Monday has dawned, at about midday, in the early afternoon, they go to the local shop. It is said that they have gone to the "opening," that they have gone "Mondaying." This "Mondaying" does not mean that they are necessarily going to shop for anything. They are merely going there to pass the time. It is customary that they do this on Mondays. They feel a necessity to gather together again. But those coming together this time are the local boys and girls, not the various sections from around the countryside. The youth of each of the sections congregate at their own store; they do not all gather together in a large group on these Mondays. Each person in his own area goes to the "Mondaying" at the local shop, and the strands of the previous conversations are tied together—the things that were discussed over there at the dance and later on Sunday. The boys and girls are sitting in couples. Some of the topics are brought to a conclusion; other topics are initiated here. Some of the young people have already made up their minds about the subjects of conversation. In those cases, they do not converse, but simply admire each other, enjoying each other's company. Others are carrying pennies and half-pennies, and they too engage in mutual admiration, buying little things for each other when they feel like it. So-and-so buys something for So-and-so. Mainly, it is the girls who buy things for each other. The boys merely sit there.

The custom proceeds in that manner in the land of the Xhosa.

I WANT YOU TO BECOME A MAN

Performance Note

Time: 2 August 1967, in the morning. *Place:* In the home of Mrs. Zenani, in Nkanga, Gatyana District, the Transkei. *Audience:* Members of Mrs. Zenani's family—her husband, her daughter, her granddaughter. (NS-10.)

The time will come when the boy grows older here at his home. His father says to him, "My child, I want you to be circumcised. I want you to become a man. I want a second man here in the homestead. I want you to be able to carry out the business of this homestead."

The boy does not answer. In the olden days, a child did not answer back when an adult spoke to him. Even if he did not like what was said, or feared it, if his father said it the boy was obedient. He would be subject to whatever his father said. The child would restrain himself, still enjoying the things of his childhood.

His father says, "I want you to be circumcised."

"All right, Father, I understand you. But my peers. . . . If I am to be a youth undergoing the circumcision rite, with whom will I be circumcised?"

His father says, "My child, if you are agreeable, let the rite be my responsibility. If it is all right with you, I shall tell the men of the village. I shall inform them that I am holding a circumcision. There are peers of yours who will also want to be circumcised."

The purpose of this ritual is to bring the child away from boyhood, to introduce him to manhood.

The boy says, "All right then, Father."

The man then addresses his wife: "Nobani!"

The wife responds.

He proceeds: "I want to circumcise this boy. Make preparations. I want to circumcise him well."

His wife says, "All right."

In those olden days, the boy would realize that his rite of passage was commencing on that day. His father would make the announcement to his neighbors in the village.

Having called the men together, he says, "Gentlemen, I have called you here because I want to circumcise this boy of mine. And I want to have the chief responsibility for the rite."

A lodge for the youth undergoing the circumcision ritual is established some distance from the homesteads; it will not be at the boy's home.

The men respond to the person who has been talking: "We have heard you, Fellow of So-and-so. We're in agreement."

Those men who wish to have their sons circumcised come out one by one. Each of these fathers contributes something to this man.

He says, "Since I am doing the circumcising, and since I am the person responsible for the circumcision lodge, I want someone to be my second."

The other men then try to decide who the second should be. The second is not an easy position; he must do certain things in his role as the second to the "Father of the Circumcision Lodge." A man who is fairly well-off is therefore chosen, and the other men agree that he is fitting to be the second. After the circumcision, that man will be very important, in the cooking for the circumcised youth, for example.

A day is fixed for the circumcision of the boys.

Before he goes into seclusion for the circumcision ritual, after the day has been fixed and confirmed and just before he becomes circumcised, the boy goes around announcing his impending circumcision to his relatives, to his aunts, sisters, the people of his mother's home. When that is over, the day of circumcision is very near.

People who are close to him come along on the day of circumcision, carrying corn, pumpkins, beans, as appropriate, because boys are usually circumcised at the beginning of the harvest, the commencement of the first fruits.

The master of the household now gathers the people of the homestead together, and he obtains the services of a surgeon. The surgeon is the person who will perform the operation. The Father of the Circumcision Lodge brings this expert to the village and conceals him.

The circumcision lodge is built by the men. The boys chop down trees in the forest and bark them; they cut a certain tree. Each boy takes his bark from the tree; it will be plaited later. When the boys have returned, the women ululate, they ululate. Meanwhile, the pots from which each boy will eat are boiling. Each boy who will be circumcised will eat from a pot in his own home; each boy will eat from a pot in his own home. After the women have cooked, the boys will be brought into the kraals of their homes—each boy into the kraal of his home, each boy into the kraal of his home, each boy into the kraal of his home.

The ululating goes on. There are many groups of people, and the ululating continues:

> [sings]
> "Iyoooooooo hweuuuuuuuhi iyooo!
>> It is getting late,
>> The sun is setting!
>> Take the axe, you women!
>> Halalaaaaaa yeha!
>> Satan has been ashamed!
>> Today we have a new man!"

A man suddenly springs up from among the men, and he sings,

> "Uuuuuuuuu hu! Uuuuuu hu!
> A thing like this has happened before!
> The cowards are getting circumcised!"

This affair then becomes festive. Someone strikes the ground, others drag their blankets along the ground. There is much noise. Some of the people weep, as if the boys were about to die, because this ritual involving the youth's movement into manhood is very serious. While all of this is going on, the boy is led into the kraal, and he sits there along with some younger men. Food is dished up for him to eat over there in the kraal. He removes all of the adornments of his boyhood—the anklets from his lower legs, for example. Everything that he is wearing is discarded; he takes off his earrings.

Then a knife is taken; it is sharpened and the boy's hair is shorn—he is now completely bald. An ox's tail is plucked, and an older aunt is brought in to plait knots in it. That bark that the boys brought from the forest is taken and plaited; a little rope that fits around the neck is made. This is joined with those knots that have been made of the hair plucked from the ox's tail. This is called "the knot," and it is worn by the boy.

When that has been done, a goat is slaughtered. The boy is now going through a rite, a kind of farewell feast. The goat is slaughtered there in the kraal. Then it is cooked. A foreleg from that goat is cooked for the boy. When the meat has been roasted, it is distributed. That is the way it goes in all of the kraals of the boys who are about to be circumcised. The other boys are going through the same ceremonies as this boy. The foreleg is given to the boy, and he eats it. When he finishes eating, he covers his head with a sheepskin cape. These capes were put together at the time the man of the household said, "Make preparations, Wife. I'm going to circumcise this boy." This wife has sewn the cape and finished it. Now the boy covers his head with the cape, and he throws away all the garments he has worn as a boy.

The boys then come out. All of them, accompanied by the men and women and their companions, pass by this boy who is the head of the circumcision lodge, this boy who is the chief circumcised youth. As the women ululate, the boy comes out, along with the others in his group. They proceed to the place where they are to be circumcised. There, a lodge is being constructed. Women transport a special grass, they plait ropes with it. Some of them pound and soften the ropes, which are actually straps fashioned from various vines. They make straps, bands for tying down the thatch on the lodge. Still others do the actual binding. The structure is then smoothed with grass. When this operation is at an end, some of the grass is put on the roof of the lodge, and it is thatched. The lodge is complete.

When the women have finished their work on this grass lodge, they go and sit at a spot overlooking the area, some distance away, together with the contingent that carried the grass.

Only the men remain here at the lodge. When the women have removed themselves, the men stay together in a group, a considerable distance from the women. Over there at the lodge, the boys who are to be circumcised are taken to a river where, out of sight, they wash. Each boy washes his body, then comes back to the lodge to sit. The surgeon comes, the boys now seated in proper order. He comes, and cuts them; he cuts the member that should be cut [the foreskin of the penis]. What remains is the manhood, what is removed is the boyhood.

After that, the men pluck medicinal healing herbs for treating the wounds of those circumcised youths. A fire is then made in the lodge. Recently married women, along with older women—but not old women—go into the forest, gathering firewood, putting the wood a distance from the lodge so that a fire can be maintained during the period that the circumcised youth, still with only their heads covered, are living there.

At that spot overlooking the lodge, the women are ululating. The circumcised youths enter the lodge, and embankments are set up, slightly elevated, as sleeping places for the circumcised youth. They are made of stumps brought in from the forest. The circumcised youths sleep on top of these forms that are made to fit the initiates.

Time passes. Young men who are wardens live here at the lodge and watch over the initiates night and day, changing shifts. This goes on until a report is sent home that the initiates will be ready the following week for a roasting ritual, the ritual during which food is roasted for the initiates. They are ready for this ceremony because they are now healed. The man who had earlier been named the second now offers a goat for the roasting ritual. This goat is driven over there to the lodge to be slaughtered. Today also, the women go to the fields to get fresh maize. On this day, the initiates eat all sorts of things for the first time. They are allowed to eat the usual things—pumpkins and beans, stamped mealies, everything that has been proscribed during this period of seclusion, including beer—and whatever else is available. Today, they are allowed to eat these foods. The women go out and roast corn, maize boiled on the cob. Fresh corn is taken to the lodge to be roasted. Then that goat is slaughtered.

A bitter tree, the sneezewood tree, is cut down, and it is used to kindle a fire at the circumcision lodge. The goat is roasted over the sneezewood, the corn is also roasted, and these bitter tasting foods are given to the initiates to eat.

After all this, the initiates can begin to eat everything.

Each woman can now cook the initiate's favorite dish. She carries it to the lodge, and when she gets there, she stands on an elevated spot, still a distance from the lodge, and shouts, "Hayeeeee! Hayeeeee!" She is doing this in order to be heard because she is a mother and dares not approach the lodge housing the circumcised youth. An initiate and his mother are not supposed to look at each other; he is not supposed to see anyone who is even an age-mate of his mother. This avoidance will go on until graduation. The initiate cannot see his mother until the day that he graduates. He is allowed to see one older female person, an aunt. Otherwise, he is allowed to see only young people, and then only in a group.[3]

---

3. Mrs. Zenani notes, parenthetically, "These circumcised youth are the type that do not do the initiates' dance."

THE INITIATES' DANCE

Performance Note

Time: 13 August 1972, in the morning. *Place:* In a fallen rondavel near Mrs. Zenani's home in Nkanga, Gatyana District, the Transkei. *Audience:* Two women and one teen-aged boy. (NS-170.)

They begin by being initiates, and when they are initiates they are taught to dance the initiates' dance. For this dance, palm leaves are taken from a wild palm tree at a river. Artisans take those leaves and make garments for the initiates, garments that are tied around their waists. Straps are tied around the waist nine times. The straps are made from wild fig trees. The strap should be big enough to fit the particular initiate. He will be involved in this ritual for a full year, beginning from the time of his circumcision, which usually occurs during the eating of the first fruits. That is in the autumn, and the rite of passage continues into the winter, right up to the spring. The initiate graduates at about the beginning of the ploughing season. At the first ploughing, the plots are cultivated by the initiates; no woman may approach them. The seed is sent to the initiates in the fields, carried by the girls. The mother of an initiate dares not go to where the initiate is, according to Xhosa custom.

It is during this period that the initiate is made to revere some things: he cannot call them by their usual names. He does not call water by its proper name. And meat: he does not say *yinyama* [it is meat]; instead, he says *yikruza*. Tobacco: he may not say *licuba* [it is tobacco]; he says *lifoza*. Even a pipe: he may not say *yinqawe* [it is a pipe], but says *lipheko*. A boy: he does not say *yinkwenkwe* [it is a boy]; he says *yinqalathi*. A stick: the initiate does not say *yintonga* [it is a stick]; he says *ngumkrolo*. Whatever something is called, the initiate does not use that name. Now that he is an initiate, all things are renamed. The time will come, of course, when he will use their usual names again, but that is only after he graduates.

The initiates dance in these palm garments that have been fashioned by the artisans who were hired for the purpose. No matter how many initiates there are, each will have an artisan hired for him. The artisan is paid for his efforts by the home of the initiate. The face covering and horns are also made from the palm tree.

GRADUATION

Performance Note

Time: 2 August 1967, in the morning. *Place:* In the home of Mrs. Zenani, in Nkanga, Gatyana District, the Transkei. *Audience:* Members of Mrs. Zenani's family—her husband, her daughter, her granddaughter. (NS-10.)

Then follows the celebration of the graduation of the initiates. They graduate, and a celebration is held after they come out of the lodge. On the day that they are to come out, the initiates go to a river and bathe. An experienced man will be chosen, a man who has done things that are recognized in the village as commendable. That man will be selected, and an oil will be produced with which he will be told to anoint the initiates. At sunrise, when the initiates are about to graduate, this man will go down to the place where they are. All night, they will have been bathing. They bathe many times in the river, repeatedly washing off the white ochre that they have been wearing on their bodies. They bathe, then observe that some of the ochre is still there, so they lather again, and bathe. At sunrise, this man will anoint all the initiates.

Then the circumcised youth return to their lodge, and they are presented with new capes, capes that have been treated with red ochre. They wear these capes now, covering their heads.

The initiates go to the home of the chief initiate, and that lodge in which they have been living is set on fire.

The circumcised youth will be told, "You must not look back and see the lodge burning!"

If an initiate should look back and see the smoke, he will have broken a taboo.[4] The initiates will therefore move on without looking back, journeying to the home of the chief initiate. When they arrive, they will find a gathering of girls and young men.

This usually occurs at night, after the meal has been dished out for them. They will be taken to the house, having been admonished and having been presented with gifts before entering.

Each man gently touches the head of each of the initiates with a spear and says, "I give you this charge today, Boy. You are a man! You have left boyhood behind." So saying, that man places the spear on the initiate's hand. He says, "You must not use this spear to stab your father or your mother. This is not a spear with which to stab anyone. I give you the spear so that you can defend your homestead with it. Place the spear up there among the weapons. Let it be a revered spear. I am bestowing on you a mind that has today left boyhood behind."

Then another man will rise and present the initiate with a gift—a goat or a cow, a fowl, money. All this takes place in the courtyard; the men are by themselves.

The initiates will then be taken to the house. The women go there too, and they present gifts. They begin with the chief initiate; they give him

---

4. The Xhosa word used for "taboo" is *isisila*, a word that literally means misfortune or unhappiness: *Lo mfana unesisila*, "This young man is unfortunate." The term has special relevance to a youth who has just emerged from the seclusion of his circumcision period.

gifts first. The chief initiate is that circumcised youth belonging to the homestead of the father who started the process of this particular circumcision ritual. Gifts are offered there.

The women make presentations to the initiates. They give the initiate a little turban, a plaited turban, to tie around his head. In those olden days, it was plaited into a little strand, then tied around the forehead. It would be said that the initiate was being presented with a gift. Another person gives him earrings; another gives him a flint, an object used to create fire. Another woman gives him a knife; another, matches; another, tobacco—it can be anything. They go to the initiates and give the presents.

This is the first time that the initiates see their mothers. They can now stop avoiding each other because the boys have ceased being initiates— they are men.

Younger members of the family come in, presenting gifts: bracelets for the ankles, the arms, rings for the fingers.

So ends the gift-giving.

Then the young men's dance takes place. It is said that the "raw" young men are being taught now. A "raw" young man is a person who is just beginning to be a man; he is now being taught by others who are already men. The dance goes on. Blankets are worn about the waist; there are no other garments. When that has been done, they are taught a song called "Nomdidiyelo," which involves a certain rhythmic movement of the foot— five steps and, as they move to the sixth, they pause. Then it is said that they have made a misstep; they have gone wrong. Of these raw young men, it is said derisively, "Yo! Smeared-stomachs! They don't know anything! They've gone wrong!"

Laughter breaks out; the young men are insulted. Abusive language is used against them; they are thoroughly ridiculed. Some of them become sullen and angry when they hear the lavish insults. But this is all by way of admonishing them, of teaching them. Soon enough, that hazing will come to an end.

Now it becomes necessary for these initiates to return to their own homes. They scatter, journeying. When they get to their separate homes, preparations are made for the coming-out celebrations. All of this is a part of the progression, the unfolding of the African's custom, as he becomes a young man.

THE YOUNG MEN'S DANCE

Performance Note

Time: 13 August 1972, in the morning. *Place:* In a fallen rondavel near Mrs. Zenani's home, in Nkanga, Gatyana District, the Transkei. *Audience:* Two women and one teenaged boy. (NS-170.)

The initiates having graduated and come out, their circumcision lodge is burned. They have now become "raw" young men. They have left their homes. It is said that they were going through a transition. Now they are young men; they have graduated to the status of being able to go to a "raw" young men's dance. This dance is not for uncircumcised boys; the dance is for "raw" young men. They go to the young men's dance with the women friends they used to take to boys' dances when they were younger. But now they have graduated, along with their woman friends.

The young women had cut their own hair, and now the hair has come out afresh, indicating that they are now young men's women.

When they get to the young men's dance, dancing takes place. The women supply the music, and they adorn themselves with bracelets— these are the "young men's women." The young men's dance starts on Saturday night, and it goes on until early Sunday morning. Sometimes it goes on until midday on Sunday, depending upon how big the party is and how many different kinds of young men are there. The young men go to various locations and villages for these dances, coming together at the young men's dance. These young men carry sticks along with handsome dancing clubs, but no fighting goes on at these affairs. These are not fighting sticks, they are not even for play. The boys' dances often end in fights, but this is not the case at the men's dances: sticks at the young men's dance are only for style. It is a dignified ornament, not a fighting weapon. The men move about with such sticks, inciting admiration from others at the dance. Some of the men are admiringly called "oxen"; others are "experts" who keep things in order according to appropriate regulations. The experts keep the oxen from overwhelming the young men's dance; they have rules that are beautiful in the sense that they exist to discipline these young men, to transform them from brawling boys to responsible men. The experts are responsible for seeing to it that these various regulations do what they are devised to do. The young women too have more responsible roles now; they are not to urge their men to brawl and stick-fight. A young man's woman is quite different from a boy's girl. This is the case even in the kind of dress that a young man's woman wears: her skirts reach almost to the ground, they are not as brief as those of boys' girls. The young men now wear little garments that have been decorated with beads; these garments are worn around the waist. The young men also put on headcloths now; the headcloths are the color of the hammerbird, they are new. Headcloths of young men may be yellow or pink, just as they are for their woman friends. One really cannot mistake a young man's woman even at a distance: it is clear that she is indeed a "young man's woman"! You can also distinguish a young man from a boy; you can tell him from his father too, because he is wearing a garment of young manhood. A gathering of young men does not resemble that of boys. They discuss things that pertain to young men.

The young men's dance, then, begins in a certain place at its own time on Saturday evening. The young women stay together in the upper part of the house, away from the door. Mats are spread out for the young men. They sit on these mats, which are made of rushes picked at the river, so that their garments will not get dirty. They sing then. The young men put the garments on their waists, and they dance around the hearth. Their woman friends supply the music, clapping their hands. The young men dance around the hearth, wearing their headcloths. In the second song, the young women remove the headcloths from the young men, and that is a beautiful thing to see: the young women move slowly, smoothly, careful not to bump the young men. The men make way easily so that the women move elegantly as they come to them. The women take the headcloths off, and, their heads bared, leave the young men at their hearth, dancing their dance.

The young men are adorned by the women who buy cloths for them. These cloths have kerchiefs placed on them. Then they bring sticks that have been decorated with beads; the young man is given this fine stick by the woman with whom he has an understanding, who is his woman friend. The woman takes the stick and gives it to the young man at the young men's dance. She gives it to him, placing it in his left hand, according to custom. Then she puts a white cloth and a kerchief on top of that; she takes another kerchief and gives it to him, placing it in his right hand. When he perspires, he wipes himself with that kerchief. The cloth and the kerchief that are in his left hand are decorations; he does not wipe perspiration with those. Crowns are also placed on the young men by the women. The crown, put on the head, has hooks attached to it. The young women also place beads on the young men, a string of beads, fashioned to be placed around the neck; this string of beads is long and fixed with large knots. Straps come over each of the young man's shoulders. The youth who surpasses the others in the splendor of such decorations is called "an ox."

"Yo! The ox is So-and-so's son! From such-and-such a section!"

There is a comparable champion or ox in each of the sections represented at the young men's dance.

When the young men's dance ends on Sunday, there is a saying uttered by the young men: "It is the coming of the kettle!"

They are referring to a certain time. When they get up in the morning and morning coffee is brought to them, this is called "the coming of the kettle." But when they use the expression here, on the Sunday morning following a young men's dance, they are using it figuratively rather than literally. That is, they are referring to the time when the kettle is brought in, not to the bringing of the kettle itself. There is no kettle here, no drinking of coffee, no eating. It is just the time that is referred to, when all of these things are done. They are going to discuss the usual things—the dance, the clothes worn, decorations, and so on. They joke and make critical comments about the dancing of others, about garments and adornments. They discuss the quality of the ox. And they contradict each other about various things. Because they meet at the time that the kettle is usually brought in, they refer to these discussions as "the coming of the kettle."

Songs are sung by the young women, songs of joy, songs that contain nasty remarks. Such a song would be known as "So-and-so's song." Each song has a name, not necessarily the name of someone who is present. But the song is directed at someone who is indeed present.

These things are done on Sunday morning, after the young men's dance, in the morning as the sun warms things. They dance vigorously at that time; they dance the various dances. And one of the young men becomes a champion—the best—in speech, in rhetoric. But he might not know how to dance. He excels in speech rather than dance.

Comments are contradicted, arguments are developed, arguments are destroyed, but all of this occurs with words only. Judgments are passed by means of words. There is no fighting.

Because argumentation becomes more important than fighting, it is understandable that gifted speakers emerge. A young man is able to develop an argument with considerable eloquence, making it very clear.

It is said, "That one is an ox!"

Now if such a man happens not to have come to the young men's dance, during the Sunday discussion period, the people say, "Yo! That young men's dance wasn't a very good one."

"That's because So-and-so's son wasn't there."

"He would have expressed everything clearly."

A young man has emerged, a young man who has become something of a wonder at the young men's dance. He has become a legend because of his speech-making ability. And he dresses well, with fine beads. But he belongs to another village, along the Qhora River. He lives on one side of the river. When he goes to the other side to attend a young men's dance, it is said, "He'll win again!"

A young men's dance was organized once, but word about the dance did not get across the river to this young man. So he did not attend. It was obvious then that the young men's dance would not be a good one because he had no peer. He dressed well, but more than the clothing he had a sharp and eloquent tongue. Whenever he came to a place, he turned all the young women around; they wished to throw their own companions away on his account. In the end, he became a significant factor at the young men's dance. The women began to avoid the young men's dance, saying that they would not dance with him because he generated confusion—confusion, because whenever he spoke to a young woman, she would desert her own boyfriend. The women said that they wanted no part of this confusion, so they left the young men's dance.

That set a bad precedent, for the young men began to quarrel: "We're not boys, we should not get ourselves into a situation at a young men's dance in which we begin to keep our sticks within reach."

"And all this because of one person who wishes to interfere with the decorum of the young men's dance by provoking fights."

"From this day, we'll never again cross the Qhora, we'll never again go over there and have a dance with him."

The young men's dance was torn by argument then, it split into two sides. Some said that the young men's dance became dull, cool, when those from across the Qhora were not present. Others insisted that it would bring them back "to a practice that we left behind in our boyhood."

"It's evident that this kind of thing makes us forget that we are men."

"We grasp our sticks aggressively because this young man has no respect for anyone."

"This will bring trouble our way."

"In our manhood, we live according to rules."

"We do not live according to sticks and fighting."

The argument divided the men. They were not boys, so they began now to go their own way.

The young men returned on Sunday morning from the young men's dance. They returned to their homes on time—a young man is not a boy, he must hurry home. If anything has gone wrong at his home, he must know about that. A young woman must also get home and work—go to the river, cook—because she has now reached the stage where she might be seen by a person and get married.

Young men behave the way their parents do because they are approaching the state of responsible adulthood. They are not quite to the stage of their parents in this regard; their responsibilities are not yet those of their parents, but they are close, they are almost there. They are now approaching the state of responsible adulthood.

A young man at home is accountable when something happens. His father comes, and the young man gives his report: "Father, a certain person came here, saying thus and so. I told this person that you were absent. Because you were not here, this is what I said to him. . . ." Father and son therefore take counsel. A boy has no such role.

That is where the distinction is made between a boy and a young man.

XHOSA CUSTOM REQUIRES TRADITIONAL RESPONSES

Performance Note

Time: 18 September 1967, in the afternoon. *Place:* In a home in Nkanga, Gatyana District, the Transkei. *Audience:* Thirty men, women, and children. (Perf. 682.)

This is how traditions in the land of the Xhosa came into existence, the way they were in the beginning.

As time passed, men wondered, "How are we going to go about doing things, since all activities require a leader?"

When this issue was raised, someone said that they ought to go to the homestead of the royal residence—that is, the royal residence for us Xhosa of Gcalekaland.

Someone responded, "Two young men should be sent. Let them go to the royal residence and ask, 'What shall we do about this?' "

A school was about to be established; this was the beginning of education. The thing called a "school" was to be established for the first time. The Xhosa had not known what a school was to this time.

Later, the men assembled here, and the young men were asked, "Did you go to the royal residence?"

The two young men who had been sent there said, "We did go to the royal residence."

"And whom did you find there?"

"We arrived at the royal residence, and the king was there."

"Who was the king at that time?"

"It was Sarhili."[5]

It happened that the name of the king at that time was Sarhili, a prince of a man.

These men had now returned, and they were being asked, "What does the king say?"

The young men said, "Well, the king says that he does not know what a 'school' is, he does not know what 'education' is. Nor does he know what 'to study' means."

The young men finished speaking, and a councillor of the royal residence, a councillor who was loyal to that king, stood up.

He said, "Well, your report sounds right. King, don't allow your blood to boil. Here in the land of the Xhosa, there has never been this 'studying.' There's never been a 'school.' We aren't accustomed to that. It's not in the nature of things to have a 'school,' as far as we Xhosa are concerned. Now then, King, you must look at this matter with care, what a 'school' and 'studying' will mean in the land of the Gcaleka, of the Xhosa. Through the

5. Sarhili (ca. 1820–1902), a son of Hintsa, was paramount chief of the Gcaleka.

years, we have felt that our traditions are strong. We never thought that we required schools. Anyone who insists that we do need schools is implying that our traditions are not sufficiently strong. What do you say to that, King?"

It was quiet then, it was quiet. After a long time, the king hesitantly stood and said, "Our land is not now what it used to be. We don't know the 'school.' And 'studying,' too—we don't know it. Now some say that we must have this 'studying.' The question is, will our traditions, will the things that we do, harmonize with that 'education'?"

From among that mass of people assembled in the royal residence, another man got up. He said, "Well, King, we understand what you're saying. But time edges forward. And it's not enough just to hear one's name. One must also be able to identify it on paper. A person should know his name not just when he hears it, but also when he sees it written. I'm a member of the Qwathi clan, and I've had occasion to go to Johannesburg. Now when I got to Johannesburg, I had to identify myself by my 'surname.' The concept of a 'surname' was foreign to me. I didn't know it. This is what they mean by 'surname': they want to know your grandmother who bore your father. I wanted to get confirmation of this, so I hesitated, I was confused. Finally, I asked some others, 'Who was my father's father?' A young man of the Mvulane clan told me that my father was borne by a daughter of the Qocwa clan. Now all this happened when I was trying to understand what they meant in Johannesburg by 'surname,' something that is not familiar to us. I pretended that I was skilled in the use of 'surnames'; I gave the appearance of being spontaneous about this. So I told them my 'surname.' I explained that 'surname' idea at my home when I returned from Johannesburg, when my contract of nine months had expired—that's the length of time we had contracted for in Johannesburg.[6] I worked at Mqandatye's.[7] I told my father about this.

"I said to him, 'Father, how can something like the matter of "surname" be taken by me to the royal residence? I don't know Xhosa tradition. I may have tampered with the traditions of the Xhosa by my actions in Johannesburg. I am a child; you are experienced. Over there at the royal residence, I'll be asked about Xhosa traditional things. Really, Father, it's more fitting that I go with you when I go to the royal residence.'

"Then my father told my mother, 'Nosenti, do you hear what this young man has been saying?'

"And she said, 'What does he say?' Then Nosenti said to her husband, 'What he is saying is this: he cannot go to the royal residence alone because they'll want to know the origin of ancient Xhosa traditions.'

6. This is a reference to a contract for work on the mines.
7. His white employer's name translates "Wages are not enough."

" 'But this young man says that he should go with me, Nosenti. He says that he should go to the royal residence to tell about his experiences in Johannesburg when he worked at Mqandatye's.'

"Nosenti said, 'No, really, this is what the young man said. This is how it is, Sozekelwa, this is what happens when our children go to find employment with the white men. Our children board the trains and go off to the white man. Then they return with things that puzzle us. Now he says that he wants you to go with him to the royal residence, so that he can explain this matter of "surnames." We don't know "surnames." You must go with him, then, and explain what this child is saying. You can fill in the gaps in the statements that he makes. And there is also the matter of the school. Here, they say that a school is necessary so that a person may know his name, so that a person may know what is being said. We do not know these things because we have never gone to any school. We talk about things in our own customary way here, and we are comfortable with the things that we speak. But if something new comes up, you should not just oppose it because you do not know how it will turn out when you have opposed it.' "

The fellow agreed with his wife, and he took the journey with his son. He agreed with what his wife, Nosenti, said in support of her son's statement.

So it was that they discussed the matter of the possibility of having a school, something that had never before been present among the Xhosa—a school, education, the idea that the people should be "taught."

When he arrived at the royal residence, he said, "Well, here we are. We're busy, we've got journeys of our own to take. We don't know why we've been called here."

"We want to know if the establishment of a school among us will prove to be dangerous to us."

A man, who was believed to be an expert on the matter because he knew what a "school" was, stood up and said, "No, the school is not dangerous."

The fellow who had come with his son and wife said, "Speak up!"

He raised his voice and said, "Well, it's only a school, where people study. That's all there is to it. There's no danger."

The other man got up and said, "Who says so? Who says that studying should take place? And what is it that should be studied?"

The expert, getting up again, repeated his statement: "No, the government says that studying should take place."

This one said, "What is the government? What is this thing called 'government'? Where is this government? Who is it, really? Where does it live?"

The other said, "No, no, the government is another great one, a great one, like you notables. The government is like you, except that he is a white person. And he does not live with you. But he does look after your welfare."

The other one said, "How does he look after our welfare? Where is he now? Because in the past, we did not have to dip our cattle. We did not have to pay taxes."

It was said, "There you are, sitting at home. And this thing comes along to the effect that you must bring your tax. Now if the government was actually there, then why didn't he help us? We're suffering. Where was that government when we needed it?"

The expert said, "No, you should know that, at the time you were suffering, the government had no knowledge that you were being harmed because you were far from him. You've never even talked with him."

This one said, "Well then, the government had no knowledge that we were suffering because we didn't speak with him because he is so far away from us. But what pains did he take to come and find out from those of us who were in the bad situation of which he knew nothing?"

That one said, "No, consider all facets of it. You ought to study in this 'school.' When you have studied in the school, you'll know how to speak with the government. You'll be able to inform him of your serious sufferings, so that he'll realize that you've been harmed. We must move quickly. Forget the irrelevant things. There's just one point at issue here. Let's not get involved in peripheral matters that will only keep us here. The question is, Should there be a school, so that a person may know his name? We'll learn soon enough what one gets out of this 'education.'"

The other said, "No, he'll *get* nothing from 'education'! But he'll be *given* enlightenment. He'll know where to go to get help, how to write, and he'll know a lot of other things. He'll be able to say what a thing is!"

Another said, "All right then, if that's the way it is. How many schools are there to be in a village?"

The councillor at the royal residence got up and said, "Well, we'll only waste time if we go on in this way. When the schools begin, there won't be nine or ten of them. One school will be established, and if that is seen to be a good thing, then another will be set up."

The other fellow got up again, and said, "My ancestral name is Mdladla. I don't want to hear something discussed in isolation, unrelated to anything else, so that we don't have a clear direction in our argument. Will someone tell me what we've come here for? People are talking, but others say that nothing has been said yet. What have we been talking about all this time? The things that are being mentioned are the precise things that should be mentioned. Now, if you don't understand what is being said, then ask your neighbor about it, someone from your own village. Ask him to listen for you. The rest of us understand that what is being said is that there should be schools. All of us, as we sit here, understand that it is being recommended that something called a 'school' should be established here. And it is said that, because of this 'school,' a person will know his name and be able to write it. It is said that he shall recognize his name when it is written. It is therefore concluded that a 'school' will help us. Some of us want others to understand how it is that we have suffered. Now, this is supposed to be a time of enlightenment. Do you refuse to be persuaded? Do you insist that you won't have anything to do with this school business? What is your position?" So he said, and then he sat down.

This fellow got up then, and said, "Well, I understand the argument, but I'm quite old already, and I've never heard of this school nonsense before! At home, milk used to be poured out into a spoon, then we'd drink it. At home, all that we talked about was in regard to what ought to be done concerning our home. If there were a misunderstanding between my aunt and my father, the people were called together and the case was judged in court. Nothing was written down. Now I wonder. You want things for writing. Is it because things will work out better then? Perhaps, without knowing it, you are misleading yourselves with all this writing business because this is how we live, according to the laws of the Xhosa and of nature and tradition.

"But I'll accept whatever you decide because it is obvious that I am alone in the matter of which I speak. But keep in mind that Xhosa custom is traditional. It is of ancient tradition, and it requires traditional responses. No young upstart dares issue a command related to the school concerning traditional Xhosa custom, and then expects that this is healthy for the society. Look. My younger sister is a doctor. And she never came close to a school! Even though she has never been to a school, she has told us significant things in that home of ours. What did she do over there in our home? Well, this is one thing that she did. When there was a falling out between our father and my uncle, she told them, 'Uncle, would you take the time to come and visit me, so that you'll have a better understanding of why you're really quarreling with your elder brother? You see, Uncle, there's this one fault in you: you do not realize that this elder brother of yours knows the customs of your home better than you do. On the day when the "sickness" took over me, you were not present—when I was in this sick state, being initiated into the profession of medicine, being developed into a fully qualified doctor. But this is how we do it in this homestead. A plant must be picked in the fields, then applied to the person. Then a white goat must be slaughtered. Now then, Uncle, you're not very close to my father, and that puzzles me. After all, I'm your daughter too. You should help to put me together. You should speak the healing word to me. But you didn't speak the healing word to me because you don't get along, you don't know how it ought to be done.'

"Then that woman's father did indeed get together with his younger brother and said, 'This woman is posing a problem for us. Clearly, she's more important than we are because she knows the traditional Xhosa mind, the origins from deep down, from long ago. Now then, how shall we approach this problem? The young woman should be summoned; the people should also be called. And this young woman should speak of this matter while the people are present, so that they may or may not concur. We don't know whether they'll agree with what she says or if they'll side with us in our disagreement with what she says."

Things went on, and the assembly was still discussing the matter the following week.

TALES

Tale 4

THE BOY AND THE LIZARD

Masithathu Zenani's Analysis: The storyteller here emphasizes the necessity of a child's absence from home during the puberty ritual, as well as the consequential role played by nature in the process. Among the Xhosa, the circumcision ceremony for boys occurs in a remote place, away from their homes. They remain in that isolated condition for the duration of the ritual while they assemble the knowledge necessary to their new roles as men in their societies.

In this imaginative account of a boy's puberty rite, the storyteller makes the link between the boy and his father an antagonistic one; this bruising relationship results in the boy's movement away from his home, into a state of nature where his ritual occurs. The father, who remains his son's antagonist well into the tale, has a relationship with his child that results in the youth's growth to manhood.

In the meantime, the boy is abandoned, discovered by a lizard, and taken by the lizard into a pool where the creature becomes his surrogate father: it does what the boy's blood father should have done, it guides the boy through his puberty ritual. The pattern of father-son antagonism intensifies when the boy returns to his home to visit his mother. In a struggle, he wounds his father on the thigh.

Mrs. Zenani provides considerable realistic detail of the boy's purification ceremony, describing vividly the initiate's dance. She works this into the story by having the youth's father as a part of the admiring audience, the father unknowingly applauding his own son. During the dance, the boy beats his father until the lizard calls him off. Then the lizard announces the end of the ritual by making the youth the ruler of his city. His father, after a long time, loses everything that he has. The boy identifies the father by the wound on the thigh; with the assistance of the lizard, he heals the still festering wound. The boy is then reunited with his family, and they live together in harmony, the youth "having been educated by the lizard."

The lizard and the father are one, models of propriety and impropriety, and through that conflict of elders the boy undergoes his ritual. In the end, nature and culture are again joined, as the boy moves into his majority.

Performance Note

Time: 12 August 1972, 2:30 P.M. *Place:* In a fallen rondavel near Mrs. Zenani's home in Nkanga, Gatyana District, the Transkei. *Audience:* Five women, three teenagers, and two children. (Perf. NS-159.)

A certain man had no wife. He sought a wife, and when he had found her, she became pregnant. When she had become pregnant, he called the men who were at his homestead.

He said, "I've called you here today to inform you that I now have a wife. You see her here, she's the one. Now I want this woman to bear children for me. She's pregnant now. But I've called you here because I want you to know this: there is one thing that I do not want in my home. I do not want a wife who bears boy children. I want no boy here at my home! I want a wife who bears girls. If she ever gives birth to a boy, I'll kill that boy! I do not want a boy."

The men who had been called by that fellow were astonished.

"How could you get married, yet not want a boy?"

"You want girls only?"

"How do you know if this woman will bear a boy or a girl? You're demanding something that you can know nothing about."

"Why don't you want a boy?"

"Surely there's never been anyone who has said, 'I don't want a son.' "

The man said, "I say that I don't want a son here at my home. Not at all! At all! I never want to see a boy child here! I do not want to see him. I don't want to see him with my eyes. I do not want to see a boy child. I want children who are girls."

They stopped discussing the subject then, but the men wondered, "What kind of man is this?"

"What is this? Not wanting a child who happens to be a boy?"

"Was there ever a man who didn't want a boy child?"

The people were puzzled. They did not know what they should do about these words that had been spoken by the owner of the homestead. So they stopped discussing the matter, and they departed.

Now, when they had departed, the woman remained there. She was very anxious. She was afraid because she did not know what kind of child she would bear. She was agitated because she did not know the sex of the child she was carrying—what sort of child it was. Because of her uneasiness, this woman after a time became thin.

The months went by, and her pregnancy was coming to an end. When the hour of her delivery was near, some women were called to help her to give birth to her child. When they arrived, she gave birth; she dropped the child. And the woman bore a big boy.

Someone said, "What will happen now?" because these women knew that whenever a woman gives birth, the husband must be told that she has borne a certain child. But these women also remembered the words of this young mother's husband; they recalled what he had said.

"Well, someone must go to him, no matter what."

"What alternative is there?"

"They journeyed a great distance." Her thumbs extended, Nongenile Masithathu Zenani suggests travelling movement.

"He must be told."

One of the women got up then and went to tell the husband.

"That woman over there, your wife: she has given birth."

The man leapt up. He stared, he listened carefully. "What kind of child did she bear?"

"Well, she gave birth to a boy."

He said, "Oh, you ass! You ass! What did you say? Say no more! Leave me, get out of here!"

The husband then called a man from another homestead and asked him to take this child off somewhere and abandon it because he refused to have a child who was a boy. He had said before that he did not want a boy child.

No matter how the father of the boy pleaded with him, however, that neighbor refused. "Never has a person who's still alive been abandoned like that!"

But in the end this neighbor did go. He agreed to go to that wife there and do the hideous thing that had been asked of him by the father.

The child was taken away by a woman. She gathered the boy in her arms because his mother was still weak—she had just given birth, after all. The woman took the child, then, and went away with him. She was walking with this man who had been instructed by the father of the boy to "go and abandon the child in a distant place. Even if this means that you won't get back until tomorrow. Abandon him in some deep pool. Throw him into the pool so that he's devoured by the creatures there. I don't want such a thing!"

They departed with the child. This man walked with the woman: they walked all that day. When the sun went down, they were still walking. At dawn, they were journeying, carrying this child. They came to a great river. They saw a path there; it was a broad path, and they could see that something regularly traveled on it, coming to this place. But they saw nothing, only the heavily traveled path.

The path was above a deep pool. They arrived there and put the child down above that pool, so that no matter what thing might come along, it would discover this child and eat him—that is, if it were a thing that eats humans. Then they went home, and again the sun set because they were so far from home. They walked on and arrived at their home on the second day.

"Well, have you abandoned him?"

They said, "We left him at a river. Which river it was, we don't know. It was at a very deep pool."

This fellow thanked them for doing that deed for him, for casting off the child who had been borne by his wife. He did not want a child who was a boy.

As for this wife, she was in deep sorrow because of the abandonment of her son—that child was her first-born. She became emaciated, aching because of what had occurred. But her husband was not at all concerned.

Eventually, she recovered from the birth, and then she became a woman who merely existed. She resigned herself and her heart to what had happened. Then, after a long time, she regained her weight. When she had recovered her health, she again became pregnant. Her stomach grew big. But during her pregnancy, the woman again became thin because of her anxiety; she feared that "I might bear a boy again, and he'll be abandoned!" This thought caused her great pain during her pregnancy.

Her husband continued to warn her, "If you conceive a boy, then *you* must leave. I don't want a person here who'll bear a boy." So said the husband, and he hurriedly married another wife. He was determined that she should also bear children, he wanted her to bear a girl. This second wife also became pregnant; this one was pregnant for five months. Then, during the sixth month, she gave birth. That other wife, the first one, was still pregnant. Now when this second wife gave birth, she bore birds! Five ring-necked ravens!

This husband went to that house then; he went to live with that wife who had borne five ravens.

He said, "She's better than the other one, the one who's still bearing boys." Boys—that is what he did not want to see.

The father of this homestead lived then in that house with the ravens. That became his favorite house. He refused even to enter the house of the great wife, the one who had given birth to the boy who had been abandoned. She was very big now with her pregnancy, and then the month of deliverance arrived. And she gave birth, she bore a girl. The husband was told that she had given birth.

The man said, "Speak! Speak quickly! What did she bear?"

It was said, "She bore a girl."

"All right," he answered. "But now I've got to the point where I really don't like that wife because I know her. I know her. When she becomes pregnant again, she'll bear a boy. I'm not pleased, even by that girl child, because it might just happen the next time that she'll give birth to a boy again. She's already done that once!"

So this woman continued to live a very unpleasant life; she was in a state of mental anguish, and she did not see her husband at all now. He was living in that house that was filled with ravens. So it went: all the nice things were done in that house of ravens. This great wife just managed to provide for herself; her husband was not interested in her.

Now, about the abandoned child, the one to whom she had given birth . . .

It turned out that, in the place where he had been abandoned, above that deep pool, there was a monitor lizard. It happened that the path belonged to that lizard, which would come out in the evening and take a walk. The lizard had two large homesteads. One homestead was in the water, at the bottom of the pool; the other was above the water, on the outside. The path connected the two homesteads, the one in the water and the one on the land. The lizard would come out of the water in the evening and go to the homestead that was on the outside, on the land. It would come out of the water in the evening.

One day, while it was walking along the path, it discovered this child. The lizard carried the child, it carried him. "What is this thing?" The lizard took "this thing" and went off with it. It arrived and put "this thing" in that homestead that was on the outside, the big homestead that was above the water, on the land. Now, this lizard had its own people, and it loved them. On the land, in this homestead that was above the water, there were two people. In the homestead that was in the pool, there were two people who prepared food for the lizard, which was actually a big man. It arrived at its homestead and gave the child to these two people.

It said, "Treat this child well. He is my son. Wash him, feed him."

So they took the child, and they washed and fed him.

The child grew up well then, a child with healthy blood. He was fed well; the food he was served was well-prepared, and it agreed with his blood.

The lizard continued to come out in the evenings, and this lizard's son continued to grow: he became an older boy.

When the child had grown into an older boy, he said to the lizard, "Father."

The lizard said, "Mm?"

He said, "I have dreamed that I have a mother who is thin. And my mother has a child who is a girl. My mother has no clothing for herself, and her daughter also lacks clothes. I dreamed that my other mother, my little mother, has ravens; it seems that her children are ravens."

The lizard said, "This thing that you dreamed, my child—where did it take place?"

The boy said, "Father, this thing that I dreamed seemed far off. But I really could go there because I saw it so clearly in my sleep."

The lizard said, "Well, then, you must go and pay them a visit."

Now this boy was very handsome, and he had fine clothing—perfect. There was nothing that he did not have.

He said, "I'm going to go then, Father. I'll take a weapon, a spear, with me."

The child got up on the appointed day; he got up and took his clothing. He dressed himself appropriately; then he took a shield and a weapon with which to defend himself. He took his shield and his stabbing weapon, and he journeyed. He walked, going to the country he had dreamed of.

He trekked to that country; he walked for two days. He walked, and the first day ended. He walked all night. Morning, and finally he saw the homestead—just as it had appeared in his dream. He went to the homestead. He arrived and saw the man who was his father, the one who had abandoned him. He arrived, and his father was sitting outside with the ravens, together with that junior mother of his. His own mother was in her house.

When he got there, he said, "Hello, Father!" So he said, and he extended his hand.

The man stood. He took his hand. "Who are you?"

The boy said, "I am yours, your first-born! Remember? When you were just beginning to sire children? You ordered that I be abandoned because I was a boy because you would not have a boy child. Now I have come to see you. Where is my mother?"

The man said, "I don't want to see you here at my home! Not at all! I don't want to see you! Get out of here! Don't stand in front of me!"

The boy said, "I cannot avoid standing in front of you. I say to you, I am your son, your first-born! When you discovered that I was a boy, you said that I must be abandoned because of your refusal to have a boy. I was my mother's first-born child."

So he said, and the boy went off. He went to his mother's house. He arrived there and found his mother with her daughter—both very ragged people. He greeted them, but they did not know him. He saluted them.

The woman said, "Where have you come from, Boy?" They could see that the boy was greeting them with great pleasure, with love in his face.

The boy said, "I am your child, Mother! The one you bore, the one who was abandoned!"

Then the woman cried, and the girl cried too. What the boy said was true, and that made them weep.

The man who was his father came along then. He was carrying fighting weapons. He stood in the doorway, and said, "Come out, Boy! Come out of the house! Go back to where you've come from! I shall never accept you as my child! I shall never have a child who is a boy!"

The boy came out then, already in a defensive position. When his father attacked him, he defended himself with his shield. They struck each other with force. They fought, and the boy stabbed his father with his spear—he pierced his father's thigh, and his father bled. When the boy had done that, some men intervened and stopped the fighting. It was clear that the boy would overwhelm his father; he had the strength to do so. The men made them stop fighting. They drove the boy away, saying, "Go, Boy! Go back to where you've come from. We can't allow you and your father to kill each other."

The boy went off then; he departed, he went back to where he had come from. Finally, he reached his home. When he had arrived, he sat there awaiting his father—because the sun had not yet gone down.

When the sun had gone down, the lizard arrived.

"Hello, my child."

The boy responded: "Yes, Father."

"So you have returned, my child."

"Yes, Father, I have returned."

"What did you find over there? Was it as you had dreamed?"

The boy said, "I saw him. I saw my father, the one who abandoned me. He is still there. And I found my mother, the one who bore me. She is still there. And I saw a girl, the one who is my sister. She is there too. I was assaulted by my father. He tried to drive me away, saying that he did not want to see me. We struggled, and I fought back. And I stabbed him, wounded him with my spear. I hit him on the thigh. Some men stopped me then. They had seen what had happened, and they drove me off, saying that I should return to where I had come from. They did not want to see us kill each other. So I went. I left that place."

The lizard said, "My child, you must remain here. The time will come when they will love you. Stay here. Do you see this homestead? Today, it is your homestead. All of it! What you see here is yours. And these two people—they are your servants. But if you decide to keep a dog, you'll have to build something for it. If you rear a dog here, you must build a big house for it. That dog should never come outside. I don't like dogs!"

The child who was a boy said, "I understand you, Father. I shall raise dogs because I like them. But I shall do as you say."

The boy did this. He raised dogs. He built a house for the dogs and closed them in. The dogs lived in a house that was closed in, so that they could not come out. They were completely confined, shut up inside. Even if they barked, they did so inside. There was no way for them to get out— in accordance with the instructions of the boy's father, the lizard.

When that was done, the lizard said, "I want to circumcise you. I want to circumcise you now. Then I want you to have the customary dance after circumcision. I'll do everything that is necessary."

The boy agreed. So it happened that the lizard circumcised the boy, and he completed all of the appropriate preparations for this ritual. When these things had been done, a large celebration took place in this homestead.

People of the countryside heard that a celebration and dance—customarily held after a circumcision ritual—were now being held over there at that homestead.

They said, "There's a boy over there who is an expert dancer!"

These things were heard throughout the land because this boy's homestead was a big one. This news finally reached his own father, the one with whom he had fought. When he heard this story, when the information about the circumcision dance was reported to him, the father had a strong desire to attend.

"There is a boy there who dances magnificently!"

He heard, too, that the generosity at that homestead was unsurpassed. So the father wanted to go and see this wonderful affair.

The boy's father went then, along with some men from his homestead. They walked over there: they slept, they got up, and finally they arrived there on the day of the circumcision dance. The circumcised youth was wearing his long palm-leaf face-coverings, those traditionally worn by circumcised youth. When his father sat down there, the boy saw him; he saw that it was his father, the man who did not want him as a son. He saw him, but his father did not know that the circumcised youth was his own son.

This boy, an initiate,[1] went over to where his father was sitting, and stopped. He danced there. As he danced, he beat his father with the palm-leaf costume that he was wearing, until his father's skin was scratched, until his father's entire body was chafed. The initiate danced, falling down on his father, blinding him with the palm-leaf face-coverings. And the father was unable to get up because he was a spectator and this dance was beautiful to watch. But although the dance was stunning, the father was getting thoroughly beaten. He was prevented from getting up. He could not bring himself to leave this dance, however, because if he departed he would not be able to observe it. So the father continued to be mauled by his dancing son, but he did not want to leave the dance because it was so splendid, because this youth was such an accomplished dancer.

Then the lizard entered at the lower end of the kraal. It arrived there, then sent one of its servants to "Call that initiate! Tell him to come here."

The circumcised youth was called, while he was still dancing, and he went to the kraal. When he got there, the lizard said, "Well, Mkhwetha."

The initiate said, "Father?"

The lizard said, "Stop beating that person. Leave him alone. Stop beating him, leave him alone. He'll punish himself. Stop beating him, he'll punish himself."

The youth went out again, but he did not return to his father. He danced the dance of circumcised youth there in the courtyard. Then everyone danced.

Finally, when it was time to go, those older men went on their way; they went home at sundown. They traveled, they slept, and on the second day they arrived at home. The father got home, and he truly had a story to tell—of a wonder so great, of a dance so magnificent, of a person so hand-

---

1. He is an *umkhwetha*, undergoing the puberty ritual.

some, of a dancer so splendid! Never had he seen such a person. He did not know, of course, that it was his own child.

The boy finished his dance. Then he came out: he was a man now. And now that he had become a man, his father the lizard sought a wife for him. So it happened that he married the daughter of a king, and now his wealth increased greatly. His homestead began to become known as the royal residence in this area.

The lizard said, "This city of mine, all of it: here is my son who will rule it!"

Because he had been brought up by the lizard, the boy was now to obtain the kingship.

Time passed, and after a long time that has now been forgotten, it turned out that the people over there at his home of birth came to lack everything. They had nothing, not even a dog. They had nothing, not even a chicken. They were destitute: they were just things. Because of his need for some nourishing food, his father left those wives of his—the mother of the raven, the mother of the boy. He traveled, then slept, getting up and going on, because he had seen that great homestead, that fine and wealthy homestead. He had seen it at the time he had gone to that circumcision dance. He moved on, walking straight to that place. He arrived there and sat at a distance, fearing to enter. Finally, this boy, who was now a young man, saw the man; he knew that it was his father.

When he saw who it was, he went and told the lizard: "Father! Father, I've seen something. It seems to me that my father, the one who abandoned me, the one I stabbed in the thigh, it seems that he is here today. There he is—that one, the one who is limping over there."

The place in which he had been stabbed by the boy had never healed, not to that very day. He had been stabbed long ago, but the wound remained. It never healed. He had become a cripple because of the stabbing inflicted on him by the boy.

The lizard said, "I repeat, my child, leave him alone. He'll punish himself. Don't bother beating him. What you should do now is take charge of him. Take charge of him—spit on your hand, touch his wound. Tomorrow, the wound will be gone."

The boy agreed. He said to his two people, the ones who had been given to him by his father the lizard, "Go, invite him to come in."

Then the father entered, a ragged one now, a cripple who did not have clothing to wear. He arrived, and the boy went to him, went to this man who was just a cripple. He went to him and spit on his hand. Then he uncovered the man and touched his wound. He left him then, and his father was given things to eat. He slept, and at dawn, he had nothing! No wound! At dawn, he was healed!

When it was dawn, he was well. He moved about tentatively, saying,

"Oh my child! What made me do those things to my child? I brought this thing on myself! I don't know what got into me. This would have been my homestead now. It would have been built for me by my child! Don't you do what I did, my child. Don't use me as a model. What I did, I did not do deliberately. I was driven to it by some outside force!"

The boy, now a young man, was quiet. Then he said to the lizard, "Would it be all right if I went and took my mother and sister, the ones who are in such sorrow—would it be all right if I brought them here?"

The lizard said, "It is very proper that you go to them and bring them here. This is your homestead. This will give them a chance to meet me as well."

The boy got up one day, and he departed. He slept along the way, and eventually he arrived at his destination. He arrived and found the mother of the ravens. His own mother was not there, nor was the girl. They had gone to gather firewood. When he got there, dust was billowing up because the ravens were scratching the earth. They were playing. The dust kept getting into his eyes. He went and sat at a distance and asked about his mother.

The woman said, "She's gone to gather firewood."

He asked about his sister.

She said, "She's also gathering wood. She went with her mother. Who are you? Why are you asking about the people of this home?"

He said, "You wouldn't know me because when I came here previously you did not speak to me. So even now, you cannot know me. Now do you mean that there are two of you here in this homestead—three, including the girl?"

The woman said, "Yes, because we don't know where the man of this homestead has gone. He went away, limping."

The child said, "What caused him to go lame?"

The woman said, "An amazing thing happened to this man. Such matters are not spoken of. He was stabbed by a boy, the son of his wife—the great wife. The boy had been abandoned. He should have been killed, but instead returned with great wealth. He suddenly arrived one day, saying that he had returned. But his father did not want him. He fought with the boy. He was supposed to have been abandoned long ago, but it was obvious that he had been taken to the home of his mother's parents instead, because we saw him arrive here unexpectedly that day. The boy happened to be carrying a spear, and when his father started fighting, the boy fought back. The boy stabbed him. He left on that day and never returned. The man had that wound on his thigh from that time. He was crippled by the wound. It would not heal. He has been limping ever since; he has been crippled. It has been like that for a long time. And now, we don't know what has happened to him. For all we know, he may have fallen into a ditch because of the wound. When he left here, he did not tell us where he was going. And he's been gone a long time."

The boy was silent. He did not tell her that he knew where his father was. He just sat there quietly. He said, "Oh."

Then his mother and sister returned, having gathered the firewood. While they were still coming, his mother said, "This is my child."

His sister said, "Really, Mother, it does seem to be my brother."

He had his back to them. They removed the wood from their heads, and then they went to him in the cattle kraal. They came to him and greeted him. The girl clung to her brother, she greeted him—she would not let him go. They stayed there, and his mother wept when she saw him.

He said, "Quiet, Mother. I'll take you now. Let us go."

The raven-mother was perplexed by all this. She did not know the correct thing to do. The others, all three of them, got up then and journeyed. The mother of the two children walked with these offspring of hers. On the second day, they arrived at the boy's homestead. When they got there, the woman at once saw her husband walking outside—not crippled! There was nothing wrong with him now.

She said, "Ehe! My child, see your father. He is not lame!"

The other said, "What do you say?"

"Mhm!"

They approached the man who was now fully healed. When they got to him, they greeted each other, then sat down. The son took all of the things that his mother and sister were clothed in, and he cast them away. He threw them into the fire. Then he gave them new garments, so that they would be worthy of his house.

In the evening, his father the lizard arrived, coming to see his son.

The youth told him, "Father, I went to get my mother. Here she is."

The lizard was very pleased. He said, "Let us take her beneath the water."

They went to the homestead that was in the deep pool. They entered the water.

As the lizard went into the pool, he said, "You'll not be drowned. You'll not be choked by the water," because at first they were afraid to go into the water.

So it was that they came to the great homestead there in the pool. The lizard was generous to them, giving them the privilege of living in style in their son's homestead. In the morning, they emerged from the water, then went to the homestead that was outside the pool, on the land. The boy's mother remained there; she was the mother of the king, her son having been educated by the lizard.

Tale 5

THE LOST CHILD

Masithathu Zenani's Analysis: One of the most durable of the ancient, fantastic images is that of the swallowing monster. It is a useful character for dramatically suggesting the before and after contrasts of a person undergoing a change. It is therefore particularly applicable to the changes of identity resulting from the puberty ritual—in this story, a girl's rite of passage.

The girl's childishness is indicated in two ways, each considered a peculiar quality by her neighbors: she is always getting lost, and her speech is "difficult to comprehend." This is an indication that change is needed, growing up is necessary. When she disappears one day, as she is wont to do, it is a different situation: she does not return for many years. This is the separation stage of her ritual. A frog is the swallowing monster—not so monstrous as it is benevolent, however. The frog becomes Mvulazana's ordeal. Mrs. Zenani emphasizes the ordeal by presenting as the tale's chief pattern the efforts on behalf of various groups to destroy the frog—as frequently happens, a song is at the center of this pattern, to call further attention to it. This pattern also points to the role played by the community in the person's gradual move to majority status. The girl, appropriately separated from her people during this time, is undergoing change, and the frog is protective of her as she goes through this exceedingly vulnerable part of her life, when she is without identity, when she is in a state of betwixt and between. Mrs. Zenani explained that she was further emphasizing the puberty ritual aspect of these fantastic activities by having the frog, after it has swallowed the girl, encounter boys who have been present at a dance that occurs during the puberty period. When the frog restores Mvulazana to her family, reincorporation into human society has occurred, and the ritual has come to an end.

Performance Note

Time: 18 September 1967, in the afternoon. *Place:* In Mrs. Zenani's home, in Nkanga, Gatyana District, the Transkei. *Audience:* Thirty men, women, and children. (Perf. 685.)

In the old days, in a certain homestead, a woman gave birth. She bore a daughter, she bore a son. This girl grew up, the boy grew up.

One day, the girl went on a journey.

She was a strange child, a child who was difficult to comprehend. She would travel, wandering about aimlessly. Sometimes she would get lost because she had walked so far. She would frequently travel from one sunset to the next, journeying interminably. This girl, whose name was Mvulazana, walked around like that. It was her habit and her peculiarity.

On this particular day, as she was wandering, she came to a certain

135

village. But she did not approach the homesteads in that village. She just continued to walk, descending, ascending, going to a place where there were no homesteads. As she drifted along, she met a frog. And when she came to that frog, it swallowed her. After it had swallowed her, it resembled a frog again.

People looked for the child. The people of her home hunted for her everywhere. She was sought everywhere. The child was always getting lost. People were always having to go out to find her. Usually when this happened, they would ultimately hear something. Then they would find her. But this time, the child was not found. They walked about, seeking her. But look though they might, the child was not discovered. They finally gave up hope for her.

And time passed.

In the meantime, Mvulazana's brother was growing up. When he had grown up, he got married. In the course of time, he built a large homestead. They had now given up hope for the lost child, Mvulazana. There were other children there at home now, and no one even thought of her anymore.

Time passed in that homestead, and one day Mvulazana's brother said, "This is a wonder because usually when a person is lost he is found sooner or later—if for no other reason because he is rotting. Now, I had this sister, and she got lost while I was still young. She was older than I. Her trail has never been found, and this puzzles me. Isn't there something we can do to find out what happened to her?"

The people came together, and they said, "What you're saying is not clear to us."

"It happened so long ago, nothing can be done about it now."

"So long ago!"

"What do you think we should do?"

"This is what I mean. I'm still anxious about this lost person. Even though we're happy here, even though we've now grown up, the loss of my father's child remains a mystery."

"What can be done about it?"

"She was lost so long ago."

"Well—"

Some people said, "No!"

Others treated what he said lightly: "He's a bit unbalanced."

"How can he be digging up such old memories?"

You will remember that this Mvulazana had been swallowed by a frog; it had swallowed her when she was descending into one of those valleys. She had come to a valley and was swallowed by a frog. And she did not come out of the frog.

When the frog got to its own homestead, it found that "Well, Friend, I can't sit down. I can't do anything. What should I do?"

The frog traveled on, and as it did so it hobbled because of the big person who was inside its stomach. It moved along. The frog traveled, and finally it came to a fork in the path. One path went down, another went up, one veered off one way, the other turned off the other way—four paths. When the frog got to the path, a group of boys came along. They were coming from a dance, a Xhosa older boys' dance. At such dances, girls and boys mingle all night, then separate in the morning. These boys were returning from such a night-dance.

And they saw this huge frog.

One of the boys said, "Yo! What kind of frog is this?"

"Was there ever such a big frog?"

"It's as big as a house!"

"This is the kind of creature that just begs to be beaten!"

The boys unfastened their fighting sticks, preparing to beat the frog. When they were about to bring their clubs down on the frog, it said,

> "I'm not a frog,
> I'm not a frog to be beaten!
> But I am a frog,
> And I am pregnant.
> I'm pregnant with Mvulazana,
> Her mother and father's daughter."

Among these boys was a child who said, "This frog has spoken a strange thing. What it says upsets me. It's talking about my father's daughter. It is said that she was lost. It happened when she was a girl, before we were born. Let's go on, let's move, Men!"

So the boys departed.

The frog moved on, passing that place. It ascended, hobbling along the ascending path. It came to another fork, again with a path descending, a path ascending, a path veering off one way, a path turning off the other way—four paths.

Some young men came along, returning from their own party. It had been a party for young men, a young men's dance, not like the party for the boys. They were traveling with their women.

When they arrived, they said, "Yo!"

"Never have we seen such a huge frog!"

"It's as big as an ox!"

"What kind of frog is this?"

One man dropped his garment, and said, "Well, this one must be killed! Really, it may hurt us."

The young man approached the frog cautiously, preparing to attack it.

The frog said, "No, Man,

I'm not a frog,
I'm not a frog to be beaten!
I am a frog,
But I'm pregnant,
I'm pregnant with Mvulazana,
Her mother and father's daughter."

The young man stepped back, and said, "Heee, this frog! It's not a real frog. Did you hear what it said?"

"Yes."

"Did you know this Mvulazana? She's the one from over there at home, the one who was lost. She got lost when we were still small—she was also a child at that time."

"This frog says that it's pregnant, that it's pregnant with Mvulazana!"

"Well, Friends, leave it! Let it go. Let's move on and do what we set out to do."

"This frog has been sent to harm us by a wizard."

"All right, let's go!"

The young men traveled on. So did the frog. It ascended that path again. The frog went up the path—the way was long.

Then the frog came to yet another fork—yes, and again the paths were four. There was one that cut right through. The frog stopped.

Some men were coming, returning from a beer party. They were traveling with their wives, coming from their parties. The frog stopped, and the men arrived.

The first man said, "Yo! What kind of frog is this?"

"It's so big!"

"Really, this frog is frightening!"

"It's not a frog to be ignored, this one! We might be harmed by it."

One of the men said, "No, let it go! Just stop a minute. Let me see it." That man looked at the frog. Then he said, "Well, let it be killed. Let it be killed. We must kill it now."

That man took his stick, and when he raised his arm to strike the creature, the frog said,

"I'm not a frog,
I'm not a frog to be beaten!
I am a frog,
But I'm pregnant with Mvulazana,
Her mother and father's daughter."

This man said, "Oh!" That man was actually Mvulazana's uncle.
"Oh!"

"Heee!"

"Well, really, I'm leaving this frog alone."

"Leave it alone!"

"All right!"

"I don't want to have anything to do with a speaking frog."

Other men said, "Why are you so sentimental?"

"You've had too much beer."

He said, "No, I haven't had too much beer! But I don't like what this frog just said. It upsets me."

The men went on their way, passing the frog by, going on with their wives.

The frog ascended. It moved along the path. Then it came to a village. When it arrived in the village, it went to the first homestead and entered the house through the door. A man who had been standing by the door ran. He stopped at the upper side of the house. He seized a spear.

He said, "Never have I seen such a big frog! Wife, come here with the stirrer. Let's beat this frog!"

As the fellow raised his arm, the frog said, "No!

> I'm not a frog,
> I'm not a frog to be beaten!
> But I am a frog.
> I'm pregnant,
> I'm pregnant with Mvulazana,
> Her mother and father's daughter."

This fellow began to cry when he heard the name—he was Mvulazana's father. He was crying, and as he cried his wife cried too—she was Mvulazana's mother. They did not touch the frog. The woman got up. The man was uneasy. He took a mat and placed it to one side so that the frog could sit. The frog sat on the mat, and when it had done so the man wondered how he would speak to the frog. He had never before spoken to a frog.

His wife said, "Father of So-and-so."

"Hmm?"

"Why don't you just call the people? Ask them to advise you. This is a real problem."

This fellow got up then. He called another man behind his homestead. He said, "Please come here."

The other said, "What's the matter?"

He said, "I'll tell you in the house."

The man went with him. They entered the house.

When they were inside, the neighbor said, "Yo! Why have you brought me into such a house? Yo! What is this, Man?" So he said, and this man ran off. He fell on his back out in the yard. He fell to the ground. Then he stood up and knocked against the other man who was chasing him. The other man seized him then.

He said, "No, don't be frightened! Stop!"

He said, "How could you call me to witness such a wonder? You called me to a house of frogs."

The other said, "No, stop! It's not a frog. Well, yes, it is a frog, but I want you to hear something. I was startled too. But it has said something that I want someone else to hear. Perhaps you'll know what to make of it."

That fellow started to go in again, but he stopped just outside the house. He said, "I won't go in! I won't enter such a house."

He sat down outside because he was afraid of the frog. He sat outside.

As he sat there, the father spoke to the frog: "Now then, Stranger, please speak. What is this all about?"

The frog said,

> "I'm not a frog,
> I'm not a frog to be beaten,
> Because I'm pregnant
> With Mvulazana,
> Her mother and father's daughter."

He said, "Yes, you're a frog. That we can see. Would you show her to us? Would you show this Mvulazana to us? What kind of Mvulazana are you talking about, this Mvulazana you say you're pregnant with? We had a child—her name was also Mvulazana—but we lost her a long time ago. It happened so long ago that we don't even think much about her anymore."

The frog got up. It said, "I want to sit on the upper side of the hearth."

They said, "Yes, go and sit there."

The frog got up and went to the upper side of the hearth. When it got there, it brought out Mvulazana.

She rolled out! She rolled out—and she was an older girl now, with breasts that had fallen. When she had disappeared many years before, she had still been a girl, not yet experienced, perhaps even a little soft in the head—because she was the child who always got lost, who did not know her own house, who, when she went away, did not know the way home. Then she came along with this frog, in this extraordinary way.

When the frog had put her down, her parents came to their senses.

"Friend, please bring a blanket. This is a guest, not a frog."

A new white blanket was brought, and the frog was covered up. A sheep was brought too.

It was said, "Let the beast be slaughtered for the frog."

The frog agreed to this, but it said, "I don't eat cooked meat. Please prepare raw meat for me. Pound it, pound it with rocks so that I can swallow it. I can't swallow it unless it has been pounded."

That was done then. The meat was pounded—meat without bones was selected, and it was pounded, it was made supple. Then the frog was able to swallow the meat as it sat there.

It was said then, "What should we give you?"

The frog said, "No, my reward is your thanks."

"We thank you then, Frog."

It went on its way the next morning.

Tale 6

THE PREGNANT BOY

Masithathu Zenani's Analysis: As the child grows to adulthood, he is caught in an identity crisis. Who am I? What is my proper social function? How do I distinguish myself from others? Stories that dramatize rites of passage of necessity emphasize questions of identity.

No longer a boy, not yet a man, he is between two states of being, a person without a role, without a defined character. He is sorting himself out, learning his limits, seeking his possibilities.

In this tale, a boy becomes a mother. He has disobeyed his parents by taking prohibited medicine. But obedience to one's parents is not the key thematic concern of the story. What is important is his uncertain gender. The storyteller emphasizes this by making the boy's womanhood the central focus—and she does this through patterning.

The two major patterns have to do first with the boy's awareness of the developing embryo in his stomach and then with his love for and feeding of the child. Mrs. Zenani thereby directs the audience's attention to the boy's womanness, his temporary state of androgyny a dramatist's embodiment of his betwixt and between state—not yet a man, no longer a boy, he is poised between male and female.

It is left to the mother to teach the boy what his limitations and possibilities are. In the end, the mother nurses the child, which is a woman's role, and the boy "became healthy again, and did his work well . . . [and] there was happiness at this home." Restored equilibrium has been achieved only after the boy understands his function as a man. The story is more than simply the dramatization of the rite. It also provides an insight into the meaning of the ceremony.

In her use of the various traditional components of *intsomi* production, Mrs. Zenani suggests the possibilities of the art form. One of the most direct and obvious ways in which she distinctly develops her images is through the use of detail, particularly in the delineation of character. Her eye is generally on the character rather than on the action, the latter being important only in so far as it reveals character. She seems to enjoy seeing a human in an utterly incongruous situation—putting him there and then carefully detailing the way he reacts.

Consider the following excerpt from one storyteller's version of the story of "The Pregnant Boy":

> When she had gone, this boy took the medicine and drank it. When he had drunk it, he went to the river, and when he got to the river, he gave birth to two children, because he had consumed the medicine. One child was a boy, the other was a girl. The boy remained there at the river with these children. Whenever he wanted to suckle them, he

said, "Breasts, breasts, breasts, be full!" And a breast would appear. Then he would suckle the children at his breast.[2]

Here is another version by yet another storyteller:

> When he returned, along the way he drank from the bottle. He was now in a certain place, and this boy became pregnant. He bore a child there, and he put it there in that place. . . . In the morning, the boy returned to where he had left the child. . . . As he was approaching, he said, "Breasts, breasts, be full! . . . Breasts, breasts, be full!" Well, the child appeared, and he nursed it with this milk, he nursed it with this milk.[3]

Finally, this is a version of the story created by Masithathu Zenani in 1967:

> When he found that his mother was gone, he looked at the medicine and said, "This medicine looks good! It probably tastes sweet!"
>
> He put the medicine into the hearth. It was cooked, and then he drank some of it. Then the boy waited, and finally his mother arrived. He gave the medicine that remained to his mother.
>
> "But why did he prepare such a small amount of medicine?"
>
> "Well, I don't know! This is what he gave me. He said that you should put it into the hearth, and then drink it."
>
> So the mother of the boy put it into the fire, and then she drank it.
>
> Time went on for the boy, time went on, and he noticed that breasts were developing on him. The boy saw that breasts were developing on him, and from time to time he felt the breasts with his hand.
>
> "Oh, I'm developing breasts!"
>
> As he was developing these breasts, his stomach became bigger. The boy was pregnant now, and he carried on in this state of pregnancy. He was constantly afraid of this pregnancy. He wrapped himself up carefully. He fastened his cape in front. He was afraid of these breasts of his and his stomach which continued to grow larger. Time went on for the boy, the months came and passed, and the boy's stomach became bigger and bigger. He remained by himself. He did not go around with the other boys because of his breasts which kept growing larger. He remained a boy who kept apart from the others. The boy continued in that state, and the months followed one another. Ah,

2. The *intsomi* from which this excerpt comes was performed on 14 November 1967, at about 1:30 P.M., in a home in Nyaniso, Matatiele District, the Transkei. The performer was a thirty-year-old Hlubi woman, and her audience was composed of twenty women, fifteen children, and six teenaged boys.

3. This performance took place on 15 November 1967, at about 12:30 P.M., in the home of Headman Thandela in Nyaniso, Matatiele District, the Transkei. The performer, a Hlubi woman of about fifty-five years, produced her work before an audience consisting of three men, five women, one girl, and two boys.

now this boy was truly heavy, and when he saw that he was so heavy with a child, he began to feel birth pains.

When the boy first felt the pains, he was away on the veld looking after the livestock, and he exclaimed, "What might have gone wrong with me?" And all this time, he was feeling the movement of the child here in his stomach. But he kept quiet. He did not speak about it. He hid it from the people. He felt that there was indeed something moving here in his stomach. He carried on like that, and when he was going through the pains, he started digging, he dug in the ground, he dug and dug, making a house, he made it well. He scooped out a hole, he scooped out a hole, he dug, he dug into an ant heap. And the boy felt these birth pains. When he at last felt that the pains were especially intense, he went into the ant heap house and gave birth. He gave birth to a girl. . . .[4]

Her concern is for character, for verisimilitude of character and motivation of a character's actions. Through the use of details, Mrs. Zenani here develops the boy's plight, and she does not fail to reflect the grim humor of his developing pregnancy, exploiting his agony. Moreover, these details, which may seem merely descriptive here, become more vividly expressive in performance. With gestures and body movements, the artist portrays the boy's enlarging body, his attempts to shield his developing breasts from the other boys, his frantic digging motions. The details provide a strong motivation for the boy's anguished question, "What might have gone wrong with me?"

Through details, Mrs. Zenani enhances the unreal. The bizarre elements of the plot are made more curious because of her concentration on the atmosphere of realism elsewhere—the long period of pregnancy, for example, and the boy's relations with his fellows. This is one of her primary artistic techniques: she achieves humor, surprise, and terror by means of this detailed and fanciful juxtaposition of the real and the fantastic. She casts fantasy in a known milieu, providing detail after detail about the realistic activities, most of which the audience knows well. This artist communicates her fascination with what occurs when the unknown penetrates the real. She does this for artistic reasons. She explained that she was not attempting here to make the boy's condition logical; she made his awkward situation more incredible by making him so real. She thereby grafted onto her immediate society the activities of the *intsomi*, no matter how strange they may be, and she was thus able to support the basic and controlling metaphor of the tradition.

Performance Note

Time: 2 August 1972, in the late afternoon. *Place:* Outside, along the side of a ridge near Mrs. Zenani's home, Nkanga, Gatyana District, the Transkei. *Audience:* Three teenagers and three children. (Perf. NS-14.)

4. Mrs. Zenani performed this *intsomi* on 13 September 1967, at about 6 P.M., in a home in Nkanga, Gatyana District, the Transkei. Her audience was made up of about thirty-five children and fifteen women.

A woman and man lived together for a long time without having children. A long time passed, but the woman did not become pregnant. No matter what cures the husband sought, his wife did not become pregnant.

After seeking for a long time, they finally found someone who said that he could cure her.

The husband told him, "My wife is not pregnant. I've tried to cure her for a long time."

This person said, "Why don't you bring her to me? I'll give her a medicine that will make her pregnant."

The husband went to him because he wanted a child.

The stranger gave him medicine that was composed of two roots; the woman was to take this medicine. The roots were put into the hearth, and, when she removed them from the hearth, she chewed and swallowed them. She pounded some of the roots and put them into a bottle. These were to be drunk.

So it was that the woman became pregnant. She became pregnant: the months went by, and finally she gave birth—she bore a boy.

This child who was a boy grew up. He grew to the age at which his mother should have another child.

But again this wife dried up. She was not pregnant.

Her husband said, "What must I do? I'm always in debt, going to the doctor to get medicine for her barrenness. This wife, it turns out, is unable to become pregnant unless she's treated. Now again, she cannot become pregnant. How can I deal with this?"

His wife said, "Really, Father of So-and-so, please go back to that person who cured me the last time. It's obvious that I am again unable to become pregnant."

The man returned to that person.

"Hello, Sir."

"Yes."

"Hm mh."

"How are you?"

"Well, I've come from home."

"Yes?"

"That person you cured before—well, she cannot get pregnant again."

"Mm mh."

"She wants some more of that medicine."

"Yes?"

"So I've come here to ask you to provide it for her."

The owner of the medicine answered him, "Well, I cannot give you the medicine again, and this is why: when I gave it to you the last time your wife gave birth to a child. He's an old child by now—he's a boy, he herds for you. But you haven't paid me yet."

"What should I pay you?"

"You should pay me an ox because I have made a child for you."

"All right, I'll bring an ox. In the meantime, will you find the medicine?"
The person said, "First, come with the ox."

The man went to his home. He explained to his wife what the man had said: "He won't give me any medicine until I give him an ox because I haven't paid him yet for the medicine that he gave us the last time, when you got pregnant and bore a child, a child who is old now. What do you suggest, Wife?"

The woman said, "I'm satisfied with his demand, Father of So-and-so. I'm content that you should produce an ox for him because I want to have another child. What can we do with one child? Give him the ox."

The man agreed. He brought out the ox. He took the ox to that fellow, and when he arrived, he said, "Here's the ox. Now give me the medicine."

The man did not refuse. He said, "Well, now, you've done what I wanted you to do. But as far as the medicine is concerned, you'll have to come and get it tomorrow. I've got to go and look for it. It doesn't grow here at home."

The man agreed. He went home.

He arrived at his home: "Wife, I didn't get the medicine. But he was pleased with the ox and said that I can get the medicine tomorrow. He has to go out and find it. But tomorrow, I'll be busy. How shall we handle this?"

The woman said, "This child is old enough now. He can go and pick up the medicine. The boy knows where the place is." She called the boy. "My child, can you go over there and get the medicine?"

The boy said, "Yes."

"Do you know the place?" his father asked.

"Yes, I know it, Father. It's over there, in that direction."

"What'll you say when you get there?"

"I'll say that my father says that I should come and get the medicine that he came looking for yesterday."

"All right. And then what?"

"When he has given me the medicine, I'll ask him how it should be administered."

"Well then, go, my child. Do you hear him? This child is really quite careful about this matter." So said the wife.

"Yes, he is."

"I told you that the child has grown up."

The next day, the child was sent.

"Go then, my child. Go and get the medicine."

The child went. He was given a cloth in which to tie the medicine.

So it was that the boy arrived at that place, and he knocked at the door.

"Come in."

The child said, "Hello."

"Yes. Where have you come from, Child?"

"I come from home. I was sent by my father. He told me to come and get the medicine that he asked for yesterday."

"All right." The fellow rose and got the medicine. It consisted of four roots. He said, "Now, Boy, tell your mother that she is to put two of these roots into the hearth. When they're warm, they should be eaten—swallowed. Tell her that these other two roots should be pounded, then put into a bottle. She should add water to these, then drink the medicine. Do you understand, Boy?"

"I understand, Father."

The child traveled then. He went home, carrying that medicine in the cloth.

As he walked along, he uncovered the medicine. He was still far from his home when he looked at it.

"Ee, this medicine looks good! These roots are nice!" He took the roots that his mother was supposed to put into the hearth, and he tasted them. "Oh! They're good! Mm! They taste good!" The child chewed them. "Hmmmm! Mm! This medicine that my mother eats is really nice! Mm!" He ate the roots. He ate them, he ate them and finished them. Then he took the medicine that was to be pounded, and he tasted that. He said, "Mh! Ptt!" He spit it out. "It's bitter! This is bitter! Mmh! No, I don't want this!" And he left those roots alone, tying them in the cloth.

As he journeyed on, the child thought, "What'll I do now? What shall I say when I get home? The man said that my mother should take one portion of the roots, roast it in the hearth, then eat it. He said that she should take the other portion, grind it, then put it into a bottle and drink it. Well, I won't say anything about these two that I've eaten."

When the boy got home, his father said, "My child, you've hurried!"

"Yes, I've hurried, Father."

"And what happened? Did you get the medicine?"

"Yes, I got it."

"Where is it, my child?"

"Here it is."

"What did he say? Did he tell you what was to be done with this?"

"He told me."

"What did he say?"

"He said that my mother should take one of the roots, put it into the hearth, then eat it. And she should take the other root, grind it, then put it into a bottle and drink it."

"Ee, he gave me four roots last time. There are just two, my child! What's the matter today? Why did he give us only two?"

"I don't know, Father. I didn't ask him about that. I didn't mention that subject. I was given these two roots, that's all. And he said that Mother should put this one into the hearth and eat it, and that she should grind this one, then put it into a bottle and drink it with water."

"Well, the directions are clear enough."

His mother took the medicine then. She took it hurriedly because she was eager to have a child. She put the root into the hearth, then ate it.

She said, "Mhm! Ee! What's the matter with this medicine today, Father of So-and-so? It wasn't like this the other time, when I ate the medicine and then as a result bore this child who is a boy. It wasn't like this at all!"

"What's this medicine like?"

"This medicine—I don't know. This one's bitter!"

"What is this woman up to now? What was it like the first time?"

"It was sweet. It was the other medicine that was bitter."

"Well, eat it. Medicines are not all alike."

"Ee!" She ate it. Then she ground the other root, and she drank it.

"What's that one like?"

"It's like the first one. The medicine that he told me to drink the first time was just like this one. It's the other one that tasted different."

"Oh."

Time passed then, and she did not become pregnant. The moon appeared and died, and she was not yet pregnant. Another moon came and died, and she was not pregnant. She drank the medicine, it was finished, but she did not become pregnant.

But the *boy* was developing breasts! The boy! He developed breasts—here, on his chest! Ee!

"This boy is developing breasts! What's the matter with you, developing breasts like that, my child?"

"I don't understand this!"

"You must press them down, press them, squeeze them. Do this to them. Squeeze them, to keep them from developing."

The child repeatedly squeezed them, but the breasts grew.

And his stomach grew too! Eee! Ik! The boy wore his blanket differently now. He made room in the front of the blanket for his developing stomach, hiding his stomach in that way. His stomach continued to grow, and the months passed by.

Then one month, he had labor pains. The *boy!* He was out in the pasture, herding the livestock, and he had labor pains. He had pains, he had labor pains. Labor pains! He came in from the pasture.

"Milk the cows, Boy."

"No, my finger—my hand, it's sore! My finger! My hand's sore!"

"What's the matter, Boy? What happened to your hand? Let me see."

"No! It's throbbing with pain! I can't milk! Oh!" He writhed in pain.

But actually this boy was having labor pains.

"What's the matter with you, twisting in pain like this? Do you have a headache, Boy?"

"No, my hand is throbbing with pain!"

"Oh!"

Time passed, and the father milked that day because the boy did not feel well. They went to sleep, and the boy groaned all night. Some medicine was ground up for him, and his hand was massaged; it was massaged. The hand was cooled, treated with the medicine.

He said, "It's throbbing with pain!"

"Ee!"

When the boy went out with the herd the next day, he moved slowly. He went out to the veld with the herd, and while he was herding, alone, he was having labor pains.

"Yo!"

He went to an antheap, and he dug into that antheap. He took a stick, and he dug and dug. He dug into this antheap which was situated beneath a cliff. He dug a small hole that went deep into the hill—a hole, like that made by bees. And the boy remained there, he gave birth there. He bore a child, a girl. Ee! Then the breasts of the boy produced milk. They dripped with milk. The boy nursed the child then, he nursed the child. He tore his blanket up and wrapped the child in it. He wrapped the child, he wrapped her and snuggled her into that hole, then he closed it up with rocks.

He turned the cattle around and took them home.

When he got home, he immediately busied himself with the milking.

"How's your hand, Boy?"

"It's better. It's healed."

"Oh, it's healed. Are you able to milk now?"

"Yes, I'll be able to milk now, Father. My hand is healed."

The boy milked then, he milked. He finished milking, and when that chore was finished, he stayed in the house. He ate. And then he went to sleep.

Yo! In the middle of the night, the boy sneaked away. He went out as if he were going to urinate. But then he hurried to the antheap, to the place where the child was. He arrived there, and the child was crying. He took the child and nursed her. He nursed her, then he wrapped her up in his blankets again and snuggled her in that hole.

He went home. When he arrived, he sat outside.

His mother came out.

"Where did you go?"

"Oh, I was just sitting outside. It's hot in the house."

"Oh."

Time passed for this boy.

He went out with the livestock the next morning. He went to herd. At midday, he took the cattle to drink, and when he returned he went to his child. He nursed her. He nursed the child, then he wrapped her up again and nestled her into the hole.

He turned the cattle around, and went home.

Time passed for the boy.

On a certain day, his mother spied on him. She said, "There's something wrong with this child."

Time passed that day for the mother. Time passed, and when he took the cattle out to pasture that morning, his mother went out as well. She went over the ridge, in a different direction, and came out below. She watched him, she observed him as he was herding there. She saw him as he ran off to the child. His mother was still watching him when he arrived at the place where the child was, as he took the child out and nursed her, nursed the child, and talked baby talk to her. He talked baby talk to his child, then he took her and cradled her. He took her and nursed her. He cradled the child, held the child close to his body. His mother observed all this, but she did not reveal herself. The boy wrapped his child in blankets then and nuzzled her into the hole, then closed it up with a rock.

He went to the cattle.

His mother ran, she disappeared. She arrived at her home and remained in the house.

The boy arrived. Mmh, he was busy, he milked the cows.

"Mm! Mhmm!" His mother did not reveal that she had seen him; she lowered her eyes and the boy relaxed.

That night, the boy again got up and went out. His mother went out also.

"What is it? Where are you going?"

"No, I'm not going anywhere. I'm just sitting here."

His mother sat outside too; she reclined.

"Why are you reclining, Mama?" the boy asked. "Why don't you go into the house? Won't you catch cold?"

His mother said, "No, I won't catch cold, my child. I was also suffering from the heat in the house. I want—I will—It's hot in the house."

The boy went in then and slept. His mother departed. She went over there to that antheap, and she took the child. She hid the child, holding her against her body. She brought the child home with her.

Ee! The boy came out.

His mother nursed the child, and the child did not cry. The mother hid the child.

The boy came outside, and his mother went into the house. The boy was not aware that the child was here at home with his mother, that his mother had hidden her. So the boy ran off and went over there to the antheap.

When he got there, he found that the stone had been removed. There was no cover over the hollowed-out place. Nothing was there! The boy cried and cried, "My child! Perhaps something's eaten her!" He cried, he cried and cried. He went into the valley, he came out of the valley, searching for his child. He wandered about until daybreak, going up and down, round and round, round and round. He could not find even the blanket of the child. He saw nothing, nothing at all. Oh, this boy cried. When the sun came up, he went home. When he got home, his eyes were bloodshot because he had been crying.

His father said, "What's the matter with you, Boy?"

"It's nothing! I just have some smoke in my eyes."

"Do you mean to tell me that smoke has made you like this?"

"It's smoke! The smoke's irritating my eyes!"

"My child, what shall we do about this?"

The mother had already told the father what had happened: "Look, this baby is the child of our child. The boy bore this child! This boy has breasts! He ate the medicine, then gave birth to this child!"

"So that's why this child has breasts!"

"Yes."

Well, time passed, and the boy was given food.

"Eat! Eat, then open the kraal for the livestock. And go and herd."

"No, I don't want any food."

"How can you go away hungry? Ee!"

Things were looking very bleak. The child was still concealed from him. He did not know what had happened.

He went out with his cattle. His father observed him. He saw his son descending and ascending, journeying up and down, seeking here, there, leaving one place, looking in another. Then the boy gave up.

His father returned: "Nobani, you must tell my child. He must be told now. You must tell him where his child is. He'll get hurt this way."

"All right."

In the afternoon, the boy returned with his cattle. When he arrived, he closed the cattle in the kraal and entered the house. Then his mother got up and went and awakened the child and nursed him. The boy saw this and stared at the child.

He said, "Oh, Mama! Mama, you have a child! You have a child, Mama!"

"Yes, I have a child. I picked this child up."

"Where did you pick her up, Mama? Hand her to me. I want to see her."

"I just picked her up over that hill there."

"Please hand her to me. I want to see her, Mama! Please hand her to me, so that I can see her. Oh! oh! The child of my mother! Isn't she beautiful? Heee heee! Yo, Mama! I'm happy, Mama! You have a child!"

His mother sat there. She was silent. She nursed her child.

His father said, "Now, my child, we were ignorant all this time that you had eaten the medicine. Well, that's all right, my child. This matter won't be talked about. We won't shame you among the other boys. This is your mother's child.[5] And you must never again eat that medicine!"

The child said, "I did eat it, Mama. I was tasting it, to see how it was, and I found that it was very nice. I didn't know then that I would end up having a child! I was really embarrassed when I gave birth!"

"Now, you see, this child is your sister. It's your mother's child. It's not yours."

"Yes. All right."

The boy was happy now. He became healthy again and did his work well. He did not become sick again. When he milked, he milked for the child, so that the child of his mother could drink milk. That was pleasant. There was happiness at this home.[6]

A WOMAN BEHAVES LIKE A MAN

The confusion of sexes in the foregoing tale is not an uncommon subject of the oral tradition, both imaginative and historical. What follows is a companion story to "The Pregnant Boy," a story that is, Mrs. Zenani noted, historical. In "The Pregnant Boy," sexual masking revealed the movement of a boy through a period of being betwixt and between into adulthood. In this historical tale, "A Woman Behaves Like a Man," an entire society is moving to a new dispensation, with the ruler in a state of sexual ambiguity. The result is the same: the androgynous person becomes emblematic of the betwixt and between state of the society. The significance of the sexual ambiguity is suggested by a member of the assembly at the end of this tale, as he refers to the son of the "king": "He has done nothing but preserve your land for you until you got through this difficulty."

Performance Note

Time: 13 September 1967, in the early evening. *Place:* Outside, in a kraal in Nkanga, Gatyana District, the Transkei. *Audience:* Fifty men, women, and children. (Perf. 624.)

Long ago, in the land of the Xhosa, a royal homestead was being established. The king took a wife, and when he had married her she bore a

5. In the 1967 version of the story (*Time:* 13 September 1967, in the evening. *Place:* In a home in Nkanga, Gatyana District, the Transkei. *Audience:* Fifteen women and thirty-five children. Perf. 626), Mrs. Zenani emphasizes the division of sexes. The boy's mother comments, "I took the child. You'll just make yourself the joke of the other boys. A boy never has a child. I took this child, she's in the house. She'll be mine now. Don't ever again say that you have a child. . . . I'll nurse her. You must dry those breasts up. Remember, you're a boy!"

6. See the appendix for an alternative ending used by Mrs. Zenani in her 1967 version of this story.

girl—the only child she had. This woman did not have a son. A long time passed, and she bore no son.

It became clear that her daughter should not marry because there was no son in this house. This girl, who did not marry, must be addressed as a prince. And, as a prince, two "wives" had to be gotten for her. So her wives were created. They were called her "wives" because she was unmarried: she was a son. These "wives" were created: one of them became the right-hand wife, the wife of the right-hand house.

This woman did not wear a skirt, she did not put on a headpiece: she behaved like a man. In those days, people dressed in skins; there were no cloth garments in those days. They wore skins of cattle and wild animals, skins that had been tanned. That "man"—the one who had been created a man, "he" actually being a woman—wrapped "his" head with the crest of an animal, as a man would.

Then it developed that both of "his" wives became pregnant. The senior one bore a boy, the junior gave birth to a daughter.

Later, once again, they became pregnant: the senior one again bore a boy, and the junior wife also bore a boy this time.

Time passed, and the children of that woman who was to become a king grew up. This woman had her councillors, because she was a son. When "his" sons had grown up and had wives of their own, those wives of the sons called this woman "Father," not "Aunt." And her father's children called her "Older brother," not "Aunt," because this person had been made a son. Later, when "he" had reached an advanced age, "he" became the king.

A certain councillor, a member of the Cira clan, had sexual relations with her. While they were having sexual relations, they were surprised by someone. Because of that, the councillor was fired. It was said that he had done something dirty. He departed; he went off and established a homestead by himself. New councillors were sought.

After a long time, this king said that it was necessary that her son now take over the kingship. So her son did take charge; he became the king. Court cases were now conducted at his home. As a plaintiff came in sight of the royal residence, he would say, "I'm laying a charge!" making that statement while he was still above the homestead. It would then be said, "Come further down!" That plaintiff would gradually come down, repeating the same thing until he reached the house, speaking in that manner the whole time. Then, as he sat there at this homestead, the councillors would come out. They would go and sit with him in the courtyard. A dried skin would be taken and put in the courtyard. The king would come out and sit on it. The plaintiff's case would be discussed.

After a long period of years, a controversy arose. This woman's son, the one who had been made the king, was harassed by his uncle's sons. They insisted that the child of an unmarried woman could not rule. This issue became a subject for debate. Important people came together to discuss the problem, to exchange opinions about this matter. The king was appealing to a higher court, against the idea that his uncle's son should take over the reign. He argued that the heirship to the kingship belonged to him. It had been so directed by the previous king.

But the uncle insisted that this man could not rule because he was a *wangu* [an illegitimate child].

He asked, "What is a *wangu*?"

He said, "I say *you* are a *wangu*! You don't belong to this homestead because you're the child of an unmarried woman!"

He said, "What am I? Whose child have I been all this time? During the period that I have ruled—isn't it because I have been formally and ceremonially appointed that I came to rule?"

"No," the uncle said. "No, if you ruled during that period, it's because everybody was still unaware of the true situation. But now you cannot be allowed to go on ruling because the children of this home have appeared. The line of succession belongs to them. You are the child of an unmarried woman!"

Then that son who was the ruler, the son of the unmarried woman, said, "Is it because the woman impregnated herself that you're digging into my background?"

The uncle said, "No, she did not impregnate herself. But even so, you are the child of an unmarried woman. Now the children of this home are here. Male children. And they should rule."

"So that is the way things are. I want this affair to be adjudicated from the beginning. I am appealing. I am arguing that I must rule. That I should not rule is impossible!"

The meeting broke up then. The people scattered.

Time passed. He was agitated now, wondering, "How is this problem to be resolved?"

He visited his friends, reporting everywhere that he was being persecuted. He was advised that the person who had been the councillor should be present—the one who had lain with the king, the progenitor of this current king. That was the councillor who had consequently been banished, the member of the Cira clan. But this Cira clansman was no longer around. He had died long ago. What, therefore, should be done?

One of his advisers told him, "At the time of his indiscretion, the Cira clansman had his own sons. Whatever sons he might have had by the king, they would have been superseded by his own legitimate children. One of his sons might still be alive. While this Cira clansman was a trusted advisor, he was hopeful. He lived at the royal residence, he married at the royal residence, he sired children at the royal residence. When he was banished and went over there to live, he departed with three of his sons. They know what he was thinking and saying in those early days. One of the sons was already alive when the tryst took place."

The son whose reign was being contested departed. He sought the place where the Cira clansman had established his homestead. It was far from this area where the dispute over the kingship was taking place. The king departed—sleeping, waking up, and finally he arrived there. He found four sons of the Cira clansman, but the Cira fellow himself was now dead.

He arrived and said, "I've come from the royal residence to visit that councillor who was your father. I realize that he himself is deceased. But I've come here regarding an important matter. I seek a child who was already alive when a certain event took place at home, a child who might have some knowledge of the day the decision was made that the woman of the royal residence should have a wife, that she herself should not marry."

The son, who was now middle-aged, answered, "Yes, Young man, there's something like that here. We were born at the royal residence, three of us, when that matter was developing. Our cousins were also there. Considerable discussion was taking place regarding that matter—the princess, she was of the great house. Since there were no male heirs, she would have to marry wives. And she did marry two wives. Our father came here and died far away from your home because he committed a forbidden act. The breaking of a taboo, Young man, was not appreciated by the king. He had sexual relations with her, he slept with the king, and he was caught at it. So he exiled himself from that house. The people were assembled, and it was decreed that he must leave. Different councillors were sought. That is the part of the situation that we are aware of. If you want me to come over to your place and testify, you are going to have to wait a while. Don't hurry me because there's some business here that we must address ourselves to."

He was referring to an important ceremony, which involved the brewing of a considerable amount of beer. There was to be a sacrifice: beasts were to be slaughtered for a deceased person. Because of these circumstances, the man of the homestead could go nowhere; such an affair was a significant one among the Xhosa, a ritual involving the healing of the sick.

The young man accepted the delay, and he departed, saying, "I shall return. I shall come to you again next month to see if the ceremony has ended. This matter is disturbing me greatly."

They agreed, and the young man left.

The ceremony proceeded. Beer was prepared in that homestead. A beast was sacrificed. The women put on leather skirts for the sake of the beast; they dressed in them as usual because there were no cloth garments in those days—skins were the typical garments at that time.

When the ceremony came to an end, the crowds dispersed.

Eventually, when he thought that the affair might be over, the young man returned.

He arrived: "I have come back. I would like you to come to my home, both of you. Your older brother too. I have found your comments enlightening, but I would like him to be there too. It is not that I do not consider you helpful, it is just that I want him there."

He agreed. "You shall see us when the time comes."

The young man departed.

Some days later, the young Cira clansman and his elder brother journeyed to the royal residence. When they arrived, they remained outside. They entered no house, they stayed at the side of the kraal.

Someone asked, "What is your business?"

The son of the king responded before the strangers could do so. He said, "These people have come here on my account. They are the ones I visited concerning this matter. Those involved in the earlier discussion must now return. I want them all to be here when the matter is discussed. It was during my appeal that I requested that the Cira clansmen be here."

"All right," the uncle said.

The people were called; they filled the royal residence.

It was said, "Let the one who wishes to speak do so."

The young man got up. He said, "I wish to speak. I want to speak because I have been called a *wangu*. You might wonder what a *wangu* is. I understand that it is a person who is borne by an unmarried woman. What I want to know is this: did this unmarried woman impregnate herself? Had she not been created by you yourselves to rule? It is claimed that she was 'created' because there was no one in this homestead who could take over the reign. Now an heir has appeared, and the situation is reversed. I pause."

"All right. Now tell us, Young man, clarify the issue. Where do you stand?"

"This is where I stand. The man whom I went to seek—let him stand. He was present at the time. He can tell us what was said when I came to rule. What was it that was said that brought me to the rule?"

"All right, stand up then, Young man."

"You can hear for yourself what is at issue here," said other members of the assembly.

The young man stood. He said, "Yes, Honorable ones, Children of great people! This is the reason I have come. This king came to me, saying that he has a problem. He complains that he is being harassed here at his home. People are claiming that he is the child of an unmarried woman. So he sought me and asked me to come here and clarify things, since my father is now dead, and since we were already living at the time the woman was 'created' a man."

"Young man of the Cira clan, can you contribute something to this discussion?"

"How old were you at the time?"

"I was already old. The discussion was held outside here, and it was a practice in those days not to drive children away when such matters were being discussed. We grew to maturity, these things being discussed in our presence. At that time, my father was still here. We sat at the side of my father. He was an important councillor here."

"Do you remember your father?"

"I do remember him."

"What did he do that made it necessary for him to leave this place?"

"My father had to leave because he slept with my grandmother and was caught."

"Who caught him?"

"My sister caught him."

"Which sister?"

"This one, from the right-hand house."

"And what did she do?"

"She said, 'They are not opening the door here. They are sharing a blanket.'"

"Then what happened?"

"The king went and blockaded him. My father said, 'Please don't even touch me, Lord! I've done wrong.' Then the king assembled the people and said that 'he' was going to exile my father."

"Oh!"

"Sit down, Young man." So said the men. Then they said, "That's his statement, Lord."

The king said, "Well, he is right. That is the way it was. Now then, what have you come here to say?"

"I have come to argue that this young man is correct. His mother was ruling. His mother—I mean, that 'father' of his, his mother is actually his 'father'—that woman who did not marry: she became a king here, and consequently two wives were taken for her to marry. And they gave birth to these sons."

"In your opinion, what do you consider is the proper thing to do now? Because the children here at home have now appeared."

"In my opinion, that would not be right. That is not the way it should be. It must be settled in some other way."

"Please sit down, Young man."

The young Cira clansman sat.

The young man who was appealing this matter was told to rise.

"What do you suggest should be done, Young man?"

"I think that if I am exiled from my home, I ought to be given my rights.

I should be given an axe if I must leave home. When I leave, I should be allowed to leave with everything that is mine, everything that was called by my name. I should leave nothing behind in my sleeping place." So said this young man; his words were addressed to this assembly.

"Now this matter is for you alone to decide. We must see where we view the matter differently. We shall just think about his words, but you might be seeing it differently."

The king spoke then. "Please make your decision. I shall contradict you if I conclude that you are not walking along the right path."

Then the members of the assembly spoke. They said, "This young man is right."

"He ought to be given a part of the nation to rule."

"He can live in that land according to the way you cause him to depart, because he has not wronged anyone."

"He has done nothing but preserve your land for you until you got through this difficulty."

These words prevailed. The young man was given a portion of the land. He was given his own land to rule over, as a *wangu*.

That is how he came to be a king with his own land. He alone ruled now, in his own district.

Tale 7

MALEJESE, SON OF A KING

Masithathu Zenani's Analysis: Before events combine to create sadness in Malejese, the son of a king, something else has happened. Two old men have arrived at the royal residence. They have led unhappy lives and arrive impoverished, asking for the protection of this king. They become accepted members of the king's household, held in affection by all but loved especially by Malejese, who refers to them fondly as "My father's old men." But then, strange things happen here. "It seemed as if a plague had struck the royal residence." Everyone dies, until only Malejese and his family remain. Malejese inherits all of the considerable livestock of his father. His own wife, before she dies, urges her husband to burn the houses and kraals and then to depart.

If there is a connection between the arrival of the old men and the death of the community, it remains somewhat ambiguous. Malejese's wife's dying wish is: "I am the last one. Now, you are left with the cattle of my father[-in-law], you are left with the horses . . . the goats . . . the sheep . . . the fowl . . . the hogs . . . , you are left with the old men of my father. . . . [Y]ou must go with these things to [your] mother's parents' place. . . ."

Now commences a typical set of activities for a puberty ritual. The young person departs. The home that he leaves is typically one in disarray, one that is tainted, or, as in this case, a dying or dead home. "Malejese cried because he was the last person, the end of the people of his home." The major pattern of the story—underscored in this case by the song at its center—has to do with a fantastic monster: ". . . a thing that turned out to be a fire, a forest, a cliff, that suddenly appeared behind me. . . ." In the world of fantasy, the regular encounters with this monster result in the decimation of his father's livestock, the remnants of Malejese's ties to his past. These are systematically eliminated as he moves further from home, further from his childhood, moving toward his adulthood and independence, cut off from his past. Literally, he is journeying to the homestead of his mother's parents, a long way off. Relentlessly, the monster demands that he "make an offering!" and Malejese, in fright, complies. He gives the monster the "goats of my father," and, as the persistent pursuer (another of the durable images from the past, capturing as it does a deeply felt fear) continues to return, Malejese gives up his father's sheep, his father's hogs, fowl, cattle. With each encounter, he must confront some aspect of this many-faceted monster—its cliffs, fire, snow, cold. In the end, he has only his father's dogs and the old men. He is loathe to give up the men, so he releases the dogs, saying, "I'll give up the old men another time." This sacrifice turns out to be unnecessary. The youth arrives at his parents' place, "cleansed of the ugly thing that had befallen him," and he is now a man.

The role played by the two old men seems significant. Their own past is

159

shadowy. They "lost count of the days" that they had been gone from their own original place. And when they arrive at this homestead, where they develop a special relationship with Malejese, people begin to die. It is these men, then, who accompany the boy as he moves to his new status. They might be, Mrs. Zenani suggested somewhat elliptically in a later discussion, from his ancestral past. There is something about them that keeps the youth from sacrificing them to the monster. They may be responsible for the destruction of the youth's home. They may be his guides to his new life as a man, as he forsakes his past, giving up his ties (the livestock) to that past.

Performance Note

Time: 11 August 1972, in the late morning. *Place:* In a fallen rondavel near Mrs. Zenani's home in Nkanga, Gatyana District, the Transkei. *Audience:* Six women, three men, and five children. (Perf. NS-148.)

The great homestead of the royal residence was an opulent one. The master of this homestead was a king, and he had his councillors and courtiers. He lived there with his wife, who had her own councillors. Nothing was lacking in this homestead—everything was there, from things that are raised to things that are cultivated. The king was kind, a constructive person.

It was during his kingship that two old men arrived at the royal residence.

The two old men accompanied one another along the way to the king's royal residence where they hoped they would be granted shelter. When they got there, they remained in the courtyard; they did not sit on the king's chair.

The councillors over there at the royal residence saw that the men were aged, and they asked them what they were seeking.

One of the old men answered, "We have come here because we are impoverished, both of us—this is my brother. We decided that we should come here to the royal residence, which is everyone's home, to become the children of this noble place. We seek refuge; we want to be protected by these women, the wives of the king. We are not going further. We have come here to stay. We are destitute."

The king heard what they said. He said, "Ask them what their clan is, where their homes are."

The old men were asked, "What clan do you belong to? Where is your home?"

The old man who had been sitting while the other was talking now spoke. He said, "Our homes are very far away, Majesty. This country we have come to today—we have been walking a long time, many many days." So he said, and he asked the other, "How many days has it been, my friend? How many days have we been walking?"

The other replied, "I really do not know. We spent some time at a homestead where there was a feast, and I lost count of the days. We spent a number of days there. We had hoped that we would not have to go on. But we did move on because the children there made fun of us, and they were not scolded for it. We saw that we would have to find a different homestead.

"That is what confuses me, my friend. It keeps me from remembering how many days we have been traveling. To me, it seems that we have been traveling for as long as a month. That is because we did not travel until the sun set. When we got hungry, we would stop at a homestead. If we got nothing there, we would go on until we got to another homestead. Then the sun would set. And so we come to the present—we have found a homestead now that seems to have respect for people, a homestead that loves all people. That is why we have come here."

The other old man said, "You have directed your words to the truth. You have hit it right on the mark. And you have reminded me of something I had forgotten—that we once stayed in a homestead that had a lot of beer, even a second brewing. What I mean to say to you, my lords, is that we just do not know how many days we have been traveling. For a long time, there seemed to be a new moon. But when we were talking about coming here, there was no moon like that—it was a piece of bread, the moon was altogether full. The real reason for our coming here, Nobles of our home— we have been living in great sorrow, we have had no relief, our home-steads are finished. We were abandoned in our village, we were like little owls in a deserted village, a laughing stock. That is why we are here. We have come here to place ourselves under the protection of the great per-son. We will stop our account there."

Then the king said, "Take them inside. They are all right. They will grace us because they are such fine people. And you, Councillor, you are not worthy of such a great person when he stays in your homestead."

They remained there then. The wives were told—they were also happy to see such dignified men who would stay at the royal residence for good. They prepared things for them. The men were given things to eat. So these old men ate, and when they finished eating they sat there like peo-ple of that home.

Time passed there, and all the normal things of the royal residence were done. Life went on as usual, year after year, and they became old men of that regal abode—the children and women and young girls referred to them as "grandfathers." They were distinguished from one another be-cause of their complexions—one was lighter than the other, the other was darker in color. Whenever they were referred to, it was said, "The grand-father who is light," or "The grandfather who is dark." And they were happy.

It would happen, while they were sitting there, that the king, when he had something to eat, would say, "My old men!"

They would respond, "King!"

And he would present them with whatever it was that he was giving them. They would take it in their hands—in both of their hands to show respect to the king.

So time passed, time passed, and the house of the royal residence gradually lost some of its members, one after the other dying in this royal place.

Now this king had a son of whom he was very fond. Because of his intelligence, this son was trusted by his father, and he was also relied on by those who were of this house because he did not go against his father's will.

This son profoundly loved the old men of his father. He would often talk affectionately with them, saying, "My father's old men. Oh, the old men of my father!"

These old men, too, were happy when they saw him. They would laugh delightedly because this king's son would speak with them. He too was happy. He would give the old men tobacco. They would smoke with flint—things that are struck against rocks, metal things that are struck against rocks to make fire. The combination of metal things and the rotten wood of trees would produce fire.

So it went then, and it happened that when the king died his wives were left behind. Nor did the wives go against the wishes of their husband, the king.

And others passed away, one by one.

Time passed, time passed, in a year perhaps one would die. Finally, in this great homestead everyone had died.

Only the son was left behind.

The king's son's name was Malejese.

Time passed for Malejese. He lived there with his wife and children. It seemed as if a plague had struck the royal residence. Malejese's family had been decimated. He was left behind with his wife. And after a time, his wife also died.

When she was about to die, his wife said, "Malejese."

Her husband, Malejese, responded.

She said, "I am the last one. I am the last one. Now, you are left with the cattle of my father[-in-law], you are left with the horses of my father, you are left with the goats of my father, the sheep of my father, the fowl of my father, the hogs of my father, you are left with the old men of my father, you are left with the dogs of my father. You must travel with those because now you are all alone. You alone have hands with which to work. Those things do not know how to work. I say to you then, you must go with these things to my mother's parents' place." She was referring to the mother of Malejese, saying that he should go to his own mother's parents'

Counting livestock

place. "I too am dying, and you will be left alone. Now, when you leave, you must burn these houses here. Burn the kraals, too. Then travel with all these things [meaning, the livestock]. They will go ahead; you walk behind them. And when you journey, you know that there are two ways. Do not travel by the upper road, travel by the lower one."

So said the wife of Malejese, and she died.

Malejese cried because he was the last person, the end of the people of his home.

He was sorrowful. He slept only that day there, that day alone. At dawn on the next day, he burned the other houses. He burned all the other houses, leaving one dwelling only, the one in which he was staying. He wondered what he would do first. He could begin with the burning of the kraals—he had not been told what he should begin with. He concluded that he must begin with the kraals, and he would still have a place to sleep. If he burned the house first, he would have no place to sleep. So he burned all the kraals. When he had finished burning all the kraals, he slept.

The next day, he burned that house he had slept in. It was the last thing.

He traveled then; he drove all the stock of his home. He walked behind the stock, moving in grief—walking, crying.

He walked on and became totally confused when he got to those paths: he had been instructed that he should travel on the lower road, but he forgot that. He traveled on the upper one, the one he had been told he should not walk on.

He traveled by a way that was very long; it went through open country.

He was pleased with this road because the stock that he drove were spread out, not crowded. He walked with pleasure along the open way.

It happened when the sun seemed to say, "Buy me" [meaning, at the most desirable part of the day], when it was about to set, there suddenly appeared a thing that he would never forget. No matter how he looked at it, it was a thing that he had never before seen. He shaded his eyes as this creature came toward him: it was a thing he had never heard about, even in stories.

On one side, it was fire only. On the other, it was rock. On yet another side, it was a forest. He saw no head, no feet. As the thing came toward him, he could feel its warmth. Nor was it disjointed in the middle—it was one object altogether. It was composed of various elements. When it was a short distance from him, it was hot to him; he seemed to be burning. But this thing was also cold; there seemed to be frost, and he felt as if he were freezing. On one side, it was a cliff; it tended to be continually falling, and he felt that he would be crushed.

The thing arrived, it stopped in front of him. Then it erupted, talking to him. It said,

> "Please make an offering,
> Please make an offering, Malejese,
> Please make an offering, Child of the king."

Malejese stopped. He was confused about how to answer this thing. But there was no room, he could not even move his foot; there was no way of passing this thing by.

The thing repeated,

> "Please make an offering,
> Please make an offering, Malejese,
> Please make an offering, Child of the king."

Malejese answered,

> "Please make an offering?
> Please make an offering, Malejese?
> The cattle of my father, I refuse to part with them!
> The horses of my father, I refuse to part with them!
> The sheep of my father, I refuse to part with them!
> The goats of my father, I refuse to part with them!
> The hogs of my father, I refuse to part with them!
> The fowl of my father, I refuse to part with them!
> The dogs of my father, I refuse to part with them!
> The old men of my father, I refuse to part with them!"

So he said, and he brought out the goats. He pushed them down the hill. As he pushed them down the hill, he said,

> "Goats of my father, take them:
> There they are!"

That creature went to the goats—the goats of Malejese's father were so many that they used to fill the kraal at his home. Malejese produced all of these goats now because he feared this thing. It was a marvel of a being that he had never before seen.

He walked on.

When the thing took the first goat, that entire goat disappeared! In a short time, the time it takes a person to blink an eye, it was approaching the second goat.

Malejese drove that stock that had not yet been surrendered, and he traveled on.

He traveled a long way, and he disappeared in the distance. That thing was still eating those goats back there, they were so many. Malejese journeyed a great distance, wondering whether it would take the entire day for the thing to eat those goats—because of their great number.

After a time, when the sun had set and it was dusk, he looked back and saw it: "There's that fire! Yo! It must be that thing again!" He moved on then, no longer rushing because when this thing traveled it moved quickly. When it reached him, he felt as if he would burn because of the fire. But there was also snow, and he was doubled up with cold. And the cliff was about to fall—it seemed that it would crush him!

That thing confronted Malejese.

It said to him,

> "Please make an offering,
> Please make an offering, Malejese,
> Please make an offering, Child of the king."

Malejese was silent, confused. So the thing repeated,

> "Please make an offering,
> Please make an offering, Malejese,
> Please make an offering, Child of the king."

Malejese repeated; he answered this thing:

> "Please make an offering?
> Please make an offering, Malejese?

These cattle of my father, I refuse to part with them!
The sheep of my father, I refuse to part with them!
The hogs of my father, I refuse to part with them!
The fowl of my father, I refuse to part with them!
The old men of my father, I refuse to part with them!
The dogs of my father, I refuse to part with them!"

He was quiet.
   This thing repeated,

"Please make an offering,
Please make an offering, Malejese,
Please make an offering, Child of the king."

Malejese took the sheep, he brought them out to the side. When he had done that, he said,

"Sheep of my father, take them:
There they are!"

The thing went to the sheep. Malejese watched, and when it got to the sheep, the creature took one of the animals. Instantly, that thing chewed the sheep. Malejese watched as the thing went to the second sheep.
   Malejese got up then; he drove the stock of his father.
   He traveled then, he traveled into the night. He was still a great distance from his mother's parents' place.
   He repeatedly looked back.
   After a time, when he was very far off, he looked back and saw it: there it was, a fire coming toward him! The thing arrived. It reached him and stood there. Malejese felt as if he would burn. But he also felt hoar frost. He was numb with cold. And it seemed as if that cliff would fall on him and crush him.
   Again, the thing said,

"Please make an offering,
Please make an offering, Malejese,
Please make an offering, Child of the king."

Malejese was silent. He was uncertain as to what he should produce now. The thing repeated,

"Please make an offering,
Please make an offering, Malejese,
Please make an offering, Child of the king."

Malejese stared. He took the hogs of his father. He brought them out; he placed them over there. When he had done that, he said,

> "Hogs of my father, take them:
> There they are!"

That thing went to the hogs. When it got to them, it took one of the creatures as Malejese watched—and it ate the hog without delay, in a flash. While the thing was taking the second hog, Malejese began to travel. He drove the stock of his home. He journeyed, leaving the thing behind eating those hogs.

He traveled and traveled. Night pushed on, it also traveled. Malejese journeyed a long time, and he continued to look behind because he was very anxious about this thing. Finally, when he looked back, he saw it—he saw that it was a fire coming toward him. That fire approached, and it burned him. As the thing arrived, Malejese felt that he would burn. Then the cold, the frost, emerged, and Malejese was numb. The cliff seemed about to fall. Malejese feared that he would be hurt.

That thing spoke,

> "Please make an offering,
> Please make an offering, Malejese,
> Please make an offering, Child of the king."

Malejese was silent; he did not speak.
The thing repeated; it said,

> "Please make an offering,
> Please make an offering, Malejese,
> Please make an offering, Child of the king."

Malejese wondered what he should do now because the livestock were diminishing. He took the fowl this time. He took all of these fowl, and he put them over there.
He said,

> "Fowl of my father, take them:
> There they are!"

This thing went to the fowl; it arrived and took one fowl. It ate the fowl while Malejese watched. Then, when it was taking the second one, Malejese got up and traveled. He drove the stock of his home; he drove that stock. He traveled with the stock again a long time, as before—journeying, driving this livestock. He traveled, he traveled, and after a time, when the night was separating itself from the day (because night too was pushing on), he suddenly saw it again. He again saw the flame. The creature approached; it came to him. And again it stopped in front of him.

This thing said,

> "Please make an offering,
> Please make an offering, Malejese,
> Please make an offering, Child of the king."

Malejese was silent; he did not speak at all.
Again, the thing said,

> "Please make an offering,
> Please make an offering, Malejese,
> Please make an offering, Child of the king."

Malejese took the cattle now; he brought out all of the cattle of his father, and he put them on one side.

He said,

> "Cattle of my father, take them:
> There they are!"

The thing went to the cattle. When it got to the cattle, it took one of them as Malejese watched. It was very painful for him to observe this. It was not because he liked doing this: he saw himself dying in some horrible way, and the devouring of the stock was the first step in that direction. He foresaw that this thing would finish him off too. He watched with tears in his eyes.

The thing ate this ox, and finished it—and Malejese continued to stare. Then it took the second one. Malejese got up then; he traveled with the old men of his father and with his father's dogs—the last of the stock. These were the only things left now, these and Malejese.

He traveled and traveled. The cattle were eaten by that thing back there. They were more of a mouthful than the other stock that he had left behind; the thing took a long time to eat the cattle. The amount of distance he traveled this time—the thing would already have caught up to him in the earlier confrontations.

Malejese journeyed on.

When morning was about to break, and the horns of the cattle glistened in the early light, when the cocks crowed in the land and it was dawn, that thing appeared. Malejese looked back and could see its fire. It arrived and stood in front of him.

It said,

> "Please make an offering,
> Please make an offering, Malejese,
> Please make an offering, Child of the king."

Malejese was quiet; he did not speak. The thing repeated,

> "Please make an offering,
> Please make an offering, Malejese,
> Please make an offering, Child of the king."

There were these old men then, these old men who had been cared for by his father—and Malejese was apprehensive about giving them up. He would rather surrender himself than see the old men of his father eaten by this thing. He could not bring himself to respond to the creature, until it had spoken six times.

The thing repeated,

> "Please make an offering,
> Please make an offering, Malejese,
> Please make an offering, Child of the king."

Malejese knew that this thing would eat him. This was the third time it had spoken, but he persevered. He was quiet; he could not decide what to produce.

The thing repeated,

> "Please make an offering,
> Please make an offering, Malejese,
> Please make an offering, Child of the king."

Malejese was silent; the words stuck in his throat.

The thing repeated,

> "Please make an offering,
> Please make an offering, Malejese,
> Please make an offering, Child of the king."

Malejese was quiet as he observed the old men—he saw that the old men of his father were trembling, afraid, their stomachs runny. They moved behind him, then in front of him. They grasped him, and when this thing spoke the old men again turned and went behind Malejese, their noses running because of their fear. They saw that it was their turn now because the stock was finished.

The thing repeated,

> "Please make an offering,
> Please make an offering, Malejese,
> Please make an offering, Child of the king."

Malejese said, "Rather than give the old men of my father away, I'll give up the dogs. I'll give up the old men another time."

He took the dogs of his father, and he put them over there at the side. Then he said,

> "These dogs of my father, take them:
> There they are!"

The thing went to the dogs. It was difficult for the old men. They could see that the dogs were being given over now, and they knew that they were next, that they would be surrendered when the thing returned from the dogs.

The creature went over there to the dogs. It took a dog—the thing tended to seize its prey by the head. Now, it seized a dog by its head. It seized the dog by the neck, and the dog bit into the tongue of this thing! It ate the tongue! And the thing quivered.

Then all the dogs of the royal residence came—greyhounds, pointers, mongrels, terriers, all sorts of dogs. They began to attack this thing, and it was hurt. The first dog was eating its tongue. The fire went out. The fire went out; it disappeared. But the dogs did not stop. They were all crowding around that first dog that was eating the tongue. The forest disappeared now; the trees were gone. Malejese saw that the trees were no more. Then the cliff disappeared. He saw that there was no cliff. He saw that the dogs were eating, and blood was seen coming out of that thing: blood poured out like a river, a continuous stream to the ground. The dogs ate. The thing was finished. Malejese could see that. He watched as the dogs licked the ground.

Malejese said, "Why didn't I think of the dogs of my father at the beginning? If only I had known that this thing couldn't cope with dogs! It turns out that it's the dogs that could have protected us from such a monstrous thing. But now my father's home is finished. Travel, Dogs of my father! Move on, Old men of my father! We're going to the house of my mother's parents."

The dogs returned; they came to him.

Malejese traveled then, still walking with these two old men of his father, those old men who had arrived at the royal residence impoverished. He traveled and traveled, and finally he arrived at his mother's parents' place.

That morning, when he arrived at his mother's parents' place, they were startled.

They said, "Nephew! Nephew! Where has the child of our daughter come from?"

Malejese explained, sitting outside, talking. He explained that his homestead was finished. His wife had been the last of the people of his home to go. His wife had instructed him to drive everything from his home and to come here with them. "But along the way, something happened to me. I saw a wonder that I have never before seen. There is no story like it: a thing that turned out to be a fire, a forest, a cliff, that suddenly appeared behind me. I had made a mistake. My wife had told me that I should travel by the lower road, but I forgot and traveled on the upper one. When that thing came to me, it said that I should make an offering. I who am the child of the king. I answered the thing: 'I make an offering? I make an offering? Here are the things of my father, take them!' That's what I said, and the thing made me give those things up, one by one. I would take one group, and the thing would eat all those things until they were finished."

He went on, "I was helped very much by the old men of my father. These old men had arrived at home, saying they were indigent, and they became a part of the family of my home. My father loved these old men. I was ashamed to hand them over to this thing. I had already decided that it should eat me instead of them—when the dog of my father helped me. The creature, it turned out, began with that dog. When the creature grabbed its head, the dog seized the thing's tongue. It went into its head and sat there and chewed. This thing shook, and all the other dogs then came to it. The fire was extinguished then, I could see that. I don't know where it went. I saw that the forest was finished. I don't know where it disappeared to. The cliff, I could see that it was finished too, and I don't know where that went. I saw blood on the ground, a continuous stream of blood. And the dogs were drinking this blood. That's the way we were saved. That thing was finished by sunrise. That's what I've been through. This is not just a visit. I have come to stay at my mother's parents' place because I am destitute."

When Malejese had finished speaking, his uncles began to feel bad about this. Moreover, here at the home of his mother, there was no longer any father of his mother, no longer a mother of his mother. A beast had to be slaughtered, to cleanse Malejese. A slaughtering took place there at the place of Malejese's mother's parents, and he was cleansed of the ugly thing that had befallen him.

He stayed there at the home of his mother's parents, and he was happy there. After a time, a wife was gotten for him by his uncles, as is appropriate for a person who had become accustomed to having a wife. So he lived happily.

Tale 8

THE CIRCUMCISED BABOON

Masithathu Zenani's Analysis: Like "The Pregnant Boy" (Tale 6), Mrs. Zenani observed, this tale, a sportive view of a male circumcision ceremony, with a woman masquerading as a male, has to do with the sorting out of male and female functions. It is a tale of growth, of movement to adulthood, and of a consequent acceptance of new roles. The story builds on a dualistic pattern: first, the baboon is circumcised; then, it is the man who is to be circumcised. The story, its motivation, and its effect depend on a contrast that is intensified, and the humor of the story generated, when the man's wife takes his place and the baboon, not fully comprehending the difference between men and women, assumes that she has been badly circumcised.

One insight into the theme of this tale was provided by Mrs. Zenani's contention that the male circumcision ceremony and female menstruation, the first menses signaling the commencement of a girl's puberty rite, are equated: bleeding in a genital region, the most dramatic indication of adulthood, unites the two.

During the performance of this story, it was clear that some members of the audience were shocked by what they considered impious references to the hallowed circumcision ceremony. Mrs. Zenani, however, insisted that she was doing what storytellers have always done: she used real world activities to get at a larger truth. She was not, she assured her audience, being derisive of the ceremony. Rather, she was using the baboon's circumcision to reveal two significant characteristics of the ritual: (a) the distinguishing of male and female roles in Xhosa society, and (b) the transition from childhood to adulthood, the dualism of the story emphasizing the meaning of the rite, the movement from animal to cultivated human.

Performance Note

Time: 15 September 1967, in the afternoon. *Place:* Along a path in Gatyana District, the Transkei. *Audience:* Five women, two men, and fifteen children. (Perf. 653.)

In a certain village, people cultivated fields which grew luxuriantly. But these fields were constantly being raided by some baboons that ate the corn and demolished the crops. They gathered pumpkins and stole off with them.

The people regularly watched out for the baboons. They feared the creatures and kept a wary eye out for them. They would frighten the baboons by shaking belts—it was thought that the baboons feared snakes, so the people would take belts and dangle them, snakelike, in the air. And the baboons did flee. But they were intelligent animals: they would watch the person with the belt, and, when he had disappeared, they would return to eat the corn.

But a certain man had an extraordinary plan.

He said to the baboons, "My friends, you've become a real nuisance."

The baboons merely stood there.

"Yes, please, just stand there, Fellows. I'll come to you."

The baboons stood there; the man approached them. He said, "Are all of you of the same age group? Is there one among you who is older than the rest?"

The baboons asked, "What do you mean, 'older'?"

This fellow said, "Isn't there a *man* among you? Because really, a man would empathize with another man. He wouldn't be such a nuisance; he would be responsible."

A baboon said, "A man? What is a *man?*"

That man said, "A man is a person who has been circumcised, who has left the things of boyhood behind—who has become, in a word, a *man.*"

The baboon asked, "And what is this 'circumcised'?"

"Well, as for this matter of circumcision, come," said the man, "and I'll show you."

So the baboon came along, and the man explained, "Now I don't want to expose my body to you. I just want to tell you about it. To become a man, one must be circumcised—with a knife. When you have been circumcised with a knife, you become an initiate, a circumcised youth. When you are an initiate, that means that you've graduated. And when you have graduated, it is said of you, 'You are a man!' You are separated from the boys then; you remain with the men. Then you get married."

The baboon said, "What good is all that?"

This fellow said, "It gives you dignity; it gives you a certain distinction. You become a person of excellence, and when people speak to you, they speak with respect to a responsible person. When you have become a man, I won't shoot at you anymore when I see you. I won't even set the dogs on you. I'll simply ask you, politely, what you're doing in my fields, Sir, and you also, you will respond politely, and I'll pick some of my corn for you, and you'll go on your way—when, that is, you are a *man.* All of this depends on your becoming a man."

"Oh," said the baboon. "Well, all right then, I think that I should be circumcised!"

Then that man said, "Yes, and even though I've said all this, I have to tell you that I have not been circumcised either. I too want to be circumcised. But I think that we should begin with you, so that you can see how it's done. I'll do it to you, then you can do it to me."

"Oh." The baboon agreed. It said, "Let's meet over there, at the place where I live." The baboon was referring to a cliff. Baboons live in cliffs, in caves.

The man said, "When should I come to you, so that we can get on with this business of ours?"

The baboon said, "Well, tomorrow is a good time. You come over there, and we'll get on with it."

The man got up the next day and went off to the cliffs. He was carrying a knife. He had sharpened it—it was really sharp! He arrived at the cliffs. He went up to the baboon and said, "Come on out, come out of the cave."

The baboon came outside.

The man said, "You must go and wash. You must wash your body first."

The baboon went; it went to wash its body. When it returned, the man said, "The other baboons, they must stand back. Over there."

They stood back, over there.

He said to the baboon, "Spread your legs. Spread your legs, don't bring them together!"

The baboon sat; it spread its legs. The man seized it then. He seized it here in front, and he cut it. He cut it and put the foreskin down.

He said, "Now, you must say, 'I am a *man!*'"

The baboon said, "I am a *man*. Yo! I didn't know this would be such a painful thing!"

The man said, "Yes, that's why we're called men. That's the way we become men in this world. Today, you've graduated from boyhood. Now you must remain here for two months. Then I'll return, and we'll have the 'coming out' ceremony. The other baboons must bring your food here. You must not go to them."

The baboon remained there. It stayed there by itself; it did not join the others. They brought it food every day. It stayed there all that time. It was an initiate—that is the name of such a person. It was said, "Food must be brought to the initiate."

After those two months had passed, the man remembered that he had to go over there to the baboons. He went there one day for the "coming out" ceremony, so that the circumcised baboon could go and join the other baboons.

The man went there.

"Oh, hello, Sir."

"Yes, Stranger!"

"Where have you come from?"

"Well, I've come from home."

"Yes."

"I've come for the purpose of taking you out. It's time now for you to go and live with the others. You're finished being an initiate."

"Oh, what am I to be now?"

"Well, for this month alone, you'll be a 'recent graduate.'"

"Oh, I'm to be a 'recent graduate' for a month?"

"Yes, then you'll be a man. After that month is over, it'll be said of you, 'Now you're a *man!* Your youth is at an end.'"

Time passed for the baboon. It was a happy creature.

That month ended, and the man returned.

He said, "Well, today you're a man! Now a date must be set for my own circumcision."

The baboon said, "Yes, that's right. That means that you'll come to me with that knife. Sharpened!"

The man said, "I'll sharpen the knife."

The man went home. When he got home, he spoke to his wife.

"Wife."

"Mm? Well?"

"Over there—I'm to be circumcised. I'll be circumcised tomorrow. A baboon will circumcise me."

His wife said, "What? What? Go on! Why are you going to be circumcised? You were circumcised long ago! Why will you be circumcised now?"

"My fields were in danger. Really! And that baboon over there—well, I deceived the creature. The reason my field is no longer being raided is because I deceived those baboons. I said that they must be circumcised. But to make my ruse work, I had to say that I too was not circumcised. I said that they must go through the ritual first, and I would be the last. This is a delicate situation. I might be hurt!"

He paused.

"Now here's my plan. You must put my trousers on. And put my coat on, too. Then go over there to the baboons. When you get there, say that you've come to be circumcised. Carry this bag of mine and my pipe. Smoke as you go. Say that you've come to be circumcised. When you've washed yourself, you must sit naked. But don't take off the shirt, or the baboon will see your breasts. Don't take off the top, just take off the trousers. Then you must spread your legs, spread your legs for him, and say that he should circumcise you."

His wife said, "Is this a good idea?" She said, "Won't the baboon see through this? After all, he has known you for a long time now, you've been seeing him so often!"

"No, he doesn't know me! I didn't take my clothes off in front of him. He won't know the difference between us. Just smear your face with mud, and he won't know you."

Well, the woman dressed then, she smeared her face. She went to the baboons.

When she came to the baboons: "Hello! Hello, all of you! Friends!"

"Yes."

"Yes, goodness!"

"Where have you come from?"

"Well, really, I've come so that we can do that . . . thing . . . now."

"Oh, it's today! Did you bring the knife?"

"Yes, I brought it."

"Did you sharpen it?"

"Yes, I sharpened it. I sharpened it yesterday."

"All right, then, go and wash."

The woman went then; she went to wash. The baboon followed. Then the baboon said, "Take off your clothes now."

The woman took off her trousers. She did not remove the top, the shirt. She took the knife and gave it to the baboon—sharpened.

The baboon approached, the woman spread her legs.

The baboon said, "Yo! Yo yo yo yo yo! Who circumcised you so badly? Who harmed you so? Who hacked you so terribly? Oh oh oh oh oh! I cannot bring myself to circumcise you! You're horribly mutilated! Go! Go! It doesn't matter, it doesn't matter, Friend, you've been done already! You've been done already!"

The woman put on her trousers, and went home. She arrived at home, and said to her husband, "Well then, Sobani, I'm circumcised."

He said, "What happened?"

"The baboon said that I've been done already. Then it ran off. It asked who had circumcised me so badly, who had hacked me. Well then, I've been done, I'm safe."

"Yo! You helped me, my wife! You saved me! I would have been murdered by those baboons—because baboons don't know how to circumcise! It would have cut me; it would have killed me! It's splendid to have a wife who's clever. I've been saved!"

Tale 9

A GIRL IS KIDNAPPED

Masithathu Zenani's Analysis: After this performance, Mrs. Zenani reflected on some of the important repeated images in her story. The opening pattern, she suggested, establishes an ominous linkage between the twelve girls and the splendid gardens. The girls find these gardens, not coincidentally twelve of them, in a forbidden forest. They are led there by a princess from the royal residence. In this initial pattern, the girls regularly and secretly visit their gardens, cultivating and harvesting them. It turns out that these gardens are a deception devised by fantastic creatures, cannibals, intent on kidnapping the king's daughter. An unknown dog goes to the princess, presumably identifying her, and a chase commences. The leader of the cannibals makes plain that he is interested only in the princess. She is abducted and is to become the leader's wife: ". . . she's going to make a fine breed of children for me." A subhuman creature is attempting to becoming fully human by aligning himself with a human being. The princess is given a new name, Nojikolo, and the chief keeps his cannibalistic subjects from devouring her. She bears two children, one who is similar to the cannibals, the other a human. The effect of this pattern is to move the princess from her home and to link her to the fantasy world of the cannibals. She has, in effect, been swallowed by these creatures—figuratively if not literally—because she cannot escape from their land. The pattern is deepened as the cannibals show a characteristic interest in devouring her: this is her ordeal.

The story's second major pattern occurs during the escape, with an old woman warning the cannibals of the flight of Nojikolo and her brother, Mbengu-Sonyangaza, who has become the means for her liberation. As they flee the cannibals' world, they take with them all of the cannibals' livestock, all of their property, and, when the cannibals attack, Mbengu-Sonyangaza destroys them in a typical fantasy image: he kills one, and they all die.

The significant aspects of this first part of the story are revealed in the patterns. It is a fantastic rendering of the puberty ritual of Nojikolo. She is spirited from her home, which is the separation phase of her rite. Her ordeal takes place at the village of the cannibals, where she must endure life with subhuman creatures. And her reincorporation into human society as a woman occurs when she escapes with her brother.

The second part of the story is a more realistic description of the girl's ritual progress toward womanhood. As a part of that process, she is ritually cleansed, the storyteller making it plain that she is to "be initiated into womanhood." With her attendants, she goes to a clay pit to dig for ochre. The ochre will be used in the rite. She leaves a garment behind, goes back to the pit alone to retrieve it, and is kidnapped and put into the villain's bag. In a typical puberty ritual tale, the initiate undergoes a change of some kind. Often, this change is suggested by a transformation from an animal to a human. Mrs. Zenani here echoes that tradition by having the girls put a raven into initiation seclusion in place of Nojikolo. The remainder of the story is composed of a single dominant pattern—the kidnapper's singing bag. The people are celebrating the approaching emergence of the girl into womanhood, not realizing that a raven has taken her place, and initially ignorant of who is in the bag of the villain. That kidnapper goes to the boys with his singing "Bird of a Great One," then to the young men, then to the men, and finally to the women. But the familiar sound of her voice, emphasizing the identity theme of this ritual, alerts her relatives to her presence, and her song alarms them as well. They send the kidnapper on a fool's errand, then remove Nojikolo from the bag. It is her emergence from the belly of a swallowing monster: she has been reborn, a woman. Her ritual is complete, and all that remains is to get rid of the several villains.

A series of minor patterns concludes the tale: in the first, the people determine what stinging, biting, poisonous creatures to substitute in the kidnapper's bag. The second minor pattern takes place as the king demands that the parents of the errant girls destroy them. And in the final pattern of the story, each of the wives of the kidnapper incurs his anger when she is stung by his bag. In a lengthy and humorous coda, he too is destroyed.

Part two of the story is a reflection of the more fantastic part one, the second part explaining and reflecting upon the significance of the first, as the girl gets rid of the ugliness within her (in part one, the cannibals; in part two, the childish girls and the kidnapper) and moves into full womanhood, with the active assistance of the members of her community, whether it be her brother, her father, or other members of her family and village.

Performance Note

Time: 13 September 1967, in the evening. *Place:* Outside, in a kraal in Nkanga, Gatyana District, the Transkei. *Audience:* About fifty men, women, and children. (Perf. 625.)

At a royal residence were two girls. They had a brother, a little boy who was the last born. The girls had chaperones—one of the sisters was chaperoned among the young men, the other among the boys.

Then it was announced, "The elder sister must be initiated into womanhood."

She hesitated for a time, then decided that she would go through the purification and initiation ceremonies during the following year. "I don't want to be initiated this year." Things were left at that.

One day, she said to the other girls, "Let's go and gather wood in that distant forest, the one that people don't usually enter. Let's go there and see this thing that is so feared in that forest. There is a lot of firewood there. I tell you, wood is really plentiful in that forest!"

Twelve girls went, two of them from the royal residence, the other ten from the village. They traveled; they went to gather firewood. They carried provisions with them—cooked maize. (Those were the days when people cultivated with digging sticks; they cultivated with their hands. There were no ploughs then; no oxen were yoked. People cultivated with their hands in those days.) Maize and millet—the girls made some loaves of millet and some of maize. They carried these with them, and they journeyed. The forest was a long way off.

They walked, they walked and walked, and finally came to the forest. When they got there, they took the provisions down from their heads and put their equipment down at the edge of the forest. Then they went into the forest and gathered firewood. When they had penetrated that woodland, they found great amounts of firewood. They gathered it up, they gathered it, then put it outside, on the rim of the forest. They stacked it there.

As they finished doing this, they saw some beautiful gardens: the gardens were twelve in number, the same number as the girls. They were elegant.

The king's daughter said, "Look at this!"

The others said, "What is it?"

"Do you see this? Such beautiful gardens! All arranged in order. Count them!"

They counted the gardens: they were twelve.

Someone said, "How did they come to be equal in number to us?"

"I don't know. My guess is that they are a gift to us, a boon from the ancestors."

One of the girls agreed: "These gardens are a gift to us from the ancestors."

"Well, let's go home now."

The girls carried the firewood and went home. On the way home, the king's daughter said, "We must steal some seeds from home. Each one of us must steal some corn seeds, some pumpkin seeds, and sugarcane seeds. Then we'll wait for the rains to come. We'll also have to hide some hoes, some digging sticks." (That is not a hoe with a metal head, the kind we have today. In those days, the hoes were made of wood. They were like wedges, and ploughing was done by putting these wedges into the ground.)

They agreed to this plan and moved on. When they got home, each girl went in the direction of her own home—one went that way, one went this way, another went that way. When they got home, they all stole seeds and hid them.

Time passed.

Time passed; then the rain fell. It rained heavily; the rain dropped like teeth. The girls came together after the rain began to fall.

"Hasn't the princess noticed that the rain has begun to fall?"

Another said, "Surely she's seen it."

They came together again, and when they had done so the king's daughter said, "It has rained. We must go and cultivate those gardens. Do you have the seeds?"

One girl said, "We hid the seeds as soon as we got home."

She said, "Now don't tell anybody about this at home. I too, I have not mentioned the subject at my home."

"We haven't talked about it."

"We haven't talked about it either."

They departed one day. They again made their provisions and went over there to the gardens, carrying the things that they would use to cultivate. They arrived at the forest. When they got there, they gathered firewood. They came out of the forest and stacked the wood; they put the firewood on the edge of the forest. They turned from where they had stacked the wood and began to cultivate. Each ploughed her own garden; each ploughed her own. They ploughed; they ploughed industriously so that they could finish quickly. They ploughed, then finished. When they had finished ploughing: "All right, let's go home!"

They went home; they walked and finally arrived at their homes.

Time passed.

Time passed at their homes. After a month had gone by, during the second month after they had returned, the king's daughter again brought the girls together. "Let's just go out there and inspect those gardens. Let's go and see if those plots of ours are in need of weeding."

"All right."

"Be sure, now, not to talk about this!"

"No, we won't mention it."

"I too, I don't talk about this matter at my home."

Well then, time passed, and again they traveled. They arrived over there; they arrived and found their corn thriving. They hoed, they hoed and hoed. When they finished hoeing, they went into the forest. They gathered firewood there, and piled it up, and they ate their provisions. Then they carried the firewood and departed.

When they got home, they stayed as before at their homes. And time passed.

Time passed; they remained at home, and it happened just as before: after a time, the girl said again, "Let's just go and inspect those gardens. Let's see what is happening over there."

They again made their provisions, and they journeyed; they went to inspect their gardens. They arrived there. The corn was now forming little ears, and the cane was in the blossoming stage. They looked around as they had before. They gathered firewood in the forest as they had before. They carried the firewood again and went home.

Time passed, they remained at home for a long time. Finally, they estimated that the gardens must be at a more advanced stage now.

Time passed.

Time passed, and the king's daughter said, "Let's go again." Provisions were prepared, and they departed.

When they got there, they found that the corn was thoroughly ripe. They arrived; the cane was also perfectly ripe. They gathered firewood for a short time, then they kindled a fire. Each one plucked an ear of corn from her own plot; each of the girls plucked an ear of corn from her plot, and the corn was roasted. When the corn had been roasted, it was eaten. When they had finished eating the corn, some of the sugarcane was picked. Each one picked cane from her own garden; each one picked cane from her garden. Then they gathered together in one place and ate the cane.

While they were eating the sugarcane, a huge yellow dog suddenly appeared. They said, "Where did this dog come from?" The dog approached. On and on and on it came. It went right up to this king's daughter; it went to her and was affectionate, wagging its tail, beating its tail, cuffing its tail against her, climbing up on her again and again, paddling its tail, waving its tail, wagging its tail against her.

Someone said, "Ee, this dog! It must be the dog of a friend of yours because it certainly seems to know you."

"And your friend's dog is just this size."

The girl said, "No, this is not my friend's dog. I don't know this dog."

"Then why?" said the other girls. "How is it that this dog is so friendly to you?"

"How can you say you don't know it?"

"Well, my friend, I don't know this dog. I don't know this dog at all, no! Besides that, I'm afraid of it!"

They hurried away. The girls got ready; they fastened their skirts. They were still fastening their skirts when they heard stalks breaking, stalks breaking there in the garden. When the girls went to look—there were people there! People they did not know! And these people had very long ears! These people—"Oh! They're cannibalistic monsters!"

The girls ran. They ran very fast; and while they were running, they were being pursued.

Among these cannibalistic monsters was a leader. He said, "Leave them alone! Leave all of those girls alone! Just grab thaaaaaat one who's in front!" referring to that girl over there, the one for whom the dog had wagged its tail—that girl over there, the one who had urged the others on. It was because of her that they had all come over here.

The monsters passed the other girls by, all all all all the other girls; they passed them by, and finally caught up with this other girl. They seized her. The girl cried out, but by that time she had been taken. The other girls were left alone; they ran on and finally got to their homes.

They arrived and said, "So-and-so has been taken off by monsters!

They attacked us while we were roasting meat! We had planted some gardens out there."

Someone said, "Oh! No one would even dare go there!"

"We must just accept the fact that she is gone, Friends!"

"Our child is gone!"

Time passed; time passed then.

The girl cried as the cannibals took her home to their kraal. As they returned, all of the monsters were staking claims to this girl, thinking that she would be slaughtered.

One of them said, "I get a foreleg, Chief!"

Another said, "Me too! I get the other foreleg!"

"Well, I have a breast!"

Another said, "I'll have a leg!"

"Chief, I'll take the other breast!"

"I claim the head!"

"I want the viscera!"

. . . until the end.

The chief said, "No! She is not to be touched! This girl will be my wife. She will be Nojikolo, She-of-the-waist-band. She will be the wife of the great house. She's going to make a fine breed of children for me. If any one of my offspring is not a thoroughbred, he'll be eaten!"

The monsters were disappointed. They had been anticipating devouring the meat that they had found that day.

A house was built for the girl. She lived in it together with that monster who was now her husband. In time she became pregnant and gave birth. She bore a beautiful child, a child who resembled her mother.

When Nojikolo had given birth to that child, the monsters said, "Chief, give us the child! We want to eat her!"

He said, "No, I cannot eat her! This child is loved by Nojikolo. My wife would feel terrible."

They left the child alone, even though they were ravenous for her flesh. Whenever the child cried, they would leap at her; they would lick her tears, they would swallow her tears. But the chief would scold them: "No! No! Don't do that to Nojikolo's child!" They would leave the child alone then and run off. But when the child was in the company of others, when she cried, the monsters would leap on her and lick her tears from her face.

"Ffffff! Mnca! Kwo! If only we could taste the girl herself! Ffffff! Mnca! Kwo!"

Time passed. Time passed, and Nojikolo again gave birth. This time she bore a child who was a boy, who resembled his father, whose ears reached to his shoulders.

And time passed.

This girl grew up; she developed breasts. She would sometimes go to

the river with the other girls to dip water, but she was so loved by her
father that she did not work at all. One day, she wanted very much to go to
the river, so she took a tin and went to the water. When she got to the river,
the others were dipping water and hoisting it to their heads.

As for her: "This tin is weighing me down! What is the matter?" Her tin
pail would not leave the ground. "Help me, someone! Help me to lift it!"

Someone said, "Yo! You're too soft!"

"You're spoiled! We all know that you never do any work because you're
so spoiled."

"You're so loved!"

"How could that thing weigh you down?"

"Too soft!"

"Spoiled!"

They left her there. The child sat down. While she was sitting there,
struggling with the tin, something in the water bubbled to the surface. A
beautiful person rose to the surface.

When this person came out of the water, the child ran.

But the person said, "Don't run! I won't do anything to you! Come
here, I have some questions to ask you."

The child returned.

This person said, "Whose child are you?"

She said, "I am Nojikolo's child."

He said, "Now, what does Nojikolo say when she swears an oath?"

The child said, "She says, 'I swear by Mbengu-Sonyangaza that I will
punish you!'"

This person said, "Do you see me?"

The child said, "Yes."

He said, "Do you know me?"

The child said, "I don't know you. But I can see that you resemble my
mother."

This person said, "How do I resemble your mother?"

She said, "You resemble her because of your gap teeth. And the point of
hair on your forehead. You also have the same color that she has."

This person said, "I am her brother. I am the very one she swears by. I
am this Mbengu-Sonyangaza about whom she always speaks. Now then,
this is what you must do, my child. Go home, carry these reeds along
with you. Put them down in the doorway of your home. Your mother will
come to help you take the tin of water down from your head. Don't let
anyone else do that. You must throw the reeds into disorder, so that your
mother steps on them. When she has stepped on the reeds, you must cry,
saying that you want the reeds replaced with fresh unbroken ones. But
again, don't agree that the reeds be picked by anyone else. Demand that
they be picked only by your mother."

Brother and sister

Well, the child did that. She took the reeds and departed with them. She got home; she arrived and put the reeds in the doorway. She crossed the reeds, one over the other, in that doorway.

She said, "Mother! Come and take the pail of water down from my head! Mother, come and take it down!"

"No! Take it down yourself! Don't be so silly!"

"Mother! Come and take it down!"

"Take it down yourself! What is this, that your things have to be taken down by me? What are you carrying?"

"I said, 'Mother, come and take it down!' "

"Oh, this child is really naughty! I'm going to have to give you a beating!"

The girl's father spoke: "No, Nojikolo! Please take the water down for the child. She's been standing there in the doorway for a long time."

Nojikolo got up then; she went to the child, scolding her. "This child is silly." She went to her angrily, and in her anger she crushed some of the reeds. Then she helped the child take the water from her head.

The child cried, "Yoooooooo! How could you break my reeds? I want my reeds! I want them! How could you crush my reeds? Go, get some more for me!"

"No, stop it, my child!"

Her father said, "Stop, my child. I'll pick some more reeds for you. I'll pick them myself."

"No! I don't want them to be picked by you, Father! They must be picked by Mother! I don't want them to be picked by anyone else. She must go and pick them! She broke my reeds on purpose!"

This happened: the child cried; the child went to bed still crying because her mother had not gone to get more reeds. Her mother angrily scolded the child for her antics. "She's mischievous!"

In the morning, the child woke up and continued to insist that her mother get the reeds. She cried and said that she wanted the reeds, that they should be picked by her mother.

"Nojikolo! Go, finally!" so said the husband. "This child will get thin if you don't go and pick the reeds for her. Go and pick them, satisfy my child."

The mother got up and went, and the child followed. When they were close to the river, the child said, "Mother, you who did not agree to pick reeds for me: do you think that I'm pushing you to this river just to get some reeds? I'm not insisting upon reeds at all. I saw something at the river!"

"What did you see?"

"You'll see it, Mother! Please go on. I saw a handsome person, handsome! handsome! handsome! He resembles you, this man. This person has gap teeth, he has a hair point, and he says that he is your brother, the one by whom you swear! He says that he is Mbengu-Sonyangaza!"

Yo! Her mother hit her. She slapped her with her open hand. "You're being ridiculous! You're naughty! What Mbengu-Sonyangaza? I'll beat you!"

"Please go on, Mother!"

She went on. When she got to the river, he appeared. She saw her brother! Yo! She cried; her brother cried. His sister cried, and the child cried too. They all wept a little over each other. Then they went up the river, moving away from the usual dipping area. They went to sit in another spot.

Her brother asked, "What happened to you, Sister?"

"I was kidnapped by those monsters. But I wasn't eaten. It was declared that I should produce highbred children, so I became the chief's wife."

"How can I help you escape?"

She said, "I'll work out a plan; I'll work out a plan."

"Do you want to come home, to come home with me now?" he asked.

"Yes, I want to come home."

"All right then, please think of a plan."

She took his garment and trampled it with mud. She dirtied it; it became muddy. She tramped on it; she trampled it. She took some mud and smeared his entire body with it, from his head to his feet. His clothes oozed with mud, and she put them on him; they were dripping wet.

Then she said, "You must crawl. Walk on your knees. And you must walk ahead of me; I'll walk behind you. I'll say that I have made you my servant. No one will do anything to you."

He went then, he went with her, Mbengu-Sonyangaza crawling ahead of his sister, creeping along, dirty. He was oozing with mud and water. His sister walked behind him.

They suddenly appeared at the monsters' place.

"Halaaaaaaaala halala! It has appeeeeeeared! My servant is here with me! Halaaaaaaaala! See! See!"

The chief came out of his house, and said, "Oh! Nojikolo has a servant! Well, what shall we do about this? Get the bad things off the path so he won't be hurt. Clear the way! Everything must be clean. Remove the doctored herbs. The little beast of the chief's wife is here! Remove the doctored herbs from the path! Clear the way for them! Bring a mat!"

A mat was put down, a new mat.

The chief's wife was pleased because of her little beast. She went around, saying, "Little beast of miiiiiine! Little beast of mine! Little beast of miiine! Little beast of the chief's wife Nojikolo!"

Mbengu-Sonyangaza went into the house. When he had entered, she made a bed for him, a bed fashioned from the mat. She made a bed for him behind the door. He remained there, his garment still dripping because it was so wet.

They slaughtered for "the little beast" then. A beast was butchered for Nojikolo's servant.

Time passed, and they were happy.

At dawn, the monsters went out to hunt people. They would return later with a dead person who would be cooked here at home. But an animal would be brought for Nojikolo, the woman, because she did not eat human flesh. They departed, they hunted, then they returned. They brought an animal along for Nojikolo, saying, "Here it is! Here's your animal, Nojikolo!"

She said, "Thank you! This little beast of mine doesn't eat human flesh either, so don't come in here with human flesh."

The "little beast" was cooked for then, and he ate with his sister. Again, they went off to hunt; the monsters went away to hunt.

The "little beast" asked, "Well, Sister, do you have a plan for our escape? How shall we do it?"

"We're going to escape today. I want us to leave this place today!"

There was a little old woman there who did not know how to walk. She had been left behind at home, this little woman who was now old; she was left alone in this homestead.

Everyone else departed—even the child of the chief's wife went on the hunt. That child, the son, went along with the hunters. The one who remained behind was the girl, Nojikolo's daughter.

Time passed, and when time had passed, Nojikolo gathered all the livestock together; she brought the livestock together, and all the goods and property were tied on a wagon. All valuable property was brought together, everything that was pleasing, everything that was beautiful—all of it. Everything was gathered together—sheep and that sort of thing, goats, cattle, horses and that sort of thing—they were gathered in large numbers behind the wagon. The wagon was inspanned; things were tied on. Then they climbed on. Mbengu-Sonyangaza was carrying a spear. They climbed up, and they journeyed.

When they had departed and were moving in the distance, the old woman of the house heard the wagon rattling far off. She slid along the ground, she slid along the ground, then appeared at the door.

"Oh!" She got to the door just as the others had reached the other side of the village.

She said, "Ee! All the property of this home! There are no people here, so who could be taking it all away? Everything's gone! Why have the goats, the sheep, the cattle, the horses all been brought together into a single group? Who's driving the livestock? And who inspanned the wagon?" She shouted, "Nojikolo! Nojikolo! Where are you? Where are you, my friend? Nojikolo! Who'll do something about this theft?"

No sound from Nojikolo.

The old woman slid along the ground, she slid along the ground, and finally she got to Nojikolo's house. Oh! even the door of Nojikolo's house had been taken!

The old woman called out, "The homestead has been rooooooooobbed by the beast of Nojikolo!"

That occurred at about the time the monsters were turning back.

"Ee! What's being said over there? It sounds like Grandmother! She seems to be shouting to us. Just wait a minute."

"The homestead has been rooooooooobbed by the beast of Nojikolo!"

"Eee! She says that the homestead has been robbed by the beast of Nojikolo!"

Yo! They hurried then, climbing up the hill to the homestead. When they got there, Mbengu-Sonyangaza and his sister had already moved out of sight. They had disappeared; they were no longer visible. They could not be seen.

The little old woman pointed: "Over that hill! Over therrrrrrrrre!"

The monsters, as numerous as an army, pursued them; they went after them.

When she saw the monsters in the distance, Nojikolo said, "Oh, Mbengu-Sonyangaza, Child of my father, what will happen to us now? Look! Over there are the monsters! Even I won't be safe today!"

He said, "Don't worry. It'll be all right!"

He had been driving the oxen, but now he said, "You drive them, Sister!" He stopped and his sister continued to drive the livestock. Mbengu-Sonyangaza stopped, and he hurled his spear at the first monster who appeared. The spear hit the monster; down it went. When it fell down, all of the monsters fell. They died as one! All of them died, even those who had not been stabbed by the spear. They all died.

Then Mbengu-Sonyangaza climbed up on the wagon, and he drove on. They went on their way and finally arrived at home.

When they got home, he said, "There she is, Father!" He was speaking outside: "I've come with her; I've brought the child and her spoils. I have returned today."

They all came outside and thanked him. The people gave thanks for the safe return of Mbengu-Sonyangaza and his sister. An ox was slaughtered, as a ritual washing of the girl's stigma of being married to a monster.

The people also knew that this was the girl who, for a long time it had been said, should be initiated into womanhood. She had responded for a long time, "I don't want to be initiated into womanhood yet!" Now it was said, "Well, she must be initiated."

She said, "I want to go to the clay pit first. I want these attendants of mine to go with me"—she was referring to those who had been girls at the time of the first adventure. They had been ten, and now they were married and living in their husbands' homesteads. It was arranged that these women should return. They should return because their leader was now here. When they were asked to do so, they returned from their homesteads.

They journeyed then; they went to the clay pit to dig clay. When they got to the pit—this daughter of the king was carrying a spear—when they got to the pit, they began to dig clay. They dug. She took off her apron and put it down on the ground. They dug, they dug for the clay. They dug, then they departed. They carried the clay and went home. They crossed a river.

When they had crossed the river, the king's daughter said, "Yo! I left my apron over there at the pit!" What should she do about that? They were far from the pit, and the sun was already setting. "No, I can't leave my apron behind. Other people might go over there and take it. I must go back, even if the sun is setting! Nomavo, please come with me!" Nomavo was her sister.

"No, Friend, I won't go. I can't go over there now. It's too far!"

"What's the matter, Child of my mother? Why won't you come with me? Can it be that even you won't come with me?"

"No, I won't go back there with anyone! At this time of night, I'm afraid!"

"Well then, if you won't come with me, I'll just go by myself. But all of you must sit down here and wait for me. I'll plant my spear here in the ground. Keep your eyes on this spear. If I should happen to stumble, it will fall, then rise again. If I die, the spear will fall and not get up. In that case, you should go home."

"We understand," and the women sat down.

She went back, having planted her spear in the ground. They watched the spear. After a time, as she neared the pit, she stumbled and fell. And the spear fell, too.

They said, "She's dead. Let's go."

They got up; the women traveled. After they had gone, the spear rose because the girl got up.

She went into the pit. When she had entered, she found that it was bright inside. It was all lit up.

She said, "Why is the pit all lit up?"

What made her think that the pit was illuminated was actually a pair of glowing eyes. She saw the eyes of some thing here in the pit. She took the apron. It was lying in the front of the thing with the eyes. But when she took the apron, this thing seized her and put her into a bag. It went away with her; it took her to its home. It arrived at its home and hung her on the upper side of the house, away from the door.

Those other women had gone home, but this girl they had left behind was to be initiated into womanhood that very day![7] What should they do?

7. The *intonjane*, or female initiation, ceremony is the subject of this story. The rite has to do with the tradition observed when a girl reaches the age of puberty, occurring at the time of her

What should they say? When they had crossed a stream, the women discussed this problem.

"We should appear at home singing an initiation song."

"We'll help to initiate the ceremonies over there at home."

"But what should we do about *her*? She's not here!"

"Well, let's just take this crab," the others said. "We'll initiate this crab in her stead."

"Crab, come here!"

"We're going to initiate you into womanhood."

The crab: "No, I have my children to think of. I don't participate in such things."

They traveled on.

"What shall we do?"

"Let's get a raven!"

"A raven likes meat."

"A raven just can't refuse."

"How shall we deceive it?"

First, a frog was caught. When it had been caught, it was held in the air as someone said, "Come, Raven! Here's some meat!"

The raven came to get the frog, and it too was seized.

One of the women said, "We're taking you to a place where meat is being eaten. You're to be initiated into womanhood! You'll get to eat meat—the small intestines. You'll eat the liver, everything, even the duodenum. You'll remain in seclusion, behind a screen."

"Don't make a sound! Just stay there."

The raven agreed, and the women went and wove a screen of reeds; this would become the initiation screen.

When they got home, the women went around to the rear of the homestead, singing a song of initiation into womanhood. The song went like this:

"You, Nongabe-ungezanga-ngena!
O yhooooo wewowe!
Yhee-e yhee-e yhee-e yhee-e!

---

first menstruation. She goes into seclusion for approximately one month in a house especially built for the purpose. No one, except a sister or a paternal aunt or paternal grandmother, is allowed to see her during the period of seclusion. Her brother will be allowed to enter the house, but her father, mother, and women on the mother's and grandmother's side of the family are forbidden from doing so. She remains behind a screen in the house, and bathes in water doctored with special herbs. Ashes in the hearth of the house of seclusion are not taken out until the end of the period. The *intonjane* custom is usually observed just before the marriage of the young woman.

This is not initiation,
It's just a little wound!"[8]

The mothers of the women also sang this song when they heard that the girl was beginning her initiation. "She" was made to enter one of the houses; they put up the screen that they had woven, and the raven remained behind the screen. The bird was hidden from those who were not involved in this conspiracy. The women who were involved would not allow others to go behind that screen and see the raven; only the ones who knew about it were allowed to go there.

Time passed, and that initiate was cared for; that initiate was cared for. At dawn, a beast was slaughtered for the initiate. The beast of the ritual-entry-into-the-initiation-house was slaughtered; then the beast of the second stage of the ceremony, the wormwood stage, was killed. The mothers of the women were also slaughtered for.

Time passed, the time of the initiate, and beer was brewed. Now the initiate would have a coming-out ceremony, an emergence-at-marriageable-age ceremony. As the beer was about to be strained on the day of that ceremony, an ox was slaughtered for the boys, an ox was slaughtered for the young men, an ox was slaughtered for the place of the initiate, an ox was slaughtered for the men, an ox was slaughtered for the women. The boys ate below the kraal, the young men ate in the courtyard, the men ate inside the kraal, the women ate in the sheep kraal, and inside the place of the initiation meat was also eaten. A great amount of smoke was caused by all this roasting of meat, and there was joy throughout the homestead because the king's daughter was being initiated into womanhood.

On the day that this feast was taking place, that noxious creature who had seized the girl over there in the clay pit took the bag in which he had placed her and carried it on his shoulders. He went off with the bag. As he traveled, he happened to see the homestead where all the smoke was, and, because the wind was coming from that direction, he smelled the meat. He sought the place from whence the smoke and the smell of the meat were coming, then he headed in that direction. When he got there, he first went over to the boys below the kraal.

He said, "Boys! Yo! You take on the whole cow! Please throw me some of the fat! And some of the lean meat too! If you do, I'll make the Bird of a Great One sing for you!"

The boys threw some meat—lean meat, fat meat. He ate it; he ate the meat. Then he picked his teeth; he picked meat from his teeth and threw the tooth-pickings over there into the bag, so that the girl inside the bag

8. "This is not initiation [lit., *intonjane*],/It's just a little wound!" The comment about *intonjane*, the female puberty purification ritual, may be a reference to the menses.

might eat. The girl had not eaten since the last time she had been home. But she refused to eat the meat that had been picked from that creature's teeth.

When he finished eating, he took a big stick and hit the girl. "Please sing, Bird of a Great One!"

The girl sang:

> "What should I say? What should I say?
> I traveled and got hurt!
> You, Bentsel'-esangweni!
> Noluhlu, won't you help me?
> Tshiiiiiii! Ngantshoooooooooo-ooo!
> Nomavo, won't you help me?
> Tshiiiiiii! Ngantshoooooooooo-ooo!"[9]

When this girl sang like that, she was heard by a little child, the child who was the last born of this home. He was here with the other boys. He recognized the voice of his sister, and he called one of his brothers. He ran. The child over there ran to Bentsel'-esangweni, a young man in the courtyard.

He arrived and said, "Brother! Brother, please come! Here's the voice of the initiate! I heard it in that bag over there! It was the initiate. She was calling out to you. And that initiate was calling for Sister, too. Yes, she's over there! She was calling for this one, the one following her in age. She was calling her by name."

The young man said, "No, don't shout like that. Please stop. Be quiet, I hear you."

The young man stayed where he was, as this other man, carrying his bag, came closer. He approached the young men in the courtyard. This boy was sitting at his older brother's side.

The man with the bag said, "Young men! You take on the whole beast! Please give me some of the fat! And some lean meat! I'll make the Bird of a Great One sing for you."

The young men cut off some of the meat and threw it to him—both the lean and the fat. He ate it. This thing ate, and when he had finished eating he picked his teeth, throwing the tooth-pickings to the girl inside the bag. But the girl refused to eat the tooth-pickings, she just stayed in that bag.

When the man had finished eating, he took his stick and hit her. "Sing, Bird of a Great One!"

The girl sang:

9. These are the names of her siblings—Bentsel'-esangweni, the name of a brother; Noluhlu and Nomavo, her sisters.

"What should I say? What should I say?
You, Bentsel'-esangweni!
I traveled and got hurt!
Noluhlu, won't you help me?
Tshiiiiiii! Ngantshoooooooooo-ooo!
Nomavo, won't you help me?
Tshiiiiiii! Ngantshoooooooooo-ooo!"

She stopped then.

When she had stopped, the man departed, taking the bag with him. He went to the kraal where the fathers were eating. When he came to the fathers, he said, "Hello, Gentlemen!"

"Yes."

"Please give me some lean meat! And some fat! I'll make the Bird of a Great One sing for you."

That young man got up and went over to his father. He said, "Father, I wonder what we have put into the initiation house? Because the initiate is there in that bag. You'll hear her in a minute. That initiate calls me by name. She calls my sister's name. You'll hear her, it's the real initiate, the one we slaughtered beasts for here at home. Now, I wonder what it is that we really slaughtered for here? I wonder what it is that we slaughtered so many cattle for?"

That person was given fat and lean meat by the men, and he ate. When he finished eating, he picked his teeth, and again poured the tooth-pickings into the bag. Then he took his stick and beat the bag, and said, "Sing, Bird of a Great One!"

She sang,

"What should I say? What should I say?
You, Bentsel'-esangweni!
I traveled and got hurt!
Noluhlu, won't you help me?
Tshiiiiiii! Ngantshoooooooooo-ooo!
Nomavo, won't you help me?
Tshiiiiiii! Ngantshoooooooooo-ooo!"

Well, he got up and went away, carrying her on his shoulder. He went to the women in the sheep kraal.

The father of the initiate got up there among the men, this thing having already been heard by all the people. "Well, it is the girl in that bag! How could this have happened?" He went over to the yard and called his wife.

"Come here!" Then he said, "Now, you mustn't cry when you hear this. The girl for whom we have gone to such expense to initiate here at home—

here she is, in this bag! Now, you mustn't show that you recognize her, not even a little. You mustn't show that you know what is going on. Just look on and pretend not to be concerned about her. We'll try to solve this in some way."

Well then, the wife sat there. Because she was a woman who easily broke into tears, she took some time to go off and attempt to control herself. Then she went back and sat down.

The man went to the women. He came to the women and said, "Women, please throw me some fat! And some lean meat! I'll make the Bird of a Great One sing for you."

The women threw him some meat. He ate, then picked his teeth. He threw the tooth-pickings to the girl, he threw her the pickings. Then he took a stick and beat her. "Sing, Bird of a Great One!"

The girl sang,

> "What should I say? What should I say?
> You, Bentsel'-esangweni!
> I traveled and got hurt!
> Noluhlu, won't you help me?
> Tshiiiiiii! Ngantshoooooooooo-ooo!
> Nomavo, won't you help me?
> Tshiiiiiii! Ngantshooooooooo-ooo!"

"We thank you, Great one! You've pleased us! Now please go and eat your meat in the kraal. Go on!"

He went. While he was eating that meat, he put the bag next to him. He was given a lot of meat, and he ate it now, not paying attention to anything else, not caring about anything now, letting his guard down.

After a time, it was said, "Now, when a person visits us here, he customarily goes and fetches some water for the king. That is the custom, the tradition for everyone who comes here. The visitor must go and dip water for the king. This is particularly the case if the visitor happens to be a man."

"All right," he said. A cask was brought, a cask that leaked. The container was very old. They gave it to him.

They said, "Go and dip some water. But do not dip in a place where frogs croak. Do not dip the water in any place that has crab holes. Dip in a place where the water is clear, where nothing stirs!"

This person went off then. When he had gone some distance, he turned and said, "My bag! You're not going to tamper with it?"

"No, we're not going to touch it. You can tie it up, if you wish."

"Mm!" He fastened the bag to a post in the kraal, he tied it tightly. He tied it tightly, he tied it tightly, then he went. When he had gone some distance, he turned: "Don't tamper with that bag!"

"No, we haven't touched a thing! It's not the kind of thing we would do. We don't handle things that belong to strangers. It's not the kind of thing we would do—tamper with a visitor's bag."

"Oh!" He went on his way, he went on. He did not turn around again. He went down to the river. The same thing happened throughout the day: he arrived at a place and, while he was dipping, he saw a frog, so he spilled the water out. Then he found that the cask leaked, and he tried to patch it. He dug some clay and patched the container with it. He went farther down the river to other places and dipped. But he saw the hole of a crab. So he again spilled the water and went farther down the river. The cask again began to leak, and he patched it. This person, this thing, went to work again and filled the cask with mud, trying to patch it.

Finally, he came to a deep pool in the river, a pool that was calm: he saw nothing. He dipped the water, then carried it. He traveled with it.

In the meantime, this girl was taken out of the bag. She was set free over there at the kraal post where the bag had been tied. She was put into a room, and it was locked. When she had been set free, the bag was put down on the ground.

They said, "Let all the animals of the earth come here!"

Quickly then, quickly the animals came, all of the animals of the earth. When the animals were there, someone said, "Will you be able to do the thing that must be done?"

They said that they would indeed be able to do it.

It was said, "Snake! Snake, what will you do?" There were even snakes there. Nothing was missing.

A snake said, "I'll just get up and bite the man, on the heel or ankle or calf." So the snake was put into the bag.

It was said, "You, Wasp, what will you do?"

The wasp said, "I'll just get up and sting him, I'll pierce him with a stinger. I'll stick it right in!" The wasp was put into the bag.

It was said, "You, Hornet, what will you do?"

The hornet said, "What will I do when what is said?"

"When it is said, 'Now sing, Bird of a Great One!' because that is just what is going to be said."

The hornet said, "I'll say,

> 'What should I say? What should I say?
> You, Bentsel'-esangweni!
> I traveled and got hurt!
> Noluhlu, won't—' "

They said, "Stop, you know what to do! Put him in the bag. You must say that when the proper time comes, Hornet."

They were all put into the bag, all the things—black biting ants, everything that bites. What was not put into the bag were the things that do not bite. Only things that bite were put into the bag, and when that bag reached the size it was when the girl was in it, it was left alone. It was tied over there in the same way that it had been tied previously to that kraal post.

Time passed then, and after some time had passed this thing arrived. He took the water down from his head, and the king dipped it and drank.

It was said, "But did you dip this water in a place where nothing croaks?"

"Yes, I dipped it in a place where nothing croaks."

Some meat was given to him then. He was given some meat and he ate it.

It was said, "You have performed satisfactorily."

He said, "I must now ask your permission to depart, Gentlemen."

"Yes."

He took his bag, then put it down and said, "But did you touch this?"

It was said, "No, nobody would tamper with it."

He said, "Please sing, Bird of a Great One!"

"What should I say? What should—"

"Stop! It's obviously you!"

He carried the bag on his shoulder and departed with it. He disappeared as he went toward his own homestead. He arrived there and hung the bag up in that very same place he had hung it on the previous day, away from the door, on the upper side of the house.

After a time had passed, there was a discussion back at the king's place about "What should be done to that thing that is in the initiation house?"

The king spoke with the fathers of all those who were being initiated into womanhood, all of them. There were eleven of them—twelve, counting the girl who was actually being initiated. One of those eleven was her sister, the other ten were residents of the village. The fathers of all ten of them "must speak up and say what they wish to say about their daughters."

"Well, King, I am offering a heifer to buy the life of my daughter."

All of them made similar offers, one after another offered the king a heifer.

But the king indicated that he did not want the heifers; he would not accept them because his child was not saved by anything that they had done. She was saved by her ancestors because she was despaired of as being dead. The king himself had lost many cattle, thinking that he had been slaughtering them for his child. He did not want cattle now. In any case, this child of his had returned with a great amount of booty when she had fled from the monsters.

"What do you propose to do about your daughters? That is all I want to know." The king went on, "Each of you must cut off his daughter's head. Each person, each father must do that himself."

"All right."

They went, then, to the initiation house. When they got there, the door was barricaded. When he found the door barricaded, Mbengu-Sonyangaza entered; the brother of the initiate went in and broke through the screen. The raven fled; it flew off. It was not touched; nothing was done to it.

He asked, "Where is the person whom you are initiating here?" and there was nothing anyone could do now.

Mbengu-Sonyangaza began with his own sister. He seized her and cut off her head; he threw the head outside.

It was said, then, that each father should go in and cut off the head of his daughter. The men did as they were told, each one entering the house, each one cutting off his daughter's head. The heads were then thrown outside. All of the heads of those daughters were cut off and thrown away. Now the initiate was left without a sister; her head had been cut off because of her part in the conspiracy.

It was necessary that Mbengu-Sonyangaza's sister enter the initiation house. She was to be brought into the initiation house by those girls who had had nothing to do with the conspiracy. She began from the beginning, as an initiate.

As this was going on in the homestead of the initiate, over there in that thing's home, he was saying, "My wives! Go and gather some firewood!" He had three wives. "Today my bird will be cooked!" He meant this girl because he thought that she was still over there in his bag. The three wives went out and gathered firewood. They came back and put the bundles of wood down. When they had done so, he said, "Put the pot there!" They put the pot in the place he indicated.

"What should be done now?"

The women had put the bundles of firewood down. They had come with the large pot.

"Kindle a fire. Make it big enough to heat this pot until it's red hot! I want to eat this bird today! It'll be baked. Bake it, so that its fat comes out of it."

The women kindled the fire; then they put that pot on the hearth. When the pot had become very hot, he said, "My great wife, please take that bag of mine down. The pot is hot now."

The great wife went to get the bag. When she arrived there, she seized the bag and her hand was pricked. She said, "Shu shu shu! Sobani! This bag of yours bites!"

The big fellow got up and beat her vigorously. He said, "Get out of here, you fool! I wasted my cattle [that is, the bridal dowry] when I married you! Now you do nothing for me! Come, my right-hand wife! I provided dowry for you with red cattle only. You take that bag of mine down for me. It's on the upper side of the house. This pot is red hot now."

The right-hand wife went, and when she grasped the bag it stung her. She said, "Shu shu shu! Sobani! This bag of yours bites!"

He beat that wife too. He said, "Go, you fool, go! Go to the other fool outside! I wasted my cattle on you! Come then, my little wife of the supporting house of the great house,[10] the one in whose house I spend most of my time. You take my bag down. This pot is red hot now!"

This wife went over there, and she took the bag. The bag stung her. When the bag had stung her, she also returned, saying, "Shu shu shu, Sobani! This bag of yours bites!"

He beat her as well, saying, "Get out! Go to the other fools!" Then he told his wives, "Now I want all of you to mix up some mud. Take the mud and close this house up tight. Lock me inside. Take the mud and plaster all the holes and cracks in the house, then close the door and plaster over it so that there is no evidence of the place where the door is. Cover it up completely! Plaster the whole thing evenly. Make the door even with the wall. Let there be no hole that the wind can seep through."

The wives did that: they locked the door, they mixed the mud, they plastered and covered all the doorway. They completely covered it. There was not even a tiny space through which the wind could seep. When it was completed and no wind could get into the house, he said, "Have you finished?"

They said, "Yes."

"Well, go and sit somewhere!"

He went then and took his bag down. The bag did not bite him, not even a little. He took the bag and removed the rope from its mouth. Then he covered the pot. He took the bag by its bottom, and covered the pot. But not one creature fell out of the bag into the pot. Instead, all of them came rushing out—all over him, all over his body! They tore into him; they ripped into him.

He cried out, "Yooooooo! Open the house! Open the door for me! I'm dying!"

The women did nothing.

He said, "What husband will you have if you let me die? Open for me!"

But the three women said, "Eat your bird, Wise man! Leave us alone! We'll just remain steeped in our foolishness. Please, please eat that wisdom of yours!"

He said, "Oh, what is this? These things have all but finished me! I'm

10. The supporting house, or *iqadi,* is attached to one of the two principal houses, the great house or the right hand house. Should there be no male progeny in the house to which the *iqadi* is attached, the eldest son of the senior *iqadi* becomes the heir.

being eaten alive! They're eating me! They're eating my flesh! Please open up!"

The great wife called out, "You said that we are fools! You are the wise one! Now you please just be eaten by that wisdom of yours! That's beautiful!"

The women sat there laughing; they laughed at him. Those beasts ate him; they devoured him, leaving only some white bones. Before his spirit left him, he threw himself. He flew out through the grass thatch of the house. He ran, he ran naked, and threw himself into a pool and got stuck there head-first: his head in the pool, his rear end directed into the air. He remained like that, frozen in that position. Some bees came along and went inside there. They made honey in his buttocks.

It happened on a certain day that some men went walking along, going about their business. As they were doing so, they saw these bees coming out of the buttocks.

They said, "It's just a stump in the pond."

They went there and took the honey out. They took the honey out. Well, Friend, it happens that bees tend to have cells in their honeycombs, and these cells are far back in the hive, the last ones; they are white, and they usually contain the honey.

While the men were taking the honey out, "Well, what's the matter?"

"My hand can't reach back far enough!" one of the men said. "It's too big!"

One of the other men had a smaller hand, and he tried it. He took out some honey, then he reached back to the last honeycomb. But then, the buttocks contracted! They squeezed! They trapped that hand!

"Yo!"

"What shall we do about this? My hand won't come out!"

"Well, Man, it must be pulled!"

They pulled it then; they pulled the man's hand—but no!

"The bones of the ass of a grown man have locked!" The dead man was speaking! The dead man was speaking and saying, inside there, "Lock, Bones of the ass of a grown man! Lock, Bones of the ass of a grown man!"

"What shall we do?"

"Well, Friend, this hand must be cut off."

One of the men took a knife, and the hand was cut off. It was left inside there, in that ass—together with the honey. When this hand had been cut off, the dead man began to force the hand out of his buttocks. "Eeeeeeeenh!" The hand flew out! It was flung out!

Well then, that man was now maimed. The men went on their way, in that condition.

Tale 10

THE TWO NIECES

Masithathu Zenani's Analysis: This story is a variation of a common African story about a good girl who is contrasted with a bad girl. In the simplest version of this tale, a good girl has a series of challenging experiences and responds to them positively; she is rewarded. A sister has the same experiences but responds to them negatively; she is punished. It is a tale with a clear moral about growing up.

Mrs. Zenani explained that she was using this simple dualism to form a more elaborate tale about the growth of two sisters. A person of their own family, their aunt, will become the differentiating factor in the story: she has become a cannibal and is a deadly threat. The story begins with a common scene in the traditional good girl–bad girl tale. An old woman asks the girls to perform a task—a nauseous task, it involves the licking of a green humor from the corners of her eyes. One of the sisters dutifully does as the old woman requests; the other is repulsed: "The elder sister retched violently; she vomited. She became sick because of what her younger sister was doing." This establishes a relationship of antagonism between the sisters as they undertake a journey to their aunt's home.

In the simpler versions of the story, the girls go on their journeys serially. Here, they go together, and the storyteller regularly returns to their antagonistic relationship. This means of telling the story enables the performer to make plain what is only implied in the other versions: the suggestion that the diametrically opposed sisters actually represent the two contending sides of the same person, a storyteller's glimpse at the internal workings of a person's psyche as she searches for her identity while undergoing the puberty ritual. It is the oral tradition's means of evoking stream of consciousness.

The disputatiousness of the two sisters makes up the primary pattern in the early part of the story, the performer emphasizing the opposition between the goodness and the petulance. The presence of the aunt creates a complementary rhythm, a pattern that continues to sort out the qualities of the puberty initiate as represented by the two sisters. Composed of the aunt's attempts to kill the children, this pattern is buttressed by the two songs that dominate the final parts of the story. The intervention of nature, in the form of the *intengu* bird, is typical of puberty ritual tales, the storyteller emphasizing the inter-relatedness of culture and nature. [In this translation of the story, I have retained the Xhosa ideophones to give readers a sense of the added dimension given to oral tales by words rich in sound.]

Performance Note

Time: 18 September 1967, in the afternoon. *Place:* In Mrs. Zenani's home in Nkanga, Gatyana District, the Transkei. *Audience:* Thirty men, women, and children. (Perf. 689.)

In a certain homestead were two girls, immediately following each other in the order of their births. They decided one day to visit their aunt, so they began their journey. They carried provisions with them because their aunt's place was far away.

As they began their journey, they had a quarrel.

One of them said, "We didn't go this way the last time we visited our aunt!"

The other said, "Yes, we did go this way!"

"No, Friend, this is not the path we took! Really, it isn't!"

In spite of their quarrel, they traveled on. They journeyed for a long time, and as they were walking they met a little old woman who had a humor at the edges of her eyes. Her eyes were full of this humor. It was green. It was in the corners of her eyes.

The old woman said, "Please come here, my children, and lick me here. Lick this humor from my eyes!"

The girls were revolted. They felt sick when they looked at this humor. But the younger girl went up to that old woman, and she dug into the humor with her tongue. She licked it with her tongue, swallowing it.

The elder sister retched; she vomited. She became sick because of what her younger sister was doing.

The girl finished doing that, and the old woman said to her, "Now then, my child, things will go well for you. You may not be aware of this, but it is the way it will turn out. You shall have the knowledge to escape dangers. Now listen, the path that you're traveling on is going to take you to places that you have no intention of visiting. I know that you're going to your aunt's place, but if you remain on this path you're going to go past your aunt's place. You'll move on to other places. You're going to find a wonder when you finally do get to your aunt's home, but the way that you're traveling is not the right way. You've passed by the path that you should have taken.

"Now then, I'll tell you what you should do. Up ahead, you must turn. Turn to the right. Don't take the path that goes to the left. Then you'll arrive at your aunt's house. You should know that your aunt was maimed sometimes back, and she is no longer human. She has become an ogre who eats people. She'll even have a strong desire to eat the two of you.

"When you return to your own home, don't go back by the path that leads directly to your home. You may have other adventures, but I say to you, my child, you'll be safe from your enemies if you humble yourselves."

These children went on then, and they came to that fork in the path, the one this girl had been told about, where she was to turn to the right.

She said, "Let's turn here. The old woman said that we should turn here. The correct path is the one to the right."

The other one said, "No, we'll not turn here! I know the way to my

"Lick this humor from my eyes!" Her face reflects the condition of the old woman; her hands, the reaction of the girls.

aunt's place! The correct path does not turn here! I know the way. No one can tell me how to get there! You were starving; you were so hungry that you would even eat that woman's humor! Well, don't make me endure the effects of your appetite! Keep it to yourself. Keep your humor in your stomach! I'll walk along the correct path, the one that leads to my aunt's place!"

They walked on then. This older sister was an arrogant person; her younger sister was quite humble. They walked on, and when they had gone a great distance, the younger sister said, "Oh, Friend! Really, Sister, I fear this journey to our aunt's place! You said that we had to travel this way. But look at where this path is taking us! Have you seen these places that we're passing? This forest—is it familiar to you? Do you remember it from the other time we visited our aunt?"

The other said, "What forest?"

She said, "That forest! Do you see? There's a river on one side. Do you see the forest on the other side? And in another place, do you see the meadow?"

"What's that?" she said. "The humor of the old woman has made you crazy! You're full of it, up to the neck! I've never seen a child lick the humor from someone's eyes! And now you don't know the way. Now you say that those are forests! You say that those are cliffs! You say that those are rivers! But it's just a path! You're crazy! I'm going on!"

The younger child walked along with her. She was silent. But she was also concerned that this other one did not see things as she did. They walked on and came to a certain place, a homestead. There was one person in this homestead—a person who stood up, who did not sit down. He did not bend down. He did nothing: he just stood upright, like a post.

This person told them that he could not bend at the neck, he could not bend at the waist, he could not bend at the knees. He said, "Yu!" That is what this person said, this fixed person, this polelike person. "Eheee!" he said. "And where do you come from?"

One of the girls said, "We're going to our aunt's place. We've come from home, and we're going to our aunt's place."

This person said, "Ee, are you on the right road to your aunt's place?"

The older girl said, "If it's not the right way, it's not the right way for a person whose aunt does *not* live over there. For those of us whose aunt *does* live over there, it is indeed the right road."

The younger sister said, "Careful, Sister, careful! This is not the right way. I told you that the correct road was the other one, the one we were told to go on, the road that went to the right. But you didn't agree. You scolded me!"

The older girl said, "You've really become crazy, Little child! I've never seen a person who eats humor! I'm not at all surprised that you're crazy! No wonder you're crazy: humor is not to be eaten!"

After a time, this person said, "Look here, Girl, I cannot bend. Look, I can't turn around. The way I am now—that's the only way I can be. This is all I can do. The only reason I'm still around today is because I'm in the condition that you see me. But you're a person who has supple limbs, who can turn around, a person who can bend her body—and I can tell you that you are as good as maimed! You're no better than I am because no one has ever traveled here before. The thing that you call a forest is not a forest. And what you call a river is not a river. What you say is a meadow is not a meadow. All of these things, taken together, form a many-spotted beast; that's what you've been seeing. Now it's asleep. But when it wakes up, you're no more than a mouthful for it!"

The little girl got up then and said, "Sister, let's go home!" Delicately, gently, she tugged at her sister's garment.

The other one shook her off forcibly. "You're silly! I've never before seen a child who's gone mad on the humor of an old woman! You're really crazy! What got into your head, to eat old people's humor? That's been bothering me! You're really insane! What's the matter with you? And why do you keep tugging at me?" So she said, and she punched her little sister in the face. The younger girl fell to the ground, then got up.

She said, "I won't fight you, Sister. But I'm telling you, we should go! That's all I say—let's go!"

Eventually they resumed their traveling; they walked on. The older girl continued to abuse her sister: "Well, where is that path, then? The real one, the one you know?"

She said, "Let's just walk on, then we'll turn at that place where we're supposed to turn."

They continued to walk, and finally they came to that tree where they had been told to turn. They did turn this time. They took the right-hand path, no longer quarreling about it. The older sister seemed to realize that the sun was setting now, that they were going to be caught by the darkness. They walked along that path. Then they came to their aunt's place.

When they got there, they found a person who had one leg and one arm.

This person said, "Yo! Where have you come from?"

They said, "We've come from home. We've come to see our aunt."

This person said, "Yu! Your aunt is a cannibal! She's not here right now. She has gone hunting, looking for humans. Now she might eat you! You should know that. I'm sorry, but that's the way it is. She hasn't eaten me because my flesh is bitter. My body turned bitter, so she left me alone. So I remain here. She'll return later, carrying a human body. She eats human flesh. But she always brings an animal along too because I eat animal flesh, not human flesh."

The children waited.

"She'll greet you, but you mustn't acknowledge her greeting. And do not allow her to embrace you, do not allow her to kiss you on the mouth, to bring the two sets of lips together. Do not let her bring her mouth to yours. If she does that, if she comes into contact with your mouth, she'll tear it off with her teeth!"

The children agreed to do as this person suggested, and they remained there. And time passed.

That person said, "Soon you'll hear her."

She was heard approaching—there was a thumping and there was a squall. A violent gusting was felt, then she arrived. She dropped something—*godlo!* It was a large man whom she had killed, a human.

The children watched her: "Yo! Things don't look good!"

She said, "Yu! Yu yu yu! Now, One-leg, what is this? What is this that smells? Who are these?"

He said, "They're your brother's children."

She said, "Yu yu! Children of my brother, oh!" She greeted the children, she greeted them. "Yo yo yo! What do they bring for me?" As she greeted one of them, she plunged her nails into the girl's hand.

That one said, "Yo! Shu! Sister of my father!"

"Yes!"

Then the aunt went to the older girl. She greeted her: "Hello, Child of my brother!"

The child of her brother went to her. The woman came close to the girl—*zum!* She clung to her—*molokonco!* Then she ripped the girl's mouth off—*vungu!*—and ate it because it was meat that she wanted.

The girl cried out, "Yo yo yo yo, Sister of my father! Oh!" And she cried.

The aunt said, "I'm *so* glad to see you! I'm just expressing my warmth and generosity, my kindness, you see. I might have overreached myself a bit there by taking off your mouth. But, Child of my home, you must understand that it's only my way of expressing my kindness, my joy at seeing you."

Time passed then, and at dusk they went to sleep.

These different meats were first cooked—the human was cooked, the animal was cooked. When the human flesh was taken out of the pot, the aunt ate it. She also dipped the animal flesh out and put it down so that it could be eaten by One-leg and those daughters of her brother.

Time passed, and, when they lay down to sleep, One-leg said, "On no account should you go to sleep! If you go to sleep here, you'll be chopped up by her, I swear! Even if you are the children of her brother."

"Oh!"

They slept. They slept and their aunt got up.

She crept quietly. She went over to where they were sleeping. She was carrying an axe. She crept quietly—*cwashu cwashu cwashu!*

But the younger sister was not asleep. She was wide awake. The older one was sleeping.

The younger sister said, "Shu! Shu! Shu! Shu! We're being eaten up by the fleas of my aunt's house!"

The aunt said, "Oh, all this nonsense about fleas! I don't know anything about it!" She threw a small blanket to the girl, and said, "Cover yourself with that blanket, too! What's this nonsense about fleas?"

The girls put on the additional blanket, and they slept.

The aunt also went to sleep in her sleeping place. She slept there, and after a time, when the girls were quiet again, she got up—*cwashu cwashu cwashu*, carrying this axe.

As the aunt approached them, the little sister again said, "Shu! Shu! Shu! The fleas of my aunt's house! Yo! How will we get to sleep? We'll never get to sleep at this rate!"

The aunt said, "What kind of little pest is this who doesn't sleep? This little pest! The others are sleeping!" She took off her short skin-skirt and threw it to the girl. The girl took the skirt and put it on top of herself. Then the aunt went to sleep again.

Later, she crept quietly back—*cwashu cwashu*.

The younger sister pinched the older one, trying to awaken her. She pinched her, and the older sister was startled out of her sleep. She said, "Why are you pinching me? Why are you pinching me? I want to sleep! Stop it!"

The younger girl was quiet. She was silent. She did not speak.

"Aunt! How is it over where you're sleeping? We're really suffering here because of these fleas!"

"Yo! This pest is still awake! This child—this child is passing strange!"

The aunt went to sleep in her place again.

Finally, it became obvious that the aunt was really sleeping. She snored. She snored in an extraordinary way: the oxen inside her stomach bawled—everything inside her stomach, including the fowl, cried out. Her stomach was all a-rumble, every possible noise could be heard.

"Oh, she's asleep!" When she was certain that her aunt was asleep, this child awakened her older sister. She roused her.

"No, leave me alone! Leave me alone! Don't keep awakening me! What's wrong with you?"

The child was quiet.

Then she again shook her sister: "Let's go now, while our aunt is asleep!"

"No, leave me alone! Stop awakening me!"

The child was quiet. She realized that the ogre of an aunt might hear them. She was quiet for a time, then she again attempted to arouse her sister.

Finally, this thing awakened—the younger sister dragged it by the legs, she brought it outside, dragging it like a sledge.

When they got outside, she said, "Yu yu yu! What is it? I try to arouse you, and you refuse to be awakened! Don't you know that we'll be harmed here?"

"What's the matter with you now?"

"Your mouth has been eaten! Why are you delaying? Let's go home!"

"No, what can we do? It's night!"

"Get up! Let's go home. It's no longer night!"

"Well, I'm sleepy!"

"How can you be sleepy?"

She finally got her older sister to her feet, and they departed.

In the place where they had been sleeping, the younger sister had placed a rock under that short skin-skirt of her aunt's. She covered the rock with that skirt and all those rags that the aunt had thrown at them when the little girl had complained of fleas. She piled them together there. She made bundles that resembled humans. Then the girls went on their way.

The younger girl had done all this. The older sister, the coddled one, had done nothing. Well, this older sister did not really know what she was doing now. She just wanted to remain there and sleep.

They traveled then, and while they were walking—oh! their aunt woke up! She leapt out of her bed suddenly—*khuphululu!*

"Yo! They're surely sleeping now! Mp!" She thought that they were sleeping, so she took her axe and wielded it—and hit against the rock!

She said,

> [chants]
> "Axe of mine, be sharp!
> I'm going to eat a person now,
> I'm going to eat all those good things!
> My axe, my axe, be sharp!
> You're going to eat a person now,
> You'll eat all those good things!"

The axe was sharp. She stood up and crept quietly to that place where the children had been sleeping. She seized the axe with both hands and brought it down on the rock—*helele!* The axe at once was blunted!

She said, "Yo yo yo! They've gone already! They left last night!"

She got up in a fury. She went and sharpened the axe again. She sharpened it; she sharpened the axe. Then she pursued the two girls. Her breasts, those nursing breasts, trailed on the ground, trailed after her on the ground—*rrrrrrrrr!* She took one of the breasts and flipped it over her shoulder—*tyu!* on one side. And she took the other and flipped it over her shoulder—*tyu!* on the other side. Then she ran, pursuing the children. She was roaring along the trail.

At sunrise, the younger sister said, "Yo! Here's our aunt! Now what'll happen to us?"

The elder said, "All I know is, I'm tired! I don't care about anything else!"

"Now, Friend, how can you say you're tired—while our aunt is coming after us carrying an axe?"

"I tell you, I'm tired! I don't care about anything else, I'm tired!"

"Yo! How can you say you're tired when we're in such danger?"

"No, let me be! I'm tired! We'll just tell our aunt that we're tired!"

"You want to say that to someone who is going to eat us?"

"Do you still regard our aunt as someone who eats people?"

"Your mouth—where is it? Let's run!"

She pulled her sister along, and they ran.

The aunt arrived. She could run like the wind, there was no doubt about that. She did not run in the usual way. She did not have the ability to do so anymore because she had become a cannibal—she ate people, while she herself was also a person.

When the aunt was fairly close to them, the younger girl said, "Oh, she's got us now!"

The aunt appeared.

"No, Noma! I won't give in!"

The aunt was there!

The younger sister spoke to Noma, her older sister:

> [sings]
> "No, Noma!
> She'll hack us up!
> No, Noma!
> With an axe that's sharp!
> No, Noma!"

Their aunt said,

> [sings]
> "That's my song!
> Who made it for you?
> That's my song!
> Who made it for you?"

She moved along—*hitsh'! hitsh'! hitsh'! hitsh'! hitsh'! hitsh'!* but she was off balance and collided with a house—*ngqiiiii!* It was her own house! The aunt tried to stop herself from hitting the house but—*ngqiiiii!* She had suddenly returned to her own house!

She said, "Yo! Heeeeee!" She said, "Oh! How did I get here? They've bewitched me! I'm here at home!"

The aunt ricocheted; she pursued them again.

When she was close, the children fled to a tree that hung there in the air.

The younger child said, "Yo! Here's our aunt again! What'll we do now?

[sings]
Our aunt's here!
No, Noma!
She'll chop us up!
No, Noma!
The axe is sharp!
No, Noma!"

The aunt said,

[sings]
"That's my song!
Who made it for you?
That's my song!
Who made it for you?"

Again, she could not steady herself, and she again ran against her own house—*ngqe!* "Ee! Yo!"

The children came to the tree, a very tall tree, and they climbed it. They went right to the top of the tree. When they had climbed it, their aunt arrived, having again pursued them, coming backwards now from her homestead.

She said, "This is more than a mere meeting. It is a major confrontation! We have really met! It's a major showdown!"

She saw the children at the top of the tree. The younger child was trembling. The damned one, the elder sister, was numb—*bhexe!* This stupid one had no idea what was going on.

The aunt said, "This is more than just a meeting. It is a major engagement!"

The child said, "Yo! What'll we do now?"

The aunt took her axe. She said, "Yahaa!" She cut into the tree—*zukhekhe!* She chopped this tree, it was ready to fall—and the girls would fall too! And the aunt would eat them!

The tree was tottering, about to fall.

A bird suddenly arrived—*thu!* The bird was called Ntengu. It swooped down—*rrrriwu!*

It said,

"Ntengu, Ntengu,[11] little wood-chips!
What have these worthy children done?

11. The *intengu* is a fork-tailed drongo or bee-catcher. The bird is said to have wonderful abilities: it can herd cattle, because the cattle mistake the bird's characteristic whistle for that of the herdboys.

> I laugh with the tree
> And it stands up again—*gomololo!*"

Gomololo! The tree stood up straight again. *Gomololo!*

The aunt said, "Oh! What kind of bird is this? Yo!"

She pursued this birrrrrrrd!

She caught up with the bird; she seized it and ate it—*shwam! shwam! shwam! shwam! shwam!*

But there was a feather, a feather that the aunt had not got into her mouth. She gobbled everything, even the feathers, but there was one little feather that had fallen to the ground, unknown to her.

"We've met!"

Again, eee! the tree was about to fall—*tya tya tya tya!* And when the tree was about to fall, that feather flew—*phe phe phe phe,* gently flying, gently floating—*lenye lenye.*

It said,

> "Ntengu, Ntengu, little wood-chips!
> What have these worthy children done?
> I laugh with the tree
> And it stands up again—*gomololo!*"

Eeeee! The tree stood upright!

Yo! The aunt pursued the feather. She pursued it. She seized the feather and ate it. She finished it off, then she again returned to the tree and chopped it—*rrr!* There was no bird now—*rrr rrr!* Then: *taaaaaa!* a small scrap of flesh from that bird flew from between her teeth as she was chopping, a small scrap of flesh from that bird. *Taaaaaaa!* the scrap of meat flew from between her teeth because of the force of her chopping. Eee! *Taaaaaa!* The scrap of meat flew—*rrriwu!*

> "Ntengu, Ntengu, little wood-chips!
> What have these worthy children done?
> I laugh with the tree
> And it stands up again—*gomololo!*"

Gomololo! The tree stood upright. *Gomololo!*

The aunt said, "What is it that is saying these words?" She could not even see it this time. "What is it that is saying this?" But she could not see this scrap of flesh. It was so small, it was almost not there. She did not see it at all.

And, well, the tree stood upright—*gomololo!* No matter how hard she chopped, this scrap of meat would speak. But she could not find it.

Up above, in the tree, the younger girl said, "Mbambozozele! Ntu-mntumshe! [She calls her dogs by name.] Please hurry! Come for us!"

The dogs of their home came. Two of them were greyhounds—there were greyhounds and pointers, there were mongrels and terriers. The ones called greyhounds were lean and tall. They rushed furiously to the trees, and they ate the girls' aunt! They ate her. They finished her off. All that remained of her was bones. The dogs gnawed the bones but did not break them. A dog took one of her breasts and ate it. It wrenched the breast whole from her body! It took one buttock and went to eat it over there. Another dog took the other buttock and went to eat it over there.

All that remained of her was bones—white, pure white bones—*mpe!* That is what remained of the children's aunt.

"Eee, now then, let's go!"

The girls came down from the tree. There was their aunt, lying on the ground. When the girls came down from the tree, their big brother was also there. He had come with the dogs. Now the girls and the dogs went home with him. Along the way, they told him about their travels, and how they had argued along the way. It was the fault of this younger sister that they had quarreled, but even the older one now agreed: "I was almost hurt badly because I contradicted this child. I knew this as things developed."

Tale 11

A GIRL CUTS OFF A MAN'S EAR

Masithathu Zenani's Analysis: An unusual fog carries the central character from her home. In an alien land, where she and her family are not known, she undergoes change: in a homestead not her own, she is brought up. She becomes a woman.

It is, said Mrs. Zenani, a world of fantasy that she has entered, a world that seems opposed to her own home, yet it is, in the prismatic world of the story, a mirror image of that home. This is the ordeal stage of the three-tiered puberty rite, the three stages being separation, ordeal, and reincorporation.

She has been separated from her home, and the villainy in this remote place is in the figure of a suitor who happens to be a member of a group of cannibals. But he has disguised himself as a human, and he courts the young woman. Her surrogate parents, who know of the presence of these deadly cannibals, having lost members of their own family to them, leave her alone for a time, and the masquerading cannibal comes to her. This is her ordeal; in the ensuing struggle, she cuts off his ear. At a dance, she meets an apparently different young man, not realizing that it is the same person in a new disguise. When he is alone with her, he reveals that his ear is gone, gives her a chance to pray, telling her that she has seen the sun for the last time. But the ancestors preserve her: he falls asleep, and she escapes.

Her ordeal at an end, she can begin the reincorporation stage of the ritual. The arduous journey is undertaken with her surrogate father, and she finally returns to her home. She has gone through an ordeal and has become an adult.

The connection with the ancestors is an important part of this story; it supplies the puberty ritual with religious sanction. It is the ancestors, and their connection with the cultural past, who make it possible for her satisfactorily to complete the ceremony.

Swallowing monsters take many forms in the oral tradition. They are effective symbols of change: the central character is engulfed as a child, for example, then emerges as an adult. In this tale, the cannibalistic youth is such an ogre. Even though he does not physically swallow her, proximity is enough: the effect is the same.

Performance Note

Time: 13 September 1967, at night. *Place:* Outside, in a kraal in Nkanga, Gatyana District, the Transkei. *Audience:* Fifty men, women, and children. (Perf. 628.)

Long ago, in a certain village, some children went out to play. They were in the habit of playing in one particular place. Their games were

"Morning after morning, the fog remained with her. It was in her eyes."

varied—they made clay wagons, pots, that sort of thing. They made dolls, too, and horses.

One day, while they were playing, a fog appeared. The fog descended, the sky became overcast, and suddenly it was dark. They could not see where they were going. They could not even find the path leading to their homes. They ran.

One child said, "This is not an ordinary fog!"

"We've never seen such a thing," said another.

The children ran. Some of them fell over cliffs, others stumbled into strange homesteads. Some, fortunately, got home safely.

One child did not reach her home:

She hurried along, crossing rivers, pushing on. Morning after morning, the fog remained with her. It was in her eyes. She went to sleep at night; every morning the fog was in her eyes. It had singled this child out from among the other children. She hurried along.

On the third day of her wandering, she came to a homestead. She stumbled against it in the fog.

Someone asked, "Where have you come from, Child?"

She said, "We were playing, and the sky suddenly became dark. I want my friends!"

"Where are they?"

"I don't know. We scattered and ran. I don't know where they are."

"Where have you come from, Child? We know every child around here. But we don't know you."

The country that she described to them was not known here at all. What this child was saying was a wonder to them.

They asked who her father was.

She told them his name.

They did not know her father.

Was there not, in her country, some other person—an elder who was very, very old?

"Just name him."

The child named one such elder, an old man from another homestead.

He was not known here at all.

They asked her "the name of a river in that country of yours."

"What's its name?"

The child named a river.

It was not known.

Someone said to this child, "Now just think a minute, my child. What day was it when you were playing and the fog came?"

"When you were separated from the others?"

"When you were forced to try to find those others?"

The child told them.

They said, "Oh, shame! Do you mean to say that this is the fourth day that this child has been wandering around?"

"Where have you been sleeping?"

She said, "I just slept whenever I got tired, wherever I was. I slept on the ground."

"What did you eat?"

"I didn't eat at all."

They hurriedly prepared something for the child to eat; she was given some food. But the child could not keep the food down. So they ground her some millet porridge; they made it with water so that she would be able to swallow it more easily. The child was able to digest it: she swallowed some of the food, then rested; she swallowed some food, then rested. It had been a long time since she had eaten. She continued to swallow, then rest; swallow, then rest.

Finally, she said that she was satisfied, she had had her fill—but she was not actually sated. She said that she was because she was embarrassed about her inability to eat properly.

A woman of this home, an older, experienced woman, said to the girl, "Rest, my child, you can eat some more food later. This is not at all surprising, considering that you haven't been eating all this time. It's your hunger that makes you eat like that."

The child rested for a while. Time passed, and she again took the porridge and ate. In the end, she really was satisfied.

Time passed in that way then.

Time passed for that child, and she grew up. She grew up. She became a child of this home, one who had been picked up—an orphan. She became a child of this home.

They continually asked about her, inquiring if there was anyone who had lost a child. But that quest resulted in nothing, and this child grew and became older.

When she was older, a grown child now, she went around with others from this area, participating in the things that they typically did.

They went to parties. At these gatherings, when the dancing came to an end and the people had gone home, the girls, because they were traditional Xhosa,[12] would pair off with the young men. She too had a young man with whom she attended these events.

This young man said to the girl, "I'm really very attracted to you. I believe that I'll court you. I want you to be my wife."

The girl said, "Well, if you wish to court me, that's all right."

But when they started going together, people began to whisper against this young man; they whispered against him.

They said, "He's not a successful sexual partner."

"He has sexual inadequacies."

"His women leave him."

So the girl rejected him; she refused to accept this young man. She left him; she parted from him.

Time passed, a long time passed, and this child was happy. She was treated like the other children of this home.

In this home where she now lived were two girls. There had been many other children in this household, but there were only two left now. The others were dead.

There was a certain person who came from a group of cannibals—they

12. Literally, Xhosa of the red ochre people, that is, people who dyed their garments with red ochre, as the Xhosa traditionally did.

were creatures that moved about stealthily. When the people were away, when there were no adults at home, this cannibal would come along. He would not go to a place where there were a lot of people.

At that home one day, they said, "Today, we're going to the sea. The house will not be locked. We'll leave this adopted girl behind at home."

They went to the sea. The family went to the sea, and when they had departed this child slept there.

They had said, "When you go to sleep, lock the house."

But she was not told what frequently took place at such times. This had been hidden from her.

All they said was this:

"Since you're going to be alone, my child, take care that you lock the house when you go to sleep. Open the door only in the morning. Lock up when you go to sleep."

"And don't go to sleep before you've locked the door."

"We'll return in about a day."

"Oh."

They departed. The child was left behind. She remained in the house by herself. The sun set, and, when it had set, she closed the door and went to sleep.

But she forgot to lock the door. She forgot that; she did not lock the door, she only closed it.

She went to sleep.

Then she heard something approaching the house. She heard it clearly; she heard a thing coming, a thumping sound. She got up; she got a big knife that was at the upper side of the house. She took the knife and went toward the door. She could not find the key. She knew that there was no time to look for it. She went to the door and stopped.

This thing arrived. It opened the door. As it did so, as it stuck its head inside, she leapt forward with the knife. And she sliced off its ear. The ear fell inside the house. The monster pulled back, it pulled back. She closed the door. It was only then that she was able to find the key. She locked the door.

She locked it. Then she went to sleep, red with blood. She slept until morning. She would not open the door, even the next morning.

She saw that "This is an ear that has fallen down here, this thing that bled so much on me."

She did not open the door. The morning passed, and she refused to open the door. She refused to open it because she did not know if this thing was still outside.

Time passed then. Time passed for her in this way.

In the afternoon, the people of her home arrived, returning from the sea. They arrived and found her locked inside.

They were on the outside, and they said, "Yo! What's all this blood?"

"Yu! What's been bleeding so much?"

"Oh, my friend, has this child been devoured?"

They tried to open the door.

"It's locked!"

She said, "No, Mama, I'm here!"

So saying, she opened the door. When she had opened the door, she said, "Look! the blood of that thing that tried to get in here! I forgot to lock the door. This thing came. It came and wanted to open the door. I took a knife because I knew that I wouldn't get to the key in time. I was afraid when it opened the door, so I acted as if I were going to hit it. The knife cut this ear off. That's why there's blood here. The monster fell back, and when it had done so, I closed the door. It was only then that I was able to lock it. The reason I didn't open it this morning is because I was afraid. I kept thinking that maybe that creature was here again at the door."

"You did well, my child. That is the thing that destroyed my children! When I told you to lock the door, I avoided telling you that there is something that has been killing the children here. You did well to cut off its ear."

"Oh."

"It's all right. Relax, my child."

The child was washed and scrubbed, and she became beautiful. Her beauty was restored, and the ear was thrown away.

Time passed then. Happiness returned to this household; everything went well.

There was another dance, and this child attended it. A young man came to the dance. He arrived in the morning. When he got there, he sat down. He did not dance; he just watched. When the girls had departed, along with this girl, the young man approached them.

He said, "Where does this girl come from? This one, who's cast a spell on me?"

The girls asked, "How has she cast a spell on you?"

He said, "She's cast a spell on me; I'm attracted to her!"

The other girls said, "She's from our place."

He said, "Oh!" He called to her, "Come here, my girl!"

The dance was ending now; they were all going home. As they were going home, he stayed with this girl; he delayed her. The others went ahead. He kept her behind.

He sat down. He said, "Sit for a while. I have something I want to discuss with you. I want us to explore some things together."

The child said, "But the others are leaving me behind."

This young man said, "No, please stay here. Don't worry about being left behind by the others. You'll catch up with them. I have something I want to discuss with you. You'll catch up with them later."

The child said, "But what will they say at home when they've learned that I've remained behind? I can't stay here."

This young man said, "No! No, my girl. Really, I want to say something to you. I want you to be my wife. I don't appreciate your fear of being left behind by the others. I'm in love with you, so you shouldn't be afraid to be seen with me. When they ask you at your home why you delayed, you can say that a young man was speaking with you, a young man who wants you to be his wife."

This girl said, "Oh, well then, all right. Why don't you come along to my home?"

The others were leaving her behind. They had disappeared a long time ago.

"All right then," this young man said, and he stood up.

Then he said, "Girl!"

The girl said, "Hnn?"

He said, "Do you know me?"

The girl said, "No."

He said, "Look for the last time at the sun. You shall never see another sun!"

The girl said, "Why?"

Then this person, who she thought was a young man, removed his headcloth—and she saw that his ear was not there!

He said, "Where is my ear? Where is my ear?"

This child said, "Oh! Wait, please wait! Since you insist that I'm seeing the sun for the last time because of your ear, give me a chance to pray."

He said, "You may pray."

The child knelt and said, "Gods of my home, be with me. I thought that I was removing the ear of a monster. Had I known it was a human, I would not have cut off his ear. I did not know whose ear it was. I did not know what this person wanted. He did not come back the next morning to discuss the matter, but he wants to talk about the affair of the ear today. So that I should know that the gods of my home are watching me, let them preserve me today as they preserved me on the day that I removed this ear."

This young man became drowsy then; he went to sleep. The girl got up. She saw that he was asleep. She moved a little farther away from him. Then she looked again; she saw that he continued to sleep. She moved a little farther; she looked again to be sure that he was sleeping. She moved a little farther; she moved over there. Then she ran.

She went over the hill to the place where the others had disappeared, running the whole time. When she had gone over the hill, she caught up with the others. She was crying by then, while those of her homestead awaited her. They waited for her, and she caught up with them. She was crying.

She said, "Yo yo yo! How could you leave me behind with such a person? A person who was going to kill me? You think he is a young man, but he was asking me about an ear! He showed me the only ear he has. He said that I should look at the sun, that I'd never see another. This same person had earlier said that he wanted me to become his wife, but he doesn't want that at all. Yo! My ancestors have preserved me today. This is not the first time that they have saved me."

"Wo!" The sisters joined in the exclamation, and they supported her conclusions: "She's right!"

"Let's go, Child of my father!"

"The ancestors are with you!"

In the meantime, the young man was startled when he awakened. Indeed he was. "There's no girl here now. She must have left a long time ago!"

He went home.

The girls traveled on. They finally reached their home. They arrived and reported this matter to their parents. That ended well: the parents were relieved, though alarmed. Things ended well, because she had not been harmed.

This child said, "Father, I want you to help me now to find my home because I know that eventually something bad is going to happen to me. Really, we must go. Maybe if we were to go together, we'd find my home."

That fellow agreed to go with her, and he said, "Well, all right, Girl. I'll help you to find your home."

They prepared their provisions. Then he and that girl went on their journey. They traveled, sleeping along the way, seeking her home, moving on again, sleeping, seeking.

Whenever they came to a place, the man would ask, "Well, my child, have you ever set foot in this place?"

The child would try to recall. She would say, "It does seem to be familiar. I think I did pass through a place like this." And they would go on.

Finally, they arrived at her home.

When they got there, they found her father, mother, and all her family. They greeted them. Her mother saw immediately that this was her child.

She said, "Yuuuuuu! My child!"

It took her father a little longer to recognize the child. Then he said, "Where has my child come from?"

The stranger explained what had occurred, that "This child came to me. She said that, as the children had been playing, a fog came up. The children lost each other as they went to their homes. On the fourth day, she finally stumbled on to my home. When the child got there, she could not eat. Porridge with water was made for her, but she had difficulty swallowing it. We repeatedly urged her to rest. Finally, the child was able to eat until she had had enough. She became well. She has encountered several hazards during the period that she has been absent from this home. Once, I left her alone in the house and went to the sea. When we left her there, a certain thing that we knew about came along. You see, we chose to leave this child behind at our home rather than one of our own children. We told her to lock the house. The child forgot where the key was when that dreadful thing arrived. But she took care of herself with a knife. While that thing was terrorizing her, she cut off its ear. After that, she went around with the other children, and finally she was courted. She would have gotten married, but the man she was to marry was whispered about. When she heard about this, she rejected him. On another occasion, the child encountered a young man at a dance. He arrived there but did not dance; he just sat there. When she was leaving this dance with the other girls, she saw this young man approaching. He said, 'This girl has cast a spell on me. Where is she from?' The girls asked him, 'What do you mean, "cast a spell"?' He said, 'I've fallen in love with her!' And when the dance ended, he accompanied her; he spoke about courting her. So she was left alone with him by the others—left behind there, sitting. The others had left her behind. When her friends had disappeared, the young man stood up. He said, 'Look at this sun for the last time today! Where is my ear?' So saying, he showed her the ear that was not there. The child said, 'Oh, leave me alone, Friend, let me pray. I did not know that I cut off your ear.' While she was praying, the young man slept. That's how she got the chance to escape. Finally, the child thought that I should help her to find her home. That's why I've brought her home. I'm happy that I've found her homestead!"

The owners of that homestead thanked the stranger. They gave him an ox, thanking him for what he had done, showing their gratitude to him for watching over their child.

Tale 12

SIKHULUMA, THE BOY WHO DID NOT SPEAK

Masithathu Zenani's Analysis: "Sikhuluma" is a tale that treats a boy's movement through puberty and beyond, to his marriage. Rites of passage always emphasize crises in people's lives, as they move from one state of existence to another, and the resultant changes of identity. These rituals are periods of transformation, of change, in individual lives, as biological changes are made harmonious with social needs.

Sikhuluma, derived from the noun *isikhulumi*, means an eloquent, loquacious speaker. This is somewhat ironic because Sikhuluma does not speak at all in the early part of this tale. But later, when he does speak, it is to save lives, befitting a future leader. And when he returns to his home at the end of the first part of the story, he speaks splendidly; the reason for the lengthy retelling of the events that have occurred is to emphasize this eloquence, suggesting that Sikhuluma, born not speaking, has now come of age. His movement from muteness to eloquence is a dramatic revelation of his move from childhood to adulthood.

The story is in three parts. Part one has to do with the quest for birds and emphasizes Sikhuluma's puberty ritual. The old man reveals this when he derides the boys, insisting that chasing the birds is an act of manhood. Part two centers on the quest for the fabulous river monster and signals the end of Sikhuluma's puberty, the preparation for marriage. In part three, the bride quest is central, Sikhuluma is married, and he ascends the throne.

The second section is the pivotal part of the narrative. The cape made of the skin of the monster enables the puberty ritual to end (only then will Sikhuluma emerge from the circumcision lodge) and the marriage rite to begin. The two rituals overlap in part two. The river monster's skin becomes Sikhuluma's protection during his bride quest. The skin symbolizes the satisfactory completion of the puberty ritual and saves the wearer in his mature life. The suggestion is that properly and successfully experiencing the puberty ritual preserves one as he moves into adulthood and its many dangers. In the end, Sikhuluma dies, is swallowed (the traditional symbol of death and rebirth), and is reborn a man.

Mrs. Zenani noted that parts one and three are connected in a rather complex manner. The relationship between Sikhuluma and Sitshalotshalwana in part one is equivalent to that between Mangangedolo and his daughter in part three. In each case, a struggle between good and evil is dramatized, with Sikhuluma emerging victorious in the first part, Mangangedolo in the third. Mangangedolo is, as are many villains in the oral tradition, both life-giving and death-dealing; he is death-dealing in his persistent efforts to destroy Sikhuluma, and life-giving in his daughter, who is, in the language of the tale, his extension. Father and daughter form a pair, a life-giving/death-dealing pair. Similarly, Sikhuluma and Sitshalotshalwana, the brothers, are a contrasting pair, a dramatization of the struggle occurring within the initiate as he moves to manhood. But the key here is the parallel between the two parts, as Mrs. Zenani dramatically parallels Sikhuluma and the woman, clearly moving this story beyond a typical male puberty ritual. Women are important in this version of the story. A hero and leader like Sikhuluma, Mrs. Zenani is implying, does not achieve his triumphs alone: he has the active assistance of women, his sister in part two, the bride in part three. But she argued that she was going even further, equating the male and female rituals.

Performance Note

Time: 15 September 1967, in the afternoon. *Place:* Along a path in Nkanga, Gatyana District, the Transkei. *Audience:* five women, fifteen children. (Perf. 656.) Another version of this story, also performed by Nongenile Masithathu Zenani, can be found in Richard M. Dorson, ed., *African Folklore* (Garden City, N.Y.: Anchor Books, 1972), "Sikhuluma," pp. 525–61.

A man and his senior wife: the wife gave birth; she bore a child who could not speak. In time, when his playmates started talking, it became clear that this child did not know how to speak.

He spoke with his hands: whenever he referred to something, he would point to it.

He spoke with his hands: he did not hear with his ears, he did not speak with his tongue.

When it was time, he was weaned.

That wife again became pregnant, and again she gave birth to a boy. That boy grew up. He learned to speak in the normal time.

He was a child who was able to speak.

The name of the child who did not know how to speak was Sikhuluma; the name of this child who knew how to speak was Sitshalotshalwana.[13] These children grew up, they became big boys.

I

These boys had a grandfather, the father of their father. That old man enjoyed sitting outside at the cattle kraal, relaxing in the sun, and many boys stayed there too, passing the time.

One day, some birds passed by. They appeared suddenly, moving from the left to the right side. They flew by in a thick flock. Then another flock of birds appeared from the same side, going to the other side.

13. "Sitshalotshalwana" is probably derived from the ideophone, *tshalu,* meaning a momentary appearance, a passing flash, which might refer to Sitshalotshalwana's brief effort to overthrow Sikhuluma. It might also be a reference to him as a quick, impatient talker.

When a fifth flock of birds had flown by, the old man said, "Ee! In the old days, when we were boys, those birds wouldn't have dared to do a thing like that. Passing above us like that. We boys wouldn't let those birds pass by without going after them and beating them. What's happened to these modern boys? If only I could be a lad again!"

When Sitstalotshalwana heard that, he turned to the other boys. "Did you hear Grandfather? We must find sticks and throw them at those birds!"

The boys went to Sikhuluma, the youth who did not know how to speak. They gestured with their hands. They gestured as they usually did when speaking to him; they gestured until he understood what their motions meant. This boy who could not speak also took a stick; he was a good shot. The boys departed; they went after the birds, hurling their sticks at them, moving to the side that the birds were on. When one flock of birds left the boys behind, another flock appeared behind them, flying toward them. Then that flock too moved to the other side. The boys went on, striking at the birds from morning until sunset. They kept moving on; they did not turn around.

When they came to a certain place, the younger boys, those who were small, were told to find firewood and to kindle a fire, "so that we can roast these birds and eat them." They had killed so many of the birds that they were weighed down by them. The boys relaxed here. A fire was built; the birds were roasted and eaten. Then they went to sleep.

They awakened in the morning. They awakened, and the birds were doing the same thing they had done the day before—appearing suddenly from this side, then flying to that side.

The boys said, "Let's get started again."

They traveled with those birds once more; the boys journeyed, striking the birds, crossing river after river, passing place after place, traveling through country after country, beating those birds. But the birds seemed endless. When one flock flew by, another took its place. The sun set again; the boys were still throwing their sticks at them.

They said, "Let's sleep. We'll roast some of these birds. Boys, gather firewood."

The words were addressed to some of the smaller boys who then gathered the firewood. The fire was kindled; the birds were roasted and eaten. Then the boys went to sleep.

They awakened in the morning. They awakened, and the birds were forming the same procession that day, too.

Again, it was said, "Let's take up the chase again."

They got more sticks. They walked on; they pulled sticks from trees and added them to their arsenal. New sticks were added as the other sticks were thrown at the birds. So they moved on with the birds.

When they were far off, the sun set. At dusk, a homestead was seen

Performers

glimmering a long distance away. They saw the fire, even though it was off in the distance.

"Let's go over there. To that homestead."

"It's getting tiresome, sleeping at night in the cold."

"Let's go and sleep in that homestead."

"Let's ask for a place to spend the night."

It was on that day that they first heard this boy speak—the one who did not know how to speak. In his first speech, Sikhuluma said, "No, Sitshalotshalwana, my little brother! Don't take the children to that homestead because no one sleeps there. That homestead is not to be entered. If we go there, the children will die."

Sitshalotshalwana stood up. As he stood, the boys said, "Yo! At last, the king has spoken!"

"My friends, has he been able to speak this well all this time that we thought he couldn't speak?"

"We did well to beat these birds. We finally heard him speak."

Sitshalotshalwana said, "Nonsense! Nonsense! What is he saying? He's telling us that we shouldn't sleep over there! He knows nothing! This is, after all, only the first time he's spoken. Now, suddenly, he's such an old man, a grown-up person! He's only beginning to speak! He doesn't know anything! He doesn't know the proper way to say things! Don't listen to him! Let's go!"

They did go. Sikhuluma was silent; he did not speak again. They walked on; they went to this homestead. They came to the homestead and found that no one was there. When they arrived, they found only some dishes, and all of the dishes contained food. These boys were twelve in number, and it turned out that there were also twelve dishes.

As they went in, Sitshalotshalwana said, "Do you realize that we almost didn't come here because of Sikhuluma—because of this Sikhuluma, who's just learning to speak, who talks about things he knows nothing about? Look! We've been provided for! We've been expected here! Look at our dishes; they're the same number as we are—twelve! Look! One, two, three, four, five, six, seven, eight, nine, ten, eleven, and twelve! Don't you see? Food has been cooked for us! Let's eat, my friends!" So said Sitshalotshalwana.

Sikhuluma spoke: "No, Friend, don't tell the children to eat that food! That food is not meant for us. It belongs to the owner of the house, and she'll arrive in her own time. I've already warned you that no one should sleep in this house. The children will die!"

The boys stood up and whistled, calling each other.

"The king has spoken well!"

"It's a good thing for us that the birds came along because we've at last heard him speak!"

Sitshalotshalwana said, "Don't be foolish! Sikhuluma doesn't know what he's talking about. He's talking nonsense again! How can he say that the food on these dishes is not meant to be eaten? These are clearly our dishes! Eat!" He said this, then took one of the dishes and ate.

The boys ate too because they respected Sitshalotshalwana, and also because it was only Sikhuluma who spoke against him. Since this was the first day that he had spoken, what could he know?

After they had finished eating, they slept. During the night, while they were sleeping, Sikhuluma just sat there. He was not sleeping.

The others, including Sitshalotshalwana, slept.

Then he heard someone coming into the house.

When this person had entered, she said, "Yo! Who's this? Who has eaten my food? All of it eaten! All twelve dishes!" Then she said, "Ah, but I've got a boon here! I'll begin with this one, then I'll go to this one, then this one, then this one, then this one, then this one, then this one, then this one, and I'll finish with this juicy child!"

Sikhuluma sat there all that time and listened. The boys were sleeping. Sikhuluma moved over to them and pinched one boy. He pulled him; he pushed him. The boy was startled.

That woman went outside; she went outside.

Sikhuluma spoke: "Get up! All of you!"

All the boys got up.

He said, "The thing that Sitshalotshalwana wanted to happen has happened. The owner of this house has come; she wants to know who has eaten her food, all twelve dishes. She said that she has got a treasure-trove: she said that she'll begin with this one, then go on to this one, then to this one, then this one. And she said that she'd finish with me! We must remain awake now; we mustn't sleep. We must stand up. Take your sticks, and let's go!"

The boys agreed.

They said, "We're thankful that you can speak!"

His little brother, Sitshalotshalwana, got up and said, "Nonsense! You always do this! Do you boys like what Sikhuluma has said? He knows nothing! He's just learning how to speak! He knows nothing! Who's this person who's supposed to have said these words? Only Sikhuluma saw her! He alone heard her speak! But we didn't see her! When this boy talks, he knows nothing. He just babbles."

The boys said, "No, let's go!"

"All right, if that's what you want."

The boys walked on then, and when they had been traveling for a time, they saw a broad road—a big white road—and a village with many homesteads. But they saw no living being. In all those homesteads, there was no one there—no dog, no ox, no sheep, nothing, only these houses.

One homestead did, however, appear to have someone in it. It was the homestead in the front, a white house. There was smoke in front of the house. It seemed that it was the only homestead with someone in it.

Sitshalotshalwana said, "Let's travel on this road. We'll pass by that homestead. We're thirsty now."

Sikhuluma spoke again: "No, Sitshalotshalwana, don't go on that road. It's dangerous. These children will all die if they travel on that road. There's some long thing there that has destroyed people. That's the reason there is no one in this village: they've been destroyed by the thing that lives over there in that house."

"We thank you, King!" the boys said. "You speak well. The things that you've said have all turned out to be so."

His little brother, Sitshalotshalwana, said, "Nonsense! Why are you thanking him? What does he know? He knows nothing! Travel on! Let's go!"

He said that, then went to that road. All the boys did the same, and Sikhuluma also traveled on that road.

They had been traveling for a short time when one of the boys died. He lay stark dead there on the road.

They walked on. No one spoke now. These boys seemed to understand that they would all die.

A short time after the death of that first boy, another died. They left him there; he lay stone dead.

They journeyed on; they continued their traveling. After a short time, another boy died.

They traveled on, and another boy died a short time later. Four of the boys were now dead.

Sitshalotshalwana was getting nervous. He seemed to understand that—well—his turn would also come. He too would die because it was clear that any person who stepped on this road would die, no matter who he was.

They moved on; they traveled for a short time, then the fifth boy died.

They pushed on, leaving him behind, exposed there on the road. They themselves were ignorant of where this road led; they did not know if the road led to their home because they were uncertain of the direction from which they had come. Those birds had made clear to the boys the location of their homes, but the birds were not there now, they were gone. The boys were traveling alone. They journeyed through other places. They traveled in darkness, not knowing the countryside. They did not know how to get back to their homes.

Again, they moved on, and the sixth boy died.

They walked on, and a little farther along, the seventh boy died.

They were far from that house now. It was clear that it had been that house alone that had contained a person. The village was huge, but nothing had come out of it; it was empty.

They moved on, and the eighth boy died.

They went on again for a short time, and the ninth boy died. They walked sorrowfully—the ninth boy had died, and they journeyed on.

Then the tenth boy died.

Only the two of them remained now, Sikhuluma and Sitshalotshalwana. Sikhuluma and his little brother remained.

They walked on. Then Sitshalotshalwana said, "Sikhuluma, I'm going to that homestead. I want to see this thing that's killing the people, that puts something in the road to make people die. It makes no difference if I die now."

Sikhuluma answered, "No, Son of my father, don't go over there. We're as good as dead; we shall die as all those children have died. It makes no difference now. We'll return alone. Let us die on this road. Don't go and bring that thing out of the house!"

He said, "You see, you're still speaking nonsense to me. You speak foolishness to me, even now that we're alone. I'm going there! You go on with your foolishness! I'm going. I want to see this thing." He said this and went over there.

He arrived at the house. He arrived.

The thing was sleeping in a room. When Sitshalotshalwana arrived, he saw this thing and also discovered a person there who had one arm and one leg. This person was a woman.

When he entered, she said, "Oh! What kind of person is this? Was there ever such a person in this country?"

Sitshalotshalwana said fiercely, "Give me some water! I'm thirsty!"

This person said, "Oh, worthy child, but why? I don't want to watch someone die! Well, go outside. I'll give you some water."

He said, "I won't go outside! Give me some water, I'm thirsty!"

She dipped some water. This woman gave it to him, and he drank it.

He said, "This thing that's sleeping here, is it the thing that destroys people? This thing that's sleeping here?"

He stabbed at it with a stick. The thing got up. It got up and broke his backbone. It broke his backbone in two, then it put him down. He died.

Sikhuluma knew that his brother was dead. He walked on. He did not go to that place to which Sitshalotshalwana had gone; instead, he walked on. When he was in the middle of nowhere, he turned from the road and took a footpath. He walked along that path, then became thirsty. He came to a river; he looked for water to drink but found none. As he leaned on his stick, he heard something below in the mud, saying "Sikhuluma! Sikhuluma, you're stabbing us with that stick! Walk on, there's water on the upper side."

He was surprised: "What was talking down there in the mud?" He had not seen anything. He pulled the stick from the mud. He carried it in his hand; he did not lean on it again. Sikhuluma went to the upper side and found water. He drank. When he had finished drinking, he stood up, then went on his way.

He was still walking when his dog suddenly appeared, the dog he had left behind at home. It suddenly appeared, wet and hungry. It trailed its tongue, panting. The dog came to Sikhuluma, wagging its tail at him. As it moved ahead, Sikhuluma followed. He knew that "If I'm going to find my home, I'll have to follow this dog. I don't know where the house is anymore." He walked behind his dog; he journeyed with that dog.

The sun set. He slept, tired. The dog slept at his side. At dawn, he trekked on with his dog. He walked and walked; he walked all day.

The sun set, and he slept. The dog slept at his side.

He traveled again at dawn, and then he saw that "This is my country! But I'm still far from home." He walked on. The dog traveled; Sikhuluma journeyed in his own land now, that was clear. This dog was leading him to his home.

Finally, he did arrive at his home. When he got there, he did not enter any house.

He cried.

While he was crying, his grandfather came to him and started to speak to him with gestures, remembering that Sikhuluma was unable to talk. He gestured, he gestured with his hands.

But Sikhuluma spoke: "Grandfather, all of those with whom I traveled have remained behind because of Sitshalotshalwana. Because of Sitshalotshalwana alone. He has remained behind also; he brought himself into the thick of it.[14] The others are no more. I alone have returned. You should call a meeting. The fathers of those children should come and hear the reason for the absence of their children."

Sikhuluma was quiet then; he did not speak again.

The people were asked to come.

Those who were the fathers of the children arrived.

Someone said, "Let the king speak."

Sikhuluma stood and explained, "On a certain day, we departed from home, pursuing flocks of birds. There were twelve of us. Those boys, all of them, are now no longer here. This includes my brother; he was the last one.

"At the beginning of the third day, we saw the glimmer of a homestead in the distance. Sitshalotshalwana said, 'Let's go!' It was on that day that I began to speak. I said that we should not go to that homestead. If we did go there, I warned, we would all die. The boys were happy. They said that it was a good thing that those birds had come along: they finally heard me

14. Literally, "He even brought himself into the skin."

speak. But Sitshalotshalwana stood up and said, 'Nonsense! You're a fool who has never spoken before, who doesn't know what you're talking about! Let's go!' They went on then, and I remained quiet. We were going to sleep in that homestead. When we got to that place, no one was there. Some dishes were there, twelve of them, matching our number. Sitshalotshalwana said that we should eat. I spoke up again, and said that we should not eat. 'This food belongs to a person who'll be coming along,' I said. The boys thanked me for my speech, but Sitshalotshalwana insisted that I continued to speak of something I knew nothing about. Didn't I see that these dishes belonged to a person who was expecting visitors? Those dishes were the same number as we. They went to sleep, but I didn't sleep at all that night. Then the owner of the house arrived. She said, 'Yo! Who has eaten the food that I prepared for myself? Who are these people? I'll start with this one, and then move to this one, then this one, then this one, and I'll finish with this little juicy one!' She was referring to me. I was awake, and I tried to awaken the boy who was next to me—I pinched him, dragged him, trying to rouse him. When he woke, I said that all the boys should get up. Then that woman, the one who had spoken, went out. I reported to the boys what I had seen. Sitshalotshalwana said that I was lying, that I was speaking of things that I knew nothing about, that I was even now speaking foolishness. 'There's no one here!' How could it be that a person was heard by me alone, while the rest of them slept? I urged that we move on. We should take our sticks and move on. He didn't agree. 'Let's stay. No one's going to move!' I said that we should go. And the boys said, 'Well, let's go!'

"We left then. We saw a road. I warned them that we should not travel on this road, that it was dangerous, that if we traveled on it the children would die. The boys thanked me, but that brother of mine said that I was delirious. 'Over there's a homestead! See the smoke?' He wanted to go to that house. We journeyed on that road then, and almost immediately after we had set foot on the road, one boy lay stone dead. He died there; we left him behind. And that is what continued to happen: dead boys formed a kind of procession, until we came to that homestead. When we neared that place, Sitshalotshalwana said that he was going over there. I said that he shouldn't go, but he insisted; he wanted to see this thing in this house, this thing that destroyed people. He went; I didn't go. When he got there, he asked for water. A certain person said that he should go outside. I was unable to hear their conversation. I did hear Sitshalotshalwana say, 'Give me some water! I'm not going out!' He drank, and when he finished drinking, he said, 'Is this the thing that destroys people?' He attacked it with his stick. The thing got up and broke his back in two; then it put him down.

"I traveled on then; I walked alone. Then I came to a river. When I jabbed at it with my stick, something below, in the mud, spoke and called me by name. It said, 'Sikhuluma! Sikhuluma, stop stabbing us! You're stabbing us with your stick! Go to the upper side; there's water on the upper side!' I pulled my stick up then and went to the upper side and indeed found water there. I drank the water, and, as I was getting up, I saw my dog coming toward me, wagging its tail at me. The dog was wet. It helped me to find my way home."

And that is what Sikhuluma said.

The weeping of women, the weeping of the mothers of the children could be heard. There was deep mourning for the children.

The men said, "Do not blame this on a single person. All the boys together were involved in this affair when they died. They died while completing their assignments, killing the birds. They did it on their own. No one pushed them into it; they pushed themselves. We're thankful that this child of the king has returned, that he was saved, so that we might know what happened to the others, so that we might know why they aren't here."

That is what the men said. Then the gathering was dispersed. That was the end of it.

II

After a brief time, Sikhuluma, the king, said, "I want to be circumcised. I want to be circumcised; I want to become a man."

"Well, all right, King."

The men were again assembled.

It was said, "The child of the great one wants to be circumcised."

"All right, but how shall it be done? The boys are not here now."

According to the custom of the Xhosa, the king is never circumcised alone. Because he is the son of a king, he must have supporters while he is in the circumcision lodge—one supporter stays on the lower side near the door, the other on the upper side, with the king between the two.

"Well, the additional boys will have to be selected from among the young boys." They would have to find the best of the younger boys to be Sikhuluma's supporters.

They assembled then; everyone was present. The people brought the boys out, so that "this child of mine might be circumcised. When my king is circumcised, he must not be left alone. He must have supporters. Even though the boy who is to be the supporter is very young, he'll do."

Finally, there were as many boys as there were fingers on the hand of the king; they were ten. And there were the two who were to be Sikhuluma's supporters.

They were circumcised. The king underwent the ritual and became an initiate. Oxen were slaughtered. The dried ox skins would be used in the circumcision lodge—the doorways of these lodges used to be closed with the skins of oxen.

There were wardens there who were boys. And there was one warden who was a girl; she was in charge of the food of the king, that king who was an initiate. She remained there at the lodge.

Time passed then; time passed for the initiate. Finally, it was said that the boys, now young men, must come out of the circumcision lodge.

That king spoke again. He spoke rarely, only when it was necessary that he say something. He spoke again: "I am not coming out of this circumcision lodge. I shall come out when I can put on a cloak made of the skin of a water monster. Otherwise, I am not coming out."

Someone asked, "What's that? What is this about a water monster?"

He said, "I'm speaking of a fabulous monster that lives in the river; it lives in the water. It must be drawn out from the depths, from the deep pools. I want it to be skinned, then tanned and made into a mantle for me. If I don't get the mantle, I'm not coming out, not under any circumstances!"

"But what can we do about that?"

"Who can go into those deep pools again and again to find this monster?"

"How can such a thing be?"

"Well," said Sikhuluma, "this is what you'll have to do: prepare some loaves of corn bread. Fill three baskets with loaves that have been baked, so that someone can go to these places and find the pool that contains a water monster."

"But who can do this?"

"When this water monster comes out, won't it eat people?"

"Isn't it dangerous?"

Sikhuluma said, "If it comes out, it will attack a person, chew him up, and swallow him. And then that person is gone! But I insist, I want that water monster! I want its mantle!"

"Yo! This is a difficult matter!"

"Let's consider this carefully, from the beginning. Let's ponder it."

He said, "I don't want any pondering from any beginning! I say that I want the water monster, and that is that!"

The other boys came out of the circumcision lodge on the following day.

"That's all right," said Sikhuluma. "I'll just remain here. Even if the house is burned down, I shall remain.[15] I shall never go home. Not until that mantle is here."

Someone said, "All right then."

15. The circumcision lodge was burned down following the emergence of the young men. The burning of the lodge was a part of the ritual, signifying among other things the break with the childhood past.

They dispersed; they all went home.

They went home; then the corn was crushed. The corn was crushed; the loaves of bread were made. The baskets were filled, three baskets filled with baked corn bread. Then Sikhuluma's sister, the warden who had stayed at the circumcision lodge cooking for him, took the baskets.

She said, "I shall go. I shall find the mantle for the son of my father, the cloak that he wants to come out with. I want this thing that devours people to eat me. It must begin with me! I am going. I shall take these loaves along with me." Those were the provisions for a traveler.

So it was that this child journeyed, carrying these loaves.

When they were far off, they saw a large river. They went to this massive river. They arrived there and threw a loaf of bread into the water.

They said, "Water monster! Water monster, come out and eat me!"

There was silence. They journeyed on, beyond this river.

Someone said, "It's not in this river."

They moved on for a long time, seeking another big river. Again, they found a huge river. They sought a deep pool in this river. When they found it, they again threw a loaf of corn bread into the water; they threw another loaf into the water.

When that loaf of corn bread had been thrown, someone said, "Water monster! Water monster, come out and eat me!"

There was no water monster there.

They passed beyond that river, traveling again for a long time. They were seeking yet another large river. Little rivers were crossed, rivers having small pools that did not seem to contain the creature they were seeking.

Finally, they came to another big river, and again they stood above a deep pool. They tossed a loaf of bread into the water.

They said, "Water monster! Water monster, come out and eat me!"

The water in that pool was in tumult; it stirred, then it roiled, the water churned—it was brown, then red, then green.

The girl said, "Run! All of you! Take this bread with you! Make sure that you can see me at all times! Don't let me out of your sight!"

These others fled; they departed. They ran, continually looking back, constantly watching her.

The water monster came out of the water. When it came out, the girl ran. The thing that came out—it was huge in a way that she had never seen before. It was not like a horse; it was huge. It was not like anything else; this thing was gigantic. Colossal. As big as this: if it entered a kraal where cattle stay, it would fill that kraal by itself. That is how big it was.

This child ran. The water monster ran after her. It did not move with great speed, but it went steadily, moving easily. She ran, she ran and ran.

When she was far from the water monster, she sat down and rested.

When it came near, she put a loaf of bread down on the ground; then she ran on again. The water monster stopped, chewed the bread, and swallowed it. Then it pursued her once more. But it did not run, it just walked.

Finally, she was a short distance from those men who were waiting for her.

When they saw what was happening, the men said, "Well, we won't stay here!"

"This thing's getting closer!"

"We're on our way, we must escape this thing!"

"You stay here with it yourself!"

"A thing so terrible!"

"A thing so big!"

"Yo yo yo!"

The men went on, leaving the child behind.

The child said, "You're leaving me behind, but would you please try to keep an eye on me? Please, when you're far off, watch me, so that you'll know if I've been devoured by this thing, so that you'll be able to report at home that—well, I've been eaten. Please don't let me out of your sight! Stay in a place where you can watch me."

The men agreed to do this. They hurried off; the child moved on. She waited for the water monster, and it approached. When it was a short distance away, she put a loaf of bread on the ground. Then she again went on her way. She left the water monster behind; she ran. The creature came to the loaf and chewed it. When it had finished, it took up its pursuit of her. She was again resting. When it was a short distance away, she put a loaf of bread on the ground. The loaves in her basket gradually diminished, until finally only one loaf remained. The beast came along and ate that loaf.

She ran; she hurried to these men. She replenished her supply of loaves; she poured loaves from their basket into hers. It was full again. Then the men hurried on—the thing frightened the men; they did not even want to see it. This monster was dreadful.

When the creature was near, the child again put a loaf of bread on the ground. She ran; she ran a distance, then sat down. The water monster came to the loaf and ate it. The child went on.

She came to the men and said, "Travel on now! Go home, tell them at home that they should borrow a gun. A gun should be sought, so that this thing can be shot. But no one should come near it! Shoot it from a distance! If they can get a number of guns, so much the better. We don't even know if a bullet can penetrate this thing."

The men hurried on, leaving that child behind. The girl moved on, leaving a loaf of bread on the ground. The water monster was a short distance away. She hurried on; she was not far from home.

When the men reached the homestead, they reported what the girl had asked them to say. The guns were borrowed, they were loaded, they became heavy. They were cocked. Most of the men were carrying guns now; those not carrying guns had spears.

Time passed, the sun set, and finally, a short distance from home, the girl appeared. The water monster came after her, that thing was approaching. She arrived at home; she hurried into the kraal.

She told the men to go into the houses. The water monster would enter the kraal because it wanted this girl.

"Go into the houses so that it won't see you! It will come into the kraal. When its back is turned to you and as it approaches me, come out with your weapons and go to work! I'll come out at the other end of the kraal."

The men heard. They went into the houses; all of them went into the houses. The girl arrived; the men saw her as she stood in the courtyard, just above the kraal. They were looking through some small holes, trying to see this thing.

When they saw this creature approach, the men cried out, the women cried out, the dogs howled, everything there at home fled. The dogs ran, they disappeared on the other side. Everything in this homestead ran— the cattle fled when they saw this thing coming. The water monster resembled nothing but itself, its like had never before been seen. The people in the houses shrieked. They were inside; they had closed the doors.

The water monster did not bother about those wailing people at all. It was face to face with this girl. It came up to her. She entered the kraal, and the creature also went in. When it had done so, the people came out, coming to assist the girl in the kraal. All of them came with their weapons. Twelve men began to shoot. They shot; they went through their ammunition. The thing stirred; it wanted to move on. Twelve other men came out, and they shot until their ammunition was also finished. It was clear that the water monster was wounded. It moved there on the ground, but it was unable to stand up so that it might escape. The men with spears threw them; those men were some distance away.

The water monster would never survive this. When it collapsed, the kraal was broken down; it was shattered. The men shot repeatedly, and then the thing was dead. It had been penetrated by the men.

When they felt certain that it was dead, they skinned that thing. When the skinning was completed, the cloaks were divided. The water monster provided three cloaks, the number that they had hoped for. The boy second in rank to the initiate would put on a mantle similar to his, and the companion on the other side would also wear a cloak resembling the king's. The three mantles were tanned by the men.

The flesh of that water monster was put outside, because they did not know if it was edible. They threw the flesh away, outside. It was a windfall for the dogs and pigs; they ate that meat all month. When the second month appeared, it was still not finished; it was being eaten by all the dogs of the village and by all the hogs of the village.

After a little while, when the cloaks had been tanned, the people went to Sikhuluma. A song associated with the initiates' coming out of the circumcision lodge was composed, a song about the emergence of the initiate. He was taken out then, covered with that mantle. The mantle was turned inside out because when the fur was on the outside it had such a fearsome appearance that nothing would approach it: everyone would run, they were afraid. It was therefore necessary that he wear it so that the fur side was next to his skin. That is how all three of them wore their mantles as they came to the homestead. They arrived and remained in the yard. They sat in the yard. A mat was placed there, and they sat on it. The newly initiated young man was admitted into manhood as the people presented him with gifts. All the people presented him with gifts, celebrating his transition to manhood. They acclaimed the king, they acclaimed the warden, they hailed the second warden, they extolled that one who was on the upper side. All of the twelve initiates had come here, and they were all admitted to manhood. Now it was necessary that they go to a house, that they remain in the house where something would be prepared for them to eat. They would anoint their bodies with red clay, according to the custom of the Xhosa.

III

When Sikhuluma emerged from the circumcision lodge, he spoke: "I am not going into the house. The others can go in, but I am not entering the house. I shall stay out here; I shall not go into the house. I shall go in only when I have a wife."

"What is it now?"

"Has there ever been such a thing? A person who refuses to go into the house?"

"A person who will enter only when he has a wife?"

But Sikhuluma sat there, refusing to eat. He would remain there, he would not go into the house.

He did not speak again: he would speak just one thing, then he would not speak again. He would speak again on the day that he next spoke.

"What'll we do?"

"What is this, Friends? Now he won't even answer us!"

"When he speaks, he speaks!"

He did not speak again.

"Yo! This is difficult!"

It was proper that those young men entering manhood should go to the house, and the others did so. They arrived; they were anointed with red clay. Food was dished up for them, and they ate. All the things of young manhood were done for them. Songs were sung for them; they were also taught songs sung at a men's party, dancing songs.

Sikhuluma sat in the kraal.

Food was brought for him in the kraal, but Sikhuluma said, "I am not eating. I told you that I shall eat when I have a wife. I want a wife. I want one of Mangangedolo's daughters as my wife."[16]

Someone said, "A wife from Mangangedolo's place?"

"How can anyone want to go there?"

"Men who seek brides at Mangangedolo's place are finished!"

"The bridegroom who goes there does not return!"

Sikhuluma did not speak again. He would speak in his own time. He slept here, not eating.

At dawn, the men were called.

It was said, "He says that he wants a wife. The people must go with him as always. They must go and ask for that daughter at Mangangedolo's place."

"This is only the latest of unusual happenings here at home. Now, this child wants a daughter of Mangangedolo's place!"

The men said, "When he says something, that is what must be."

"No one will forsake his king!"

"Those boys who died didn't die because of anything he did. In fact, he was warning them."

"They died because they disregarded his words."

"Well, we shall not disregard his words. We'll bring out our young men. They'll go along with him to look for a wife wherever he sees fit."

Five young men were brought out then; Sikhuluma was the sixth. The supporters also accompanied them, so that they were eight in all.

They traveled then, going to Mangangedolo's place.

Along the way, they met a mouse. The mouse crossed the road; then, when it had crossed, it returned to the other side. It stopped there on the road and said, "Sikhuluma!"

He said, "Hmm?"

"Child of the king, slaughter me. Put my skin in your sack and travel with it. I'll advise you when you get to your destination. You can hide my flesh here in this tuft of grass."

Sikhuluma said, "I shall put you into my bag, as you have instructed. But do you know where we're going?"

"You're going to ask for a daughter of Mangangedolo's place. Now then,

16. The name "Mangangedolo" means "as big as the knee." This dangerous wizard kept his magical concoctions in his knee, which was therefore very big.

let me point out Mangangedolo's place to you. Do you see that hill in the distance there? On the upper side of the homestead?"

He said, "Yes."

"Those are heads over there. The heads of people who have come to ask for Mangangedolo's daughter! Your head could also be thrown onto that hill! But if you put me into your bag, I'll tell you what to do when you get there."

Sikhuluma was quiet. He took a knife, killed the mouse, and skinned it. He skinned it, then took its flesh and hid it in the grass. He took the mouse's skin and put it into the bag. Then he went on his way; he walked on.

As they approached the homestead, the mouse said, "Sikhuluma, consider this. You'll be escorted to a beautiful house over there, a very attractive house. Don't agree to enter that house! Say 'We don't stay in such a beautiful house.' Tell them that you want to stay in a house in which calves are tethered, a house where the fowl sleep.

"They'll bring a new sleeping mat to you. Say that you don't use such mats. Tell them that you want an old mat—the mat of a young mother, a mat that's in tatters.

"Then food will be brought to you on new plates, with new utensils. Say that you won't eat food on such plates. Say that you eat on leaky dishes; you don't want new ones.

"Now, during the time that you're over there, do not walk on mole hills, walk on the grass instead. Never walk in a place where there is no grass.

"They'll tell you over there that the bridegroom's party should assemble at the cattle kraal. Enter through the gate of the kraal, but when you're ready to come out, come out on the other side. Don't come out through the gate.

"Also, when someone over there says 'Hello' to you, say, 'Mmhmmmm.' Don't say, 'Yes,' say 'Mmhmmm.'"

"All right."

"Now put me in the bag."

Sikhuluma put that mouse into the bag, and he traveled on. He walked a great distance. When he arrived at that homestead over there, he walked on the grassy areas; he walked on the grass.

He arrived. He sat in the yard at the place where the bridegroom's party stays. The thumping steps of the owner of the homestead could be heard. Mangangedolo arrived. His knee was huge. He arrived, stomping on the ground; he stomped and stomped.

He said, "Hello, Party of the bridegroom."

They said, "Mmhmmm."

"I say, 'Hello, Party of the bridegroom!'"

"Mmhmmm."

"What is this? Don't you know how to say 'Yes'?"

They said nothing; they were silent.

He said, "I greet you! Hello—especially you, Bridegroom!"

He said, "Mmhmmm."

Mangangedolo said, "Ah, this is a unique groom's party." He was quiet then. He chatted with them, asking, "Where have you come from?"

Sikhuluma explained, "I come from my home. I have come here to seek a wife."

He said, "Select for yourself from among the daughters of my home. There are many. Let them come and greet the groom's party."

The daughters were called. They came to greet the groom's party. Sikhuluma selected a wife for himself.

He said, "It's that one. There is my wife!"

Mangangedolo laughed. He said, "Ha ha! I've never heard such a forthright groom! Well, I see how it is with you, Husband. We'll meet again; we'll see each other again! Now, please tell me, on what basis are you claiming her?"

He said, "I do so with cattle. Just tell me the number you want as far as this daughter is concerned."

He said, "Do you have eighty head of cattle that you can bring here for my daughter's dowry?"

Sikhuluma said, "Even above that number! Ask whatever number of cattle you please for your daughter."

He said, "All right then, I want those eighty."

He said, "They're as good as here."

That fellow said then, "Go, Women, make arrangements for the groom's party."

They went; the young women left the groom's party.

That daughter rose and grasped her groom's hand. Sikhuluma took her hand; he took her hand, not certain that he should do so—wary, not sure if this might be the cause of his death. But he took her hand anyway. Then the young woman departed.

Those young women went and prepared a house for the bridegroom. The house in which the women would sleep was beautiful. That is where the groom's party was taken. Someone told the spokesman to bring the groom's party along, and he did so, bringing the group to that house.

When Sikhuluma appeared in the doorway, he said, "No! I'm not entering this house!"

"Why not?"

"Why won't you enter this house?"

"Are you staying outside?"

"What kind of bridegroom are you?"

He said, "No, I have never stayed in such a house. The houses at my home have pillars supporting the roof. And the houses at my home are made of mud. They have pillars; they are thatched with grass. We sleep on the floor with the calves and the fowl. Take me to the house in which the calves and fowl sleep."

They said, "Yo yo yo!"

"Never have we seen such a bridegroom!"

"This is an extraordinary groom."

He was quiet; he did not speak again. He was taken to a dirty house. It had manure in it; there were fleas and bedbugs in it. The calves were sleeping there, the fowl were sleeping there, hogs were coming in.

A bed mat was brought; it was new. They said that they were making the bridegroom's bed.

He said, "No, I'm not sleeping in a bed like this. I want an old mat, a young mother's mat, a tattered mat. At my home, they do not put down a mat like this. I'll not sleep on such a mat!"

"He's doing it again!"

"Really, this groom is unusual!"

"We're accustomed to groom's parties here at home, but we've never seen anything like this one!"

A tattered bed mat was brought; it was put down for him. He sat. They sat on it. They turned their mantles inside out, they turned them inside out; they turned them so that the fur was on the inside, the fur of the mantles was next to their skin—they did not wear them with the fur on the outside.

"Never have we seen such a groom's party!"

"We could see at once that they were strange—they were wearing long skin skirts!"[17]

Sikhuluma sat, and food was brought on new dishes with fine new spoons. The food was put down there, and he said, "No, go away with this food of yours. We don't eat from such fine dishes; we fear them. We eat from dirty dishes, leaky ones, and we eat with dirty spoons. We don't know these things; we won't eat with such things."

"Heeee! Never have we seen such a groom's party!"

"This is strange."

"What kind of groom is this?"

They went away muttering. "This is really a marvel!"

"Today, my father has come face to face with something unique!"

"Something that's really weird here in our homestead!"

"Take it! Here's the food!"

17. Women wear long skin skirts. This is meant as an insult. The men are actually wearing cloaks. But the members of the groom's party will turn the insult to their own advantage later, when they insist that they wear the young women's modesty aprons.

"The groom's party doesn't want this food."

"They say they want leaky dishes over there!"

"Yo!"

That is the way the groom's party became a wonder to the people in this homestead.

Leaky dishes were obtained, and the food was dished out. Dirty spoons were brought. Sikhuluma ate. From the time that he had come out of the circumcision lodge, this was the first time that he had eaten. He ate, he ate, and when Sikhuluma had finished eating, the members of the groom's party were told that they were wanted at the cattle kraal.

He said, "All right, I have heard."

He went there; he went to the kraal. They entered the kraal through the gate. They arrived and sat.

Mangangedolo turned to Sikhuluma and said, "Now, let's discuss our business. Because we were alone when we spoke earlier, repeat in the presence of these men what you told me earlier."

That groom answered, "Yes, all right, Father. I repeat that eighty head of cattle is satisfactory to me. I want your daughter to come to my home and kindle a fire."

Well then, his words were heard.

"All right, you may go into the house."

A trap had been set at the entrance to the kraal, so that when the members of the groom's party went out, they would die there at the gate. Sikhuluma got up. He went to the other end of the kraal; he went out at that end.

Someone said, "Oh! Why don't you go out at the other end?"

He said, "This is the way we do it at home. We do not enter through the gate, then go out again through the same gate. We enter through the gate, then go out at the other end."

Someone said, "Yo! This is really a unique groom's party!"

"It's a wonder!"

"This thing's really strange!"

So it was that Mangangedolo's medicine did not work in the gateway.

Time passed. That night, they went to sleep.

The mouse said, "Sikhuluma! Take me out of the bag. Hang me over there, above the door, so that I can maintain a lookout for you. While you sleep, this is going to happen: the young women will come here, to sleep with you. Each man will sleep with a woman. This is what you must do: all of the men should take the women's modesty aprons and put them on. The men should say that they are borrowing the aprons from the young women, that it is their custom. You and your wife should remain idle. Do nothing. In case I should happen to fall asleep, just turn your mantle over, this cloak of yours, so that the fur is on the outside."

"All right."

In the night, the young women came in. When they had entered, each woman went to bed with her appropriate young man. All the young women did that, and the bride went to sleep with her groom, Sikhuluma.

A member of the groom's party said, "Women, we have a custom. We usually have a marshal. Do you know what a marshal is?"

The young women said, "No, we don't know."

"What's a marshal?"

"A marshal is a man who arranges things. He orders people about; he prepares the young women. He takes the women's aprons and puts them on the members of the groom's party." He said, "Now, one of us will play the role of the marshal."

So one of the members of the groom's party became the marshal.

The young women agreed to the arrangement, but they said, "Yo! This is really strange!"

"Never have we been in such a situation!"

"We're used to having bridegroom's parties here, but we've never seen a groom's party that takes women's aprons and wears them!"

"A wonder!"

"You're a peculiar groom's party!"

"This groom may be handsome, but he should be rejected by this woman!"

"He's made up for his strange ways because he's so handsome."

"But these habits of his!"

"No, no! We just don't understand them!"

The women unfastened their aprons, they gave them to the members of the groom's party. Then time passed for this groom's party. Sikhuluma and his wife did nothing. They slept—they chatted, then they slept.

While they were asleep, Mangangedolo came along with the weapon which he used to destroy people: a huge knife with which he cut off the heads of the members of grooms' parties. He stepped heavily; he stood at the door of the house of the groom's party.

The mouse said, "Return! Return, Mangangedolo, return with that magic! Return with it!"

"Oh!" Mangangedolo ran! He stomped as he fled; he stomped, he stomped, he stomped. He arrived at his house and said, "Mmhmmmm! Do you know that they're awake over there in that house? Someone said, 'Return with it, Mangangedolo. Return with that magic!' We'll have to try something to make them sleep!"

They worked with their magic to put them to sleep over there, to put them to sleep. They worked with the magic; they worked with it.

"You go this time, my wife."

Well, his wife went. She threw her breasts over her shoulders and walked with a swaying gait. She arrived and stood in the doorway.

Before she could enter, the mouse said, "Return with it, Wife of Mangangedolo! Return with that magic, return with it!"

"Yo!" She ran! "Oh! oh! oh! Do you know that they're not asleep in that house? Someone said, 'Return with that magic, Wife of Mangangedolo!' "

The man said, "I told you so. They're awake in that house. These are strange people. It'll soon be dawn, and they're still awake!"

"Mm."

They decided that the dog should go over there this time. There was a big dog in this homestead, and hanging from this dog were concoctions and bottles and capsules—all sorts of things.

"Please go, my dog. Go now. If they escape from this dog, they're beyond us."

This shaggy dog went then; it arrived and stood in the doorway.

It barked, "Nhu nhu!" It leapt there at the door.

The mouse said, "Return with it, Dog of Mangangedolo! Return with that magic! Return with it!"

When the groom saw that this dog was going to enter the house by force, he turned his mantle around. He knew that there was nothing that the skin of a mouse could do to this dog. He turned his mantle so that the fur was on the outside. He was lying at the extreme end of the house, the others were on the upper side.

The dog barked, "Nhu!" It barked, "Nhu!" It leapt and charged at Sikhuluma, but the mantle of the water monster immediately began to maul the dog. It pummeled the dog, it ripped into this dog, it tore the dog to shreds, to shreds! To shreds! It tore the dog up—all all all of it! Even the legs! It lacerated the dog. Then it took the dog and put it in front of Mangangedolo's house. The mantle returned to Sikhuluma, shook itself, then covered its owner once more.

They slept.

In the morning, the young women awakened. They awakened, took their aprons, and went out. And they saw a real wonder in their homestead, a marvel having to do with the dog.

"What could have dismembered it like this?"

"Did you see the dog come to that house?"

The young women said, "It didn't go there!" The women had been asleep; they did not see it. It must have entered the house while they were asleep.

"This dog didn't go there!"

"Why was it ripped up?"

"We were just sitting! When our father went to that house, we were still awake. We heard our father!"

"The groom's party was asleep then, but we were awake!"

"But this dog! It didn't go to that house!"

"Well, this is a mystery!"

"What kind of groom's party is this?"

"Well, we must try something else now."

"Don't bother them; let them sleep."

In the morning, the cattle kraal was about to be opened for the cattle.

A member of the Mangangedolo's home said, "We've come to visit the groom's party."

"We've brought them food, so they can eat."

"Now the members of the groom's party must go out with the cattle, they must herd the cattle."

"They must herd the cattle. That is the custom in this home."

Sikhuluma said, "All right, we want to follow your customs."

"Yes."

The food was brought to them, on leaky dishes. They ate the food; they finished.

Someone said that they should move on, so they went to the kraal to take the cattle out. A trap was sprung. A trap was sprung; it was sprung on the lower side as the groom's party entered the gate. Previously, they had refused to come out through the gate. They insisted that they come out at the lower end of the kraal. So this time a trap was laid there at the lower end.

It was said, "Go into the kraal and bring the cattle out."

The groom's party entered the cattle kraal; then they brought the cattle out through the gate. When they had driven the cattle out through the gate, they also came out through the gate—on the upper side of the kraal. They did not go out on the lower side.

"Why have you come out through another place?"

"You said that you come out on the lower end."

Sikhuluma said, "We go by our customs, you go by yours. We do it this way at home."

"Yo! This groom's party is an odd one!"

"It is a wonder!"

"Travel on, herd those cattle."

Far from this homestead was a plateau.

Someone said, "Go and herd the cattle over there on that plateau."

They traveled with those cattle. They went to herd them on the plateau. Sikhuluma had his bag with him on that plateau, the skin of the mouse was with him.

The mouse said, "Sikhuluma! You're as good as dead!"

"What must we do?"

"Do you see that cow over there? The one with the big udder?"

He said, "Yes."

"Go over there. Get under that cow! All of you! All of you, all eight of you must get over there under that cow. Grab its legs. Some of you seize its tail. The others, grasp the neck. Keep it stationary. A cloud is going to appear suddenly; this cloud will thunder. That thundering will be sent by Mangangedolo. Because you triumphed over him at his home, he wants to destroy you by lightning. He wants you to be killed out here. The cloud will pass by. When it passes, you'll see some women approaching with bags. They'll want to pick up your heads."

"All right."

The cloud suddenly appeared. When the cloud had appeared, the members of the groom's party grasped that cow. They seized that cow over there. All of them. Some grabbed it by the neck, others seized its horns, others grasped it by the legs, others clung to the tail; they went beneath it. They also clutched the cow by the udder. The cow stood, and they remained there.

Then it thundered; there was a mighty thundering. The sound was engulfing, unsurpassed in volume. Other cattle were struck by the lightning.

The storm passed over. The sun came out and shone brightly. When the sun had come out, some women suddenly appeared, carrying bags.

When they got there, they said, "Heeeeeee!"

"Mmhmmmmmm!"

"Such a rain!"

"Sheeeeeee! Didn't it reach you?"

"Such a great storm!"

"Ehee! You're safe!"

Sikhuluma said, "If you think that you've come here to take the heads from me, you're wrong! You'll have to take manure, you'll not be taking any heads from me!"

"Well now, what is this groom saying?"

"We've just come to gather manure, that's all."

So they said, and the women gathered manure. The groom's party went on its way, taking those cattle back to the homestead.

Yeeeeee, when the groom's party had returned, Mangangedolo said, "Well, I'm giving you your wife. Now you can travel on out of here."

He brought that wife out. When he had done so, he told her to go along with her groom's party.

Sikhuluma, the king, said, "Well, that's fine. That's all I wanted anyway. All the time that I've been here at this homestead, that's all I wanted."

"Mmmm!"

They traveled then, the wife with this groom and the party. The young women of the bride's home accompanied them, showing the groom's party the way.

After a time, they turned around: "Well, In-laws, we're going back."

"All right."

The young women turned around; the members of the groom's party traveled on with this wife of theirs.

After a time, Sikhuluma stepped on a place that had soil, even though he had been warned by the mouse that he should never tread on earth, that he should always walk on a place that had grass. If he walked on earth, he had been warned, the result would be disastrous.

Mangangedolo traveled. He went after them, seeking the groom's footprint. Finally, he found it; he came upon it by surprise at that place over there where Sikhuluma had happened to set his foot.

He said, "Yo! Thank you! I've found his footprint!"

Mangangedolo took it up, he took that footprint from the earth there. He went home where he worked his magic. He worked on this groom with his magic. He spread the earth out; he spread the footprint out.

As Mangangedolo was carrying on in that way, the groom said, "I'm hurt."

The mouse said, "Yes, you're hurt. You stepped on earth! You forgot what I told you, so you're hurt. If there's anything I can do nothing about, it has just happened. This is it. What can I possibly do about this?"

Sikhuluma said, "No, I'm the one who forgot."

The mouse felt very bad about this matter. It had helped Sikhuluma so much, and now, this close to home, he is about to die.

Sikhuluma went to that place where he had hidden the mouse's flesh. He took it and put it into the skin of the mouse.

The mouse arose and said, "Well, Sikhuluma, now, you're dying."

Sikhuluma said, "Yes."

The mouse went on its way.

As they traveled on, Sikhuluma said, "My body feels run down."

"What did you say, King?"

"My body is run down."

"How is it run down?" his wife asked. "How is it run down?"

"My body is run down; I'm weighed down by the mantle."

His mantle dropped to the ground.

He said, "Pick it up, pick it up, old friend."

A member of the groom's party picked it up and carried it. They walked on.

He said, "My head is in pain."

"What did you say, King?"

"I said, 'My head is in pain.'"

His stick dropped.

"Pick it up, pick it up, old friend."

Another member of the party picked it up and carried it. They traveled on.

He said, "My back is in pain, my legs hurt, my feet are aching."

His penis cover fell to the ground.

"Pick it up, pick it up, old friend."

Another picked it up and carried it.

He said, "I'm thirsty."

He was obviously giddy, feeling faint. He walked on.

"There's a pool up ahead."

He went to that pool; he went to the pool and drank. He drank and drank, then disappeared. He disappeared completely; he was not seen.

They considered the possibility of going into the water to bring him out, even if he was dead. But they did not see him. They saw some horned elands emerging from the pool.

The groom's party traveled on. His wife walked on too, crying for her dead husband.

She said, "Yo! I don't want this! I don't want to go home!" She sat down and said, "Let's just sit down. I'll try to do some of my father's tricks. I know them. The things he does, he does in our presence. We children know all about his activities. Heeee!"

The bride took out a bottle from her bag; she opened it. She lit a fire, then heated the concoction. She threw it into the pool; when it was hot she threw it into this pool.

The elands came out; they came out. She seized one of the elands and said, "Gather some firewood. We'll roast this eland. This eland—here's the king, in this eland! He's here, in the stomach of this eland."

"Oh really? Is that true?"

She said, "Yes, here is the king. Inside this eland."

They kindled a fire. All of these people grieved here, but they wept inside because they were men. They kindled a huge fire. Then they cut the eland's neck; they skinned it.

And the king emerged. He emerged alive. He was sick; he was not well.

She said, "Roast this eland and eat it."

It was roasted; it was eaten here by all of them. They ate it. The wife and her groom did not eat it, however.

When all that had taken place, she took an ember from the fire. Then she opened another bottle. She blew on it and said, "Go, Spirit! Go and scatter that earth. There it is, the earth of the king's footprint. It has been spread out by my father near the cattle kraal. When you arrive over there, become a whirlwind!"

The spirit traveled then. It was not visible; there was no wind. When it arrived over there at the side of the kraal, it became a whirlwind. It went off with the earth that Mangangedolo had spread out on a patch of cloth. It flew off with it, then scattered it and threw it away—far off, along with that patch of cloth.

In the house, Mangangedolo said, "Yo! Hasn't that wind passed by yet? Hasn't it caused me some damage?"

He stepped heavily and went to the side of the kraal. When he got there, he could no longer find the patch of cloth or the earth.

He said, "Yo! Satan is alive. He's active wherever he is!"

Sikhuluma, the king, was now well; he was as he had been before. Now he went home with his wife. When he got to his home, he sat outside by the cattle kraal. He said that his wife should sit at the side of the house; she should not enter the house. As for the rest of the people, they should go into the house. His second in rank would stay with him outside by the kraal; both of the seconds would remain with him.

The others went into the house and said, "The king is outside."

They went out and asked, "King, when will you come into the house?"

He said, "I am not entering the house until I have my own house! I shall go into my own house, I cannot enter any other house!"

"Oh, King! That house—When must you have the house?"

"Your house is being built as quickly as possible! But it takes a long time to build a house."

"It takes days, months to build a house!"

He said, "My house will not take months to build. The house must be built! Then I'll go in. Speak to this wife of mine. Ask her what sort of house she wants."

They went to his wife who was at the side of the house. "Woman, please tell us what sort of house you want—how big you want it to be, where you want it to be."

The bride answered, "Well, Father, I want the house to be on the upper side of the sheepfold. And I want it to be big, because it's going to house a family, and because you too may stay in it when you wish. I shall build the house myself, the way I like it."

"All right then. When will you build it?"

She said, "All I need is permission; then I shall build it."

It was said, "All right then, build."

The bride opened her magical kit. She took something out that was not seen by the other people. She put it down.

She said to them, "Move over there."

The people went to that place that she indicated. Then she put the thing down over there. She said that all the people should look to one side. The people looked to one side, in the opposite direction. When the time came for them to look back, they saw a house that had six doors. It was a wonder.

Then she said, "Let us go into the house."

They entered the house. In that house, every kind of bedding could be found. Everything necessary for making a bed was there. There were things to sit on, things for standing, things for sleeping, things for clothing, things for eating, things for washing.

"Well, we've seen the house."

She said, "Tell the king that he can come into the house. His house is ready now."

They went and told the king. He got up from the side of the kraal, with those people on either side of him. He went into the house.

So it was that he sat as a king. When it was dawn, he was given his cloak; the mantle of kingship was transferred to Sikhuluma from his father, who was then pensioned. His son became the ruler.

In the morning, a huge meeting was held, and the authority was officially transferred to his son. This son was the king; he took charge.

And they all lived in happiness.

Tale 13

THE BOY WHO DID NOT WANT HIS SISTER TO MARRY

Masithathu Zenani's Analysis: In this tale, the storyteller weaves a complex kinship web. Vel'ekhaya, whose name suggests that he was born at his mother's home of birth rather than her home of marriage, is the son of his classificatory sister. This story is a working out of that relationship, to avoid the scourge of incest.

The pattern describes a slow progressive movement to a solution. Vel'ekhaya's eloquence convinces others, and it is his rhetorical grace that reveals his manhood, much as Sikhuluma's brilliant oratory in the preceding tale is a visible manifestation of his manhood. This is underscored by the storyteller in this narrative, as she has Vel'ekhaya undergo his puberty ritual, at the urging of his mother. He has demonstrated his readiness to take on an adult role in his society.

Apart from the immersion in the complexities of kinship relations, the story is a realistic version of the puberty ritual. Instead of a fantastic ordeal, this youth's ordeal is his elocutionary struggle against the adults in his society. When he shows his intellectual depth, he is accepted as a man, and the literally rendered puberty ritual at the end of the tale is simply an acknowledgement of his achievement. The lengthy and arduous study of Vel'ekhaya's relationship with his mother also emphasizes, albeit in a realistic rather than fantastic way, the question of identity that is so crucial in tales treating the puberty rite. The establishment of his legitimacy, his lineage, is of immense significance in the puberty ritual because it goes to the heart of the question, Who am I? a crucial part of the movement to adulthood.

Performance Note

Time: 18 September 1967, about 1:30 P.M. *Place:* In a home in Nkanga, Gatyana District, the Transkei. *Audience:* About thirty men, women, and children. (Perf. 684.)

There were a woman and a man. That woman gave birth to two children, a girl and a boy. The girl was older than the boy; the boy was the younger of the two. The girl grew up then; both of them grew up.

The girl gave birth here at the home of her birth. She gave birth and was not married. She bore a child who was a boy. This child was named Vel'-ekhaya.[18] This Vel'ekhaya was regarded as the child of the father of that girl.

---

18. The literal meaning of "Vel'ekhaya" is "He appeared at home," that is, he was born at the home of his mother's birth, rather than at her home of marriage. His mother was unmarried when he was born.

251

"No, Father, I don't want my sister to marry." Determination, uncertainty, and respect are revealed in the combination of words, body, and facial expression.

Time passed for them, then. Much time passed.

The young woman was sought after by some suitors. But this child, Vel'ekhaya, who was older now, had something he wanted to say about this matter of the young woman's suitors.

He said, "My sister [that is, his mother] cannot marry, because I am here! My sister must remain here at home."

The girl's father said, "Vel'ekhaya, how can you say that your sister should not get married because of your presence here? Remember that this sister of yours is my daughter. It is proper that she marry, so that I can get something [that is, a dowry] on her account. I have got nothing from you, Vel'ekhaya!"

Vel'ekhaya said, "No, Father, I don't want my sister to marry. When I was born, you said that I am your child. But if you wanted my sister to marry, you should not have said that I am your child. You should have said that I am the child of my sister."

His father said, "Vel'ekhaya, how can you insist that I say that you are my child, when by so doing I'm throwing away that child of mine? How can you place me into a situation in which one of my children is not my child?"

Vel'ekhaya said, "Listen, Father. What you're saying is contradictory. It cannot be. My sister gives birth to a child—me, Vel'ekhaya. Then you say that I'm your child. Yet my sister still has a chance to get married. I tell you, Father, my sister cannot marry! There's only one thing she can do: she must remain here at home with you and me."

Vel'ekhaya's grandfather said, "Vel'ekhaya, whose child is this sister of yours?"

Vel'ekhaya said, "She's your child, Grandfather."

"And you, Vel'ekhaya, whose child are you?"

"I'm your child too, Father."

"How is it, Vel'ekhaya, that you don't agree that I should give your sister in marriage?"

"It's like this, Grandfather. My sister was unmarried when she gave birth to me. She bore me at her home of birth. Now, what does my name mean? It's the reason you gave me a name like that to begin with. You gave me a name that reflected my situation at birth: your daughter had a child while she was unmarried. Grandfather, you yourself said that I am Vel'ekhaya."

"Yes, my child, I did say that you are Vel'ekhaya," said his grandfather.

"Then, Grandfather, why do you ask me what I mean when I insist that my sister should not marry? Why do you object to that?"

"Well, Vel'ekhaya, here's the reason for my objection. Simply because you were named Vel'ekhaya does not justify your conclusion that my daughter should not get married. I had meant that you were born at home, my daughter not having been married at the time. And so I said that your name is Vel'ekhaya. But now you're arguing that your sister cannot marry, and that argument I cannot accept, Child of my daughter."

Then Vel'ekhaya said, "No, Grandfather, I didn't know that you would ever agree that my sister should marry. I say that she shouldn't marry because I'm here—I, Vel'ekhaya. I didn't think that she would ever marry. I thought that she would remain here without getting married. But go on, marry my sister off, Father. You marry her off. But you should also know that I have a cause for complaint. The women who are here, even though they're mothers, cannot be like my sister in their responsibilities for looking after me. They'll regard me as the child of an unmarried woman. Only you, Grandfather, pretend that I'm a child who's not the child of an unmarried woman. Only you accept that."

Vel'ekhaya's grandfather said, "Well then, Vel'ekhaya, your sister will marry. And, because you were borne by her when she was not married, you are my child. Your sister got hurt [a euphemism for pregnancy] here at home. My child, listen to what I am saying. I am telling you that you were named Vel'ekhaya because your sister became pregnant here at home without being married. She bore you while she was in an unmarried state. You came into the world when she was unmarried. Now you are my child because today she has a chance to get married; she is being courted."

"Oh," said Vel'ekhaya. "All right then, Grandfather, but this might just be the cause in the future for something unfortunate. My sister, having become married, may be bothered by her conscience because she gave birth to a man-child before she left home to become someone's wife. Over there at her house of marriage, she might bear other man-children. Or she might not be treated properly by those people. Then she'll begin to think of me, her first-born child here at the home of her birth. Even though I am not your child, she has the memory of her first pregnancy. I agree then, Grandfather. Marry her off."

Time passed. During the days that followed, this person considered what had been said by Vel'ekhaya, the child of his daughter.

He thought about that for a while, then said, "Well, really, I must call the neighbors [the extended family, clansmen]. They must help me to consider the words that have been spoken by this child. It sometimes happens that what a child says turns out to be true—when we have already forgotten it."

He called his clansmen. They filled his homestead. He called all of them, including his father's brothers, people from his mother's parents' place, the old man himself, and also people from his home: the totality of the extended family. The invitation knew no limits; it crossed the river. Everyone was brought; all were summoned. They were told the day that they should arrive at this home.

On the appointed day, they came to the homestead. When they had arrived, he said, "You're not all here yet. I want everyone to be here. This child spoke threateningly to me. He said things to me that I don't know. I don't want to have a confrontation with this child by myself. I want you to hear for yourselves what this child says to me. But there's still someone who's not here, someone who is very close to us—the son of my eldest brother. I want him to be here too. He'll arrive next week."

That fellow did arrive during the following week. His name was Qhusheka [the name means to hide or conceal]. When he arrived, he said, "Now what's the problem here at home? I had to leave my own duties to come here, and my duties are very pressing right now. The activities in which we involve ourselves require that we remain close to home. But I'm here now. Please go on, so that I can get back to my own business."

When he had spoken, someone else said, "Vel'ekhaya! Come outside, my child."

Vel'ekhaya came outside, and a little time passed as he approached them. He stood there at the side of the fence, and he said nothing. He just stood there, silent. He was silent, and the men waited on each other to speak first. They were puzzled. They did not know how to begin to talk to Vel'ekhaya. But Vel'ekhaya did not speak either; he too was silent.

After a very long time, one of the men said, "Why are we waiting so long? The boy is here, yet we say nothing!"

Then the father got up and said, "I don't know. I thought that when this boy came out, he would say what is on his mind."

Another man said, "Was he to speak first?"

"Does he know what he should say?"

Another man was getting up, but Vel'ekhaya, at the side of the fence, broke his silence: "Wait, Fathers! Please wait. Wait for me, Fathers, even if I am young. You must all be familiar with the subject of this assembly. Why must I speak further? I am arguing that my sister should not be married off. I have told my grandfather, 'Grandfather, why are you marrying my sister off? She's already given birth to me!' But my grandfather disputes this. He insists that I'm a child of this homestead. The reason I am opposed to my sister's marriage is because I am a child who is a man. Now it might happen that, after she marries, she will again give birth, perhaps bearing male children again. That might be the occasion for trouble for me in this house [inheritance problems, for example, might result]. And I don't want any trouble with my grandfather. Nor do I wish that my sister be troubled. She gave birth to me; I don't want her to be troubled. I have never been against her marrying. I have simply tried to make certain that they understand what they are doing. Do they know into what homestead she'll marry? Do they know what kind of child she will bear? But I can see that this is not what this meeting is concerned with. The meeting has come to a standstill. They have made me the first speaker. They put me first despite the fact that I last spoke at home. I spoke there when the decision had been made that my sister should marry. The focus is on my objection alone, but it should be on what will happen to my sister. That was the purpose of my statement, and I am still arguing about that same point. I am not saying that my sister should not marry. I only ask them this: Do they understand that she has given birth to a child who is a boy, and who will become a man? Do they know where she will go when she marries? And whether or not she'll bear a man-child? Then there will be a struggle over the inheritance, or she'll be treated badly by the man-child she may bear. In that case, I'm the proper person to whom she should appeal at her own home. I am the right one to appeal to because I am her brother. But there can be no appeal here, because I came from her stomach! Please unravel that problem, Men. That's what I have to say."

A man got up and said, "Have you heard this child? What he says is important; it enters your head. It comes into your head, to your brain."

One of them spoke for the first time: "Yes, what Vel'ekhaya has said does enter the head. Vel'ekhaya speaks about some comment his father has made. What does all this mean? It means that you should listen to what the child has said. The implications of his speech may be momentous. His words should not be taken lightly. We must not forget anything that this child has said regarding his home. This youth is not lodging a complaint against his father. He's not even complaining about his mother. He complains about one thing: that his sister might marry while he is present."[19]

"Oh, that's the way it is."

"Yes, that's the way it is," said another man. "That's the way it is. You ought to focus on what Vel'ekhaya is saying."

"Well, Vel'ekhaya, what is your understanding? Is it your view that your sister should not marry? Or that your sister should have her own house?"

"No, as far as I'm concerned, I don't want to contradict my grandfather's words, I don't want to interfere with the conclusions that he has made about his offspring. What I'm concerned about is this: when my sister marries, they must understand that I am not denying the fact that I am his child [his grandfather's child], and I'm not denying my sister either. But let the matter of my sister's marriage be frankly discussed, so that I can understand it. Then my sister can go on and get married."

Those men who were in the court said, "Let someone speak!"

Another man got up, and said, "All right. What Vel'ekhaya is saying is becoming clear. The intelligence of people who wear skirts [women] is limited. If this mother of Vel'ekhaya had brains, this matter would have

19. That is, his very existence may prove to be an obstacle to her marriage.

turned out all right. But because of her sex [literally, "tying on a dress"], the issue has developed complications. The child is shedding light on it. We're coming to understand that this matter has its consequences. What I mean to say, Vel'ekhaya, is that, as far as I'm concerned, you're right. I say this without going over to check with the chief. I say you are right. It does not matter to me what the chief is going to say. I do not care. You are correct in saying that when your sister marries, it must be clear that she is leaving you, Vel'ekhaya, behind here at home. But in this home, you are the child of her father because she bore you at her home of birth. This should be clear to you, Vel'ekhaya, our child. Your sister is an unmarried woman. You were conceived, and no reparation was made when you were conceived.[20] It is only now that your grandfather will get something by reason of your mother.[21] So you must be patient. Be patient. Let your sister be married off by your father. But this should be clear to you, Vel'e- khaya: when your sister marries, she is giving up nothing on your account because never, at any time, were you hers. You were the child of her father. She is going there for your good; you should be able to take her there."

Vel'ekhaya said, "But it is not like that at all! I am not at all persuaded that it can turn out like that because I, Vel'ekhaya, am a child who is a boy here at home. I have never seen anything handled in this way. It was said, 'Let Vel'ekhaya be called first.' How can I be sure that if my sister marries and if trouble arises regarding her, I'll not be called again? And it'll again be said, 'Let Vel'ekhaya be called.' Only yesterday, my sister was sick here, and no one told me anything about her sickness. They just wondered what I could possibly do about it. And today, when I speak, you say, 'You, Vel'ekhaya! Everything will work out all right for you.' I am not convinced of that, even now. It seems to me that you have deceived me. It is not going to work out all right for me at all. But if my sister is persuaded by what you say, then that is all right. If she is satisfied, I am content. I am not pleased either that my grandfather is going to end up with a bad attitude toward me. I'll become someone who is competing with him in this homestead. I want to be in my grandfather's good graces."

The discussion went on in that manner, and it appeared that Vel'ekhaya was winning his point by his eloquent speeches and the reverence that he was showing for his father and mother.

Then Vel'ekhaya's sister came to the court. She had been listening to the proceedings while inside the house; she sat by the door with her mother, listening.

She said, "Father, please wait. I have heard what has been said here,

20. No dowry negotiations took place, and no fine was paid to the father for the illegitimate birth.

21. He got nothing for you in the form of reparation for the dowry he would lose because his daughter is not a married woman.

even though I have been over there in that house. Vel'ekhaya does not want me to marry. And I can see what is concerning him. It is not that he does not want me to marry. It is just that he fears what might happen when I am married. Something may happen, in the course of time, that will present him with problems—or present me with problems, not him. Then I will not have the right to come to Vel'ekhaya. This is what I think should be done. If you marry me to that man over there, Father, Vel'ekhaya should be the negotiator. Make my child a man. I have borne him among you. He is my brother because I bore him at home. Make him a man, so that when negotiations for my marriage take place, he shall be the negotiator, and therefore he shall be here when I marry."

The men agreed: "You're right, young woman. We wanted to hear where your heart was in this matter being discussed here. Tomorrow, discussions will begin for your marriage preparations. Vel'ekhaya's boyhood must come to an end. He must be circumcised whenever he decides that he wants to undergo that ritual. He must be included in these marriage discussions. This matter must not be overlooked. As you know, during marriage negotiations, things come up for discussion: certain days must be remembered, along with people who were present on the first day that a certain thing was discussed. My daughter, this Vel'ekhaya is still to be called by the men. It will be said, 'Today is such-and-such an occasion.' On that day, Vel'ekhaya was present. Now I wonder if he'll remember what was said—the first word and the last? Will he remember what was spoken?"

The girl said, "Yes, Father, Vel'ekhaya will remember what came first. You are here right now because of him. No man said, 'What is Vel'ekhaya doing here regarding the marriage of his mother?' Vel'ekhaya did not say, at any time, 'It's my mother who is getting married.' He only says, 'Should my sister marry while I am here? After all, she bore me at home. I do not know what is going on here. Do you know how her marriage will turn out, whether or not she will bear male-children over there at her house of marriage? Is there contention over the matter of inheritance? What if they treat her badly? What will happen to her if I never come to know what you know?' I agree with what he says—I, the person who was burdened with this child for nine months. What Vel'ekhaya says is true. Heed what he says. And straighten it out. Put it in the appropriate terms of the homestead, so that things will go well for me if I marry. Should I refuse to marry, should I refuse to allow myself to be married off by my father, I would in effect be disowning my father. I could not do that. If there were not mutual satisfaction between my father and me, I would have no home, just as Vel'ekhaya has no home." So said the young woman.

After she had spoken, her father got up, and said, "No, my child, stop. Really. You have been heard, your words have been heard. The institution of marriage establishes a pillar for a woman, whose nature is to lean on a man. That is why you must marry. Now, as for Vel'ekhaya, we want him to be the master of ceremonies at the wedding. He'll know everything that occurs when you are married. You'll be sent off with a bridal party, you'll kneel at the kraal, there'll be dancing in that homestead. The women must borrow some leather skirts."

Time passed. They borrowed the skirts for the members of the bridal party who were going along to effect the marriage, according to the story.[22] Enough skirts were borrowed for the bridal party. Men were also needed for the party, and two men were found. And it was said that Vel'ekhaya must be the master of ceremonies, so that he might know how to keep the rules. Vel'ekhaya agreed to this. He became the master of ceremonies. He went to negotiate on behalf of his mother. Because he was the negotiator, when the first ox of the wedding ceremony was slaughtered, it was said that the skin should be given to him.

But even then, there were rival claims regarding the master of ceremonies' ox-hide. Someone insisted that "There's no skin of a master of ceremonies for a mere boy!" That was the claim of the two men who were in the bridal party. But the bride, the person who was the reason for the marriage rite, this mother of Vel'ekhaya, said, "Not at all! Now just take this matter back to the beginning. You are going to disrupt this marriage party! Vel'ekhaya has been included in this group because of certain ground rules that were established at home. It was determined that he should be the master of ceremonies. Therefore, the skin of that ox that has been slaughtered for the wedding is rightfully his, so that he will know how to preserve everything. That was the decision, you will recall. Now do not start disrupting the hospitality of this homestead [the groom's home]. Do not come and argue afresh matters that have already been debated and dispensed with. Give Vel'ekhaya his skin."

"Well," the two men decided, "let's leave it at that. This skin should be Vel'ekhaya's because it is clear that this argument will go on and on until it is heard in this strange homestead [the groom's], and then they'll conclude that these people who are guests from another homestead still have something to quarrel about."

---

22. Mrs. Zenani reminds her audience that she is telling a story, not describing an actual marriage ceremony.

Tale 14

A COURT TRIAL

Masithathu Zenani's Analysis: This is another tale that is more realistic than fantastic. It begins with the puberty rites of two brothers, circumcised at the same time. The father secures a wife for one of the sons, but not for the other. This leads to an altercation, and the youth lays an official complaint against his father. At the court trial, the ordeal of the young man is, as in "Sikhuluma, the Boy Who Did Not Speak" (Tale 12) and "The Boy Who Did Not Want His Sister to Marry" (Tale 13), not a fantasy ordeal; his ordeal has to do with his eloquence at the court trial. Again, identity is at the core of the ordeal, as the elder brother struggles to establish his claims and argues their legitimacy. His success signals his movement to manhood.

Performance Note

Time: 19 September 1967, in the late afternoon. *Place:* Outside Mrs. Zenani's home in Nkanga, Gatyana District, the Transkei. *Audience:* fifteen women and thirty children. (Perf. 710.)

There were a man and his wife. The wife gave birth. She bore four children: two were boys and two were girls. Those children grew up.

Then the father told the oldest child that he wanted to send him to the pastures to increase the size of his livestock. The father built a homestead far from home. He built it just north of a large forest. He erected a fence there. He built one house. He brought out the stock that he possessed— oxen and goats and sheep—and then he turned to his son and told him that he should herd these stock. He had constructed an outpost, and now this older child stayed there with the livestock.

Time passed, time passed over there, and that son remained at the outpost.

The two sons were circumcised then. They were circumcised at the same time. The father said that one of them should be circumcised at his mother's home—otherwise they would fight each other. The other was circumcised at his homestead. So they both became men.

The father was living with the younger son, so he took a wife for him. The elder son, who was at the outpost, had no wife yet.

The elder son asked, "What's the matter, my father? My young brother has a wife, and I don't have one yet—even though we were circumcised at the same time."

The father did not respond to these questions. He would not be questioned on this subject. He had taken a wife for this younger son. He had obtained a daughter-in-law who could help his wife and give her some

260

rest from her work. But this angered the elder son because he now saw himself beneath the younger son in status.

The mother supported her elder son: "Well, really, Father of So-and-so, you haven't done this properly. If you had done it the right way, you would have gotten them wives at the same time because they were circumcised at the same time."

So it was that this fellow and his wife quarreled.

He said, "You're trying to get me to fight with my children. I can see how this is going to turn out."

The wife became impertinent then, and said, "You love the younger son more than the elder."

It was clear that the mother and her elder son had the same view about this. The elder son then looked for some people to mediate between him and his father.

The people whom he sought arrived. They came to his home. They did not go to the outpost; they arrived at his proper home instead.

His father asked, "Who gathered you together here?"

The first person to answer said, "Your son called us, saying that you were asking for us, that you desired to see us."

"Where is this son now?"

They said, "Well, that's the thing. We don't know where he is. Your son came to our homes to ask us to come here."

The son did not come to the house. He remained at the outpost. He awakened in the morning and opened the kraals for the livestock. He herded the stock, then again shut the stock up in the kraals. Only then did he go home.

At dusk, he arrived at his home, coming to see the people he knew were there. When he arrived, the people were waiting for him.

His father asked him why these people had been summoned to this homestead.

The elder son said, "I called them."

His father asked, "How did you dare to call them without first consulting me?"

The son said, "I called them to your homestead because an injury has been done."

His father said, "Who's been injured? Who in my homestead is troubled?"

The child said, "You have troubled me."

His father asked, "You? What are you?"

The child said, "I am I! I am your son! Though I'm away from home, out there at the outpost, living on the other side of the forest, I am still your son. I am your son, yet I can see that you discriminate against me. I want this matter to be rectified."

The issue was thereby raised.

His father said, "If something is wrong, I should not hear about it from you. You cannot call a meeting unless I have called it. You should begin by lodging your complaint with your mother. I should have discussed this with your mother first."

The young man said, "You almost beat my mother when she raised the question. I did speak to her about it, told her this very thing for which I have now summoned the people. Speak, Father. I want to know what I should do."

The matter was discussed, and finally it was decided that it should be taken to the royal residence, where offences such as this were judged. If a person wanted to appeal a disciplinary matter from his home, he would go to the royal residence where people lay charges against each other.

They went to the royal residence now.

His father said, "This matter is too much for you, my son. I don't want a meeting here at home if I myself have not called it. Where will you go now?"

The son said, "Father, I'll find a place for myself. It doesn't matter where I go. I'll find a place; that's not a problem. The main thing is, I don't want to be disowned by you. You've done wrong, and I want you to straighten this matter out. But you, of course, don't see it that way. You don't think that you've wronged me."

His father said, "I say to you, go away from this home!" He sent the people away: "I did not call any meeting!" The people went home that very day.

At dawn, the son journeyed. He went to the royal residence where he lodged a complaint.

At the royal residence, they asked him what he was bringing an action for.

He said that he was laying a charge. His father had done something, and the son wanted it set right.

It was asked, "Who exactly are you accusing? Are you complaining about the soil that is on the ground in the courtyard?"

He said, "No, I am not complaining about the soil. I am complaining about my father. He has done me an injury, and now he refuses to allow it to be discussed."

It was declared, "Let the young man go home. The offense will be heard tomorrow."

The king's messengers were sent out; they went and summoned that father, informing him that his son had brought a case against him in court.

This father went to the court, and the case was discussed.

The son was addressed: "Please state your complaint about your father, Child."

The youth said, "This is my complaint against my father: even on the day of my circumcision, I was not satisfied. I have a younger brother. We were circumcised on the same day. My father did a strange thing on that day. He took my younger brother and circumcised him at the home of my mother. He said that we would fight if we were circumcised in the same place. We might fight each other, and such a dispute might lead to one of us burning the other in the circumcision lodge. One of us might go mad because an older and a younger son were circumcised on the same day. I've never liked that. I don't say that we were kicking each other, and I don't say that we were not kicking each other. The way I see it, my father did not even like the idea that he had to circumcise me because, after the ritual was over, he went and built an outpost on the north side of the forest and put me over there along with his cattle. I alone was to herd them. He said that he was breaking up his outpost and making several out of it. He wanted to increase the number of his cattle—and that could not happen on a single outpost. Well, I agreed to this. But after he had done that, he took a woman and made her the wife of his younger son. How much do I have to endure? Must I be quiet when my father does such an insensitive thing to me? That is why I called his people together, I hoped that they would clarify the matter. I hoped that they would determine who was wronged, my father or me. But my father did not agree to this. He dismissed the assembly without any discussion. I did not want to come here to the royal residence: I have been patient. But now, I have decided to come to the royal residence because I do not know any more where this matter will end."

They asked the father, "Have you heard what your son has said?"

He said, "Yes, I hear him. I hear his words. Children! They're so impetuous! So anxious to speak! I hear him, but I do not pay much attention to what he says!"

They said, "But is he correct? Are you aware of the situations he is talking about?"

"Yes, I am aware of those matters. But he went and called the men together—my homestead was full of people! I did not know why he called them together. So I took a wife for his younger brother. I did not take this boy's oxen. I told this child—"

It was said, "Stop! Do not say things until you have been asked! Respond only to what you have been asked. This court has asked you, Are you aware of the situations spoken of by this young man? Now continue, speak the facts as you know them."

"Well, King, I told him that I married this woman to his younger brother because his mother is old. I did this so that there would be a young person there in the homestead who would cook for his mother. I do not understand why this should have distressed him. The minds of children are puzzling."

"No, Fellow, do not jump around so much. Keep to the subject, and when you have said what you have to say on the subject, then stop. Do not talk so much. You talk about everything!"

That fellow said, "Well, if I speak interminably, it is because of what this young man has said. He says that he could see a long time ago that I did not like him. He claims that I have damaged many things, and he even goes on to charge that I muddled the circumcision ceremony when I built the outpost. Could such a thing have happened? Who would tell someone he did not like to go off and herd his cattle?"

"No. Do not speak in that way. Respond according to the style of this court. You have not come here to scold your son. Your son has made an accusation against you. Answer the question. Do not scold him here."

"Well, I do it because of what my son has done. This is wearisome. I could see what was happening when he summoned the assembly at home."

The matter was discussed. Then the youth was questioned again.

It was said, "Young man, your father is not cooperating with this court in the matter that you have laid before us. It is therefore fitting that, because you have brought the matter to the court's attention, we analyze it according to the customs of this court. There is no time here for a person who comes and has tantrums. No matter what has happened, it is customary in this court that a person is quiet, that he responds to what is spoken to him. Now, for a long time, your father has displeased you."

The young man said, "Yes, I have noticed the things my father habitually does. When those things are all put together, I am not pleased with the result. I saw what he was up to when he circumcised me and my younger brother on the same day, something that has never happened before among the Gcaleka: it has never happened before that a younger and an older brother are circumcised on the same day.[23] As if that were not enough, my father built the outpost for me on the other side of the forest—for me alone. He said that he had made the outpost for me. And then he took somebody's daughter and made her the wife of my younger brother. And I did not yet have a wife. I complained about this. I asked him about it. I consulted my mother. No large assembly was gathered when I first raised questions about these matters. But my father became intemperate. When I gathered the kinsmen together for him, so that they should plead my cause, so that they might investigate and determine whether or not I had a cause, my father sent them all home. He even disowned some of them. He said that he never wanted to see them again because I had called them together. Now I ask you, how much of this injustice must I endure from my father? I have tried to go through the proper channels, but it turns out that that is not possible. I am not complaining with the hope that he shall be arrested. I have come to complain because he broke up a meet-

23. The Gcaleka are a Xhosa people.

ing of his kinsmen, a meeting that I called to discuss in detail the things that disturb me about my father. I'll stop there."

They said, "Now, Friend, have you heard what your son has said?"

This fellow said, "Well, it's only words spoken by a child who's carried away by his eloquence. When he speaks, he is very fluent. There's no doubt about that. But he flattens what happened through his fluency. He never said that he did not want to go to the outposts when I broke the livestock up into smaller sections. He was happy about that. But he saved it, he put it into a purse, so that he could use it against me later, so that he could accuse me of something when I married that woman to my younger son. There is nothing to his accusation; it's empty! A ceremonial beast was slaughtered for the wedding—he even ate some of the meat, and he was happy. But now he's nursing a grudge, he's carrying me on his back. Well, I care nothing for what he thinks. Let him go the way he wants to go."

The court came to its conclusions. "What do you 'care nothing' for? Your son? Or this court? You should realize now that you are not speaking to your son. You are addressing an august body. You are speaking with the king and the court of justice. Now then, which is it that you 'care nothing' about? One or the other! Please be clear."

He said, "No, no, I do care about the king and this court of justice! What troubles me is the matter of this child, what he's indicating through his speech. It surrounds me! He wants the homestead to be his, even though I am still alive. I can see what he's up to. He's being deceived by his mother. They have a habit of asking the same kinds of questions."

The case was dismissed then; it was dismissed.

The king said, "Go and get a wife for this young man. This is my judgment. Go and marry him a wife. When you have done that, remove him from the outposts, and send your younger son there. An older son is never made to leave home. You have regularly distorted things. You have placed the heir, the eater-of-the-inheritance, in the outposts, while it is the younger brother whom you should have put out there."

The man got up and kissed the hand of the king because he had not been fined. He had been judged according to the law. He thanked the king. He said, "All right, King, I'll do this. I thank you." So he said, and he went home.

When he got home, he told his wife of the decision of the royal residence. He said, "I was told that I must find a wife for this young man. All right then. This matter of your son and you, it has ripened. You've got your way. The court has determined that the younger son must go to the outpost. Now I must get a wife for this other young man."

A wife was sought then. The bridal party was assembled. She became his wife. He married according to Xhosa custom. Then she went to live at his place.

The younger brother was thereby brought down. He went to the outpost with his wife.

Part Three: Marriage

INTRODUCTION

MASITHATHU ZENANI ON STORYTELLING

Time is a key to understanding the mechanics of this aesthetic system, Mrs. Zenani said. She discussed at some length the different temporal experiences that occur in her performances. Real time is independent of the performance, for example, and within the work of art is narrative time, chronological time involved in the linear movement of images between an initial conflict and an ultimate resolution (there may be minor resolutions along the way). Performance time is real time; it is the time that it takes for the performance itself to be externalized.

Time within the narrative can be said to approximate real time as it exists outside the narrative, in the sense that narrative time is telescoped real time. But in order for the narrative to establish any significant relationship with the objective world, a unique bond, necessary to the goals of oral performance, narrative time must be broken up. Otherwise, image plotting becomes the object of the performance: a good story is told, but no real message is experienced. Narrative time must seem to be ruptured. This is achieved through a trick that the art tradition plays with time.

Few concepts of time in oral narrative are more important than repeated time, the sense of time created by the repeated images. When these image sets are the same, and when identical patterns force into alignment sequences in which images are not the same, then they are in a sense without time. Each is the same; each achieves its temporal dimension only when plotted in a continuum in a performance, performance time itself assuring that temporal dimension. These repeated image sequences contain the potential for the breaking up of the linear surface, one kind of time (actually the absence of time) apparently shattering another kind of time (narrative time). Because repetition creates tensions with narrative time, it is possible for the manipulation of image plotting to occur without doing damage to the essential chronological movement of the narrative.

Narrative time is continuous; it is a movement, no matter how circular, from a beginning to an end. But this linear movement is a unique one: it is accomplished by means of repeated image sets. This is the key to the message-making capabilities of the oral tradition. Narrative may seem to be disrupted, but in fact it must remain uninterrupted; to interfere with its motion is to transgress one of the cardinal tenets of storytelling performance. It is real time that is being manipulated—or, at least, there is an illusion of such manipulation. The almost identical repetition of image sequences plays havoc with the audience's experience in real time. We keep arriving back at point A, it seems. The image set begins: it moves from point A to point B to point C. Suddenly, the sequence begins anew, and we are back at point A. That is the experience in real time. But in narrative time, that irresistible movement from conflict to resolution retains its integrity; each image sequence (the movement from point A to point B to point C) moves the narrative ahead slightly toward the denouement. Each image sequence (A, B, C) adds new information to the accumulated experience of the members of the audience, even when the image sequences remain identical. The first repetition of a sequence provides a context for the second, so that the audience's second experience of a series of images is altered, if for no other reason than that it follows the first.

Real time and narrative time come together in this attractive manner to enable the surface of the narrative to be fractured even as narrative time remains inviolate. Repetition is thus at the very heart of oral narrative tradition. There is an amassing of identical image sequences (A, B, C), even as narrative time flows on uninterrupted (A, B, C/linking details/A, B, C/linking details/A, B, C, etc.).

The temporal elements are complemented by a spatial dimension in such performances. As with the temporal, spatial characteristics have an existence outside the narrative. And, as with time, real space is telescoped within the performance. In the story, spatial relationships exist between actions and between patterns. The space between a set of patterned images can be as significant temporally as the patterns themselves. Space in this sense becomes indistinguishable from time.

The plotted images themselves have spatial characteristics that give clues to the structural composition of the performance. These include the central physical movements of the story. In many oral tales, such movements consist essentially of a shift from the security and familiarity of the home to the veld, the wilderness, the out-there where all is unfamiliar, dangerous, unknown—fantastic. In some Xhosa performances, for example, this pattern of physical movement becomes a journey from the central character's house of birth to her house of marriage, a trip that Xhosa women take when they marry. In oral narratives, that movement is frequently a perilous one, a traversing of the threatening land that lies between the protagonist's parents' home and the uncertain life at the home of her husband. In other narratives, the movement is between a home of birth and a surrogate home of birth, as when children are physically removed from tainted households or societies to be reborn in a state of nature. The movement dealing with women will often become a narrative with a theme of marriage; that concerned with the surrogate house of birth, a theme of purification, of passage from childhood into adulthood. Many narratives depict a journey from the home to the threatening veld, where strange creatures lurk, most of them with cannibalistic designs on humans.

The regular spatial movement becomes a pattern that also constitutes the physical, imaged axis of the narrative. Temporal regularity provides the rhythmical structures within which the spatial patterns move. This regularity leads to a receptivity on the part of the members of the audience for certain repeated image alignments. This receptivity and structural expectation have been developed in audiences from childhood. Every child's narrative, while it may have no profound theme to communicate, nevertheless describes an essential spatial movement against a regular temporal grid. The child internalizes these spatial and temporal dimensions of the tradition, as he experiences them in diverse performances. As the narrative image sequences become more complex, the movements become more and more functional. Actually, it is not the image sequences that become more complex; it is, rather, the combination of spatial and temporal patterns in separate narratives. Plotted imagery remains generally the same, although a greater emphasis on detail may occur; and with the emphasis shifting from surface repetition to structural patterning in the intricate performances, repeated identical image sequences become less frequent. Repetition on the narrative surface is deemphasized in favor of the more subtle rhythmic patterns revealed beyond the level of plotting.

Because of the experience of patterns, because of the rhythmic expectation, the audience participates in bringing the performance to a halt temporarily, in real time, and spatially. Even as the movement of the narrative is through time toward a resolution, even as it moves from one locale to another, an accumulation of image sequences of like composition is occurring. These structures become sufficiently numerous to require sorting out.

The identical experience of spatial movements has the effect of stopping time. The audience experiences the same movement, again and again, and in that sense there is no time uniting like image patterns. Its members shuttle back and forth across the same time line, back and forth between identical locales. Even when locations change, the basic pattern does not. What gives these like experiences a feeling of temporality is the linkage in the performance of the repeated image sequence. This connecting of nontime identical image sets in a continuum, plus performance time, gives the whole a sense of chronological time—but it is an illusion.

So the movement continues, and because the rhythmic patterning is regular, certain image sequences begin to layer, to pile one on top of the other despite the linear arrangement of images. This piling or layering effect is necessary to the establishment, by the plotted images, of timeless forms. Only when the members of the audience feel the similarity of these frequently diverse image sequences can they begin to sense the identical structures underlying each. When this occurs, the formal patterns themselves become clear, and their relationships are revealed.

COMMENTARIES

MARRIAGE IN THE EARLY TIMES

Performance Note

Time: 19 September 1967, mid-morning. *Place:* In a home in Nkanga, Gatyana District, the Transkei. *Audience:* About thirty men and women. (Perf. 702.)

Regarding the marriage of a young woman: when a young man wanted to take a wife, he went and asked for the young woman at So-and-so's place. The family was told that it was fitting that this young man get a wife. No young man would ever say to a person older than himself, "I want a wife." It was his father who would reach a certain point at which he would say, "I must get a wife for my child. He's old enough now." That was the normal procedure.

When the people had assembled, that father said, "Fellow clansmen, I want to get a wife for my child. The young man's old enough now, and I want us to consider this matter."

The elders and the people talked back and forth then.

Someone said, "Yes, you're right."

"That's the way it should be."

"You're right, Fellow clansman."

"Yes, really. He's old enough now. It's just about time."

But it was not the marriageable son who got up and did something about it. He just stayed there; nothing in the conversation was directed at him. He was just there; he was not consulted about anything. In time, he came to realize that his fathers were discussing this matter, even though he did not know the details. No one, not a man or a woman, was told what these elders were discussing at this home.

When all that had taken place, this elder, the head of the household, said, "Now I ask you, So-and-so," and he addressed a man who was mature, "I want you to seek a wife for my child. The homestead that I prefer is So-and-so's"—he named the homestead and the village where the homestead was located. He named the homestead and village when he was sending people to seek a wife for his child to marry, according to the ancient custom of the Xhosa.

These men set out—perhaps two men, perhaps three. They traveled, carrying black sticks that were given particular names to distinguish them from other sticks. It was said that the men were carrying sticks for the purpose of doing something special, for carrying out the business of their home. Those men arrived at this homestead. They sat in the courtyard.

272

They did not enter the house. Anyone could see that they were there on some kind of business, an important matter, for they were sitting in the courtyard.

Then one man from this homestead went to where they were sitting and asked them, "Where have you come from?"

They answered. The oldest man among them said, "We've come from our home. We've come to ask for a spear."

They talked in that way. Then the man who had gone out to interrogate them got up and went to the house, to the old man of the homestead.

He arrived and said, "These people who are visiting this home have come to see the great man." But this man did not say here in the house what the strangers had come for.

That fellow of the homestead got up and went out to the men. He greeted them; they responded. He sat down and said, "Now these gentlemen here, where have they come from?"

The older one among those in the groom's party responded, "We have come from our home to visit you, Sir. We have been sent by the old man of our home." He called that old man by name. "That old man said that we should come to you carrying a lotion with which a woman is washed on the day that she is to be married. He sent us here to ask for a spear."

The man said, "Mm! Has the spear that you're seeking at this homestead been seen? Or has it not been seen?"

The visitors responded, "Really, Father, as far as we can gather from this father of ours at home, it was seen once. It appears that she was seen once. And that old man says that he wants a spear from this home."

"Mm, well, he had better point out the house where he saw the spear. As you can see, there are many houses in this homestead."

In the olden times, men used to have, say, two wives—maybe three, four, or five wives. One husband. And each of these houses had daughters, so that there were many daughters from a number of wives in the homestead.

The visitors answered, "The old man said he saw the spear in this great house."

The other said, "Well, he can get the spear that he wants. But we're not giving that spear away for nothing; it's not a gift."

These men had been told before leaving home that they should keep to a certain amount in the dowry negotiations, that they should not go beyond a certain number of cattle in the negotiations with the bride's people. The men of the groom's house might make an offer of cattle right there in the courtyard. They negotiated with this representative of the bride's house. They made an offer of cattle—maybe six, maybe eight, whatever the number, according to the preference of the groom's father. When the negotiating ended, the people from the groom's home departed, saying, "We have accepted you."

That is how it was done.

Then this man went to the house. He did not mention anything; he spoke of the conversation to no one. Not a person knew what had occurred, not his wife, not his son. The only person who knew what was said was the big man. No one went near during the discussions that had taken place in the courtyard among the older people.

After a while, when they were alone, the man whispered to his wife, "Nobani, our daughter has been seen by a certain person. I have accepted him because I like him. I have asked for dowry—cattle. You must prepare the proper things for the young woman's departure."

That wife said, "When will she be going?"

The husband told his wife the time his daughter would depart.

When the groom's party returned to its homestead, preparations were made for the approaching bride.

Long ago, that is how it was done.

On a certain day, these groom's people returned to the bride's home, to determine the state of the business that they had been negotiating. Again, they carried those special sticks; again, they sat in the courtyard. As before, someone came to them, to ask them where they had come from.

They explained their situation: "We have come to determine the state of the business we've been negotiating. How long must we wait?"

"We would like this matter to be completed next week."

The owner of the home answered, "All right, that's all right. I shall send her then. I shall send her to the home of her sister by marriage, or I shall send her to her mother's parents' home, and you can meet her along the way."

The girls did not know that this particular woman was going to get married. She was not told herself. She was taken to wife without knowing anything about it. She found herself being taken, and in the end she would become a wife of that country without ever being told that she was going to be married.

The groom's party departed and waited for the day that had been decided upon.

"We'll send this child. Watch out for her."

The groom's party returned to its home. Some young men were sent out. They were told to go and lie in wait for this young woman on a certain road. She would be sent along a certain road, and they were to stay in such-and-such a place and wait for her.

"Then you must take her."

The young woman went that way, and the young men waited for her along the road. She walked along; she came upon them suddenly. She was going along, not thinking about anything special, not knowing what was happening.

When she saw them, she greeted them. "Hello."

They responded, "Yes."

"Say, Young woman. Can you give us some tobacco?"

"I don't have any"—if she did not have any tobacco. If she did have some, then she produced it and gave it to them.

These young men came close and asked, "Where are you from?"

They walked close to her, accompanying her, chatting with her.

As she was going along, it was said, "You've been walking a long time."

"Turn here. This is the way we're going."

She said, "No, I'm going the other way."

"No, you're going with us."

"Now you're a wife of our home."

The young woman said, "No! Leave me alone! Leave me alone! Where are you taking me?"

They said, "You're going with us!"

The young woman screamed and kicked, scratching them, biting, trying to get away, angrily accusing them of behaving brutally toward her.

They slapped her.

All of this was according to custom. They were expected to beat her, so that she would become afraid of them and would then agree to go with them. And she would fight back until she finally realized that "Really, I'm being beaten! There's no mistaking it!" Then she would stop fighting and go along with them. She would go along, crying, throwing away her garments; they would pick her garments up and carry them. She would continue to cry until she arrived there and was put into a house. She would know nothing, she would not know whether or not this abduction was connected with her father.

On arriving, she was put into a house. Then a girl from this homestead or a young married woman took a black cloth and put it on the bride's head, veiling her head to the eyes. She covered the bride's head to the eyes, then tied the cloth under the young woman's chin.

They said to the young woman, "You've married into this homestead now."

She repeatedly pulled the cloth off, saying, "I'm not getting married!"

Were she to continue to resist the marriage, it might happen that she would ultimately leave this homestead without getting married. In that case, another young woman would go through the same ceremonies and be married.

After a while, the people of her home came and borrowed this young woman; she was borrowed by her father.

"Please lend me that woman."

The father of the young woman sent messengers; he would not yet go himself. And, of course, they released the young woman to him. Her father then began to do those things to formalize this marriage arrangement, to marry her properly, formally and truly.

When she returned to her home of birth, many things were done. The father had told his wife, "Prepare the marriage things for our daughter."

So that appropriate marriage items might be fashioned, some things were picked in the pasture, others gathered from the rivers. Whatever was required for this person was gathered—from the rivers, the forests, everything that was needed to provide the elegant wedding objects in those olden times. In those days, there was nothing that shone—no buckets or pots, nothing like that. All such vessels were made of clay. Artisans made such vessels. They knew how to make them very well; these objects were regarded as beautiful.

The women, girls, and men of the bridal party set out, and two beasts were driven along—one was the bride's beast whose tail would be plucked whenever the bride was unwell.[1] The hair from the tail of this bride's beast would then be put around the bride's neck. The other beast was called the bridal party's beast.[2] Early in the morning, it would be slaughtered in the homestead to which the bridal party was going.

The young woman returned to her parents' home, and time passed in that way. Preparations were made. Beer was brewed for a great feast; everyone gathered for the marriage of a daughter.

At her home of marriage, preparations were going on as well because the bridal party was expected. Preparations here included maize that was being ground, and there was dancing.

On the appointed day, in the afternoon, the bridal party departed from the bride's home of birth. The party arrived in the evening, at the time that it was supposed to arrive. It was necessary that the bridal party arrive in the evening when people were having their evening meal. When the members of the party arrived, they sat at the top of and just beyond the homestead. In the meantime, the groom's household was keeping watch for the bridal party, for it was expected; this was the day it was scheduled to arrive at this homestead. The dogs were heard barking, announcing that some visitors were approaching. And the person who was responsible for keeping watch went out to meet them.

It was said, "The bridal party is here!"

---

1. This was the *ubulunga* beast. It was presented to the bride by the members of her home of birth. It symbolized her connection with her home of birth and the consequent protection while she was living in her home of marriage. It belonged to her alone and could not be taken from her by anyone.

2. This was the *impothulo* beast. It was meant to be slaughtered and eaten by the bridal party during the marriage negotiations at the home of marriage, before the bride officially became a part of that home of marriage.

Someone else said, "Go, ask the members of the bridal party where they have come from."

Someone went out and asked the bridal party where it had come from. He began, "I greet you!"

The bridal party responded, "Yes."

The young women, including the person-of-the-meat, the bride, had their heads covered. All the others' heads were uncovered.

The interrogator asked, "Where do you come from?"

The spokesman for the bridal party said, "We've come from home. And we're traveling with a child who is not well. We're looking for a place to spend the night."

"Do you know anything about this homestead at which you're asking for a place to spend the night?"

That question was not unexpected. The people of whom it was asked were known to this interrogator; the questioning was a part of the formalities, the ritual. It is Xhosa custom. He was supposed to be asked if he were familiar with this homestead. Everyone knew that he was familiar with the homestead; the members of the groom's homestead knew him, too.

"No, we don't know it. It just happens that this homestead was near the road. That's why we happened to come to this particular home to ask for a place to spend the night."

"Well," the representative of the groom's party said, "I'll take your answer to the house."

So he went to the house and explained that "These people say that they're looking for a place to spend the night. They're from far away. They're tired. But they say they are unfamiliar with this homestead. They're just looking for a place to sleep, nothing more."

Their house had already been prepared here at this homestead. It had been thoroughly arranged: the floors and walls had been plastered, because visitors were expected. The floor was coated with cow dung. Firewood had been gathered; it was stacked near the door, just inside the house. A fire would be kindled with this wood as soon as the bridal party entered the house. And they would want to make a fire in the morning, too. On the day of their arrival, the fire was built as soon as they got there.

A woman from the groom's homestead went to light the fire in that house that the bridal party would enter.

The interrogator said, "You're instructed to go to that house."

The members of the bridal party followed him and entered that house. When they had entered, they said, "We ask you, Friend, do not go out right now." They said this to the member of the homestead who had ushered them to this house. "Don't go out right now. We have some calves here that we're traveling with. We want to request that you put them into your kraal because we obviously do not have a kraal here. They might run away."[3]

This was a part of the ritual as well. The fellow agreed to keep the beasts in the kraal. They opened the kraal, and the animals were put in.

In the morning, the members of the bridal party said, "We'd like to borrow a rope—and a person who can help us."

Such a person was offered to them; the people of this groom's home produced young men and boys for use by the visitors. The bridal party's beast was seized that morning, and it was slaughtered. A side of the carcass was taken to the groom's people; the other side was taken to the bridal party. Its skin was taken to the house of the groom's party.

Time passed, and when the days during which the meat of the bridal party's beast was eaten had passed, the parties moved toward the marriage itself here at the groom's home.

The real marriage involved the emergence of the bride. She went to the cattle kraal with her head covered. The groom came out of his home and went to the kraal. They were arranged in proper order—the groom was on one side with his party, and the bride was on her side with the members of her own group, those who had come with her in the bridal party.

The unveiling ceremony followed—the disclosure of the bride's face.

And the master of ceremonies was mocked: as they were going to the cattle kraal, they said to him, "Go on, you with such buttocks!"

"Don't shake your buttocks here!"

"Keep them under control when you're with that child!"

He was in the front.

They said to him, "You with the bald parched head!"

"You with the yellow ass, as if you've just shit!"

"You're acting so arrogant!"

"As if this child you're walking with were your own!"

The master of ceremonies did not answer because that derision was also a part of Xhosa custom. The fact that he was being mocked did not mean that there was a quarrel between them; it was customary that he be treated like that.

They entered the cattle kraal, and when they got there a mat was spread out. The young women arranged themselves in order there, with the bride in their midst. Then the uncloaking took place.

The people said, "Yo! Isn't she beautiful?"

"Reveal her again!"

They said this because she had been veiled again by the master of ceremonies. Again and again, she was covered, then uncovered. Then they

3. This is a continuation of the fiction that the bridal party is only stopping by here temporarily to spend the night because one of its members—the bride—is ill.

left, and the bridal party too departed, leaving a shilling on the ground at the place where the bride had been kneeling. In those days, various kinds of money were the currency—gold pieces, ten shilling pieces, pound pieces, and they were all gold. They were the moneys in those times; that was before there was paper money.

They moved away from there and went to sit in the courtyard, before the women. When they got there, a mat was spread and they knelt again. Again she was unveiled, that person-of-the-meat now being shown to the mothers-in-law.

Again, it was said, "Yo yo yo! She's beautiful!"

"Just reveal the legs!"

Then the members of the bride's party rose and stood on their feet. A woman put their clothing in order. The master of ceremonies—the fellow who was in the front, the one who was being mocked, the one they said had a bald parched head, a yellow rump like a yellow-eye canary, the one with the dry scaly buttocks—went on adjusting things. Then the young women of the bridal party exposed their legs, catching their garments delicately, lifting them high. All the young women did that, and so their legs were seen. Then they were again covered. The bridal party departed, and went to the house.

When the Xhosa bridal party arrived at the house, blankets were taken out and put down. Then the skin skirts were put on by members of the bride's party. They covered their heads with shawls, because they were now going outside, to the river. The buckets had been put into the proper place by young married women of the groom's homestead. Hoes were also brought and twice stuck into the ground.

Members of the groom's party said, "Here at this home, ploughing is done."

"We work in this homestead."

"We do all sorts of things."

Members of the bride's party went and dipped water. They returned from the river, keeping to the north of the homestead, avoiding the homestead, walking behind the houses, going to put the water that was in those buckets and clay pitchers over there. When they got there, they took the vessels down from their heads and sat down.

The next day, it was said, "Today, we're going to dance. We're dancing at this home because we've married the daughter of So-and-so."

The groom was naked; he was just the way he was born—with nothing on. He wore a penis sheath in front. Behind he wore an animal skin, from the neck down. In front, he was completely naked; even his stomach was exposed. He was wholly naked.

They carried the special sticks, together with sharp weapons.

It was said, "They are dancing!" They danced nude, gesturing with spears.

They formed a line in the courtyard. The bride wore a skin mantle.

It was said, "Today, they've put on the skin mantles for the dance," to confirm that this woman had truly married into this home: she was a woman of the marriage dance. That bride had a skin mantle on her back, but she was covered with a skin skirt, and she was also wearing a breast cover.

They danced then, the dancers danced. And this affair had its bulls [meaning, champions]: there was competition among the dancers. Some of them danced better than others; some of them received tobacco, an acknowledgement of their skill. In those days, people smoked horns, cows' horns. There were no pipes then; this occurred before the skill of pipe-making was developed.

When all that had been done, the dancing ended. When the dancing had ended, the bridal party went to get water. They also gathered firewood. On the next day, the bridal party would break up and go home. All the young women would go home, along with an elder woman.

The bundles of firewood were put down. Then the members of the bridal party asked for permission to depart.

But this is what was said concerning that bride: "No! This woman cannot go in this way! The people of her home have come to see her married, but she has not yet been made to drink milk.[4] The bride must drink the milk of a goat."

The first part of the marriage ceremony included all those things, all the cattle. But in spite of what had already been done, the actual marriage was not yet complete.

"Now the gelding of a goat must be taken, so that the real marriage can take place."

"Oh!" and the visitors agreed. They sat down again.[5]

The next morning, the goat was taken and slaughtered. They took an old milking bucket and the strap with which a cow was tethered when it was milked. That strap was put around the milking bucket, then milk was poured into the bucket from a milk sack. The mouth of that milk sack was untied—milk was stored there in the skin of a beast, the skin having been sewn. The milk was poured into the milking bucket. The meat of the goat that had been slaughtered was prepared. The meat around the kidney, on the right side of the goat, was taken and cut in the proper way. Then a fire was kindled in the house of the bridal party, and the meat was roasted in the hearth by a fellow from this groom's homestead, the home into which the girl had married.

4. And therefore no marriage has yet taken place.

5. They would sit down again because they had got up to leave. Doubtless, this was also a part of the ceremony. They pretended to prepare to leave, knowing that this essential part of the ceremony had not yet taken place.

The strap was then placed around the neck of the woman who had come to marry. A small piece of the meat was dipped into the milk that was in the bucket.

Someone said, "Eat, Young woman. You're now a wife of this home. Never be troubled in any way. We want you to bear children here at this home. Bear a boy, bear a girl."

That part was finished then, all of it.

The next day, the bridal party asked for permission to go home.

The members of the party went out and sat in the courtyard. They said, "Now give us what is ours because we're asking leave to go."

The groom's people then produced the beasts of dowry for this woman. The cattle were placed in front of them, and they drove them and went home.

Before they left, they said, "We're leaving this child behind here. We leave this child."

The bride was taken away along with her goods; she was put into a house at her groom's home, at her home.

"We leave this child with you, and as we do so let us tell you about any illness that she might have, so that if she contracts an illness you'll know what it is. We leave her with you without any chronic illness. She is not a sickly person; nothing troubles her. But, of course, like anyone else she might get sick. But she has no illness now. She has no chronic illness."

What is the purpose of this speech? What does it anticipate? When the bride has been left there, if she contracts some new illness, the groom's homestead should know that it is something she has never had before, that this is the first time that she has had it. And what does all of this suggest? Should she become ill at sometime in the future, then it will be known by the groom's people that it is something that had been mentioned by the bridal party, that there is an illness that sometimes afflicts her.

The groom's party thanked them for that good speech, agreeing that, when the bridal party leaves its child behind, it should mention any sickness that she has so that the groom's people will know about it.

Then the bridal party said, "Over there is the gelding of an ox, her bridal beast, which we have driven here. If she is troubled by anything, she need not return to her home of birth to have it attended to. Some hair should be plucked from that beast's tail; it should be plaited, then put on her. While the hair is being taken from the beast's tail, a word should be uttered [meaning, an exorcism should be made], and the plaited hair should be put on her so that the illness might abate—if it is not too serious a malady."

So it went. The bridal party departed, and whenever something was wrong with her, hair would be plucked from that beast. When that hair

Going to the market

had been pulled out, an exorcism would be uttered, and she would be told: "This is the beast of your home. It was left here by your people. We have been told to take hair from it when we see that your blood is a little disturbed. Get well now; we are plucking hair from this beast for you. It is as if you have actually returned to the home of your birth because you were given this cow by your own people. It has privileges by virtue of its entering this homestead."

After she had been living at the groom's place for a time, it happened that, in spite of plucking hair from the beast and putting it on her, the sickness did not pass. Although they took the hair, although they applied it to her body, the illness persisted. Then it was discovered that the cow had to be returned to her home of birth, then brought back again to her home of marriage. The bride was herself at her home of birth now, and over there at her parents' home a goat was slaughtered for the cow.

It was said, "We release you, Cow! Go, and heal this young woman over there at that homestead." These words were spoken to the beast by the father of the bride.

After beer had been brewed for this ceremony, after millet had been cooked, the bride departed.

That is how they did it in the land of the Xhosa years ago.

When the bride returned to her home of marriage, the beast was again taken into the cattle kraal. Then a goat was slaughtered.

It was said, "We're admitting you into the kraal. We've accepted you, to do what it was said you should do at your home."

Beer was also brewed there, and millet was cooked. Beer was drunk; millet was dished out.

Time passed, the young woman began to get well. She did everything that she was supposed to do, and she begot children. Her children were healthy because the customs of her home had been observed.

NONGENILE MASITHATHU ZENANI GETS MARRIED

Performance Note

Time: 12 August 1972, in the morning. *Place:* In a fallen rondavel in Nkanga, Gatyana District, the Transkei. *Audience:* Five women, including her sister, two teenagers, and three children. (NS-156.)

Another version of Mrs. Zenani's autobiography has been published: "And So I Grew Up," transl. Harold Scheub, in: *Life Histories of African Women,* ed. Patricia W. Romero (London: Ashfield Press, 1988), pp. 7–46.

It happened that she [Nongenile Masithathu Zenani] was taken to her homestead of marriage to be married. The bridal party was composed of two young women, one of whom was her sister who came directly after her in age. The bridal party was composed of that sister of hers who came directly after her in age along with another young woman from the village. There were also two older women and two men—an older and a younger man, an older woman and an unmarried woman who was still young in comparison with the other.

As they traveled there, they followed a road that used to be a wagon road and crossed the Qwaninga River. That group of visitors journeyed, going to form the bridal party at Nkanga, at a place called Ngqaqini, the headman being Mabala. They traveled along a certain road, and when they came to curves in the road, they followed a footpath that was a shortcut. So they journeyed: they took a footpath, leaving the wagon road, moving in a direction that brought them to navigate a certain little valley— it happened to be a valley without any water. As they traveled, they were driving a bridal party's beast; according to Xhosa custom, it was an animal that was driven by the bride when she was going to her new homestead of marriage. When she got to that homestead, that ox would be slaughtered on the morning following the evening of the bridal party's arrival.

Then that ox, the yellow ox that they were driving, whose name was Selani, ran off—it was an ox that was being driven in the front while the family of the bridal party followed behind. It was being driven by the second man here in the bridal party. This ox, Selani, began to run wildly, bucking. Because it was evening, the ox got lost in the high grass of this area—this country had trees, thickets, and tall grass, as well as many ditches, and these made it possible for something to disappear at dusk. That man pursued the ox, wanting to bring it back to the road, but he was unable to find it. The beast was lost. The man turned around and went back to his group. When he arrived, he said, "Ahee! I don't see the ox! Perhaps it has turned back. It doesn't know the place we're going to. It's an old ox, and it's in the nature of the beast that it does not like to be driven alone, without other oxen."

The members of the bridal party agreed with him, saying, "Yes, this is the kind of thing that might happen because the ox was traveling alone. When it becomes dark and the eyes cannot see, it might just decide to go back. It's likely that it has gone right back home."

The members of the bridal party stopped.

Someone said, "What shall we do, now that we don't have the ox?"

They discussed the matter and concluded that they should go on because a bridal party, once it has begun its journey, cannot turn back. It was necessary that it go on. Then, when it arrived at that homestead, its destination, the negotiators of the bridal party would leave early in the morning; they would go back home to see if the ox was there. The ox would miss the day it was to be slaughtered; it would have to be slaughtered on the second day. When they had taken counsel in this way, they proceeded along that road that would take them to their destination. They went over a hill, the first hill; it was called Nqangana. There was a quarry on one side, on their left side; they came to the quarry and rested. They sat down in that place, and those who were smokers smoked their pipes. It was already getting dark. Time passed, and after a while, it was said, "Let's go." They went on their way; they went to the curving road and ascended. The bridal party was now fairly close to the homestead to which it was going, but, when it arrived at a junction, it became clear that no one knew which road was to be taken to this homestead. But I, the bride, who was going to the homestead of the groom, knew. An older woman in the bridal party asked, "How could you leave us to wander around like this? You're about to be married, and you don't tell us the way! Why do you let us wander around at night? Do you think that this will help you to return to your home?"[6]

I kept quiet. I, the one who was taken to be married, did not say a word.

They went on, but I saw that this road that they were taking was not the proper one. Now they were going right over toward the Nkanga shop. That shop was beyond a ridge, at a place that was at a bend. When one

---

6. Initially, Mrs. Zenani was not in favor of this marriage.

goes over there to the shop, one keeps close as if one were going down. The name of the white man who owned the shop in those days, in those years of my marriage long ago, was Ben. The name of the white man of that shop was Ben Blaudin. I watched this group of people as they headed toward the shop. There was a homestead to the north of the shop; the homestead belonged to Gomomo of the Qwambi clan. Now, when the people were at a certain curve, just before they were going over the hill at Nkanga, they stood and said, "Well now, it seems that the homestead is not in this direction."

Others said, "Is that not it, the homestead overlooking the shop?"

Another person came up and said, "It seems that the homestead we are seeking is down below, the one that we are looking for is large. Besides, it's a homestead that has wagons and a lot of livestock." By the standards of those days, it was a large homestead.

Another person said, "Why don't we turn back? Let's go over the hill."

So the bridal party went over the hill on the wagon road. If you were to see it in the days of which we are talking now, you would not recognize it. In those days, it was not as it is today. In these days of tractors, gravel has been dug and piled up, as if it were from a quarry. Those things were not present in those days; at the time of my marriage, there was nothing like that. In those days, a road on which automobiles would travel was still being made in this way: men would be employed, and they would dig the road with picks, all the while singing a work song. Keeping in time, they would raise their arms, steadily singing,

> "You're heaving it!
> I'm heaving it,
> This arm of mine!"

The picks would rhythmically follow that pattern; the workers did it like that. It was before there were any buses, before there were these myriads of things crawling over and mixing with each other that we see today. In those days, the little motorcars were not like those that we see now. When we saw such things, it was a surprise; they were rare. We called them "motorcars." What was commonplace at that time was a cart drawn by two horses.

We were sitting next to what is now the quarry—it was not there then; there was only grass in that place. We could see the glint of a fire, blinking some distance from us. The young man who was the master of ceremonies was told to go to that homestead where the light shone and ask anyone[7]

7. Mrs. Zenani used the word, *umnyatheli,* literally, "one who steps," a *hlonipha* word or term of reverence for *umntu,* and explained parenthetically, "an *umnyatheli* is an *umntu* in

there the directions to the homestead to which we were going.

That young man went then; he went to this homestead. We all sat down and waited.

He arrived. When he had knocked, it was said that he should enter. He said, "Come out. I am a traveler. I want to ask something."

A young man whose name was Ngodwana appeared in the doorway. He said to him, "Where do you come from?"

This master of ceremonies said, "I am a person who comes from afar. I am looking for a homestead that I intend to visit." So he said.

This young man said, "Where is this homestead?"

The other answered, "It is in this area of Nkanga, at the Ntlane clan."

The young man said, "Oh, you must be the guests we are expecting. The homestead is across the river." It was already early evening, deep dusk. It was meal time for those who ate early. He said, "You won't be able to see the homestead tonight because there is no moon. The homestead you are looking for is really quite near. If I shouted, they would be able to hear. But it would be far for you, because you're a visitor. Where are those with whom you're traveling?"

The young man said, "The ones I'm traveling with are here. They're on the top, over there. I told them to stay there while I came here to ask."

So he said, and the other young man said, "We should go to them, I'll accompany you."

This young man traveled then, chatting with the master of ceremonies, that member of the bridal party, saying, "You are guests of our home. This place where you're going is also our home. The bride whom you're taking there is going to my older brother. I'm his younger brother. We are Ntlane by clan. I shall accompany all of you right up there."

The master of ceremonies came then and found us sitting like that. He came with this person, and, as they were approaching, we heard them conversing pleasantly about that matter. They were laughing. They arrived, and the master of ceremonies said, "Get up and take your loads." He was referring to the goods that we were carrying—pots, drinking vessels, billycans, dishes, and what not, all the things that were common in those days when I was married. There were no boxes yet at that time, nor anything that resembles a chest; all the goods were carried in shoulder bags and in buckets; some of them would be wrapped in mats, some would be carried in kerchiefs.

We traveled then. We traveled with this young man. We turned around because the road cut below Nkanga hill, and we went below Nkanga. We crossed a streambed, then another place that was like a streambed—but

---

Xhosa." *Hlonipha* is a system of respect and reverence shown by Xhosa women toward their in-laws who are male. It involves a substitute vocabulary for words normally spoken.

these only resembled streambeds; it was the way the land was shaped. When one says, "across," it does not mean across a river, it means across this depression of the land. Because it was already dark, there was the danger that we might get hurt in these depressions. It began to seem as if we were traveling over cliffs.

I was robed in my new cloak, the one that had been wrapped around me at home, the one that I am still wearing now. We walked on there; we skirted that place. As we neared this homestead to which I was being taken, there were bushes, shrublike trees.[8] There were cabbage-wood trees,[9] and there were thickets. These thickets were on either side of the road. Beyond the thickets were peach trees that we came to realize were a part of the orchard of my homestead of marriage; my father-in-law's orchard had been there a long time.

We traveled there. We women were treated delicately because the person who would marry was in the bridal party: she was cared for with special attentiveness, so that she would not stumble and fall and be blemished. She was taken care of particularly. Someone would repeatedly come to me, and I would be held so that I would not get hurt. We traveled to this place, coming down from above the homestead; we arrived and sat at a spot overlooking the home. Dogs came out. They barked; they were barking.

When we had settled down, this young man who had accompanied us, the young man of the Ntlane clan, went ahead to the house because it was also his home. He explained that I had arrived with some visitors. The many dogs in this homestead were barking at this group of people sitting above the homestead.

A young married woman came out of the house.[10] She went to us and asked, "Where have you come from?"

Someone said that we had come from across the Mbashe River and were on our way to the Nciba River. "We are benighted, and we have a child with us who is not well. We're asking for a place to spend the night."

The young married woman casually hopped around in her response because such comments are a Xhosa custom. That is how it is done; even though everyone knows what is going on, including the young married woman, the game must be played through.[11] She said, "This particular

---

8. The *umbongisa* is a shrublike tree, Royena lycioides, *D.C.*, and Royena pallens, *D.C.*

9. The *umsenge,* the cabbage-wood tree: Cussonia spicata *Thunb.*

10. An *inkazana* (pl. *amankazana*) is a woman living at her father's place. She might be a married woman who, for whatever reason, has parted from her husband. I have translated the word as "a young married woman," but the inference that she lives at her father's home rather than at her husband's place should be understood.

11. The bridal party always makes up such an exaggerated and fictional story, thereby inventing an excuse to stay the night at the groom's homestead.

homestead, of all the homesteads around here,[12] is the one in which you're asking for a place to spend the night?"

It was said in answer, "Well, really, it's just that it happens to be this time of day. And the health of the child is a consideration: this child hurts, she is limping. When one is limping, it's difficult to travel in the dark. More than the darkness, there are cliffs. For a long time, we've been carrying her on our backs, and she is heavy."

That young married woman said, "Oh, well then, I'm going to report this matter to the house." So she said, and she departed, and we sat there. My head was covered with a new cape that was being worn for the first time. Actually, all of us had our heads covered, including those women who were accompanying me. One of those women was my sister, coming after me in age. The women were on either side of me, my sister was next to me. The other young woman was from another village. She too had her head covered. We sat there in that way.

After a time, that young married woman returned. She arrived and said, "Rise. It is said that you should go to that house."

We got up as one, our entire group of people. We went to that house. When we entered the house, we found that the furniture had been taken out.[13] The house had been daubed; this house was plastered with cow dung. There was firewood in a corner by the doorway; some had been chopped, some had not been chopped. A fire had even been kindled in the hearth, probably by the young married woman. We arrived, and mats were spread out. We sat. An old cloak of one of the men with whom we were traveling was made into a curtain, and we sat over there on the other side of this curtain.

After a short time, there was a knock on the door, and food was brought in. It was stamped maize; it was cooked with beans, and it was dished out. Dishes were put down, and we ate there in that house.

Then the master of ceremonies said that we had a request concerning something that we had lost. We requested that the master of ceremonies be permitted to depart for a short time in the morning, so that he could return to our home to get information about the loss of that thing that we had been carrying with us. The reference was to the ox that was lost at a fork in the wagon road as we were leaving the Qwaninga River area. Both homesteads had respect for each other, so there was no undue concern about this request; it was not suspect. The request, therefore, was agreed to. As the young married woman went to explain that matter in the house, the bride's party had to wait. But the hosts had a suspicion that this re-

12. A member of the audience comments, "Oh, you're *hlonipha*-ing. Is that the way you create an *intsomi* [fantastic tale]?" *Hlonipha* language is reverential language, substituting for normal speech.

13. Probably to make way for daubing the floor.

quest, which was presented with the urgency of a demand, might possibly have to do with the bridal party's beast, this thing that the bridal party had lost. Because of this urgent request, they reasoned, it was time to consider the bridal party's beast.

The bridal party was patient, waiting.

Before it was time to go to bed, another member of the groom's home came there and knocked. A member of the bridal party said, "Come in." He entered and was asked, "Is this person of this homestead bringing us any word?"

He said, "Yes, I am speaking. I've been sent from over there at the house. Because there is something that we do not know. It is said that a man from this group should come outside for a short time to identify a certain object. This might be what you say was lost as you traveled. But we do not know what you have lost, what it looked like. What we wish to identify arrived here before it was dark; it arrived early in the evening, after the livestock had been locked up. Please come and look."

Immediately, a member of the bridal party got up, and this young fellow and the old man of the bridal party ran over each other, going to look. They arrived and the member of the bridal party saw that it was that ox that they had driven, its name being Selani, the yellow ox. They were amazed that it should have preceded them here; it had been here for a long time.

They said, "This is what we have been speaking about!"

It was said then at the Ntlane homestead, "This ox has been here for quite some time. When you arrived, it was already here. It got here when we were putting the livestock into the kraal. It lay down in the kraal—in the middle, between the posts, in front of the entrance. It faced the entrance of the kraal. I tell you, it lay between the posts. At first, we regarded it as possibly some ox from around here," because at that time this homestead had much livestock—it had cattle, horses, sheep; it had wagons, it had all the things of those days. Were an ox to come around here, no one would take any notice. Sometimes, it would even be thought to belong here. No one would take notice or raise a question as to where it had come from.

The people returned from outside. They said, "Heee! It's amazing! This ox turns out to be the very one! When we were going over to Nkanga and lost our way, when we wanted to cut by the shop, it knew where the homestead was. It parted company with us over there at Ndlambe's place because we were going the wrong way, we were driving it to where it was not intended to go. So it left us; it decided to come here by itself, to rest here and leave us to wander aimlessly alone."

The members of the bridal party laughed. From time to time, they came back to this subject and laughed. They chatted about it until morning.

Eventually, as morning was approaching, before dawn, the master of ceremonies got up and asked members of the groom's homestead to help him to slaughter the bridal party's ox. It was fat now, it was extraordinarily fat. I am not just speaking subjectively; it was amazingly fat! It was surpassingly fat. Its fat would fill billycans.

When everything was ready, the scheduled events occurred: "Bring down from the mountains,"[14] water for the bridal party, everything that was a part of the marriage ritual. Beer was ground for the celebration; for the festive gathering, much beer was prepared. There was a lot of beer, beer for which maize was brought to the house of the bridal party. Grinding stones were brought in, and the maize was roughly ground. The initial stages of brewing took place, then the dough was transported. It was the young women in the bridal party who ground it. I also ground maize, along with my companions in this house, so that the dough might be taken away by this young man of the bridal party. When we finished grinding, at dusk, he took the dough to the main house. Then, when people were sleeping, the young married woman again knocked—had it not been a young married woman, it would have been a young, recently married woman. When she knocked, it was said, "Come in!"

She was asked where she had come from, and she said, "I have come to borrow the young women." When she said, "the young women," she meant me together with the young women who were my companions, according to Xhosa custom. One of the young women was my sister, the other was from my village. It was that way with the groom as well, this was the proper form. He was treated in the same way as I. My groom had companions, two men; one of his companions was a Ntlane clansman, the other was a Dala clansman. So it was that this young married woman said that she had come to borrow the young women.

It was said, "We cannot produce the young women. We do not have such a custom—that, before the women are viewed formally, they already go to sleep with the men."

Because this matter of sleeping with men was a Xhosa custom, it was necessary that it be done. The master of ceremonies had to come out with a mat, and go with these young women of the bridal party, taking them to the house where the groom and his companions were. When the women arrived, the groom slept with his wife on his own mat, and the companions slept on their mats. It was necessary that, when the horns of the cattle glimmered at dawn, the young women should come out, and the bride and her party should return to the house of the bridal party, along with the master of ceremonies. They carried buckets, and went and washed their

14. That is, bring the members of the bridal party down from the place above the homestead, where they have been waiting, into the groom's homestead.

bodies. Then they returned and waited. Now, if they happened to oversleep, if it happened that this washing did not occur, if they did not get up at dawn, if they were still sleeping at daytime, if they overslept and it was light outside, the groom's party would be fined; the groom's party had to produce money for sleeping with people until the requisite time had passed without having been given leave to do so. These are requirements because this is where the master of ceremonies gets his money: if the young women oversleep, the master of ceremonies gets money by fining the groom's party—that money is his.

When we left the bridal party's house, the master of ceremonies urged us to oversleep so that he could get his fine money. "Don't keep saying, 'We want to go now!' You must oversleep!" Otherwise, this master of ceremonies would leave without having obtained any money.

We went then. When we were over there with the groom's party, the groom and I did not trouble each other, we just slept there.[15] But these companions were rowdy. They were grappling with each other because there was much sexual, amorous interest among them.

One said, "Yo! This young woman! If only she wouldn't go home, if only she were mine!" That resulted in a lot of commotion in this house.

The groom repeatedly said, "Don't be rowdy over there!"

That went on. Time passed; it went on, and things fell into place, and finally we did oversleep. My groom and I were wide awake, but the others were fast asleep. Remember that they had been roisterous all night. As the night went on, there was merriment, and when they did finally go to sleep it was almost daybreak.

I said to my groom, "Well, let's go now, wake up the others."

He said, "Oh, well, all right."[16] The reason the groom said that was because the larger share of the money would come from him, even though he had done nothing; he had just let it happen.

The master of ceremonies arrived and knocked at the door. When he entered, he said, "Ho! So that's the way it is! Who gave you these women?"

They rushed to get up.

"Yo!"

"No!"

"Pardon! Pardon! Pardon!"

"Really!"

He said, "I told you! Pour! Pour! Pour!" He was saying that they must pour money into his hand.

The groom's party begged, "No, really, you'll get it when we go to the house!"

15. That is, there was no sexual intercourse or wrangling.
16. He seems somewhat reluctant.

Then they went to the house. We did not bathe that day when we went into the bridal party's house.

The master of ceremonies said, "Well done, my girl! Now, do that again when night comes!" He had his eye on more money.

The money arrived then—the money of the companions was a half crown each, that of the groom was six shillings. So it was that time passed; the money of the master of ceremonies being uncontested,[17] and he had the intention of getting still more.

Time passed; that is the way things were.

As the celebration of the marriage went on, the reveling intensified, and it was finally necessary that the bridal party should come outside to be seen. The wind that day was very strong, Friend, the wind of the Ntlane clan. I can comment on the wind because I now belong to them, to the Ntlane clan.[18] Now, this wind of the Ntlane clan, really, was beautiful; it was a good omen: there was no lightning, there were no overcast skies, no thundering—nothing like thunder. It was a wind on a clear day.

The people in this homestead were observing this, and they took calabashes and faced them into the wind. They closed the mouths of the calabashes to produce musical notes there. As they watched, the members of the bridal party whispered critically about these activities. It was said, "Yo! This wind has some significance here in this land, but it has none for the bridal party. You see, they make calabashes and face them toward the wind."

The ceremony was moving toward the cattle kraal, but there had been delays. Repeatedly, someone was being sent from the house, saying, "When will the bridal party come out?"

The answer was, "No, we'll be there! We shall be there!"

This happened repeatedly—a person would come: "Say, when will this bridal party here at home come out? Is this wife yours, that you don't want us to see her?"

"No no no, we'll be there, Honored sir!"

The fellow returned. The thing that was delaying the bridal party was the washing and cleansing of the entire body. Then the hair was combed so that it was flat [literally, that it should sleep], then they worked the hair into a chignon, the hair being plaited and made into a rope. Sometimes, there were three ropes inside, and sometimes there were four that made up this topknot in the hair. The woman who wanted such a chignon selected her own style. On the neck were shells that were gathered on the seashore, picked up on the seashore and smoothed on rocks; two strings were made for the shells, and they were worn around the neck, hung in a

---

17. Literally, it sat quietly in his purse.
18. Literally, now I belong to them, and I understand what it is all about.

chain in front, coming down to the breasts—those shells looked marvelous. Another adornment was a necklace of green beads, sometimes called dove beads. These beads were arranged into a pattern which was then rolled into a long coil that had a loop that reached to the thighs when a person knelt. Those beads would be looped around the neck, and the bride would not have a breast cover; she would not wear anything, she would just stand naked in the kraal wearing a little loin cover. There were varieties of attire. She would emerge with her head covered with a turban that had been unrolled and just put on the head with no knots. This turban would be held in place by a cape that was thrown over her shoulders, and she caught hold of it in front. That kept the turban in place so that the wind would not blow it off.

Friend, I tell you, that is how it was in those days of my marriage.

The master of ceremonies was going to be in the front—he was that young man, not the old man here in the bridal party. The young man was the man who was in front, and he was followed by a young married woman behind. This young married woman glanced about and, when she saw that there was something that should be put right—making certain that the heads of all three of us were covered, that I was in the middle between my sister in front and the other young woman behind me, that our capes were not dragging on the ground lest we step on them—she whispered from time to time to the master of ceremonies. Then it was necessary that we stop, and the young married woman stopped. She turned around to correct whatever had to be corrected. Either she or the master of ceremonies would adjust the capes, pulling them here over the feet and shaking them, pushing them back a little. She whispered as she got up, "Don't raise your feet! That way, you step on your capes and pull them off. Shuffle your feet so that you don't step on the capes. Otherwise, we'll have to keep adjusting them."

So that she would not be heard by the other group over there, she spoke softly when she instructed us.

Those people over there were using abusive language, cursing. That is what they were doing over there. The women of the groom's side were in the cattle fold, and the men were in the courtyard. The bridal party was coming in a procession, slowly, with the young married woman and the master of ceremonies attending to their chores, helping the bridal party along, pulling up the capes, moving across the courtyard to the kraal where the groom's party was awaiting them. The bridal party was in the middle of the courtyard, and the groom's party was also in a procession, coming out of the house, also three in number.[19] That groom of mine was

19. The women and the other men of the groom's side were waiting for the two parties in the kraal, as the bridal party walked in a procession from one side and the groom's party from the other.

also put in the middle, and when I looked I saw that their order was a mirror of ours, his party being led by a Ntlane clansman, that clansman being followed also by someone from the village,[20] the groom in the middle as I was in the middle of our party.

They came into the kraal and sat on the right-hand side. It was not customary to sit just anywhere. Even the seating arrangements were according to Xhosa custom. It was necessary that they come in, then turn to the right and sit on that side. All the men in the house sat on the right-hand side. As we were being put right—our garments, or whatever—we walked very slowly. If you saw it, you would become dizzy with boredom, it was a slow process. The party did not advance very rapidly. Each one stepped in the same place as the person who went before, and we arrived at our destination after a very long time. And, I tell you, the master of ceremonies was being abused throughout all of this. Relatively casual insults were directed at the young married woman. The ones who did most of the reviling were the women.

They said to the master of ceremonies, "You with these hip bones! Don't get in our way as we gaze at those children!"

"Why do you keep looking at them, you bony, awkward thing?"

"We don't want you!"

"We see you busy-bodying around them with those scaly feet of yours! Hurry up with those children!"

"He is really a wonder! Where did they pick up this fool?"

"This thing looks like The-one-who-peers-nosily-in-there!"

The master of ceremonies paid no attention. He happened to be a flamboyant fellow. He stared at them, and sometimes he made faces at them if he felt like it, because this irreverent language of theirs was not really serious. This tradition of abusing the master of ceremonies does not worry anyone. No one takes it seriously. It is a custom that he should be so derided. Xhosa custom is being observed when they do that.

In the end, the bridal party arrived at the cattle kraal, the cattle fold. The master of ceremonies was going in front, removing every piece of dry dung. And there, in the kraal, he was even abused by the men.

"Go on! Go on, you young man!"

"What's all this? When will you get here if you keep wasting time being stylish, an exhibitionist?"

"You nobody, it's possible that you do not even have a wife, strutting like this in front of these women!"

"Is that your mistress [referring to the bride] whose eyes you keep looking so intently into, with whom you are being so familiar?"

---

20. As in Mrs. Zenani's bridal party, in which one of the women in attendance was a member of her village.

The men said this, but the master of ceremonies did not care. In the end, when they were in the center of the cattle fold, in the middle of the kraal, the party did not sit just anywhere. The master of ceremonies arrived there, and he spread things out, made things ready so that we would take our positions properly. Then he covered us; he busied himself around us, his penis cover bouncing as he hurried about, dangling his penis cover and his inner groin in our direction, running around, his hips and his buttocks facing the other people. He was naked because he was stepping on his cape with his feet, and his legs were spread wide. He covered us so that we should be inside the covering with him; he was hiding the bridal party from the groom's people.

The young married woman made us sit; she made us kneel. The garments were taken and put over the thighs; the body was exposed from the navel up, all the area down to the navel. It was necessary that the body from the navel up be exposed, that the entire top portion of the body including the breasts be seen. The black head coverings were removed and placed on the ground. We kept our heads low; we bowed reverentially toward the people that day. Yes, I bowed my head, being a young woman who was perfect in my home. My sister too was fine; she had a good complexion, even better than mine. So we were on our knees, facing the men, and the men burst out and said, "Yo yo yo yo yo!" There was even a man who went further, who said, "My daughter-in-law, we loved her even before we saw her!"

In the meantime, the master of ceremonies was thrusting his buttocks and hanging his testicles in our direction. He deliberately closed a blanket around us so that the groom's party could not see us. And he was again verbally abused: "Let us see her again!" But he would not let them see us.

The groom's party joined us. The members of that groom's party also had hair ornaments. They put on beaded necklaces; they wore shells and capes. They were bareheaded, while we had our heads covered with black turbans. At the feet, on the calves where the lower leg ends, entering the feet, we wore boots; over the boots were black beads, rows of black beads inside and white beads outside. Those beads were worn by a bride who was still young. At the time of my marriage, they were worn by the bride until the time when she stopped wearing her turban just over her eyes. She wore her boots until she took off the cloth that was tied around her waist. She wore her boots constantly until she became a young married woman. And when these boots wore out [literally, became lazy], they wore out when she was a beer-party-going woman. Even when she was a beer-party-going woman who was aware of herself, a woman who dressed well, people knew her by those boots. And there were the chains, together with all the other things that adorn a person. Today, that custom is no more; it has fallen into disuse. This is today's practice: boots are worn on that day only, on the day that the bride is viewed, for the last time. Never again will she wear boots.

That was the custom when I was married.

When we came out from the men and went to the women, this master of ceremonies was abused by the women. We had left a shilling at the place where I had been sitting in the kraal among the men. We carried another shilling; this would be left under me also, when we went among the women. When we were before the women, we went down on our knees in the same way as we did in the kraal before the men, there were the buttocks-thrusting activities of the master of ceremonies, and we were again exposed and naked, shown to the women as we were to the men earlier. We went down on our knees and faced the women. The master of ceremonies uncovered us, and when he had done so it was said, "Yo yo yo! She is beautiful, Friends!"

"Yo!"

So they said, those who were being hypocritical as well as those who were in earnest.

When we were covered, the master of ceremonies made us stand because we were going to the house.

The women said, "The legs! Show the legs, lest you should bring us a cripple!"

We were turned toward the east, our movements orchestrated by the master of ceremonies, and now the young married woman and the master of ceremonies helped each other to expose our legs for the women. The garment was lifted.

"Yo yo yo yo!"

So it was that they observed that there was no cripple. Still, even when they had suggested that, they really knew that there was no cripple. Even suggesting that was a mere matter of form.

The top portion of the body was exposed as well as the lower.

We went on very slowly again, but now we were going to the house. When we arrived at the house of the bridal party, we undressed. Skirts were there already, and we put on the skirts; we put on the skirts.

The naughtiness of the young married women of this place as well as their daughters was legendary.

Hoes and buckets were now brought. There was much noise. Now the young married women came; they said, "At this home, the land is cultivated," and they struck the ground.[21]

"At home here, water is dipped."

Others chopped wood: "At home here, wood is gathered."

---

21. That is, to show stylistically and symbolically how the hoeing was done.

They demonstrated everything, mixing up all of these activities. They were noisy.

Then, the master of ceremonies came out of the door, and he took a strap, he took a billycan, and sat in front of them. He squatted and put the billycan between his thighs, then imitated the milk when it struck the can when a cow was being milked. He milked, going through the motions, all the while saying, "At our home, before any milking is done, you have to produce cattle so that we can milk and plough and do what not."[22]

That is the way this portion of the marriage ceremony worked. The young married women departed, and we put on our skirts and began to put on our breast covers. These young married women took off their breast covers, and we put ours on. We covered our heads to the eyes and knotted our turbans under our chins. We looked like lumpy-headed hammerbirds with the turbans on our heads. We went to the river. There we were, going to the river, lined up and shawled. Then we came back from there and put those buckets down circumspectly, going around the homestead, avoiding the courtyard.

After that, there was the actual marrying.

"Master of Ceremonies, the ceremony has now taken place."

The master of ceremonies came out then, and a bar was put across the entrance to the cattle kraal. He put money there for the removal of the bar. When the bar had been removed, they delayed killing the ox, because they wanted the money of the spear from him. He provided the money of the spear, and the ox was slaughtered. This part of the ritual is called "The marrying of me." That is what they were saying: they were marrying me by means of this ox; that is how I became a wife of this homestead.

We ate that meat then, portions of which went to the people of the homestead [the groom's homestead], to the guests, and so on, the meat of the home being helped along by appropriate payments of money. After that, it was said that I should undergo the ritual of drinking milk from this cow. Then there was some confusion. On the day that I married and became a wife, my people said, "A beast of marriage [the *impothulo* beast] that has traveled all over the land shall not be the one with which the bride shall undergo the ritual of drinking milk. We shall not allow it to happen! The ritual of drinking milk can only be done by means of a goat that is suitable for this custom. An ox—never! An ox is for celebration, not for this milk-drinking ritual." Yo! They said, "This may be what they have

22. The master of ceremonies, representing the bride's home, may be suggesting that provision of the rest of the dowry must be completed before the bride can do the chores being demonstrated by the in-laws. The pretense of milking by the master of ceremonies may be a not so subtle way of reminding them that more cattle are necessary for the dowry, that the full dowry has not yet been provided.

done in the rituals of others, but they won't get away with it in our case!"[23]
Then the bridal party said, "You did that to those people of Tsomo area,
but we're not those people! This young woman will have the correct milk-
drinking ritual! You won't trifle with us with an ox! What you're doing is
foolishness. It's certainly not the ceremony of drinking milk."

At length, my groom surrendered his goat, a gelding of a goat, and the
ceremony of drinking milk was performed. Now, the meat of this beast
was finished, and the ceremony was performed. They brought a strap
along with a bucket that had milk in it. A slice of meat was roasted, and
brought. The strap was soaked in the milk. A mouthful of meat was soaked,
and I was made to suck on the strap. I was given that mouthful of meat
that had been soaked in milk. It was a really disgusting thing to taste, but,
because it was the custom, it was acceptable, so I swallowed it. We ate the
meat then; the meat of the homestead of the groom's people was sent and
accepted.

This was the procedure: the skin of the goat slaughtered for the milk-
drinking ritual belonged to the master of ceremonies. These things were
carefully distributed. They were not casually thrown this way and that;
they were allocated here in the house in an orderly way, according to
protocol. The master of ceremonies was the young man who ran errands,
going to see to everything, in this house of the bridal party, and he was
sent to the groom's house.

Time passed, and the money of the young married women was now
demanded, along with the money of the homestead. On the occasion of
my marriage, there was no money that was not forthcoming. But it was
clear that the bridal party should return home quickly: my father, a Christian convert, was ready to produce the necessary twelve pounds, saying
that, because obligations must be discharged according to social procedures, all the money required should be produced. He did not know if
twelve pounds would be enough, nor how the twelve pounds would be
distributed to meet the demands.[24] That money of the young married
women is distinct, it has its own name. It is called "the money of the
young married women," and that is all. It is fixed; it cannot be used for
anything else. The women of this homestead of mine did not share the
money of the women with any other group. The three pounds earmarked
for this purpose were distributed within that group. The smaller currency

23. That is: "This is the kind of thing they did when others in this groom's family got married. They got away with it with those others, but they won't get away with such cheap, non-
customary actions with us!"

24. The father, a Christian, seems to be in a hurry to get things over with, to complete this
non-Christian custom. He is willing to accept the custom, to pay the requisite amount of
money; he is at his home, not here at the marriage ceremony, but it seems that he wishes the
entire tradition to be completed quickly.

was distributed, according to their status, among the women who happened to be present in this homestead.[25] The daughter-in-law had no part in the share of the married women. The older brother and the young brother[26] are those who were privileged to have a share of the money. The distribution of money goes all the way to the aunts and whoever—except for the daughter-in-law.

The activity proceeded in that way; then the marriage ceremony ended. At the end of the ceremony, the people went home. Before that happened, I was taken to the main house with all of my belongings. I came out of the house of guests and went to put the things in the main house of my new home. My father-in-law and mother-in-law and older brother were not in the main house of my new home; only the wife of my older brother was there, in place of the parents.[27] She presided over the preparations, making things right. The bridal party now went outside to the men. It departed with four cattle because the six had already gone, to make up a dowry of ten.

When they had departed, I stayed in the homestead of the groom as a married woman. I lived well. I was treated properly by the wife of my older brother [meaning, her brother-in-law], and I also honored her completely. Now, she is deceased. While she lived, we were never separated; we never talked in an ugly way to each other, we did not use bad language or strike each other. She was the person who took the responsibility. When I was a little older, at the time of the birth of my third child, it became clear that I, the wife of her younger brother, should build my own homestead. I asked her to give me leave to go and set up a house on my own, but she resisted this for a long time. Finally, she agreed. She was willing to provide me with the wherewithal to set up housekeeping on my own, so that I should live well, so that I did not have to borrow anything from anyone. She offered to give me her grinding stone; she gave it to me so that I might have a stone and not have to grind at other homesteads. She offered me her little pot so that I could cook and not have to ask for anything from other homesteads. That was the evidence of the mutual respect that there was between us because I had put myself under her completely, even after she had a daughter-in-law. Her child was circumcised under my eye; he married, and she had a daughter-in-law. The daughter-in-law bore a child, and I had still not moved out and set up my own homestead.

25. That is, the money is all apportioned. It is distinct for each purpose; it cannot be used for any other purpose.

26. The older brother's wife? The young brother's wife? It is customary to refer to the woman according to the title of the husband.

27. Her older brother was apparently dead. Her sister-in-law took the place of the parents.

A MOTHER WHO HAD NO SON

Performance Note

Time: 10 August 1972, late morning. *Place:* In a fallen rondavel near Mrs. Zenani's home in Nkanga, Gatyana District, the Transkei. *Audience:* Two women. (Perf. NS-140.)

This is a story about another time.

A man once said to his wife, "Wife, the fields are not yielding much. I think that I should take another wife. She can be the right-hand house, the wife of the right-hand house."[28]

His wife said, "I am opposed to a second wife in this homestead. It will not be a congenial arrangement. We'll irritate each other."

The man said, "No, you won't resent each other. This institution of the right-hand house is only one section of the home. I shall build her homestead for her in another place. But it shall also be one of my homesteads. It shall be built in the same way as we built this one. When that wife has become accustomed to our ways, we shall give her the wherewithal to establish a homestead and to build it up herself."

The wife said, "How will that be done?"

"Well, she'll be given a heifer. From the small stock, she'll be given, say, a sheep or a goat. She's being given a heifer so that she can become my other homestead, the second homestead."

His wife said, "Oh, Sobani, if that's to become your homestead, then who'll remain here? Who will stay here with me? Which man will be my husband?"

The man said, "Well, you shall be my 'great' wife. You shall be honored and deferred to by the junior wife. She'll be important only in her section."

The wife said, "Are you trying to worry me?"

He said, "No, you won't be inconvenienced. Can't you see the number of wives over there at the royal residence? As many as eight wives to one man. And those wives have status."

"What will that wife do for me?"

"She will become your supporting house. If something goes wrong for you here, she'll be the one who rushes in to help you with whatever is causing damage. If it's something that causes you joy, you'll celebrate with her. You'll help each other. It'll be as if she were your sister. She is the stick

28. "The second married wife of a commoner the *umfazi wasekunene* (Right Hand Wife). . . . has a very important status. It is second only to that of the *umfazi omkhulu* (Great Wife) and she therefore exercises great authority in the *umzi* [homestead]. She is not wholly subservient to the Great Wife, and has an independent status. . . ." (J. Van Tromp, *Xhosa Law of Persons* [Cape Town: Juta and Co., Ltd., 1947], p. 88).

The storyteller in a didactic mood

to guard your back where you cannot see. And, similarly, you're the stick to guard her back where she cannot see. You'll live together cooperatively, advising and helping each other."

That wife remained quiet for a long time without responding. She was troubled because her husband was going to marry another wife. She thought about it, then decided that she should visit the home of her birth regarding this matter. She should go home and recount the strange thing suggested by her husband.

One day, she said, "Sobani!"

Her husband responded.

"I miss my home. I want to visit my people. It's been a long time since I've seen them."

"But who will you leave behind?"

She said, "I'll return promptly, I won't sleep overnight."

Her husband gave her leave to go. "Go then. But return before nightfall."

So the woman departed. She went to her home, and when she got there she greeted everyone.

"Where have you come from?"

"Well, I've come from home."

"What made you think of us at this time?" her father asked.

"Well, Father, I thought of you on this day, but I did not come to ask you for anything. I'm paying you this visit because I'm trying to understand something. I want to have a conversation with you, Father, and with Mother. Over there, by the kraal."

When she had said that, they hurriedly went over, eager to hear what their daughter would say.

When they got to the kraal, her father said, "Speak then, my daughter."

"Father, I'm visiting you because of a strange thing that my husband has been talking about. I want you to assure me that such a thing is proper because when he mentioned it to me, it disturbed me. I don't understand how a second wife can be desired. He has never shown any dissatisfaction with me. Now he says that he wants a woman to become the wife of the right-hand. He says that the right-hand wife will be one side of the home, that he'll build a homestead for the right-hand wife. She will be my rear guard, he says. If she notices something that I haven't noticed, something that might cause me trouble, she'll set it right. I'll do the same for her if I should see something that might trouble her. And on happy occasions, we'll also cooperate.

"That's what my husband says, Father. He told me that a heifer and perhaps a young female goat would be taken from my stock and given to that woman. He says that this must be done so that her homestead becomes just like mine. Now, this has not pleased me. But my husband cited the fact that the king over there at the royal residence has eight wives. It has become clear to me that this husband of mine wants innumerable wives.

"When he told me all this, I didn't respond. I decided that I should come here and seek counsel from you, to see if what he is doing is correct. That's why I've come here, to see if you can understand it. It troubles me. I don't understand it at all. It seems to me that my husband is being critical of me, although he hasn't indicated this in our talks about his strange desire to have another wife."

Her father said, "Wait, my daughter. Please wait. If you speak at too great length, you won't recall what your first word was. Now then, did you say that this matter is strange?"

"Yes, Father, that's what I said—in my heart."

"Well, Child, when you concluded that this is something that is unheard of, weren't you able to see with your own eyes that there are as many as eight wives at the royal residence?"

The daughter said, "Yes, Father, I can see that they are there."

"Well then, my daughter, from your own observation, what fault do you see in these eight wives?"

The daughter said, "There's no fault that I can see, Father. But it is also obvious to me that some of those wives are mere things, objects, not especially honored by that king. They are objects called 'brooms' for sweeping up the dust.[29] I have no desire that my husband have another wife."

Her father said, "My daughter, according to Xhosa custom, you are honored when your husband thinks about doing something in his homestead, especially with respect to taking a wife. He does not usually condescend to discuss such matters with his wife. He more often discusses them with the male members of his clan. He tells them, 'I want another wife. You must help me to find a homestead with a suitable woman.' He takes counsel with the appropriate men of his area. But you have the unusual distinction of being consulted by your husband before he goes to the other men of his clan. If you were sensible, if you were not a woman,

29. In addition to the great house, right-hand house, and supporting house is the *ixhiba*, the house of the wife called "the broom": "This is a house found among Chiefs only and not among *abantu abamnyama* (commoners); and the establishment of the *xhiba* wife is not in the same *umzi* or kraal as the establishment of other women may be. The status of this wife differs from that of any other house of the husband. It is not under the control of either the *indlu enkulu* [great house] or the *indlu yasekunene* [right-hand house].

"The *xhiba* house is sometimes spoken of as the *indlu yendlu enkulu*, meaning that it is the House of the Great House, thereby indicating that it is the house of the Chief's father. It must perform certain sacrificial ceremonies for the spirits of the forefathers who have occupied it. . . . The *xhiba* wife is married after the fourth wife [among the Xhosa], and usually is the fifth wife married by the Chief (J. Van Tromp, *Xhosa Law of Persons* [Cape Town: Juta and Co., Ltd., 1947], pp. 91, 95–96).

my daughter, you would have exchanged opinions properly with your husband. Look, you already have five children. That means that you're a well-established woman in your homestead. It's about time your husband thought of taking another wife. You don't have a man child; you have borne only girls. It might be that your husband is hoping for a child who will have a testicle. That may be why he is thinking of marrying another woman.

"This will be a way for you to grow old gracefully. After you've grown old and have lost your vigor, your children will be unprotected because there is no man child. If there were a man child, your children would have someone to look after them, someone to do for them the things that they need—because by that time you won't be able to work anymore. My opinion, then, Daughter, is that you should not be worried. Let your husband take that wife. When he is about to brand the ears of his livestock, he'll call the men together and speak with you first. Then he'll mark the stock with his brand. These are the marks of ownership, my child: he'll take the heifer and give it to the wife of the right-hand. In time, a kraal will be built for that heifer in the homestead he has constructed for that wife. Then he'll enclose that beast that he marked on the ear, and it will give birth to calves there. Various gifts that are presented to her will be placed in that kraal, and the heifer and subsequent gifts will be distinguished from your stock by these ear-marks."

Then that man turned to his wife, the woman's mother, and said, "Well, Nobani, do you agree with what I have said to your daughter?"

"Yes, Sobani, I agree."

"If you agree with it, what comment would you like to make? This child has come here so that we might explain to her whether or not her husband is doing the right thing. But you shouldn't be influenced, my wife, by the fact that I never took another wife for you. Your reaction to this situation should not contradict Xhosa custom. Remember that, in your home, you had more than one mother. You had more than one mother at your home, my wife.

"Now you must clarify things for this child. What do you, the mother, have to say? Remember that children are often confused by the ideas that they get from their mothers. I am glad that my child came to both of us when she was seeking enlightenment regarding this problem. I am pleased that she came to us and brought the two of us together as soon as she arrived. I am happy that she did not take you aside by yourself, so that she might get your response to the problem before I got to see her. You might have said injudicious things to her.

"All right, respond to her now."

The wife remained quiet for a time, then said, "Well, Nobani, I hear all that you have said. And she also understands what you have spoken.

Now I want you to know that it would be quite proper for you to look around for a young woman for this homestead. The work around here is breaking my back. Really!

"I would never say anything contrary to this child. I'd never tell her something that contradicts what you have already told her. Yes, her husband should take another wife, because my daughter hasn't given birth to a male child. That is a fact. Let me say this, my child, about the words your father has spoken. Don't hope for other words; these are enough. Let your husband find another wife. Pay no attention to what you've seen at the royal residence. It's been a time-honored practice over there—you know this—that some wives are, from the start, regarded as 'brooms' of the great house. Sometimes it turns out that the 'broom' is the more loved and honored of the wives, but sometimes that 'broom' is never favored by the king—and she actually becomes little more than what her name implies: a thing for sweeping. [See the appendix, "The Broom," for Mrs. Zenani's story about a "broom" wife.] Now don't allow that to cause you anxiety. Just let things be.

"Look at me. I've had three mothers. When you visit the home of my birth, you never notice anything untoward, my child. You find happiness there and mutual love.

"And another thing. Over there at my home, you get what you want from one of the other mothers if my own mother doesn't have it. That's because of the reciprocal understanding among the mothers.

"Men aren't the same either. They don't all ignore the first wife when they take another. Some men know how to live with the institution of the wives. You might feel inside that the institution is not quite right, but the actions themselves demonstrate that it is indeed proper."

So said the young woman's mother.

Then the man said, "Heed those fine words that your mother has spoken. She's saying precisely what I said. And I repeat: don't balk the next time your husband tells you that he wants another wife. Let him seek her. And you should be well disposed to such a woman, because she'll be taken into your house. Treat her well; admonish her. And don't take exception if once in a while she goes on a journey with your husband. Don't let that distress you. She should be able to take journeys with her husband just as you do."

Then the young woman said, "All right, Father, that was the only reason I came here. I came to find out what I should do about that matter, to discover whether it's right or wrong. Since you're of the same mind as my mother, I'll depart now. But you should know that, if this second marriage is a distressing one for me, I shall no longer be a wife to him. If things turn out not to be as you have described them, I shall not be a wife to him any longer. I shall not become a mere plaything after having built up the homestead and reached this status."

So saying, the young woman departed.

As she was leaving, her mother said, "Don't you even want some ochre? Since you're not staying overnight?"

Her father said, "Give her some ochre."

Her mother took some of the ochre that is applied to garments and gave it to the young woman. Then the daughter departed; she went home.

When she reached her marriage homestead, she sat down.

Her husband said, "Nobani, I don't understand why you came back so quickly. Didn't you find your parents at home?"

"Yes, I found them there; they hadn't gone anywhere. But I didn't go there to ask for anything. I merely went to visit them for the day. I told you that I intended to return by nightfall."

Her husband said, "I thought you just said that in passing. I really thought that you would stay overnight. After all, sometimes you say that you'll return by nightfall, then sleep over anyway."

Several days passed, then her husband said, "Well, Wife, concerning that matter that I mentioned to you: I have some young men, they seem quite judicious and mature. I've sent them to find that wife for me, the one I spoke to you about. I've sent them to a home that I already regard with favor. And the people over there seem to be pleased because they know this homestead. Now it's necessary that you make the preparations because the guests are arriving today."

The wife said, "What preparations am I to make?"

He said, "As you know, the visitors should find firewood here when they arrive. And there should be a pot ready, so that food can be provided for them. I'm going to slaughter a little lamb for them to eat, that's the customary practice. When the guests have come, it's usual for them to have a little chicken [a euphemism] prepared for them, so they can eat something before going to sleep. A dish should also be ready. That is the custom. And when you dish the food out for them, they'll be expecting you to say, 'Pluck off the feathers, here's a fowl!' But a fowl is not really what is meant. What is meant is that you should take some 'lamb,' be it of sheep or goat."

Then the wife said, "Where will that 'lamb' be obtained?"

He said, "I told you about this before. I told you about the marking of the ears, that when I marry this wife these things will be obtained from you. I won't ask for anything from any other homestead. I'll take it from the fold here. I'll choose one beast and then go and perform that ritual."

His wife said, "All right, do as you see fit. I'll cook the food because I was going to cook anyway. As for the firewood—well, there's wood on the woodpile."

He said, "Yes, it's true that there's wood on the woodpile. But I meant that you should also prepare the guest room. You understand that they won't be put into the main house. They'll be lodged in another house, then come to the main house in the morning, when they're about to depart. I want you to know all of this, my wife, so that you'll understand just what I'm doing.

"Then I'll provide the dowry. I've already sent them six head of cattle. I've taken these six cattle from your kraal here. Because I've done that, this is what will happen: I have taken these six cattle from your kraal. If this woman produces a living thing when she becomes pregnant, and the child grows up, then that child will be yours—whether it's a girl or a boy. It shall become yours. That is how the cattle of your homestead will be repaid to you."

Then the woman said, "Ha! Do you really think such a thing is possible, that a woman would allow her child to become the child of someone else?"

Her husband said, "It will indeed happen. It is law. It is custom. If such a child refuses to live with you at your home, and if she happens to be a girl, when she marries the dowry knows its rightful home—that will be undisputed. All of it will be yours, for the firstborn child."

His wife said, "Well, go ahead then, Fellow of my father. We'll see."

As the sun was setting, the people accompanying the bride arrived. There were two of them. When they arrived, they were taken to the house which the wife had prepared. Time passed. The guests remained in that house. And the wife dished out the meal as she had been instructed by her husband. She brought the guests' dishes in, and they ate.

When they had finished eating, the husband said, "Now it's time for me to send that 'lamb' over to them."

The wife said, "All right."

A neighbor, a man of the same clan, was present. The two had been sitting together in the house.

"My brother, go and look for that 'lamb' we were talking about, and take it to these guests. Tell them, 'The old man of this homestead says that you should pluck the feathers off this "fowl" and eat it before going to sleep.'"

The man got up and went to the kraal, the fold for the small stock. He chose a suitable beast, fit to be sent to the guests. He took it with him and knocked on the door of the guest house.

"Come in."

He went in.

He was asked where he had come from.

"I come from home. The old man sends me to you to say, 'Pluck the feathers from this fowl. There's really nothing to eat at this home. But please take this, so that you'll have something to eat before going to bed, so that you won't be too critical of us. It does sometimes happen that a traveler comes to a homestead and gets only a place to sleep—in a dirty house. Bear with us.'"

When he had finished talking, the guests said, "We thank you. Convey our warm thanks to the old man over there. The dearth is widespread in all the land, wherever one goes."

"He's done a great thing for us. We can never forget you. But please lend us someone to do this task for us."

The fellow went out then with the beast. He took a knife and cut its throat. He flayed it, then took it back to the guests. The meat that would be given to the homestead—the foreleg and the viscera—was prepared. What was to be cooked was cooked: the lower portions, the backbone. When it was removed from the fire, the guests sent the gift of that meat which had now been cooked over to the main house.

They were again thanked.

The next day, the guests went to the main house. When they got there, mats were spread out for them, and they sat down. When they had done that, they were asked if they had anything to say.

They said, "We do have something to say, Mathile clanspeople. Actually, Sirs, we're hurrying toward our departure now, and we're going to leave behind the one whom you have provided with a dowry. We've come to you now with the intention of describing her to you. She has no scar; there's nothing the matter with her. Except for the usual things that come and go, there's nothing wrong with her. And now, we must depart."

The man who had been with the owner of the homestead said, "What you say is acceptable. You're saying the kind of thing we like to hear. When someone is leaving a child behind, he should make a statement concerning her. That is something we would have asked you about, and now you've already made the statement. Convey our thanks to the people of your homestead. We know that this young woman was duly admonished when she departed from her home. We hope that she will follow those admonitions closely."

So they departed. And she remained behind, to be a newly married bride. Time passed for that woman [meaning, the first—or great—wife], and she observed the words that had been spoken to her at her home. She looked after the new bride, talking helpfully to her about everything, teaching her the customs. She told her that she should go to the river at dawn, and the young woman went to the river at dawn.

In time, the younger wife became pregnant; she became large. The months went by; she was a woman who enjoyed mutual love, and there were no problems. She and the older wife looked after each other well.

When she took a journey, the senior wife would say, "My sister, I'll be away for a while. Take this key for the special house, and I'll leave the box key with you as well, so that you can set things in order."

She kept no secrets from the junior wife, and they loved each other.

When the time came, the younger wife bore a child. She bore the child in the older wife's home, and not in her own. She delivered it right there at her husband's wife's house, and her first child was a man child.

"What a good thing!" said the older wife. "Today, I have gotten a son."

It was all very pleasant: the words that had been uttered on the first day had come to pass—"Perhaps she'll bear a boy!" That had indeed happened; a boy had been born. Now the things spoken by her husband and father were confirmed; she had heeded their words, and these things were now coming to fruition. She loved that child and carried him on her back; she nursed him. And he spent much time with her while the young bride was busy working. The infant spent so much time with the older wife that it was not readily apparent that the younger wife was its mother.

Time passed; the years rolled on and on. The child was weaned, and soon it became evident that the mother was again pregnant. When she was big with the child, still enjoying a good life, she bore a daughter.

The older wife said, "Now I have a daughter!" because, as you know, it had been said that the new wife's first children would belong to the first wife, and she was glad about that too.

Again, life was pleasant, and she loved this child. The child so enjoyed being with its older mother that she went to her own mother only to sleep. Once again, the husband brought up some of the things that had been discussed on the day that they had agreed he could take another wife.

He spoke to the senior wife: "Nobani."

She responded.

"Wife, I think that we should give this wife an 'axe.' This 'giving of the axe' means that we should build for her her own homestead, the homestead of the right-hand house."

The wife said, "But Sobani, what will happen if a homestead is built for this young wife? Who shall remain behind here at home? Who shall be the young wife? You took this woman to wife when I was still vigorous. I'm not as active as I once was. You've spoiled me with this young person who can move so quickly around the homestead. What will happen now? It won't be long before the girls get married, and I'll be left alone at home here."

The husband paused, not answering. After a time, he said, "Nobani, I must take another wife. She'll be your supporting house."

The wife answered, "Oh! You're going to marry another?"

"Yes. As you know, a supporting house will never leave, she won't go anywhere. In time, the right-hand will also have a supporting house attached to it. It will be called 'the supporting house of the right hand.' It's necessary to have one wife who'll not depart from here, who'll be your supporting house."

The wife was quiet for a while. Eventually, she spoke: "Now this is something else that you're talking about, Sobani. Does this mean that you're going to subtract even more cattle from among the stock of this homestead?"

Her husband answered, "I'll not be diminishing any cattle. That new wife will be yours, she'll add to your strength. She'll never leave you. Even her children will be yours, all of them, because she is a supporting house. If she bears a boy, he is yours."

The wife replied, "But you also said that the boy borne by the right-hand wife would be mine. How does it happen now that the supporting house will bear children for me? Aren't you deceiving me?"

The husband said, "Of course, that one is more senior because she came to you before there was a supporting house. Now, this one is a supporting house. She'll be junior to that one, a younger sister, because she came when the senior one was already here."

The wife left the matter at that. But when she thought about it again, she decided to visit her home, to go and consult about it once more with her father and mother—to see if they concurred again. She went there in a great hurry, not even asking for permission from her husband.

She got there early, when people were still rousing themselves from their sleep. She greeted them and knelt.

Her father said, "What's the matter, my child? Why are you kneeling?"

"Well, Father, I wanted to come home immediately. I didn't even tell my husband that I was coming here. I had to hurry, to come at once. He wasn't at home when I left. I plan to be back there by the time he gets home. Let's talk together."

They went outside, she and her mother and father.

"Well, speak. What is it?"

"Father, you're the one who said that I should agree that my husband take a wife of the right-hand house. We haven't quarreled about anything. I haven't even quarreled with this wife. I have had no misunderstanding with her yet. But now, my husband says that he wants to take another wife. He says that he's setting up a supporting house. He'll take my cattle again. He says that this other wife should be 'given an axe,' so that she can go and build her own homestead. What do you think of that? Is such a thing correct? Do you still think that what he is doing is proper? Is it good that one's cattle be decimated like that over something one doesn't even understand? I ask you, Father."

Her father answered, "Yes, my child, that is the truth. It's still the truth. I tell you, this child is really loved by her husband! Did you hear this, Nobani?"

The wife said, "I heard it, Sobani."

"This child is truly loved! He is right, my daughter. That's the way it is. The supporting house is you. She will never leave you, that's the family of your own house. She, this supporting house, has no other place to go. If there are children in that house, they'll all be your children. Even if the supporting house produces a boy, he will become the junior brother of that one who is being grafted on to you—you having no male child. That one of the right-hand house is still to bear for us a boy of the right-hand house, if she has another child. So you must calm down. Don't become so heated. Abate your passion for the sake of your husband. Bitter talk causes misunderstandings between a woman and her husband. Don't use crude speech—speak smoothly, gently."

"Well then, that's the only thing I came here for. It's all right," said the daughter. "If that's the way it is, then it's all right. I must go now."

Her mother said then, "Your father is right, my child. Your husband is not treating you shabbily, he is correct. Nothing that he has said can be disputed. Your husband has thought of a really imaginative solution— when he releases the wife of the right-hand house, he provides you with a new bride."

She departed; she went home, having heard those words at her parents' place. When she returned to her homestead by marriage, she found that her husband had not yet come home. He arrived after she did and did not know that she had been away. Nor did the junior wife mention anything about her absence.

Time passed, and they were content.

One day he said that it was necessary that a site be found for a homestead for the right-hand house. The site for the right-hand house was duly marked, and a homestead was erected. Two houses were built, and this wife of the right-hand took her clothes and mats and left for her own homestead. She remained there, visited by her husband on the appointed days, as he took turns visiting his wives. Sometimes he would spend an entire week there, then come back here to spend a week.

So it went on. Everything was satisfactory, and the right-hand wife would sometimes come along to spend time chatting with the senior wife. The senior wife also would visit the right-hand house to converse—the two were very pleasant to each other.

As time went on and months passed, the husband took a young wife, wishing to install her as the supporting house of the senior wife. She became a bride who lived here with the senior wife. Time passed, and they were happy. They got along well together, and the senior wife treated the bride as if she were the young wife of a son. The bride in turn was subject to the aging wife, as if she were her mother. The older woman was kind, loving, and solicitous; she admonished, she was attentive to this young wife about everything. And she came to understand that—well, this institution of the supporting house is really quite useful, and one can live amicably with it.

Time passed in that way, and everything went smoothly. The supporting house addressed her as "Sister." So time passed, and this wife also became pregnant. When she delivered, she gave birth to a man-child as her firstborn. The senior wife rejoiced, remembering what had been said to her: if the supporting house should bear a man-child or whatever she bore, it would be the senior wife's own child. Any child of the supporting house would be hers. And the male child of the right-hand house would be the senior brother to the one born of the supporting house.

This went on, and the junior wife bore several children. The right-hand wife went on bearing children.

When the right-hand wife had borne four children, her husband said, "Nobani, you have reached the stage now that the right-hand wife should have some livestock marked for her. It is time for her to have her own stock."

The wife agreed.

The husband then called together the men of the village, along with his brother, and said, "I have gathered you together for this reason: the right-hand wife has set up house by herself, but she has not yet had stock marked for her. I want some stock to be branded for her today."

The men agreed. "Granted, but you've already delayed too long—that there should be as many as four children, with no branded stock!"

So the right-hand wife had stock branded for her: from the kraal, a goat; from the fold, a bovine heifer. They were marked, designated for her. The husband began to build a kraal for the right-hand house: he made a little kraal for this house, and those two animals were taken to be herded over there in the right-hand house by the boy of that house.

One day, the senior wife said to her husband, "When will this child, whom you say is mine, come here to me? Why does he herd over there at the right-hand house? Why does he sleep over there? When will he begin to stay here?"

The husband said, "Well, he'll be responsible for herding all the livestock, of course. It's just that, when he brings them back from the pasture, he'll take those that belong here into this kraal, and those of the right-hand house he'll take to that kraal."

The wife said, "But when will he begin to live here himself? When will it become plain that he belongs here? If he stays here, it'll be abundantly clear. It will be obvious from his habits that he belongs here."

"It doesn't matter where he stays. Children, after all, tend to follow their own inclinations and stay in a certain homestead which they are not known to belong to. This causes no problems. In itself, it is of little consequence. No customary practice is thereby compromised. Customs are definitive."

Time passed. That woman kept quiet and left the subject.

Her eldest daughter had gotten married and had become a wife in her own homestead. This boy of the right-hand house was still young. There was not yet much that he could contribute. But the boy grew and became older. At length, he was circumcised. He became a man and he worked; he had his own property which he purchased because he worked so well. He bought cattle. He bought small stock—goats, sheep. Then the girls of his homestead began to marry—all of them. The first to marry was the eldest. She came back from her home by marriage in ill health; she came home and explained, "I am not well. I am ill. I am troubled because I have not yet undergone purification [*intonjane*, the puberty ritual for girls] and been properly married. These things all trouble me."

Her father explained to his son of the right-hand house: "Well, my son, your sister is here because of ill health. She requires the custom of purification. After the ritual has been completed, she will have to be married in the appropriate manner. All these things are your responsibilities—you, her brother—because you are my senior son, the heir. That is because your senior mother has never borne a man-child. You were the first man-child born in this homestead. That means that you must do something with regard to your sister's problem. You are the proper person to perform it: it is your privilege, your duty."

The son listened, then said, "I hear you, Father."

He went home after a time, to the right-hand house. When he arrived there, the young man explained this to his mother.

"Mother."

"Yes?"

"Father says that my eldest sister is here. She has come here because of ill health. Now, Father has told me that these things must be done: she must first undergo the purification ritual. After that, she has to be married properly, with a bridal party. Father says that such matters are my responsibility because I am a son to the senior mother, since she has only borne girls. I am designated as the son of the great house."

They were speaking by themselves, mother and son. His father was not present.

His mother replied, "Oh, that will never be! At this rate, you'll never get yourself a wife! What they're demanding is difficult. We have built this homestead from nothing, and now they want you to have nothing. Purification requires goats—it requires three goats! And it requires a fourth creature, a cow! Then you'll have to scrape around for a lot of goods of various kinds for when the daughter returns home. Where do you think you'll get all those things? Not only that, your father wants you to organize the bridal party when you've finished the purification ceremony. That means two head of cattle for the bridal party. Then there's the endless amount of money—money for the women living at their father's homestead, money for the beard, and what not. Consider, further, the accessories of the bridal party. It's equivalent to the price of a beast.

"Now you can see that we still have only three beasts here at home. The burden your father is imposing upon you will wipe out everything! And when all these cattle are gone, you'll have to work to eradicate the many debts that you will have incurred in addition to the things you've already been told about. I shall have no part of that, my child. No woman ever bears children for another!

"Now, you may say what you wish to say."

The young man said, "Well, Mother, what must I do? I have accepted the obligation that my father has presented me. What can I do to escape this obligation?"

"Well, there's one thing that you can do. Depart, leave, hide, don't do these things! If you don't want to hide, then just keep quiet, act dumb: don't answer them, no matter what they say. Just keep quiet. Then they'll see for themselves what they can do about this matter."

The son said, "Well, I hear you, Mother. But over there at the great house, preparations are already being made for the purification ceremony. It will be initiated with the slaughtering of a beast. This is because the father has now reached an understanding with his son, who has agreed to what his father has said. He is not aware of what we've been talking about."

People were called together. Women came. At sunset, the appropriate song was chanted, and the person who was to undergo purification was secluded. A curtain made from grass in the customary manner was hung in the room, and the initiate was placed on the other side. Another young woman was chosen to be a chaperone.

The next day, the young woman's father waited to see if the son would act on the business that they had discussed. But the son did not come there. He did not depart from the right-hand house and come to the main homestead. He left the right-hand house and, in an unprincipled manner, went away so that his father would not see him, so that no matter where they sought him they would not find him.

They attempted to find out where this son was. The sun went down, and they failed to find him. His mother insisted that her son had not told her where he was going: "He didn't tell me. I don't know where he's gone."

Time was running out for the slaughtering ritual—a goat was to be slaughtered, a part of the ritual involving the young woman's entry into seclusion at the beginning of the purification ceremony. But the young man was nowhere to be seen. Finally, it was determined that the ritual of the entry into seclusion would have to be postponed. The next day, they would get together with the young man so that he might explain where he had been.

"I don't know. Perhaps this young man went off to get a goat that will be large enough. Maybe there is such a goat over there at his home, but if he doesn't have one, and if there's one here at this homestead, then he should have asked me to loan him a goat so that he could fulfill his obligation."

When his father had said that, the men said, "It might be a good idea to question the mother closely about the young man's absence. It's possible that she is the cause of all this."

"He knew what was to take place today. Why has he failed to appear all day?"

The right-hand wife was summoned by the men, and they asked her if there was "anything you might know" about this young man.

She said, "Anything? Like what?"

It was said, "Perhaps he mentioned some place to you. Or perhaps there's some place that he regularly goes to in this manner."

The young man's mother said, "No, I know nothing. He didn't say a thing. I just saw him go out. I thought that perhaps he had come here. I had no idea that he wasn't here."

After the mother had been dismissed, the men summoned a little girl from the youth's home—a sister of the young man. The girl arrived, and the men said to her, "Little girl."

The little girl responded.

"Tell all you know. Were you present over there at your home when the young man was explaining to your mother that there was to be a purification ceremony here?"

The child said, "I was there."

"Proceed, my child. What did he say?"

The child said, "My big brother said to my mother, 'My father says that my sister has arrived. She is going to undergo purification. She is not well. And when she has completed the purification ritual, she will be sent away with a bridal party.' Then my big brother said to my mother, 'My father says all of that is my responsibility because I'm the senior son, because my senior mother has no man-child.'"

"How did your mother respond to that, my girl?"

The child said, "My mother said, 'Yo! Can you possibly shoulder all that responsibility? We've only begun to accumulate stock. How can it be that, before we even have a complete homestead, you're ordered to take these three head of stock? All three of these beasts will be swallowed by this affair! And that's not all. You've not fully discharged your obligation yet. You're to sink deeper still into debt because of all the items required for a bridal party. The money of the women living at their father's homestead, all kinds of money! You'll end up in so much debt that you'll never accumulate anything! When will you be able to get a wife?' My big brother then said, 'What should I do, Mother?' Mother answered, 'You should just hide. Just don't be there. Then they'll have to see what they can do.'"

The men then said, "You may go, my child. That is enough."

"We were correct in thinking that the mother was behind this."

"Have we not been proven right, Men?"

So they said. The evidence was plentiful, but it was decided to adjourn and return the following morning.

For what purpose?

"To give you, Father of the homestead, an opportunity to meet with your son tonight regarding tomorrow's business."

"When we return tomorrow morning, you two should have reached some conclusion about the appropriate preparations."

The young man's father agreed. Then they dispersed.

At sunset, the girls at the place of purification were chanting. At night, the young man returned.

When he came to the place of purification, he greeted them: he spoke; he went into the seclusion area and chatted with the initiate.

His father heard that the young man was over there at the place of purification, and he called him. The young man went to his father, and, when he entered the house, he was asked, "Why weren't you here, my child, all this morning, until sunset? Because of your absence, the day's business could not be performed."

The son said, "Well, I took a little trip to a certain place. Father, I completely forgot about this ceremony. I thought it was tomorrow actually. I didn't remember that it was today."

His father said, "But you see now! It will be held tomorrow, in the morning. You ruined it yesterday. Tomorrow, you must go nowhere! You get up and be here early!"

The son departed then when he had concluded that exchange with his father. He went to his home. People slept; morning came. And again the people gathered as had been arranged. The women arrived and chanted.

But the young man was not there.

It was determined that someone must go to him before the livestock was taken from the kraal to the pasture. A messenger was sent to the right-hand house, but he found that the young man was not there.

His mother was asked when she had parted company with the young man.

She said, "I left him here at home. I didn't realize that he would not go over to the main house. Even now, I was wondering if that's where he was."

Time passed.

"What shall we do about this now?"

A man got up and said that a goat should be seized. The goat was seized, and they performed the ritual of the entry into purification seclusion. The beast was slaughtered, and the meat of the ritual of the entry into seclusion was eaten.

At sunset, after the people had dispersed and departed, the young man arrived.

Again, his father heard that he had arrived; and again, he called him and asked him what had happened.

The young man said, "I was looking for a goat. I went to a homestead where I once saw a large one. But when I got there, I couldn't find the people of that homestead. So I left."

His father said, "My child, I can see that there's nothing you will do regarding this affair. I'm becoming very suspicious about you. Now then, after eight days, the marriage will take place. We'll need a beast to be slaughtered for the initiate. And don't you say that you're going off to look for the beast!"

The son said, "But I don't have a beast for the occasion. The cattle of my home are few, and they're with calf."

His father said, "Well, what do you have to say to those who do have cattle? Because whatever it is, it's yours—if you claim it in the right way."

The son said, "I don't want to go into debt. I don't want to owe anyone anything. When I don't have something, I don't have it."

On the eighth day, the father informed the men of what his son said in justification of his inaction during the ceremony of the entry into seclusion.

"There is something, Gentlemen, that you ought to know. You know how I established status for this child in this homestead—I did so in the presence of you men. Now, considering how he has been carrying on, I put the matter before you again, Gentlemen."

The men heard him, then answered, "Perhaps he's just immature."

"In time, he'll understand his obligations."

"Just go on with this rite concerning your child."

The man took a beast for the marriage ceremony of the initiate. The rite was performed at the place of purification, and it was completed.

When it was over, on the twelfth day, the initiate emerged from seclusion. When she had emerged, the mat that she had used in the place of purification was burned. When that had been done, it was time for her, in the company of the bridal party, to return home. To insure that all those pains that had been plaguing her should come to an end, it was essential that everything that remained to be done be performed.

Things went on.

The father again called the young man: "Your sister has now emerged from seclusion. We must now make preparations for the bridal party, so that she can return home, to her marriage home. There should be no interruption after she has undergone the purification ritual. Everything should now be pressed to a conclusion."

"I hear you, Father."

"Concerning the bridal party, then, my son: your mother must make household items that are constructed of grass—mats, blankets, strainers, grinding mats. And it is your duty to provide articles of clothing—all of them, along with eating utensils. These are the necessities for a bridal party. You should also have money—about ten pounds—to cover currency demands that will be made of the bridal party. And you know that the money for the women living at their father's homestead is another expense—the usual three pounds. Get all that together quickly because the young woman's in-laws will soon come and fetch her."

The young man agreed with all the words spoken by his father.

His mother then prepared the things that were her responsibility—all of the grass items. She worked carefully, stacking the things until she had completed what was required. The mother finished the items pertaining to women.

There remained the things pertaining to men.

The senior mother said, "Ee, Sobani! We now have all the things for the bridal party—as far as the female section is concerned. The male section hasn't done its part yet. This child will soon be fetched by the people of her home by marriage. The things that you men are responsible for can be obtained ready-made. But the things I must prepare are made by hand, and they take a long time to make. I have completed my task but have not yet seen a single item prepared by the men."

The husband said, "Yes, I agree. But here's a strange thing: I haven't heard this young man say a thing. And I see nothing that he has produced. I'll call him and ask him. I want him to explain to me what he's been doing."

He called the young man then. He also called a few men together. He said, "Please ask this young man for me exactly what he's contriving. In which direction is he pulling? Let him explain."

The young man was asked, "Young man, you've heard your father. He asks what your purpose is. What are you scheming? Explain it to him. We were here on the day the ritual of the entry into seclusion should have been performed for the initiate. For two days, your father hunted for you. And in the end, you didn't do what you were supposed to do. Again, on the day of the wedding, we were here. And again, your father hunted for you. But you didn't even make an appearance."

"Finally, when your father asked you to explain your behavior, you merely said that you have no cattle."

"You said that you don't want to go into debt and borrow a beast."

"Then your father himself seized a beast. We know all about that. What we don't know, young man, is this: do you understand that these matters are common knowledge?"

The young man answered, "Had he loaned me the money, I would have been able to do it. But I gave no thought to borrowing because it's hard to take out a loan when one is just beginning to accumulate things."

His father said, "Be certain that you are making a loan—a loan!—and that you'll pay me back! Because this affair is your responsibility!"

The young man said, "I am taking out a loan."

His father said, "When will you pay it back?"

The young man said, "The first time I take a train and go off to seek work, I'll repay to you all that I borrow."

So the father gave him the money needed to cover all that business. The young man took the money and went to get the necessary things for the bridal party. The bridal party would carry with it the money that remained.

On the appointed day, the bridal party departed, taking the young woman to be married properly.

His father asked the young man if he was taking as a loan the two head of cattle that would be driven by the woman—the beast of the bridal party together with the beast of the bride.

The young man said, "Yes, I'm taking them as a loan. I'll repay them the second time I go off to seek work. My first job will pay for the items for the bridal party; the second will be for these beasts."

These were presented to him in the presence of the rest of the men, and the bridal party departed.

It proceeded in the customary manner in all particulars. Dowry was provided for the woman: eight head of cattle. Those who were to return to the main homestead arrived, having departed from the bridal party. The young man ordered that the dowry cattle be taken to his home at the right-hand house. That, he said, is where they belong.

"What do you mean, your home?"

"I mean, the place where I live."

The men said, "Where you live? Don't you recall that you were told that you're the senior son because there's no man-child in the great house?"

"Why, then, do you insist that the dowry cattle be taken to the right-hand house? You don't belong to the right-hand house."

"You belong to the great house."

The young man said, "I want them to stay where I can keep an eye on them, in case they attempt to run away."

The men contradicted him: "You watch over all the cattle, young man. Even if they remain here, you're the one who takes them out to pasture, and you're the one who brings them back. What you suggest is inappropriate."

The young man relented, and the cattle were taken to the great house.

In time, he boarded a train and went off to work.

After he had gone, another daughter, coming after the one who had just been married, underwent the purification ritual. When the young man was told of this, he said that his father should proceed with the affair. He would repay him everything. All of this was the young man's responsibility.

His father went ahead with the arrangements because it is difficult to carry on a discussion with someone far away while things are pressing here at home. So his father went ahead and completed all of the necessary rites.

The young man returned. When he had come back, it was time that yet another girl have certain rites performed for her. This was a different rite than the puberty purification. It was the first rite, a rite performed for a child. It was completed for the child as a propitiation, and a beast had to be slaughtered.

When this matter was referred to the young man, he said that his father was the appropriate one to perform this rite of propitiation: "I'll be responsible for the larger rites."

His father responded, "As for the two occasions involving the oldest daughter: you said you would repay all the money after your first period of work. But," and he turned to the men, "he has paid back nothing. I report this sad news to you, Men, because all of this has unfolded before your eyes."

The men remembered the occasion well because they were present when these things occurred. Repeatedly, they had been called together.

The father named a day on which the propitiation rite would be held.

That day arrived. The men came, and the rite, including the slaughtering of the beast, was performed for that little girl of his. The meat was consumed. That event passed.

When it was over, the young man again boarded a train to go and seek work. While he was away at work, his father fell ill and died, leaving the mothers behind. The young man came back from work.

He had three mothers—his own mother of the right-hand house, his mother of the supporting house of the great house, and his senior mother, the one of whom it was said he was her son. They all remained behind now, alone. The mother of the supporting house had a man-child, her firstborn. The senior mother had no man-child, only girls. This young man had been created her son.

Now, when this young man returned, he went back to his home; he went to the right-hand house when he came back from his job.

The men wanted to know why, since his father had long since died, he returned to that house instead of going to the place where there was no male. Over there in the right-hand house, he had a younger brother, a man-child. He should have come home to the great house; he had, after all, been created the senior son, the heir.

The young man was very vague about such matters, just as he had been unspecific about other things.

Time passed. Time passed, and then the young man sought to appropriate the dowry cattle of his oldest sister. He wanted to bring them to the right-hand house.

As he was driving the cattle, the old woman—his senior mother—stood in the way. She said, "No, you won't do this! You would drive these cattle away, even though your obligations regarding them have never been discharged! You have the brazenness to attempt to drive these cattle away!"

The young man confronted his senior mother; they quarreled, as she contested his insistence that the cattle were his. Then she went and laid a charge against what her son was doing.

The men of the village were called together, along with the headman, and the case was discussed.

It was said, "Proceed, woman."

The woman said, "I accuse."

"What is your complaint?"

"I am a plaintiff against my son: he is seizing my cattle. He is taking them to a homestead that will never to anything for me. He himself has not done all the things he was supposed to do."

"What sorts of things?" asked the men. "Don't be nervous, Woman. Just go on. We're not asking you difficult questions. Speak clearly."

The woman said, "As you know, I bore children who were all girls. I never had a man-child. My husband sought a second wife, so that when our energies began to ebb, there would be a man-child here. Perhaps this second wife would bear a male. That child would then look after my other children and see to it that they are not treated badly, and so forth. But when occasions arose during which he was to see that they were made whole, he did nothing. Today, his father is dead. When he died, this son had not yet paid him back what he owed him. The men had gathered, and when this child had been argued with and finally convinced regarding our customs, he said, 'Just loan me the money, I'll pay it back.' But he has never paid it back. Even today, things are outstanding: there is a rite that he has not yet performed. Now he has returned, but all he has done is to attempt to drive away the cattle, taking them to a place where it is said he does not belong. He is mine. By taking the cattle, he is wresting them from me. He is taking them where they do not belong.

"Those are the grounds for my complaint."

Then it was said, "Young man, have you heard these words? You've heard your mother's words. How do you plead?"

The young man said, "Yes, I did say that my father should loan me those things, that I would work to pay him for them. But I came back with no money. And I asked him to loan me money a second time. I told him that I would pay it back. But that cannot now be held against me because it was decided that I am her son. What kind of son am I if there are no cattle that I can turn around and drive to my home?"

The person who next spoke said, "Do you understand, young man, that you are the son of this woman who has laid a charge against you?"

"Yes, I understand."

"Do you understand, young man, that of the things that you were supposed, like any child of her home, to do, you never did one?"

"Yes, I understand. But I did do something: I took out a loan, and as a result the daughter got married."

"You took a loan. But did you pay your father back?"

"No."

"Are you paying him back now?"

"No, I'm not paying him back. I'm merely herding."

"Is herding any different when the cattle are here?"

"No."

Another man said, "No, drop this argument. Concentrate on statements that are not contested. Isn't there anyone here who knows what happened on the first day, when all of this started?"

Someone who knew what had happened on that first day was asked. He recalled how the young man was called from the place of purification and asked about not fulfilling his obligation, and how the youth had temporized and given no definite statement about anything.

"We think that this matter should be referred to his paternal uncle."

They turned to the young man's uncle.

"You've heard your young man, Uncle. Do you have anything to say?"

The young brother of the youth's father said, "I want the word to come from this woman because this young man has proved too much for us. He was too much even while his father was alive. His father had really been quite disgusted with this young man. When he died, he had derived no satisfaction from anything that this youth had done. It doesn't really help. It's no use our trying to patch things here and there. It's preferable that we turn to his mother, to find out what she thinks about his turning these cattle around."

There was a pause.

Then they turned to the senior mother, and said, "Say something, Madam. We are about to adjudicate this dispute. From your vantage, what do you suggest should be done?"

The woman answered, "The problem, as I see it, centers on this business of the senior son. The idea of a senior son, an heir who is the owner of the property, is premised on his habits and deeds, the things that he does to help people. He is supposed to be a person to whom one goes for protection, a person with whom complaints are filed, a person who comforts the grieving and rears the young and does all necessary things. Only when he does these things do the people who are his live well, believing in him. When we do not trust this young man, what can we do? In this case, we began to distrust him while his father was still alive. Who does he honor and respect now? He showed no respect at the time when he should have shown respect. He did reprehensible things while the person he was supposed to revere was yet alive. I see what you men do not see. It is clear to me that you are currying favor. But I am not doing that. I refuse to seek favors even though I have no man-child. I seek favors only from those who seek favors from me. I want this to be done: I refer now to that child over there in that house, the new bride, the one who is the supporting house. Make an arrangement with her because she has given birth to a man-child. And she will probably have more because she still has only three children. But she has a man-child now; he was born after the birth of one of her daughters. I will have my man-child from that house. If I don't get him from the supporting house, it'll just be my bad luck. But I say that it is better that I take the child from that house, from the supporting house, because she is not an independent part of this homestead. It was stated that the right-hand house is indeed an independent section. It has now become clear what is to be: the right-hand will promote itself at my expense, without doing a thing for me."

So the lawsuit was settled in that manner.

"This woman is right. It is clear that this is how this thing must be settled."

The verdict was given.

Then it was said, "Well, Madam, this young man has already borrowed so much, saying he would pay it back. What do you say about that?"

The woman said, "I don't care. I don't care how much he has failed to return. That was all arranged by the child's father—but that child was never worthy from the beginning. I want nothing to be returned. He is nothing to me. He is of the right-hand house."

All agreed, and it was said, "The woman is right."

All the men in the court agreed. Even the woman's younger brother agreed, and her older brother, and the younger paternal uncle of the young man. He said, "The woman is accurate in this matter. She has viewed it properly. No one can improve on what she had said."

The young man was told that, from that day, the right-hand house was to be independent and distinct. It was never again to touch anything in the senior house, the great house, without specifically being directed to do so, without being sent for by that house. He was now the right-hand, the section that acted upon invitation. "But you remain responsible for the great house because both of the houses proceed from the stomach of the same man. You should build each other up. But you have demonstrated to them that you are an ogre. From this time, you must never do anything here at the great house without clearing it with them."

So they were happy.

He too was happy, in his own home.

But it developed in time that they could not get along together because the mother of that young man, the senior wife learned, had again convinced her son that he should not do anything to help the great house.

Time passed, and they accumulated some wealth, but they were abased. In the great house, however, the people were raised in stature, their goods increased, their stock was abundant. And they became more and more comfortable. But the young man was able to do no good work; he was not admired by the people. Nor did he get any better, no matter how hard he tried. As time passed, instead of increasing, his stock diminished.

TALES

Tale 15

A POOR GIRL MARRIES A KING

Masithathu Zenani's Analysis: This is a story about Mityi (see also Tale 23, "The Tree That Could Not Be Grasped") who, in other tales in Mrs. Zenani's repertory, is an epic hero. In this story, Mityi plays a melancholy character who is treated badly by her stepmother.

This is what moves this tale: two parallel positive patterns are paired against a negative pattern. The most obvious repetition, the first pattern, connects Mityi to her dead mother; the stick given to her by her mother becomes her fantastic tie to her past. The stick is the means of her survival. The first pattern is matched by a second, that having to do with the suitor who, seeking a wife, refuses to be persuaded not to marry Mityi. Those are the two positive patterns. The antithetical pattern has to do with the cruel treatment of Mityi by her stepmother and her children. As is usual in stories, the interaction of the patterns reveals the theme.

There is an ample supply of wish fulfillment in this tale; it acts as a motivating force. The two affirmative patterns establish the two positive influences on Mityi's life, that of her mother and that of her husband-to-be. That rich set of linkages, Mityi's connections with past and future, is threatened by present villainy, as Mityi makes the psychological journey to womanhood. She has the active assistance of her mother and her future husband as she weathers her ordeal.

In the end, the positive patterns dominate the story, and Mityi is happily married. The connection with the mother remains a key thematic image in the story; the performer is analyzing the relationship between the living and the dead, and assuring her audience that benevolent ancestors are looking out for us, no matter how miserable our circumstances.

Performance Note

Time: 2 August 1972, in the afternoon. *Place:* Outside, along the side of a ridge, near Mrs. Zenani's home in Nkanga, Gatyana District, the Transkei. *Audience:* Five women, five children. (Perf. NS-13.)

There were a woman and a man. The woman became pregnant and gave birth; she bore a daughter. She gave birth a second time; she bore a second daughter.

Then her husband took another wife, and the second wife also became pregnant; she too bore a daughter. When this wife had given birth to a girl, she lost her health. She was loved very much by her husband; he

"Even the child's name was forgotten." The words are given resonance in the body.

lived in her house. She was ailing—year after year, she remained ill. The husband took his loved wife to a doctor, but her illness continued.

Finally, she died.

Her little daughter lived in sorrow because of her mother's death.

The husband went to live in the great house with the wife who had given birth to two daughters. He lived there now, and the dead wife's daughter lived in grief. She was treated badly. She had no clothing; when her garments were worn out, she was dressed in skins, in old rags, in dirty things that were picked up for her. That is the way this child lived.

She was taught to cook at an early age; she became the cook in this homestead. Her function, she learned, was to cook. It happened that her father's livestock was increasing, and a herdboy was needed. So she also became the herdboy. The child would get up in the morning, take the livestock out of the kraal, then go and herd it out in the pasture. She would herd; and then, in the afternoon, she would hurriedly drive the stock home so that she could prepare the evening meal. If the preparation of the food took too long, she was beaten and sent to bed without food. They would ask, "Why didn't she cook the food in time?"

Even the child's name was forgotten. She did have a name, it was Mityi. But they came to refer to her as Roqololondini, Ragged One. They did not call her by her real name.

Time passed, and the child continued to live that melancholy life: she was thin, her body was covered with sores; she was hungry, cold, her body was dirty, there was dirt on her feet. Because of the unhappy circumstances of her life in this home of hers, she did not have time to make herself presentable.

Time passed, and the child remained there: she knew of no other place where she might go. She did not know where the home of her mother's parents' was. She often thought about secretly running away from this place, but she did not even know in what direction she should flee. Because her mother had been so deeply loved by her father, that mother had never gone back to her home. Consequently, this child did not know the location of her mother's parents' place.

Time passed; a long time passed, and this child continued to grow older. She reached the age at which girls played a variety of games. But when this girl played such games, she was unbecoming. She had nothing with which to protect her body, and she was thus handicapped because she was so neglected.

That is the way she lived.

On a certain day, the people went to the fields. When the mothers returned from the fields, they brought beautiful things for the children. Mityi also went out when all the other children ran eagerly to meet their mothers—the mothers were carrying sweet sugarcane. When a mother's child arrived, that mother would give the child some cane. Mityi arrived, and stopped in front of the women. Her mother was walking with the women of other homesteads; Mityi was with her sisters, the daughters of this mother who was alive. She gave her own children the sugarcane.

Mityi stayed there, holding on to her mouth.

Her mother then said, "You ragged one! Holding on to your mouth like that! Do you think that there's enough sugarcane for you too? Get out of the way!" and she kicked her. The girl fell a distance away. She got up and walked off in sorrow. She went to her home.

She told her father what had happened: "When I went out to meet the mothers, Father, my mother kicked me. She did not give me any sugarcane. When I stood there, she said, 'You ragged one! Do you think that there's enough sugarcane for you too?' and she kicked me. And I fell."

When the child had said that to her father, the man was pained. He turned to his wife.

"Why did you kick her when she followed you? She just wanted what you were giving the other children."

His wife answered, "Don't annoy me about this ragged thing of yours. Even though she was given something, she denies it. I did give her some cane!" So she said, then she leapt up and beat the child, hitting her in the face with her hand. Her husband intervened, even though he did not care very much.

So it went with the child. She herded the livestock, she ate with the dogs, with the hogs. And when the others finished eating, she was the one who washed the dishes. When she finished doing that, she had to scrape the pot. Then the food that was scraped from the pot was poured into the hogs' trough. She was told to go and eat with those hogs; this child had to go and eat with the hogs.

When the child went to herd the stock, she frequently ate resin from trees. She ate the resin regularly because she did not want to eat the dirty food she was given at home.

Time passed for this child; time passed.

One day, as she was walking about, she suddenly saw a thing that was unearthing itself. Something sprang up from her mother's grave. While the thing was emerging from the earth, it said, "Take me, here I am!" She looked for it; she looked for the thing that was speaking but could not actually see it. The thing said, "I say, Take me, here I am!" She finally saw the thing—a tiny lump, a tiny black lump, a stone, that moved on the ground. The child took the lump. It said, "Put me—" The child stopped. The thing repeated and said, "Put me in your other hand!" The child put it in her other hand. It said, "You see, I am your mother—the one who died. Now, my child, Mityi, here is a stick. Take it. Hide this stick. Never show it to anyone! The day that you show it to someone, things will go badly for you. This is what you should do with this stick. I'll tell you what you must do with it. Beat here on the ground and say, 'All that I deserve, let it come out!'"

The child beat the stick on the ground and said, "All that I deserve, let it come out!"

When the child had said that, a table came out, a bathtub came out, and all the foods proper for the table came out. The bathtub came out, containing water that was lukewarm.

"All right now, bathe." The lump that was in her hand spoke.

The child entered the bathtub, she washed herself. She washed, then anointed her body. When she had finished anointing her body, she saw some dresses and she put them on. She dressed herself, and when she had finished dressing, the lump said, "All right, undress." The child undressed. It said, "Eat now." And the child ate; she ate and ate. When she had finished eating, the lump said, "Are you satisfied?"

The girl said, "I am satisfied, Mama."

"Then beat again on the ground. Say, 'Let all these deserved things go down.'"

The child beat the ground. She said, "Let all these deserved things go down." The things disappeared. Suddenly she did not see them.

The lump said, "Put me down now. You'll never see me again."

The child cried when the lump said this.

It repeated, "Mityi!"

The child said, "Mama."

"Don't cry. I tell you, you'll never see me again. Hold on to this stick. Hide it in some place that you alone know. Rely on the stick. Carry it. Whenever you're confronted with something difficult, come to this stick. Hold it in your hand, tell it what you want. I have finished now. I am your mother; you'll never see me again."

The child stopped crying then. She took the stick and hid it. She hid it in her own place. When she had hidden it, she went home. She went home satisfied, not wanting a thing. She arrived and went to the livestock. She brought all of the stock home and put them into the cattle kraal.

Today, she had not cooked at all. The time for doing the cooking had passed. The time when she should have been cooking had been taken up by her conversation with her mother. She was very anxious now because she knew that she would be beaten that day. She shut the stock in the kraal—the cattle in the cattle kraal, the sheep in the sheepfold. Then she went to the house.

When she got to the house, the mother said to her, "Where have you come from?"

She said, "I've come from herding the livestock."

"Why haven't you cooked the food?"

"The stock gave me trouble."

"Yo! You'll go to sleep without your meal! You can eat your wandering!"

Mityi was quiet because she was full today. She sat there as the food was ladled out. They ate. Today, the girls who were her sisters did the dishing out of food. They ate, they ate, and they finished. When they had finished eating, the girl washed the dishes. Mityi washed the dishes. She washed them all. Then she went and threw the water into the trough. She returned and sat down.

It was said, "Why is it that you're not eating with the hogs tonight?"

She said, "I don't want any."

"Why are you full?"

"I am full of resin."

"Where do you get it?"

"I take it from trees."

The child sat, and time passed.

Many days later, it was heard that there was a man who was seeking a wife. He wanted a wife who was an orphan because he had had a wife and she had died. Now, he was seeking a wife who had experienced grief, so that they would be able to comfort each other. The man sought such a wife, and he finally happened to arrive at the home of this child.

When he arrived there, he announced that he was seeking a wife.

Her father, because he disliked Mityi, said, "These are my two daughters. Choose between them."

The stranger said, "No, I cannot choose just any woman. Let me explain to you: I want a wife, a woman who has grown up in adverse circumstances. Perhaps you can advise me."

The father answered, "Here is a young woman who grew up in difficulty," and he again pointed to those daughters of his whose mother was still alive. He wanted the man to marry one of them.

The fellow said, "No, really, why is it that they seem to come after each other in birth? Why does it seem as if they were borne by this woman?"

The man said, "No, they were not both borne by this woman. It's because they look alike. This young woman has no mother." But even as the father was saying this, the daughter who truly had no mother was not present. She was herding the livestock in the pasture. Only the other two young women were here. While the father was speaking, that ragged one appeared, a skin wrapped around her. She was driving the cattle because it was afternoon. She was in a hurry, returning early so that she could do the cooking—because these chores were done by her alone, all of them. When she got there, she put the livestock into the kraal.

The stranger said, "Yo! It is she! This is the one, the person who must become my wife!"

The father of the young women said, "How can a thing like that be your wife? That thing's not worth anything! It doesn't have any sense, that thing! It's a fool, just a fool! She's so stupid that she brings the wrong livestock here! She has no sense. She's just a thing! You'll see her. Just now she'll eat with the hogs! She's not altogether a person, that one!"

The fellow sat and chatted. He did not pursue the matter. He spoke of other things, and so time passed.

Mityi arrived; she made the livestock enter on the other side of the kraal, the side near her home. The child returned then, and she entered, a ragged person. She went to greet them.

"Hello, Father."

This fellow then put out his hand. He wanted to greet her.

"No! No!" her father said. "No! Don't greet such a thing! What's the matter with this child? How could you extend your hand to a person, you being so filthy?"

The fellow took her hand. When he had done so, the child got up. The child got up and went about her usual business. She took a pot and washed it; she washed it thoroughly. The stranger watched her, wondering if she would do a proper job of cleaning the pot, since it had been said that she had no sense. But she did wash it. She washed it, and the pot became flawless. She rinsed it, and it was clean. She took everything and dried the things. She cooked. The stranger observed this person who, it was said, had no sense. She cooked, she cooked, and this fellow sat there. When the pot became hot, the child ladled the food out, and they ate. The people ate, and food was also dished out for the stranger. When they had finished eating, she still had not eaten.

The stranger ate. Then he said, "Here you are, my child."

The child stood up, she took the food with both hands. The fellow observed the child as she took it with both hands.[1]

Her father said, "Well! Don't give it to that person! Leave that to someone else!"

The stranger said, "No, let her take it."

The child took it then. She thanked him, having bent her knees slightly. Then she went to eat; she ate and ate. She concluded things and went out.

Her father said, "Why are these hogs eating alone, while you're sitting here? When will you eat?"

The child said, "I have already eaten."

"Oh."

After a time, the stranger got up, and said, "I request permission to leave now. I'm certain that I've found the woman I've been seeking. I say to you, Master of the homestead, this is the one. I don't care if she has no sense."

"How could you want such a thing? Here are the *women!*"

"No, no, I don't want these, really! I want this one, the one who seems somewhat vacant."

Then that fellow traveled. He said that he wanted to marry this young woman. What would happen was this: when the wedding was to take place, he would simply announce that there would be a wedding that day.

"What is this? What is the correct thing to do?" asked Mityi's father.

Time passed for Mityi, and one day while she was herding, while she was with the livestock, still a dirty and ragged person, the fellow appeared.

"Hello, young woman."

"Yes, Father."

"Are you herding?"

"Yes, I am herding."

"What has your father said about my desire that you become my wife?"

"I don't know," the child said. "I don't know, Father. Nothing has been said to me."

"Why has nothing been said about it?"

"I don't know, Father."

"Would you be satisfied if I took you away from such things as herding this stock? Would you be satisfied to be my wife and not a shepherd boy? Would you be satisfied to remain in the house?"

---

1. It is polite practice to accept a gift with both hands extended.

The child said, "I would be satisfied."

"All right then, I want to tell you the day that you are to come to my home. Once you're at my home, there's no way that your father can reclaim you."

The child said, "Speak then, Father. When must I go?"

That fellow said then, "On the week after next, on Saturday, I want you to come to my home, in the morning. At midday, I'll slaughter an ox. I'll slaughter an ox and say, 'I am marrying my wife.' "

The child said, "All right."

That fellow departed then; he went home.

Time passed, and the child continued to herd. The time came when she had to go home with the livestock. She went home and allowed the stock to graze in a pasture near home, so that she could go and cook, at the same time permitting the stock to wander about since it was too early in the day to put the cattle into the kraal. She went to the pots. She went to cook as was her habit. She cooked; she finished that. Then she dished the food out, and the people ate. She washed the dishes and went to pour the remains in the trough for the hogs; she went to eat with those hogs.

The next morning, at dawn, she took the livestock out; she went off with the cattle. Then she recalled that "I picked up a dirty, little, round stone. When I took it, it said, 'Put me in your other hand!' So I put it in my other hand. Then it said, 'I am your mother. I will not be here again after today. You must hide this stick. You'll never see me again. You'll never see me again. I'll never be with you again—so you must rely on this stick.' " When the child remembered that, she went to the place where she had hidden the stick. She got there, she arrived and took the stick. She remembered that her mother had said that she should beat the ground with it and say, "All that I deserve, let it come out!"

Everything came out then, exactly as it had the first time. There were the table, the water, that food. She washed, she washed and washed. When she had finished washing, she dressed and ate. When she had finished eating, she again soiled herself in the dust, so that she was dirty. She was dirty, and then she again said, "Let all these deserved things go down!" She beat with that stick, and everything disappeared. She again hid the stick in that secret place. She traveled and went to the livestock. She turned the stock around and went home with it.

She arrived at home, then pushed on with her work. She cooked. She did all the usual things—she dished the food out, the others finished eating, then she washed the dishes. When that was finished, she took the water and poured it out for the hogs. Then she returned. She went to sit in the house.

Her father said, "Why are you sitting in the house? Why aren't you out there eating with the hogs?"

"I'm full."

"How can you be full, you ragged one?"

"I'm full of resin. I ate resin from the trees, and I'm full now."

"This thing will suffer from hunger at this rate! You untidy one!"

The girl stayed there, she did not speak. They had finished eating, and now they slept.

The morning comes without refusal. The weeks tumbled by—until the appointed day arrived. On that day, the child went out with the livestock. She went in the direction of the pasture. She went out to herd the stock. In a little time, she remembered that "That man said that today is the day I should go over there. He's going to marry me. He said that my father would have to accept that. Yo! What shall I do with the livestock?" the child wondered. "What'll I do with the stock?" Well, she just faced the livestock toward home, and she left them that way.

She walked away, she went to get her stick. She took it and said, "Stick of my mother, stick of my mother, today I am traveling. Today, I'm going away. Today, I'm going to be married. Now, all that I deserve, stick of my mother, the things that are known by you, the things that a person like me should have, all things proper to a person who's going to be married—I know nothing about such matters; you're the one who knows about the necessary things—let them come out, let those things that are fitting come out."

So she said, and she beat the ground. When she had done that, everything emerged from the ground—wedding garments, garments to change into later during the marriage ceremonies, tea dresses, all the proper things.[2] There were a wagon and a span of oxen. It was a covered wagon full of goods—all, all, everything! Nothing was omitted. There was a white cloth on the first pair of oxen [signifying a wedding wagon]. And there were two beasts, an ox and a heifer.

She got up and climbed on the wagon. Then the wagon moved along, not being driven by any person; it just traveled along the way. Finally, it arrived at that homestead. The wagon arrived there, then stopped in the yard. The husband came out. He went to the wagon and greeted that wife of his. The people there were witnessing a wonder. They did not know the wife; they had not seen the woman, the one who, it was said, would be married here at home. They saw that the wagon was full of things, but they saw only one person inside. The wagon was full, and no one was driving, and there was only one person inside.

Then they saw a wonder of a person, a beautiful person—they had never seen such a person, not in all the world. She was a person who was grandly polished. It happened that the girl had a gap in her teeth.

2. The wedding, as described earlier in the narrative, would be a traditional Xhosa ritual, but these changes of dress are contemporary.

After a time, the husband brought out some men.

He said, "I'm marrying today. Let the women ululate. Some should become members of the bridal party; others will be members of the party of my home."[3]

The two parties assumed their roles: they separated, one group here, one group there, each doing the proper things—the things that belong to the bride, those that belong to the groom. So they were married, and the young man then slaughtered an ox. He also slaughtered an ox which came with the bride. Those two oxen were slaughtered, and the man and woman were married.

Regarding that marriage: that child lived in elegance, surpassing even that of her home. She became the mistress of this home; she lived there doing nothing. Things were served to her; she became an important person. It was as if that mother who was no longer present had risen.

Time passed; time passed, and the fellow said, "Let me say this to you, Men of my home. I want twelve beasts. You must drive them to my wife's home. Give them to her father. Tell him that she has not been lost to him, that he should not miss her. I took this child of his from the stock she was herding, that ragged one of his who was dressed in skins. She is here now. She is my wife. There are the beasts. I am providing them for her dowry."

Those men went then. They traveled to her home. When they arrived there, they explained the matter. Her father was happy that day. She was such a ragged person. He did not know that she would bring him so much dowry. He thanked the men, realizing that she had done well to be found by this fellow who had discovered her in such difficulty.

The fellow lived happily then with his wife.

3. Since Mityi had no bridal party of her own, some of the people of the husband's home would act as members of her bridal party; others would act as the members of the groom's party.

Tale 16

THE BABOON'S WEDDING

Masithathu Zenani's Analysis: This is the singular story of a human's encounter with a group of baboons. The baboons wish to engage in human activities; in fact, the baboon chief is about to marry his daughter to humans. They want the hero of the story, Jojothwane, to be their human go-between, to answer questions about human culture of which they are ignorant. As happens at times in oral tales, the baboons are attempting to achieve full humanity by becoming a part of human culture through one of its rituals, in this case, the marriage rite. Jojothwane helps them to work through the complexities of the ceremony, including developing the network of connections established by the symbolic provision of gifts. In the earlier pattern, Jojothwane assists the baboons to become a part of the human world. But Jojothwane himself breaks this connection, sounding the alarm, thereby routing the baboons. When he returns, incongruously, to the baboons, he is accused of taking the baboon chief's prerogative, eating the chief's meat. The second pattern is a divining pattern, an effort to discover whether or not Jojothwane is guilty. The result is his exoneration and the death of the baboon chief. In the end, the baboons are scattered to their several natural habitations—the cliffs, thickets, meadows, forests. Initially, they moved in what appeared to be an imitation of a house ("But it was not really a house that they stayed in, a house with a wall. It was a structure made of grass and twigs").

The sorting out of humans and baboons, Mrs. Zenani said, gives the tale a mythic aura. The baboons make an effort to penetrate human society, but fail. A human being, an only child, alone in the world, traveling across the veld to his mother's parents' home, goes to a drinking party, pretends to be an adult, drinks a lot, then crosses a river and comes upon the home of the baboons. The drinking bout is Jojothwane's entrance into the world of fantasy, the world of myth. Time collapses, and he is back at the origins, the beginning of time, the time of creation. In that bizarre and wonderful world, he becomes an active participant, and in fact plays the role of God the creator as he interferes with the movement of the baboons into human society, as he destroys their chief, and as he moves the baboons into their proper places in the scheme of things.

Performance Note

Time: 14 September 1967, early evening. *Place:* At a beer party, overlooking a steep valley in Nkanga, Gatyana District, the Transkei. *Audience:* About forty women, six men, twenty children. (Perf. 646.)

There were a woman and her husband. This woman bore only one child; she gave birth to one child, a boy whose name was Jojothwane. She did not become pregnant again.

When he concluded that his wife was barren, the man said, "It's not enough to have only one child. I must supplement you. I must marry another wife."

She agreed.

So it was that this fellow took another wife—she became the wife of the right-hand house. After the marriage, this woman of the right-hand house had many children. The husband left his senior wife and went to live over there with the right-hand wife. In the process, he took away from his senior wife all of her privileges.

It was during that period that a terrible drought occurred. They were reduced to eating small roots that were dug up on the veld. The roots would be dug up, then roasted. These people lived in that way, and so time passed. Time passed for them, and they had a sorrowful existence.

Then the mother of Jojothwane died, and the boy was left alone in this house. His father, who continued to live at the right-hand house with that woman who had many children, showed no concern for Jojothwane. Time passed for this lad. He continued to live there because he did not know where his mother's home was. He had never visited the home of his mother's parents.

The boy suffered: he was hungry; he had nothing to eat. He thought and thought: "I remember that someone said that my mother's parents' home is more or less in that direction. I must just go there, even though I'm only a boy. I'll travel at night; in the day I'll sleep."

The child took his fighting stick and went off. He closed up the house, then went in the direction that had been pointed out to him. He walked and walked; he walked all night. Whenever he met an adult, he would ask, "Do you know about a woman in this area who got married? A woman who is the mother of Jojothwane?"

That person would say, "No, I don't know about such a person."

So the child would travel on. He had an old blanket with him. When dawn approached and it became light, he draped the old blanket on his body so that he appeared to be an adult man. He continued his journey; he walked and walked. He walked, and on the second day he passed by a homestead. Along the way, he slept in the forest. Then, when the sun had set, he went on his way again.

As this child was walking along, he heard a loud noise. "Yo!" he said. "It's a drinking party!" The entire village resounded with the din, and because of the noise he could tell exactly where the party was taking place. It was on this side of the village.

He went to the party. When he arrived, he hid his possessions below a kraal. Then he went to the front of the homestead. He pretended to be an adult man, a man among men.

Again and again, the people asked him, "Who are you?"

He responded, "What's the matter with you? Are you drunk? Don't you know me?"

And they would say, "Drink! Drink! Drink!"

The child drank and drank because he was very hungry. He remained there for a while.

Much later, he realized that "The dawn is coming! It'll be light soon, and they'll find out that I'm really a boy. They'll find out that I don't belong here!"

So he left and looked for a place to sleep, a thicket. He found such a place and went to sleep.

At dusk, he woke up and went on his way. There he is, crossing a great river. When he came to that river—he did not even know its name—he saw a little glowing fire on the other side. He crossed that river. He crossed and then came to the place where the fire was.

"Who are you?"

Jojothwane realized that these beings that were speaking were not people at all.

"What are these things?"

The creatures came out of the house. But it was not really a house that they stayed in, a house with a wall. It was a structure made of grass and twigs.

He said, "It is I!"

"Who are you? Who are you? Come here!"

He said, "Yo! I must go to them. If I run, they might hurt me. They're animals, after all. They're not people!"

When he came to them, he saw that they were all dirty and shaggy, and they all had tails. "They're only baboons!"

One of them said, "What's your name?"

He said, "I'm Jojothwane."

"Where are you from?"

He said, "I come from far away."

"Where are you going?"

He said, "I'm going to my mother's parents' place."

"And where is your mother's parents' place?"

He said, "It's in that direction, ahead."

"Mm! Whose homestead is it?"

"I don't know the precise homestead of my mother's parents. I do not know if there's a tree in the yard."

"Which place?"

"Up ahead."

"Please come in. You've been summoned by the king."

The child entered. He was trembling, afraid, because he did not know what they would do it him when he went in. He carried his fighting stick with him.

When he had entered, he said, "Here I am."

The king said, "Please speak with him. Speak with him because my daughter has got to be going tomorrow."

Someone said, "Sit down."

"The king says that you must be in the bridal party."

"You must be in the bridal party of the king's daughter."

"You'll be the master of ceremonies: you know Xhosa customs."

"The king is marrying his daughter to the Xhosa at the royal residence."

He said, "Well, that's all right." But he did not say this with his heart: he said it out of fear, realizing that there was no way he could get out of this. He said, "Well, that's all right."

"Sit down then."

When he sat down, he asked, "Do you have all the things of the Xhosa, the things that I must have when I go to the groom's place to speak with the Xhosa?"

"What kinds of things, Jojothwane?"

He said, "Mats and baskets, blankets, bottles, all the vessels proper to a bridal party, beaded necklaces, everything like that. Shells."

The king said, "Bring them. You know the things that are needed. All we say is that you must go with the bridal party."

He said, "Is there any red ochre? The bride's body must be anointed so that it has a red complexion."

"Go and get the red ochre, Jojothwane."

"All we say is that you must go with the bridal party."

He said, "Well then, all right. I'll just go and look for those things."

Even as he said this, he had no idea about how he would get the necessary objects. He went out. When he had gone, the baboons stood outside there; Jojothwane realized that he would never be able to outrun them because they took such great strides—they could take one step to his three.

He said, "Now what shall I do?"

He went and crossed that same river. He went back to the side he had come from. He went to the homestead at which the party had been held the night before—when he had pretended to be a man. When he got to the homestead, it was night. He mingled with the people there and, yes, he drank some more.

Someone said, "Who are you?"

He said, "What's the matter with you? What do you want? What have you lost? Why are you continually asking?" And he would go to the woman's side of the homestead again and again.[4]

---

4. The homestead was composed of a number of houses. He moved from one of them to the next.

Finally, he came to a house that was on one side. It was clear that "Everyone's drunk here!" so he went up to that house. It was locked. He broke in—he tried to open the door and broke it. When he went inside: "Ah! the goods of this homestead have been placed in this house!" It was clear that this was a celebration for a bride's party. So he took all the things necessary to the bridal party—bottles, he examined them; he took out some shells, necklaces, blankets, he took various kinds of blankets; and loaves of ochre. He put those things on his back, then went to cross the river.

When he had returned, he said, "Here are the goods."

Someone asked, "Is everything here now?"

He said, "Do you have any pots? How will you manage without pots? At a bridal party, beasts are slaughtered. If you have no pots, how will you manage things? And do you have knives? How shall we manage?"

Someone said, "You know about such things."

"All we say is that you must go with the bridal party!"

He departed. He crossed the river again. The sun came up, and he went into a thicket and slept. Then, when the sun had set, in the late evening, he went to another homestead. This homestead was in another village: he did not return to the place where he had been the night before, where there had been a bridal party. He went to another village.

When he arrived, there was considerable commotion: "So-and-so has not yet returned from the party."

"Yo! Do you know that over there at So-and-so's place, the house is still locked up? They haven't come back yet."

Jojothwane carefully noted the houses that were being referred to, the ones to which the owners had not yet returned. Then he went to those homesteads. He broke into them and entered. He found beer in one of the homes; he spilled it out on the ground and took the pot the beer had been in. He opened a chest in one of the houses and took out a large knife. Then he departed.

He returned to the place of the baboons.

"Oh, Jojothwane! Do you have everything you need now?"

"Yes, everything is here."

The bridal party would leave the next day.

The next morning, Jojothwane said, "You must anoint yourselves. You cannot leave until late evening, so that people won't see that you're walking on all four legs. If they see you walking on all four legs, they'll know that you're a bridal party of baboons. And you must arrive over there at the groom's place when it's dusk. I'm the only one who should be clearly seen because I'm a human. The bridal party will be told to go into a certain house. Now you must remain behind when that person from the house comes to call you. If you do go with me, then I must try to cover you."

"All right, we'll take our cues from you."

The next day, in the evening, they departed. There they go: they helped him to carry all those things on a horse. They walked along the side. The baboons practiced walking upright, on two legs: sometimes a baboon is able to stand on two legs. They continued to practice, then they got tired and walked again on all four legs.

Finally, they arrived at the groom's homestead. They sat just above the homestead. There was silence. But the baboons constantly said, "O-o!" And Jojothwane would say, "No! You'll be heard! Don't make that noise! Be quiet! I'll be the only one who speaks! They can hear you already!" They were very quiet then.

A person came to them: "Where have you come from?"

"Well, Friend, we've come a great distance."

"Mhmh!"

"And we're asking for a place to spend the night."

"Mhmh!"

"This young woman too, she's asking for a place to spend the night, here at the royal residence."

"Yo! What shall be done about this? Mm!"

This fellow went to the house, then returned. "All right, just follow me."

Jojothwane said, "No, you go on. You go on. Just tell us which house we're to go to, and we'll go there."

He said, "All right, it's that one at the end."

"Oh."

The fellow left them then, and he went to another house. But he sat outside, fearing that the strangers might be bitten by the dogs.

Jojothwane said, "Now we'll do it this way. Stay together, keep yourselves hidden. I'll take the blanket and spread it out a little, so that he won't see that you're so short."

"All right, Jojothwane."

He spread the blanket. Then they went into that house. When they had gone in, the curtain of the bridal party was prepared; when it had been hung, all of them went to one side of the curtain.

He said, "No one should speak. Don't let anyone hear your voices. They'll know that these are the voices of animals. I'm the only one who should talk here. Now someone's going to come and say that he wants to borrow the young women from our party. I'll say that, according to the custom of our home, young women do not go to the groom's people before they have been seen."

"All right, Jojothwane."

"That's why we got you, Jojothwane, so that you can teach us these things."

"We don't know Xhosa practice."

Time passed.

"Then they'll come for the money-of-the-urination here. And I'll explain to them that the money-of-the-urination, according to our custom, is produced after the wedding, on the second day—according to the custom of our home."

"All right, Jojothwane."

Time passed, and some people arrived. They knocked.

"Come in."

"Mm!"

The older women and the young women of the groom's party entered and sat over there.

Jojothwane said, "What brings you here?"

"We've come from the house."

"Yes."

"We've come to ask urination."[5]

"Yes?"

"That's it."

"Well, pardon me. Pardon me, we do know about that custom. No one denies it; we want to fulfill the custom. The money-of-the-urination won't be difficult to produce. But according to the traditions of the royal residence where we've come from, at the home of this king's daughter whom we have brought here, the custom is that all things are produced on the day following the marriage day. All the money, including the money-of-the-urination, is right here. We have it. How much do you expect as far as the money-of-the-urination is concerned, Young women?" So said Jojothwane.

"Well, it's sixpence."

"And you, Women?"

"A shilling."

"Is that all you ask?"

"And there are the little children to be considered—that's threepence."

"Well then, all right, we understand."

They left then. They went and reported what had been said in that house.

The king said, "Well, sit down then, if that's the way things are. They aren't going anywhere. Just sit down and don't worry about the money-of-the-urination. They'll produce it before they go."

Time passed, and beer was brewed here at this place. The dough was brought to the house of the bridal party to be ground: "It's our custom; the bridal party must grind on occasions like this."

---

5. That is, they have come to ask for the money-of-the-urination, one in a series of symbolic acts that create a network of linkages between the two marriage parties.

An evening dance

"Excuse us. These things are not done this way where we come from. That's the custom. Each person has the unique customs of his home."

"Oh, it's all right then."

So the dough was taken back; they went back with it. It was Jojothwane who took it over to that house. Then he returned to the baboons.

It was announced, "The king's daughter will be seen tomorrow."

"All right."

The next day would come. The wedding would take place, and this bridal party would come outside before the wedding occurred. And the bride would then be seen.

"Oh."

Then it was time for the young woman to come out. The men had filled the homestead. There were crowds of people who had come to the royal residence to see the bridal party and attend the big celebration.

Then a little cloud appeared. But it was not a small rain that fell—it was a different kind of rain. It really poured! The earth opened up; it was a flood. The kraal was completely filled with water.

The king said, "Now really, the king's daughter must not be made to walk through mud." He spoke to the people who had come to the celebration: "Please go home. The bride will be seen when the sky clears up. But because you have come here for meat, let the ox be slaughtered—that brown one, catch it and slaughter it. We'll have to take another ox for the wedding itself. But these respectable people who have come must not go away without having at least something from this royal residence. Let the beer be brought out too; they should drink."

The beer was produced then. Some of it was sent to the bridal party. And the celebration went on. Nothing was demanded of the bridal party on this day because all of these activities were being done for the sake of the people who had come for the celebration; the wedding itself would take place on the next clear day. When the meat was brought in to the bridal party, the baboons rushed for it because it had not yet been cooked, it was still raw.

They said, "Oh! Jojothwane, oh!"

And he said, "No! If you persist in doing that, I'll just go outside and report that here in this house there's a bridal party of baboons. And I know that they'll shoot you then."

"Oh no!"

"No no!"

"We've stopped, Jojothwane!" And they settled down.

Then the meat was cooked, and Jojothwane cut it into pieces. He cooked it and sprinkled some salt on it. He cooked the meat, and it was done— and the baboons were quivering. They wanted the meat raw. Over there in the cliffs where they lived, they were not accustomed to cooking their meat; they ate their meat raw.

"Watch out then! Someone might just come along and find you chewing on raw meat. Leave the meat alone, so that I can cook it."

"Oh."

That night, Jojothwane said, "Look here now, all of this meat should be cooked. We should get out of here before the dawn comes because you really can't afford to be seen. If you should just enter that kraal, you'll be closed in—you'll die in this homestead. Maybe only I will escape. Then again, I may not escape. I may be the first one to die because they will wonder why I, a human being, have brought such a thing to this homestead."

"All right, Jojothwane. We know that we're in great danger here."

"We might get hurt."

"Let the meat be cooked."

All of the meat was cooked that night. Jojothwane took some off the fire, then put another piece on; he took that off the fire, and put more on. He regularly sprinkled it with salt, cooking it and taking it off the hearth. All the containers were stuffed with this meat, the containers they had brought along as part of the materials of the bridal party—the pots and baskets, everything was filled with this cooked meat.

Then, in the middle of the night, Jojothwane said, "Let's go! Let's go now. It's time!"

"Yes, let's go now while the others are still asleep."

"Not even a cock is crowing."

The blanket was taken down, the one with which they had fashioned the bridal curtain; the meat was tied up. And they left. They went in a zigzag way, carefully avoiding the people of the groom's homestead.

Then, when they were a distance away, Jojothwane said, "Run now! I'm parting company with you here. I'm going to my original destination now. Run!"

Oh! Oh, the baboons ran, galloping, strutting. When they had gone down into a valley and had ascended the other side, Jojothwane shouted, "There's a baboon's bridal party here at this home! There's a baboon's bridal party here at this home!"

Someone said, "What's he saying?"

Dogs were barking.

"Go and look in that house!"

Someone went to look—"Yo! There's nothing in the house anymore! Only a pot remains! Only a pot—that's all, that's all! There's no meat! There's no one!"

"Yo!"

Someone said, "Close off the fords!"

"Close off the fords!"

People came out from all the ridges, on all sides, trying to close off the fords.

"An alarm has been raised at the royal residence!"

The king said, "How could I ever slaughter my ox for such an unworthy affair?"

Jojothwane went on his way, and the baboons went on theirs. Toward dawn, Jojothwane turned around and went back to the baboons. He found them.

He went to them and said, "Did you manage to escape?"

"Why did you say that we were a bridal party of baboons?"

He said, "Well, I was designing a plan that would enable you to escape and not be traced. No one would even know where you had come from. Just remain here. They dare not come to your home!"

"All right, then, leave him alone."

"Get the king."

A little time passed, and Jojothwane said, "Take the king's meat that I brought for him, the choice meat that I wanted him to eat—put it aside."

That meat was taken by the baboons and put into a pot at the back of a house. While they slept, the baboon king, for whom the meat had been brought, sneaked about; he went to that pot because he had not yet had enough to eat. He took off the lid slowly, then ate the meat. He ate it, he ate it, and left only a white bone. He put the bone back into the pot and closed it. Then he went to his house and slept.

The next morning, he said, "Please bring me my meat."

Jojothwane said, "What's that?"

Someone said, "He's referring to his meat, Jojothwane."

"The piece that you put away for him."

"Mm!"

Jojothwane opened the pot: "Oh! Who has eaten the meat? Just a bone remains!"

The baboons said, "You ate it, Jojothwane!"

"We would never take the meat of our king!"

"It was eaten by you!"

"You are the one who said you were giving it to the king as a gift. But then you went back and ate it yourself!"

Oh! All the baboons rushed at him, shaking.

The king said, "No! No! No!"

They wanted to kill Jojothwane.

"No! No! Please leave Jojothwane alone! Let's try to discover who has eaten my meat!"

"No! No! No, it was Jojothwane!"

Jojothwane said, "Don't you have diviners here? Diviners who can find out what's happened to this meat? Before you do anything to me, you should first bring a diviner into the case. Then, when he has made his decision, you can do what you must do. I'm not satisfied with your conclusions right now. You suggest that I put the meat over there, and then, when it was gone the next morning, you concluded that I ate it. Yet I was the one who put it there in the first place!"

"He's right!"

"We do have a doctor," they said.

"Do you hear, King?"

"He says we should go to the diviner."

"Yes."

"All right, let's go and divine this."

So they got together.

"Let's go!"

"Let's go and divine!"

"What'll we do, how shall we carry out this divination?"

Jojothwane said, "Don't leave the king behind! It's his affair!"

Then it was said, "No, the king can't go. He's too old."

"Well, he had better totter along with us," Jojothwane said. "No one can be divined for if he is not present. Who will raise questions for him?"

Yo! He tottered along with them. He stumbled along, and they arrived.

The divination would take place at a pool, in a river. They sat above the broad pool, near a rock. This is how it is done: a person speaks and speaks, then leaps. The one who has done nothing wrong will manage to jump right over, from the rock to the shore, and not land in the deep, broad pool. But the one who has been smelled out will sink in the water and die there.[6]

Someone said, "Let the divination proceed."

Jojothwane said, "Divine now."

He was told, "Jojothwane! Divine!"

He said, "I don't know how to do that. You do it first. You do it first—show me how."

One of them began. He said,

> [sings]
> "It's all Jojothwane's fault:
> He ate the king's meat!"

The baboon leapt from the rock and successfully landed on the other side.

Jojothwane said, "All of you do it now. All of you do it, to the last one of you. The king and I will be last." Jojothwane had a suspicion that the meat had really been eaten by the king. He was very suspicious, but he did not want to say anything.

So another of them climbed to the top of the rock:

> [sings]
> "It's all Jojothwane's fault:
> He ate the king's meat!"

He leapt, successfully.

And so it went, until only the king remained.

"Get on with it, King!"

"No, Jojothwane must do it first!"

So Jojothwane went up on the rock. He said, "Must I mention my name in the song too? Should I call my name?"

They said, "Yes, all of us must call your name!"

> [sings]
> "It's all Jojothwane's fault:
> He ate the chief's meat!"

Jojothwane leapt and got to the other side.

The baboons were disappointed. They said, "Now how has this happened?"

Jojothwane said, "Get on the rock, King. It's your mystery!"

---

6. "Smelling out" is the process whereby a diviner determines the identity of a person who has wrought some kind of mischief or evil.

"No, why don't we just drop this?"

"It cannot be dropped!"

The youth produced his club and said, "I'd rather die! I'd rather die now. This king cannot get away with this. Let him climb on the rock now. This thing happened because of him."

So the king went on the rock. And when he had gone on:

> [sings]
> "It's all Jojothwane's fault:
> He ate the king's meat!"

He leapt! And when he leapt, he went up into the air—then came down headfirst into the pool. And he sank, head first. He got stuck in the bottom. He did not come to the surface.

After a time, it was clear that the king was dead.

"Yo!"

They said, "Oh, pardon us, Jojothwane!"

They were crying. "Pardon us, Jojothwane!"

"Really, we didn't know anything about that!"

"If the king had confessed, if he had said that he had eaten the meat, then we wouldn't have come here!"

"He's the one who got up and asked for it!"

"Pardon us because you really have helped us a lot!"

"We ask your pardon!"

"Today, we're separating."

"Those baboons of the cliffs are returning to the cliffs because our king has now died."

"Those of the thickets to the thickets!"

"Those of the meadows to the meadows!"

"Those of the forests to the forests!"

So the baboons scattered. They scattered.

As for Jojothwane, he walked on.

He finally arrived at the home of his mother's parents.

Tale 17

HAMIOSE, THE WIFE WHO WAS CREATED FROM A TREE

Masithathu Zenani's Analysis: This tale, a story of marital infidelity, has to do with a young woman who is created from a tree by a lonely man. When he drives a nail into the carefully prepared tree, the tree becomes a beautiful woman. The first part of the story tells of how the husband, not a wealthy man, attempts to establish a homestead for his wife, to clothe and feed her. To do this, he must leave home to find work. During his absence, another man spirits her away and marries her. The remainder of the story, dominated by a pattern with a song at its core, has to do with the gradual divestment, by means of helpful pigeons and doves, of the young woman's clothing. Finally, they remove the nail, and the woman becomes a tree again.

It is a failed marriage, Mrs. Zenani pointed out; the man has fulfilled his obligations to his bride, but she, in her unfaithfulness, abdicates her responsibilities. The pattern of the story, developed in leisurely fashion, emphasizes her perfidy and reveals her infidelity, as the birds remove the items that are tokens of her husband's contrastingly proper behavior. In recalling these items of clothing and jewelry, the husband is exacting revenge—with the help of nature, in the form of the birds—at the same time that the storyteller is making a statement about the necessity of proper relations between husband and wife.

It is out of love and loneliness that the man fashions the splendid wife: he is her creator. She is meant to have no life, no will of her own. In her own loneliness, she allows herself to be seduced by another man. The storyteller is emphasizing the sanctity of marriage, but there is a subtext here as well, and that has to do with the view of a wife as having little choice in the matter of her married life. The husband made her, the husband can destroy her. That is the terrible effect of the pattern that largely composes the tale. Mrs. Zenani seemed to be of two minds about this married couple. On the one hand, she argued that the story was meant to uphold the tradition of marriage, and the dominant pattern, she asserted, channeled the audience's attention to that theme. But she also made the comment that in some respects the woman's marital situation was similar to her own, when, as a young woman, she was caused by her father to marry a man with whom she was not in love.

Performance Note

Time: 13 August 1972, about noon. *Place:* In a fallen rondavel near Mrs. Zenani's home in Nkanga, Gatyana District, the Transkei. *Audience:* Three men, three women, four children. (Perf. NS-173.)

There were a man and a woman. The woman was pregnant, and she bore a child—a son. Time passed for them. They were paupers. They had nothing; their lives were hard. There was nothing there, nothing at all; they barely survived. In order to eat, they had to work very hard, and this child of theirs grew up in hardship.

Finally, the time came when the parents were no longer there, and the son was left behind. The mother disappeared first—she died. The son lived on for a time with his father. They lacked everything; they had nothing to eat. Their clothes were rags; they had no decent clothes because of the great difficulties they experienced. And they had nothing to sell, nothing at all. That is the way they lived. People gave them old garments, even ragged clothing, to wear.

Time went on then. Time went on, and finally the boy's father also died. The lad was left behind, alone in that house of his. Time passed for him there, and one day, after he had thought long about how he might change his sorry state, after he had thought and thought about it, he took an axe. He honed the axe; it was sharp. Then he closed the door and left home.

He came to hard, stony ground among trees in a forest, and he looked around for a time. Then he chopped a tree down, a cabbage tree. He cut it down neatly, making certain that it was equal to himself in height. Then he barked the tree, peeling the outer bark in strips with the axe. He peeled that cabbage tree carefully; he peeled it, and it was smooth. Then he left it there—it could not be lifted, it was so heavy.

He went home. He stayed at his home, allowing the tree's bulk to decrease so that he might finally lift it, so that it might be placed in an upright position. That took a long time. After a time that has taken a long stride, he went back, and he attempted to raise the tree. Finally, he was able to stand it up. The problem now was how to get it home. He barked the tree flawlessly then with his axe.

He was wearing two bracelets on his wrist. He took one of the bracelets and stretched it out. He put it on a rock and beat it, straightening it until it resembled a nail. When it was straight, he took it and drove it into this tree that he had barked. He drove it in on one side. He drove it in, saying, "I want a wife." When he had driven it in, it disappeared completely in the tree.

Suddenly that tree spread out. It developed arms and legs, breasts, buttocks, the whole person, complete. The tree had become a beautiful person, a splendid person.

He said to it, "My wife."

And the tree said, "Hnn?"

He said, "I want us to go home now. I want to go and find a little job because I want you to have things to wear."

The tree said, "All right."

He went with the tree. He took a worn garment that he was wearing and put it on this tree. The lovely woman walked on then, and he went into the house with her. She remained there.

Then he said, "I'll look for work."

He went away, and she stayed behind—this cabbage tree, his wife. He traveled. He went to look for work in places that employ people and pay them for their work. Finally, he was hired by a king.

The king said, "I want you to herd these cattle. Is that satisfactory, Young man?"

He said, "I'm satisfied to herd the cattle. I want to be paid at once. I can't stay at home because local employers pay so little. I'll finish my work. I must be paid now because of a pressing problem that I have over there at my home. I have a wife who is inadequately clothed. And I do not have sufficient clothing either."

The king said, "All right, I can pay you, to enable you to overcome these pressing problems of yours."

The young man was paid by the king. When he had been paid, he looked around for women's wearing apparel. He sought cotton capes, he wanted a cotton skirt, a breast covering; he wanted petticoats, kerchiefs, necklaces, armlets; he wanted rings; he wanted neck-beads; he wanted metal chains so that those who saw his wife would know that she was a complete woman, a woman with whom no one could find fault. Only he would know her origins. He also looked for garments for himself, and he found those as well.

So he worked there at the royal residence of the king, herding cattle. He herded in the daytime, then returned with the livestock. He then went to sleep at his own house. At dawn, he got up and came to take out the livestock and herd it. He spent all day with the livestock at the royal residence, at the place where he had been hired. And he spent the nights at his home.

Things went on like that for the young man. He clothed his wife; he put necklaces on her; he put rings on her. Armlets also he put on her. He put foot-chains on her; he put long cotton skirts on her, petticoats; he put boots on her; he put on her everything that a woman should wear—earrings, everything. She had handbags like any woman and the things pertaining to handbags.

The villagers now saw her. This was a homestead that had hardly been noticed in the past—it was not much of a homestead, really. But now it was noted that a person was there: she walked about, she made fires, she cooked there. She was a wife. In the past, there had been no wife in that homestead. The neighbors knew that. Then, suddenly, one day a person came there from the river.

They wanted to see this person who had appeared from the river, to find out where she had come from. Whenever someone was going some where, that person would purposely pass by that homestead to gaze about, to see what was happening there.

"Well, hello there!"

"Yes, hello."

"Mh! Where have you come from, Friend?"

"I'm from here!"

"Whose wife are you?"

"I am the wife of the young man of this homestead."

"Oh! You're a daughter of what place?"

"Well, my home is far away, I'm a daughter of a distant place."

"Oh! How could he have such a beautiful woman? This is a wonder!"

She continued to be seen by the other people. They would go by her homestead and invite her to accompany them when they went to gather firewood.

One day, the husband said to his wife, "My wife, I don't want you to travel about with just anyone. I want you to stay here at home. There have never been many people at this homestead, even when my mother and father were still alive. You must stay here by yourself. You mustn't get into the habit of traveling around, going to all these homesteads. That's not to be done."

Now, the wife did not know that she was a woman who had been created from a tree. She saw herself as just a woman.

She acceded to her husband's admonition.

A year passed, and the husband continued to work at the royal residence, herding the cattle. Again, the king wanted to pay the young man.

The young man said, "When you pay me this time, pay me in edible things."

So the king brought out food, all sorts of food—corn, beans, sorghum. He gave the young man food equal to the value of money that was owed him. The young man and his wife carried off those edible things, transporting them to his home. When he had taken the things to his home, his work commitment at the royal residence was at an end.

He said to the king, "You see, King, I want to leave this place now. I'm going to get a job far from my home. When one works too close to home, he gets reports of troubles.[7] It is better that I seek work in another place, far from home. There are no hard feelings. I'll come back when I've finished in that other place."

The king agreed, and the young man went on his way, going off to work, leaving his wife at home.

He first instructed his wife, "Now, I'm going to look for work. Remember what I told you: this home is not to become a congregating place for groups of people. I know that they all come to admire you. But when my mother and father were alive, there were never idle gatherings in this

---

7. Troubles that require money and his presence.

house. Nor did they travel around to other homesteads, going from house to house throughout the neighborhood. I want you to stay here. I'll work for perhaps a year, then I'll return. But it may not be a complete year."

The wife agreed. She and her husband understood each other completely. There was no suspicion between them, only mutual understanding.

The young man went off to work, and he found a job. He found work, and, while he was working in that distant place, his wife remained at home. She was also happy.

Time passed. Time passed for that wife.

After her husband had been gone a long time, she became more and more familiar with the neighbors, continually going about visiting.

Then a young man was seen—not far away, just on the fringes of activities in this neighborhood. This young man was the same age as the woman's husband, and he began to make oblique references when speaking to that man's wife, wondering how such a beautiful woman could belong to one who was so ragged, "considering that the rest of us are available."

He initiated the relationship; he cajoled her. "You can't be married to a thing that doesn't even have cattle, a thing that has no sheep, a thing that has nothing. I'll marry you right now! What can have entered your mind, to be attached to such a man?"

This young wife was pleased with him, and he urged her on. She accepted him; they became lovers. He married her, and she became his wife. Remember, this new husband had no wife: he began his married life with a wife whom he married in her husband's absence.

Time passed, and it happened that her husband, in that distant place, heard that "Your wife has left you. She's become the wife of another man."

This news alarmed the young man because he had found his wife with such difficulty. So he returned to his home, not having completed his job. When he arrived, he found that his wife was not there with her little garments. He slept alone over there at his homestead. He remained there; he remained some days, thinking. He thought as deeply as he had that time in the forest when he had made the decision to fashion his wife from a cabbage tree.

Then one day, he said, "I'm going to call the pigeons and doves. I'll ask them to come here."

He called them, and those birds came. He was still there, at the side of the place that would have been a cattle kraal—if he had one.

The birds arrived and perched in front of him.

He said, "I'm sending you to do something for me."

They responded.

One of them said to the other, "Say to him: what will he give us for that?"

The other bird turned to the young man, and said, "*Vukuthu vukuthu!* It is said, 'What will you give us for that?' "

He said, "I can give you some corn."

The first bird said, "Do you think that we have throats large enough to swallow corn?"

The second bird said, "*Vukuthu vukuthu!* It is said, 'Do you think that we have throats large enough to swallow corn?' "

The young man said, "I can give you some millet."

The second bird said, "He'll give us some millet."

The first said, "Do you think that we have throats large enough to swallow millet?"

This second one repeated, and said, "*Vukuthu vukuthu!* Do you think that we have throats large enough to swallow millet?"

The young man said, "I can give you small seeds."

The second bird said, "He says he can give us small seeds."

The first one said, "Tell him that he should show the seeds to us; let us see them."

This second one said, "*Vukuthu vukuthu!* Show them to us; let us see them."

The man went into the house; he took down a tin dish containing the seeds. They are from a certain plant that has black seeds; they are sometimes culled in the forest and are loved very much by birds. He dipped into the dish with his hand and poured some of the seeds out.

The birds ate the seeds. They bowed their heads to pick them up. They said, "*Vukuthu vukuthu!* More!"

He dipped some more seeds and poured them out. They ate and ate; then they had enough. They began to speak again.

"Well, proceed, young man, tell us what course you're sending us on, so that we can get on with it."

The young man said, "Go, take the cotton cape from my wife."

The doves got up then, and flew off—mprrrrrrrrrrrrr! They went to that homestead. They arrived there and stopped at the cattle kraal.

"Here are some doves!"

"Beat them! Here are doves!"

They took sticks with which to beat the birds. One of them came toward the birds with a stick, and the birds spoke to her. They said,

[sings]
"Hamio! Hamio! Mio! Mio! Miose!
We were sent by your husband, Miose.
We were told to take the cape, Miose.
Yo! Help us, Child of our father, we love you.
Yo! Help us, Child of our father."

The new husband said, "What is this? Have there ever been doves that speak? Hee! Isn't this strange? Birds that speak?"

The birds flew off, wiuuuuuuuu. They stopped at the entrance to the house, and it was quiet now because the husband and wife were puzzled by what was going on, by birds that speak.

The doves repeated,

> [sings]
> "Hamio! Hamio! Mio! Mio! Miose!
> We were sent by your husband, Miose.
> We were told to take the cape, Miose.
> Yo! Help us, Child of our father.
> Yo! Help us, Child of our father, we love you."

They were puzzled. Within that house, the wife was sitting on one side, the husband on the other. The birds suddenly perched on the shoulders of the wife—one perched on one side, one on the other side.

They said,

> [sings]
> "Hamio! Hamio! Mio! Mio! Miose!
> We were sent by your husband, Miose.
> We were told to take the cape, Miose.
> Yo! Help us, Child of our father, we love you.
> Yo! Help us, Child of our father."

Then they climbed on her head. They took the cape on both sides. They seized the cape, then carried it off neatly with their beaks. And they departed with it. They went out of the entrance to the house—prrrrrrrrrrr!

They returned to this home. They arrived, and the young man was sitting outside his house. They put the cape down there.

"Here it is, here's the cape."

They stopped.

He said, "Go back and get the long cotton skirt."

They returned—prrrrrrrrrrr!—and they perched on the kraal gate.

One of them said, "Hee! The doves are back! Did you see them disappear with that cape? Hee, really!"

"I don't understand what's going on!"

The birds repeated,

> [sings]
> "Hamio! Hamio! Mio! Mio! Miose!
> We were sent by your husband, Miose.

We were told to take the cotton skirt, Miose.
Yo! Help us, Child of our father.
Yo! Help us, Child of our father, we love you."

He said, "No! It doesn't matter that the doves have come! Just give them this cotton skirt. I'll buy you another."
The wife remained silent. The doves flew and stopped at the entrance.

[sings]
"Hamio! Hamio! Mio! Mio! Miose!
We were sent by your husband, Miose.
We were told to take the cotton skirt, Miose.
Yo! Help us, Child of our father.
Yo! Help us, Child of our father, we love you."

They were quiet; they were silent. The birds stood in front of her. The woman sat down then, and they climbed on her legs.

[sings]
"Hamio! Hamio! Mio! Mio! Miose!
We were sent by your husband, Miose.
We were told to take the cotton skirt, Miose.
Yo! Help us, Child of our father, we love you.
Yo! Help us, Child of our father."

They began the operation on her waist, untying the long cotton skirt, and they flew off with it. They went out of the doorway, peeeeeeeeeeee! Trrrrrrrrrrrriii! And they arrived at the home of that young man.
They arrived and spread the skirt out before him.
They said, "There's the long cotton skirt. What else is to be done?"
He said, "Go and get the petticoat."
They departed, twiiiiiiiiiii! They got there; they arrived and stopped in the yard.

[sings]
"Hamio! Hamio! Mio! Mio! Miose!
We were sent by your husband, Miose.
We were told to take the petticoat, Miose.
Yo! Help us, Child of our father.
Yo! Help us, Child of our father, we love you."

Silence. No one spoke here at home anymore. The birds ascended, coming to her. They sat in front of her.

[sings]
"Hamio! Hamio! Mio! Mio! Miose!
We were sent by your husband, Miose.
We were told to take the petticoat, Miose.
Yo! Help us, Child of our father.
Yo! Help us, Child of our father, we love you."

The birds took the petticoat off, the clothing beneath the long cotton skirt, and they flew away with the petticoat.

The man got up then; he took another garment and clothed the woman in it.

Twiiiiiiiiii! The birds returned to the young man, and said, "Here it is!"

The young man said, "All right, go and get the breast covering."

Oh! They departed, twiiiiiiiiiii! They arrived over there; they stopped at the entrance.

[sings]
"Hamio! Hamio! Mio! Mio! Miose!
We were sent by your husband, Miose.
We were told to take the breast covering, Miose.
Yo! Help us, Child of our father.
Yo! Help us, Child of our father, we love you."

Silence.

They moved on; they climbed on her. The man did not come out—he remained, filled with wonder. The love fever was abating.

Silence.

One of them climbed on her.

[sings]
"Hamio! Hamio! Mio! Mio! Miose!
We were sent by your husband, Miose.
We were told to take the breast covering, Miose.
Yo! Help us, Child of our father.
Yo! Help us, Child of our father, we love you."

Then they took it; they untied the covering, they pulled it off. They pulled it from her chest. And they went off with it, trrrrrrrrrrrr! They arrived at the home of the young man.

They said, "Here's the breast covering. What shall we do now?"

The young man said, "Go, and take the foot-chains."

They departed—trrrrrrrrrrrr!—and arrived. They stopped at the entrance.

[sings]
"Hamio! Hamio! Mio! Mio! Miose!
We were sent by your husband, Miose.
We were told to take the chains, Miose.
Yo! Help us, Child of our father.
Yo! Help us, Child of our father, we love you."

Silence, They went to her, to her feet. They arrived there and sat.

[sings]
"Hamio! Hamio! Mio! Mio! Miose!
We were sent by your husband, Miose.
We were told to take the chains, Miose.
Yo! Help us, Child of our father.
Yo! Help us, Child of our father, we love you."

They removed the chains. And they departed with them, trrrrrrrrrrrr!
They came to the young man. He was sitting at the site of the cattle kraal.
The birds threw the chains down.
   "Here are the chains. What shall we do now?"
   "Go and get her boots."
   They departed, trrrrrrrrrrrii! They landed in the entrance.

[sings]
"Hamio! Hamio! Mio! Mio! Miose!
We were sent by your husband, Miose.
We were told to take the boots, Miose.
Yo! Help us, Child of our father.
Yo! Help us, Child of our father, we love you."

Silence. They went to her ankles.

[sings]
"Hamio! Hamio! Mio! Mio! Miose!
We were sent by your husband, Miose.
We were told to take the boots, Miose.
Yo! Help us, Child of our father.
Yo! Help us, Child of our father, we love you."

Those are boots we're talking about: they untied them, and they departed with them, twiiiiiiiii! When they got home, they threw the boots
down.
   "Here they are!"

The young man looked.
They asked, "What shall we do now?"
"All right, now go and get her apron."
They traveled, trrrrrrrriiiiiiii! They arrived; they stopped in the entrance.

> [sings]
> "Hamio! Hamio! Mio! Mio! Miose!
> We were sent by your husband, Miose.
> We were told to take the apron, Miose.
> Yo! Help us, Child of our father.
> Yo! Help us, Child of our father, we love you."

Silence. In that house there was wonderment. No one conversed. They were utterly astonished, aware now that their affair was at an end.

And there were the birds. They went to her loins. They arrived there and remained at her loins.

> [sings]
> "Hamio! Hamio! Mio! Mio! Miose!
> We were sent by your husband, Miose.
> We were told to take the apron, Miose.
> Yo! Help us, Child of our father.
> Yo! Help us, Child of our father, we love you."

They came to her loins and removed the apron. They took it, helping each other. Then they departed, trrrrrrrrrrrr!

When they came to the young man, they threw the apron down.
"There it is! Now what shall we do?"
The young man thought. "Go there, go and take the armlets."
Yes! Trrrrrrrrrrrr! When they got there, they arrived and stopped at the entrance.

> [sings]
> "Hamio! Hamio! Mio! Mio! Miose!
> We were sent by your husband, Miose.
> We were told to take the armlets, Miose.
> Yo! Child of our father.
> Yo! Child of our father, we love you."

Silence. They came to her. They looked at her arm.

> [sings]
> "Hamio! Hamio! Mio! Mio! Miose!
> We were sent by your husband, Miose.

We were told to take the armlets, Miose.
Yo! Child of our father.
Yo! Child of our father, we love you."

They unfastened the armlets and slipped them off. They departed with them. They arrived and threw them down.
"Here they are! What shall we do now?"
The young man said, "Return. Go and take the rings."
They departed, trrrrrrrrrrrrr! They arrived, and stopped at the entrance.

[sings]
"Hamio! Hamio! Mio! Mio! Miose!
We were sent by your husband, Miose.
We were told to take the rings, Miose.
Yo! Child of our father.
Yo! Child of our father, we love you."

They went to her. They arrived and sat near her arm.

[sings]
"Hamio! Hamio! Mio! Mio! Miose!
We were sent by your husband, Miose.
We were told to take the rings, Miose.
Yo! Child of our father.
Yo! Child of our father, we love you."

They began the work on her fingers. They drew the rings off, drew them off, drew them off, drew off the rings. Then they parted.
"Hee!" The man said, "It doesn't matter. I'll buy others for you."
The birds departed, trrrrrrrrrriiii! They arrived; they arrived and put the rings down.
"Here are the rings!"
"Well, go back. Go and take the armlets [from the forearms]."
Trrrrrrrrrriiii! They arrived and stopped at the entrance.

[sings]
"Hamio! Hamio! Mio! Mio! Miose!
We were sent by your husband, Miose.
We were told to take the armlets, Miose.
Yo! Child of our father.
Yo! Child of our father, we love you."

Silence. Those persons inside did not speak. The birds ascended; they went to the woman, perching near her arm.

> [sings]
> "Hamio! Hamio! Mio! Mio! Miose!
> We were sent by your husband, Miose.
> We were told to take the armlets, Miose.
> Yo! Help us, Child of our father.
> Yo! Help us, Child of our father, we love you."

They began to remove the armlets. They took them off; they slipped them off. Then they went away with them, trrrrrrrrrrrrr! They arrived, they arrived.

And they said, "Here they are!"

He said, "Return. Go, and take the neck-beads."

Oh! They departed, trrrrrriiiiiiiiii! They stopped in the entrance.

> [sings]
> "Hamio! Hamio! Mio! Mio! Miose!
> We were sent by your husband, Miose.
> We were told to take the neck-beads, Miose.
> Yo! Help us, Child of our father.
> Yo! Help us, Child of our father, we love you."

Silence. The birds ascended, they arrived and perched on her shoulders.

> [sings]
> "Hamio! Hamio! Mio! Mio! Miose!
> We were sent by your husband, Miose.
> We were told to take the neck-beads, Miose.
> Yo! Help us, Child of our father.
> Yo! Help us, Child of our father, we love you."

They took the beads from her throat, and parted with them—trrrrrrrrrrrrr! And they landed at home. They put the beads down in front of the man. This property was now heaped up; the things that had been removed from that other place by these doves, those things were heaped up in front of the young man.

"Well, what shall we do now?"

"Return, go and get her kerchief."

They departed, trrrrrrrriiiiiiiiiii! They arrived, and they stopped in the entrance.

> [sings]
> "Hamio! Hamio! Mio! Mio! Miose!
> We were sent by your husband, Miose.
> We were told to take the kerchief, Miose.
> Yo! Help us, Child of our father.
> Yo! Help us, Child of our father, we love you."

Silence. The birds traveled, they ascended. They arrived and climbed on her, perching on her shoulders.

> [sings]
> "Hamio! Hamio! Mio! Mio! Miose!
> We were sent by your husband, Miose.
> We were told to take the kerchief, Miose.
> Yo! Help us, Child of our father.
> Yo! Help us, Child of our father, we love you."

Abruptly, they took the kerchief from her head. Then they parted with it. She was left behind just like that, without a kerchief on her head. Trrrrrrrr! They arrived and put it down.

They said, "There it is then. We're finished. She has nothing now. She is without clothes. All she has now are the clothes of that homestead."

The man said, "Now take the final property from her. Return, take the final piece of equipment. Now you will take her life, her life. That life is in her head. Pluck it out, bring it back here."

Eheee! The doves traveled, trrrrrrrr! They arrived; they stopped at the entrance.

> [sings]
> "Hamio! Hamio! Mio! Mio! Miose!
> We were sent by your husband, Miose.
> We were told to take your life, Miose.
> Yo! Help us, Child of our father.
> Yo! Help us, Child of our father, we love you."

The man said, "Well, there's nothing here now. There's nothing; everything's been taken! Where is that life?"

The woman said, "No, I have nothing now! I have nothing! There is nothing to be taken now. Everything has been taken! I have nothing, nothing now!"

They ascended. The birds arrived and sat at the upper side of the house. Then they perched here on her shoulders.

They said,

[sings]
"Hamio! Hamio! Mio! Mio! Miose!
We were sent by your husband, Miose.
We were told to take your life, Miose.
Yo! Help us, Child of our father.
Yo! Help us, Child of our father, we love you."

Then they perched on her head:

[sings]
"Hamio! Hamio! Mio! Mio! Miose!
We were sent by your husband, Miose.
We were told to take your life, Miose.
Yo! Help us, Child of our father.
Yo! Help us, Child of our father, we love you."

Then they pulled out that nail that had been driven in by the young man when he had barked this tree, when he had created a wife for himself. They pulled it out. As soon as they had removed the nail, the tree snapped open. Its roots appeared, the house filled up! Then the other one, the man, was raised up by the roots of the tree, by the branches and the leaves. The house filled completely. Even the door was shut, and the tree returned to its original condition: it was now a huge tree.

The doves parted; they flew off, and they arrived.

They said, "There's the life then!" and they put down the nail fashioned of the bracelet.

The young man took some seeds and put them down there; he poured out seeds for the doves. And the doves pecked them up. They ate the seeds and were satisfied. He fed them. They thanked him; then they departed. The man thanked the birds. He helped them by giving them food.

He said that he would not want to go to all the difficulty of creating a wife for another man, to create a wife and then find that he did not have a wife anymore: "Now let us see if that man will be able to take that tree over there and make it into a human being."

Tale 18

THE MAN WHO BEAT HIS WIFE

Masithathu Zenani's Analysis: The opening pattern of this story establishes the conflict: a girl who is a musician is a thief. As a punishment, she is beaten by her father, who then turns on his wife and beats her severely when she intervenes on her daughter's behalf.

Mrs. Zenani noted that the story has to do with proper relations between husband and wife. At the heart of the story is a dualistic pattern: the beating of the wife, the beating of the husband. The retaliatory punishment of the man is meant to argue for the proper respect of the husband for his wife. Her humane efforts to prevent harm to her daughter by the angry husband call down his anger upon her. In the end, the husband must learn how to treat members of his family. The opening pattern, that describing the activities of the thief, is only the motivation for the real point of the story. As his angry wife, on a brief return visit to her home of marriage, tells her husband, ". . . the beating that you received was your own fault. You were thrashed because you had beaten me on the head. A wife is never beaten on the head by her husband. You were punished so that our marriage would not be disrupted." Finally, the husband apologizes and gives up cattle as a fine. His wife returns to him, and "they lived together in happiness . . . ," the husband having learned a lesson. The wife, though living at her home of marriage, remains under the care and protection of those of her own home of birth.

Performance Note

Time: 15 September 1967, in the morning. *Place:* Along a path in Nkanga, Gatyana District, the Transkei. *Audience:* Five women, fifteen children. (Perf. 649.)

In a certain village was a large homestead. A girl who was very much a thief lived in this homestead.

During this time, calabashes were made of cowhide: the skins were fastened together at the throat of the vessel. When milk was to be poured out of such a calabash, the rope at the neck was first untied. Then, when the child had finished pouring the milk, she fastened the rope at the neck once again.

Now this girl was an expert thief. No one was her equal: she stole from the entire village. It happened that she wanted a stringed instrument, an *isitolotolo.* She was a fine *isitolotolo* player.

One day, she went to gather firewood. As she was returning, she passed a certain homestead. She put the wood down by the side of that homestead and went inside. She poured some milk from the calabash in this

With the music of the words, the body of the performer shapes the emotions of the audience into an attractive artistic form.

home and drank it. Then she fastened the calabash again and went on her way.

At the same time, the owner of that homestead, a man, was approaching. He said, "Yo! That child over there, she's robbed me!"

When he got to the house, he went straight to the calabash. He found no milk in it. She had already departed with her firewood, and he pursued her.

When he got to her home, he said, "I've come about this child! You should see what she did at my homestead!"

The girl's father said, "What did the child do?"

"She drank the milk from a calabash! I saw her coming out of the house as I was approaching, still far from my home."

"How could she have done that? Why didn't you chase her? Instead, you come for her at her home—even though you saw her in the act. You're going to have a weak case."

"But I tell you I was still far from home when I saw her coming out of the house!"

Her father said, "Girl, is this true? Did you really do this?"

"No, he's lying! I didn't go over there at all! I went to gather firewood, and I carried it home."

"Where's that firewood?"

"Here!"

"Well, Stranger, your accusation is not substantiated. Here's the child's firewood. Whether she's a thief or not, the fact is that you're accusing her falsely today."

The man went home, saying, "Just wait! In time, you'll see!"

He said, "All right, wait and see."

The man went home then. This child remained there at her home. Yet, even at her own home, she habitually engaged in thievery and was not found out. It was known that this child played the *isitolotolo* very well, but no one was aware of her stealing.

After a number of years, she was caught in another homestead while in the act of fastening a calabash. A woman of the homestead entered while she was doing that and said, "What are you doing here? What? What are you doing?"

She said, "I'm hungry!"

"You say you're hungry! What business do you have here?"

"I became hungry as I was gathering firewood."

"Why did you set out without eating first at your own home?"

"There wasn't anything to eat at home yet. Oh, please let me go, Mama! Forgive me! Let me go!"

"Why should I let you go?" So saying, the woman went to the door. She closed the door, then took a stick with which to beat the child.

The child said, "Stop, Mama! I'll play the *isitolotolo* for you!" She took the instrument from her bag.

The woman said, "Well, please play it, Daughter."

[The storyteller reaches into a billycan, takes out an *isitolotolo*, and proceeds to play it.]

"Well, my child, I'll forgive you. But you must never do this again. You've played the *isitolotolo* often, but we really didn't know that you were so talented."

"Yes, Mama."

"Bring that ladle over here, and I'll pour some milk for you. Your song was a beautiful one."

She took the ladle then and poured some milk for the child. The girl drank it; then the woman fastened the calabash. The girl went on her way; she returned to her home. The woman followed her, and, when she arrived at the girl's home, she said, "Do you know that this child stole that calabash over at my place? I caught her! But when I had seized her, she begged me to forgive her. She asked me to forgive her, saying that she'd never do it again, that she had been hungry. She had left home without having eaten. She said to me, 'Oh, what is it, Friend? Mama, leave me alone, and I'll play the *isitolotolo* for you!' I agreed. She played the instrument, and I forgave her. But she must never do this again. And she should never come back to my home. This child will teach other children her bad ways."

The child's father thanked the woman: "I thank you, Woman. I want to punish this child now, in your presence. I'm really tired of the things this child has done!" As he said this, he took a grass rope. He seized the girl. Then he beat her severely, beat her on the buttocks, saying, "Why do you steal?"

"Oh! Father! Father, stop! Stop! I'll never do it again! I'll never steal again! Stop, my father!"

He said, "Why do you steal? You're ruining my name! No one in this homestead has ever done such a thing! Why do you do it? What kind of omen in this? Whom do you take after, Child?"

He beat her. Finally, the child's mother intervened: "No, leave her alone now! You've punished her enough. The child won't be able to sit down. You're breaking her skin!"

The man then leapt over and began to beat his wife. "I'm beating this child for doing something bad! How dare you suggest that she not be beaten? Do you approve of what she's done?" He beat the wife violently while she sat on the bed. She moaned. Her head was bleeding.

His wife departed. She went to her own home, to her home of birth. When she got there, she showed the people the beating her husband had given her. He had beaten her on the head; he had given her head wounds.

She was told that she must not return to her home of marriage, not until her husband himself—"the one who beat you in this way"—came to this home.

Her husband was anxious, afraid to go to his father-in-law's place to bring back his wife.

Time passed; time passed, and he was uneasy. Finally, he went; he gave up and went there. When he arrived at his wife's house of birth, he was made to stay outside.

Someone said, "Let only the women go to him. No man should go to him because he has no character. No man should go to him. He must be questioned by the women."

The women of that village gathered then: "The husband of this little girl has arrived—the one who beat her."

"Come!"

The women gathered then; they went to him.

Someone said, "Let's ask him!"

The women carried sticks. They stood in front of him.

One of them said, "Where have you come from?"

This fellow said, "Oh, what is this, that the women are questioning me?"

One of them said, "What are you? Are you a man?"

"I thought I was a man."

"No! You're not a man! You're another woman! You've met with some other women today, the ones you beat and give head wounds! There must be another administration of wounds today!"

So saying, the first woman got up and hit him on the head. He fell. Now he too had a head wound.

He got up and said, "How could I be beaten by women?"

Meanwhile, the men were witnessing these activities from the doorway. They did not go over there. They just spoke to the women: "Cut him up!"

"Cut him up!"

The women beat him then, and the husband fled. He even left his garments behind; he was running naked.

The women were beating him.

He finally arrived at his home in that condition, unable even to cover himself. They had retaliated for the beating he had given his wife.

His wife remained at her home of birth, and, when she had recovered from her wounds, she said, "Friends, I must go home now. I have children there. That man won't come here again."

Her father said, "Sit down. Stay. We want cattle from that man over there, to make up for the beating he gave you."

"No, I'll return. I'm going to have a look, Father. Really, my children are alone." So she said, and that woman traveled then. She went home. She went to her home of marriage.

When she got there, that man was still in pain because of the head wounds he had received.

Her husband asked, "Are you returning today?"

She said, "Yes, I am returning."

"If you are indeed returning, then where are my cattle? It was an outrage to beat me until I was in this condition! Yet you have the nerve to come home."

His wife said, "No, the beating that you received was your own fault. You were thrashed because you had beaten me on the head. A wife is never beaten on the head by her husband. You were punished so that our marriage would not be disrupted."

"Oh, you mean that you might stay here at home with me then? Even though I've been beaten at your home? And you'll be my wife again? No, I shall be content to take another wife. You can go home. I want my cattle."[8]
He said that, and the wife went home.

When she got to her home, she said, "That man over there says that he wants my cattle because he was beaten here at home. He wonders how I could ever return to his home again."

8. He demands cattle as damages for the crime that he feels has been committed against him.

"What do you say?" her father asked. "What do you say should be done then, my daughter?"

"I want him to be given his cattle."

"You want him to be given his cattle?"

"Yes."

"But can he be given cattle after he almost killed you? You have been hurt badly, yet he wants his cattle?"

"Well, if he is not given his cattle, Father, it means that I shall have to live here. Because I can see that the man over there no longer wants me in his homestead."

"Well, sit down."

"All right."

"We'll see."

The young woman remained in her home then. Her small children came to her, taking turns carrying each other on the back. They arrived at their mother's home of birth, and when they had arrived: "Hello, Mama!"

"Yes!"

"Well, Mama, we have come to fetch you."

"What does your father say?"

"He says that we should be the ones who come because he is afraid to come here."

"Go home, then, my children, and tell your father that I shall not come home. He must come here himself. My father insists that he pay the damages, that he make amends with an ox. Explain that to him. Then I shall want to go home, too."

Those children returned to their home, and, when they arrived, they said, "Father, our mother will not return. She says that Grandfather wants cattle because you beat her. You must produce two oxen. That, they said, is the condition for her returning. You must go yourself and bring those cattle."

"Well then, all right, my children. I shall bring those cattle in the morning. My property has been spoiled. I want my wife to return. We quarreled, but now I am quarreling no longer. It's over."

In the morning, at dawn, the man asked another man to "help me to drive these oxen. I want to go and get my wife."

They traveled then, the husband and his neighbor, helping each other to drive those two oxen.

When he arrived over there, he sat in the yard. Someone asked him where he had come from.

He said, "I come from home. And really, I have come here to ask my father to pardon me for the wrong that I did."

"Yes."

"When one is angry, one perceives things wrongly. Then, when one is calm again, one can understand things properly."

"Yes."

"Now, I'm bringing these two oxen so that he'll let me have my wife back [literally, "so that he will loan me my wife"]. My property is deteriorating."

"Yes."

"Well, really, Father, I regret what I have done. I repent. I have reproved myself now that I understand the bad thing that I did. I was overcome with anger."

"Yes."

"Today, I am asking your pardon."

"Friend, if you want my pardon, I always have it ready. You're the savage one, almost killing my daughter like that. I'll just lend her to you for a little while. Then we'll have another meeting, to see if you've talked sense to yourself, or have gone back to your bad habits. I shall loan her to you. But you must return to your home alone. Your wife will follow later. Go home. She'll come to you next week."

The man went home then. He was thankful. He raised his hand to his father, thanking him. Then he went home.

When he had gone home, time passed for him. The following week, things returned to normal—his wife returned to his home. All kinds of beautiful things were prepared for her because she was returning after a long stay at her father's home. The following week, she went to her home of marriage, and her husband was happy when she arrived.

Now they lived together in happiness, peacefully, saying pleasant things to one another so that the wife would not hold a grudge.

Part Four: Maturity

INTRODUCTION

MASITHATHU ZENANI ON STORYTELLING

Contemporary images and the physical bodies of the members of the audience are introduced into a closed world of art. Anything considered superfluous by the artist is omitted, as images from the real world dramatically touch ancient images and gestures fertile with compressed experiences. Gesture is now harnessed to thought, to feeling, not to physical action. Gesture now responds to an imaginative story, not to the bewildering open-endedness and uncertainties of the objective world. Already, familiar physical movements are being transformed simply because they occur in new, artistic environments. Life in the world of the imaginative narrative flows evenly and predictably within culturally sanctioned patterns.

The artistic experience molds our feelings in youth, organizes them in images, then nourishes and expands those trapped feelings (remembered feelings, mementos of one's artistic and social experiences) as we move beyond youth into adulthood. The narrative experience catches feeling and, engineering it through patterns, gives it meaning. The narratives can have no impact if they are not constructed on and of human feelings: uncertainties, fulfillment, suspense, expectation, hopes, fears. Feelings are held in images and gestures, shaped by patterning which is itself composed of such feeling, then brought into contact with other feelings caught in other images and gestures having to do with characters and actions. In the juxtaposition, feelings are controlled, imbued with message.

The ancient, familiar images and patterns give meaning to experience by shaping feelings, by providing order. Images are the repositories of emotion; they evoke, surround, trap feeling. In a performance, the members of the audience are immersed in images. They move through the network of body movements and sounds, and, to an extent, they themselves control this patterning. Nameless and diffuse emotions are tied to patterns and are brought under control through expectation, suspense, fulfillment. In the act of being controlled, the same feelings act as the motor of the tradition; they make the narrative move. All—gestures, movements, images—are constructed of human feelings.

A cannibalistic creature evokes and holds a certain feeling. So does the image of a hapless, homeless young mother. Bring the image of the terrified woman, which contains a particular feeling, into narrative relationship with the image of a fantastic cannibal, also evoking a specific feeling, and the artist has already begun to mix and channel emotions, to give feeling form. Simultaneously, the sensations involved in uncompleted models continue in the background, so that both feelings are being called forth, the abstract and generalized emotion, and the more particular emotion. This process, of course, becomes exceedingly complex as more and more images are introduced into the performance and as other patterns follow the initial one. Varied patterns may also occur, making the experience ever more intricate.

Mrs. Zenani directs the rhythmic movements of the narrative with her hands, her forefingers often outstretched, a supplementary movement when mimetic gestures are not being employed. It is an abstract movement, frequently growing out of very particular, complementary movements. Her hands also act as directors; she moves things about in the space that she has claimed for herself and her performance, an aesthetic space existing in a familiar cultural place. She moves characters into the space, out of this space—characters from the real world, characters from the world of fantasy. She constructs things here, brushes actions into being, burnishes characters, orders complex movements and patterns. Her hands also, usually in abstract fashion, indicate the passage of time. Complementary gestures become more important as she herself takes on the roles of the characters. She points to the various personae, gives directions, alludes to things that are outside the range of her charted territory. She reveals the dimensions of people, things, sketches in the contours of events. When the attention is on a character, she becomes that character, gives it flesh and breath. When she is not performing the actions of a character, she assumes the role of storyteller; it is in this role that she moves things, people, and events about her space. At times, she is both simultaneously—commenting on the action at the same time that she is depicting it.

These two roles define the artist's functions in the performance, and this dual role distinguishes gestures and body movements also. When she is acting out a character, her gestures are primarily complementary; as the storyteller, she is more apt to use symbolic and abstract gestures and movements. There is a full range of movements for her storyteller's role— emphasis, punctuation, repetition, patterning. It is in this role that she raises the expectations of the audience and fulfills them, deviates from them, causes friction, controls and channels these automatic audience responses. A hierarchy of gesture and body movement, based on the artist's body and its proximity to what is transpiring in the narrative, is established. The strictly complementary movement (the acting out of a character, for example, by means of the artist's body) gives way to the ushering in and out of characters, now more removed from her body, gestures thus becoming somewhat abstract, and the manipulating of the story's events against a rhythmic, patterned background that is wholly abstracted movement.

Narrative images are very old, a central part of the memory of a culture. They tie the present audience to the past. Body movements and gestures link performer and members of the audience in a physical and emotional bond. Contemporary images in the narrative flow from the physical beings and presences of artist and audience. But their relations one with the other undergo alterations during an imaginative performance. Normal gestures are stylized; common movements are cradled in attractive rhythmic cycles. The contemporary world moves through these assembled bodies and is ordered in several ways. It is organized by the nonverbal patterning; the physical bodies of the members of the audience are enticed into, then trapped in, the regularity of movement. That regularity is particularized and linked to the verbally evoked images which the artist is selecting from the mythic past. But the relationship is more complex. As the body provides the rhythmical grid against which the ancient images are externalized, so also the body and gesture provide the keys for the deciphering of the venerable images—that is, for revealing their important relationships with the contemporary images brought into the performance. There is a joining of ancient and contemporary images largely because of the silent movements, a dance unifying artist and audience and making possible communication of a message that is, in essence, a renewed sense of order.

COMMENTARIES

SETTING UP THE HOMESTEAD

Performance Note

Time: 13 August 1972, in the afternoon. *Place:* In a fallen rondavel near Mrs. Zenani's home in Nkanga, Gatyana District, the Transkei. *Audience:* Three women, three children, and two teenagers. (NS-174.)

This is how the Xhosa set up their homesteads:

A man takes a wife, and they leave the premises of their parents' homes, preparing now to establish their own homesteads just as their fathers and mothers did before them.

The man's first duty is to dig the foundations of the house at the appropriate site. He digs the foundations. After he has finished the digging, he seeks poles and cross-bars that will be placed against the wall. When the digging is completed, the man takes a spade and makes sod bricks. Lines have been drawn, marking the outlines of the house, and he proceeds then to pile the bricks along these outlines.

The first house to be built in a homestead is the homeowner's private room. A small house is built first; then the great house will be constructed. During the period of construction of the larger house, the man and his wife will live in the smaller structure. When the great house has been built, the small house will become the crib for storing maize.

If a man does not have sufficient time to cut sods from the earth and construct the walls of the house, if at the same time that he is digging the foundations of the house he is inspanning the oxen to till the soil, then the wife herself will cut the sods, pulverizing the earth with a hoe so that she can knead it into bricks. The woman then transports water from the river and prepares the mud to make little loaves of mud which are called bricks, molding them, arranging them, and drying them.

The man will then put those bricks one on top of the other, until they become a wall. When he has completed that, his work will be at an end. Then the wife takes over.

The wife will mix the mud and plaster the wall on the inside and out. She will plaster the top of the walls as well. She arranges things in proper order on the floor of the house, then prepares the mud and daubs the floor. She does all that by herself; it is her work.

The husband must obtain the poles for the roof. He places them on the wall, then finishes the job with cross-bars. As far as this part of the construction of the house is concerned, his work is again at an end. His

A Xhosa homestead

concern is with the framework of the roof. The woman takes over: with a sickle she cuts grass, then returns with a particular type of grass. Some of the grass is used to plait a rope. She makes bundles of grass, transporting the bundles, carrying them on her head. She puts the bundles here by the side of the wall, and the grass piles up. Then the woman divides the grass, putting it into piles. That is a demanding job. It may take her until sunset, day after day.

If the man feels like it, he will take an axe and help her to trim the grass. But this is entirely voluntary: it is woman's work. When the grass has been trimmed and shaped, it is time for the man to go to work again. The fellow of the homestead must now begin to sew the thatch of the house: he will sew all that grass onto the roof of the house. As he does this, it is said, he is sewing the rondavel.

Should the man wish to build yet another house, he will dig another foundation. He will again go to the forest to chop wood for the poles and cross-bars, the various items necessary to the construction of the roof of the house. The man again makes the roof for the top of the house. It becomes known as a house with a thatched roof. It becomes a house. Then it is again time for the woman's work: she transports water, mixes mud, plasters. She takes the sickle, goes and cuts grass, trims the bundles, transports them, returns to the house. She puts the bundles in order, makes small piles of them. Or she will prepare grass for binding the roof

of the house. Very soon, she will trim and transport more grass—for reinforcement, for strengthening the house. All that is woman's work: plait-
ing ropes for reinforcing, weaving ropes for cross-bands for thatching,
other ropes for strengthening the walls and roof. All that is the work of a
woman.

WOMAN'S WORK

Performance Note

Time: 13 August 1972, in the afternoon. *Place:* In a fallen rondavel near Mrs.
Zenani's home in Nkanga, Gatyana District, the Transkei. *Audience:* Three
women, three children, and two teenagers. (NS-174.)

Other woman's work: water should always be available here at home.
Wood for kindling fire is always here. The woman continually goes to the
forest to gather wood; she carries it on her head, then stacks it in one place
outside the house. The woman sweeps, and she sometimes takes wet cow
dung and coats the floor of the house. Such work does not require a man.

The woman should also see to it that there is food for the man. She
knows the kinds of food he likes to eat. When the children are hungry,
feeding them is not the obligation of the man. The woman must go out to
seek food. All of this is the work of a woman. She must do all the domestic
chores.

Sleeping mats: the woman should see to it that her own mat has been
prepared, that there is a mat for her husband, mats for the children, mats
reserved for guests. When there are overnight visitors, she should take a
mat and place it before a guest: the woman's work. When any kind of rite
is to be performed in the home, she must make the appropriate preparations because a woman should know that such-and-such a rite is to take
place.

If a big beer party is to take place, the woman brews the amount of beer
befitting the occasion. These occasions have special names: the celebration centering on the female purification ritual, the celebration accompanying male circumcision ceremonies. Or she brews beer for the "whip"
ritual. Beer is an important part of these events. During such activities,
the woman is busy all the time; she is constantly on her feet, working until
all the people arrive: they will be able to tell whether or not the woman has
done her work. [See the appendix, "Beer Making," for Mrs. Zenani's
account of the preparations for a beer party.]

The woman prepares the beer with her hands. She solicits the assistance of others. But the man has no responsibilities in this regard. She
might enlist the help of other people, of women from other homesteads: "I

have come to ask you to help me to prepare beer for a special occasion that's taking place at my homestead. Nobani, will you come and help? You can help me to prepare the beer. And your children, the girls, perhaps they can help too."

Because the girls are unmarried and living at home, they are expected to be trained in women's work—because a woman starts off as a girl. Some young women are open to criticism when they get married. When a young woman marries into a homestead, she might not know what a woman's work is because she has not been trained by her mother. Such early training accustoms her to woman's work. When her husband returns from some place—say, he comes home from chopping wood, for that is a man's work—his wife should have his food ready for him. The food should be completely prepared, so that the husband does not have to sit around hungry. If he must do that, then she has not performed a woman's work properly.

If a woman is negligent in regard to her husband, then she is not a wife at all, according to Xhosa custom.

She must pay heed to her husband; it is especially important that she carry out her husband's desires. If the man should say, "I don't want my wife to go to beer parties," then that woman should remain at home; she should contain herself, even if she would like to go. She should do what he wants her to do; she will have broken the requirements for a wife if she does not abide by her husband's directions.

When the husband has established the site for the house, when he has chopped wood for the poles and cross-bars, he will have completed the man's work as far as the home-building is concerned. The man is also responsible for providing the door to the house. Those are the man's obligations regarding the house, according to Xhosa practice.

At the farthest point from the door, inside the house and on the floor: these are the woman's responsibilities. It is her duty, moreover, to obtain a cooking pot: that is not the man's responsibility. The wife might even have to go to her home of birth to ask for something that she needs, if she does not have it. Or she will find other ways to obtain the various things that she requires. She should be aware of a vessel that is wearing out, that is beginning to leak. And she must find a way to obtain dishes for her homestead. The man has no part in this. The woman is expected to be solicitous of every person who comes to her home, assuring that such a person has something to eat. She should know what she will give to the visitor. This does not require a man. According to Xhosa custom, the man's responsibility is only to ask the visitor where he is from and what his business is.

The man will chop wood for building his kraal. His wife has no part in this. It is the man who must do the chopping. What the woman must do is cook, dish up the food for her husband. And the man will herd his cattle.

If there is no one else in the homestead, the woman will require some help from the man. But that too depends on the husband's initiative and inclination. The woman will help him, allowing the calves to meet the cows. But, according to Xhosa custom, a woman does not set foot in the kraal. She does not open the entrance to drive the cattle from the kraal. However, if she is able and if she is alone in the homestead, under such circumstances and if things go wrong—if, for example, the cattle gore each other in the kraal—then, had her husband been at home, he would have gone to the kraal and taken the cattle out. But he is not at home, so it is necessary that the matter be discussed: "The woman is alone." The usual thing is that the men in the homestead assist her. A woman has no part in this; it is not a woman who does anything for another woman. It is the role of the man to say to the woman, "Take off the bracelet from your wrist"—or some other bangle. "Come here, Woman." And the woman will go to the kraal. When she gets there, it will be said, "Come in." The man will give way, and the wife will go in and place that bangle at the entrance to the kraal, near the posts—just as I am doing. That is the custom that enables a woman to move into a category of work not usually hers. She is initiated into such categories in an orderly manner, according to custom, because she lacks someone who can do these things for her. The woman then begins to be a woman who can go into the kraal, according to this rule that has been established in her homestead of marriage. The woman's normal role is to keep a distance from the courtyard. She walks between the two kraals, she "cuts a path" between them, according to Xhosa tradition. She must either go above or below the kraal. That is how it is; that is Xhosa custom.

MAN'S WORK

Performance Notes

Time: 13 August 1972, in the early afternoon. *Place:* In a fallen rondavel near Mrs. Zenani's home in Nkanga, Gatyana District, the Transkei. *Audience:* Three women, three teenagers, and three children. (NS-174.)

The man's work, from that point on, involves the making of yokes and pegs and things of that kind—such things are prepared by the husband. He will do the inspanning of the oxen if the fields are to be ploughed. The field for cultivation itself will be procured by the man; he goes to the royal residence to ask for land. This activity does not require a woman; it is a man's work.

The man usually asks for a plot for cultivation: "I need a plot of land because I have my own homestead now. I've left my parents' home." He will be asked what land he prefers. He will himself already have surveyed the land and will respond that such-and-such an area is very good for a field. He will point it out. Sometimes, the place that he indicates is near plots belonging to other people who are already well-established—whereas he himself is only beginning. It is necessary that he get along well with the people of his village. They should know that a certain man will now also have a plot of land.

A plot will be apportioned for him beside that of a certain person. The men of the village will come together, to testify officially that "We know him." That is the custom for the men. It is the way homesteads are established by the Xhosa. This is the way the Xhosa build up their homesteads.

A man's work starts from the time that he requests a site upon which to build. He goes to the royal residence and is asked, "Are you known by the Board?" And he replies, "Yes." It is necessary that the ruling be known in the village where he will live. He should be known by the people as well, or introduced to them—the people beside whose fields his own plot will be located, according to the practice of the men. These activities are ordered in that way. That is the procedure for a man.

When all such matters have been taken care of, the limits of the field are marked. A man acquires his field as a man; yet, in the normal order of things, a field is obtained on the basis of his having a wife. A man without a wife can have no field, since he has no homestead. And before a man builds a homestead, he gets a wife.

That is the work of a man and the work of a woman in the establishment of a homestead.

WORKING IN THE FIELD

Performance Note

Time: 13 August 1972, in the early afternoon. *Place:* In a fallen rondavel near Mrs. Zenani's home in Nkanga, Gatyana District, the Transkei. *Audience:* Three women, three teenagers, and three children. (NS-174.)

When all of this has been accomplished, the man inspans oxen and hitches up a plough. He goes off to the fields with his children—or, if he has no children, he goes off with others whom he has asked to assist him. He may even make a special plea that his wife help him, though her normal work is to cook for the people who work with the oxen. Still, she may join these people, if she wishes to help. It is, however, a man's work, remote from the work of a woman. The wife will achieve a unique distinction in this way: she does not sleep because she is making the preparations for the cooking of the next day's food, and on that next day she will go and help her husband with the oxen.

When the field has been measured, when a field begins to exist for him, and when the food is being prepared, this begins to be a homestead. Everything is in operation, the woman helping the man.

Sometimes, the woman may learn how to plough on her own. If her husband happens to be absent from the homestead, the woman will gather her children together and plough the field on her own, without the help of any man—because she will have gotten practice when she helped her husband with the ploughing in the past. She becomes accustomed to such work after a time. There are also women who know how to construct the walls of houses because they and their husbands work harmoniously together, without coercion. They speak decently to one another: the woman does this and that, and when her husband says, "Put it here," that is where she puts it. Or, the husband will occasionally ask her to do a certain thing, and she will do it—calmly, unhurriedly. If she is alert, it will soon become evident that she is beginning to measure up to the work that is normally that of a man.

That is how it is done.

Building the homestead is the first thing. Sometimes a garden is cultivated before the field is developed. We used to call a garden a tobacco patch because it was a little plot where only tobacco was grown. Then the garden became more diversified, as we slowly gained knowledge about other things that might be planted there. We did not know that there was such a thing as a potato, which is edible. Nor did we know about the cabbage, also edible. We did not know that a person might plant an orange tree. And we did not know that a prickly pear could be planted. Enlightenment came slowly, as the saying goes. The first people were in darkness, but we are enlightened. We know that there are such things as potatoes.

As the woman continued to till this plot over the years, the garden became something uniquely related to women. It was the woman who specialized in the development of the garden. The woman would learn of some new crop: "Father of So-and-so, such-and-such a thing is edible. They have it over at So-and-so's homestead, I saw it. I even tasted a little of it." Then the woman would take a hoe and extend the cultivated area so that she could plant this new thing that she had seen. Eventually, the man came to appreciate the woman's deep knowledge of the garden.

The field, too, by ancient precedent, is a woman's specialty. But it is a man's work. It is the man who inspans the oxen, who goes to plough in the fields. The woman specializes in cooking food for the workers in the fields. That is how it is.

Again, a man's work: when there is scarcity of food, or starvation, he

Evening chores

must go into debt so that the family will have something to eat, so that the family will not starve. That is the obligation of the man. The woman's relatively minor obligation is as follows: if she knows someone, a person whom she is not afraid of, she might explain to him that "Yo! The starvation is too much for us over there at my home!"

"But what is your husband doing if, as you say, you are starving? Is he a responsible fellow?"

Then this person will give the woman sufficient food for her to cook.

If food is scarce, the woman will go into debt for the man. She gets food by taking loans from people: "Lend me some food. I'll return these things on the day that I buy something."

The husband may buy, say, a bag of corn on credit, thinking that it is for his homestead. But when people from whom loans have been taken are paid back, the corn is exhausted. This emphasizes that such activities are a man's work. The main burden is on the husband. The wife takes what comes in and cooks it. Her responsibility is to look after the family so that it will not starve, and she does this by taking a little of the available food and cooking it.

THE RITE OF THE SITE

Performance Note

Time: 13 August 1972, in the early afternoon. *Place:* In a fallen rondavel near Mrs. Zenani's home in Nkanga, Gatyana District, the Transkei. *Audience:* Three women, three teenagers, and three children. (NS-174.)

A homestead does not become a respectable one if the woman does not like people. If she is to make it into a real homestead, she should be fond of people. If the woman does not like people—you can see for yourself—that homestead will have no visitors. Its owner will always be alone; people do not like to stay with her because she does not like people.

A woman and a man will help each other to manage the homestead, so that it develops into a real homestead; it takes shape as a real home. Whenever someone visits it, that person should feel relaxed.

Respect and deference are shown toward the side where the older brother sits. The wife of the younger brother does not sit on that side, according to Xhosa custom: "You, Daughter-in-law, are not to sit on the side of your husband's father." Nor does a daughter-in-law hold the hand of her husband's father. If she should deviate from this custom, she is said to be without character. She has no sense, no respect; she has no regard for people who are senior to her. And she will be dismissed with the words, "She'll never amount to anything." People do not speak well of her.

That is how it goes.

When the site has been established, the house constructed, the kraal built, the people live in the homestead for a year. Then it becomes necessary that a goat be slaughtered for the homestead.

An announcement will be made: "This homestead has been built by this young man of So-and-so."

In the Xhosa idiom, it is said, "A person is now making his whereabouts known to his people and his ancestors, so that it will not be said, 'We do not know him.'"

On the appointed day, people will go to the homestead. When the goat has been slaughtered, it is said, "With this goat, we inaugurate this site, so that anyone can know that So-and-so is here." He should live well. He should develop this homestead; it should not seem that he has stolen it. These are Xhosa customs.

Xhosa practice dictates that other rites cannot be performed unless "the rite of the site" has been observed: "You cannot perform a rite before you have indicated where you are."

BRINGING UP THE CHILDREN

Performance Note

Time: 13 August 1972, in the early afternoon. *Place:* In a fallen rondavel near Mrs. Zenani's home, in Nkanga, Gatyana District, the Transkei. *Audience:* Three women, three teenagers, and three children. (NS-174.)

When that man and his wife have completed these observances and activities, they will bring forth children. In the process of producing these children, each discovers his or her role: the one who begets, begets; the one who does not, does not. When the child has been begotten, the man of the homestead will, by slaughtering the goat, already have gone through the rite of the site. If that has been done, then the man can slaughter a beast for his child. At that time, it will be said, "He is dedicating." That too is Xhosa custom.

When the man of the homestead gets older and the time comes for the ceremony of the female puberty rite, he will undertake that ritual properly because he has initially performed the rite of the goat. That is how it goes.

The children are born, and they are different. One may be a boy, one a girl. Even at the beginning of her socialization, the girl learns to be aware; she knows how to "Bring such-and-such a thing here." Her training begins at that point. A child is born, then sits, crawls, stands uncertainly, then walks and is weaned. She early begins to know that, when she is given something, she should "Take it with both of your hands." She is admonished when she takes it the wrong way, and finally when it is said, "Cup both of your hands," she does so.

In time, when the child is told, "Bring me some water," the boy or girl will bring the water.

At this early stage, sexual roles are still undifferentiated as far as work is concerned. But such differentiation begins for the girl when she is told to clean up the dust. If something has been spilled on the floor, she is ordered to "Take the broom and wipe it up." A girl will initially be taught to use a little dish, a dish appropriate to her size; she is shown how to dip water with it. She will also be taught how to take, say, a piece of corrugated iron and cut vegetables, then strap them to her back, perhaps with a kerchief.

If she has been sent on an errand, the adults will begin to ask her what delayed her. She might even be punished and trained to "hurry when you've been sent on an errand by an adult!" She is trained not to answer back when scolded by an adult; she should not talk back to an adult.

She is taught to take mealies and grind them on a stone. Maize is ground on a stone to provide food for the people.

Tasks that match her strength and ability are set for her, right up to the time that she reaches adulthood. She is taught to pound maize, to daub the floor with fresh cow dung, to wash and clean the dishes—and not to wash the dishes with dirty water: "When the water gets dirty, you must throw it out." She is told, "Pour fresh water in." So she will pour it in and clean the dishes.

"Wash your hands." And the child will wash them. "Don't handle anything with a soiled hand."

So she will be trained.

"Get up and wash your hands and face."

"Where is the wood?"

"Make a fire." And the child will kindle a fire.

As she is learning to gather wood, she might on occasion pick up wet wood, whereupon the child's mother takes that wood and breaks it, saying, "Now go and get some other wood."

In that manner is a girl trained, and eventually she reaches marriageable age. By that time, she will have been trained in the proper work done by a woman.

A boy is trained to herd. He is taught to milk, to know the proper time for milking. In time, he learns. And when he is bigger, he is instructed in the use of the axe, and he learns to chop trees. If the cattle lack a place to sleep, he is taught how to provide them with such a place. He will fill wagons with chopped wood, and he learns how to inspan those wagons.

Eventually, he will become a man, knowing boy's work, learning, with an eye to the work of a man.

PROFESSIONS: MEDICINE

Performance Note

Time: 2 August 1972, late morning. *Place:* In Mrs. Zenani's home, in Nkanga, Gatyana District, the Transkei. *Audience:* Members of her family—her husband, her daughter, and a granddaughter. (NS-11.)

This is the way an African becomes a practicing doctor:

The ways of becoming a doctor are varied, but they merge at one point. A doctor is a person who has become troubled by certain pains; she is troubled by pains, and, although she is treated in every possible way, there is no relief. Or, she is a person who has no pain but who is suddenly absent from her home. When she returns, she is very uncomfortable with things.

This is the way it begins: a person develops a kind of nervousness that causes her to become excitable. It is accompanied by chest pains. It narrows the mind's scope; she loses her appetite, she becomes incompatible with anything that is evil. This nervousness causes her body to quiver when she sees a vile person, or when a person possesses something that is odious.

In those old days, when things were beginning, people said, "What is the matter with this person, Friends? She is not like other people."

"What sort of person might she be?"

"This person who is so excitable—"

"This person who does not eat—"

"This person who cannot stand filth—"

"What kind of person is she?"

"She tends to avoid other people."

This went on for some time before it was understood precisely what it was about. The ancients diligently sought a solution to it. They sought, until they found an answer. They found a solution by means of a doctor who, at the beginning of the institution of doctoring, turned out to be a person who was missed at his home. He was missed and was not seen again. There was speculation that he might have fallen into a quagmire— or perhaps he was dead, perhaps something else happened to him.

Actually, he had remained a long time in a forest, eating the leaves of trees, satisfied with that, not wishing to be seen at home. During the second month that he was missing, his paternal aunt dreamt in her sleep that she saw him in that forest. He seemed to be saying, "Chant a song for me."

The old woman, his aunt, spoke of this: "I'm always dreaming of this young man of this home, the one who is missing. He seems to be in the forest."

Because the ancients took dreams seriously, they considered the dream and concluded, "Well, it might just have some truth in it."

"Why don't you act on this matter that you're always talking about?"

"We who have lost our child are pained. We're pained because you tend to leave things only half said instead of discussing them in their totality."

"We are depressed."

This aunt thought and thought, then decided to call some girls [later identified as the children of her brother]. She told them that they would spend the night with her in her home. She daubed her house with cow dung and said, "At dawn, awaken me. I have a song to chant, and you must accompany me, Children, by clapping your hands."

In the middle of the night, this aunt got up and chanted the song alone. The children were unable to follow it.[1] She chanted the song, and the

1. "It was," Mrs. Zenani commented, "an *umhlahlo* chant, the first part of which is called the *intsusa*." The *intsusa* is the preface to an *umhlahlo*, a meeting ordered by a chief when someone is ill; the purpose is to discover, by divination and the dancing of a doctor, the identity of the person suspected of causing the sickness.

children clapped their hands. But they could not follow the song, nor sing it. They just did the clapping; they did not sing the song.

Then the aunt took an old dried cowhide, the kind out of which a skin skirt might be made; she took it and put it on the ground. She took a stick, an extension of her hands, so that the noise would be even louder, so that their chant could be heard more clearly. The stick supplemented the clapping; she beat the cowhide with the stick so that the volume of the clapping would be increased. The children clapped, and the woman chanted. This song is the first chant of the ritual.

After she had sung it for a time, she rested. She said, "Be appeased, be appeased. Children of my brother, why should your hands burn? You take sticks too, and beat this hide."

The children took the sticks and drummed on the hide.

Meanwhile, the night was moving on toward dawn. Eventually, they saw a shadowy person moving toward them, his head covered. They recognized the form of a person who was entering the house. But as the form approached, they continued their ritual; they did not stop. He danced around the hearth. He danced and they pounded harder without stop.

After a while, he said, "Peace!" Then he said, "I thank you, Aunt! I thank you for this chant. How I wish the darkness would flee and the light come. In the morning, Aunt, you must go and get fragrant leaves for me.[2] Then go and dip water at the waterfall. When you've done that, don't look back. And Aunt, don't take the water to another house. Put it over there in my parents' house. Oh, and look for a stone over there at the falls. Seek it a little lower down, in the water. The stone should be of the right size for pounding the fragrant leaves."

The aunt said, "Be appeased."

She thrummed again on the cowhide and chanted the song once more. She did this, and he danced until he was wet with perspiration.

Then she said that she was stopping, and the chant ended. The young man did not leave the house. He remained in that room until the morning.

His aunt went to the main house, to her brother. She said, "I've seen a strange thing. The young man's in the other house."

The young man's father was startled. "What are you saying?"

She said, "He's in that house! He came in during the night because of my nocturnal chants. When the first light glistened on the horns of the cattle in the kraal, he had already entered. He danced in that house, then stopped the proceedings and thanked me for my chanting. He instructed

---

2. Mrs. Zenani is referring to *ubulawu*, "fragrant powder made of the dry leaves of *umtombhoti, intombhotshane, igusawa, umto, umdiza, umxobho, isifikane, ityeleba, igqoqina* or of the root of *ingqawane*, and used as a perfume for the body; a lotion secretly used by chiefs for evil purposes; a lotion with which a girl is washed on the day when she is sent to be married" (Albert Kropf, *A Kafir-English Dictionary* [Lovedale: Lovedale Mission Press, 1915], p. 213).

me to dip water at the falls. He told me not to look back while I'm carrying the water. He said that I should put it here in the main house. He instructed me to gather fragrant powder leaves and pound them for him. He asked me to get a stone from a place a little lower down from the waterfall. And he told me to take a grinding stone from that spot. I decided to come here and report this strange thing."

Her brother said, "It's truly a wonder! I'm afraid to go to that house. Did he say anything more?"

The aunt said, "No, he said nothing more. He said that everything else that I am doing should be stopped, that his instructions should be given my full attention."

"He'll have to speak through you again. I'm afraid to interfere with this affair."

Time passed, and his mothers and fathers said nothing. Then his aunt departed. She went to the waterfall. She dipped the water and took it to the main house of the young man's homestead; she put it at the upper side of that house. Then she went to pick the fragrant leaves of the family; these leaves were from a family tree that grew in the forest. Usually, a person of the home ate its leaves, saying, "It is from the ancestors." It was the natural tree of the homestead. His aunt got there and plucked the leaves from that tree. Then she went farther downstream and looked for a stone. She found a stone that was of a good size for grinding. She also sought a small one to use as a hand-stone.

She took the stones home and put them beside the medicine. But then she had a problem: she did not know what to do next. She put the stones down, then went to her house.

When she got there, she sat beside this young man and did not speak.

He said, "Aunt."

She responded.

"Have you now picked the fragrant leaves?"

She said, "Yes, my child, we've just returned from picking them."

"And the stone? Did you get the grinding stone? And the hand-stone?"

She said, "Yes, I got them."

"Well, go now and get a short branch."

"A short branch?"

"A short branch, Aunt, of the thorny shrub."[3]

This thorny shrub has fruit on it which is eaten, but the shrub belongs to the forest.

He said, "Look for a branch that is forked, then cut it. I'll use it to churn

3. She calls the shrub *isibetha-nkunzi*, literally, the bull-beater. "Carissa arduina *Lam.*, a thorny shrub with small bright red edible fruit. The [Africans] entertain the notion, that when the bull is beaten with this shrub, he becomes excited and seeks his mate" (Kropf, *Kafir-English Dictionary*, p. 33).

that medicine so that I can eat it. Then you should do this—" and he demonstrated for her. "You should go there and pound it, and when you have pounded it, beat it. Beat it, and when the foam comes up, sing that chant again. Take this cowhide with you."

His aunt went to pluck that short branch, that stirrer, in the precise way she had been shown. She returned, then entered the house. She pounded the medicine, she pounded it, she pounded, pounded that medicine, and put it into a billycan. Then she put the stirrer in and churned the mixture; it foamed up. Much foam came up. When she saw that the billycan was full, she put it outside and took the cowhide drum and called all those children. They beat on the hide, and they again sang the song. Then the young man came in.

It was now in the afternoon. As they performed this chant, all the people of the homestead gathered, observing this wonder, this strange thing having to do with the person who had long ago disappeared. They wanted to see if they really would see him here.

"What is this?"

"We'll see."

The young man came in and danced; he danced and danced. When he had finished dancing, he said, "Be appeased!" He stopped and said, "Aunt, thank you for doing this, for pounding for me the leaves of our special tree. I was pressed into service by the sacred animals of my home. What's been the matter with me all this time? I lacked an escort, someone who would accompany me. I would have been a doctor long ago. This is what must be done for me: my sickness must be accepted. It requires that a pure white goat be slaughtered. Beer should be brewed; sorghum should be cooked. Before the billycan is taken into the house, its contents should be pounded in the kraal on the very day that this goat is to be slaughtered, on the eve of the consumption of the beer. This rite is to be accompanied by a chant. The cooked food is to be eaten at the time that the beer is drunk, as soon as the meat has been taken from the fire. My special animal is in the forest."

The assembled people made the appropriate response to what he said.

Then he said, "Let me add this: I'll be able to confirm others who are sick. They'll not have to go through what I experienced. I myself shall enable them to become doctors, those whose vocation is medicine."

He said that the song should be chanted again, and it was. The young man danced and danced. Then he went to that billycan; he reached for it. He took the stirrer and churned the fragrant leaves. The foam came up; he ate it, he ate and ate.

Meanwhile, the sun was setting. He ate, and when he had finished eating, he took his blankets and covered his head. Then he went out. He went to wash near the kraal. He returned and sat in the house. He did not return to the house of his aunt. He remained in the main house of his homestead.

Time passed, and he began to make his divinations.

A certain person was in pain.

Now when he felt this pain, it was said, "Let's go to that young man whose chant was accompanied by the drumming of a cowhide."

"Let's see if he can divine which part of the body is paining me."

A part of that person's body was hurting him: he had chest pains, palpitations, headache.

He went to that doctor.

"We've come to pay a visit."

"Yes."

"We've come to this person because we want him to clarify for us what we do not understand."

The young man immediately went into a convulsion; he groaned and bellowed, once again doing things that were unfamiliar, things now occurring for the first time. He repeatedly howled, saying, "Hheeeee! ee! hheeeeee, hheeeeeee! Eee!" gradually approaching the person who was in pain. He reached him and touched his hand; he touched his neck, his chest. He touched the ground with his hands, then went and sat down.

He said, "This person has a headache. More than a headache, he has chest pains. He also has an aching body. But above all, he has palpitations, a certain nervousness. It happens that he has the sickness of his people. This means that his sickness is an indication of his vocation for medicine, and it must now be made possible for him to become a doctor."

The people said, "Yes! Yes, that's the way it is!"

He said, "Don't say, 'Yes, that's the way it is!' If I say something that turns out to be the truth, you should say, 'We throw!' "

So the people said, "We throw!"

He said, "You must get a doctor for him. The doctor can confirm him in this vocation and give him the fragrant leaves of his people."

The people asked how he would be confirmed.

The young man said, "He'll dance to a chant and a song. He'll dance and consume from a bottle a concoction made of fragrant leaves."

"Will he then become a doctor?"

"He'll become a doctor. You did not realize, did you, that I am able to speak about something I have not seen?"

"We throw!"

"Won't you work on him yourself, confirm him yourself?"

The young man said, "When you say such things to me, you should say, 'We are going up the arm' " [meaning, "We ask for more."].

So the visitors said, "We are going up the arm!"

So saying, they gave him a spear and said, "Here is the spear, to signify that we say, 'Heal!'"

The young man took the spear and poured ashes on it. Then he put it down. They left the patient behind there and went home. The young man treated the patient, preparing him to become a doctor.

This is the way he treated him:

He said, "A billycan must be prepared for you at your home. You should be kept in seclusion, so that this matter can proceed properly."

That was worked out.

The two of them went to the house of the patient. The doctor put the patient into seclusion (this seclusion procedure has no special name), then worked with his medicines, keeping the patient isolated. He shut him in darkness.

When the sun was hot, he took the patient out and administered a medicine. The patient retched. Then the doctor washed him with the medicine, a medicine he had obtained from a black root in the forest. He cut the root up, then tied it to the patient with a strap made of a creeper also found in the forest.

When he had finished doing this, he said, "You must not go to the river for six days." He could go on the seventh.

So the patient remained there without going to the river.

Time passed. On the seventh day, he went to the river.

The doctor then prepared a billycan for his patient. He prepared this billycan with the fragrant leaves of this home. He confirmed him in this way, repeatedly putting foam on the patient's head. The patient ate the foam. When he had done this, visitors began to appear to this patient in his dreams. He was seeing things.

The doctor told him, "I'm cleansing you. I'm making you retch. I'm purifying you so that things pertaining to divination might appear to you."

When the patient slept, therefore, he began to have impressions of himself in various places; he could see himself digging up medicines and pounding them. He could see himself treating another sick person, giving him medicine to drink. And he would wake up and report the dream to this doctor, who said, "Those are the things that I told you about. I told you they would appear if I treated you with these medicines; I told you that you would become a doctor."

He was an initiate now, an apprentice to the doctor, an intern. He was being confirmed. The young man who had become a doctor was now said to be the doctor of this patient.

THE INSTITUTION OF MEDICINE GRADUALLY EVOLVED

Performance Note

Time: 2 August 1972, late morning. *Place:* In Mrs. Zenani's home, in Nkanga, Gatyana District, the Transkei. *Audience:* Members of her family—her husband, her daughter, and a granddaughter. (NS-11.)

The practice of medicine proceeded in this way:

The institution of medicine gradually evolved. In certain circumstances, the vocation to become a doctor surfaces for some people with mental illness: a person suddenly becomes mentally ill and is sent to a mental hospital. But he is not cured when he gets there. Instead, his illness becomes worse.

Another person called to the practice of medicine does not become mentally ill; he just becomes sick. He is bedridden with pains. It is clear that he is not well.

The institution of medicine originates from a talent bestowed upon a person by his ancestors. That ancestor is an original person, a first person who died long ago, a person about whom it is said, "That person died and was buried." It is said of him, "He has gone to heaven." He returns to you as a spirit, in your sleep. He tells you what you must do. When you have done what he has told you to do, things turn out as you envisioned them in your sleep.

We Xhosa say, "It is the ancestor."

Regarding this phenomenon of the ancestor, we say, "It is God," because God was the first being. He created the human. After that, the human himself named it: he said, "There is such a thing as Ancestor."

There are various areas in which a doctor may specialize. He may specialize as an examining doctor. He only examines; he does not prescribe medicines for healing the patient.

Another doctor specializes in both examinations and divination. The latter occurs when people come from a great distance, by themselves, leaving at home the person who is ill. They go to a place where there is a doctor. When they get there, they sit down, saying that they want information.

The doctor says to them, "You've come from over there. You've come to learn about that person at your home who is sick. You left him behind. He has a certain illness," and he diagnoses it as this or that, or that, or that. So saying, the doctor enumerates all the things that are troubling that person who was left behind at home. This is the process of divining.

As for examinations—a person sets out on foot and goes to the doctor, and tells him, "I've come for an examination." The doctor will examine him and describe the parts of the body that are hurting. He will say, "You suffer from such-and-such." This is the examining doctor. He is not an expert in divining.

Another doctor examines, divines, and also has the gift of healing. He cures people who are ill.

There are thus several degrees of medical competence. The gifts associated with medicine are not all the same. One person may be able only to examine patients. That doctor cannot divine; all he can do is examine. And there are various kinds of such doctors.

There is another kind of doctor who, after he has examined his patient, draws out with his mouth the thing that is inside the patient, that is hurting the patient; he extracts it with his mouth. This is the single competence of that kind of doctor. He is a doctor who draws out what is hurting the patient.

Another doctor, one who cannot examine a patient and who does not draw out with his mouth what is hurting the patient, who does not divine, does none of the things performed by those others. He has one specialty— to cure.[4]

And there is the doctor who, when he has finished divining, becomes an exorcist. Among those people who are sick, there are those who have been stricken by practitioners of evil, along with destroyers of the flesh. A person might be sick because a spell has been cast on him by the possessors of secret knowledge. The doctor who practices exorcism casts off that spell. He is distinct from the others.

MASITHATHU ZENANI BECOMES A DOCTOR

Performance Note

Time: 12 August 1972, in the morning. *Place:* In a fallen rondavel, in Nkanga, Gatyana District, the Transkei. *Audience:* Five women, including Mrs. Zenani's sister, two teenagers, and three children. (NS-156.)

It happened, when I was living at my own homestead, that I became ill with the white sickness. I had nervous palpitations. I felt congested and missed my periods [literally, "the turn of womankind"], the change, and I was in the grip of that. I became awkward to my husband. That is how I became. I had been a person who loved a man greatly, who desired him

4. Mrs. Zenani calls this kind of doctor an *itola*. According to Kropf (*Kafir-English Dictionary*, p. 417), the *itola* is "A rainmaker, soothsayer; one who regulates the conduct of war. . . ." This doctor's function, Kropf argues, is "To render warriors invulnerable (and thieves undetectable) by making them pass through the smoke of certain herbs and sprinkling them with the gall of certain animals given as offerings to the doctor," p. 177).

with vigor, but, because of this white sickness, I lost the taste for it. That was puzzling. It was clear that this matter puzzled my husband very much. I did not eat. I had these palpitations; I had these places that were congested, that are never congested normally in a human being.

My husband took me away by night, now traveling, now causing me to rest by putting me on his back—sometimes I could not walk because the palpitations, when they affected me, caused me to have shortness of breath, and my body felt debilitated and weak, and I could therefore not walk. Once, when we had to go up a steep incline, we had to rest four times. Finally, we came over a ridge to the homestead of an old doctor who had been there a long time, who is now deceased; he has been dead for three years. I was examined there: it was an examination by the doctor to diagnose this sickness that I had, to ascertain what kind of sickness it was.

The doctor exclaimed, "This person is a doctor! She should have become a doctor a long time ago. The problem is, there has been no person to tell her how that congestion can be alleviated. What is troubling her is the lack of such advice. Her body and everything that is clogged up in her—this is caused by her vocation to be a doctor. The way to solve it properly is this: she should be treated with medicines appropriate to her. She is a white person."

My husband said, "Continue your treatment," because he was weary of the continual sickness. But he did not speak much; it was his nature not to talk much. He had taken me from place to place, hoping that maybe this thing would come right. But it just had not worked out that way. He said, "I am leaving her here so that you can treat her. I hand her over to you now."

The doctor asked him, "Observe this closely: a person who is being treated, who is like this, should not have requirements imposed on her from all directions. It is necessary that she have a single directive.[5] Will you acquiesce in this matter?"

The husband answered, "I shall comply with your instructions because I'm tired of this. It has gone on for such a long time. I have taken this woman to a person over at Mboya. We went to several people, taking long journeys. I was puzzled by the state that she was in. One person did diagnose the problem. But, because I disliked the fact that he lived so far away from my house, I did not take his advice and leave her with him. I shall observe the matter closely."

When my husband had finished saying that, the doctor said, "I am charging you at once a pound for preparing the medicines, so that I can grind them immediately." He took ten shillings for the medicine so that it could be pounded then; my husband would produce the other ten shillings some other time.

---

5. That is, no one must interfere with this doctor's prescription.

He left me there, and I was treated by the doctor. He did all sorts of things to me, giving me medication for my body, a medicine that itched like a fantastic tale. I took this itchy medicine at sunset, and I took it again at dawn. At night, the chanting and singing of the medical initiates took place. At dawn, it was time to take the medicine, and again there would be chanting and singing. For a long time, the medicine worked on me, and I reacted to it uncomfortably. That is the way it was for me. I was caused to vomit. I drank from the bottle of medicine that was always there. Sometimes, medicine would be pounded. Medicine would be ground, and we initiates would eat it.

We initiates were many now. I observed the group that was there; this was the procedure in this doctor's place. Those who were of this area had become accustomed to the procedures, and, when I arrived, I watched them to see how they did things.

Time passed. There were people who came to be examined as I had come to be examined. After a time, it was said that I should do some examining. One day, I examined a patient for the first time. I was in the land of Mfuno, where we had looked for my doctor; it was a place called Mathumbu, across the Qwaninga River, down below. A person came to the doctor, bringing along another person who was in pain. In that area, a person carries a black stick when he goes to be examined.

It was said to me, "Masithathu, here are some people. Go and examine them."

I was already feeling it; one feels this thing of being a doctor, one feels it in one's body as the person is approaching. This is the way it happens: if this sickness descends on you, then you have a sense of the thing. No one else will diagnose the sickness for you, you simply have a sense of the sickness of the person you are examining. When I got there, I examined that person and diagnosed his illness. He gave me money for the examination, and I took it into the house. I was too shy to put it down, so I went to the further side of the house and put it there. I put it behind a bag of maize. Then I went to sit down because I was rather apprehensive. I was afraid that people would laugh at me regarding this matter because I had done this, I had examined someone. I sat down there.

There was also another woman, a woman from Ngcobo District. She was a Mpondo woman; she was also being treated here. But she had already become accustomed to these matters. She had arrived there before I had. She had been there a year ahead of me. After a short time, this woman said to me, "Where did you put the money?"

I was quiet; I said nothing. I told myself that I would inform her when she went out of the house. I would then tell her where I had put it. I did not want to answer in front of everyone.

Then another initiate spoke—also a new initiate, but a little more advanced than I.

The doctor saw the people whom I had been examining come in. They sat in a room. They were asked where they had come from, and they said that they wanted a bottle of medicine from the doctor who had been examining them, so that they would be wet inside.

My doctor was a member of the Nqaba clan of the Thembu people. His name was Ngedelele. He was a Thembu clansman. He said, "Who is examining these people?"

The others said that they had gone with Masithathu.

He said to me, "Masithathu."

I said, "Doctor."

"When you examine people, why don't you put the money on the hearth?"

I did not know how to answer the question. "Because I didn't know, and I was afraid. I just went and put the money up there. I was afraid."

"Where is the money?"

I said, "I put it over there, in back of that bag, up there."

The doctor scolded me. He said, "Take that money. Why are you putting it in the mealies? Is it for buying bags of food during a famine?"

I took that money and put it on the hearth. When I got to the hearth, I saw all the money that was put down there and saw that ashes were poured on the money. So I put the money there and poured ashes on top of it. That is the custom of being a doctor, and the way in which I, Masithathu, also became a doctor.

This went on, and other people arrived, people who had come to be divined, who were carrying sticks.[6] They arrived and sat in the cattle kraal. Now those with the sticks were sitting in the kraal, jostling each other, each one saying, "Let's go!" each one saying "Let's go!" Here at the doctor's place, when people came to be examined, they sat by the kraal. When this happened, it became necessary that an initiate—one who had come to be treated, who was being initiated—get up and go to the sick people over there by the kraal. When the initiate got there, she spoke to them there. If they were too many, she returned to the house and said, "I could not cope with it." If she finished her work with the sick people and brought the money in, when she came with the money, she was given a little money—six pence—to go and buy beads, and they were tied in a knot on her.

So it was in my case: the first set of beads was tied on my head, in a knot in my hair. The second knot of beads, when I was beginning to study to be

6. The sticks were apparently used in the divination procedure.

a doctor, indicated that I was under treatment. Those beads were put around my neck. Time passed. Then the beads were put on my calves. It became clear that, well, many people were coming here because they knew me and were satisfied with what I said and with my diagnoses of their diseases. When they came, they would say, "We want Masithathu."

"Well," the doctor said. "Well, Masithathu, I'm loaning you the stone so that you feel at home, my child. You have the stone at home."

My stone had to be picked up at Qwaninga, in the river.

He said, "I'm loaning you this stone. Go and put it in your house. Learn now to pound medicines with the stone without transgressing on my prerogatives. The person for whom you grind medicines should get well. Because you have not transgressed on my prerogatives, because you have not stolen from me the right to do these things, you have received the knowledge and the permission to use it from my own hands, and the person will therefore get well under your care. Sometimes I shall entrust him completely to your care and will not see him until you have cured him completely."

That went on. When money was given as a payment for healing someone or from a person who came to divine, I took the money to that doctor who had made me into a doctor. When I got to him, I said, "Be appeased, Doctor. I have brought this money. People came for such and such a thing, and then they asked for medicine. I gave it to them. One of them got well and gave me grain [a euphemism for money]. Another one said, 'Be appeased, Doctor!' I had to do a divination in a certain way, and another patient came to me and was divined in the same way."

If it happened that I used the money without taking it to the doctor first—if, say, some emergency arose, and I took the money and used it for the emergency—then I explained the situation over there to the doctor, that money had come in, money amounting to such and such a figure, and that I used it on account of some emergency. I reported that the money had been used in that way, and the doctor was appeased. There is no surreptitiousness, no deceit in this business of being a doctor. One should not steal. There is no stealing at the doctor's place. If one takes anything, it is necessary that one explain why one took it, so that the doctor releases one from any blame, so that one has good fortune.

So it went, and I went from grade to grade as a doctor. It became clear that I was progressing as a diagnostic seer and as a doctor.

Then it became necessary that I go into seclusion. That was another stage in a doctor's initiation. I went to be kept in seclusion in a house on the doctor's compound. A long time ago, I was put into seclusion at this home, and, that time long ago, I was given a charm at this home—the tail of a goat was plaited into a rope necklace and placed around my neck. The ritual for this rope necklace: beer was prepared for it and food also, boiled sorghum. A necklace fashioned of the tail of a white goat: hair of the tail was plucked and plaited and made into a charm; all the time I was propitiating, saying "Be appeased!" on account of this white sickness.

Once, because of a misunderstanding with my husband, I wanted to become a Christian convert and go to church, so I went out and tore the necklace off and threw it away into a bush below my homestead. [The bush, Mrs. Zenani said, was called *ndincazele*, literally, "Give me tobacco."] I even threw out that necklace, the symbol of a medical doctor. I just snapped it and those knotted beads, and I threw them away.[7]

Then there was a time when the illness that I had earlier been afflicted with, the white sickness, resurfaced [because she had left the doctor's trade and become a Christian]. But it resurfaced in some other way, because it was not able to do anything to me, to make me sick, because the rituals and the treatment had been done. So it attempted to resurface in other ways.[8] It became clear that I had arrived at the stage of being able to dress like a doctor.[9] I was a doctor now. I put on my official doctor's uniform, the skin skirts that I was able to obtain only after journeying far from home—various skins of animals went into making the skirt, genets, animals from a far off place, genets along with leopards.[10] At the time that I had obtained those skirts, it was clear that my medical reputation was immense, reaching beyond my area. I had no match, no equal in doctoring. It was clear that I should then put on the appropriate regalia that was of the same rank as the doctor who had initiated me. This uniform was put on me, that doctor being present, and we became equal in rank. Those animal skins were put around my waist whenever I danced the dances of doctors.

In my practice as a doctor, I treat those who are sick, all of them. It does not matter what illness they have. I can also diagnose anyone who has the vocation to be a doctor; I can see that such a person wants to be a doctor, and I treat him and he becomes a doctor also. It sometimes happens that someone is sick with an illness I cannot treat, according to the will of God. But I am still a doctor, a reputable, notable doctor.

---

7. Apparently the misunderstanding was over differences between the traditional doctor and Christianity, with the husband in favor of Christianity. Mrs. Zenani finally gave in, and dramatically threw away the necklace, the symbol of the doctor.

8. That is, she was having a bad reaction to her conversion to Christianity, and the sickness, that could not return in the same way as it had originally afflicted her, was seeking to resurface in some other ways.

9. This is not entirely clear, but it seems that she gave up the conversion to Christianity and returned to the medical practice.

10. She said in an aside, "Here is the skirt, even now." She was wearing it at the time of this commentary.

A NEW KIND OF DOCTOR

Performance Note

Time: 11 August 1972, in the afternoon. *Place:* In Mrs. Zenani's home, in Nkanga, Gatyana District, the Transkei. *Audience:* Four women and three children. (NS-149.)

Something began to be seen here in the land of the Xhosa that was never before known, something that was strange: it was a kind of doctor unlike any known in the past.

This kind of doctor proceeds in a strange manner. He knows things not known before, things that are not as they were at the beginning. A medicine—an herb that has been powdered—is swallowed. This is swallowed; the hands are crossed and the powder is poured on the backs of the hands. A person picks up the powder with his tongue, then swallows it. Some time after the powder reaches the stomach, it comes back up to the throat. When it gets to the throat, the person who swallowed it knows nothing: the powder speaks for him. Even though his mouth is moving, the sound of his speech is not normal. He speaks a language that is not exactly Xhosa. What he says can be understood, but it is in some tongue other than Xhosa.

When he speaks, he says, *"Yetsho phela!"*[11]

This is something that we Xhosa do not know.

When this thing speaks, it says, "My medium, this is my medium!" referring to the person from whom the voice emanates.

This is a very strange thing. We are still amazed at it, because this is only the fourth year that this phenomenon has existed among us. It is still very unusual. No one can speak authoritatively about it; it remains vague, confusing.

By means of this prodigy, a person may become a kind of doctor, but not the traditional kind. Special songs are associated with this form of doctoring, and people dance to the music of the songs, a unique style of dancing, also quite distinct. The clapping of hands is different, the chanting is different. Since they are doctors, they charge fees, but even the fees are different in kind from the traditional, natural ones.

This kind of doctoring has various levels. A person may one day have a beer-drink, and when a beast has been slaughtered, it is said, "There is a marriage. Notables are being 'married'!" It turns out that these "notables" are really that powder that is poured on the back of the hands, then swallowed. When it has gone to the stomach, it comes up again. Then it speaks; the person speaks with his mouth, but the voice is not his. It is this "thing"

---

11. The expression, *Yetsho phela*, is similar to the Zulu expression *yebo phela*, "Yes, indeed."

that speaks. And this person faints while this is going on; he struggles with death while it is going on, groaning, "Hrm! hrm! hrm! hrm! hrm! hrmm! hrmm! he! hm! hm! *Yeeeeena phela!*" The thing is giving a greeting. This thing is called "the notables"; that is the name by which it is known. It goes on and on, until the various rituals called "It is a marrying for them" have been completed.

The old traditional doctors have nothing to do with this. They do not know how it works. They keep at a distance, merely observing. The newer doctors dance to the beat of drums that are closed.[12] Large cans are closed up, then struck, and the noises come out.

If such a doctor is troubled by something, it gets to his very essence, and he seems about to die. The powder comes up from the stomach, and he becomes a person who meanders about: it is said then that his powder has been annoyed, the powder on whose account he is a doctor.

This is a new thing. It has been among us for three years, this is the fourth. It has been observed, but it is not known where it comes from nor the direction in which it is going. The result of such doctoring, what it will eventually do to the person who harbors it, is unknown. And it is quite pervasive; this kind of doctoring is prevalent. It is danced to in that unique way.

The process resembles a fantastic tale; it is so unusual.

This is the way it works: if a person becomes ill and goes to such a doctor, the doctor makes that patient an initiate, a person just like him. He provides the powder and administers it to the one he is treating. Even if a traditional doctor should become ill, if he is taken to such a person, that person will say that the notables have taken a liking to him. That thing may enter a person, even if he is normal. It will simply be said that it took a liking to him.

The name of this is "the notables," and its songs go something like this:

> What will become of me, Young man of the rendezvous?
> You are calling me.
> Come, let us go, Young man of the rendezvous!
> You are calling me.
> You are calling me from the rendezvous,
> You are calling me.

This is not known here in the land of the Xhosa. It is something that those in that group do by themselves. It is quite different; it is unique.

12. A closed drum is contrasted with the typical drum which is a dried skin that has not been worked into the cylindrical shape of a drum.

TALES

Tale 19

THE JEALOUS CO-WIFE

Masithathu Zenani's Analysis: The conflict in this story has to do with jealousy, of one co-wife for another. The pattern has to do with the repeated efforts of the senior wife to kill the junior wife. These deadly plans become grotesquely comical, as the senior wife, following the instructions of an advisor, seeks poison pumpkins. She feeds the pumpkin to the junior wife, assuring her that the food will make her healthy. It does. The senior wife, more determined than ever, seeks a different kind of pumpkin, a mature one. Again, it does not have the effect on the junior co-wife that she envisions. Then she is told to get two pumpkins, a green one and a white one. But this food, too, only makes the junior wife healthier. She then sprinkles her junior wife's blankets with poison, but a fantastic voice warns the intended victim to burn the blankets rather than use them. In the end, the senior wife gives up.

As always, the pattern reveals the theme. The necessity for harmonious relationships among co-wives, Mrs. Zenani explained, is at the heart of the story, and the persistent, intensifying efforts of the senior wife, her ridiculously futile efforts, have as a clear, underlying theme the dangerous and ultimately vain impulse of a jealous person.

Performance Note

Time: 15 September 1967, about noon. *Place:* Along a path in Gatyana District, the Transkei. *Audience:* five women, two men, fifteen children. (Perf. 652.)

A certain man married two wives, a senior wife and a junior. Because she was excelled by the junior wife, the senior wife was jealous. She longed for something that would help her to surpass the junior wife.

This younger wife became pregnant, and she gave birth. While the junior wife was still nursing her child, the senior wife called on various people, asking, "What can I do with this woman? I want her dead! My husband loves her, and I cannot bear it!"

One person whom she spoke to, her brother, said, "Get a pumpkin for her. Cook it, then tell her that this plant will make her breasts yield a lot of milk. Tell her that you want her baby to grow and be healthy. You must prepare the pumpkin yourself, but don't you taste it! Dish it up for her, and let her eat it."

402

"I want her dead! My husband loves her, and I cannot bear it!" The eyes, the mouth, and the abrupt movement of the left hand betray malevolence.

The woman did as she was advised. She journeyed all day, seeking this plant in the forest. But she could not find it. She returned.

On the following day, she went back to her brother.

She said, "In which forest exactly is this plant? I looked for a long time in that forest over there, but I didn't find it. I went all around that forest. I went all around seeking this plant. But I couldn't find it! In which forest is it?"

The other said, "Go to that great forest. Look just beneath a cliff there. That's where you'll find it."

The woman went to that place, and she looked and looked. She found a pumpkin, and she picked it. She took it home and worked at it. She worked with this pumpkin; she worked with it. She cooked it; she ground it into meal and poured it out. She let it simmer, then said, "Now, my sister, I'm coming to you today with some food that'll make your child's blood healthy. Your child will grow. Your child will be satisfied because this plant will help your breasts to provide milk."

Oh, the young woman was happy about this.

"You're really helping me, Sister!" ("Sister" is what she called this wife of her husband whenever she spoke to her because she was the older woman.)

She took the food out of the pot, then poured it neatly into a dish. When she had poured it into a dish, she cooled the food so that the junior wife might eat it comfortably. She gave it to her, and the young mother ate it.

Oh! It was good!

"This is the best food in the world! It's the first time I've tasted it! I've never tasted such food! Sister!" she said. "Sister, this food—where did you get it?"

"I journeyed over there to the great forest to get it for you. Someone told me that a nursing mother should be fat, so that her baby will grow."

The young mother continued to eat that food.

"Sister, what's this food called?"

"Well, it's a pumpkin. It's name—oh, it's a pumpkin. Yes, that's what it is."

"Yo! It's good! Oh Sister, please! You taste it too."

She said, "No, no! I won't eat with you now, not from the first pot. I'll eat with you later, from another pot."

But she spoke knowing that, when the young woman finished eating this, she would die. And this senior wife did not want to put this food into her own mouth.

The nursing mother finished the food . . . and she did not die.

The next morning, she was still alive. She had not died. She did not even have a pain. She felt nothing at all. And the milk in her breasts increased.

"Oh Sister, when will you get some more of that food for me?"

The senior wife again went to see her brother.

She said, "Now look! I gave her the food. I prepared it for her, but she hasn't said anything yet!"

"Has she felt anything?"

"No, she hasn't felt a thing!"

"Doesn't she feel any pains at all?"

"No, not yet."

"She doesn't even have pains?"

"No."

"Not even dysentery?"

"No."

"Well, Friend, then you probably picked a fresh one, one that's not yet potent. You must go and find a big one, one that seems to be mature. Don't pick a fresh one this time."

She returned, determinedly going to that forest. She journeyed; she walked and walked. She ignored some of the pumpkins. She was looking for an old one, the one that would make that junior wife die—today.

Finally, she came to an old one, and she picked that one. She took it home. When she arrived at home, she was very happy because she knew that she had found the right one this time, the mature one.

When she arrived, "Mmhm! Yo!" the nursing mother laughed. "Sister! You found another one?"

"Yes, I've found another."

"What shall I do now, Sister?"

"I want you to be happy, that's all. You always stay in the same place, and you're hungry. I want to make you happy."

"Yo! Well, Sister!"

"You say it's nice, my little one?"

"Oh!"

She cooked it, she cooked it. She prepared it carefully; she ground it into meal. She brought it to a simmer; then she stirred it. She ladled it out. She did not taste it herself because she knew that it was a killer. She did not want to die. When she had finished cooking it, she cooled it, then gave it to the young mother. The mother ate it. She ate until her stomach was big.

She said, "Yo, Sister! This one's even better than yesterday's! Oh! Mh mh! Lord! My sister's constantly bringing me such find food—it's a miracle!"

Well, the young mother's blood was warming because the food that she was eating was so good. She ate it with great appetite.

Morning came, and the nursing mother was not dead. Heee! The woman wasn't even in pain. Not a thing was wrong with her. This young mother did not have dysentery—she was happy, that's all!

The senior wife said, "Hee!"

She walked off alone. Friends, what can one say? Why is it that the nursing mother did not die?

She went again to her brother.

"Now, Friend, that nursing mother's still alive! She's not dead! I gave the food to her, and she ate it. It was an old plant, a mature one. But she did not die!"

"But Friend, you must pluck two plants, obviously. Mix them together; cook the two of them. She will not die, she just won't, unless you pick a green pumpkin and a white one, then mix the two of them together."

The woman slept then—sleeping quickly, on her knees, so that she could go off to pick these pumpkins. She journeyed; she went to this forest. She arrived and looked; she looked and looked, and she found a green one. She carried that one on her back, while she sought a white one. She wandered about here in the forest. Then she found the white one, and she picked it.

She went to her home. She arrived and cooked for the nursing mother.

That young mother laughed gleefully when the older wife was still approaching.

"Yo! Sister! You've found another one!"

"Yes, Child of my father, because I want you to be fat, so that your child will grow."

"Oh!"

She cooked the pumpkins; they were well-cooked. Then she ground them up. She stirred them, but she did not taste them. She strained them, and the young mother ate the food. The young mother ate and was satisfied. Some of the pumpkin was left over, and she said, "Put it over there. I'll eat more of it when I'm hungry."

Time passed, and the nursing mother did not die.

In the morning, she was not dead. Instead, she became plump. The nursing mother became more beautiful. She was nourished.

The senior wife returned to her brother.

"Friend, what is this? Why didn't you tell me that you want me to nourish this young mother? I asked you for a medicine that would kill this person who's favored by my husband. And you keep saying that I should cook a certain thing for her. She just keeps getting plump! I'm tired of cooking. That woman is plump. Healthy! She's not dying at all. She doesn't even have a headache. She just sits there. What are you doing to me? What can I give to that person to make her die? I want her to die!"

"Well, it could be—look, let's the two of us go over there and pick those plants."

They traveled and arrived in that forest. They arrived, and there were some other people there who were also picking these pumpkins.

They asked the others, "Why are you picking these things?"

They said, "This is food for the blood. It makes one plump."

This woman said, "And you told me that this stuff kills. What is this? Here I was, carrying food for this person, feeding her—and all the time I was fattening her rather than killing her."

"No, I heard that the pumpkin of the forest kills. I've heard it said that it is deadly. A certain woman ate it, and she died. I thought that this would happen in this case as well. Obviously, that's not happening. What should we do?"

"No, Child of my father—"

"Let's give it up."

"No, let's try something else."

"What do you have in mind?"

"Well, something else must be tried. Let's just think of another plan, something that we can do."

Time passed, and she sought some medicine that could be sprinkled into the nursing mother's blankets—so that she would not be desired by her husband, so that she would not be wanted by anyone here at home.

The young mother was sleeping. As she slept, she heard a voice: "Something is going to be poured into your blanket, and the result will be that you'll no longer be desired by your husband. You'll be made to leave this home. It will be poured into the blanket that you will have spread out earlier. You must take this blanket and burn it."

She slept on, and in the morning, when she got up, this medicine had already been poured into the blanket, it had been poured while she was asleep. She got up that morning, then folded the blanket carefully. She held it guardedly.

The other one, this sister of hers, the one who had poured the medicine, said, "What are you doing? What are you doing? You'll make the child cold this way, Woman. You're going to make the child cold. What are you doing?"

"No, I won't make him cold. I'm just removing this blanket, that's all."

"What are you going to do with the blanket?"

"I'm going to spread it again."

The nursing mother took the blanket then. She wrapped it up. She wrapped it up, then tucked it under her arm and took it outside. She set it on fire.

"Why are you burning this blanket?"

"I don't want it anymore. I'm setting it on fire because I don't want it. I don't want to spread this blanket now. It disgusts me!"

Oh! This is a strange person!

Again, the senior wife went to her brother.

This is a strange person!

She went again to her brother's place.

"Friend, I poured that thing into that nursing mother's blanket. And do you know what happened? She took the blanket outside and burned it. Who tells this woman what we're going to do to her? I did that when she was asleep. I was certain that she was sleeping. I tiptoed and poured it into the blanket. But she wakes up, then goes out and burns the blanket. No, I don't understand her. Because I certainly didn't meet her. I wouldn't tell her what I was about to do. I want her to leave! I don't want this junior wife with my husband. I wouldn't tell that person a thing."

Then she went out, away from the nursing mother, and she sat outside with some other people.

The young mother's child grew up.

The senior wife gave up hope because whenever she tried to do anything, it came to nothing. Whenever she tried to do anything, she failed. She became a sulky person, despairing, at a loss as to what she might do. The young mother continued to be loved very much by her husband, as she had been formerly.

Eventually, she weaned the child, and then the young mother again became pregnant. She continued to surpass her sister, and that senior wife finally gave up.

Tale 20

THE CHILD WITH THE STAR ON HIS FOREHEAD

Masithathu Zenani's Analysis: The central pattern of this story has to do with a series of animals—a hog, a heifer, a horse, a crab—that swallow an abandoned child. This pattern, Mrs. Zenani argued, has to do with the jealousy of the barren wife's sister. The destructiveness of this character dominates the action, from her preying on the unhappiness of the husband to her persistent efforts to destroy the child whom the sister finally bears.

When the child is given into the care of a crab in a river, he has his surrogate home, and he is brought up there. In the benevolent swallowing of a child undergoing a transformation, the main pattern of this story is similar to that in Tale 1, "The Frog and the Child without Limbs"; in the description of an unhappy home life that drives a youth into nature where he is nurtured into manhood by a creature of nature, the story echoes Tale 4, "The Boy and the Lizard." In Tale 4, the emphasis is on the puberty ritual of the boy. In this story, although it is certainly present late in the story, the puberty ritual is less emphasized. The performer focuses the audience's attention on the unhappy relationship between the wives of a callous husband. It is essentially the same story as "The Boy and the Lizard," but the pattern shifts the focus. That pattern has to do with nature intervening in the unhappy human affair, revealing a struggle between humans out of harmony with nature and a woman who has no such dissonance. The boy's growth into manhood flows out of this unsettled relationship, and in the end solves the problem.

Performance Note

Time: 19 September 1967, in the afternoon. *Place:* In Mrs. Zenani's home in Nkanga, Gatyana District, the Transkei. *Audience:* Seven women. (Perf. 712.)

In a certain homestead lived a man and his wife. That woman could not become pregnant at all—at all. She was a woman without children.

So time passed for them.

The woman grew older, and it happened that one of her sisters came to visit her at her home of marriage—not for any special reason, simply because she wanted to come and stay at her sister's place. That sister remained there, and she was very friendly with her brother-in-law.

Now it was during that period when she was so friendly with her brother-in-law that the other one, the real wife, took a journey and went to her home. She went to the home of her birth, going to visit some people there. She left her sister behind, with her husband. This wife remained over there at her house of birth for some days, remaining there until she had seen and visited with the people of that area.

In the meantime, the brother-in-law began to have a certain feeling as he stayed there at home with his sister-in-law, the sister of his wife. He began to experience a disturbance of the spirit.

So he approached his sister-in-law with a bit of deception: "Now, Sister-in-law, I really should marry you because your sister is unable to become pregnant."

"How could you, Brother-in-law? How could you even think a thing like that? Saying that you might marry me! Even if my sister can't become pregnant! You'll turn my sister against me. She'll become suspicious of me."

The other said, "No, she won't suspect you of anything. I'll marry you, without apology, because there's nothing that I can do with her. She's no woman. She's a gelding because she's unable to become pregnant. She does nothing!"

"No, there must be a better way than that. You must come to me by some other means. Don't marry me. Don't make me your wife. You are perhaps pleased with me, but you don't know me. You don't know if I would be able to have a child."

So they secretly developed a plan. They would have an affair, living together in secrecy.

The real wife completed her visit, and she returned to her home of marriage. But when she got home, she became suspicious: "This sister of mine is up to something with my husband. I haven't seen it with my own eyes, but something around here is very strange."

She became a changed person. She was not the same person she had been. She became ill-disposed toward her sister, but she tried not to let her sister see that she harbored such feelings.

She said to her husband, "Please go and look for a beautiful round stone for me at the sea. It doesn't matter how little you trust me. If you do that, I'll bear a handsome child for you."

Her husband said, "What are you saying, Woman?"

She said, "Yes, please go and find a beautiful round stone for me at the sea. Take it from the water. Don't take it from outside the water. It doesn't matter how little you trust me, I'll bear a handsome child for you."

"Do you say that you'll bear a child?"

"I'll bear him. If you come to me with that stone, I'll bear a child for you."

The man went to the sea and did what his wife asked him to do. He went to the sea and sought the beautiful round stone. He even went into the water, and he looked around on the outside of the water. He looked carefully. The water of the sea was clear. He could see what was in the water. If you are really looking for something, you cannot miss it in such clear water—if you are really looking for something—like a beautiful stone.

"There it is!"

And he went into the sea. He went in and got this stone. It fit into his hand; he was able to hold it. He clenched it in his fist, then returned with it.

He brought the stone and said, "Here it is, Wife. Your round stone. I've come with it from the sea. Now I want that child you said you'd bear."

"No, I didn't say that. I didn't say that if you went to the sea, you would return and I'd have a child. This is what I said: Go, seek a round stone in the sea for me, and I'll bear a child for you. Moreover, he'll resemble you. You don't have confidence in me, but my heart will enable me to have a child." These words were uttered by a woman who was much distressed because her husband was having an affair with her sister; he no longer cared about his real wife. This woman believed that her heart would cure her, that she would become pregnant by means of her husband.

Time passed for that woman. She had not gone to any doctor. She had not gone to anything. She took the stone and put it in the house. She did nothing with it. Time passed for her.

During this time, the brother-in-law was just sitting around. He was bored; he had no spirit. He was happy only when he was talking with his sister-in-law. The rest of the time he was bored. But he enjoyed conversing with his sister-in-law.

Time continued to pass for this wife of his, and then she noted that the time for her menstrual period had passed. This month passed, and again the time for the menstrual period went by. That month also passed, and the time for the menstrual period passed again. This month passed too, and then came the fifth month.

The husband saw that "Really, something's happened to this woman. She's not usually like this." He made this comment because this woman, his wife, began to have a radiant face. Her blood became healthy again. He noticed that she began to like certain things, and that she began to dislike other things. He saw that something was happening within her.

Friends, is it possible that this woman might indeed be pregnant? After all, she had said, "I'll bear a child who resembles you."

Now, just ask me what this husband was like. He had a star here on his forehead, and he had a crescent, the sliver of a moon, here on his chest. These were natural birthmarks.

Time passed for the woman then. She became big. The woman became big. She became larger, and finally the month arrived, the month when the woman must give birth. She was in labor.

She said to her husband, "I'm having labor pains. I don't know who'll be my midwife."

The husband said, "How could you ask such a thing? You'll have no difficulty whatsoever in that respect because your sister's staying with you, staying at your house. You'll have a smooth delivery because your mother's own child will act as your midwife."

The woman said, "Well, I don't want to comment on that. But I guess what you say is true." So she said, and she sat down. But she had a knot in her heart—she knew that this sister of hers had already "stabbed me in the back!" Her labor pains continued. She was in pain—really in pain. This was no pretense. She was in pain now; she showed all the signs of giving birth. She remained in the house that her sister had prepared, had swept, and that sister was the one who was to help her to deliver her child. Both of them stayed in that house. The sister-in-law kindled the fires for her sister.

This wife was about to deliver her firstborn child, and her sister said to her, "Daughter of my mother, you're bringing forth your firstborn child. Now, if you're to give birth properly, there are certain things that you must not see. Give me that turban of yours, and I'll tie your eyes with it. It's not desirable that you bear a child with your eyes open."

The other said, "But people have been bearing children for a long time. Do they always have their eyes closed? Are they all blindfolded with turbans when they're about to deliver?" This was her first delivery, so she was somewhat confused. Every woman goes through this. She was in labor now, and she did not know whether or not she would survive. Remember that she had never given birth before. So she agreed to do as her sister instructed. She gave her the kerchief, believing that when she was blindfolded the birth would be easier, the pain would end. The sister tied this wife with the kerchief, tied it over her eyes. She wrapped it around her eyes with a double fold.

The sister put the double folded blindfold on the wife when she realized that she was going through her final exertions. She bound her sister with that blindfold just as she was beginning to perspire. She bound her and saw that she was about to bear her child. And she gave birth: she bore a child who was a boy—with a star on his forehead, the crescent of a moon on his chest, just like his father. This wife had said, "I'll bear you a beautiful child, and it will resemble you."

This sister-in-law took the baby and put him into a blanket; she rolled him in the blanket, then put him somewhere else. When she had hidden this child, having rolled him up in that way, she took a kitten from a cat that she had seen giving birth in the garden. She took one of the kittens, and put it in the place where the newborn child had been. She rolled the kitten in the blood of childbirth, and so on. She rolled it, she rolled it, and it began to appear as if the kitten had been borne by this human mother. It looked as if it had just been born.

When she had completed all these arrangements, this sister said, "Yo! Hee! Scandalous! What strange thing have you brought forth? You're going to see something strange! I've seen a wonder that I've never seen before—a person who has given birth to a cat!" So saying, she removed the blindfold. "Let's remove this blindfold, Girl, and see the thing that you have borne."

When the blindfold was removed, the mother said, "Oh! But the thing was crying just like a child! Is this it?"

The other one said, "Yes, when it was first coming out, you heard the crying. Strange, the cat opens its mouth just like a baby! I ran out at one point because I was frightened by this cat!" She was referring to the time that she had gone out to hide the child.

"No," said the mother, "it doesn't matter. It doesn't matter. Here I am, suddenly pregnant with a cat—but I have never come together with any cat."

That nursing mother lived in pain then, and, although she was suspicious about what had happened, she said nothing about it. She suspected that something untoward had occurred. Time passed for her, and she took this cat, continually examining it, staring at it. But she saw nothing. She stared at the cat. She examined the cat, and she lived with the cat.

She said, "To bear a cat! This is painful! I wonder what's going to happen to me now? because I told my husband to find a round stone for me at the sea, and he did come with the stone. I told him I would bear a handsome child for him, that this child moreover would resemble him. And all those promises only resulted in this: I was going to bear this cat." So she said, and she cried and cried.

Her sister said, "Sit down, Child of my father. Don't kill yourself over this matter. What God has given you, you should accept. Put this cat in your lap. After all, it's all you've got."

The husband was not present at this time. He returned, stamping vigorously on the ground, going into that house.

"Mhmm, Brother-in-law, your wife has given birth. But she has given birth to a strange thing. This puzzles us because we have never seen a person who has borne a cat. It's the first time we've ever seen such a thing. And your wife did it! These strange occurrences at your homestead have filled me with fear. I'll just go home. I'm afraid of these scandalous goings-on."

Her brother-in-law also wondered about such happenings. "How could such a thing happen?"

"Well, it happened."

He said, "I knew this would the result! I told you that you should become my wife. I said that to you. But you said it wouldn't be right. But I knew that this other one was not a real wife. There she is now, giving birth to a cat! Is that a wife? Now what do you say about my comments? Just let that wife stay there with those cats of hers!"

"Well, all right. It doesn't matter."

"Mh mh."

"All right. I didn't realize either that this thing would give birth to a cat. And I despaired too when I saw that thing." She changed now, she began to play the role of a wife. She began more openly to be the wife of her brother-in-law. She was the wife now. She acted the part unmistakably in every way. And that sister of hers remained only a nursing mother. No kindnesses were shown to her because she was no longer regarded as anything of significance. Finally, she stopped being a nursing mother, producing much milk. That cat's real mother had given up on the kitten. The cat did not even miss the kitten; it had other children. One of her kittens had been taken from her, and it had been placed at the side of this mother while she was blindfolded. Time passed for the mother, and then she came out of her confinement.

She went outside, staying with this cat.

Then that sister took the real child. She said, "Hog, swallow this child!"

There were hogs at this home that were big. The hog swallowed the child; the hog swallowed it.

Time passed for this woman then, and the hog grew bigger because that child inside it was growing bigger. This hog trailed its stomach on the ground because it had swallowed this child. And this was not a female hog; it was a gelded hog.

The real wife had now become the servant of her sister, and that sister had become the wife of this homestead.

When the sister saw the hog, she said, "Well, we had better slaughter that hog. I would die if I didn't taste the liver of that hog!"

The man said, "Which hog are you talking about?"

"That one, that great gelding dragging its stomach so pathetically. Let it be slaughtered. I want its liver now!"

"All right. If you say so, then it'll have to be slaughtered."

When the hog heard that it was to be slaughtered, it went to an ox. It said to a heifer, "Swallow this child! I've learned that I'm to be slaughtered."

The ox swallowed the child then, and the child remained there in the beast. The hog was slaughtered, but the child was not found in its stomach.

The woman immediately said, "Heee, where has the child gone, Friend? I made this hog swallow the child. We've slaughtered the hog, but the child is gone!"

She watched carefully, then saw that "There's a heifer, falling over itself. It's clear that the child has been swallowed by this ox."

She repeatedly told her husband, "I want the liver of a beast, of that beast that's so weighed down in the stomach. I'll die if I don't taste it!"

Her husband agreed. He said that the beast must be slaughtered. The ox heard these words, so it went to a horse. It told the horse that it must swallow this child because the ox had learned that it was to be slaughtered the next day. So it was that the ox was slaughtered, but there was no child in its stomach. The liver of the beast was eaten.

"What kind of beast is this? Where has the child gone? When the ox was slaughtered, there was no child in its stomach!"

As had happened with the ox, the horse became burdened, it was weighed down by this child that it had swallowed.

The woman said, "I want the liver of that horse!"

The man asked, "Have you always been like this? Is the liver of a horse ever eaten?"

"The liver of a horse? Yes, it is eaten!"

"Never have we seen such a thing!"

The horse was caught and slaughtered, but the child was not there. He had been sent away to be kept by a crab in the river.

Time passed, and this mother continued to suffer because of her connection with that cat. Her sister was happy because she was now married in this homestead. She was living a good life, but the original wife was being eaten up by her great sorrow. Time passed for her, time passed. Yes, time passed . . .

"What shall we do now?"

She saw that "Well, this child is not here! Perhaps the hog chewed him up, and I've now swallowed him by eating the hog's liver."

The child grew up at the crab's place, and finally, the crab decided to send him home.

"Yes, I want to send you home now."

So the crab brought that child home. It took him to his home. They arrived, and the crab greeted the people there. It sat at the door, greeting them. It shook hands.

They asked, "Where have you come from?"

It told them that it had come from the crab's place, the homestead below the neighboring hill.

"Yes."

The crab said, "Well, this boy has come with me. I brought him here. He says that he wants to visit here for a while. He wants to see if there is someone he knows in this homestead." The crab said this.

When the child took off his hat and put it down, his father saw the star on his forehead and was greatly startled. His mother had been crying from the time the child had appeared. Then the child took off his jacket. He flapped it open—and they could see the crescent of the moon.

This fellow leapt up and gathered the child in his arms. He said, "Whose child are you?"

The child said, "Where were you when I was borne by my mother? Her sister took a cat from the garden and rolled it in my place. She blindfolded my mother, so that when she gave birth she would not see a person. Instead, she substituted a cat, then told my mother that she had given birth to a cat. Don't you see my mother? So thin? Unkempt? Unfed like this?"

Well then, it was said that this sister should be taken and killed. They seized her, and she was killed. Her body was deposited in a barren place. She was not buried.

The wife began to be happy again, and she occupied her former position.

Tale 21

A MAN HIDES FOOD FROM HIS FAMILY

Masithathu Zenani's Analysis: Some roots, a cave, a pair of fantastic creatures, a miraculous flying rock, a weak husband: How are these places, objects, and characters organized in an oral performance to communicate a complex message? Physical action by the central character of the narrative links these entities and others in a tightly constructed performance in which everything is involved in a regular, physical movement from a house of marriage to the lonely, forbidding veld. These are the major spatial poles of the tale; they establish a pattern, a repeated movement, the crucial organizing activity. The basic movement flows through the three parts that comprise the story, with one significant alteration: at one time, the quest for food takes the central character from the house of marriage not to the veld but to the house of his wife's birth.

The main narrative conflict is the drought. But this is not the message of the performance. Drought is the conflict that moves the various characters in a patterned set of actions, and it reveals important relationships.

Because drought is the conflict, the problem of food—milk, roots, pit corn— is developed at some length. Food is a key to the message of the tale, providing insights into the crucial relations between the husband and his wife, between the wife's house of birth and her house of marriage. The root is not proper food, but it helps to overcome hunger. It can be eaten raw, but if roasted it resembles natural food: "When it is cooked, its quality as a plant comes to an end."

The major physical movement of the performance involves the journeying from the man's home to the veld, where he herds cattle and where he now seeks roots. These are the poles. The veld is not home; it is unfamiliar, a wilderness. It is therefore understandable that the roots, not a normal food, are found in this strange place. It is also plausible to assume that curious creatures will be encountered out there in that unusual setting. When the husband returns from the veld with his roots, the movement is complete: the move to the veld, where roots are hunted, and back home again with the unnatural food, not really a human food.

The narrative falls into three parts: the first deals with the drought, and the husband's journey to his in-laws' place to get food; the second details the man's relations with the fabulous clinger; and the final part describes his encounter with the unlikely rectum-snatcher. In part one, the husband behaves deceitfully toward his wife and son. In part two, the clinger takes over the husband's function, sucking the life out of him as he, in effect, sucked the life out of his family in part one. To reinforce this, Mrs. Zenani adds a third part: the rectum-snatcher behaves toward the husband as the husband behaved toward his wife and son. He has torn his family apart, as the rectum-snatcher is tearing him apart. Parts two (the clinger) and three (the rectum-snatcher) are meant to comment, metaphorically, on part one (the husband).

417

They are mirrors of part one; in a fantastic way, they explain the significance of the husband's antisocial acts in part one.

Things go well in the home until the drought occurs, and it reveals the husband's flaw, his lack of responsibility. His hunger drives him to deceive his own family, to abdicate his role as provider, father, and husband. The roots make it possible for the people to move from a drought to a period of sufficiency, even though the roots are a substitute food. They are not real food, but they act as a mediator, moving the family from no food to real food. There is a concomitant movement, in which the wife takes the family from instability to stability. The in-laws' food makes it possible for the wife to move to a position of superiority in her husband's homestead. In this sense, the roots and the in-laws' food—real food, but it is not food from the man's homestead, and therefore it is equated with the food of the veld—are the same structurally, as are drought and the wife's initial position in her husband's homestead, as are plenty and the wife's new position in that homestead. It is the logic of this narrative that the food sent by the in-laws (normal food—corn, etc.), which might understandably be thought of as the food of normalcy, is actually emergency food, substitute food. The story's culinary code requires that roots mediate between drought and sufficiency. Because of the role that it plays here, the food of the in-laws functions in the same way as roots. It is substitute food, sent to enable the family to survive the food crisis, like the roots mediating between drought and normalcy.

The movement to the veld is extended at one point to establish a connection between the house of birth and the house of marriage, so that the presence of the wife's blood relatives is strongly felt in the latter. The relations between a man and his wife, between a homestead of birth and a homestead of marriage, are explored and revealed by means of food and hunger. The roots become a means of communication between the couple. And when the husband substitutes fake roots for real food, his relationship with his wife is ruptured.

The second and third parts of the tale also examine these husband-wife relations. The fantastic creatures in the narrative play crucial roles. The clinger keeps the husband from the tree resin and becomes a part of the husband, twisting the life out of him. The rectum-snatcher requests roots from the husband and damages the husband when he refuses to provide the food. In each case, the wife heals the husband. These second and third parts of the tale parallel the first, probing and explaining the significance of the first.

The wife brings into her house of marriage the force and presence of her house of birth. Her role is also that of the roots—mediatory, like the food of the in-laws. The fact that the in-laws' food is seen not as the food of normalcy but as food of emergency brings the in-laws' efforts into alignment with the role of the wife, and with the function of roots, also the food of emergency. The in-laws and the wife are equated in their functions. The husband is more and more aligned with the drought, with the withholding of food, the withholding of truth. The wife unmasks him, denudes him; the wife is the responsible one, the one who feeds her family, who plays the role of the husband. She finally restores the husband to his proper role. The wife, then, is at the opposite pole of the husband, identified with food of normalcy, with sufficiency.

The husband is damaged by his irresponsibility; he becomes powerless, impotent, in the same way that his family is powerless. In narrative logic, the husband becomes the drought; the wife becomes the instrument for change. In association with her own parents and home, the connection made by their offerings of food, the wife will move the husband toward plenty, toward normalcy. She takes over her husband's functions. With the help of her blood relations, she establishes the influence of the in-laws here in the land of her husband, in his homestead. The food is in this respect an extension of the in-laws, of the house of birth, a chain connecting the wife to her house of birth. The narrative focuses on the transition of the wife from her home of birth to her house of marriage, her establishment as a force for normalcy in her homestead of marriage. The husband is seen as an adversary, a negative force, to be cured of his irresponsibility, to be brought into the framework of the house of birth. The move to the house of marriage is a move into a drought-stricken area where she and her children are at the mercy of her husband. Only when the presence of the house of birth is felt in the house of marriage is harmony achieved. The ties with the wife's house of birth are purposely broken by the husband: the food chain connecting the two houses is severed when he moves the food into the cave, sending the in-laws' representatives back to their homes. The kinship system will not allow this deception to prevail. The food, the channel with the in-laws, must be kept open, or drought will destroy everything. The force of the wife must be formally and firmly established in the homestead of the husband.

It is a narrative of transition, a drama of conflicting powers; the final argument centers not so much on drought and plenty, or even responsibility and irresponsibility, though these are obviously involved. Primarily, the narrative focuses on the establishment of the presence of the in-laws in the house of marriage, for the protection of the woman and her children, for the protection of the in-laws themselves. In the process, the role of the wife is emphasized.

Mrs. Zenani explained that the veld, home of the roots, is the transitional area, the area between the home of birth and the home of marriage. The roots are transitional food, making it possible for the family to move from drought to sufficiency. The food of the in-laws is also transitional food, enabling the family to move from a state of dependency on the husband to a state in which its interests are protected by the presence of the in-laws. The wife is transitional; she makes it possible for the husband to move from irresponsibility to responsibility, recognizing his role in a system in which he is not dominant.

The audience is moved from the literal level of the performance—drought, danger of death through starvation, an irresponsible and weak husband, fantastic and dangerous creatures of the veld—to the level of relationships between the various elements of the performance, the level on which the message is felt. The connections between the two levels, the elements that make it possible for the level of relationships to be experienced, involve the complex functions played by food in the tale. The audience emotionally apprehends linkages, relationships between husband and family, between husband and wife, between man and clinger, man and rectum-snatcher, man and in-laws, ultimately between house of birth and veld and house of marriage. These relationships are experienced in an organized, logical fashion because of the identical nature of patterns that occur throughout the performance, patterns based on space, patterns that are felt and that lead the members of the audience into an emotional experience of connections between narrative entities, the ultimate message of the work of art.

Performance Note

Time: 10 August 1972, late afternoon. *Place:* In a fallen rondavel near Mrs. Zenani's home in Nkanga, Gatyana District, the Transkei. *Audience:* Five women, five children. (Perf. NS-142.)

There were a woman and a man. It happened that this woman gave birth; she bore some children, including a boy. The children were of various ages, the boy a little older than the others.

Time passed then. Time passed at this home of theirs.

After some time had lapsed, the people ate the crops that they had cultivated. They harvested the crops. Then winter came—and these activities were all repeated.

During all these times, that woman lived happily with her husband.

Time passed, years followed years, and eventually there came a season of drought. Everything was parched. The trees lost their leaves; rivers dried up. And as the rivers dried up, it became obvious that there was nothing to eat. People resorted to eating old food: pit corn was dug out of the corn pits; sour food was now being eaten. Some of the pit corn had maggots in it, it was so old. And the people were not fond of it. They would sometimes develop stomachaches, caused by the corn that was three or four years old—it had finally rotted in the pits. Yo! What will be done with this corn?

The man of this homestead had some livestock—some milk cows, a few milk goats. There were corresponding calabashes for the stock, a separate calabash for the goat milk, called "the calabash for children." And the calabash for cows' milk was called "the calabash for the older people," the mother and father. Milk would be poured on the pit corn. Or the pit corn, having been ground up, would be cooked, then milk would be added. On another day, to give their stomachs a break from the pit corn that was so old and rotten, they would shift to milk.

Time passed in that way, and the family continued to eat these rotten mealies. Time passed, time passed, and this man regularly went out to herd his livestock. But whenever he saw some people, he would go to them, leaving the cattle behind. He would go to them, greet them, and they would converse, discussing the drought.

"This is awful for us, too."

"We've stopped eating those bitter mealies."

"The food has rotted. It's developed maggots."

"Now we're eating roots."

The man asked, "What are these roots?"

They told him about the root: "Well, it's something that's dug up in the pasture."

"Then it's roasted and put into the hearth. But you can eat it when it's raw too."

"But it really should be roasted, so that it settles well in the stomach. A fire should be kindled, and it should be roasted to remove the rawness."

"When it's cooked, its quality as a plant comes to an end."

The man asked them to point out the roots to him, because over there at his home starvation was imminent. All they had was milk. Milk was the only thing they had in their stomachs. It was as if one drank milk and nothing else: "No matter what one pours the milk over, it's as if one has eaten only milk. He tastes nothing else."

When the conversation was at an end, the people helped the man to find some roots.

One of them said, "There's one!"

They showed him where it was, so that he might dig it up himself.

One of them said, "Dig it up."

Then they told him to taste it, to see what it was like, so that he would be able to identify it.

All day he dug these roots, and at last he was able to identify them properly. And he began to dig for other roots. He put them into a bag. He had a goatskin bag that he had tanned and provided with some pockets. In the pockets of the goatskin bag were places for putting things, one could force them into the pockets. That is what he did.

At length, these roots were a bundle, and he put them down. Then, when it was time to go home, he turned the cattle around. He went home, and, when he got there, he put the cattle into the kraal.

His child, this boy, said, "Mama! Mama, look! What's Father carrying?"

His mother said, "What is he carrying, my child?"

"He's carrying something. But I don't know what it is. He's carrying something on his shoulder. Maybe he's bringing some corn."

His mother said, "Mhm! I wonder where he got them from, my child?"

They sat in hope, constantly looking out at him. He put the cattle into the kraal, and, when he emerged from the kraal, he went into the house.

He dropped the load.

"Nobani, kindle the fire."

"Mhm?"

"Please kindle the fire so that the children can have something to eat. How have things gone today?"

His wife said, "We've been hungry all day. Even my breasts are dry. Nothing comes out of them because I'm so hungry."

"Kindle, kindle the fire, Wife. You'll be satisfied today."

The wife got up and got some firewood, and she built the fire. Then the man uncovered his load, he poured the contents out on the ground. He divided these things, he divided them, saying, "These on this side are yours. They're for you and the children," and he snuggled the roots into the hearth. He showed his wife and son how they were to be roasted. They continued to push the roots into the hearth. When they had been properly put into the hearth, the roots would whistle. Then they would burst. The members of the family would take them out, allow them to cook, then they would eat them.

This went on, day after day. Soon, the threat of starvation had been alleviated. When they drank milk, they drank it when it had been poured over these roots.

Whenever this man left home, he would dig for these roots. Whenever he herded cattle, he would dig for roots. Every day, he dug up these roots.

So it went. A month came to an end; a second month appeared. The family was beginning to feel that "Really, these roots aren't corn."

"This is a plant."

The root began to be felt in the stomach. It began to show evidence that "I am not really corn. Even though I'm eaten, I'm just a plant." And that plant became tiresome. But there was nothing that could be done about it because it did remove the feeling of giddiness that the hunger caused.

The wife said, "Sobani, please go to the home of my birth." She said, "There's never been this kind of starvation at my home. Many crops are cultivated there—corn and pumpkins, beans are grown there, millet is grown. And because so many things are cultivated, it's unlikely that there's nothing left over there. I'm a nursing mother, so I cannot go. Please go for me, my husband. Go to my home."

The husband said, "But Nobani, with whom will I leave the cattle?"

His wife said, "I'll just put my child on my back. I'll find time to go and herd while you're gone. I can't herd the cattle for the entire day, but I'll do it part of the time. This boy and I will help each other. Now please go! I have a little baby here. I can't go. We'll all die because of this hunger."

The man journeyed then. He got up the following morning and did what his wife had asked. He went to his in-laws' place. He traveled; he walked and arrived at his in-laws' place. When he got there, he knocked at the door and greeted them.

They responded, asking where he had come from.

He said that he had come from his home, that he had been sent here "by my wife. She said, Father-in-law, that I should come here to her home. My wife has given birth to a child, and the starvation is about to kill her—it's especially difficult for her because she has just given birth. Her child is also in danger of starving. In that entire land of ours, no one visits anyone else anymore. All we do is eat roots that are dug up on the veld. They're put into the hearth and roasted. We've been eating roots for two months now. And we've come to realize that this root is only a plant; it's not corn."

The mother-in-law and her companions were concerned. "Yo! How could she give birth while she was starving? Well, you'll return to your home in the morning."

His sisters-in-law were there, and there were some young men there too, and boys; his father-in-law was there and his mother-in-law.

"You can go back tomorrow. The young women will accompany you."

Before the husband went to sleep, a beast was slaughtered for him there at his in-laws' place. He gorged himself. He kept one side of the beast, from the foreleg to the hindleg. He kept that. He would take it home with him. He would take it to his own homestead.

At dawn the next day, the man was ready to go home. Various things were prepared for his journey: he was given corn, beans, and millet, all in equal quantities. And there was also the whole side of meat.

When everything was ready, when the food had been prepared, the husband said, "Mother," speaking to his mother-in-law, the mother of his wife.

His mother-in-law responded.

He said, "We're also lacking a pot over there at my home. The one we used to have is broken. My wife asked if you would lend her one. And, because of the problem of starvation, there isn't even any salt. We use salt on nothing now. Please give her some salt, too."

All this was done for the husband. He was given some salt; he was given a large quantity of salt that would last a long time. And he was given a small pot. These things were tied into three bundles so that he would be able to carry them more easily.

He was accompanied by the young women. They helped him to carry his load. They were told to accompany him right to his home.

He traveled with those young women, walking to his home. There was a river that had to be crossed. When they got to the river, the husband said, "Well, my in-laws . . ."

The young women answered, "Brother-in-law?"

"Please stop here, my in-laws. Stop. Really, it's all right now. Just turn around and return to your home. I'm fairly close to my own home now. You don't have to accompany me further. Just take these loads to the other side of the river and deposit them over there. Then you can turn back. I saw the amount of work that has to be done over there at your own house, work that you're needed for. Now I've left the land of my in-laws. The country on the other side of the river is mine. I'll tie the bundles together and carry all three of them myself. I won't be laughed at for carrying such a big load, not on that side of the river—because, really, I was born in that country. Turn around, my in-laws."

These young women said, "How can you go home carrying such a big load? What will our sister say? She'll wonder why we left you, why we didn't help you to carry such a burden."

The man said, "No, my in-laws, really, I cannot accept further help. I have already been assisted greatly by you. And because of that, no one can say anything negative about my in-laws. Turn around, go back."

The young women turned around then, and he remained there. When the women had disappeared in the distance, this fellow took the three bundles, one at a time. He began by taking the corn. He ran with the bundle. He hurried with the corn and went into a forest—there was a forest not far from his homestead. He got to the forest; there was a little cliff there. He looked around for a cave. He found one, then put the load down in it. When he had put the load of corn into the cave, he returned; he went to pick up the load of beans. Again he ran, and he put the beans into the cave also. Then he returned once more. The load of meat and the load of millet were still there at the side of the river. He ran and put these into the cave as well.

When he had satisfied himself that all was well, he thought, "I'll just go back and pick up the pot and the salt."

He returned to the river. Then he ran and put those things in the cave.

When he got back to the cave, he began his first task. He took the millet, then looked for a stone. He ground the millet thoroughly. He ground it, he ground it. Then he moistened it with water and molded it into little loaves—the loaves were the same size as roots, the roots that are dug up in the pasture. He took eight of these loaves, and put them into the fire. Then he cut the meat and roasted it in the fire. He roasted it, he roasted it, and he ate quite a lot of it—until he was sated. Then he took the little pot. He went to the river and dipped water. He returned. He drank this water. When he was finished, he departed.

The sun was setting now. There he is, going toward his home—and he was not carrying even one of those things that he had been given by his in-laws. He had left all that food behind in the cave.[1]

When he was fairly close to his home, he looked about for roots. He dug them up. He dug, he dug these roots. Then he took them to his home, and he threw them down near his wife.

---

1. But he is, as shortly becomes clear, carrying the "roots" made of millet.

He said, "Yo! You made such a fool of me! Sending me so far! And for nothing. They're really starving over there. Yo, they're starving. They're really starving! They have nothing to eat at all. They eat roots. There's nothing, nothing at your home! You sent me there for nothing. I looked like a fool! So I just went about, scavenging along the road." So saying, he threw the roots down, then brought the cattle into the kraal.

His wife said, "Didn't you even get some millet at my home?"

He said, "No."

"Weren't there even some grains of corn?"

"No, there was nothing."

"Not even a few beans?"

"No."

"Didn't you even get a pot at my home?"

"No."

"This is a sad affair." The wife sat down. "My hopes have been foiled. I did not think that you would return home with nothing. I hoped there would be some relief."

Time passed. She kindled a fire. These roots sizzled. They were snuggled into the hearth and roasted.

As for the husband, he put his "roots" on his own side of the hearth. But his wife caught their scent.

"What kind of roots are those? They have a peculiar smell. And why don't your roots whistle? What's the matter with them, Sobani?"

Her husband was evasive. "Well, really, your roots are of the variety that belongs to women. Mine are the kind that belongs to men. The two kinds are not the same. Yours—well, you know that you tend to char them badly. That's the reason for the difference. You women overheat them. They get burned on the outside and aren't cooked on the inside. We men put ours under the ashes."

His wife was quiet. This fellow ate his roots, eight of them.

Again, his wife said, "Ee, Sobani! Why is it that your roots don't crunch when you chew them? Yours are quiet; ours crunch!"

"What's the matter with this woman? I tell you, you must remember that you women overheat the roots, then take them off the fire while they're still raw. Mine get well-cooked. I put them in the hearth, then pile on the coals so that the roots become nice and soft."

His wife was quiet.

The next morning, the fellow took his cattle out to the veld, leaving his family behind, hungry. They had to resort to drinking milk. This fellow went off, and when he was a distance away, the wife said to the boy, "My child!"

The child: "Hmm?"

"Have you noticed that your father hasn't roasted as many roots for himself since his return from my home? Since the day he got back, there's been a change in the amount of roasting that he does. He just roasts two roots. What does he eat? Sometimes he doesn't even drink milk. And milk is plentiful at home now. What is your father eating?"

The child said, "I don't know."

She said, "Your father is eating something. Now you stay here for a while with the baby." So she said to the boy, who took the child and remained there at home with it.

The woman traveled. She walked and walked, keeping to the shadows. She went over there to the mountains, far in the distance. She looked carefully, going to the places where the man usually herded the cattle.

Then she saw him—and she noted that he was looking around. He was looking around furtively. He ran then and disappeared in a cave.

The woman came away from the mountains, then went back another way. She arrived, and when she got there she saw smoke coming from inside the cave. She stood at the outside and heard someone saying, "Be on the lookout, my penis cover! Is anyone coming? Is anyone coming?" Then she heard the sounds of grinding. And she knew that he was grinding.

The woman looked around for a rock, a big round rock that would stay in a track, that would be certain to hit him, to smash him over there. She aimed the rock—the woman knew that meat was being roasted inside the cave, she could tell by the smell. So she rolled the rock, she kept it straight in its course. She rolled it, and the stone flew over there to the place where the man was roasting the meat.

Suddenly the man heard something in front of him—*nqhooooooooo!* He was startled. He ran, leaving his clothes behind. He fled—naked! And whenever he looked back—Yo! This rock! Here was this rock, "coming straight at me!" He ran; he ran and ran. He looked back each time he crossed a river, and—"Yo! This rock! Here's this rock, coming straight at me!" The man ran, and the sun went down, and he was still being pursued by the rock.

In the meantime, this woman went into the cave, and when she got there: "Oh, here's meat! And here is corn! And beans! Millet! And here's the pot!"

The woman took these things. She made several trips. She traveled with those foods, a bundle at a time—walking with them, going to her home with them. She arrived, put the bundle down, then went back to get another. And she put that one down, then went back to get yet another. And she put that one down too.

She sat. And when she saw that the sun was going to set, the woman took some corn and cooked it. When it was cooked, she took it off the fire. She ground it, then poured milk over it for her children.

And they ate.

Then she put the pot over there, in the house. The woman did not hide these things—she carefully put them in the upper part of the house, in full view, so that her husband would see them when he came in.

The woman cut the meat into pieces, put the pieces into a pot, and cooked them. The meat was cooked.

And they ate it.

She and her children finished the meat, and she took the bones and put them in the upper part of the house. She did not hide them. She wanted them to be seen.

The great man arrived after the sun had set. He was driving his cattle. He closed them up in the kraal, then returned to the house. He returned, bruised—he had lacerations on his feet, his legs, everywhere, even on the thighs. He had been scratched by trees, pricked by things as he fled from that rock, as he ran and stumbled. His feet were in pain, and he was limping.

His wife said, "What's the matter? Why are you limping? What has happened?"

"No, no, I was looking for the cattle and couldn't find them, that's all."

"What happened to the cattle?"

"They just wandered off. They went to graze far off. I was looking for them."

"Oh, and you got all scratched up like that just because you were looking for the cattle?"

"Yes."

"Oh."

She took a dish and dipped out some corn for the children; they ate the corn, and so did the woman. This fellow poured out his roots, and his wife said, "Just eat those roots of the kind that belongs to you, to men! My children and I will just eat the kind that belongs to women. As I was going about seeking food, hungry, I found some roots of the kind that belongs to women. You eat yours. You eat the kind that belongs to men!"

The man had a problem. What could he do about this? Here in the house, he could see all the things that he had hidden away in the cave. But he could not understand how his wife could have found them. And he was afraid: he feared that his father-in-law and others of his in-laws would hear about this. What would they say? After all, he had come to them with a special plea for food for his wife. Then he had not given her any.

This fellow was silent.

After a long time, in the morning, he was hungry, and he said, "Oh, Nobani, won't you give me just a spoonful, to satisfy my heart?"

She said, "Never! Not until you bring back to me the thing I sent you for, the thing you were to have brought from my home! Not until you learn to give me a full account of what happened, and say things were like this and like that. Then I'll give you something to eat. Then I'll share those things with you. But until then—never!"

So he sat there, suffering, unable to eat anything at all.

Time passed.

Time passed in that way for this fellow, and he was very hungry. The others in the house went on eating. His wife and children continued to eat this fine food, without ever once giving him any. He was hungry. He lost weight: hungry, drinking only milk, eating roots and nothing more, eating resin from mimosa trees and nothing else, fighting with the monkeys over that resin—that is all he had.

After a while, a long while, it became clear that the supply of food at home was diminishing.

Then it was gone.

One day, this man was walking, herding his cattle in the usual way, eating this resin, and he found that the mimosa trees had been cleaned out. He had been constantly rifling through the trees, combing through them for resin. The day before, he had gone through these trees, and some days before that, and now today as well. The resin had no chance to grow, to ooze out. And the man was getting hungrier and hungrier, a little hungrier each time he looked for the food. He walked a great distance, seeking resin, finding none. He traveled all day.

Finally, he came upon a tree that contained an abundance of resin. But there was something that was clinging to it, something that was clinging to the mimosa tree.

He said to it, "Get down! Who are you, clinging to this resin? Get down. Let me get some of it!"

The thing said, "I'll never come down! Who are you?"

Again this fellow tried because he could see that the resin was plentiful here. He knew that he would be satisfied, if only he could get to the resin. He went to some other trees in the area. He went to other trees, but then he returned.

He looked closely at this thing.

He said, "Say, Friend! I told you to get down from there, so that I can get some of this resin."

The thing said, "No one has ever made me get down."

Again, he said, "Come down from that tree. If you do, I'll let you suckle on this cow of my home. Look, that one with the big teats. If you'll come down, I'll carry you on my back."

The thing said, "Nobody carries me! I'm The-Clinger-I'll-Cling-to-You! That is my name, and I can cling to you too!"

The man said, "No, my friend, please come down."

It was getting late. The sun was about to set. It was time for him to return to his home with his cattle. But the man was vexed by hunger pangs, and he was afraid to go home. He was hungry. He wondered how he would be able to go to sleep in such a state.

So he again begged, "Yo, Friend! Please come down. I'll let you suckle on this cow—you'll be satisfied; the cow is in milk." This fellow said that. Then he went and brought a cow from among the cattle. He brought the beast close, holding the cow, saying, "Look! Look, this cow is in milk! Come down!"

The thing said, "I told you that I've never been made to come down."

"Come down, Friend! I'll carry you! Please come to me. I'll carry you— just let me get some of that resin. Please, it's getting late."

"I'm The-Clinger-I'll-Cling-to-You! And I can cling to you too! All right, I'll come down."

The man turned his back. He turned his back to this thing. He moved toward it backwards, moving with his back toward the thing. Then he removed his garment. The thing detached itself from the tree, and it clung to the man's back; it clung to his back. It held on tightly with its claws. It had long claws; it held on with its claws. It had four legs, and its claws sank into the man's flesh. They sank into his flesh. The thing clung to this man.

The man said, "Get down. Get off my back! Get down, get down! Get down! Get down! Yo yo yo! I'm dying! Get down!"

The thing said, "I told you that I should not be carried! I am The-Clinger-I'll-Cling-to-You! You told me to get down from that tree!"

The man traveled then, a crumpled figure—powerless. This thing was trying to destroy him; its claws had disappeared into his flesh. Its claws seemed to be reaching to his very liver and lungs, reaching inside him. He was doubled up as he walked. He was scarcely able to walk at all as he drove his cattle. He moved slowly, and he had not even eaten any resin. The thing had come down from the tree. It had detached itself from the tree and then with its claws attached itself to the man—so that he was unable to eat the resin. This thing was causing him intense pain.

The man drove his cattle. He went home with them.

As he was coming along, his wife said, "What's the matter with this man today? Why is he walking so slowly, doubled up like that?"

The boy appeared, and he said, "I don't know what's the matter with him. He's so doubled up! I don't know what's the matter with him."

"Yo!" said the wife. "He really has peculiar habits. Knotted up like that. What's the matter with him?"

In time, the man entered; he came into the house, bent over in pain. He sat in the room, but he did not come close to the others that day—he sat at a distance.

His wife said, "What's the matter? Why are you sitting so far away from us? What's the matter now?"

"No, no, nothing's the matter."

"Are you cold?"

"No, I'm not cold."

"Oh! How can you not be cold? It's not hot, yet you're not cold!"

"No, I'm not cold."

The man continued to sit over there, and the others ate their corn.

Then the wife said, "Why don't you roast your roots? Here's the fire."

"No, really, I'm not hungry."

"Oh, what have you eaten?"

"I ate some resin from the trees."

His wife said, "Oh, is it your practice to fill yourself with nothing but resin? Without roasting roots?"

"No, no, I'm full."

His wife did not bother him further. But when they went to sleep that night, it was clear that something was on this man.

While he slept, he kept saying, "Mmmh! Mmh! Mmmmmh! Mmmmmh!"

His wife said, "Sobani! Sobani!"

"Mm?"

"What's the matter?"

"What are you talking about? I'm only dreaming."

"What is the matter? Why are you making such a noise? Why this groaning? What's the problem? Where are you aching?"

"No, I'm not aching at all! I'm just stretching."

"Mh!"

"Nothing's wrong."

"Oh."

Time passed for them, and when it was morning he got up and departed. It was difficult for him to get up. He was doubled up. He walked off slowly to let the cattle out of the kraal. And his wife and child stared at him. He walked away, going to herd the cattle. So time passed for him.

His wife said to the little boy, "My child, please follow your father. Observe him. Find out what is wrong with him. He has become such a stiff thing! Watch him. See if you can discover what it is he's hiding. But don't let him know why you're following him. Just go."

The child went. He walked over there with his father.

"Go home! Go home, Child. Go home."

"No, Father. I'll turn the cattle and keep them from straying."

"Go! Go, my child. Go home. You must be hungry."

"No, Father, I'm not hungry."

The man left him alone. The boy went about repeatedly, herding the cattle. Whenever his father disapeared somewhere, the boy would watch him. The child observed him when the man disappeared to one side. He watched as his father let his garment fall, as he exposed his shoulders.

He said, "Please come down, Friend! Please come down! Come, let me suckle you. Here's some milk! Yo! You're killing me!"

The thing said, "I told you that I'm The-Clinger-I'll-Cling-to-You! I'm not to be carried on the back!"

As soon as he saw the thing that was on his father, the child ran. He headed for home. He arrived there and went to his mother.

"Mama! I've seen the thing that's on Father! He's got something that's monstrous! It's on his back! He keeps saying, 'Come down, Friend! I'm dying! Get down! It's painful!' And that thing says to my father, 'I told you! I said that I'm not to be carried on the back! I'm The-Clinger-I'll-Cling-to-You!' Father's all swollen! The thing that is clinging to Father is causing him pain!"

The mother of the child said, "Be quiet, my child. Don't speak of this again."

The child sat then, and the man herded his cattle the whole day, not realizing that his secret had been discovered. Because of the pain, he was no longer even digging up roots. He was bent over. He went home. He took the cattle home. When he arrived, he shut the cattle in the kraal, then went to the house. He sat down.

His wife dipped out some corn and ate. When she had eaten her corn, she gave some to her children. And they ate.

"Why don't you roast the roots?" she asked. "Why don't you eat over there on your side of the hearth?"

The man said, "No, I'm full."

"What are you full of?"

"Resin."

"Oh, what kind of resin is this, that you're full day after day? You don't eat here at all."

"No, there's nothing."

"Why are you so doubled up? You can't walk properly! You even have difficulty wrapping yourself in your cape! You can't make your bed! What's gripping you? What part of your body is aching?"

"No, there's nothing wrong with me! There's nothing wrong with me!"

"Mm?"

"There's nothing wrong with me!"

The woman closed the door and said, "You're going to tell me what's wrong with you! What is the matter with you?"

The man lacked strength because of what this thing was doing to him, so he gave in at last, and said, "Well, Nobani, just sit down here. I'll tell you."

His wife sat.

"I was eating resin, Nobani. And while I was eating it, I suddenly saw something that was clinging to me. This thing had attached itself to me. It clawed me. It refused to get down. It tortured me. Now I'm swollen. This thing is painful—it's painful!"

"When did this happen?"

"Yo! On some day or other."

"Why didn't you tell me about it? What's this all about? How can it be that you took such a creature from a tree? You worthless thing! You low person! I send this miserable thing to my home, and it proceeds to eat the food in a secret cave! And now, you go about getting these things from trees and putting them on your body! What kind of brain is that? Now uncover yourself. Let's see this thing."

The wife uncovered him and found that her husband was badly swollen— with this weird thing clinging to him, sinking its claws into him. This thing was alive.

The woman said to the thing, "Get down! Get out of here!"

The thing said, "I will not come down! I have said that I'm The-Clinger-I'll-Cling-to-You!"

"Yo!"

The woman wondered what she should do. Her husband would die at the hands of this thing. She boiled some oil, she boiled some oil. She heated it. She heated the oil, and it was very very hot.

Then she said, "Get down!"

The man uncovered himself, and the woman quickly poured the oil. She poured hot oil on this thing.

Yo! The thing now began to peel off. It peeled off along with the man's flesh. Then it fell to the ground. The woman killed it and threw it outside. Then she began to heal her husband, and he became well again.

When the man was healed, the wife repeatedly assailed him for the things he had done, those despicable things.

This man went out and again herded his cattle as he had in the past— herding the cattle, digging roots.

One day, something said to him, "Please give me a root."

It turned out to be a person who had only one arm.

The man looked at this person, and said, "What's happened to this person, a person with only one arm who goes about saying that he should be given a root? What kind of person is this? He has only one side!"

The thing said, "You too could come to have only one side! Just give me some roots. I am unable to dig for roots."

This fellow refused. He said, "Go on! I don't have time for that!"

He said, "Come and sit by me. You'll see better that I have no arm."

The man approached, and when he came near to this creature: "Oh, this person does resemble a human being, except that he has only one arm, there's only one eye! One leg! And the thing doesn't move from this place! He has only one finger on his hand, one finger with a long nail!"

The man squatted then and dug for roots. And this thing suddenly moved its nail, and ripped off the man's rectum, throwing it over there.

It threw the man's rectum over there.

This fellow said, "Yo! Dear friends, what is this that I've come to now? What will my wife think of me?"

Then he ran. He headed over there—and his rectum was making a noise: "Hooooooo! Hoooooooooo!" Each time he took a step: "Hoooooooo!" When he ran, his rectum moaned: "Wo wo wo wo wo!" And when he stood still: "Wooooooooo!" And when he ran: "Wo wo wo wo wo!"

He said, "What am I to do now? And my wife! Today I am bringing yet another problem to her. She just finished with that other thing that was on me!"

This fellow took his garment then. He took his cape and tore one side of it. He stuffed it into his rectum. He stuffed it—stuffing it, molding it into the shape of a rectum. And he put it where his rectum should have been. He made it firm, so that it would stop making this noise. Then he went on his way.

Again, as he neared home, he heard the sound: "Wooooooo!" So he again stuffed a part of his garment into his rectum. "Wo wo wo wo wo!" He tore the garment once more, the cape gradually diminishing in size because he had been tearing and stuffing it. That thing was heard making the noise, and again he tore the garment and stuffed it into his rectum.

"Well, my cape is getting smaller."

The garment was indeed getting smaller, and finally there was only enough material left for settling on his shoulders, then the neck—it was as if it were a mere scarf now. The fellow went on his way and arrived at his home. He put the livestock into the kraal.

His child said, "Mama! Mama! Just look at Father! He has no clothes! He's naked!"

His mother said, "What's the matter with him now?"

"Just look at him!"

His mother appeared in the doorway.

"Well, what's the matter with this man? Why is he naked?"

The man secured the livestock in the kraal, but he was afraid to go to the house—afraid of his wife. So he tarried, moving about here and there on the outside. He did that until it was dark, then he went into the house. As he was entering, his wife said, "What's the matter with you? Why are you naked? What has happened to your clothes?"

"Well, this is how it happened. While I was rounding up the cattle, I got caught on a tree stump. My clothes were torn and were left behind there. Then, when I was chasing the cattle at another place, my cape tore and remained in a thicket over there, among thorny trees. I was pricked by those thorns. The shrubs clung to the garment. My clothes were ruined!"

The woman said, "Heeee! I'll find out about this! I'll find out what kind of man we have here! This is a strange man that we've got here in this house. I can't understand him."

Time passed for this woman, and the man went to sleep. The woman loaned him a garment, and he went to sleep.

In the morning, she took the garment back, and said, "Go, go with that rag of yours!"

When the husband had taken the livestock out and he was going down the hill below the kraal: "Woooooooooooooo!"

His wife said, "What's making that noise?" She and the child listened.

The cattle were very troublesome that day, straying this way and that. The man frequently had to run to turn them around, to bring them back. As he rounded up the cattle on this side, as he pursued them, this thing would make that noise: "Wo wo wo wo!" with each step that he took.

She said, "Heeee! Something's moaning, it's coming from this man! This is a mystery!"

The man went on. He gradually brought the livestock together. He herded the cattle; he herded and herded. Then he went to that thing.

He went over there and found that thing sitting—that person with one arm, with one eye, one leg, the person with one finger on his hand—and one long nail.

"Hello there, sir."

"Yes?"

"Please give me back my rectum. My clothing is finished."

The thing said, "Come here so that you can see me better, so that you can see that I'm a human being. Because when you're standing over there, you can't see so well. Please come here."

The man said, "When I came close to you before, you tore off my rectum. And now my clothes are gone. I ask you to give me back my rectum."

The thing said, "I said, please come here."

But this fellow refused to approach. He was in great pain because of this thing.

He went and herded his cattle. In time, he turned them around and went home. All the while, his rectum kept making that noise. And he stuffed it with cloth, again tearing off a piece of what remained of his garment. He stuffed it into his rectum; he stuffed it, he stuffed it.

Finally, he came to his home. He closed the cattle in the kraal, then went to the house. The woman closed the door behind him. He stood there in the doorway.

She said, "Now tell me, what's making that noise? You're going to tell me about it today!"

Her husband said, "Mhmm! This is what happened to me, Nobani. While I was digging roots the other day, I encountered someone. Now this person told me to give him some roots. I said that I had none, but he kept begging me. I asked him who he was. And he told me to approach so that I could see that he was really a person. I went to him, and while I was digging, he suddenly ripped off my rectum! But this person wasn't a proper human being! He had only one arm, one leg. He had one hand, one finger—with one long nail. Now, when I left that place, my rectum began to make a noise. So I tore off a piece of this garment, and that's how it came to be finished."

"Oh!"

"Yes."

"All right then, this is what you must do. Give me your garment," said his wife, "and I'll take the cattle out tomorrow morning. You remain behind. And if you should happen to go out of the house, pretend to be some other person. Loan me your garments, and your knitted hat, and that bag of yours, the stick for digging roots."

"Oh!"

Well then, the next day, in the morning, the wife went about the business very purposefully, taking a stick, taking an axe, the digging stick, the man's clothing, his knitted hat, the bag into which the roots would be put. And the woman went on her way, taking the cattle out to the pasture.

The woman traveled, going out with the oxen in the customary way. When she had gone off with the cattle, she herded them out there on the veld.

She had said to her husband, "Don't come along." He was to keep his distance, and he did indeed stay far behind.

She traveled. The woman went ahead. She walked a long way, herding these cattle, walking, digging for the roots, until she finally came within sight of this thing. When she saw it, she continued walking, digging, getting closer and closer to it, approaching it little by little.

This thing said, "Just give me a root."

The woman said, "Oh, who are you to say that I should give you a root?"

The thing said, "Please come here. Come to me, and see for yourself. You'll see that I'm a person, and you'll know me and give me some roots."

The woman said, "Well, I know that you're a person. I can see that. As for the roots that I've been digging up—I've got responsibilities. I need them for my family at home. I didn't dig them up for you. But I'll give them to you on one condition—that you not insist upon them, that you not demand them forcefully."

This thing said, "All right, I won't demand them forcefully. I say to you, please give me those roots."

The woman said, "I'll give them to you if you follow my custom. You must turn around and ask for them with your back toward me. And I too,

I'll respond to you with my back toward you. We'll approach each other in that way. Then, when I get to you, I'll turn around and face you."

So this thing turned around. Its back was toward her. The woman watched carefully.

The thing said, "I say, give me those roots."

The woman walked slowly, and she said, "Yes, I'll give you the roots when you ask me for them, when you beg me. I'm digging them up for the people of my home who are in dire need of food."

The thing said, "I'm in dire need, too. I'm very hungry. But I don't have a digging stick."

The woman said, "I have a digging stick. If you follow my custom, I'll give you roots."

This thing said, "I'll follow your custom."

Little by little, she was getting nearer.

"I'll follow your custom, yes."

The woman said, "When I hit against you with my back, I'll go around to the front of you. Only then can you have the roots."

The thing said, "All right, fine. Hit against me; let it happen. Hit against me, behind me, then I'll see you finally when you come around to the front."

The woman came to the thing in that way—it still had its back to her. But she came straight to it. She did not turn her back to it. She did not move backward as she had said she would. But it had its back to her, not looking at her, not seeing her.

When she got to this thing, she cut off its head. With a cutter, with the axe that she was carrying.

And she found her husband's rectum, just sitting there. The thing was not being especially careful to guard the rectum, so desperate was it to get the roots.

She took the rectum, then called her husband.

The thing was dead.

She said, "Sobani! Sobani!"

The man responded.

She said, "Come and see where you left your rectum."

The man came, running hard. He arrived and found that the thing was dead. His wife was now carrying this rectum in her hand. She pulled the rags from her husband's buttocks and replaced his rectum. It fit tightly. Then she threw the rags away, and they left that creature there. They returned to their home. They went, going home with the cattle, going together now, looking for roots.

The man said, "Yo! My wife, you've really helped me! It's not the first time either. You've been helping me for a long time! But today, I've learned my lesson. I'll never go near such a thing again. All day, I've been remembering the time I was pursued by that stone that you threw at me when I returned from my in-laws'. I returned deceitfully, hiding the food that had been prepared for you. I also recall the day when I was almost dead of hunger because of what I had done. Then I peeled off The-Clinger-I'll-Cling-to-You from the resin, and it settled on my back. I groaned with it for a whole year. I was in great pain! Then, today, I was called by a thing that was lying on the ground, a thing that I did not recognize, a thing that demanded that I give it roots. In that situation, too, I was helped by you. I shall never go against your commands again, my wife."

Time passed, and they came to their home. When they got home, they closed up the cattle and went into the house. They roasted the roots; they drank milk.

The man was ingratiating himself with his wife now. He did not want these things to be mentioned—the things that he had done, the things that had happened to him. In particular, he did not want his in-laws to learn of his actions, of the contemptible things that he had been doing.

Again and again, he said, "My wife, don't mention that, please!"

His wife said, "I'm really disgusted with you. I loathe you because—"

"No! No, don't talk about that!"

So they were happy. The man began to have confidence in her because the woman had more brains than he had.

Tale 22

NOMANASO

Masithathu Zenani's Analysis: This rather complex story about the relationship between a mother and daughter is based on a very simple tale. That tale, occupying the second half of this narrative, is a venerable one about a persistent pursuer; it describes the insistent aggressiveness of a monster that is kept at bay as long as the victim has materials to feed it. When she runs out of such material, her life is forfeit. The persistent monster becomes Nomanaso's transformed mother in this story, to give insight into the troubled relations between the two women.

In the first part of the story, a boy is almost choked to death by his sister, as he accompanies eight young women on the wedding day of Nomanaso, one of the eight. This event establishes Nomanaso's "dewy brain," as her mother later characterizes it. She marries, and this is the conflict: she does not return to her home until her fourth year of marriage. Then she finally takes her child and goes to visit her parents.

This somewhat elaborate opening establishes the conflict between mother and daughter. When Nomanaso goes to visit her parents, she overhears— while in a tree—a coven of witches, among whom are her mother and sisters, discussing such matters as the mother's decision to kill Nomanaso. A poison called Let-not-the-sun-go-down is prescribed, and the meeting breaks up. Nomanaso puts the poison in her mother's meat; her mother dies. A fateful relationship between mother and daughter is thereby established.

It is in the final part of the tale that the persistent pursuer image becomes patterned. The deceased mother is transformed into a deadly dish that regularly menaces Nomanaso as she makes her way back to her home of marriage. As the dish nears Nomanaso, it transforms into the mother's head. The head utters the word, *"Krwebede,"* and Nomanaso proceeds to give it parts of her property—a dish, loaves of bread, a mat, a cape, skirts, a calabash dish, her child's blanket, her head covering. Finally, she has nothing left to give the monster. So she begins to dismember her child—she tears off an arm and throws it to her mother, then the other arm, the leg, the other leg, then the body, the head. This macabre exchange is intensified when the young mother debates with herself whether to throw the body first or the head. Her jewelry is thrown, and finally, covered with the blood of her child, she is rescued by some chiefs. Her mother remains at bay, and the storyteller concludes, "It doesn't matter that the baby has disappeared, so long as our child [Nomanaso] is here, so long as this one whom we know has escaped. As for that other one, the baby, we didn't know its potential."

There is something strange and indecipherable about this beast called Krwebede. It arrives when a mother and her child are on the vast, forbidding veld; it only utters its name, but its intentions and needs are clear, as it regularly returns to the hapless victim. In the end, the victim is left with nothing, but still the beast persists in its pursuit.

To place a mother into the position of this beast, as Mrs. Zenani does here, dramatically alters the traditional way the story is told, as it simultaneously invigorates and gives fearful meaning to the relationship between a mother and her daughter, the jealousy a mother might feel regarding her daughter's marriage, the indifference a daughter might feel for her parents after she has left home. The fact that the storyteller dispenses with the child in what appears to be an offhanded, even merciless, way, is a storyteller's way of focusing attention—not on the dead child but on the struggle between mother and daughter. The mother's fierce temperament is first glimpsed when she decides that her daughter must die, but in the fantasy part of the story it is deepened and made mythic when the mother becomes the fabulous beast.

This is one of the potent aspects of storytelling. A traditional image, such as that of the persistent pursuer, is linked to a more contemporary figure, in this case, a distraught mother, and the mother takes on all of the emotional history of that most ancient image of the culture. It is a story of a woman's relationship with her home of birth, and the tensions attendant on this relationship.

Performance Note

Time: 19 September 1967, in the late morning. *Place:* At her home in Nkanga, Gatyana District, the Transkei. *Audience:* Seven women and two men. (Perf. 708.)

Eight young women went to dig for red ochre.[2] They traveled with a small child, a boy.

When they had gone a good distance from their home, one of the young women said to the boy, "Child, where are you going?"

He said, "I'm coming along with you, Sister. I'm going to the ochre pit, too."

"And what are you going to do in the ochre pit? You'll only get tired! It's so far to the pit."

"No, I'm coming along. I want to see the ochre pit."

They beat the child. They took a whip and beat him.

One of the young women said, "Go back!"

"You're a naughty boy!" said another.

"It's too far to the ochre pit," said a third.

The boy cried and ran off. But he turned around and hid himself as the young women walked on. They thought he had gone home.

But when they were far off, they saw the child coming again. They waited until he caught up with them.

"Where are you going, Child?"

"Didn't we tell you to go home? The place we're going to is too far."

---

2. The ochre is to be used for ritual purposes during the wedding ceremony.

"No, Sister! I want to come along. Leave me alone! I want to come along to see the ochre pit."

"I'm going to hurt you! That's what's going to happen, I warn you."

So she said. Then she began to choke him. She took her head covering and tied it around his neck and choked him; she choked that child. As he struggled and was about to die, she loosened her grip. When she saw that the eyes of the child had changed, she became fearful. The boy collapsed.

She hurriedly got some water. "Yo! What'll they do to us at home, my friends?"

She sprinkled water in his face, and the child regained consciousness. He was dazed. He did not know where he was. When he was asked something, he replied incoherently. It was clear that his mind had not yet fully returned to him. He would wander off the path with a dazed, meandering gait. If he kept going like that, he would surely fall into a ditch.

The young women tarried there, afraid of what they saw happening to the child, waiting for his mind to return to him.

They remained there and time passed; time passed for them. They called out the boy's name again and again. But when he was called, he would look back and say something that no one understood.

"Yo!"

"What'll we do about this child?"

Well, the young women stayed there—time passed, the sun set, and they had not yet gone to the ochre pit because of the strange way the child was acting. The boy had almost died. That much was clear.

The young women continued to sprinkle him with water, and they washed him.

"What shall we do about this child?"

"Let's go home."

They wanted to go home. It was already evening.

Then the boy said, "Sister! Sister, where's the ochre?"

His sister said, "No, we didn't go to the ochre pit."

"Well, why don't you go there now?"

"There's a good reason why we shouldn't go to the pit now. I almost choked you to death. I was provoked when you ignored my orders. Then you collapsed. Now we don't know what to do about you. We're afraid to go to the ochre pit."

He said, "I'm all right. I'm all right now. Go on to the ochre pit. But I'll not be left behind. I'm going to the pit, too."

The child went along then; they traveled with him. They arrived in the vicinity and slept beneath a huge tree. Now, among these eight young women was one who was going to be married, one of the two senior young women—her name was Nomanaso.

They stayed beneath that tree and slept until morning.

Babysitter

In the morning, they got up. They rose early.

One of them thought, "My mother whispered to me that Nomanaso is about to get married. In fact, this is her wedding day. What shall we do about this?"

They went to the ochre pit then and dug the ochre. When they finished, they began their journey home.

But Nomanaso had left an earring behind. When she had gone into the pit, the earring had got loose from her ear, and now it was missing.

When they had crossed a river, she discovered this and said to the others, "Eee! I left one of my earrings behind, over there at the clay pit. And that earring isn't mine. I have to return it. My friends, come back with me."

The others said, "Never!"

"We're not going to sleep away from home two nights in a row."

"We slept away from home yesterday."

"Today, we've got to get home."

"I know that I'll be scolded by my mother if I stay away from home another night."

The young woman who had lost the earring turned around. As she was doing so, the boy said, "Stop! I'll go and get it for you. You can't move fast enough."

"Child, could you possibly go so far by yourself?"

The child said, "I can go!"

So he ran—he was the one they had been choking, the one they had almost killed. The child traveled and finally arrived at the ochre pit. He found the earring, then returned to the others in a great hurry. He was dripping with perspiration when he arrived.

His sister took the earring and kissed him.

She said, "Oh, Child of my mother, the one who almost died. You have such courage!"

She kissed him on the mouth; she kissed him on both cheeks. Then she took her kerchief and covered him.

She said, "Cover up. You'll catch cold, Child of my mother."

They went on their way then and arrived at home. It was not too late for Nomanaso's marriage. There was still time. The young woman was sent to another homestead.

The people of the groom's home lay in wait for her; they had come to abduct her into marriage that day. So she was abducted and taken to her homestead by marriage.

Nomanaso remained in her homestead by marriage in great happiness. She was so happy, in fact, that she remained there a full year and did not miss her home of birth.

The second year came, and still she did not miss her home. This woman had been the fourth girl child of her mother; in age, she was in the middle of the other girls. They all got married in the end, including the last one, the one who came after her in age.

The last-born one got married too, but she did come back to her parents' home. She did miss her home of birth after a certain time. Then, having visited her parents, she returned to her home of marriage.

Much later, she again returned to her parents' home, this time coming with her child. She came with her child. She was "repeating the way"— returning to her home of birth from her home of marriage. When she got to her parents' home, a beast was slaughtered for her. It was said that the beast was slaughtered for the child who came with her because it was the child of another homestead.

That is the way things went with them. Time passed, and everyone was happy.

In time, that other woman, Nomanaso, the one who had not missed the home of her birth, got up over there at her husband's homestead, and she said to her husband and her mother-in-law and father-in-law, "I miss my home. It has now been three years since I married, and I haven't gone home yet."

It happened that this Nomanaso had recently given birth.

Her mother-in-law said, "No, my child. You're still a nursing mother!

You can't travel by yourself. Where will you get a second person, a companion, to go with you?"

The young woman said, "No, really, Mother, my child is fairly old now, so it doesn't matter too much. It's not really a problem." She was a lying-in mother, but she was already up and about.

She went on her way then, having been given permission at her husband's homestead, permission to go to the home of her birth.

It had been a long time since she had been to her home of birth. Remember, this was the beginning of the fourth year that she had been absent from her parents' home. As she journeyed, therefore, she tended to lose her way. She missed the paths that went to her home. She would hesitate. She would take one path, then she would realize that "This is not the right path to my home!" So she would turn around. She would go back and reconsider. She would look intently at the way she was traveling. Then she would walk on again.

The sun set. It happened that it set when she was in a bleak area. She was now traveling in a place where there were no homesteads at all. Not one home could be seen across the river. Or anywhere.

She saw that the sun was setting, but she knew that she had come too far to turn back, to return to her home of marriage. To get back to a village that she had already passed through, she would have to walk the entire night.

"There's nothing I can do!" she concluded. "Nothing at all! I'm in a bad situation. I give up."

She went on, confused, fearing that her child would cry. And indeed, when it felt like doing so, the child did cry. Then the woman would despair. She would take the child from her back when it cried: "He's making too much noise. He'll be heard. Something might hurt me!"

She walked on, and finally, as she journeyed on flat land, she came to a tree—just a tree, by itself. She climbed the tree—it was deep dusk now. She climbed the tree. She got to the top and broke off some branches. She arranged these branches in such a way that, if she became drowsy, she would be able to recline up there in the tree. She arranged the branches, she arranged them, then she simulated drowsiness, acting it out again and again to find out if her child might slip through the branches and fall from his place in the tree. Then she picked more twigs and arranged them, and finally the reclining place was completed. She remained there, but she was not drowsy at all: she was wide awake and afraid.

In the depths of the night, she saw two people coming toward the tree. They arrived, then sat and exchanged their news. She saw some others arrive as well. They also conversed beneath the tree. Still others came—whenever someone arrived, one of them would salute the others, he would raise his hand. Finally, the space beneath the tree was completely filled.

This created a problem for the young mother. On every side of the tree were people—men and their wives, even some girls were present. It seemed that everyone was there.

After a time, she saw her mother.

"Even Mother is here!"

The only persons who were not in this company were her father and her brother. But she saw her sisters. They were there. She trembled. She was afraid; she did not know what to do. She put her breast into the child's mouth so that he would not be able to cry out, so that he would do nothing to betray their presence up there in the tree.

They remained there, and time passed. The night went on. After a long time, someone got up. Nomanaso heard him say, "All right, Friends, Honored Assembly! We are all present now. We must get on with our business, because the first cocks will crow soon. If we don't hurry with our business, the cocks will crow."

A woman rose, and said, "Yes, you're right, Mr. Chairman. We thank you for your statement. Truly, the time has come. That is clear."

The entire gathering under that tree heaved in agreement: "Mm mm mm! Yes yes yes!"

Clearly, what had been spoken by that person was the truth.

While all that was happening below, the woman sat up in that tree, not at all sleepy, so entranced was she by the marvel that was unfolding below.

Someone said, "Let four of us go to Sibanda's place. Six of us must go to Ntloko's place."

"And we want you to bring Mbongwe tomorrow."

"Oh!"

The things to be done were enumerated, they were listed, they were noted. The things to be done by this group were discussed. Then they turned to the business of counting money. They turned to this business of counting money. For quite a long time this money was counted. Then all of it was handed over to one person. She put it in front of herself; then she counted it.

Someone said, "We must go now."

"Yes."

It was time: they were in agreement that the time had come to depart.

Then the mother of Nomanaso, this person who was hiding in the tree, got up and said, "Wait! Please wait, my friends. Stop, Friends! Please stop, my homeland. I have something that I want to say to you, something that I want to say to all of you, to all of you who are gathered here. I want some advice about a certain matter. I have a child who has been married now for four years. She follows this girl in age"—so saying, she pointed out one of her daughters who was also in that crowd—"that child, that one there. Now she has come home three times. But that other one got married; she's been married for four years. I'm suspicious of her now. I'm annoyed by her because she hasn't come home at all. Now, there's no reason for such behavior. This child has nothing against me. Really!" She sat down, having said, "I want to be advised."

One of the others said, "Is that the way it is? My countrymen, this person is inviting a statement from us."

"We've never seen this child you're speaking of."

"Does she have any way of knowing about this gathering of ours?"

Her mother answered, "She knows nothing. In fact, she has a rather dewy brain. I never quite understood her. What I wanted to do with her was this: when she got a little older, I planned to work on her, because I could see that nothing stayed with the child. But she married quickly, just as I was beginning to take counsel with these sisters regarding her. I thought that she should be included in our deliberations. She was a child of whom we talked repeatedly. We concluded that, well, she must be left alone. We don't fully understand her mind yet."

"Oh!"

When her turn came, someone else got up. She said, "There's nothing to be done about that now. The time has passed when you might have developed some ritual to cure that daughter of yours. Now that she's so old, there's nothing that can be done. She's at the stage now at which she's just not malleable anymore, even with these medicines of ours. She might do something that will cause you shame, that might even shame your in-laws. There's only one thing to do now. She must be got rid of!"

Nomanaso's mother said, "That's precisely what I want. That's it. That's just what I want. I want her to be gotten out of the way! I want her to be finished!"

"Oh!"

"How shall we do it?"

"Let it be done in this way. You asked us for our advice on this matter, and here it is: you must call the daughter home from her homestead of marriage. Say that there's going to be a ritual of some kind."

"Well," her mother said, "that won't work because her father is very close to her. He won't agree to this. I can't just say that he should call his daughter home, that there is going to be some sort of ritual. If it's something that he knows nothing about, he'll just become angry with me. I can't just suddenly produce this idea. He'll insist that we shouldn't lie about such a thing."

"Well then, what should be done?"

"I think that you should advise me about what kind of medicine I might use. One day she'll come here. This is her home, after all, and she'll return. She will come, then I'll work on her. I'll let the medicine work on her. That's what I'll do. Now, the medicine that I want is called Let-not-the-sun-go-down!"

"Oh, you want Let-not-the-sun-go-down?"

"Yes."

"Well, that's all right."

"Let's consider this carefully."

So they thought about it. They worked on the medicine then and made that Let-not-the-sun-go-down of theirs. They gave it to her, and she kept it for that daughter of hers.

When the medicine had been given to her, someone said, "Now this is what you should do when she arrives. You should be elaborate in your kindness to her. If your husband is not in a hurry to slaughter a beast for her, put pressure on him. Say that she's a child who hasn't been here at home for a long time. Then, when a beast has been slaughtered for her, this is what you should do: sprinkle the viscera of the slaughtered sheep with the medicine. But don't pour the medicine on the meat of the body. Seek out especially the stomach meat. So that you'll have time to do this, send her down to the river. Then do it well while she is gone. After that has been done, put the meat where it should be, and she'll eat it. She'll eat it because, when you're all excited about seeing each other, she'll want you all to eat together."

"Yes." So said the mother of the young woman. "Yes, it won't be any trouble to get her to go to the river because she's a very industrious girl. I won't even have to try very hard to manage this because she's a woman who never sits down. I'm sure that, even in that home where she lives now, they find her a very industrious person."

After some time, the people dispersed. They dispersed with the understanding that she should keep the medicine.

"Let's go to those other places now."

When the money had been collected, when it had been gathered and was about to be given out, the cocks crowed. This speech of the woman had delayed them. They had planned to leave earlier, but this woman's problem had turned out to be a lengthy one, and it provoked a number of responses and discussion. She herself had provided protracted explanations, and now the time was getting short.

Someone said, "Well, we'll take up this business again tomorrow, that business of going to those homesteads of Sibanda and Ntloko, because it's dawning now. Look, you can see the horns of the cattle gleaming in the first light. You can see for yourselves—the redness in the east. Let the money be gathered."

Now, the woman up there in the tree was under increasing pressure to relieve herself. She wanted to "go outside"; she had been controlling herself, but she finally could control herself no longer. When she released her controls, that thing dropped among them there—it fell down twice.

Someone said, "What's that?"

"What is it?"

"What kind of thing might this be?"

"What is it? What is this?"

"I don't understand it!"

"Is it God giving us gruel perhaps?"

Then the baby urinated, because it had been a long time without urinating. They now found drops of water falling among them.

"And what would you say this is?"

"Well, look, please, and see if there's a cloud that's causing it."

"What is it?"

"Water is falling!"

One of them got up and went away from the tree to look at the sky. He said, "Well, Friend, the sky's clear. It's clear! Even at the homestead of the in-laws of dogs!"

One of the branches that the woman had broken off fell down just then. It fell on the person who was gathering the money. They ran. They really ran, and the money was left behind.

Someone said, "It's a big thing!"

They ran because they were startled by the falling branch. They did not know what it was.

"Something has clearly seen us."

"We've covered a lot of ground. It's already dawn."

They all ran. Each hurried to her own home and spoke no more of this matter.

The mother of Nomanaso was running with a knot in her turban—and in that knot was the death of her child.

When the people had all run away, the young woman, Nomanaso, was afraid to come down from the tree. The sun rose. She was still afraid to descend. Finally, the livestock came out from the homesteads. The cattle were being taken out to be herded—and she was still wary about coming down. At mid-morning, when it was almost morning milking time and the cattle were returning to be milked, she concluded that "Well, really now, I can descend." She came down from the tree; when she got down, she collected that money, all of the money that had been left behind there. She departed with it; she departed and arrived finally at her parents' place.

When she got there, she said nothing. She did not speak of this matter at all. She arrived and was greeted by them. She looked at them fondly, and she in turn was fondly regarded by her mother.

The mother embraced her child, saying, "My child whom I have not seen for such a long time! Yo yo yo! My child! She's become a mature woman, this daughter of mine! She has become a mature woman since I last saw her, Father of Nomanaso! Have you seen my child?"

Nomanaso's father was also happy. When he saw his child, he had a genuine feeling of happiness.

"Father of Nomanaso! Something must be done to show our appreciation. Nothing is too good for this child! I wonder why my child has never come home?"

Her father said, "There's no need to discuss anything. Let someone go and get the small livestock. Make blood for my child!"

Her mother was very happy about this. Her sisters were all at their homes of marriage. They met only at night in those secret places.

A short time passed. Then the stock that the boys had gone to gather was returned. A sheep was taken. It was slaughtered for this daughter. When the slaughtering was completed, food was roasted for her, and she ate. The stomach meat was chopped up, the large tripe—the meat of the viscera and the intestine—was chopped. The tripe was prepared. Salt was sprinkled on the meat. The mother tasted it to make certain that it was well cooked. She found it well cooked: her daughter, Nomanaso, watched her mother closely out of the corner of her eye, remembering what had been said the night before, watching to see if her mother was actually going to carry out the plot. The daughter observed the mother as she tasted the meat.

She said, "Mama, is it well cooked?"

Her mother said, "Yes, my child, it is well cooked. But it doesn't have enough salt."

"Why don't you add some more, Mama?" the girl said. Then she said, "Why don't you cut a piece for me, Mama?"

Her mother reached into the pot to find a piece of meat for her child. Then the daughter, without being sent, took a bucket and said, "There's not much water here, and the weather is hot. The sun is really hot!" She spilled that water outside, then took a vessel and went to the river, leaving her baby behind with her mother.

Her mother remained behind. She quickly took the potion that she had been given over there under the tree, the potion designed to kill her child, Nomanaso. She hurriedly took the meat and put it into a ladle made from a calabash. She added the medicine to the meat. She mixed it. Then she hung the ladle up. She hastily took the pot off the hearth so that the food could be eaten.

The girl's father said, "Oh, Nobani! Why do you hurry to do this? The person we've slaughtered the beast for hasn't even returned from the river yet."

"No no no, Sobani! I put some meat aside for her." She seized the meat. "Look! Do you think that I could be so neglectful that I would fail to put some aside for her? I did save some meat for her. I did put some meat by for her." So she said; then she again hung that meat of Nomanaso's up.

When these things had taken place, Nomanaso returned. When she arrived, everyone else had already eaten. Because her mother liked her meat cold, hers was still hanging above the door, cooling. Nomanaso's meat was hanging on the upper side of the house, away from the door.

They sat outside, basking in the sun, facing the sun. The young woman went into the house and put the pail of water down. Then she went out. She went outside to her mother and the others.

She said, "Have you already eaten, Mama? Did you eat already? Has the food already been dished out?"

"Yes, we've already eaten, my child. But you know me. It's the same as it was in the old days, my child. I still don't like to eat meat when it's hot. I eat it only when it has cooled."

"Oh."

"Go in now, Little mother. Go in and get your food. There it is, on the upper side, in the ladle that's hung up there."

Nomanaso went quickly into the house. When she had gone in, she looked above the door. She looked and saw that "There's some food hanging above the door." She took it down. It was in a dish. She poured its contents into the lid of a pot. Then she took the meat that was over there in the ladle, the meat that was on the upper side of the house, and she poured that into the dish. She took that dish of meat and replaced it, putting it back where it had originally been hanging. She took water and washed the ladle; she even washed it with ashes, she washed it carefully, thoroughly: she washed it with ashes, again and again she washed the ladle—hurriedly.

Her mother asked, "Are you going to eat inside the house? Don't you want the sun?"

"All right, I'm coming out. I thought that it would be all right for me to eat here in the house. I was just washing this ladle." She made certain that she had washed the ladle well, then she poured the other meat—the meat that had been her mother's—into that ladle. She went outside with it. She ate over there with the others. While she was eating, her mother continued to glance at her child, to assure that the food was really being consumed.

Is she really eating? Oh, well, she was eating. The child was indeed eating.

So time passed. Time passed, and the mother continued to stare at the child.

Heee! Why is there no evidence that she's finished eating it? But the mother remained silent. She let it pass.

Nomanaso ate the meat. She finished it completely. Then she went into the house to put the ladle away.

Her mother said, "Please bring my meat out here. It must be cool by now."

The child, Nomanaso, said, "Where is it? I don't see it. There's no other meat here. There was only my meat."

As the young woman was saying this, the mother said, "It's above the door."

The child took it down from above the door, and said, "Oh, there it is!"

She brought the meat to her mother. She gave it to her, and the mother ate the meat that had been hanging above the door. The mother ate. She swallowed twice and hiccoughed—"Hi-ih!" She said, "Mh! What is this?"

Her daughter said, "Drink some water. How could you hiccough while eating meat? It's said that a person hiccoughs only when she craves meat. Why do you hiccough while you're eating it?"

The mother took the food again. She ate more of it. When she swallowed: "Hi-ih! Eh! Mhmm! How did I do that?" So said the mother. "How did I do that, Friends?" And she hiccoughed. She said, "Mhm! How did I do that?"

The young woman said, "What's the matter, Mama?"

"No, it's nothing. Just wait a little, my child. Please stop, just leave me alone. Mh! How did I do that? How did I do that?"

The father of Nomanaso, who also happened to be there, said, "What is it, Nobani? How did you do what?"

She said, "No, no, Sobani! Please leave me alone. How did I do that, Friends? Oh, I wonder how I did that? How did I do that?" Something came up from her stomach. She said, "Oh, I wonder how I did that?" She was dazed. She vomited. She vomited below and she vomited above. Oh, she writhed. While she retched in the most violent way, she kept saying, "How did I do that?"

Someone asked, "What's the matter?"

The young woman said, "Father, let me tell you something. My mother put some meat for me into a ladle that was on the upper side of the house. She said that it was my meat. When I went into the house, I took the meat that was above the door instead and ate that. I gave her the meat from over there, the meat that she had said she had put away for me at the upper side of the house. Now let her answer her own question, when she asks how did she do that. Let her explain it!"

"Oh, no, Friends! I wonder how I could have done that? What did I do? I must have blundered! How did I do that?"

This fellow said, "Could this woman have wanted to kill my child?"

She said, "Leave her alone, Father. Let her do what she must do. Don't weep for her. I'll tell you a story that's amazing!"

The woman went on saying, "How did I do that?" until her life ended. Finally, she died. She came to an end. When she had come to an end, she was buried. A hole was dug for her.

When she was buried, her daughter said, "Now Father, before she is buried and covered over, I think that I should tell you something about this situation, so that you'll have some knowledge of it. As I came here from my house of marriage, I went to sleep—that was on the day that I was coming here. If you happen to accompany me when I return to my home, all you'll have to do is look at the side of a certain tree, and you'll see what happened on that day. As I was coming here, the sun went down because I wasn't familiar with the path that leads to this place—after all, I had not come here for such a long time. The sun went down, and I was uncertain about the path. I was far from anywhere. There wasn't even a homestead around there. Then I climbed that tree. While I was in the tree, some people began to arrive—a few at first, then later more came, including my sister, the one who's married, and even the one who comes after me in birth was there. They arrived there with my mother, this very one we're burying today. And other people were there as well. When the topics pertaining to that gathering were raised, my mother said that she wished to be advised concerning me—the one who doesn't come home anymore. The group asked her if I had a mark. The only persons who weren't there were you and my uncle, the one who's on top here. All of the people from this area were there."

Now the girl had called her father to a place below the homestead. She was saying these things at a spot that was a safe distance away from the other people.

Nomanaso continued, "All the people here at this burial—very few of them were not present that night. When my mother had said what was on her mind, she was given a potion and told to put it into the meat. My mother was to send me off to the river. Then while I was gone she was to put the poison into the meat. I did take the bucket, giving her the opportunity to put that thing of hers into the meat, so that I could turn the situation around and, in some way, give it to her instead. As soon as I had returned from the river, she told me that my meat was on the upper side of the house. As I entered the house, I looked around and saw her meat—because I know that she doesn't eat hot meat. I took her meat and placed it into a lid; then I washed that ladle that my meat was in, took my meat and poured it into her dish. I put it back in the same place. When I told her that I hadn't seen her meat, I was only pretending. I wanted her to say clearly what she wanted to say, and I wanted her to eat it. That's the meat that she ate today. The meat that finished her off is the very meat that would have killed me."

Her father said, "Thank you very much, my child, for telling me that. The hole that's been dug for her will be refilled now. Another hole will be dug for her—far away, near the forest. She's not a person, that thing." Then he went up and said, "Refill this woman's burial hole. It was an error. She'll not be buried in this place. I'm much troubled by her. She must be buried far away."

"Oh!"

"Has this ever happened before?"

"That the mistress of the house should be buried so far from home?"

He said, "That's what I've decided. That's it."

The hole was refilled, and another was dug in a distant place. She was buried there.

After that, preparations were made for Nomanaso's return to her home of marriage. Everything involved in the return journey was brought to her—beautiful things had been prepared for her, the same thing that is done for every child who goes home to her husband after her first visit to the home of her parents. She journeyed then, and her father went along with her, so that he might see the place where the tree stood. He got there, and truly he saw the branch that she had plucked from the tree, the branch that had fallen. He also saw that she had indeed relieved herself—all those were evident, all the things that his daughter had mentioned. He saw a heavily trodden place and realized that, truly, this was a place where people had congregated and sat. He confirmed that his daughter had spoken the truth. He accompanied her a little farther, then went back to his home.

When the daughter was not very far from her home of marriage, something that looked like a dish appeared—it was coming toward her from the front. Her father had long since disappeared. This thing came to her—a dish that arrived in front of Nomanaso. She was surprised as the dish came with its back toward her.

"What kind of dish is this?"

It arrived, and this thing said,

> "Hello, Nomanaso!
> Hello, my daughter!
> *Krwebede!*
> Oh, really!"

The child stood there. She was quiet. Then this thing that had been a dish was transformed—it became a head! And this head—Nomanaso immediately recognized it as the head of her mother. It was her mother!

The thing said, "I say,

> Hello, Nomanaso!
> My daughter!
> *Krwebede!*
> Really!"

The child answered, "What is this 'krwebede'?"

The head repeated,

> *"Krwebede! Krwebede!*
> Nomanaso!
> *Krwebede!*
> My daughter!"

The child did not know what she was supposed to do. She took the dish that was on top of the load that she was carrying, and she threw it to the head.

The head ate the dish. It smashed the dish, then swallowed it.

Meanwhile, Nomanaso hurried on her way. But again, she saw that thing, already in front of her.

It said, "I said,

> Hello, Nomanaso,
> My daughter!
> *Krwebede*, then,
> Really!"

"What should I *krwebede*?"

"I say,

> *Krwebede,*
> Nomanaso!"

Again, the child threw something—she threw loaves of bread this time, bread that she was carrying. This thing ate the loaves.

The daughter traveled on a short distance, but again the head was in front of her.

It said,

> *"Krwebede!*
> *Krwebede!"*

Nomanaso threw a mat that she was carrying, realizing that, "Well, this thing is coming after me. There's nothing else I can do."

It ate the mat and finished it.

Nomanaso traveled on for a very short time, and this thing again came around to the front of her.

It said,

> *"Krwebede,*
> Nomanaso!
> *Krwebede,*
> My daughter!"

The child threw something again—this time, she threw the large cape that she was wearing.

It ate the cape and swallowed it.

Nomanaso traveled on for a short time, and again the head went around to the front.

And this thing said, *"Krwebede!"*

Again, Nomanaso threw something—this time, she took her long cotton skirt, and she threw that.

The head ate it and finished it.

The girl traveled for a short time, and again this thing went around to the front, and said,

> *"Krwebede!*
> *Krwebede,*
> Nomanaso!"

"Oh!" Because all of her things were gone, this child saw that "I don't know what I should do now!" She was left with only a short skirt, an underskirt. She took that and threw it to this thing.

The head took the skirt and ate it.

The young woman moved on. A short time later, that thing went around to the front of her.

It said, "I said,

> *Krwebede,*
> Nomanaso,
> My daughter!"

"Oh, what shall I do now? Everything's gone!"

The thing said, "I said,

> *Krwebede,*
> Nomanaso!"

Nomanaso threw her own child's eating dish. The head ate the child's dish and finished it. (The child's dish was a calabash that had been punctured, and the child ate from it.)

The beast ate it and finished it.

Nomanaso traveled on. After a while, the head went around to the front of her, and said, "I said,

> *Krwebede,*
> Nomanaso,
> My child!"

"I wonder what I should *krwebede?*" She threw the child's cotton blanket, then carried the child who now had no covering.

The thing ate the child's blanket, and the young woman moved on a little distance.

Again, the head went around to the front and said, *"Krwebede!"*

No progress was being made because it was only a very short distance that she could walk before she was again intercepted, before she was again aware that the head was in front of her.

"What will I *krwebede?*"

"No,

> *Krwebede,*
> Nomanaso!
> *Krwebede,*
> My daughter!"

The woman took the covering from her head and gave that to the beast.

It ate the kerchief, and Nomanaso went on her way. The head went around to the front, and said,

> *"Krwebede,*
> Nomanaso!
> *Krwebede,*
> My daughter!"

Nomanaso tore an arm off of her child and threw the arm to that thing. The child cried out. The young mother went on her way, and the head ate the arm of her child.

The head went around to the front again, and said,

> *"Krwebede,*
> Nomanaso,
> My child!"

So the woman *krwebede*-ed and tore off the other arm of the child. The child was left with a head and legs. He was covered with blood, red with blood. And they were both crying—the mother was crying, and so was the child, the child whose arms had been torn off.

The thing ate the child's arm, and the young woman went on a short distance.

This thing again cut across in front of her and said, "I said,

> *Krwebede,*
> Nomanaso!

> *Krwebede,*
> My child!"

"Oh, what will I *krwebede?*"
It said, "I said,

> *Krwebede,*
> Truly!
> *Krwebede,*
> Now!"

The mother ripped off the leg of her child and threw it. The head ate the leg, and the mother traveled on for a brief time.

Again, it cut across in front of her and said, "I said,

> *Krwebede,*
> Nomanaso!
> *Krwebede,*
> My child!"

The young mother saw that there was nothing more that could be done. She tore off the child's other leg and threw it. The thing ate the second leg, and the child was left with only stomach and head. Nomanaso walked on with the child, and that child continued to cry because the time of its death had not yet come. He was being torn apart alive. Both of them—mother and child—cried; both were wailing. The head ate the leg, then again passed to the front of them.

It said, "I said,

> *Krwebede,*
> Nomanaso!
> *Krwebede,*
> My daughter!"

Then the mother twisted the neck of her child. She tore off his head. She seized the head—then could not decide whether to throw the body first, or the head. She took the head and wanted to throw the body. Then she stopped. She was about to throw the head instead. But she stopped and was going to throw the body and leave the head. She could not decide. In the end, she threw the body and kept the head. The thing ate the body of her child, and the mother went on her way.

In a short time, the thing went around to the front. It said,

"*Krwebede,*
Krwebede,
My daughter!"

She threw her child—what remained of her child. She threw that head, and that thing ate the head.

And the mother traveled on, despairing now, no longer having in her the strength necessary for her journey, no longer moving purposefully.

Again, the head came around to the front, and the thing said,

"*Krwebede,*
Nomanaso,
My daughter!"

She looked at herself. "What should I take from myself? I have nothing!"

She tore off the jewelry from her throat, jewelry for medicinal purposes, and she threw that.

The head ate the jewels, and Nomanaso traveled on.

While she was still traveling, and when the thing had again come around, suddenly a large number of chiefs appeared. They were coming from a mourning ceremony and were riding on horses.

The head vanished. It stopped, then disappeared, traveling on its neck.

By the time those horses got to the mother, she was standing naked, red with blood—all over. She was covered with blood because, when she had torn off the arm of the child, the blood had splashed all over her, even in her face. Everywhere. And when she had pulled off the second arm, the blood again splashed all over her. Everywhere. She was a fright, red all over because of the blood. And she was crying.

The horses stopped, and the chiefs asked her, "What's the matter? Are you a person, or what?"

She said, "Father, I am a person! The thing is, I've been attacked by something that I don't know."

"What kind of thing, Daughter?"

The child explained, "I was coming from the home of my birth. Suddenly a thing that seemed to be the back of a dish came upon me. Then, when it came to the front of me, it changed—it became the head of my mother!"

"Where is your mother?"

"She's dead."

"When did she die?"

"She died a couple of weeks ago."

"Then what happened? Wasn't she buried?"

"She was buried. The thing is, this head—it was my mother, definitely.

Even the voice was hers. But it travels on its neck. It's not a person. And I don't know where it puts all the things that it eats. I didn't see any stomach. When you arrived, it was just at the point of saying to me, 'Krwebede!' and I had just broken off my ornaments."

Yo! The people who were mounted departed on their horses in a hurry. They searched for this thing. But it was not to be found. Nomanaso pointed out the direction in which it had gone. But they did not see it, even though she tried to show them where it had gone.

Now they asked the young woman, "How far is it to this home of yours?"

The child explained, "It's still very far to my homestead of marriage because I'm coming from my home of birth."

Those people traveled with her. One man took a share of the burden and carried it for that woman because she was naked. She had nothing. Another man took his ornamental crest of feathers and put it on her head.

They traveled then. They went to her homestead by marriage. They arrived and told the part of the story that had to do with their meeting with this child. When they had explained as much as they could of the matter, they were thanked warmly by that gentleman for being so generous to his daughter-in-law, for breaking their own journey when they saw what had happened to a human being.

"It doesn't matter that the baby has disappeared, so long as our child is here, so long as this one whom we know has escaped. As for that other one, the baby, we didn't know its potential."

Tale 23

THE TREE THAT COULD NOT BE GRASPED

Masithathu Zenani's Analysis: In the process of undergoing a transformation, the central character moves into fantasy where the real world is reordered; there, this character encounters a form of evil that she cannot by herself overcome. She requires helpers, who may be realistic but are more often fantastic creatures or objects. Because of their unique qualities, their fantastic abilities, they bestride the worlds of fantasy and reality. It is a betwixt and between setting. These transitional characters and devices make possible the movement of the central character—almost always realistic, vulnerable, and often the least likely to achieve heroic status—from the one realm to the other. They also make possible the victory of the central character over the evil force or being, which is often at the very end of the central character's journey. The essence of the journey involves a movement into fantasy, where something recognizable, in this case womanhood, is achieved. The central character must learn how to behave in the nether world, or she will be ruined by the evil force. The helpers often show the central character the way and train her.

Patterns interact in this story, the theme having to do with the pattern of the bird in part one and of the bird in part two.

In part one, Mityi's harmony with nature and with her ancestral past is established in the scenes in which a bird assists her. The pattern of assistance by the bird that makes her human life happier is an imaged assertion of this harmony. The fabulous bird makes it possible for Mityi to attend the contests, more beautiful than anyone else, and to succeed in each. The other pattern in this first part is a polar pattern involving the attempt of the stepmother and stepsister to destroy Mityi.

Mityi's harmony with nature and culture, and the disharmony of her stepmother and stepsister are developed in part two of the tale. They kill her, a bird emerges from her head and informs her husband. Again, the bird intervenes and saves her. The first pattern relentlessly continues: the bird flies from Mityi's head, and in effect becomes Mityi, informing the husband of what has happened and then transforming back into Mityi with the help of her husband's love.[3]

The bird, the helper in this story, connects Mityi to her ancestral past and becomes the means whereby she overcomes those forces that would interfere with her movement to womanhood.

---

3. This story becomes the kernel for a grandly imagined epic performed later by Mrs. Zenani. The character of Mityi also appears in Tale 15, "A Poor Girl Marries a King."

"She was loved by this man." The body becomes a dance, purveyor of joy.

Performance Note

Time: 15 September 1967, in the afternoon. *Place:* Along a path in Gatyana District, the Transkei. *Audience:* Five women, two men, and fifteen children. (Perf. 654.)

A certain man had two wives, an older wife and a younger. The younger wife became his favorite. She was loved by this man. In time, she bore a child, a girl, and she did not conceive again.

The younger wife did not conceive again. But the great wife had many children, among whom were two girls. They were older than the younger wife's daughter.

Time passed, and the two wives continued to live with this husband of theirs. The man lived in the house of the younger wife, the one with only one child. He stayed in that house, loving this child very much, dressing her in fine clothes, doing all kinds of things for her. He also adorned her mother in beautiful clothes.

That is the way it was when the mother of this child became ill. This younger wife was very ill. No matter what her husband did for her, she remained gravely ill. Her sickness worsened, and finally she died.

So it was that this child, who was still very young, lost her mother.

The child grew up, and the husband left that house when his wife died. He went to stay now in the great house. He lived in the great house. It became clear that he now loved this senior wife, the great wife, because she was the only wife he had. As for that child—those things that she had become accustomed to eating while her mother was alive, they were all gone now.

Time passed for this child: she now ate only after the others had eaten. The others would eat first, and only when they were finished, only when they were satisfied, when they were sated, only then was she given food. And if the other children left no food, then this child did not eat at all. She became thin. She grew up. That was natural. But she was a thin child. She was made to herd the cattle, and she did what she had to do. She was the one who cooked the food. She herded the cattle. She would be out on the veld with the herd; then she would have to return to the homestead to cook. She was expected to be in both places at the same time, and she would have to hurry back and forth. She would leave the livestock near the house, then turn her attention to the cooking. If the food was not cooked in time, she would be beaten. If the cattle were not all together— and that included the sheep, which grazed in another area—she would be beaten. She was beaten by her father. She was beaten by that senior mother of hers. She was responsible to both of them: she was responsible to her father for the cattle, to the senior mother for the cooking.

Time passed for this child, and she was always sorrowful, always experiencing pain. Time passed for the child.

Things went along in that way. Then one day the child wandered off. She walked and walked. She walked until she came to a spot just above her mother's grave. She remained above that grave and cried.

While she was crying, a voice was heard coming from the grave: "Be silent, my child. Do not cry so much. You'll make me rest badly. I'm going to the sea now because if I stay here you'll be coming to me all the time. Tomorrow, go over there, below the field. Meet me there."

She departed, and the child was quiet. She was silent. She did not cry. She was surprised by this person whose voice was so like that of her mother. She had been separated a long time from her mother, and she did not cry now—she was quiet. She went home.

The next day, at dawn, she went out to herd. She remembered the appointment that had been made by her mother. She went beyond the fields and came to a deep pool in a river there. Her mother appeared in that pool, in the water.

The mother appeared and said, "You see, my child, I'm going to be fished out of here and eaten. I'm a fish now. Please do not cry. Do what I tell you to do. I shall be eaten over there in that homestead. You must pick up these bones of mine after I have been eaten. Don't you eat them. Don't you eat my bones. Don't eat these bones of mine, do you understand? And when you have picked the bones up, put them into a bottle. Put them into a bottle. Don't eat them. Leave the bottle behind, right there in that homestead."

The child agreed to do that. Then her mother gave her something to eat. The child ate—food that was good, the things that she had customarily eaten in the past. She ate and was satisfied. When she had had enough food, the child departed; she went home with the livestock. She arrived at home, but did not say anything about this matter. She was scolded because she was late in preparing the food. Because she had gone over there to see her mother, the cooking was delayed. She was threatened, slapped in the face. She cried and wiped her tears.

Time passed for her, time passed, and the next day she journeyed. She drove the livestock to the place mentioned by her mother, and she saw that some people were eating over there.

Then she remembered: "Mama's being eaten over there."

She went to that place and was given some of the meat. She took the meat and kept it.

Someone said, "Eat, Girl!"

"No," she said. "I'll eat it later."

They continued to throw the meat to her, they threw the bones as well, and she picked them up.

"Eat the meat off the bones, Girl!"

"I'll do that later."

She was carrying a bottle. She put the bones into the bottle, then left the bottle behind. She went on her way. When she was out of sight of this homestead, she threw the meat away. She walked on. She returned to the livestock; she turned the cattle around and went home with them. She arrived. She cooked. She did everything here. She put things right—there was nothing she did not do.

Then, the next day at dawn, there was a tree in that homestead!

It was a tall tree, the end of which could not be seen!

No one could put his hands on that tree. Whenever a man approached it, whenever he tried to put his hands on it, the tree refused to be grasped. The hand could not remain on the tree.

"Heee! What kind of tree is this that has appeared so suddenly this morning? How did this tree get here?"

The tree had sprung up at the very place where the child had put the bottle, and the bottle had disappeared.

There was only the tree.

"What kind of tree is it?"

The owner of this house, an important fellow who had no wife, said, "This is an astonishing tree! I must gather all the people together. They can try to lay hands on the tree. If it is grasped by a boy, I'll make his father rich. If it is grasped by a girl, I shall marry her. She shall be my wife."

That was done then. Word went out to the people. They were told that, no matter who they were, they were wanted there. There was to be a contest, open to everyone, to every child, every old person.

So they went. All the people assembled over there. But this child was left behind. She did not go along. She was left behind as usual. She went out; she herded the livestock.

When she had gone to the veld to herd, a bird suddenly appeared.

The bird said to her, "Why are you sitting here, when everyone else has gone to the contest? You're the only person who can succeed in that contest. Go! There's a tree now in that place where you put the bottle. It's a tree that cannot be grasped. You must also go. You must lay hands on this tree. Here you are. Here are some clothes."

The child stared. "But this is just a bird!"

Well, the bird threw the clothes to the child. The child took them. She washed herself. She washed and washed. Then she put the clothes on. She walked. She went to that homestead. She arrived, and the place was full of people—it was full! And they were all attempting to take hold of the tree that would not be grasped.

Finally, it was time for the girls to lay hands on the tree. The others had finished; the boys had finished, and so had the women and the men. Now the girls must attempt to grasp the tree. So they all tried. All of the girls attempted to do it, but there was not one girl who succeeded.

Finally, this child tried it. When she arrived in that homestead, she was not known. She was not recognized, even by the people of her own home. They did not know her at all. She was a wonder of a girl, beautiful, and it was not known where she had come from. She had never before been seen.

She went to the tree. When she got to the tree, she succeeded in putting her hands on it. To her, the tree was graspable. It yielded to her, and she kept her hands on it.

Then someone said, "All right!"

Someone else asked, "Where are you from?"

She said, "I come from the west."

"You come from the west?"

"Yes."

"And who told you that a contest was taking place here?"

"Well, I just happened to be walking by. I didn't come here especially to take part in a contest. It's just that I saw the people here, and I was curious. I thought I'd come over and see what was going on. When I got here, I found that this contest was being held. But that wasn't the reason for my coming here. I was merely passing by, that's all. I was on my way to another place."

"Please tell me your name, my girl."

She said, "No, I don't give my name to anyone when I'm traveling."

He left the girl alone then and departed. The contest was at an end. The people dispersed.

The girl went home.

She cooked the food. She had taken off the clothes and put on her own ragged things. She had also turned the cattle of this home around.

The others arrived, returning from the contest.

"Yo! You really missed it, Ragamuffin. But then, you'll never see a thing like that. Ever."

"All you know is the food that sticks to the bottom of the pot."

"You don't know anything!"

She was quiet. She was silent. She did not say a thing about what had occurred. And time passed.

The next day, a messenger came and announced that another contest would be held: "It is the ring ceremony today. Everyone must come. If the ring fits a boy, he'll become wealthy. If it fits a man, he'll become wealthy. If it fits a woman, she'll become wealthy. And if it fits a girl, she'll be married. She'll become his wife."

The people went then, falling all over each other to get there. They went to the ring ceremony in great numbers.

She was left behind again, walking, taking the cattle out, taking them to the pasture. She arrived over there in the pasture, and when she got there, that same bird came along.

"You don't know what's good for you! You spend your time with these cattle, but the game over there is for you. No one will be able to do that thing except you. Go! Go to the contest."

The bird threw the clothes to her; she took them. She washed herself; she washed and washed. Then she put the clothes on.

This time, she approached the contest from the other side. She appeared on the side from which she had departed that previous day: she went in that direction, and now she was returning from that direction. When she got there, the place was full of people.

Just as she arrived, someone was announcing, "It's the girls' turn."

The others had already finished. The girls' turn was just beginning. All the girls tried, but the ring did not fit their fingers. Whenever the ring did fit on one of the girls' fingers, it was too loose. And when the ring did not fit, it would get stuck, and the finger just would not slide into the ring. That is the way it was—sometimes the ring was too loose, sometimes it got stuck and would not go on.

Then this girl tried also. She went there, and the ring did fit her. It fit her very well.

"Where are you from?"

"I have come from over there, in the west."

"Yo! You resemble a girl who said she was going in that direction just the other day, when another contest was being held here. Aren't you the same person?"

"No, I'm not the same person. I've never been here before."

"Where are you going now?"

"Well, I'm going to a certain place. I didn't come here for this game. I didn't even know it was going on. I saw these people, and thought I'd pass by to see what was going on."

"What is your name, my girl?"

"I don't give my name to anyone while I'm traveling. I don't want my name to be written down when I travel."

They left her alone, and she departed.

This was repeated. The next day, there was yet another contest. This time, there was a shoe. This shoe had to fit someone. If it fit a young man, he would become rich; if it fit a married woman, she would become rich. If it fit a man, he would become rich. And if it fit an unmarried woman, she would become the wife in this home.

They all assembled then, and all tried But the shoe would not go on their feet. It would not fit some people's feet at all. It did fit other people's feet, but not really—it was too loose.

Then the young women of this home, the ones who were the sisters of this child, cut their feet. They sliced the flesh off with a knife, trying to get their feet to accommodate the shoe. But it still would not fit, even after all that effort. So they gave up. But their feet had been cut. That is the way they went home. They despaired of getting the shoe on their feet.

But before they went home, this girl arrived. Her bird had come to her again, and she had again put the clothes on. She arrived. She came from that same side on which she had disappeared the previous day.

"Oh, you come too, my girl."

She went there—and the shoe fit. It went on her foot. It was hers. It was her size.

"Oh, my girl, your name!"

"My name is Mityi."

"And whose daughter are you?"

"My father is here, at this homestead."

"Where is he?"

"He is here, at this homestead."

"Precisely where is your father?"

The child pointed. She said, "Do you see that man over there? That is my father. My sisters are the ones who were cutting the flesh from their feet."

"All right then, my girl. I'm going to leave you alone now. How will we manage this? Because now you are to be my wife!"

"You must work through the proper marriage channels. You have indeed found your wife."

He took the shoe from her foot and put it in a certain place. Then the girl departed. She went back to her cattle. She turned the cattle around hurriedly and went home. When she got home, she cooked the food. Then the others returned.

They returned, telling of what had happened, limping because they had cut their feet. They told about the contest that they had witnessed over there.

"And you, Fool, you'll never see anything!"

"You're a mere ragamuffin!"

"All you're good for is to stay around here. That's all you can do."

But the child did not really care.

Time passed for her, and she did not concern herself about that matter. She did not even think about it.

But it happened that her husband arrived, saying that he wanted his wife, that he had come to court a wife here at this homestead. He was seeking his wife.

The other women were called. They were told to come at once.

"Here's a suitor, saying that his prospective wife is among you."

But he said, "No, she is not among these."

All of the girls of the homestead, those who were favored, were called. The ragamuffin was not among them, however; she had gone off to herd the cattle.

He said, "No, she is not here yet. Please call that ragamuffin too. After all, is she not a person? That one, out there!"

"No, that's nothing!"

"It's just a dirty little thing who does the herding."

"Well, let her come here too!"

She came.

"Oh! Oh! How can you do that?"

"How can you ask a thing like that to come?"

The girl approached.

When she arrived, he said to her, "This one is my wife. Now I will provide a dowry."

He provided a dowry right there: twenty oxen. Then he departed with his wife, that ragamuffin, just as she was.

Someone said, "Don't go off with her now. We'll prepare her for you, so that she can go properly."

"So that she'll be beautiful."

"And well clothed."

He said, "No, I want her the way she is. I don't want her with beautiful clothing."

He departed with her, and when he arrived with her at his home, he washed her. He scrubbed the dirty scales off. He dressed her properly—as anyone would do for his wife. Because she was his wife, she did no work. She was the wife of an eminent man, and therefore had servants to do the cooking and so on. She reclined. She relaxed. She did not do a thing. She was very beautiful and healthy.

After a long time, one of her sisters said, "I'm going to take a little time off, and go and visit that sister of mine over there." The sister who was speaking was one of those who had cut their feet.

She went. She went over there to her sister's place.

She arrived: "Oh! Hello, Sisi!"[4]

"Yes, hello."

She called her "Sisi" now—even though the married sister was a child compared to her.

"Hello, Sisi!"

"Yes, hello."

"Oh! Eheee!"

"Where have you come from, Child of my father?"

"Yo yo yo yo!" This sister was being very nice. "I have come from home!"

"Yes."

"And I've come to you, my friend. I want to find out if there is a job for a charwoman available in this wealthy house. I'd like to have such a job—in the garden, anywhere. Yes, I'm impoverished. I'm really impoverished now."

"Well, all right. If you want to be a charwoman, I suppose that'll be all right. Your brother-in-law can tell you what you should do."

That brother-in-law of hers, who had been outside, came in now. He was pleased that his sister-in-law had come.

"Where have you come from?"

"I've come from home. I've come to see you, my brother-in-law."

"Yes. Well, I see you."

"I also want a job. I want to find out if I can get a job, doing the scrubbing. I go naked!"

"Yo! Sister-in-law, how can you work as a servant at your own sister's place?"

"No no, Brother-in-law! I'm willing to work at my sister's place because, really, I don't just want to join you in your easy living. I'm not asking for that. I'll work!"

"Well then, all right, Sister-in-law. My wife will show you the place in the garden where you can work. You can start in the morning."

---

4. *Sisi* is a term of respect, meaning "sister," usually employed by a younger sister when addressing an older sister.

Time passed then, and many kind things were done for this sister. Sheep were slaughtered for her, and the brother-in-law was generous to her in many ways. He even purchased for her things that she lacked. He clothed her, and she was invited to stay as long as she wished.

So she did remain there, writing occasionally to her home. When she wrote, she noted, "I'm happy here at my sister's place. I got a job as charwoman. I won't be returning home."

She was even able to send some money to her father—because her father and the others had fallen onto hard times. They were needy people now. Occasionally, she sent them trousers, hand-me-downs from her brother-in-law; these were sent to her father and the others. Things were going very well for this sister.

Then one day, an evil thought possessed this sister. Her brother-in-law was not there at the time.

She said, "Hee, Friend! Why don't I just take a little trip to my home?"
The other said, "Why not?"
"Now, if I go home, will that affect my wages?"
The other said, "No, really. It will have no effect on your wages because after all you're working for your own people."
"Well then, I'll take a little trip, Child of my father. Really, I do miss them."

She was given leave to go, and she took with her some elegant gifts for her parents.

She journeyed and came to arrive at her home. She said, "Yo! That one is doing very well! I have never seen such a wealthy homestead. I tell you, Mama, that child does not work at all over there. She just sits around, Father. You would really be awed if you were to go to Mityi's homestead. That place has everything. Everything! That homestead has wagons. She has servants—they cook for her. She doesn't cook, she doesn't hoe, she doesn't cultivate. She just sits around! Those two just massage each other all the time, she and her husband. They just look every so often to see how things are going. You'd be filled with envy."

Her mother said, "All right, sit down. You won't go back there again. She must come here. This will work out all right in time."

Time passed, and the sister did not return. She did not return: "What's the matter? Why is my sister not coming back?"

Her husband said, "I don't know."

"Now that I think of it, I did want to go and visit them anyway. Really."

Her husband said, "Whom will you travel with?"

"I'll have to go with two people."

"All right, Why don't you ride? We'll span one of the wagons, and you can take that."

She said, "All right."

She climbed on, having prepared herself for the journey. She brought provisions along for her mothers and fathers. Then she climbed on. The wagon was driven by two men. They finally arrived at that homestead.

Before she was able even to get off the wagon, members of her family were hurrying out to meet her. They helped her get down from the wagon. They admired her, waited on her. I tell you, they waited on her in every way, as if she might fall down and break. They outdid themselves. They fawned on her: "Yo yo yo! This big! She's grown so big!"

"She's so beautiful!"

Time passed, and she remained with them. She slept. Then she said that she wanted to return to her home of marriage on the next day.

On that day, her mother said, "Please come here. Let me delouse you. Don't you have any lice on your head?"

The other said, "No, I don't have any!"

"My child, I miss doing that. I miss crushing lice on your head. I'll feel better if you let me do that. Please lie down."

She reclined then, putting her head on her mother's lap. The mother massaged her with her hands, here on her head. As she massaged the young woman's head, she took out a needle—a sharp pin. She slid that pin into the young woman's brain. She pushed it in so that it disappeared.

The young woman died.

A bird came out of her head as she died, and this bird flew away.

The young woman was dead—this bird fluttered about; the bird was her life. The bird flew off. It went to her homestead of marriage. It arrived at that homestead. It entered the garden. It perched on a tree in the garden. It happened that the husband was there in the garden.

The bird cried out, it cried out. It flew around, it flew around the man.

He said, "Now what kind of bird is this? It keeps flying to me!" He repeatedly waved it off when it perched on his shoulder.

He said, "What's the matter with this bird?"

The bird would climb on his head, then fly off; it would fly to him again, and then it would fly off to the house. When it had gone inside, it would perch on the upper side of the house. Then it would fly over and perch on the door.

He said, "This bird seems to be trying to tell me something. I wonder what kind of bird it is."

The bird flew off again, and time passed. People slept.

Then a letter arrived: his wife had died suddenly at her home of birth. They had not yet discovered what she had died of. They did not know what caused her death. She had not complained of any pain. As for the men who had traveled with her, she was already dead when they saw her.

People were saying, "Yo yo yo! What was the matter with her?"

"We thought that she was just resting in the sun," the men said. They had been talking with some other men at the time and were amazed at what had occurred.

The husband went with a group of men to the home of his wife; he went to learn about the strange thing that had happened to his wife.

And the wife was buried.

Time passed, and the husband suffered deeply. He went home, and the wagons were also brought home. Those men who had accompanied his wife came home too. Time passed at that homestead. Time passed.

He thought and thought: "Now this bird, this bird is a wonder."

The bird was now in the habit of sitting on him. It would perch on him even when he was sitting outside. It would come to him and cry out, cry out. And it would then perch on him. It would sit on him. It would perch on his hand. Finally, he seized it one day, and when he had done so, he examined it carefully. He examined it; he looked closely at its head. He continued to examine it here on its head. He blew gently on its head, and he saw the pin.

He drew the pin out—and when he had done so, the bird was transformed. It was his wife!

He said, "What's this?"

The other one said, "I don't know what happened. My great mother pounded a needle into my head. She said to me, 'Come here, I want to delouse you.' I said, 'But I have no lice.' She said that she missed me, that she just wanted to massage my head a little. So I gave in, and reclined, thinking that I'd humor her. She massaged my head, and then I felt the needle sinking in. And I lost consciousness."

"All right," he said. "I'm not going tell those people over there at your home what has happened. I'm not going to tell them that you're alive, that you've risen from the dead. What I'll do is this: I'll call your sister, the one who was working here. She wants to be my wife. I'll call her. Now you must let me carry out my plan. Let me hide you in a safe place. You'll have to stay there for a short time—say, for two weeks."

The woman agreed, and he took her and put her in that place.

Then he called his sister-in-law at her place. The sister-in-law reacted very favorably to the plan, and she went to him immediately.

He said, "My sister-in-law, now I'm alone. Why do you do this to me? You know that I'm alone now. I'm even more alone because you do not come to me. I have no one now."

"Mm. Well, all right, Brother-in-law. I was already on my way to you."

She stayed with him then. Yo! She was happy! He treated her well, and she became healthy. She regained the plumpness that she had when she was a charwoman there.

That is the way it was.

Then the man ordered some servants to chop firewood; they should chop it from a mimosa thorn tree.

The young men cut the firewood from the mimosa thorn tree.

He told them to kindle a large fire, a fire that fit into his plans. This woman must not be killed: she must die on her own. She would be suspended above this huge fire, a fire kindled from the wood of a mimosa thorn tree, and, when the time came for her to die, she would die on her own.

A great fire was kindled then, made of the wood of the mimosa thorn tree. The husband built this great fire.

Then the woman was tied up, and, when she had been undressed, when she was naked, she was suspended above the fire. She hung above the flames. She turned red, she screamed. She screamed, she screamed.

Finally, the screaming stopped.

She was dead.

When she had died, her flesh was roasted. She was cooked. Her flesh became dry and hard. She was red, well-cooked. Her body was taken down. The entrails were removed and thrown away. The liver and kidney remained. These were placed in order. They were arranged in an orderly way. Then they were covered, and the flesh of the sister was cut into very fine pieces. That was then baked. It was cooked; it was finely chopped and placed in a container. Only the head and feet and hands remained. These were left behind. The other things were prepared.

The wind was sent for, and the things were put on the ground.

"Wind, take these to the home of my wife. I'm giving them this meat—a gift to the people who, when my wife was gracious enough to come and visit them, pounded a pin into her head."

The wind traveled; it arrived and put the meat down.

It said, "Here's some meat that you've been given. It's a gift from the husband of your daughter. He asked me to bring this meat."

They said, "Please thank him for us. Thank you very much, Sir."

"You've really helped us!"

The packet was opened; the meat was seen—but not the hands and feet.

After a time, the husband surmised that "By now, they must have finished eating the meat that we sent them."

So he sent the head now, together with the hands and feet. These were tied up and sent to them.

He said, "Take this, Wind. And say to them, 'There's the head. Those are the last pieces of meat that we're giving to you.' "

The wind traveled; it arrived and put the meat down.

Then it said, "There's the meat that has been given to you by your son-in-law. He says it's the last of the meat that he's giving to you."

There at the in-laws' place, as soon as this packet was opened up and that meat was seen: "All this time, we have been eating—our child!"

"Yo yo yo! What will be done?"

They cried. They lamented in loud voices. But they were helpless. They could do nothing. Those pieces of meat—the head, the legs, hands—these were thrown away.

Then the wife came out of her hiding place. When all of these things had been done, she returned. Her husband told her everything that had occurred. He told his wife that "I have paid them back in kind. I paid them back for what they did to you when you visited them—after I had helped them so much. I did good things for them, provided them a dowry, even though they treated you shabbily in the past. But they continued to treat you that way, then went so far as to kill you. They put a pin into your head. I have paid them back in kind. They have eaten their child, their favorite child."

Tale 24

THE BARREN WOMAN

Masithathu Zenani's Analysis: This story could, perhaps, only be told by a doctor. It is a tale that has to do with a husband's proper relations with his wife, but also a man's correct behavior before a medical doctor. Mrs. Zenani clearly has in mind the latter theme here. She builds the story around barrenness, a common theme in her tales, and around the consequent straining of relations between the husband and his wife. But the pattern of the story is, as always, the key, and it has to do with the repeated trips to an increasingly frustrated doctor. Taking the place of fantasy in this tale is the unique ability of the doctor, her insights and her remedies. The husband takes the role of villain, his wife the victim. It is the doctor who sets things right, providing the medicine that gives fertility to the woman, providing the lecture that brings the man into harmony with his culture.

Performance Note

Time: 19 September 1967, mid-morning. *Place:* In a home in Nkanga, Gatyana District, the Transkei. *Audience:* Another woman. (Perf. 701.)

In a story, a woman and a man.

It happened that the woman could not become pregnant; she could not bear children at all. The woman and her husband remained together a long time, and during that period the wife remained barren.

The man waited a long time for his wife to become pregnant, but it did not happen. Finally, he determined to marry another woman and drive this present wife away. She would amount to nothing at this home because of her inability to become pregnant. After all, when he had produced cattle for her dowry, his intention had been to get a child.

In sorrow, his wife returned to her home. Perhaps she could be sent to a doctor who might devise some medicines to cure her. When her father heard his daughter's sad story, he took her to such a doctor. As they walked along, that father carried a spear, nothing else.

When they arrived, he said to the doctor, "I've brought this child of mine to you. Please examine her, and see if you can find out what's wrong."

The doctor said, "Come here, Woman. Let me look at you."

The young woman went to her, and the doctor touched her. She touched the woman: she touched her head, she touched her on the breast, she touched her on the waist, she touched her at the bottom of her stomach.

Then she said, "Now go and sit over there, Woman."

The woman got up and went over there and sat down.

473

Visiting

The doctor spoke: "Well, this person is indeed unhealthy. The problem is her stomach. Her womb needs to be dehydrated."

The father said, "I understand. Will you attempt this dehydration?"

The doctor said, "I do not know if it will work. I have tried it with others—sometimes it is successful, sometimes it is not. I can try."

The father's decision was, "I'll leave her here with you. Please try to cure her."

His child was left at the doctor's place, and the doctor worked on her with various medicines. She treated the young wife in her customary manner, doing the things that she usually did, the kinds of things she would do to anyone she was treating.

Finally, she said, "Now go home, Woman. And take these medicines with you. Use them as I have prescribed."

The woman went home, and, when she got there, she told her father, "The doctor told me to take these medicines."

Her father said, "All right, my child. Go home now. You can take these medicines in your homestead."

The wife headed to her homestead by marriage. When she got there, she took the medicines as her doctor had prescribed. Then, when a month had gone by, she discovered that she did not do the thing that she normally did. And it happened the next month, before she was visibly pregnant: a second month went by, and again she found that she was not doing the thing that she normally did. It turns out that the woman did not know what happened when one became pregnant; she had no idea what pregnancy was because she had never before been pregnant.

The woman said to her husband, "Well, I don't know what this is all about, my husband, but this is the second month that I haven't gone through a change. Don't you think that I should go and tell my doctor? She might want me to continue taking these medicines regularly. Or she might tell me to leave the medicines alone now."

Her husband said, "All right, then. I don't know anything about these medicines either. Go on over there to the doctor's place and find out what you should do with the medicine that remains."

The woman went to the doctor, and when she got there, "Be appeased, Doctor!"

The doctor said, "Be appeased, my daughter! Where have you come from?"

"Well, Doctor, I have come from my home."

"Yes, my child."

"This is the second month that I have not undergone a change. There's still some medicine left over, and I don't know what to do with it. Should I take it, or not? I've come to find out whether it's all right for me to continue taking it."

The doctor asked, "The medicine that is in a large tin—have you replenished that water?"

The woman said, "No, I didn't add any water because there's still a little left over from the first water that I put in."

Again, the doctor asked, "The medicine that is roasted and chewed—is there any of that left?"

The woman answered, "I finished that during the first month."

"Well then," the doctor said, "well then, Daughter, if that is the way it is, then leave those medicines alone. I shall make another medicine for you."

She got up and took an implement with which she dug medicines. She departed, saying, "Wait for me, I shall be right back."

The wife sat there and waited while the doctor went to dig medicines. After a time, she returned. She arrived and prepared the medicine; she poured it into a large tin.

Then she said, "Do not cover this medicine. It should not be covered. If you do cover it, it will ferment quickly."

The woman agreed, "Be appeased, Doctor."

Every time the doctor spoke, the woman would respond, "Be appeased, Doctor." She took the medicine and went home.

When his wife returned with the medicine, her husband said, "You've come back from the doctor's place. What does she say? Is there something in you, or not?"

She was silent. Then she said, "I don't know what you're talking about."

Her husband answered, "I'm asking what the doctor said. Are you, or are you not, pregnant?"

The woman answered, "No, my husband. I'll explain what the doctor said. She said that I should no longer take the medicine that I've been using. And she made this new medicine for me. Now I'm not entirely clear about this matter because she didn't state definitely that I'm pregnant. Nor did she say clearly that I'm not pregnant."

The man suddenly raised his voice, angrily, "What! How could you go to the doctor, then return and not know what the doctor meant by her instructions? Why did you go there? Now go right back! Go to that doctor and find out whether or not you're pregnant! You've delayed me enough! I want a wife!"

The woman cried. She cried and said, "This is agonizing! How can I be held responsible for my barrenness? How can this turn on me, as if I had done it deliberately? How unpleasant it is to be disliked by one's husband. He doesn't care about you. He doesn't even care if you're not feeling well. I might as well return to my home!"

Her husband answered, "You're crying in vain! I sent you to the doctor, and you came back with a statement that's not clear. The fees for these consultations are high. I have to pay them! And it cost me a lot to provide you with a dowry too, when I took you from your home. I paid all that money, yet I'm not getting what I married you for! You're not meeting your obligations to me!"

The woman walked away, crying. She felt very bad. Then she went again to the doctor's place. She knocked.

Someone said, "Yes, come in."

"Be appeased, Doctor!"

The doctor responded, "Be appeased!"

Then this wife sat there and cried.

The doctor said, "What is wrong, my child? You were here just yesterday. And now today, you have come here again, crying. What is the matter?"

The woman answered, "Yes, Doctor, I'm crying because my husband is treating me badly. He's upset because I returned from here without finding out clearly whether or not I'm pregnant. But I didn't hear you mention a thing about pregnancy. That's what I said to him. Now he says that I'm mere chaff at his place. He wants me to go. He's driving me away! He claims that I'm costly to him. It's better that I go home if I don't know what I came here for. I've returned to clarify this matter because the situation at my home of marriage requires that I do so. I've never wanted to return to my home as a young married woman.[5] Now then, Doctor, I ask you—am I pregnant? Or am I not pregnant?"

The doctor said, "Be appeased, my child. The reason I told you to stop taking that first medicine was because I concluded that you are indeed pregnant. Your husband annoys me when he causes you needless trouble, when he makes your blood leap. He is doing that for a reason. He is trying to interfere with what I have already achieved in you. Be quiet now; do not cry. Stop crying. I advise you now to go and tell him that you have been pregnant for two months."

The young woman went then, not altogether pacified because she did not know how her husband would react.

When she got home, she said, "The doctor says that I'm pregnant. She says that it's the second month. And the doctor was annoyed, my husband, because you've been troubling me. She was not pleased that I arrived at her place in tears. She says that this may cause a premature birth, that while she had made progress in treating my condition this might result in a regression."

The husband was quiet, silent. He did not speak.

Finally, he said, "Well, it's your inability to speak clearly that caused this

5. A "young married woman," an *inkazana*, is a woman living at her father's place. She may be a woman who was married and, for some reason, has now returned to her home of birth. Or she may be a woman who has given birth to a child out of wedlock. In either case, she is not living with her husband or the father of her child.

misunderstanding. I asked you what the situation was, and you didn't know. You didn't even know how many months you were pregnant, even though you had just returned from a person whom we both hold in respect. Now settle down. Let your blood be calm. Don't allow your blood to overflow on account of this disagreement. After all, I've also wanted you to become pregnant."

Time passed then. Time passed, and the wife became big. At the end of the ninth month, she gave birth to a boy. During all this period, her husband refused to believe that she was in fact pregnant; when he was assured of it, he began to take a renewed interest in her, and he started to love her again. He forgot about marrying someone else because of his wife's barrenness. So it was that this wife lived with her husband now, and they made each other happy. She was a nursing mother, and her child grew up. When he had grown up, he was weaned.

And this woman became pregnant again; she no longer had to return to the doctor for medicines. But it happened that, when in the ninth month she gave birth to a child, she had a bad delivery. Only the child emerged. There were other things that did not come out.

It was said, "What shall we do now?"

The husband's mother said, "Now really, my child, you have a doctor for this wife of yours. When something goes wrong, she ought to go to that doctor to be examined. We hope that the doctor will discover where the problem is. It makes no sense to go to other doctors while we have our family doctor right here at home. It would be costly to consult someone else. You should try the family doctor first."

The young man went to the doctor then, and, when he arrived there, he knocked hesitantly.

Someone inside said, "Yes."

He said, "Hello."

When he said "Hello," someone said, "Yes."

The husband sat down, and his wife's doctor looked at him coldly. She asked, "Are you not the husband of that young wife who comes here repeatedly?"

The young man said, "Yes, I am he. I'm her husband."

The doctor said, "Why do you greet me in ordinary Xhosa? That is not the formal greeting for a doctor."

The young man said, "I really don't know the proper thing to say when I'm greeting you, Mother."

The doctor said, "Since I am your wife's doctor, I am your doctor, too. When you come to me, you should say, 'Be appeased, Doctor!' "

The young man said, "Pardon me. Be appeased, Doctor! Be appeased! These things have become unfashionable for us, and we sometimes remember them only haltingly, and in fragments. We've forgotten that everyone must say, 'Be appeased!' We thought that the only person who says 'Be appeased!' is the one who's undergoing treatment."

The doctor said, "When a relative of yours is being treated, you are being treated as well. You are being treated because you are the one the treatment is for. You are the one who is affected by it."

"Yes," the young man said, "I understand, Doctor. Please forgive me. I appease you."

The doctor said, "I am going to fine you, young man, because it is clear that you do not even care to pay me my ox as payment. That is because you do not appreciate me, even though your wife already has had a child. And now she has a second child, and still you are disrespectful of me. It is proper that I should begin by attempting to wrest my ox from you. I shall never get it otherwise. I am fining you, then. You must, in addition, give me a young she-goat because when you came here you exhibited poor behavior."

"Oh," the young man said, "I appease you, Doctor. That's all right. I'll produce the young of an ox that I owe you because my wife now has two children. I'm pleased. Really, I'm happy, because now I'm just like the others. I'm like my peers who have many children. For a long time, I was without a child, but now I'm just like my age-mates." Then the young man said, "I beg your leave to go now, Doctor."

He departed then, having asked the doctor's leave to go. He said, "I'll come back later to talk about the subject I originally came to discuss with you."

So he arrived at his home.

"Father, that doctor over there fined me. She fined me for something that I was ignorant of—that I should appease her too in her presence. I just said, 'Hello,' and the doctor did respond to me. But when she responded, it was clear that she was upset about something. Then she raised the point, and we argued about it. But I did not dispute it too much, Father. I pleaded my ignorance. I told her that I didn't know that I was supposed to appease her. Then she told me that, whenever she treats my wife, she's also treating me. That's why I have to pay the fees. A person must appease when he is the one who is responsible for sending a relative to a doctor. I concluded that what she said was correct. So she fined me, she charged me the young of a goat for my bad behavior. She said that it was obvious that I would not pay the debt owed to her, even though I had obtained what I had wanted from her—because my wife now has two offspring."

His father answered, "That's right, my child. These doctors are people who must be treated with delicacy because they've gone through an initiation. They've been trained. They're people who have their directives. A doctor will be pained internally if you don't respect her, and if she is pained in that way then she will not prepare your medicines properly. You must give her respect, so that she'll make good medicine for you. Now take that she-goat to her before the sun sets. Take it now, so that she'll know that you've really been affected by what she said to you, so that she'll calm down and restrain herself."

The child said then, "Thank you, Father. You've helped me. Thank you, and remember me still in the future. My troubles have resulted from mistakes I've made because of my youth. Please don't be impatient with me, Father." He said that, then took the goat to the doctor.

When he arrived at the doctor's place, he stood in the doorway with the goat. He knocked.

She was inside.

He said, "Be appeased! I'm outside here. Be appeased. I have come here to Mother, to Mother the doctor, and ask that she come outside and see what I have brought, in accordance with the penalty that was levied against me this morning. I was troubled by that and realized that I could not live well because I had annoyed the doctor. Now I request that you come out and be satisfied."

The doctor appeared at the door, and said, "Be appeased! Be appeased, young man! A person punishes himself; a person is not punished by others. You pull the switch from the tree, and the tree is the person who is to be punished. Then you flog him with that very switch. I say, you have taken the switch from my hand, and you have put it aside. Now I am in harmony with you because my words have obviously touched you deeply, in the blood. Be at peace, then, young man. I am satisfied. Go well." The doctor said that, then took ashes from the hearth and poured them on the goat's back. She said, "Let it go." She spoke to her children: "There it is, Children. You should get to know that goat. I shall have my husband brand it on the ear, but he is still at a coming-out party. Young man, if this goat should run away and return to your place over there, if it escapes from the care of my children, please tether it again with a rope and bring it back here."

The young man answered, "Yes, Doctor. Be appeased! I hear you. I'll do that. I bring this goat to you with a heavy heart because my wife is still ill. Her situation requires that the doctor be free, that she not be pained by something I have done which is not relevant to my wife's illness. If the goat runs away, you'll see me here. If it doesn't get lost in a herd of other goats, I'll return it."

The doctor said, "Be appeased!"

Then the young man said, "I'm going home now, Mother."

The doctor said, "Be appeased, young man. Go. There is nothing wrong now. Everything is all right. We shall see each other again."

The young man said, "Be appeased," and he departed. He went home. When he got home, he told his father, "I met with the doctor. She was calm. She smiled while I was still approaching with the goat. When she got up, I could see that she was happy, Father. This woman smiled; she laughed. I saw that, well, she was happy. And I too, when I left, I was also happy. We had a pleasant conversation, and everything's fine now."

It appeared that everything was now going well with his wife also.

She said, "My husband, I must laugh when I remember how abrasive you were when I first returned from the doctor! Now you understand what this is all about. I almost died here because of the mystery of my barrenness—as if I were the reason for my inability to conceive."

Her husband said, "Don't bring up something that's over. How can you do that?"

EPILOGUE—DESTINY

THE END OF THE AFFAIR

Performance Note

Time: 13 August 1972, in the early afternoon. *Place:* In a fallen rondavel near Mrs. Zenani's home, in Nkanga, Gatyana District, the Transkei. *Audience:* Three women, three teenagers, and three children. (NS-174.)

If a young person happens to become sick and die, no more would be done for him than is done in the case of the death of an adult. According to Xhosa custom, a grave is dug for a person, and his body is placed into the hole. If he is sufficiently grown to be carried, others transport his body to the grave. If his weight and size require that he be carried by many people, many men will transport him. In the old days, a person's body would merely be put into the hole. A compartment would be constructed, an underground extension to the hole. The body was placed there, then the hole was covered.

If the dead person happens to be an old man, then the person who is left behind—his son—performs certain Xhosa customary rituals. After the funeral, according to Xhosa practice, a beast is slaughtered. This is called "the washing of the hands." Corn is cooked, and that is the end of the affair.

Sometimes, mourning or fasting follows this ritual, again according to Xhosa custom. In perhaps two, three, or four years, something that has been forgotten or omitted will still be spoken of. A beast is therefore slaughtered, and they sit down and hastily eat the flesh of that beast. They proceed carefully. It is said, "A beast is being slaughtered"; this ritual is called, "He is being turned over," he is being offered something. There is much beer drinking, skin skirts are worn by the women, bundles of wood are fetched, the people are all well clothed. Everyone is splendidly attired. It is very pleasant in that homestead: there is no sleeping; they chant all sorts of songs of joy. They drink the beer; they eat the meat that is being roasted in the cattle kraal. Some of the meat is roasted near the threshing floor in front of the house, in the nearer kraal. That is the women's meat. The men's meat is cooked in the cattle kraal. When the meat is removed from the fire, it is not removed at different times. The ritual follows this pattern: when the beast is about to be slaughtered, a song is chanted—this is called "the chant of the homestead." There is dancing, and the people go outside. The person who occasioned this feast is called by name: it is said that the slaughter is taking place in honor of him.

A dance before dinner

It is then said, "Let the unmarried women enter the kraal." (These women are usually those who are related to the homestead that is performing the rite, but other villagers are also present.)

A steak is placed on the branch of a tree, and it is eaten there. A billycan of beer is dipped and brought from the house. These are consumed there in the kraal. Some is given to the unmarried women, some belongs to the men. When this is completed, the roasting begins, and anyone present is allowed to begin. All taste the meat. In the evening, a special meat is cooked. This meat is cooked as something extra; the fire has been revived. When this meat has been removed from the fire, it is given to the women who are sitting in their own house by themselves—the unmarried women, on the other hand, sit with the men in the men's house. So it will go on. Tobacco is exchanged only among the people of the homestead, the women excluded.

The next morning, the chanting begins again, just before the meat is taken from the fire. When the people awaken, "waking-up" billycans are dipped, and the drinks and the men's meat are transported to the kraal; the women's meat is taken outside and cooked. Then, when the food has been cooked and just before it is dished out, it is said, "Women, to the house!" The matrons come out of their house and enter this one, coming now to sing songs. They are wearing skin skirts. However, they will not dance. They will sit down. The owners of the homestead go around the hearth, dancing and chanting and singing.

Then they pause and say, "We do this to insure good health!"

"We desire maize."

"We desire a child."

"We desire herds."

"Our wives should conceive children."

"Let the homestead be in good health."

The others respond, "Be appeased! So be it!"

"Be appeased!"

"Be appeased!"

"Fellow of So-and-so, we hope that it turns out that way!"

It is a very festive occasion. Some wish that it would not end. It is held to honor a person who died long ago. The ritual is performed for some ancestor, so that all bad and painful things here at home will come to an end, so that all will be well.

The people sing and dance and form a procession: this is the chant of the homestead, a song and dance called "Magwaza" in this home and sung to the beat of a drum. The procession moves outside, as a talented woman sings. They all go outside, the men weaving and dancing rhythmically, their chest muscles rippling, their big stomachs shaking, others quivering. They move slowly to the accompaniment of the song, going toward the cattle kraal. When they arrive at the entrance to the kraal, the women, as is proper, keep a respectable distance. They begin to gather there at the entrance, not going in, stacking up there—generally in the area of the fireplace where the meat is being cooked. These women do not venture beyond the fireplace; they do not go into the kraal. They continue to sing the chant—the unmarried women, the girls of the homestead— and, when they are all together, move gracefully with the men of their home. It is a very satisfying thing to witness. The people of this homestead are the ones being sung for.

Then the man who is carrying the spear stops the proceedings. He is the one who stabbed the ox for the feast, a beast that is not merely stabbed by anyone. Someone special has to do that. A certain form must be followed, a prescribed way of doing it. The person who does it, the one who kills that beast with a spear, is specially chosen. The use of the spear must be authorized; it takes an exceptional talent. A certain person is appointed for this specific task. The one who wields the spear belongs to the royal residence, and his appointment depends on his seniority.[1] That man will stop the proceedings. He says, "Today, I am making this offering to So-and-so. I am dedicating this occasion to So-and-so. I am 'turning him

---

1. That is, on how long he has been married.

around,' so that he will look on us with favor: we desire corn, we desire offspring, we desire stock, we want our wives to be pregnant, we wish to be real men so that when we work we earn substantial wages. May all evil things depart from this homestead."

The people respond: "Be appeased! We appreciate what you are saying."

Another man supports the words of the first speaker: "Be appeased, Fellow of So-and-so! May even invalids who are always being troubled by certain parts of their bodies be well today. May even the trouble that we have not yet experienced come to a proper end, so that it does not catch us by surprise."

All of these speeches are made in raised voices.

"Now, let the women go to the house!"

So the women go into the house. When the women have gone in, the unmarried women go into the house where they sleep—the same house occupied by the men, the house from which the meat has come. The girls, the unmarried women, the married women will gather outside. They sit there, girded in their skin skirts. Those who belong to the village but not to this homestead, the ones who have merely come as visitors, are not dressed in skin skirts; but they are well adorned, they wear fine garments because this is an important festive and ritual occasion.

Then the young men, also well dressed, get up and transport beer to the cattle kraal. When that task is complete, they take the beer that belongs to the women to the women's kraal. The billycans are prepared by the unmarried women who bustle around. But no woman goes near the beer; even the woman of the homestead does not touch anything connected with the beer because she is behaving very properly, containing herself, remaining seated, touching nothing that is dirty today. She is showing respect, following Xhosa custom; she is being reverential, solemn. If a woman gets any beer at all, it is because an unmarried woman has dipped it and given it to her. If a woman is thirsty, she must get the attention of an unmarried woman and whisper to her, "My friend, I'm thirsty!" and the unmarried woman will devise a plan—because she herself is nearer to the business of men when this kind of ritual is being performed.

The unmarried women finish washing the billycans, which are carefully watched by the men: they watch to see if they are finished, if there are enough of the cans. Then these cans are taken by the men, and all the men of the district enter the cattle kraal. This beer is drunk inside the kraal, and there is no talking; all they do is dip into the beer. This is the Putting-the-head-in-and-letting-go ritual. There is no ceremonial talking; they just put their heads into the can and pass it on. The beer is not accompanied by words; no one says "I'm giving this to you." This is because the beer has been presented to the one about whom the occasion is centered, the one who is dead.

The food will also be dished out and placed there. It is said, "Drink! Drink!" and the women perform the same activities with their apportioned vessel of beer, sitting according to the regions from which they have come. Each region dips a billycan, then puts it down; each dips a billycan, and so on.

The beer that comes from the men is given to the unmarried women by the men in the appropriate vessel. The women likewise dip beer from their apportioned vessel and send it to those unmarried women. The meat is handled in the same way when it has been taken from the fire; the men give it to the unmarried women, and the married women give it to the unmarried women.

The beer is drunk and finished, and in the late afternoon they go into the house. The villagers go into the house, which is small, and drink until it is time for them to go home. The house may well be full, for when a person performs a rite like this, he invites his kinsmen, wherever they may be, and they all come and fill his homestead. There is generally not room for the villagers who do not belong to this homestead. They must be satisfied with being treated courteously; then they will depart. They can see that there is no room.

But if the house is only sparsely occupied, some of the visitors also enter, until the room is filled. The people will also sleep over, and it is a very pleasant experience.

The next day, the meat is cut up—the meat that is left over. This includes the leg, the backbone, the head, hooves: the day is called "Seconds," the second day of the ritual occasion. The meat is cut up, and that which belongs to the kraal—the hooves and head, and portions of the leg—is taken to the kraal. For the women, the meat consists of the backbone and the duodenum and other portions that might have been left on the carcass. Then they all sit, and the meat is cooked. When it is ready, it is removed from the fire to the accompaniment of a chant. All that is said is that the leftovers are being cooked, "The *ummiso* is cooked." *Ummiso* is the name of the feast that day. It is taken off the fire, all of it is removed from the fire at the same time. The men take the meat off the fire, and they give some to the unmarried women; the married women too give some meat to the unmarried women. After the meat has been eaten, there are the billycans of the *ummiso* and those of the porridge, and there is also the straining of the husks for the second time. This is the beer that remains, a weaker form of beer. The husks are taken and poured out in the courtyard because the courtyard is said to be the hearth. They are poured out there, and at dawn the unmarried women wash the vats that have been borrowed from other homesteads. They also wash the pots borrowed from other homesteads, so that these vats and pots will not be returned still covered with the residue of this occasion. They clean these things; then the vessels are taken home.

Those who are prepared to depart ask leave to go, and they go to their various homes. Those who are left behind are the people of the homestead. When the next day dawns, they tidy up. The branches on which meat had been placed and the bones are burned. The bones of that ox are collected and are burned in the cattle kraal. It is said, "The bones are being burned." When that has been done, the viscera are roasted. They are roasted on the Day of the Bones, then eaten by the few who are still there. This is the Smoking of the Bones.

APPENDIX

THE PREGNANT BOY

In her 1967 version of this story (Perf. 626), Mrs. Zenani ends with a lengthy segment having to do with the unique destiny of the child born to the boy. This alternative ending is given below.

This child grew up, this child grew up, and when she became a young girl, this child became a doctor, a person who, while she sleeps, learns things that will occur in the future. She dreams it, and it happens. While she sleeps, she learns which medicine she should go and pick, a medicine that will cure a certain disease.

So this child of that boy became a doctor. She had to be treated in a special way.

When this man learned about that, he said, "What shall I do about this? Mm, the child has already made a beginning."

This is the way she began:

"Father, a thick fog is coming! With cold rain! And hail! Put the lean livestock into the house because the storm is going to cause damage! It will come on such-and-such a day."

So it happened.

On another occasion, this child said, "This year, there will be no rain at all. The grain must be conserved by anyone who has it."

So it happened.

And again, the child said, "A person who is in pain must go and dig for medicine beneath a certain cliff."

Then this child went to dig for that medicine. She saw it in her sleep, and that is the way she treated the person who was in pain. He did what she told him to do: he went and dug for that medicine.

In the morning, when she got up, she cured this person. He was well.

"That's the way it happened."

"She must be a doctor, beyond any doubt."

A doctor is a person who knows all things, and this became a habit with the child.

Once she said, "An army is coming! If that army happens to come here, don't confront it. Just dig a certain plant beneath that cliff over there. All of you must wash it, and the army will then pass you by."

What she ordered was done. It happened as she said it would.

"Now then, this is what I have surmised from all of these activities of this child. All these things that she has done perplex us. The things that have appeared to her while she was sleeping are things that we do not know. She even tells us things of the old times which we do not know—things of the ancestors. Now, I have gathered you together here, People of this home."

The people answered, "Well, a white goat must be slaughtered for her, and a skin that she can use as a bed must be made from it, a skin that she can lie down under, or on top of. She must wear the distinguishing white beads of the doctor, on her neck and arm. The beads will help to clarify the future when she dreams of what will happen."

So it was.

So it was with the child of this boy. And that boy began to prosper because people who had puzzling diseases traveled to come to this child.

When a person came to this child, the child would sleep. Then, when the child got up in the morning, she would say that what was good for this person was such-and-such a medicine that must be dug up in a certain place and prepared in a certain way. When this procedure was followed, the person would be well.

So the wealth here at home increased, and that boy prospered until he was finally circumcised, until finally he too had taken a wife.

He lived with this child in this home.

Then her grandfather said, "Something ought to be done for this child. She should have her own homestead so that the things that she does might be clearly seen. Here at my home, the things that she does are mixed up with other things, and they're not so visible."

A homestead was therefore made for this child, this child who was a girl. A homestead was built for her, and she remained in her homestead together with this boy. He also stayed in her homestead.

There were happy people in this homestead . . .

THE BROOM

The "broom" is the wife or house that is created as an adjunct to the main house or main wife. "Broom" in this sense means the one who does the work; or, in the case of a childless or male-childless great wife, the *ixhiba* is the "broom" in the sense that again it does the work of the great wife, to relieve the great wife or to act in her stead. But the idea of the *ixhiba* seems to indicate that it never reaches the heights of prestige and influence of the great wife and the main house; it exists purely as an adjunct, a broom.

Performance Note

Mrs. Zenani's story, "The Broom of the Great House" (*Time:* 18 September 1967, in the late afternoon; *Place:* In a home in Nkanga, Gatyana District, the Transkei; *Audience:* Thirty men, women, and children. [Perf. 688.]), is given below.

A certain homestead was very large; many people lived there. Three women were there, including a girl wearing a jersey. This girl was not altogether a woman: she was a servant who cooked the chief's food.

Time passed, and after a considerable length of time, the great wife said, "I want to have a subsidiary house, an *iqadi*. There is this girl who cooks for me at home."

The wife second in rank, the wife of the right-hand house, said, "I'm not pleased to hear you say that you want an *iqadi*."

The chief said, "No, it's right that this be discussed because there are sometimes four wives. These women have names. The *iqadi* has a designation, the right-hand house has a designation, the *ixhiba* has a designation. The *ixhiba* is 'the broom of the great house.' Now, what this wife desires must be done. The one who has been requested should be there. That girl is just a cooking object here. Now, in what house is she to stay?"

"Yes. Now, that woman—" so said the fellow who was chairman of this meeting there in the courtyard where the great wife's speech was being considered. He said, "Well now, that woman should be placed in the great house. Her designation is *iqadi*. *Iqadi* becomes significant when the people in the great house are, for some reason, all gone. If this were to happen, people would say, 'Wasn't there an *iqadi*?' If the members of the great house are, for some reason, gone, then it's proper that the new great wife be drawn from the subsidiary house, the *iqadi*, into the great house. The *iqadi* becomes a feeder for the great house if something goes wrong in the great house."

A second speaker asked, "What about the third wife? What'll happen to her?"

"Well, this third wife is the right-hand house, and it is independent. It has nothing to do with the great house, it is independent of the movement into the great house. Unlike the *iqadi*, it does not feed into the great house."

A third speaker said, "That third woman is independent. She has no say in the matters of the great house. She too will one day have an *iqadi* of her own. The right-hand house will have its own feeder, its own *iqadi*. But this *iqadi* of the right-hand house is independent of the *iqadi* of the great house. And, as time goes on, it might become necessary to establish an *ixhiba*."

"*Ixhiba*—now, what does that mean?"

"The name, *ixhiba*, in Xhosa, means 'the broom of the great house.'"

The speaker said, "The broom of the great house. What does such a person do? What is her function? Speak clearly. Make your definitions cogent and precise."

"Well, the broom of the great house. . . . When these people are dead, then people wonder, 'Wasn't there something that could act as a broom for cleaning up what has happened in the great house?' It means the wife who has become the most fitting. She occupies a place in the right-hand house similar to that of the *iqadi* in the great house."

"Oh, what do you call that person, Fellow?"

"She is called the *ixhiba*. The *ixhiba* is under the *iqadi*. From another perspective, it is above the *iqadi* because it stakes no claim to anything. The *ixhiba* is the great house. Sometimes all the people of the great house die: in that case, the *ixhiba* rules. This is the royal manner of coping with such a situation. The *iqadi* will tend to lean on, or cling to, the great house; it will tend to be close to the great house. When the *ixhiba* becomes the great house, the pillar that holds up the falling roof of the great house is the *iqadi*."

They struggled with this problem. They turned it over and over, examining it carefully.

"Now, what would be done if there were no heir in the great house? And if there were no child in the *iqadi*? The only house to have produced a child was the *ixhiba*."

"All right, let's get on, Men."

Time passed then, time passed.

Year followed year, and the people were getting older.

Year followed year, and the people became aged.

The child of the *ixhiba* had grown up. He was circumcised. He became a man, and finally he had a wife.

The old chief was still ruling. He was sixty years old.

What must be done now?

"Well, the chief ought to be pensioned."

However, it was said, "Well, really, he can still talk. He doesn't muddle things. Let him continue in the chieftaincy to his seventieth year, if he lives that long."

He did indeed live to be seventy years old. Then it was necessary that he be pensioned. But there must be a child who could be installed as chief. And he had no offspring at all, none at all.

He did have a child of the *ixhiba*, however, in that homestead that is called "the broom of the great house," the house that is greater than the *iqadi* of the right-hand house.

The entire country that was ruled by the chief assembled to discuss the matter.

When everyone was present, it was said, "The reason we are here is to consider an issue of great urgency. Our chief is getting very old now, and it is not clear to us who shall rule after him. We are concerned about this. We want to be ruled by people of royal blood."

"Oh, a person a royal blood."

"Where is he?"

"The one who was royally sired by the chief, that's a person of royal blood."

"This is what we must do. Many people must come here. They should fill this place, for the purpose of installing the heir to the throne. We all agree that nothing can ever be done by a person who is not of royal blood."

"There's no disputing that."

"Go, summon the people."

There was a place known as Hohita, [King] Sarhili's royal residence.

They said, "Someone should go to Hohita."

That is where Xhosa himself originated; it is the reason this area became known as the land of the Xhosa.

"Before we discuss this matter, call the two men from Hohita, our two men who have been staying at Hohita."

Messengers were sent to that country. The two men were summoned at Hohita. One of them was a Maya clansman, the other a Cira clansman. When the messengers got there, they were asked where they had come from.

They said, "We have come on instructions. Something has happened at home, and the decision was that we should come here."

"There is a need to know the fundamental customs of this homestead. We have been sent because of this need."

"We have come here for that reason."

"All right, we recognize that you have come here with a weighty matter."

"No matter how complex it may be, it is not too difficult for us. It will be dealt with by men of experience."

"We shall not treat it lightly. We have already heard of your problem."

They returned with the messengers, and a meeting was then assembled.

"Speak now, Fellows of Hohita! What do you know?"

"What kind of place is this Hohita?"

The Maya clansman got up and said, "Well, Sir, if you know where Queenstown is, Hohita is near Queenstown, if you understand what I am saying. It's all the way to Qamata, at the railroad station in Qamata."

The chief asked, "What is a 'railroad station'? We don't know such things, Child. When we were born, there were no such things. There was no railroad station then. When we were born, we walked, unaided. On foot, eating meal made from roasted maize. When we went to Johannesburg, we went on foot, my child. We traveled on foot, the months rolling by as we went to Johannesburg. Now, what is a 'station'?"

The young man said, "Well, Father, a railroad station is something that we're only beginning to experience ourselves. It's a relatively new thing. It's called a 'railroad station.' The train comes to it."

The chief said, "What is a 'train'? It is a 'train' that I don't know anything about, my child. Even though you speak in Xhosa, you are telling us things that we don't know. Well, what are 'trains'?" [These comments about trains and automobiles may initially seem to be a digression, but they fit neatly into the old people's suspicion, later expressed, of the modern generation. But it is Maya, a member of the modern generation, who provides the solution to the problem. The two clansmen have left Hohita and returned to the royal residence of this minor chief. Men were sent to fetch the clansmen and to bring them back so that they could bring their expert experience and knowledge gained at the royal residence at Hohita and apply them to the problems at their home.]

The Maya youth answered, "Well, Father, it's a thing that is ridden. It's ridden by people. It's a thing that has been made—well, I don't know myself how it is made. It appeared and we rode it, that's all. It just came about. It's a thing that goes on the ground; it goes on the ground. It has wheels."

He asked, "What sort of thing is it, my child, in comparison to a motorcar that I once saw? I hear it said that there is a motorcar now at the general store in Gatyana." [Europeans refer to the small village of Gatyana as "Willowvale": it then had a population of about three hundred and is approximately twelve miles from Mrs. Zenani's home.]

"No, Father, I don't know what a motorcar is. But this train has hard wheels [as opposed to the rubber wheels of the automobile], it doesn't resemble a motorcar."

"Well, all right, my child, we must leave that subject. We don't know those things. But we want to speak of our Xhosa customs. What you are talking about only confuses me because I don't know anything about it."

The child said, "Well, pardon me, Father. I didn't know that trains have not yet been seen here among the Gcaleka. I thought that you had seen them. But really, we've seen them only recently ourselves. I'm here by order of the chief. We were told to come here."

"Refresh our memories about the customs [literally, names that speak]. We've come because something important is being discussed here."

"Then please speak, Young man. Tell us what you know. You've been sent here. You must know something. Now, according to the fundamental custom that dates from the beginning of things for us Xhosa, what steps does a person take when he is born, when he becomes a man, when he is married? [He has referred to three of the four significant rites of passage of the Xhosa people.] How do these steps progress?"

The young Maya clansman said, "I'll try to answer that question, Father. I would never claim to be an expert, but I do know that a man sometimes marries a great wife, and after the great wife he marries the wife of the right-hand house. After the wife of the right-hand house, he marries an *iqadi* of the great house. After the *iqadi* of the great house, he marries the *iqadi* of the right-hand house. And after the *iqadi* of the right-hand house, he marries the *ixhiba*. That *ixhiba* becomes the *ixhiba* of the great house."

"Stop there, Maya, my child. If a man has five wives, what is the position of the *ixhiba* among them?"

"Yes. Well, Father, according to Xhosa custom, even if there are as many as ten wives, however many a man wishes to have, it sometimes happens that the wife who is the *ixhiba* is called 'the broom of the great house.' "

"Yes, go on, my child. Why is she called 'a broom'?"

"Well, Father, in relation to the other four wives, she is a baby. All of the others must go before she counts for anything, before she obtains her rights. In order that she get her privileges, there must be no one in the right-hand house, and there must be no one in the *iqadi* either."

"Please repeat that, Young man. I didn't quite hear what you said."

"Oh, pardon me, Father, I made a mistake in my comments about the right-hand house. I meant to say that the *ixhiba* will not get her privileges if the *iqadi* of the great house is not there. If the *iqadi* of the great house happens not to bear a male child, then the *ixhiba* takes the reins of the great house."

"Now I hear you, Young man! What does all this add up to? We're here to receive that knowledge."

"When we were summoned, we were told to come here, that there was a problem here, that we should come and explain what we know. That's how it is."

"All right, Young man."

The youth of Hohita said, "Assembled people, you who have heard!" and he sat down.

Then a certain man from this royal residence got up and said, "This youth has finished. Even the words that he has not spoken, he has as good as uttered them, because we seek the fundamental custom of the Xhosa. We are already being deceived by our children because they are more enlightened than we are. But these practices of the children will spoil life because they make us strangers to the things that are happening these days. Well, it looks all right, my son. Go over to the kraal and look for a fat beast. Slaughter it for these young men from Hohita. Their work here promises to end well."

The young man went to the kraal. He seized a goat, a well-developed one—all eight teeth—and he brought it into the house.

It was said, "Take it over there to the *ixhiba* because of what has been discussed today. The *ixhiba* house has been the topic of conversation today. So that we may be faithful to the law, anything that is done should now be done in front of that house."

The young man took the goat to the *ixhiba* house. He slaughtered it there.

The right foreleg of the goat was referred to: "Cut, cut, Young man. Cut a little piece of meat from the foreleg of the goat and roast it for him. Then present it to him ceremonially, because when a beast is slaughtered for someone, he must be the first to eat of the meat, according to Xhosa custom. When the others are eating the meat, the person for whom the beast was slaughtered should already have tasted it. He should not be tasting it for the first time while the others are eating it."

BEER MAKING

In the story given below Mrs. Zenani describes the preparations for a beer party. The context of the brewing of the beer is as follows. The cattle are returning from the harvest, and a ceremony, called the "whip" celebration, is about to take place. At the same time, a respected woman of the area is soon to speak about her initiation into the medical profession. The wife responsible for the brewing of the beer is instructed by her husband that the beer must be brewed by the time this woman arrives to speak.

Performance Note

Time: 18 September 1967, in the afternoon. *Place:* In a home in Nkanga, Gatyana District, the Transkei. *Audience:* Thirty men, women, and children. (Perf. 682.)

The women were told, "Moisten the malt; soak it in water. Pour the corn into the water; let it become swollen."

The corn was poured into the water, and it swelled. After it had been in the water for some time, a woman removed it. That was on the fourth day. She put it in a warm place so that it would become stale and sprout. It did sprout, and she kept it there for eight days. On the ninth day, the malt was taken out. It was mature now. Then it was spread out to dry. For a full month, it dried. Then they spread it in the house and left it for six days. On the seventh day, it was taken outside, put in bags, and hung on the walls of the kraal. After it had been on the fence for some time, it dried.

The owner of the homestead took the matter up with his wife.

"Well, Nobani, what the initiated young woman is saying must be coordinated with the state of the malt. By the time we're ready to meet concerning this woman, the malt should be ready. You should so time the completion of the malt that it is ready when this meeting takes place."

The wife shook the malt in the bag to determine the state of its maturation. She felt it. She took a grain and put it in her mouth. She tested it with her teeth, to see if it was dry. When she was satisfied that it was indeed dry, she squashed it.

She said, "Father of So-and-so, the grain is dry."

The man answered, "All right. Then that business that we spoke about, the issue raised by this young woman, can proceed."

The wife said, "Well, Father of So-and-so, it's all dry now. The malt is clearly ready for the next stage."

Keep in mind that in those days beer was brewed. Men and women would come and drink beer in a certain person's homestead and also hear what was being spoken of in this homestead. There was no white man then, nothing from the outside—only the Xhosa. That is the way it was.

After all that, it was said, "Woman, thresh the grain if it's ready, so that what must be done can be done, so that this woman may say what she wishes to say."

The wife threshed that grain. She threshed it and finished the task. Then she gathered some women together, saying, "The grain must be ground so that the people can be assembled."

When the women had come together, they said to her, "Ee, Friend! Big sister!"

"Big sister!"

She said, "Hnn?"

"Ee!"

"Big sister!"

"Hnn?"

"Will the men know what we've come here to do? Have you told them?"

She said, "Yes, they've been told. The man of this homestead knows what we're doing. If he hasn't told the other men, then he's the one who has failed. I have told the women."

"Oh, well then, Big sister, let's grind."

"Today we're making beer."

Do you know what is done when beer is brewed? Corn that has been roughly ground on a millstone is poured into barrels. Then the malt is ground. Dishes of corn are measured out, and this is also put into the barrels. Pots of water are then boiled, and when the water is boiling it is poured into the barrels. The grain is stirred then, and covered.

The women did all that, and they covered the barrels. Then they had to go and dip water for cooling. They went to the water. They dipped it with a bucket. They returned. They poured it and cooled what had to be cooled. The younger women all got together and ground the grain. When they were all together, they worked that dough on the millstone.

I tell you, they were really dressed up. They had cleaned themselves. They were filled with awe; they were profoundly reverential. They were proud of themselves; they were preparing the beer.

When the grain had been ground, the dough was poured into the barrels.

The women of the homestead said, "Well, it has cooled. Bring cold water; cool it."

Seven young women got up, carrying buckets. They went to dip water. This cold water was poured into the barrels, and the barrels cooled.

At dawn the next morning, it was said, "Just look. Look and see if the yeast has fermented."

Someone looked. "It's fermenting."

The pots were gathered by the younger village women who had been called together. They, along with the younger women of this homestead who had come to grind, gathered the pots. They ground the grain, and that task was finished.

The yeast fermented, and it was said, "Well, let it be cooked." The women picked up dried cow dung. They took stalks of corn from the fields. And the beer was brewed. It was well brewed. Then it was removed from the fire.

"What shall we do now? There are no dishes for distributing it."

"What shall we do?"

"What shall we do now? We must find some way to do it." So said the great wife of this homestead, the one who had called the other women to help her complete this work. She said, "Go and gather some fresh cow dung. There are the cattle, sleeping. Over there. Gather fresh cow dung, and daub one side of the floor of the house. Then take the pots off the fire and pour the beer there."

The contents of these pots were poured into pots in that part of the house that had not been daubed.

The women went to gather fresh cow dung. Then they returned and daubed the floor. They daubed half of the floor of the house. They took all the pots from the fire and cooled them.

The yeast was prepared. It was made at the bottom of the barrel. The malt that had been ground into meal was put in. One pot of gruel was taken and poured in, the intention being that the beer should boil by the following day. When that had been done, on the morning of the second day the women who had cooked the beer returned.

"We've come to put the malt in." So they said, and the woman of the homestead gave them the malt that was now to be ground and put into the beer. The young women ground it into meal, and it was strained. The beer that was at the lower part of the barrel was strained. Traditionally, this was done by means of a sieve that was made of rushes—rushes are picked in rivers. When these rushes had been picked, they were dried. Then they were combined and plaited. These rushes were made for filtering Xhosa beer among the Gcaleka long ago. The young women strained the beer then. They put one billycan of beer on the upper side of the hearth; they called that container full of beer "the homecoming," "because we've just finished the straining."

They said, "We've strained a pot full. It's full," referring to the pot that was filled with beer that had just been strained.

Time passed, and the straining of the other beer progressed. After the straining was finished, it was said, "Leave a little. Leave a little; leave some beer for yeast to leaven the next brewing."

The owner of the house said, "Get moving, Young women. Dip the gruel that's in the pots in that part of the house that has not been daubed. Pour it into the barrels. The declaration that was made here yesterday is about to commence."

The women dipped the gruel. They poured it into the barrels. And the barrels were full. They leavened it, and the beer brewed. While they were brewing it, someone called on the young woman to make her speech.

When her speech had been made, someone said, "Well, Young woman, you've been heard. We couldn't halt the drinking of beer because of what you've said. We had meant it for another occasion, but we beg you not to be offended by that. We didn't know."

"A doctor should not be provoked in her own home. Be appeased, Young woman!"

This brewing of beer was called "a whip," beer that was brewed when the oxen were returning from the harvest.